The Mediterranean Response to Globalization Before 1950

This volume explores the economic challenges and opportunities presented by globalization prior to 1950, and identify how countries around the Mediterranean have responded. It examines key factors such as international trade, migration, capital flows, diffusion of technology and policy response, from the start of the world globalization boom in the 1850s, through the disaster of the great depression in the 1930s which heralded a global retreat into autarky, and beyond.

In addition to close examination of a wide range of related topics, such as the causes of Mediterranean backwardness, international shipping, and the impact of price shocks, this volume presents detailed case studies of Spain, Italy, the Balkans, Turkey, Israel and Egypt.

Offering both comparative assessments of regional performance and a wealth of historical material, this book will appeal to the economist, the economic historian, and any scholar who seeks to illuminate the current policy debates over globalization through deeper understanding of the past.

Şevket Pamuk is Professor of Economic History at Bogaziçi University, Istanbul, and sits on the Executive Committee of the International Economic History Association. He is a renowned authority on Ottoman and Middle Eastern economic history.

Jeffrey G. Williamson is the Laird Bell Professor and Chairman of Economics at Harvard University. He has written more than twenty books and nearly one hundred and fifty articles on economic history and development, and was recently elected President of the Economic History Asssociation.

Routledge Explorations in Economic History

The Mediterranean Response to Globalization Before 1950

Edited by
Şevket Pamuk and
Jeffrey G. Williamson

London and New York

First published 2000 by Routledge
11 New Fetter Lane, London EC4P 4EE

Simultaneously published in the USA and Canada by Routledge
29 West 35th Street, New York, NY 10001

Routledge is an imprint of the Taylor & Francis Group

Typeset in Baskerville by Bookcraft Ltd, Stroud
Printed and bound in Great Britain by TJ International Ltd,
Padstow, Cornwall

British Library Cataloguing in Publication Data
A catalogue record for this book is available from the British Library

Library of Congress Cataloguing in Publication Data
The Mediterranean response to globalization before 1950 / edited by
Şevket Pamuk and Jeffrey G. Williamson
    p.   cm.
  Includes bibliographical references and index.
  ISBN 0-415-22425-X (alk. paper)
  1. Mediterranean Region—Economic conditions.
  2. Mediterranean Region—Economic policy. 3. Globalization.
  4. International trade. I. Pamuk, Şevket. II. Williamson,
  Jeffrey G., 1935–
HC244.5 .M413 2000
338.91'.09182'2—dc21   99-053473

ISBN 0-415-22425-X

Contents

Figures

Tables

Contributors

Ahmet O. Akarli is a graduate student completing his thesis in the Department of Economic History, London School of Economics, London, United Kingdom.

Giovanni Federico is Life Fellow in the Department of Modern and Contemporary History, University of Pisa, Pisa, Italy.

James Foreman-Peck is Professor in the Department of Economics at Middlesex University and Economic Adviser to HM Treasury, London, United Kingdom.

Gelina Harlaftis is Assistant Professor in the Department of Maritime Studies, University of Piraeus, Piraeus, Greece.

Vassilis Kardasis is Associate Professor in the Department of Economics, University of Crete, Rethymno, Crete, Greece.

Pedro Lains is Research Fellow at the Instituto de Ciencias Sociais, University of Lisbon, Lisbon, Portugal.

Jacob Metzer is Professor in the Department of Economics and Dean of the Faculty of Social Sciences, Hebrew University, Jerusalem, Israel.

José Morilla Critz is Professor in the Department of Economics at the University of Alcala de Heneres, Madrid, Spain.

Alan L. Olmstead is Professor in the Department of Economics and Director of the Institute of Governmental Affairs, University of California, Davis, California, USA.

Kevin H. O'Rourke is Lecturer in the Department of Economics, University College Dublin, Dublin, Ireland.

Şevket Pamuk is Professor in the Department of Economics and Director of the Ataturk Institute for Modern Turkish History, Bogaziçi University, Istanbul, Turkey.

Ramon Ramon-Muñoz is Lecturer in Economic History at the University of Barcelona and Researcher at the European University Institute, Florence, Italy.

Jaime Reis is Professor in the Department of History and Civilization, European University Institute, Florence, Italy.

Paul W. Rhode is Associate Professor in the Department of Economics, University of North Carolina, Chapel Hill, North Carolina, USA.

Joan Ramon Rosés is Assistant Professor in the Department of Economic History and Institutions, Universidad Carlos III de Madrid, Madrid, Spain.

Blanca Sánchez-Alonso is Associate Professor of Economic History and Institutions, Universidad Carlos III de Madrid, Madrid, Spain.

Jeffrey G. Williamson is Laird Bell Professor in and Chairman of the Department of Economics at Harvard University, Cambridge, Massachusetts, USA.

Tarik M. Yousef is Assistant Professor in the Department of Economics, Georgetown University, Washington DC, USA.

Acknowledgments

Drafts of these papers were first presented at the Old Ottoman Mint, Istanbul, Turkey, in June 1998. We are grateful to participants who improved the quality of both the debate and the papers in this volume, especially Konstantinos Kostis, Gigliola Pagano de Divitiis, Socrates Petmezas and Insan Tunali.

The editors split the organization of the Istanbul conference into two parts. The local arrangements were handled by Şevket Pamuk, who wishes to thank our host institutions in Istanbul, Bogaziçi University (Işik Özel in particular) and the Economic and Social History Foundation of Turkey (Bariş Altan in particular), as well as Yapi ve Kredi Bank of Turkey, which made a generous grant to the conference. Without the support of these individuals and institutions in Istanbul, the conference could never have taken place. They have our warm thanks. The program was constructed, the papers were processed and the conference booklet was produced at Harvard University by Jeffrey Williamson, where his then-assistant, Elin Lee, played her usual cheerful and competent secretarial and editorial role. In addition, we wish to thank many who helped us reach other scholars with interests in Mediterranean economic history but who were previously unknown to us. They are: Engin Akarli, Mine Çinar, Metin Cosgel, Roger Owen, Leandro Prados, Alan Richards, Dani Rodrik and Sadek Wahba.

Andrew Dunbar and Elesia Bennett helped whip the book manuscript into shape at Harvard, and, in response to an electronic crisis, Ann Flack, Elin Lee and Jane Trahan pitched in too. And when the deadline seemed an impossible goal, Nancy Williamson made it possible using her evenings and weekends. Elcin Arabacı, Cem Emrence, Tulin Kabacaoglu, Yektan Turkyilmaz and Gulay Yilmaz, graduate students at the Ataturk Institute, Bogaziçi University, prepared the index. We are grateful to all of them.

ŞP, Istanbul, Turkey
JGW, Cambridge, Massachusetts, USA
January 2000

Part 1

Introduction

1 Globalization challenge and economic response in the Mediterranean

Şevket Pamuk and Jeffrey G. Williamson

As the process of economic integration between Europe and the Mediterranean advances into a new century, it becomes increasingly urgent for economic historians to try to shed more light on current policy debates by improving our understanding of the past. As if in response to this call, recent research on the economic history of Spain, Portugal and Italy has exploded. Alas, the same cannot be said of the rest of the Mediterranean, since the long-run economic experience of what are now called the Balkans, Turkey, the Middle East and North Africa remain too little studied by economists and economic historians.

This fact motivated our organizing a three-day conference which met at the Old Ottoman Mint in Istanbul on 4–6 June 1998. The guiding focus common to all the papers was to better understand the globalization challenges and opportunities that the Mediterranean faced prior to 1950, and how the region responded to them. This focus included dimensions of international trade, international capital mobility, technology diffusion, and policy response. Furthermore, the papers tried to assess country performance comparatively. Our goal was to provoke new research on the region, research which was more quantitative and analytical than has been true of past scholarship, and more comparative as well. Certainly the time is ripe: if economic history is going to inform policy around the Mediterranean, and between it and eastern and western Europe, a collective debate about the sources and impact of Mediterranean economic change over the past two centuries must begin now.

We hope that this volume will serve as a beacon for more analytical and quantitative work on the economic history of the Mediterranean basin. The thirteen papers deal with a number of interrelated themes regarding long-run economic change, but globalization issues are common to all of them. The first three of these focus on the performance of the Mediterranean in relation to the rest of Europe (Part 2). The Mediterranean countries all had a large agrarian base during the nineteenth century, with industrial activity becoming significant only towards the end of the century, and in many cases even later. Thus, this volume dwells more, although not exclusively, on the economic performance within sectors rather than on industrial revolutions and structural transformations. Documentation is difficult, but the most ambitious collection of world income statistics compiled by Angus Maddison (1995) does not point to any ubiquitous pattern of convergence between the southern and western European countries after 1850, or even between 1870 and 1914, when the first great globalization boom took place. In fact, as Gabriel Tortella (1994a) has emphasized, the gap continued to widen after 1870 and southern European countries like Spain, Greece and Portugal did not begin to start catching up with the leaders until 1950, although Italy showed some signs earlier.

Why southern European economic backwardness persisted for so long has inevitably attracted considerable attention in recent years. Jaime Reis (Chapter 2) compares the performance of southern European countries after 1850 with another group in the European periphery: the Scandinavian countries. Using various proxies (including real wages) for the missing per capita income estimates, he concludes, in contrast to the arguments put forward by Paul Bairoch more than two decades ago (1977 and 1979), that a sizable income per capita gap had already emerged within the European periphery by the early part of the nineteenth century. This finding is consistent with those of Jeffrey Williamson in this volume, and with a recent paper by Robert Allen (1998a). With the Scandinavian countries growing at rates above the European leaders before World War I, this gap became only more pronounced by 1914.

Reis only touches on the possible reasons for this divergence in performance: demography, accumulation, and natural resource endowment. He concludes by pointing to the advantages of thinking in terms of two convergence clubs for the nineteenth century, not just one.

Jeffrey G. Williamson (Chapter 3) also underlines the existence of a north–south gap within Europe and the relatively poor performance of the western Mediterranean basin during the wave of convergence around the Atlantic economy from about 1850 until 1914. Making use of real wage data that were recently compiled or that remained under-utilized for such comparisons, he first explores the origins of the great divide between the north and the south. Williamson, like Allen, shows that the wage gap did not emerge solely in the aftermath of the Industrial Revolution. Instead, it was also the product of two earlier events: the pre-industrial success of Britain and the Low Countries coupled with southern European retardation during the seventeenth and eighteenth centuries.

Williamson then moves toward the eastern Mediterranean. In the tradition of Arthur Lewis (1969, 1978a, 1978b), he explores how the eastern half of the Mediterranean fared after 1870 and whether this region, with even lower wage and per capita income levels compared to the poor western Mediterranean, was pulled up during the pre-World War I globalization boom. Making use of new wage, price and land-rental data, he finds the evidence from the Balkans, Turkey and Egypt quite consistent: while there was no catching up, there was no falling behind either; that is, it appears that the eastern Mediterranean was pulled along by economic growth in industrial Europe and North America. The forces of globalization had another large impact on the region as well. Evidence from Egypt shows that the growth of trade led to a spectacular fall in the wage/rental ratio as the cotton boom drove up land values and rents, leading to growing inequalities. Other indicators constructed by the author confirm rising inequality everywhere in this part of the Mediterranean from 1880 to 1938, and it seems very likely that it was globalization forces yielding that result. Williamson also speculates that since the countries around the eastern part of the Mediterranean, like Portugal and Spain in the western half, did not participate in the intercontinental waves of labour migration before World War I, "under"-emigration may explain, at least in part, the persistence of the real wage gap between the eastern Mediterranean and the rest, as well as some of the rising inequality. In this sense, his results are consistent with those of Blanca Sánchez-Alonso in this volume.

Measuring comparative growth performance is hard enough; explaining it is far harder. Economic historians have always emphasized institutions and technologies in searching for those explanations, and the paper by James Foreman-Peck and Pedro Lains (Chapter 4) is certainly in that tradition. The authors employ a model to explain why countries in the Balkans and Iberia showed no ability to catch up with the European leader, the United Kingdom, between 1870 and 1910. The paper is in the tradition of the new growth empirical work on the late twentieth century by macroeconomists like Jeffrey Sachs, Robert Barro and others. However, the authors also use the model to infer what played the biggest role in suppressing late nineteenth-century growth in these two parts of the Mediterranean. Their conclusions are that the lag can be explained largely by high tariffs, poor natural resource endowments and low literacy, conclusions that sit very well with most of the rest of the papers in this volume. The toughest challenge, of course, is to show why remedial trade and education policies were rarely used in the Balkans and Iberia to overcome these disadvantages.

With the stage set by these three comparative macro-assessments of long-run Mediterranean growth, the volume then moves on to the two country studies in Part 3, one from each end of the Mediterranean. Stretching from Macedonia in the west through Anatolia to Syria in the east, economic growth in the Ottoman Empire was linked, above all, to the performance of agriculture, since industrialization remained limited until World War I. Ahmet Akarli (Chapter 5) emphasizes that our understanding of the Ottoman economy during the nineteenth century has improved considerably in recent decades. Within the context of free trade, growing commercialization, infrastructure development and consolidation of European financial control, it now seems more plausible than it was two decades ago to link Ottoman growth with its integration into world markets, a theme that permeates so many papers in this volume.

In the absence of production statistics, Akarli strives to measure the performance of the agrarian economy of Ottoman Macedonia around the turn of the century. He cautions that fiscal data may be a questionable source for constructing production and national income estimates since the government's capacity to collect taxes may have changed. Nonetheless, fiscal data and consumption-based estimates both show that the rapid decline in international cereal prices after the 1870s damaged Macedonian agricultural producers and pushed them into the production of other cash crops. In that, they must have been successful since Akarli's series suggests that agricultural production in Macedonia experienced rapid growth up to 1905. However, there was a slowdown and decline thereafter, results that lead Akarli to question the optimistic estimates of overall Ottoman agricultural growth after 1890 first offered by Vedat Eldem (1970). Unless there were faster rates of growth in per capita income in urban regions and non-farm sectors, the increases in Ottoman per capita income implied by even the optimistic agricultural scenario must have been below 1 per cent per annum, lower than the rates experienced in industrial Europe before 1914, and below the catching-up rates achieved around the European periphery (e.g. Scandinavia, Ireland and Italy). But suppose there *were* faster rates of growth in non-farm regions and sectors, and suppose further that the poorer agriculture sector was shrinking, both of which would have been the expected responses to increased agricultural competition from abroad. Such facts would imply more rapid rates of Ottoman GDP per capita growth, rates more consistent with the real-wage growth documented by Williamson in this volume. In any case, available evidence suggests that the eastern Mediterranean did not belong to the Atlantic economy convergence club before World War 1.

While Akarli deals with agriculture in the eastern Mediterranean, Joan Ramon Rosés (Chapter 6) deals with industry in the western end. Rosés investigates the different technological choices made by Catalan, Lancashire and New England cotton textile producers and the implications of their choices for Catalan competitiveness during the mid-nineteenth century. From the early stages of industrialization, American, Spanish and Italian cotton textile mills tried to adapt British technology to their own needs as a consequence of differences in Spanish relative factor scarcity. By the 1850s, these followers had cut the technology gap with the leader. However, Rosés points out that choice of technology and output quality mix were closely related in cotton textiles; early technological choices had important long-term consequences not only for the choice of inputs but also for the quality of the final product. Coarse cloth used raw material intensively but labour less intensively, while the opposite was true of finer qualities. On average, Catalan textile firms produced a cotton cloth that was between the unskilled-labour-using and raw-materials-using coarse cloth of New England versus the skilled-labour-using and raw-materials-saving fine cloth supplied by Lancashire.

Rosés also introduces several new questions into the debate over the sources of Mediterranean retardation relative to the industrial leaders. He argues that Catalan industry could not compete in international markets over a broad range of products because of the high cost of energy and raw materials, as well as the superior productivity of British mills. He concludes that a less ambitious cotton industry in Catalonia, employing imported yarn and specializing in quality differentiated products, might have had lower costs and greater competitiveness in international markets.

As should be apparent, one of the main themes of the Istanbul conference was the role of globalization on Mediterranean economic performance. Transport revolutions in international shipping had a spectacular impact on commodity price convergence and trade in the world economy at this time, as two of the authors in this volume have shown elsewhere (O'Rourke and Williamson 1999, ch. 3). The Mediterranean was certainly part of it, and this fact justifies the appearance of the next three papers in Part 4, which deal with trade and transport costs from the 1870s to the 1930s.

A major Mediterranean nineteenth-century export commodity was olive oil. Together with wine, vegetables and citrus fruits, it was one of the few commodities in which most Mediterranean countries enjoyed a comparative advantage in world markets until World War II. Ramon Ramon-Muñoz (Chapter 7) shows that there emerged three well differentiated world markets for olive oil. He also documents the existence of a well established hierarchy among the Mediterranean suppliers by the early part of the twentieth century. France and Italy occupied the top rung of this ladder, specializing in the export of high-quality products while Greece, Turkey, Algeria and Tunisia occupied the low-quality end of the market. Spain was in the middle, exporting products for both ends of the market. Ramon-Muñoz explains this specialization pattern not only in terms of relative factor endowments but also in terms of other factors emphasized by the new theory of international trade – consumer preferences, product differentiation and path dependence. Ultimately, however, the hierarchy established in olive oil reflected the differences in the levels of economic development around the Mediterranean. Ramon-Muñoz points to the existence of similar hierarchies in other export commodities from the region, such as wine. One might conclude that the Mediterranean countries were exporting similar goods, but they tended to cover different market niches.

José Morilla Critz, Alan Olmstead and Paul W. Rhode (Chapter 8) examine an interesting phase in the globalization of the Mediterranean economy, and from an unusual perspective. In 1880, the vast majority of the citrus fruits, dried fruits and nuts entering the European and North American markets originated in the Mediterranean. These crops frequently accounted for a significant fraction of export earnings, and they had strong linkages to financial, manufacturing and transportation sectors. The economic performance of these sectors, and the world market conditions they faced, had a profound impact on the Mediterranean economies themselves. This was certainly true in the half-century following 1880, when a number of new areas – most importantly California and Florida, but also South Africa, Australia and

Brazil – began to specialize in these crops, vastly increasing world supplies. These new areas wrested commercial leadership away from traditional Mediterranean producers whose reliance on export markets meant that, unlike the producers of grain, they could not benefit from tariffs and thus they had to absorb the full impact of increased world competition. Drawing from six country histories, Morilla Critz, Olmstead and Rhode explore how the emergence of the new producers substantially reduced the expected benefits of specialization and trade for the traditional Mediterranean producers, and, in some cases, led to outright economic and political crisis. The authors estimate that in the absence of American supplies, the revenues of Mediterranean traditional producers would have risen sufficiently to support approximately half a million persons at prevailing income levels on the eve of World War I.

Gelina Harlaftis and Vassilis Kardasis (Chapter 9) examine the development of bulk sea trade in the eastern Mediterranean and the Black Sea regions. The half-century before World War I was characterized by revolutionary declines in freight rates and the rapid growth of deep-sea trade dominated by a small number of bulk commodities. Indeed, it was this revolutionary change in transport technologies that lowered the cost of trade and generated the globalization boom. Grain from the Ukraine, southern Russia and the Danube, plus cotton from Alexandria, were shipped to British and northern European ports, with return cargoes from the British coalfields going to Mediterranean cities and coaling stations. The opening of the Suez Canal in 1869, in conjunction with the introduction of steamships in the area, also gave Mediterranean sea routes a primary role, a role they had lost three centuries earlier as the economic centre of gravity shifted to the Atlantic. The result was an exponential increase in trade and shipping in the eastern Mediterranean during the second half of the nineteenth century.

By the last decade of that century Istanbul became the meeting point for all western European and eastern Mediterranean shipping and seamen, where all the necessary information about purchases and sales of ships, of chartering, insuring, financing, manning and equipment purchase could be found. The internationalization of the port, however, depended almost entirely on the transit bulk sea trade and its destinations in western Europe. When the sea routes to the Black Sea were blocked soon after the beginning of the Balkan wars, when Soviet grain ceased to be exported after the Revolution, and when Romanian and Bulgarian exports dried up after World War II, the port of Istanbul declined in importance.

One of the big winners from the development and the internationalization of bulk trades in the eastern Mediterranean was Greek shipping, which grew by carrying grain, coal and cotton between southern and northern Europe, and in the twentieth century by carrying the same cargoes along the Indian and Pacific routes as well. The increase of shipping thus made maritime communities in some Aegean and Ionian islands highly prosperous.

The next four papers deal with policy choice and the political economy of growth. The two in Part 5 explore pre-1914 experience with Italian protection and Spanish "under"-emigration. The two in Part 6 deal with interwar policy debates in Turkey and Egypt, the former focusing on the 1930s and the latter on internal transport and the unification of national markets.

Giovanni Federico and Kevin H. O'Rourke (Chapter 10) examine the impact of Italian protectionism that began in 1887 when the fear of foreign competition for wheat induced many landowners to relinquish their traditional free-trade stance and to side with the industrialists. Adopting a general equilibrium model to assess the economy-wide impact of the tariffs, they compare the effects of protection with a variety of alternative policies that might have been. Under standard comparative static assumptions and constant returns to scale, the authors find it unlikely that protection had a significant negative effect on aggregate welfare either in the short or the long run. The static impact of a move to free trade is estimated to increase real GDP by less than 2.6 per cent, more than other static models predict but still a lot less than the controversies over Italian trade policy might suggest. Even the dynamic effects of protection on real GDP were small. Their results are fairly robust and they appear to cast doubt on the importance of Italian trade policy. Federico and O'Rourke also suggest that while protection did matter for individual sectors – it benefited wheat and sugar, but lowered the output of Italian textiles – the impact of protection on income distribution was small and protection did not seem vital for any large social group. The authors also argue that even large changes in the output of individual sectors could not have had a significant impact on the regional distribution of income, since wheat-growing was widely diffused and the losing and winning industries were both concentrated in the northern triangle. These results may help explain why, unlike Germany or Great Britain, protection was not a big political issue in Italy.

Blanca Sánchez-Alonso (Chapter 11) asks why emigration from Spain was so low compared with Italy, another southern European country. What was the obstacle that was present in Spain but absent in Italy, even in very poor southern Italy and Sicily? The existing historiography is based, implicitly or explicitly, on a sector-specific model that singles out the tariff on agricultural imports as the key to the low response of Spanish labour to better foreign jobs, the tariff favouring agriculture and retaining labour there as a consequence. In contrast, Sánchez-Alonso uses Heckscher–Ohlin thinking which considers land as the relatively scarce factor and labour as the abundant factor. She argues that tariffs on wheat must have reduced the returns to labour, the abundant factor, and should have increased emigration. What explains the difference between the Spanish and Italian rates of emigration was not the tariff, therefore, but something else. Sánchez-Alonso argues that the something else was the depreciation of the peseta after 1895 which increased the cost of moving for the income-constrained emigrant: potential emigrants, who were very poor, found an investment in the move simply too expensive. Sánchez-Alonso's empirical work shows that the Spanish and Italian rates of emigration would have been similar in the absence of Spanish rejection of the gold standard and acceptance of currency depreciation. Thus, Spain failed to take advantage of a global economy friendly to labour migration: when mass migration was playing a critical role in fostering convergence of poor emigrating countries on rich immigrating countries in the Atlantic economy, Spain opted not to participate. Spanish emigrants had to wait until 1950 and the start of the second age of globalization to make their move to better jobs in more labour-scarce parts of Europe.

Many developing countries around the world experienced a turning point during the 1930s. The contrast between the world economic environment before and after 1929 may often be exaggerated, but there is little doubt that in many parts of the periphery the decade witnessed a retreat from free trade and open capital markets to import substitution and capital market restriction. The world crisis changed the nature of political power by weakening large landowners, export-oriented interests, and the commitment to a liberal order. In many countries, political control fell into more populist hands, turning the wheel towards autarky and import-substituting industrialization. Perhaps the best example is offered by Latin America, a region that was hit hard by the Great Depression and responded with aggressive inward-looking policies. Those Latin American countries that rejected globalization first seemed to recover soonest and fastest from the Depression. The shift towards fully interventionist regimes was completed after World War II, when export pessimism and structuralist arguments dominated the rhetoric of the day.

Around the Mediterranean, the impact of the Great Depression as well as the policy responses were diverse. Southern European countries tended to remain fiscally conservative while embracing protectionism and stronger bilateral relations with Germany. In fascist Italy, the government moved slowly towards a controlled economy. An orthodox policy of tight money was accompanied by tariff measures to protect those domestic industries that stood to lose the most from an overvalued currency. In Greece, macroeconomic policy was more expansionary. In addition to providing early support to tobacco and wheat producers, the government moved away from the gold standard in 1932, the first country in the Balkans to do so, and adopted exchange controls the following year. With the advent of protection and other forms of government support for import-substituting activities, the Greek industrial sector registered during the 1930s one of the highest rates of expansion anywhere in Europe.

Şevket Pamuk (Chapter 12) examines the economic policies and the performance of the Turkish economy during the 1930s from this comparative perspective. The Great Depression was sharply felt, especially in the foreign-trade-oriented regions of the country. In response the government, controlled by an urban-based bureaucracy, pursued strongly interventionist policies. Protectionist measures of the early years were followed in 1932 by the adoption of etatism or import-substituting industrialization led by the state.

Government intervention was not designed, in the Keynesian sense, to increase aggregate demand through the use of devaluations and expansionary fiscal and monetary policies. Instead, it was designed to create a more autarkic economy with more central control through the expansion of the public sector. Nonetheless, supported by the strong performance of the agricultural sector, the recovery from the Depression decade was stronger in Turkey than in most countries around the eastern Mediterranean. The legacy of the 1930s profoundly influenced attitudes toward international trade in Turkey. The economic model created during the Great Depression was retained, for the most part, until the end of the 1970s.

In contrast with the aggressive interventionist polices pursued in Greece and Turkey, the colonial administrations in Syria, Lebanon and Palestine did relatively little in response to the Depression; nor did the countries of the Maghrib: Morocco, Algeria and Tunisia. Egypt also rejected interventionist policies during the interwar period: it was governed by a liberal economic ideology that fostered the growth of free markets and narrowed the role of the state to building the legal institutions and physical infrastructure; it was also a policy favoured by cotton textile interests in Britain and land-owners in Egypt.

Tarik M. Yousef (Chapter 13) argues that while a great deal has been written about the failure of Egypt's liberal policies to foster industrialization, structural transformation and growth, little has been written about its success in creating an integrated national economy. He focuses on the question of market integration and its implications on efficiency and competitiveness in local trade. Specifically, Yousef examines the operation of markets in Egypt by investigating the law of one price during the interwar period. The various measures for market integration he calculates for interwar Egypt compare very favorably with those obtained for the United States for more recent years. The fact that a very large part of the population lived in the Nile Delta and along the narrow Nile Valley undoubtedly contributed to this pattern. However, Yousef also finds that government policies and the revolution in transportation and communications contributed to the creation of a nationally integrated economy with a high degree of efficiency and competitiveness. He concludes that previous notions of segmented markets in Egypt must be revised in the light of this strong evidence to the contrary, and further, he offers a critique of the perceived failure of economic liberalism in the interwar period.

A paper by Jacob Metzer (Chapter 14) concludes the volume. The author examines the economic performance and trade patterns of Mandatory Palestine from a Mediterranean-wide perspective. Income per capita grew faster than anywhere else in the Mediterranean during the years between 1922 and 1947. He also points out that the direction and intensity of swings in economic activity, and the volume and patterns of external trade, set Palestine apart from the rest of the Mediterranean during the 1930s. Exports and imports, and their ratios to GDP, rose from the 1920s to the 1930s. The growing volume of merchandise exports was due primarily to the massive expansion of citrus crops, which accounted for more than three-quarters of the country's exports during the 1930s. In the second half of the 1930s, Palestine surpassed Italy and became, after Spain, the second-largest citrus exporter in the world. For its part, the Mandatory Palestine government did not pursue an active macro or trade policy and allowed a mostly uninterrupted movement of goods and capital in and out of the country.

What distinguished Palestine from the other countries of the Mediterranean, and contributed to its atypical record, was the massive inflows of people and capital, most of them Jewish. The distinction is especially notable during these three decades when the world economy collapsed and economic autarky ruled the day.

What is the agenda for the future? Each of the papers in this volume has tried to embed its own agenda in its text, but this introduction offers a slightly broader vision.

To those who feel that the regions of the Mediterranean are poorly documented, thus making serious empirical economic history impossible, this volume should serve as a bracing antidote. The comparative assessment of long-run growth performance is quite possible, as the papers by Akarli, Foreman-Peck and Lains, Reis and Williamson clearly illustrate. These comparisons are not only possible within the Mediterranean, but also between the Mediterranean and the Atlantic economies. It is even possible to make very detailed microscopic assessments of sectoral productivity and choice of technique, as the study by Rosés on cotton textiles shows. Furthermore, the data are available to make comparative assessments on which regions adjusted in which ways to the globalization shocks which occurred in the world economy between 1850 and 1914. The papers by Ramon-Muñoz, and by Morilla Critz, Olmstead and Rhode, both document this performance in detail for traditional Mediterranean exports like olive oil, fruits and nuts, while the paper by Harlaftis and Kardasis documents the performance of the Mediterranean maritime fleet carrying this trade, and the freight rates charged. Not everybody played the globalization game with enthusiasm prior to 1914: Federico and O'Rourke find enough evidence to apply a computable general equilibrium model to debates over late nineteenth-century Italian tariff policy; and Sánchez-Alonso finds enough macro time series information to unravel econometrically the puzzle of low emigration rates in Spain but high emigration rates in Italy, and exchange-rate-policy matters. There was a variety of policy responses to the Great Depression around the Mediterranean: to illustrate, Pamuk offers an empirical assessment of Turkish active intervention while Yousef offers one for Egyptian passive liberalism. Even Mandatory Palestine's unusual economic experience with wide-open global commitment during the 1920s, 1930s and 1940s is well documented by Metzer.

This volume illustrates what is possible. We hope it encourages scholars to fill more of the Mediterranean knowledge gap about its long-run economic change prior to 1950, and to do it as soon as possible. Economic history needs to inform policy debate in the Mediterranean as it enters the twenty-first century, and understanding how it has responded to globalization challenges is a perfect place to start.

Part 2

Long-run growth

A comparative assessment

2   How poor was the European periphery before 1850?

The Mediterranean vs Scandinavia

Jaime Reis

Introduction

Among the countries that form the subject matter of the modern literature on historical convergence and long-run economic growth, one group has received particular attention. No precise, generally accepted definition of the periphery exists. However, as one of the two basic terms in the classical comparison between that part of Europe which embarked early in the nineteenth century on the Kuznetsian process of modern economic growth and that part which only caught up much later with these "leaders", its indispensability hardly needs stressing. By consensus, several ingredients help us to identify the economies that belong to it and even endow the concept with some explanatory power as regards their long-run performance. To begin with, these are countries which developed comparatively late, which had a strong agrarian base for a long time, and whose industrial activity only became significant towards the end of the nineteenth century or even later (Pollard 1981; Cameron 1985). On the whole, they were weakly urbanized and they specialized in the export of primary products to the markets of the "core", of which there was usually a single, dominant one (Federico 1988; Arrighi 1985). Indeed, some authors have argued that they were incapable of growing in a sustained fashion without demand impulses such as those which came via foreign trade from the rich countries at the centre (Berend and Ranki 1981). Geographically, they lay on the rim of Europe relative to the core of more advanced, richer and mostly larger countries, such as Britain, France, Belgium and Germany. The most important of their common characteristics, however, was their relative poverty prior to being swept along by the process of long-run growth which set in at some time during the second half of the nineteenth century. Prados and his collaborators (1993) have gone so far as to quantify a threshold for membership of this group in terms of real income per capita, but most other authors have been content to refer to them with a sentence such as "the poor countries round the European periphery" (Williamson 1996a).[1]

One of the interesting features of these economies, when viewed as a group, is the divergence in the rapidity with which they grew and drew nearer to Britain up to 1914. The available evidence shows that while a full sample of European economies clearly converged over this period, the group that consisted only of the countries of the periphery did not (Prados *et al.* 1993). Thus, from being "poor" during the early 1800s, Denmark, Sweden, Norway and, to a lesser extent, Finland had by 1913 reached levels of GDP per capita which placed them in a category with advanced "catchers-up" such as Germany, France and Belgium. In the European growth sweep-stakes, they were the countries that grew at rates above the norm and justified the view that this was a period that fostered convergence between the core and the periphery. In the meantime, Spain, Greece, Portugal and possibly Italy, which were poor in the 1850s, continued to be so comparatively speaking six or seven decades later. The trend line of their per capita incomes relative to Britain evolved over time in the opposite direction to those of their northern counterparts (Tortella 1994a).

Why such a divergence should have materialized over the long run contrary to the prediction of the Solovian model, in spite of the common low-income starting point, is something which has quite properly deserved some research (O'Rourke and Williamson 1997). A satisfactory explanation still seems to be lacking, however, for the number of outliers that emerge in this analysis, even after the introduction of various kinds of conditionality into the convergence model. Several circumstances may be responsible for this. One of them is the obvious difficulty in quantifying adequately some of the factors used as control variables, e.g. natural resources, social capability or institutions. To this may be added the lack of satisfactory data for other ones, e.g. human capital and savings rates. A second difficulty lies in the possible endogeneity of these influences, which renders the model immensely more complex to understand and specify. A third one is introduced by the recent "convergence club" literature, according to which, rather than a single equilibrium solution to the convergence problem, there could be several, with some countries being caught in "development traps" and others not (Amable 1993; Ben-David 1995; Quah 1997). Membership of such clubs would depend on countries exceeding or not the minimum threshold value for certain conditional factors, such as human capital or financial development, to have their expected impact on long-run converging growth. Given that these conditions might also have to be cumulative in order to be effective, a number of outcomes would be possible, even for countries with similar starting levels of real income per capita (Berthelemy and Varoudakis 1996). The result, as was noted already some years ago by DeLong (1988), is that when countries are ordered by their starting per capita income, convergence over the long run can occur between members of a club but does not necessarily happen between those of different clubs.

Although clearly of great potential for solving the above-noted problem of outliers, this approach faces two difficulties, however. One is that the helpfulness of the notion of "convergence clubs" depends very much on the development of an explanation about how and when individual economies progress from one club to another, an area which to date seems to have been little explored (Baumol *et al.* 1994). The second is that at present we still do not possess sufficient knowledge regarding early nineteenth-century income levels in the periphery to be able to start defining these clubs and therefore to make much use of the concept. The comparative study of these income levels and of their various implications for the analysis of long-term growth in Europe constitutes the theme of this chapter.

In the following section we discuss briefly what is currently known about the real income per capita of peripheral countries during the decades prior to the onset of modern economic growth, i.e. around 1850. Having identified the difficulties raised by these data and their associated methodologies, we go on to consider other ways of arriving at least at a ranking of and, better still, also at an order of magnitudes for this variable. Rather than the usual exercises in retropolation, which start from generally accepted levels at some point in the twentieth century, we try instead to arrive at a set of benchmark estimates for several indirect measures of real income per capita. In this way, it is hoped that coming at the problem from different angles can attenuate the shortcomings of each individual indicator. In this spirit, the third section discusses the use of "representative wages" and suggests reasons why, for this period, they may involve distortions. The fourth section presents data based on agricultural activity that contrasts with the picture offered by currently available quantification of GDP across the range of early nineteenth-century peripheral economies. This and the wage-based estimation are then put to the test of other indirect indicators of real income, such as are provided by research on consumption and demography. The fifth section proposes a new ranking of income per capita for the periphery and discusses its implications for long-term economic growth in the region. The origins in time of the differences found among countries constitute the concluding part of the chapter.

Estimating real income per capita

Notwithstanding its importance, the estimation of real income per capita in the periphery for the years before 1850 has been beset by contradictions, ambiguity and deficient data. For a long while, it was accepted with little discussion that the periphery consisted of more or less uniformly poor countries. That the southern rim of Europe belonged in this category was never in doubt, but it also came to be assumed that, prior to their strong post-1850 performance, the Scandinavian economies were equally so. This was particularly the case after Lars Sandberg's famous 1979 paper on Sweden as an "impoverished sophisticate", which stressed the country's pre-take-off poverty. Sandberg was hardly precise about what he meant by this, but the idea gained currency and was extended to the other countries in the region, it being plausibly supposed that they would be on roughly the same level.[2]

The possibility of this being wrong subsequently received some support from different quarters. It has been shown that Swedish economic growth after the middle of the century was slower and that the starting point at mid-century had therefore to be higher than used to be supposed (Krantz 1988), a fact which also implied a widening of the assumed distance relative to Mediterranean Europe. The fact that the contribution of human capital to the process of convergence may have been small in this region (O'Rourke and Williamson 1997) has further weakened Sandberg's claim regarding the contrast between Sweden's poverty and its sophistication around 1850. This in turn raised the possibility that Sweden may have enjoyed other growth-inducing advantages connected to a relatively high initial income, in other words that it may after all have belonged to a rich-country "convergence club".

The available macroeconomic data is not a great deal of help in clarifying matters. As can be seen in Table 2.1, Bairoch's (1976a), Prados' (Prados 1998) and Maddison's (1995) figures not only show quite different rankings but also fail to coincide as to whether there was a "rich" periphery and a "poor" one. Prados' two poorest countries in the south (Greece and Portugal) do quite well in Bairoch's league table while Denmark, a star performer according to Maddison and Prados, comes out in fifth position in Bairoch's estimates. In column 1, Germany and France appear on a par with a group consisting of Italy, Spain and Norway, with Denmark, Sweden, Finland and Greece getting left behind by a differential of 25 per cent or more. On the other hand, in columns 2 and 3, Denmark appears as the only peripheral country that can vie with Germany and France, while all the others are relegated to more or less distant positions towards the tail of the list. Broad regional areas are blurred. Averages for the southern and northern peripheries are quite close in every case but the two groups lack internal homogeneity, with the lag between "leaders" and "laggards" varying between 1.5:1 and nearly 2:1. In terms of income per capita, it would be more logical to group Denmark and Sweden with Italy and perhaps Spain, on the one hand, and, on the other, Norway and Finland with Greece and Portugal. Under the circumstances one might wonder whether it is at all meaningful to speak either of a single periphery or even of two regional ones.

The GDP data set for Europe before 1850 is not only troubled by contradictions such as these. Some doubts must also be raised regarding the reliability of its contents, owing to the methods employed to put it together, and therefore regarding also whether we can use these figures for the comparisons we wish to establish. Bairoch's estimates have not been revised since their publication in 1976, in spite of a great deal of work in this field having been done in the meantime. Their greatest weakness lies, however, in the obscurity of some of the sources employed and in the unjustified arbitrariness of the assumptions behind their utilization (Bairoch 1976a).[3] In the case of both Maddison and Prados, question marks hang over a number of the individual country series used in both collections. In the cases of Denmark and Portugal, the methodology employed is open to criticism on account of strong possible biases, whereas the Norwegian levels of GDP prior

Table 2.1 Estimates of 19th century real income per capita

	1850[1]	*1860*[2]	*1870*[3]
Core			
Britain	458	952	3263
Germany	308	603	1913
France	333	791	1858
mean	366	782	2344
Scandinavia			
Denmark	256	685	1927
Sweden	211	566	1664
Norway	350	n/a	1303
Finland	227	381	1107
mean	261	544	1500
Mediterranean Europe			
Portugal	260	493	1085
Spain	313	568	1376
Italy	277	585	1467
Greece	215	440	n/a
mean	266	522	1309
Mean of the periphery	263	524	1404

Sources:
1 Bairoch (1976) in 1960 US dollars.
2 Prados (1998) current PPP (USA = 1 000).
3 Maddison (1995) 1990 International dollars.

Note: Averages are unweighted.

to 1865 are also less trustworthy because they are derived using the Swedish GDP figures. The lack of adequate agricultural statistics for much of the nineteenth century remains a problem for both Greece and Spain, which has been solved by extrapolating output figures from consumption estimates, an unavoidable but not altogether reliable procedure. Lastly, in the case of Maddison's figures, it may be questioned whether these can serve for a period as remote as the one we are considering, given that they are the result of a retropolation of GDP carried out over 150 years on the basis of an unchanging 1990 set of purchasing power parity converters. In the absence of suitable intermediate benchmarks, this defect could induce large distortions (Szirmai *et al.* 1993; Williamson 1995).[4]

In view of these deficiencies, we try in the next two sections to find alternative evidence from independent sources that may constitute acceptable proxies for national per capita income levels. The countries which constitute our periphery are those presented already in Table 2.1: to the north, Denmark, Sweden, Norway and Finland, and to the south, Portugal, Spain,

Greece and some pre-Unification Italian states.[5] The decades we focus on are the 1820s, 1830s and 1840s, a period which, in comparison with the turmoil and dislocation of the late eighteenth and early nineteenth centuries, can be considered reasonably stable in most economic and political respects. It should be stressed that the approach we propose is hardly revolutionary; it was used by Bairoch (1977 and 1979) twenty years ago. What is new here is the data we have gathered for the countries in the sample and the effort to use them more systematically. In what follows, we shall consider five different indicators: wages, the output of agriculture, the consumption of certain income-sensitive articles, the statures of males and infant mortality.

Real wages

Wage rates for specific occupations and under certain conditions have been used for quite some time as a tool for measuring both historical levels and the long-term evolution of global economic activity per capita in Europe (Bairoch 1977). Several recent studies provide evidence of the endurance of this approach. Williamson (1995) has used it to confront convergence in the Atlantic economy, O'Rourke and Williamson (1977) have employed it to rank countries according to their respective real GDP per capita during the nineteenth century, and Allen (1998b) has adopted real urban wages as a proxy for real per capita income for a variety of countries over several centuries. In the related field of agriculture, both Buyst *et al.* (1995), in the case of early nineteenth-century Holland, and Clark (1987b), for a broader sweep of pre-industrial economies, have claimed a close relation between wages and labour productivity over long periods. Although criticized on various counts and indeed open to valid objections (O'Brien and Keyder 1978; Scholliers 1989), wages are indeed a suggestive source of information in the absence of better alternatives and therefore deserve to be tried out in the present context.

Table 2.2 presents data on wages for a variety of daily tasks over the period 1820–60 for all the countries of our sample except for Greece. They cover skilled and unskilled work carried out both in agricultural and in urban settings and were paid in cash, exclusive of any accessory remuneration in kind. Although several authors have stressed that the urban unskilled rate is the most representative of all wages, it was deemed preferable to consider here also the rural unskilled, since we are dealing with economies that were still essentially agrarian. The argument adduced for one of these countries during this period seems applicable to all of them: agricultural wages are probably a good indicator of the general wage level in different parts of Sweden since a large majority of the wage earners were engaged in agriculture. The agricultural sector also supplied the expanding sectors with labour and it is therefore reasonable to assume that agricultural wages were used as norms of comparison for other groups of workers, particularly unskilled labour (Jørberg and Bengtsson 1981). Although for the most part they

Table 2.2 Wage levels in the periphery, 1820s–1850s (grams of silver per day)

	Denmark	Sweden	Norway	Finland	Portugal	Spain	S. Italy
(1) Agriculture							
Unskilled							
1820	—	—	—		5.4–6.5	5.5	—
1820s		4.3	—	4.4	5.4–6.5	3.7–4.4	4.7
1830		4.2	—	—		4.2	
1830s	2.6	4.1–4.6	—	4.5	5.4–5.9	5.5–5.9	4.8–5.7
1840	4.8	4.7	—	—	5.1	4.2–5.3	—
1840s	4.0	4.1–5.7	—	4.7	4.9	5.9–6.7	4.4
1850	5.1–6.2	4.8	6.0–7.9	—	3.1	4.2–5.5	—
1850s	4.2–5.1	5.9	7.4–7.9	4.7–6.3	4.0	—	4.6
(2) Urban (capital city)							
Unskilled							
1820s	—	3.9	—	6.2–8.1	7.3	—	—
1830s	5.8	4.2	—	6.2–8.1	7.3	—	—
1840s	6.3–7.4	4.8	—	6.5–8.1	7.3	—	—
1850	6.3–7.4	6.0	6.0–7.9	6.0–7.0	7.8	—	—
Construction							
Journeymen							
1820s	—	—	—	—	10.3–13.6	17.7	9.1–10.7
1830s	11.6	—	—	—	10.3–13.6	15.3–17.7	9.8–10.7
1840s	11.6–12.6	—	—	—	11.9–16.2	15.3–17.7	9.8–10.5
1850s	14.4	—	—	—	13.0	16.6	10.5–10.7
Carpenters							
1820s	—	—	—	5.6–6.3	—	—	—
1830s	—	—	—	5.6–6.3	11.9–14.1	16.6	—
1840s	—	—	—	6.3	11.9–14.1	15.4–16.5	—
1850	12.3	—	—	7.1	13.6	16.6	—
1850s	12.6	—	—	11.5	—	16.6	—

Sources:
Denmark: Pedersen (1930); Christensen (1985); Boel (1985); Christensen (1992); Falbe-Hansen (1889).
Sweden: Hoppe and Langton (1994); Jørberg (1972); Bengtsson (1987); Soderberg (1987).
Norway: Scholliers and Zamagni (1994); Historisk Statistik: 1968 (1969); Minde and Ramstad (1986).
Finland: Suomen taloushistoria (1980–3).
Portugal: Coelho (1859); Reis (1982); Godinho (1955); Justino (1990); Documentos da Casa Real, ANTT; Martins (1997).
Spain: Sanz (1979–1980); Sanz and Garrabou (1985); Garrabou *et al.* (1991); Ruiz (1979); Flores (1986); Reher and Ballesteros (1993); Bringas (1998).
Italy: Storchi (1981); Rollo (1965); Palumbo (1979); Carani-Donvito (1933).

Note:
S. Italy comprises Tuscany, the Pontifical States and the Two Sicilies. Urban wages are for Florence and Rome.

cannot be claimed to be "national" in any sense, it is important to note that where data existed for various regions, large inter-regional differences on the whole were not apparent. The urban wages collected refer always to the capital city, where at this time a large fraction of the non-rural population was concentrated, and the rural ones are drawn from various parts of each country.[6] In the case of Sweden the coverage is wholly national and in that of Spain it is partially so.

The original figures were obtained at current values and in order to make them comparable they were converted into a common standard of measure, in this case their equivalent value in grams of pure monetary silver. This was determined in accordance with the legal metallic content in each country at the time the wage was paid (Bauer 1882). It has been argued that in such situations purchasing power parities should be used instead, but the difficulty in securing a suitably comprehensive price set and in determining a basket of goods that is appropriate for the exercise renders this procedure less advisable. Indeed, given the large differences in the pattern of food consumption (something like three-quarters of total consumption) between northern and southern Europe at the time, any effort at establishing a common basket of goods is likely to engender pronounced distortions.[7] It is not clear therefore that the result would be superior – even if it were different – to that of an approach, such as ours, based on official exchange rates. Another alternative, employed by Bairoch, to convert current values by expressing them in the number of kilos of bread they could purchase, seems also unsatisfactory. The problem here is the considerable difference in prices of the main cereals in the diet of different parts of Europe – rye in Scandinavia, wheat in Spain and southern Italy, maize to a large extent in Portugal. On the other hand, it should be noted that using an exchange-based conversion method for this period is perhaps less distortive than it would become later.[8] All the countries contemplated were on a metallic standard. Both their exchange rates and their domestic price levels exhibited little volatility during the 1830s to 1860s, capital movements were small and unlikely to affect the situation either, and governments as a rule did not interfere in monetary conditions.

Although the evidence is patchy, the picture that emerges from Table 2.2 for the second quarter of the nineteenth century is fairly clear. Whether one takes the more frequently used unskilled urban wage rate, the rural unskilled or the skilled urban rates, it is hard to say that, by this measure, there was a clear difference between the southern and the northern peripheries.[9] The first of those rates was generally of an order of 4–6 grams of silver, the second was slightly lower, whereas skilled workers in the building trades generally earned at least 10 grams a day, more in Iberia than in Scandinavia and southern Italy. Unskilled work was paid slightly more in the city than in the countryside and over time there appears to have been no evolution in this differential. Both aspects reveal a contrast with what was happening in contemporary advanced economies such as Britain and Belgium, where wages for the same tasks were a good deal higher and the skill differential was not as pronounced (Uselding 1975). The conclusion one is tempted to draw from these data is that in the period prior to the onset of rapid and sustained growth in the periphery, there were no appreciable differences in terms of levels of GDP per capita between its main components. This contradicts what we are led to believe by Table 2.1 and before we take this jump it is worth considering, therefore, whether the assumptions which underlie a fairly close connection between wage and GDP per capita levels are warranted in this particular historical context.

The first question that arises has to do with how well labour markets functioned and whether the wage rate reflected the marginal productivity of labour. After all, these were economies in which transport costs were high and factor mobility was low, and a reasonable doubt may be raised as to whether labour markets were integrated. Moreover, a large segment of the population consisted of smallholders or peasant cultivators who participated in them occasionally or not at all. If they did, this would allow us the supposition that the wage rate would reasonably mirror their self-imputed remuneration on their own farms; if they did not, the representativeness issue could be serious. It is difficult to be categorical about this but there are indications, however, that landless day labour was commonly employed by smallholders in Denmark, Tuscany and other parts of the periphery (Schousboe 1983; Pazzagli 1973). This suggests both that an implicit wage existed for the work of the farmers themselves and that it would not diverge substantially from that earned by hired workers.[10] At the same time, there are positive signs regarding wage flexibility. Prior to the 1820s, during times of monetary turbulence and, particularly, of inflation, nominal wages were very variable in all of these economies and closely tracked the rise and fall of prices (Feliu 1991; Romano 1976). Once stability returned, this high nominal wage variance ceased but, on the other hand, in many places a high degree of seasonal fluctuation continued, not only in the countryside but also in the city, something which related quite clearly to the number of hours in the working day. In Norway, where the working day in summer was 20 per cent longer than in winter, the wage differential between the two seasons was of the order of 50 per cent in the 1850s (Historisk Statistik: 1968, 1969). Finally, the low urban/rural differential for unskilled labour, which was present everywhere, may be taken to indicate a good degree of communication between these two markets and therefore encourage the notion of quite a high degree of integration between them.[11]

Even if we accept the "representative wage" as an adequate proxy for the annual per capita earnings of labour, this still does not warrant that it should be a good proxy for income per capita itself. This depends on a further assumption, namely that factor shares across the sample of countries are roughly the same too, otherwise distortions and loss of comparability will arise when we "gross up" from labour earnings to the earnings of all factors of production. Evidence on factor shares at this time is unavailable and the earliest data available comes from the estimates by Taylor and Williamson

(1997), admittedly for the early twentieth century. They provide some support for this assumption. For Denmark, Portugal and Spain, labour's proportion was 0.5, but Norway's deviates markedly from this standard since it was 0.645. Clearly, more information is needed on this score.

The existence of pronounced differences of income distribution between the economies we are studying would also upset the assumption we are trying to test here. There are some grounds for plausibly accepting that these may not have been very pronounced, but there is contradictory evidence in this case too. As van Zanden's (1995) recent work on the Kuznets curve has shown, prior to the industrial era, two of the main factors affecting income distribution were the degree of urbanization and the extent of the development of commercial capitalism in these societies. The greater either or both of these indicators, the more the distribution might be expected to be skewed in favour of capital. The countries we are considering were alike enough in terms of their ratios of urban to total population in the first decades of the nineteenth century – something of the order of 10–20 per cent – to warrant the expectation that large differences would not have arisen from this quarter (Lawton and Lee 1989; Hohenberg and Lees 1985). As for the relative extent of commercial capitalism, all we can say for the moment is that the low export ratios generally present in these economies would seem to indicate that its advance was still quite limited in the cases considered. In contrast with this, however, what is known about wealth distribution in Scandinavia around 1800 suggests that at least in this respect – and probably therefore in that of income distribution as well – considerable variation existed among them. The Gini coefficient calculated for this purpose by Soltow (1985) comes to 0.59 for Finland, 0.73 for Sweden and 0.85 for Denmark.

Even if the two preceding assumptions were nevertheless ratified, a third one still remains to be satisfied, if we are to accept wages as a reliable indicator for the level of income per capita. The question here is whether there was much divergence, over the course of the year, in the degree of employment of the labour force earning the daily "representative wage". Given the overwhelming importance of agricultural employment in these societies – it is estimated, at mid-century, in Norway, at 75–80 per cent, in Sweden at 76 per cent, in Italy at 70–74 per cent and in Spain, in 1877, at more than two-thirds of the labour force (Bairoch 1989a) – it is on this sector that we must focus our attention. The issue then becomes whether the average number of days worked per year by the members of the respective agricultural labour forces of these countries were likely to be comparable. To a large degree, this would depend on the structure of agricultural output and on the seasonality of the labour requirement of each product. Agricultural unemployment was a widespread feature of nineteenth-century Europe and, typically, in an official enquiry carried out in Spain in 1850, the extent of begging and/or lack of occupation in rural areas was strongly linked to the seasonality of the crops prevailing in each region (Ruiz 1979). The obvious distinction to be made in this connection is between vegetable production, with its peaks of labour

Table 2.3 Composition of agricultural production, *c*.1850 (per cent)

	Denmark	Sweden	Norway	Finland	Portugal	Spain	Greece
Animal production	46	47	51	54	35	26	29
Vegetable production	54	53	49	46	65	74	71
	100	100	100	100	100	100	100

Source: Table 2.Al.

Notes:
Animal production comprises milk, meat, butter and cheese. Eggs are excluded for lack of consistent information.
Vegetable production comprises grain, wine, olive oil, pulses, potatoes, rice, fruit (where available) and industrial plants.

requirement at harvest and sowing time, and animal production, with its fairly constant demand for labour throughout the year.

Table 2.3 reveals just how diverse the situation was in the periphery from this point of view around 1850. The Scandinavian economies show a near-perfect balance between vegetable and animal production, whereas on the Mediterranean rim animal production was 2.5 to 3 times less than vegetable production. The implications in terms of rural unemployment are obvious: simply taking wages as a measure of per capita income could be hazardous when comparing the northern and the southern peripheries. It is far from evident therefore that we can conclude from Table 2.2, without further corroboration, that much homogeneity existed between these two blocs of economies, as the data there seems to suggest. The following section examines four other indicators that might help in clearing up this uncertainty.

Agricultural activity and other indicators

The first possibility to be considered is the estimation of agricultural output at current prices for each one of our eight countries. Being a sector that accounts for an important share of national product and an even larger proportion of the labour force, this should serve as a useful starting point for the quantification of GDP at this time. Contemporary statistics of physical output in this sector are hard to come by and are not wholly reliable. The ones we have used are mostly official in origin but appear to be confirmed by other sources and can be regarded as roughly correct in terms of orders of magnitude. They do not include forestry and fishing, which are far harder to determine with reasonable accuracy. Physical product is valued at market prices, usually of the capital city, and they can be deemed quite reliable. Since farm-gate prices are not used, we may consider that our estimate also includes a significant share of the income and employment from trade and transport.

Table 2.4 Agricultural output and GDP/capita, *c.*1850

	1 Total agricultural output (local currency)	2 Total agricultural output (million grams of silver)	3 Agricultural output/capita (grams of silver)	4 Agriculture/ GDP (%)	5 GDP/cap. (grams of silver)
Denmark	126.9	761.6	586	39	1503
Sweden	257.7	1545.9	468	31	1510
Norway	99.5	598.9	461	43	1072
Finland	132.8	597.7	398	37	1076
Portugal	50	1356.7	399	41	973
Spain	1634.2	6863.8	437	41	1066
S. Italy	1376	5744.8	402	46	874
Greece	91.9	383.7	354	46	770

Sources:
For columns 1–3, see Table 2.A1.
For column 4: Hansen (1984); Krantz (1997); Hodne and Grytten (1994); Hjerppe (1989); Prados (1993b); Zamagni (1993); Kostelenos (1995). As there are no data for Portugal, the same ratio was used as for Spain.

Notes:
Column 1 is expressed in millions of units of the local currency, i.e. kroner for Denmark, Sweden and Norway; marks for Finland; mil réis for Portugal; pesetas for Spain; lire for Italy; and drachma for Greece. The Swedish share of agriculture is from Krantz (1997) after deduction of forestry and fisheries according to the proportions in Schön (1995). The Italian share is for the entire country; that for Greece is an overestimate because several non-agricultural subsectors were left out of the GDP estimation that underpins it. The Norwegian share, from Hodne and Grytten (1994), has been corrected to take account of the housing sector, which is absent from their calculation. The Swedish proportion for this, of 13.9 per cent of GDP, was used.

In order to make the country results comparable, we have converted them into monetary silver equivalents, as was done above with wages.

The values for agricultural production around the middle of the last century, both in local currency and in grams of silver, are presented in Table 2.4, in the aggregate and also per capita of population (columns 1–3).[12] Owing to problems with the availability of the raw data, the estimates in Table 2.4 do not refer exactly to the year 1850. They are treated as comparable here on the assumption that the period is too short for any major productivity changes to have occurred. The immediate impression is of a not too surprising dichotomy in per capita terms between Scandinavian and Mediterranean Europe, with differentials which run from the hardly discernible 5 per cent between Norway and Spain to the quite large, i.e. 65 per cent in the case of the Denmark–Greece pair.[13] Each of these groups is in itself quite homogeneous, though Denmark's leadership by a difference of

20 per cent over Sweden must be noted. The only true outlier, from a geographic point of view, is Finland, which by this measure really belongs in the southern group even if physically and in other ways it is far removed from it. A second point worth making is that the clear hierarchy that emerges from these figures – Denmark followed by Sweden and Norway, then Finland and the southern economies, with Greece last – contrasts with the far more level picture that can be drawn on the basis of wage levels alone, as in Table 2.2.

Agricultural output per capita by itself could be a reliable indicator for international comparisons of GDP per capita only in the event that the share of agriculture in the total output of goods and services was the same throughout the sample. In this particular case, although the ratio between these two magnitudes is universally large, it is far from being the same for every economy, its range of variation going from 31 per cent (Sweden) to 50 per cent (Norway) (column 4). But, on the assumption that they are reasonably accurate, once we have these ratios we can use to them to "gross up" from agricultural production directly to total production at current prices. The results of this exercise are displayed in column 5 of Table 2.4 and provide us with the best available alternative estimate of GDP to the wage-level approach that has been mostly in use thus far.[14]

The overall picture this gives us now of the GDP per capita of the periphery at mid-century hardly resembles that suggested by the wage data of Table 2.2. On the contrary, it exhibits much more the hierarchical structure presented in Table 2.1 and derived from the work by Prados (1998) and Maddison (1995), although the order within this structure is hardly the same. Denmark and Sweden are decisively ahead, with little to distinguish between them, and are followed by a fairly homogeneous group consisting of the Mediterranean economies and the two remaining Scandinavian ones. The gap between leaders and laggards is quite large and variable – between 40 and 95 per cent – but does not split along geographic lines as might have been expected. A group consisting of Finland, Norway and Spain emerges as the better-off of the poor-economy contingent while Portugal, southern Italy and Greece constitute the tail of the ranking. Greece appears so far behind as to constitute almost a category on its own, but it is well to note that this may be an illusion, given that in this case our estimate for GDP per capita is almost certainly an undervaluation.[15]

Since these findings are based on somewhat shaky statistical foundations and on assumptions that may not be entirely solid, it is important to seek confirmation for them in other data, preferably using independent sources of information. The first such effort relies on import data and is inspired by the considerable literature on the standard-of-living debate as it refers to early European industrialization. In particular, it draws on Mokyr's (1988) attempt to construct an indicator of the standard of living in England from the consumption of certain exotic luxury goods. Our approach likewise consists in examining the consumption pattern of a number of articles of food

Table 2.5 Consumption of luxury goods, 1840s (kilos/cap/year)

	Denmark	Sweden	Norway	Finland	Portugal	Spain	Sicily	Naples
Meat	53	40	37	35	29	29	n/a	n/a
Tea	0.9	0	0	0	0.03	0	0	n/a
Coffee	2.3	1.0	0.9	1.0	0.3	0.06	0.5	0.07
Sugar	5.4	2.5	1.1	1.0	2.9	1.6	1.2	0.4
Chocolate	0.03	0	0	0	0.04	0.35	0.3	0.01
Tobacco	1.2	0.5	0.5	0.8	0.2	0.2	0.1	n/a

Sources:
Table 2.4.
British Sessional Papers. House of Commons, Consular Reports.
Cohn (1957–8).
Statistik Tabelvaerk (1845).
Historisk Statistik för Sverige (1959).
Alvarez (1993).
Prados (1988).
Justino (1988).
Lains (1990).
Suomen Taloushistoria (1983).

which are commonly held to have had a high sensitivity to the level of real income in the countries of this study. It is based on the assumption that, during the nineteenth century, even across so wide a geographic area as Europe, consumer preferences in many respects would have been essentially the same, particularly when it came to what were then understood to be luxury articles. The advantage of this approach is that food in general took up a very considerable part of personal consumption and that the articles in question are easy to measure since they were imported and taxed.[16]

The articles referred to in Table 2.5 were consumed in small amounts, were highly priced and had a high income-elasticity of demand.[17] Some of them, such as coffee, tea, sugar or chocolate, were acquired mostly by a fairly high stratum of society and were unavailable to the mass of the population (Essemyr 1989; Justino 1988). In considering the consumption of luxuries, one has to be careful to avoid an excessively strict comparison among countries, given that national cultural inclinations come into play here and that natural conditions very much affect what is considered a "luxury" and what is simply ordinary fare. Thus, wine is not included in our list of goods, since it is a commonplace in the south and expensive in the north; and likewise milk and butter, which had the status of dietary staples in Scandinavia and were much sought after in the Mediterranean region. Meat was widely consumed but in varying quantities and was recognized at the time as a realistic indicator of the standard of real income. Tea, coffee and chocolate are interchangeable as hot, exotic beverages, with the Spanish having a clear preference for chocolate, in contrast to the other four countries where tea and/or coffee were preferred. Lack of data prevents us from taking relative prices into account, although on the scant evidence available, this would seem not to have been all that important, at least judging by what happened with sugar in the cases of Denmark and Portugal. These two countries are interesting because they were at opposite ends of the consumption spectrum and because the ratio of sugar prices to those of a basket of cereals in either was very similar. Relative prices therefore do not explain why the Danes should have consumed twice as much of this article as the Portuguese, which leaves income as the principal reason.

In its general lines, Table 2.5 displays interesting parallels with our earlier GDP per capita figures, although the match is not perfect. In each category, it provides broad confirmation of the ranking established by Table 2.4, notwithstanding the existence of some outliers whose position may be attributable to particular relative price situations or to certain countries' specificities as regards their food history. It should also be noted that import data for the 1830s and 1840s are hard to come by and in several cases we have had to resort to British sources, which may be less than accurate. Meat consumption was high in Denmark and Sweden and low in the Mediterranean countries, in accordance with their respective incomes, with Norway and Finland rising above the level of the other similarly "poor" countries probably because their meat was rather cheap compared to cereals.[18] Exotic hot beverages – tea, coffee, cocoa – and their sweetener – sugar – were in strong demand in Denmark but Sweden presents a situation that is hard to explain. Generally, the southern countries' standards were much lower, as one would expect, though there were exceptions. One was Portugal's high sugar consumption that may be ascribed to habits developed when it had extensive colonial production of sugar. For similar reasons, cocoa was only drunk in significant amounts in Spain, and also in Sicily, an area of earlier Spanish occupation, but to the detriment of coffee and with a corresponding weak use of sugar. In the absence of appropriate price data, the fact that in this respect Norway and Finland appear above the income per capita norm is surprising but may simply be due to climatic circumstances which encouraged the consumption of hot drinks in the north, in contrast to southern Europe, where wine fulfilled this role. Finally, tobacco equally presents some deviance, with Sweden having a low per capita importation of this luxury and Finland a high one. Again, this could be an effect of differences in price relatives but it could also reflect smuggling or strongly rooted habits for which we do not have any evidence.

The second area of research which may be of assistance in testing the GDP per capita ranking under consideration also comes from the standard-of-living debate and concerns its biological and demographic dimensions. The first of these can be analyzed in terms of its by now classic yardstick, the height of young males of conscript age. This is an indicator which has met with varying degrees of criticism (Crafts 1997) but which also has its

Table 2.6   Average heights of young males, *c.*1850 (in centimetres, for age approximately 20 years)

	1	2
Denmark	165	166.1
Sweden	169.4–167.4	168.2
Norway	168.6	168.6
Portugal	162.0***	n/a
Spain	160.6*–162.7**	n/a
Italy	162.2	n/a

Sources:
Column 1: Johansen (1998); Historisk Statistik för Sverige (1959); Floud (1984); Carrión (1986); Anuario Estadístico de España (1860); unpublished data in Portuguese military archives.
Column 2: Crafts (1997).

Notes:
* For Murcia, 1845–9
** for all of Spain, 1858–61
*** for 1857–9.

defenders (Floud 1984; Drukker and Van Meerten 1995) and if sensibly used can yield useful additional perspectives. Its advantages are that the data is relatively abundant and precise in nature, that it is suitable for international comparisons, given the similarity of procedures used to measure it, and that there is a large body of evidence that links heights with real income per capita. On the other hand, allowance must be made for the fact that other circumstances, such as the disease environment, the work effort and dietary differences, can distort the perception of the relation with income.

Bearing this in mind, it is interesting to observe, in Table 2.6, the evident split between northern and southern Europe, the gap being of a substantial size. The difference in average heights, at mid-century, between Spain, Italy and Portugal on the one hand, and Sweden, Denmark and Norway on the other, was something like 5–9 cm, an amount which normally takes decades of social and economic improvement within a single country to bridge. This finding replicates, to some extent, the GDP per capita ranking observed in Table 2.4, and therefore corroborates it. At the same time, it also clearly exaggerates the distance between the two groups of countries in the sample while it fails to reflect the variations within them. Thus, according to the extrapolations worked out by Steckel (1995), the former group of statures would correspond to an income per capita of approximately $1,000 (1985 US dollars), while the latter would correspond to one of between $3,000 and $4,000, an obviously unrealistic situation. On the other hand, it does not pick up any of the income differences of Sweden and Denmark *vis-à-vis*

Norway, while Spanish and Norwegian statures hardly appear to correspond
to economies with similar incomes per capita.

One aspect that can help resolve these discrepancies is regional differences in diets and, indirectly, the resource endowments that explain them. It
is more than likely that, independently of income levels, the greater consumption of protein-rich foodstuffs like meat and dairy products in Scandinavia was more favourable to human growth than the more cereal-intensive
pattern of the south. Indeed, recent research has established that in the
same period, in Bavaria, the average heights of recruits varied positively with
the consumption of milk in their home regions and that this could be translated into a more than 1-cm gain or loss of stature (Baten 1997). In the case
of the Norwegian singularity noted above, this reasoning may be reinforced
by the unusual importance of this country's fish catch for the home market,
a significant additional source of protein and therefore of human growth.
The supply of this foodstuff was several times that of the other countries
considered and particularly in comparison with Sweden and Spain.[19]

Both infant and global mortality are widely considered to relate also to the
standard of living and therefore to reflect real per capita income, as well as
various environmental conditions (Mokyr 1993; Johansen 1998). The death
rates shown in Table 2.7 suggest similar conclusions as before, in particular
the existence of the two blocks of the periphery that we detected earlier, and
lends further plausibility to the GDP per capita ranking presented in Table
2.4. The Danish–Swedish versus Spanish–Italian–Portuguese contrast unmis-
takably signals this, even though it is probably reinforced by the relatively
somewhat higher urbanization of southern Europe, which is usually associated with higher mortality figures. Finland appears with a poorer record
than its neighbours, as befits its poverty relative to the regional standard, but
in terms of infant mortality resembles Spain, the southern country which is
closest to it in income. Once again, the difficulty in putting together data
that are both reliable and correspond to roughly the same years, in a field
where a certain degree of change was occurring over time, may introduce
some distortions. Norway's outlier status – low mortality but only average real
income per capita – may be due to the later date for which we have statistics,
although it seems not unlikely that the considerable dispersion of its population could also have contributed to this result by engendering a less lethal
disease environment.[20]

Whether taken singly or together, the indirect indicators of material
wellbeing examined here strongly suggest that on average real GDP per
capita was unevenly distributed throughout the periphery around the
middle of the last century. They also help to make a convincing case for the
results established in Table 2.4, not only the ranking of countries but also the
quantification of this variable. They are certainly at variance with the picture
one could draw alternatively from the wage data in Table 2.2 that pointed
unequivocally in the direction of uniformity between and throughout Scandinavia and southern Europe. We would therefore submit that the set of

Table 2.7 Mortality rates in the 1840s

	1 Infant	2 Global
Denmark	144	21.2
Sweden	153	20.1
Norway*	107	18.8
Finland	173	23.0
Portugal**	>200	30.3
Spain	174	28.4
Italy***	226	30.3

Sources:
Johansen (1985).
Historisk Statistik för Sverige (1959).
Koskinen et al. (1994).
British Sessional Papers. House of Commons, consular reports.
Ferro (1995).
Reher(1990).
Zamagni (1993).

Notes:
* Refers to 1860
** refers to 1801
*** refers to 1871.

figures arrived at in Table 2.4 for GDP per capita constitutes a plausible benchmark and should be preferred to other solutions arrived at by more indirect methods.

A new income per capita ranking

These new estimates for an early nineteenth-century GDP per capita benchmark for the European periphery allow us to draw two conclusions. The first one is of a factual nature, the second is methodological. Insofar as the latter is concerned, this study questions the usefulness of employing real wages for establishing cross-country comparisons of real GDP per capita for this period.[21] If we compare the wage rates in Table 2.2 with the GDP per capita estimates in Table 2.4, the pitfalls associated with this approach become evident, even when simply trying to rank countries with this yardstick. At least for the earlier nineteenth century, very little connection seems to exist between the two realities, whichever wage rate is adopted as an indicator. The problem is considerably greater in the case of urban wages, the rate of which has been preferred hitherto by the economic historians working in this field. If we were to use Allen's (1998a) approach in the present study, for example, we would find ourselves with Scandinavia a much poorer region than Iberia in the 1840s. The implication of this is that if a wage-based meth-odology is to be adopted for income estimation, then at least unskilled and rural labour unit costs should be favoured, although they may be harder to find. Nevertheless, when following this path, formidable difficulties have still to be met, the greatest being undoubtedly those caused by rural under-employment and the seasonality of work in agriculture. For societies such as these, where these features were pronounced, wages will always be a poor measure of income unless we can take into account as well the amount of time worked over the course of the year, a datum that in the present state of knowledge is bound to prove elusive. The link between wages and the mar-ginal product of labour is undoubtedly a strong one but it captures the day-to-day reality, whereas the temporal context for GDP is a year-long one and therefore the two approaches are incompatible.

The main factual aspect of our conclusions is that around 1850 the set of countries under observation was anything but homogeneous from the point of view of income per capita. In other words, there was not a single "poor" periphery; rather, it covered a fairly wide range of income levels, with a ratio of 2:1 between the extremes (Sweden and Greece). As far as blocks are con-cerned, the respective averages of the northern and southern terms of this comparison were also quite far apart – a 40 per cent difference – with the Scan-dinavian economies much the richer of the two. Indeed, in Sandberg's sense, the latter were undoubtedly sophisticated but they were far from poor by con-temporary standards. "Mediterranean Europe", by contrast, was prevalently composed of countries which were both "impoverished" and "unsophisti-cated". All of this contradicts the impression derived from all three authors represented in Table 2.1, in particular Bairoch's finding of a slight superiority for the Mediterranean countries, but also Maddison and Prados, who show the two groups as distinct but quite close as regards average GDP per capita.

If we now consider only the ranking which emerges from our results, the view is practically the inverse of Bairoch's, who put Norway in the lead, fol-lowed by Spain and Portugal, and gave last place to Sweden. As regards Maddison's and Prados' lists, the differences are much less stark. The leaders – Sweden and Denmark – and the laggards – Greece and Portugal – are the same, while Spain and Norway appear as intermediate economies. Italy cannot be placed because we have considered only its southern half and that certainly belongs with Greece, at the tail end. The only sharp discrepancy concerns Finland, which was a laggard according to Maddison and Prados and enjoys third position here.

Further departures from established views are encountered when we move onto the more debatable ground of the actual figures for GDP per capita. If we take Denmark as the numeraire country, the first surprise is to find that by 1850 Sweden was slightly ahead, when other authors have placed it second and between 20 and 50 per cent lower. The second surprise in our data is to discover Norway and Finland together and considerably further away from the leader, whereas Norway has tended to be seen as a good second or third

Table 2.8 GDP per capita: benchmark estimates for 1850 and 1913 (Denmark = 100)

	GDP/capita 1850, Table 2.4 estimate	Annual growth rate (%,1850–1913) (Prados, 1993a)	GDP/capita 1910, Prados (1998) estimate	GDP/capita 1913 estimated from cols. 1 and 2
Denmark	100	1.48	100	100
Sweden	100	1.36	93	93
Norway	71	1.04	96	54
Finland	72	1.39	65	68
Portugal	65	0.66	58	37
Spain	71	1.03	78	54
Greece	51	0.96*	57	37

Sources: Table 2.4; Prados (1993a and 1998).

Note: * Estimated from Kostelenos (1995).

and Finland as a far poorer economy than the rest of Scandinavia.[22] A third novelty resides in the fact that Portugal and Spain are both in the group of intermediate economies and come very close to Finland, the poorest peripheral country to have subsequently achieved that convergence with the core economies that eluded these two southern countries throughout this period. Greece's poor showing has been previously noted, although in Prados' recent tables it makes a considerably better showing than Finland. It probably comes as no surprise that if the states that composed southern Italy had remained politically separate from the rest of that country after 1861, they would have been among the poorest of the European periphery and indeed of the northern rim of the Mediterranean basin.

The analysis of this new 1850 benchmark raises two further questions with regard to the study of long-term growth and convergence. Even without running a convergence model with this new data as its starting point, it is evident from Table 2.8 that it fits awkwardly with a pure Solovian framework and will require very strong conditionality to be statistically significant. If we adopt the national growth rates for 1850–1913 currently in use – for example, Prados *et al.* (1993a) – the most convergent economies tend to be those with the highest starting GDP per capita and inversely. This suggests that the notion of convergence clubs, which was raised at the beginning of the chapter, may indeed be useful in this context, with their membership being determined by the level of income already achieved prior to the convergence period. Thus, some of the Scandinavian countries might already, by mid-century, belong to the core country club, while the southern ones would not, and this would make a difference over the long run in terms of catching up with Britain or the USA.

The second question is whether this new benchmark is simultaneously compatible with available 1913 benchmarks, and with the already mentioned set of growth rates that can be found in the literature at the moment. To answer this the relevant figures are presented in Table 2.8, where column 3 represents the latest estimate for 1913 GDP per capita and column 4 the implicit point of arrival given these growth rates and the 1850 benchmark constructed here. No great discrepancies emerge for Sweden and Finland, but all the other countries of the periphery are far off the mark. In the latter case, Prados' (1998) estimate is always much higher – by between 44 and 78 per cent – which means that to arrive at his GDP per capita levels in 1913, Norway, Portugal, Spain and Greece would have had to exhibit much faster growth than has been supposed to date. If this change were to be admitted, then these higher growth rates by poorer economies would render the fit of the convergence much better and require less "conditionality". On the other hand, this would require a substantial revision of how these rates have been estimated, an exercise which clearly does not belong here but should perhaps be placed on a future research agenda.

To finalize, a word is in order regarding the origins in time of the income gap that we have detected here. Recent studies have shown that, over the long run, output per capita and productivity growth in Europe have existed well before the nineteenth century, and that when they occurred, this was characterized by very low average rates (Maddison and van der Wee 1994). In another chapter of this book, Jeffrey Williamson poses the connected question: when did the gap that is so obvious by the late nineteenth century between Britain, the industrial leader, and the Mediterranean region open up? And, in the same vein, Allen (1998a) has asked when was the time when real incomes were similar across Europe and at what stage did differentials arise between north and south, or east and west? The results obtained in the preceding sections obviously lead to a parallel interrogation, although with reference to a somewhat different geographic context, that of the northern and southern peripheries of Europe. In our case the issue is, when and how did Denmark and Sweden build up the income per capita advantage of some 50 per cent over the rest of the rest of Scandinavia and the Mediterranean economies which was patent already by 1850, that is, before the Kuznetsian process of modern economic growth started in earnest?

The answers vary, with Williamson focusing on the century before 1850 and Allen carrying his analysis back to the sixteenth century. Ours, here, can only be summary in nature but some clues can nevertheless be given. In view of the prevalence of agriculture in the productive structure of these economies, once again it seems best to concentrate our remarks on this sector, particularly as its labour productivity is bound to have been an important determinant of overall economic efficiency (O'Brien and Prados 1992). Higher productivity of labour in this area, which for comparative purposes can be proxied by our figures for agricultural output per capita, usually meant a greater division of labour, specialization of tasks and market oriented activity. And, in this period, in the absence of major rapid technical change, these were the main instruments whereby pre-industrial economies achieved lasting gains in income per capita.

As regards Mediterranean agriculture, the current view seems to be that very little changed in per capita terms over the century from 1750 to 1850 (de Felice 1965; Federico 1986; Simpson 1997).[23] Output expanded quite substantially but gains were wiped out by population enlargement. In contrast, some long-run productivity increase can be detected for Denmark over the same period, at a rate not exceeding 0.4 per cent a year (Jensen 1991–2; Christensen 1983).[24] For Sweden, it was probably somewhat less.[25] If this picture were to prove correct, it would mean that, retropolating their respective agricultural outputs per capita to 1750 would leave them somewhere in the region of 400 grams of silver. Assuming little change there, the equivalent Spanish, Italian, Greek and Portuguese variable would lie in this region too. In other words, the observed divergence in agricultural performance, and indirectly in real per capita income, was probably mostly the work of the hundred years before 1850 and therefore does not have to be sought much further back than the mid-eighteenth century. The view is thus also confirmed that some degree of consistent improvement in economic efficiency was taking place long before the classic process of growth and convergence of the 1870–1913 period, and, like it, it was not convergent either. Since it occurred under rather different technological and economic circumstances from those that later conduced to globalization – it was based on the primary sector – its analysis requires a different approach and is likely to yield different conclusions. This is not the place to carry this out, but it seems clear that further enquiry into the origins of backwardness in the European periphery must proceed, in a comparative perspective, in this direction by focusing primarily on the determinants of agricultural productivity in the long run.

Appendix: estimates for agricultural output in the countries of the periphery, *c.*1840–50

Table 2.A1 contains the total value of agricultural production of the eight countries studied in the main text, that is Denmark, Sweden, Norway, Finland, Portugal, Spain, southern Italy and Greece in the middle of the nineteenth century (southern Italy, for this purpose, comprises Tuscany, the Papal States and the kingdom of the Two Sicilies). These are expressed in local currency and also in the equivalent in grams of monetary silver. For each country, the value of output at current market prices is also given for each of the main products of agriculture, in local currency alone. Prices are three-year averages centred around 1845 and, whenever possible, they refer to the largest market in the country for agricultural goods, i.e. the capital city. In some cases, certain items are absent from the table because they are not produced in a particular country, e.g. olive oil in Sweden. In others, we were unable to obtain their value, e.g. fruit in Portugal. Both situations are

Table 2.A1 Agricultural output by value, c.1850

	Denmark '000 krone	Sweden '000 krone	Norway '000 krone	Finland '000 marks	Portugal million reis	Spain '000 pta	Greece '000 drach	S. Italy '000 lire
Grain	58 885	96 805	13 354	45 779	25 890	882 026**	28 600	1 376 000
Wine	0	0	0	0	10 958	1 280 985	18 000	—
Olive Oil	0	0	0	0	3 036	110 803	8 900	—
Potatoes	7 445	31 299	14 972	9 593	3 078	43 197	0	—
Pulses	3 900	8 058	642	3 027	369	113 100	600	—
Vegetables	0	0	0	0	0	0	2 500	—
Rice	0	0	0	0	376	10 613	0	—
Meat	35 085	62 821	18 114	19 425	11 107	301 063	22 400	—
Milk	12 988	40 595	17 200	41 274	3 869	11 911	4 800	—
Butter#	10 640	18 080	15 300	13 733	2 392	2 761	0	—
Fruit	0	0	0	0	0	0	4 300	—
Industrial plants	0	0	0	0	0	0	1 800	—
Total	126 942	257 657	99 477*	132 831	49 969	1 634 230	91 900	1 376 000
Total ('000 grams of silver)	761 652	1 545 942	596 865	597 739	1 356 658	6 863 770	383 700	5 744 800
Total per capita (grams of silver)	564	468	461	398	399	437	354	402

Notes

* Increased by 25 per cent to take account of tax evasion, according to Hodne and Grytten (1994).

** Corrected value – see notes.

Butter includes butter and cheese.

Table 2.A2 Stock of farm animals, c.1850 ('000s)

	Horses, mules, donkeys	Bovine	Pigs	Sheep	Goats
Denmark	326	858	237	1 645	0
Sweden	422	1 807	555	1 547	0
Norway	132	843	89	1 447	291
Finland	236	686	199	802	0
Portugal	232	522	858	2 417	1 044
Spain	2 997	2 967	4 351	22 468	4 552
S. Italy	927	970	2 526	6 066	1 419
Greece	103	103	55	2 186	1 720

expressed with a zero. When necessary, grain was converted from volume to weight using the ratio of 75 kg to 1 hectolitre. Corrections suggested by the literature have been introduced for two countries – Spain and Norway – and they are duly noted below. The per capita figures were calculated using population data from Mitchell (1992).

As can be seen in the explanatory country notes, vegetable production has been derived directly from the statistical sources employed. Animal production, in most cases, has been estimated using technical coefficients applied to the statistics for the stock of farm animals for each country. In order to render the way in which these results were arrived at more explicit, Table 2.A2 shows the numbers for these stocks.

Notes and sources for Tables 2.A1 and 2.A2

Denmark

Crop production for 1838 is from *Statistik Tabelværk* (1842). The animal stock is obtained from Johansen (1985). Meat and butter are estimated using the technical coefficients given by Hansen (1984) and assuming that half a million cows were milk producers, as is stated in *Statistik Tabelværk* (1842) (cheese is not mentioned by Hansen). Milk output is derived from butter production using the coefficient employed for Norway. Market prices are given by Hansen (1984).

Sweden

Crop quantities are from *Historisk Statistik för Sverige* (1959). The animal stock is from the same source and also from Mitchell (1992). Dairy and meat products were retropolated from the figures for 1871/5 in *Historisk Statistik för Sverige* (1959), it being assumed that "other products" corresponded to mutton. Prices are taken from Jørberg (1972), those for the county of Stockholm having been used. "Mixed grain" has been valued at the price for rye. As the price of potatoes is not available, it was interpolated from Danish prices for the same date, i.e. 40 per cent of the price of rye. The price for mutton was similarly estimated from the price of beef using Danish data, as was milk using butter as the reference. The price of horse meat was assumed to be 20 per cent lower than for beef.

Norway

Most of the data for both output and prices are from *Historisk Statistik: 1968* (1969) for 1845. Values for milk are from Dyrvik (1979), and refer to 1855 but have been adjusted on the basis of the earlier size of the cattle herd. Data on butter are not available and therefore were estimated using the Danish coefficients from Hansen (1984) and assuming that 70 per cent of cattle were milch cows. Meat was estimated on the basis of the same coefficients, i.e. 25 kg of meat per head of total bovine stock; 72 kg per head of the pig stock; 14 kg per head of the total stock of sheep. The price of pork was estimated from that of beef using the proportion between them in 1845 for Denmark. The same was done for the prices of wheat, rye and barley relative to oats, and likewise for milk relative to butter. None of these prices is directly available in *Historik Statistik: 1968* (1969). The value of total output was corrected upward by 25 per cent according to the suggestion by Hodne and Grytten (1994).

Finland

Quantities and prices are from *Suomen taloushistoria* (1980–3). Evidence for potatoes is not available for the 1840s but only for 1871. It was assumed that the consumption rate of 100 kg per capita for 1880 applies for this earlier date, which almost certainly leads to an overestimate. Meat and milk are estimated using the technical coefficients for Denmark. Prices correspond to 1851 or 1852, the earliest that are available. That of milk is derived from the "skimmed milk" price, which is known and transformed by the coefficient between the two for 1901–6. The price for barley is derived from that for oats using their 1901 ratio. Only the "rye meal" price is available and this was arbitrarily reduced by 10 per cent to obtain the price of rye. Meat production was estimated from Hansen's (1984) coefficients. For butter and milk, it was assumed again that 70 per cent of the bovine stock are milch cows and the Danish coefficients from the same source were used. The quantity of skimmed milk was assumed to be given by the total volume of milk minus the volume of butter.

Portugal

Crop quantities are from Lains and Sousa (1999) and are three-year averages centred on 1850. In the cases of barley, oats, pulses and rice, which are missing from this source, they were extrapolated from Morais Soares' (1873) figures for the decade 1861–70 using wheat as the reference. Meat production in 1852 is from Lains (1990) and the stock of animals is from Justino (1986). We used cheese production as it was estimated for 1870 by Morais Soares (1873), who was unable, however, to provide a figure for butter. We have assumed the latter was of the same value as the output of cheese. Prices are taken from Justino (1990). They refer to 1850 and are a national average, with the exception of those for butter, milk and cheese, which are from the royal kitchen in Lisbon and are taken from "Documentos da Casa Real" (1800–1910). The mutton price is extrapolated with reference to that of beef from Morais Soares (1873). It is assumed that goat meat had the same price as mutton.

Spain

Spanish crop quantities refer to 1857, a generally recognized bad year, and are from Tortella (1987), who considers the order of magnitude correct nevertheless. We have introduced an upward correction of 87 per cent for grain. This was calculated by comparing the official wheat output figure in 1857 with the average for 1850–9 estimated by Simpson as more realistic and presented in Tortella (1987). Total agricultural output is thereby raised by 30 per cent, a more plausible result but one that is still a far cry from Simpson's (1989) own later estimate which would place Spain in the same category as Denmark. Quantities of milk and meat were estimated from the coefficients provided by Prados (1993), who does not give any indication for butter, and from the stock of animals taken from GEHR (1985). The meat production data in Prados (1988) were not used as they would imply a per capita annual consumption of 50 kg that would put Spain ahead of Denmark and Sweden, an unlikely event. Butter was estimated in proportion to the amount of milk produced on the basis of the equivalent proportion in Swedish statistics. Prices are for 1850 and are given by Barquin (1998). They are national averages. In the case of pork, mutton and goat meat, they are extrapolated from Portuguese prices using beef as the reference. Horse meat was arbitrarily valued at 80 per cent of beef. For butter and milk prices, Portuguese data were used, converted by the exchange rate.

Italy

The value of total agricultural output is given by Zamagni (1993), who does not provide a breakdown by product either for quantities or for values; it corresponds to 1857. The stock of farm animals is from Svimez (1961).

Greece

Values and quantities are provided by Kostelenos (1995), who presents a detailed discussion of the sources and assumptions on which these results are based. They are for the years 1858 and 1859. The stock of farm animals, for 1835, is from Strong (1842).

Notes

The author wishes to thank, for their help, Joan Rosés, Dan Andersen, Jorgen Peter Christensen, Hans Christian Johansen, Jan Tore Klovland, Joaquim Costa Leite, Paulo Fernandes, Leandro Prados, Ramon Marimon, Ilka Nummela, Sofia Martinho and Jeffrey Williamson.

1   Prados' definition of peripheral countries is those which by 1950 had not yet reached the UK's level of real income per capita in 1913 measured in PPP US 1990 dollars.
2   That this continues to be the case can be seen in a recent major work of global economic history where it is stated that Scandinavia was "desperately poor" and the late industrializers of Mediterranean Europe were also "poor", the crucial difference between the two regions being their "cultural preparation". See Landes (1998).
3   They are still found useful by some authors nevertheless. See Landes (1998: 232 and 248).
4   For a recent critical overview of historical national accounting in Europe, see the special issue of the *Scandinavian Economic History Review* (1995), LVIII, n.1, edited by Bart van Ark.
5   The aim is to represent here the equivalent of today's Mezzogiorno, that is the Mediterranean part of Italy, out of recognition that the northern part of the country had already then considerable affinities with core countries such as Germany or France. To this end we have selected for inclusion in the sample a region consisting of the kingdom of the Two Sicilies, the Pontifical States and Tuscany, although the last of these for various reasons is a less obvious choice. In some instances, we have had to use data for Italy as a whole.
6   Urban wages have to be handled with care in this type of exercise because, as we are reminded by Allen (1998a), within the same country, they can vary quite a lot according to the size of the city and the place it occupied in the urban hierarchy.
7   Two baskets of goods, which have recently been proposed for the nineteenth century, illustrate this problem. Williamson's (1995) is an average of seven different national baskets around the early twentieth century and includes high-income countries such as the USA, Britain, France and Germany. Both these facts render it a far call from what was happening, for example, in the early nineteenth century in the Mediterranean region. Allen's (1998a) reflects spending shares in mid-eighteenth-century Strasbourg. Among the difficulties it raises are the absence of milk, a major article of consumption in Scandinavia, and a meat share which severely underestimates the consumption pattern of the northern periphery. A similar attempt by van Zanden (1996) yielded a "price set [which] is a very hybrid one and therefore not very satisfactory perhaps".
8   It has been used recently by van Zanden (1995) for a similar historical context.
9   This finding extends, beyond the Mediterranean region, to the whole of the European periphery and would seem to confirm Williamson's impression (Chapter 3) that real wages were roughly on the same level at this time. On the other hand, it may also help to answer his question: was the similarity of wages over such a wide area, throughout the southern periphery, due to "shared shocks" or was it the result of integrated labour markets? Given that the area in question here is even wider, the explanation may be that it was neither. If we assume that wages reflected the marginal productivity of labour, perhaps one ought to consider instead that it was a consequence of a similar efficiency of labour in the low-technology agriculture that was the predominant activity of the time in all these countries. Given the different natural endowments and capital/labour ratios in the north and the

south of the periphery, this may seem surprising but it fits with the earlier observation by Clark (1987b) on the uniformity of wages for raw labour in agriculture across continental Europe during the same decades.

10 This assumption about the labour market has been strongly criticized, notably by Ebeling, in Scholliers (1989).

11 Hoffman (1996) uses Paris wages as a proxy for wages in the agriculture of the Parisian basin during the *ancien régime* on the grounds that by then the two markets were closely integrated.

12 Spain covers the interval 1857–65, Greece 1858, Italy 1857, Sweden, Finland and Portugal the mid-1840s, and Denmark 1838.

13 It should be noted that Sweden's agricultural output is considerably higher than the recent estimate by Schön (1995), which was made using a completely different methodology, based on consumption rather than production estimates.

14 Van Zanden (1996) has recently employed a similar approach to a group of eight countries, in 1810, of which only one, Spain, is in our sample. Spain's GDP per capita here comes out at 61–7 per cent of Britain, while Poland is only 30–1 per cent of this standard.

15 Our Greek estimate is based on 1858 figures constructed by Kostelenos (1995). Several manufacturing subsectors are missing from this effort and therefore his GDP figure is lower than it should be and the resultant agriculture/GDP ratio is higher than in reality. On the other hand, if we apply the ratio used for Spain and Portugal (41 per cent), Greece continues to be placed at the tail of the country list although less far behind, with a GDP per capita of 863 grams of silver instead.

16 Around 1850, whether in Norway or in Spain, food and drink took up as much as 75 per cent of the expenditure of families (Reher and Ballesteros 1993; Minde and Ramstad 1986). In Denmark, this has been put at around 60 per cent (Hansen 1984).

17 Clark, Huberman and Lindert (1995) have estimated these elasticities for working-class families in England in the first half of the nineteenth century. Heikkinen (1996) has done the same for Finnish elasticities for *c.* 1900 and they tell a similar story: for coffee, tea and cocoa, 1.34; for sugar, 1.77; for meat, 0.88; and for cereals, 0.21.

18 Meat/cereal price ratios were calculated from the data in the appendix and were usually of the order of 3:1. In Norway and Finland this was 20 and 40 per cent lower respectively.

19 The Norwegian fishing sector's output represented 11 per cent of GDP in 1845, of which 80 per cent was for export. This leaves 2.2 per cent for domestic consumption whereas in other countries the fishing sector was always less than 1 per cent.

20 For the relations between mortality and environmental differences, see Schofield *et al.* (1991: 7–13).

21 For a spirited defence of an opposing view, see Williamson in this volume, who, it must be stressed, is more interested in factor prices than in macro aggregates.

22 For a specific Scandinavian comparison, see Krantz and Nilsson (1974).

23 Further evidence on this comes from Allen (1998b), who shows that both Italian and Spanish agricultural output per capita declined during 1750–1800, while Williamson (Chapter 3 in this volume) shows that there was no real wage growth in the Mediterranean region between 1775 and 1850.

24 This evolution has been challenged recently by Andersen (1996), who thinks the estimates of agricultural production for 1759 are exaggerated.

25 For Sweden, we only have data for 1800–50 (Schön 1995) which imply a growth rate for agricultural output per capita of 0.4 per cent per annum. This would bring the Swedish figure to *c.* 400 grams of silver at the 1800 mark, which could mean the same for 1750 if no change occurred during the second half of the eighteenth century. We have no evidence for this at the moment but using data for grain and meat production provided by Johansen (1998) for the whole period, one can infer an evolution similar to the Danish one.

3   Real wages and relative factor prices around the Mediterranean, 1500–1940

Jeffrey G. Williamson

Convergence and divergence before World War I

Two important features of the world economy since 1970 also characterized the economy in the late nineteenth century. First, there was rapid globalization a century ago too: capital and labour flowed across national frontiers in unprecedented quantities, and commodity trade boomed as transport costs dropped sharply. Second, the late nineteenth century underwent an impressive convergence in living standards, at least within most of what we would now call the OECD club, but what historians call the Atlantic economy. Poor countries around the European periphery tended to grow faster than the rich industrial leaders at the European centre, and often even faster than the richer countries overseas in the New World. This club excluded most of eastern Europe, the Mediterranean, and the Third World. Even in this exclusive club there were some poor countries who failed to catch up. Nonetheless, the Atlantic economy countries who played the globalization game converged.

It was not always that way: divergence was the case earlier. The Atlantic economy in the first half of the previous century was characterized by high tariffs, modest commodity trade, no mass migrations, and an underdeveloped global capital market. Two profound shocks occurred in this environment still hostile to liberal globalization policy: early industrialization in Britain which then spread to a few countries on the European continent; and resource "discovery" in the New World, set in motion by sharply declining transport costs linking overseas suppliers to European markets, so much so that real freight rates fell by an enormous 1.5 per cent per annum between 1840 and 1910 (O'Rourke and Williamson 1999, ch. 3). These two shocks triggered a divergence in real wages and living standards across the Atlantic economy that lasted until the middle of the century (Williamson 1996a).[1]

Figure 3.1 shows that the striking convergence which started in mid-century continued up to 1914: a plot of the dispersion of real wages is given there, documenting what the modern macroeconomists call sigma-convergence. The line with the diamonds on the upper left of Figure 3.1 is based on a thirteen-country Atlantic economy sample including Australia, Belgium, Brazil,

Figure 3.1 International real wage dispersion, 1854–1913.

Source: Williamson (1995), Table A2.1; revised in O'Rourke and Williamson (1997).

France, Germany, Great Britain, Ireland, the Netherlands, Norway, Portugal, Spain, Sweden and the United States. The dashed line in Figure 3.1 documents convergence for an expanded seventeen-country Atlantic economy sample, now including in addition Argentina, Canada, Denmark and Italy. This measure shows the convergence tide ebbing around 1900. If we exclude Canada and the United States, two "exceptional" rich countries which bucked the convergence tide, convergence continues rapidly up to 1914 (the fifteen-country sample plotted with the triangles). If we exclude in addition two Mediterranean countries which failed, Portugal and Spain, convergence up to 1914 is faster still (the thirteen-country sample plotted with the squares).

The western Mediterranean did very badly during this age of convergence, as Gabriel Tortella (1994) has recently summarized so well. Spain and Portugal fell far behind the growth rates recorded in the rest of the European periphery, defined here to include Denmark, Ireland, Italy, Norway, Portugal, Spain and Sweden, and apparently the same was true of the Balkans (see Chapter 4 in this volume, by James Foreman-Peck and Pedro Lains). Real wages crawled upwards at only about 0.4 per cent a year in Iberia, while they surged at almost 2.3 per cent per year elsewhere around the periphery (O'Rourke and Williamson 1997, Table 2). Thus, workers in Spain and Portugal missed out on the first great growth and convergence boom. Foreman-Peck and Lains suggest that Balkan workers also missed out (Chapter 4). A wide growth gap also appears for real GDP per capita (Maddison 1995), which averaged 0.9 per cent per annum for Spain and Portugal and 1.4 per cent per annum elsewhere around the periphery, but note that the growth gap was much bigger for wages than for GDP per capita, implying that Iberian workers suffered the most.[2] Italy in the central Mediterranean did somewhat better, but even that performance fell below the average for the periphery. Italian real-wage growth was 1.7 per cent per year, below the 2.3 per cent achieved everywhere else around the non-Iberian periphery, while the real GDP-per-worker rates were 1.3 versus 1.7. Furthermore, the really impressive growth in Italy was in the industrial triangle in the north, the south lagging far behind.

So it seems that the western Mediterranean failed to share in the late-nineteenth-century Atlantic economy's growth and convergence, and that the centre only shared in part of it. What about the eastern Mediterranean? How did the Balkans do? What about the shrinking Ottoman Empire, the core that eventually became modern Turkey? What about Egypt? Did communities around the Mediterranean undergo very different growth experience? And if so, why?

These are the questions that motivate half of this essay. They are in the tradition of W. Arthur Lewis who posed with such clarity the question as to whether the core pulled the periphery along during this first great globalization boom (Lewis 1969, 1978a, 1978b). It was he, together with Alexander Gerschenkron (1952), who first tried to break economic history's tenacious fixation on the industrial leaders, Lewis focusing on the Third World and Gerschenkron on European latecomers like Italy and eastern Europe.

The other half of this essay asks when the great divide between the north and south first appeared. By the end of our period, there were huge gaps in living standards and GDP per capita between the agrarian Mediterranean basin and the industrial northwest of Europe. When did the great divide open up? During the late-nineteenth-century growth boom? During the first industrial revolutionary decades between 1780 and 1850? Even earlier? And what are the explanations? The timing and location of industrial revolutions, population growth, globalization, the collapse of efficient political systems, or all of the above?

These are not questions that could have been attacked very well even only two decades ago, since the data had not been gathered in such a way as to make these comparative judgements possible. Now we have enough to make some real progress, although it will have to wait for another paper: this one dwells instead on the new factor price and living-standard data, and the agenda they suggest for the Mediterranean.

Convergence and divergence of what?

Most economists who have written about the comparative growth of nations have used GDP per capita or per worker to measure catching-up and convergence. This and other essays of mine favour instead real wage rates (purchasing-power-parity adjusted, and typically for urban unskilled workers). I can think of at least four good reasons why it is a mistake for the convergence debate to have ignored wages and other factor prices, especially for the previous century and earlier.

First, the pre-World War I real-wage data are of far better quality than the

GDP data, and they are certainly available for a wider sample. Indeed, Angus Maddison (1995) is able to document real GDP per capita starting only with 1900 for Egypt and 1913 for both Yugoslavia and Turkey. Even when Maddison's data are available for countries around the Mediterranean, there are enormous gaps in the time series: for example, the Italian series leaps from 1820 to 1870 and the Spanish from 1820 to 1850. As this essay will show, real wages for northern and southern Italy can be documented from 1500, Spain's from 1500, Turkey's from 1527, Portugal's from 1850, Egypt's from 1858, and the Balkans' from 1867. Furthermore, these time series are typically available annually, so that epochs and major turning points can be identified with much greater clarity.

Second, income distribution matters, and wage rates (especially when combined with other factor prices) offer a window to look in on distribution issues. Real people earn wages or skill premia or profits or rents, not that statistical artefact known as GDP per capita. GDP per worker-hour may sound like a good measure of aggregate productivity, but surely the living standards of ordinary workers as captured by real wages are a better indicator of the economic wellbeing of the vast majority in any society. By averaging all incomes, macroeconomists (and economic historians who mimic them) throw away valuable information.

Third, factor-price movements help us understand the sources of convergence or divergence. For example, productivity catch-up in a poor country is more likely to increase all factor prices equally than is mass emigration (easing population pressure on the land) or an export boom for agricultural products (increasing the demand for land). The open economy forces which were important in driving late-nineteenth-century convergence – trade, migration and capital flows – operated directly on factor prices, and thus only indirectly on GDP per capita.[3] An exclusive focus on GDP per capita misses most of the story.

Fourth, and possibly most important, economic change nearly always involves winners and losers, a fact which is crucial in accounting for the evolution of policy and the survival of empires. Changes that would increase GDP per capita but would also cause losses to some politically powerful group are often successfully resisted, and examining the behaviour of factor prices is a good way to start the search for the sources of such political resistance.

The real-wage hierarchy around the turn of the century

Table 3.1 puts together three sets of estimates of the real wage structure around the Mediterranean and between it and the European industrial leader, Britain. Sad to say, these competing estimates do not always agree, suggesting that a resolution be made top priority in future research. The assessment is made around the turn of the century. Panel A offers some estimates from three parts of the Balkans as well as a weighted average of the three regions that made up the much-diminished Ottoman Empire at that

Table 3.1 The real-wage hierarchy near the turn of the century

Region	Real wage relative to Britain (%)			
	1867–1901	*1890–1899*	*1900–1913*	*1909–1913*
A. *Prevailing exchange rates*				
Centre–East Balkans	33.5	—	—	—
West Balkans	32.8	—	—	—
South Balkans	45.1	—	—	—
Ottoman Empire		40.0	41.0	—
B. *PPP-adjusted "late" benchmarks*				
Turkey	17.7	17.3	16.1	16.9
Serbia	19.0	16.1	15.2	16.7
Egypt	10.8	10.9	10.1	10.9
Northern Italy	38.7	37.7	47.4	54.7
Central Italy	—	—	—	37.6
Southern Italy	—	—	—	20.1
Portugal	28.1	23.6	24.9	24.6
Spain	33.0	27.0	31.1	38.7
C. *PPP-adjusted "early" benchmarks*				
Turkey	63.4	—	—	—

Sources:

A: The three entries for the Balkans are from Berov (1978), relative to Bowley's (1900) London figures, master masons' wages. The Centre–East and West Balkan ratios reported in the table are taken directly from Berov's Table 5, and appear to be calculated at prevailing currency exchange rates. The South Balkan ratio is based on Balkan regional relatives reported in Berov's Table 3, and are based on silver wages. The entry for the Ottoman Empire is from Boratav *et al.* (1985, Table 2), weighted across three major Ottoman regions and composed of skilled construction workers (weighted by 2) and common labour (weighted by 1), and relative to the Brown–Hopkins (1955) figures for building craftsmen and laborers in Southern England. Calculated at prevailing gold standard rate of exchange. Boratav *et al.* (1985, p. 389) are critical of Berov's (1978) estimates, which seems a bit odd since Berov's skilled nominal wages rise by 50 per cent between 1825/49 and 1900/12 in the Centre–East Balkans, while the Boratav *et al.* Figure 1 (p. 386) implies an increase of about 66 per cent, not so different from Berov.

B: The entries for northern Italy, Spain, and Portugal (all relative to Great Britain) are taken from revisions of my 1995 estimates (Williamson 1995, revised in O'Rourke and Williamson 1997), unskilled urban workers, purchasing-power-parity (PPP) adjusted. The entries for central and southern Italy are calculated using the 1911 Mortara index of development (Hatton and Williamson 1997, Table 3) where those regions are reported relative to the north, and where the ratio is then applied to the northern Italy entry for 1909–1913. The entries for Turkey, Serbia and Egypt are benchmarked relative to each other and to Spain, based on the Maddison (1995) GDP per capita estimates for 1913 (all PPP-adjusted at the GDP level). They are then backcast to the earlier periods using the real-wage series reported elsewhere in this essay.

C: The figure is taken from the last column of Table 3.3 and it refers to an Istanbul versus London comparison 1850–1899.

Notes to Table 3.1 are on the next page

Notes to Table 3.1:

Regional definitions:
Centre–East Balkans = Turkey in Europe (including Constantinople), Bulgaria, and Macedonia in Yugoslavia;
West Balkans = remainder of Yugoslavia (e.g., Serbia, Croatia, etc.) and Albania;
South Balkans = continental Greece and Thrace;
Ottoman Empire = limited to (weighted average of) northern Greece, northern Syria and present-day Turkey;
Turkey = present-day Turkey;
Central Italy = unweighted average of Tuscany, Marches, Umbria and Lazio;
Northern Italy = unweighted average of Piedmont, Liguria, Lombardy, Veneto and Emilia (all compartimenti north of Tuscany and Marches);
Southern Italy = unweighted average of Abruzz–Molise, Campania, Apulia, Basilicata, Calabria, Sicily and Sardinia (all compartimenti south of Lazio).

---

time. The Balkan estimates are taken from Ljuben Berov (1978), while the Ottoman estimates are taken from Korkut Boratav, Gunduz Ökçün and Şevket Pamuk (1985). All of the estimates in Panel A calculate urban wages from this part of the Mediterranean relative to urban wages in Britain. More importantly, all the regional wage relatives in Panel A are calculated at the prevailing exchange rate. It is well known that the use of exchange rates, dominated by tradable goods, is inferior to the use of purchasing-power-parity, the latter constructed from workers' market baskets. Panel B uses purchasing-power-parity constructed from a "late" benchmark of 1913. According to Panel B, Turkey had a real wage only 17.3 per cent of Britain's in the 1890s, while Panel A suggests it was 40 per cent for the Ottoman Empire. The difference is big. Similarly, Panel B reports that on average Serbian real wages over the three decades 1867–1901 were 19 per cent of Britain's, while Panel A reports a figure of about 33 per cent for the west Balkans (which includes Serbia). Again, the difference is big. The exchange-rate-derived figures in Panel A seem too high, but are the purchasing-power-parity estimates in Panel B too low? It seems likely given that the alternative purchasing-power-parity estimates for Istanbul based on an "early" benchmark in Panel C are 63.4 per cent of London's in the late nineteenth century! This 63.4 per cent figure is taken from Table 3.3 where the "early" benchmark is for the sixteenth century. It will be discussed below, but it is apparent that these competing estimates must be resolved in the future. Still, we can make a lot of progress now even as we await the resolution. In the meantime, I will favour the estimates in Panel B.

The real-wage hierarchy *within* the Mediterranean around the turn of the century is clear enough, and those estimates in Panel B of Table 3.1 seem to be consistent with qualitative accounts. Northern Italy was, of course, at the top of the heap and industrialization had taken a much firmer root there than anywhere else, perhaps only with the exception of Catalonia. Real wages in northern Italy were from a third to a half of those in Britain, depending on whether we look at the 1890s or at the immediate pre-war years, the fifteen or twenty years in between allowing for some impressive catching-up in the Italian north and for some serious Edwardian failure in Britain. Spain and central Italy were tied for second, neither much more than a third of British real wages. (Note that Spain had also improved its relative position considerably from the 1890s to just before World War I.) Portugal was next, at about one-quarter of Britain. If Portugal was poor, Serbia, Turkey and southern Italy were even poorer, barely a fifth of Britain. Egyptian city construction workers were at the bottom of the hierarchy, with real wages only about one-ninth of those earned by their counterparts in urban Britain.

Thus, by the end of the late nineteenth century, there were huge real-wage and living-standard gaps between the Mediterranean periphery and the industrial core in northwestern Europe. Furthermore, there were huge gaps around the Mediterranean itself. Real wages earned by Spanish workers were at least twice those earned at the eastern end of the Mediterranean. The gap between northern Italy and the rest of the Mediterranean was even bigger, ranging from about five times Egypt, 3.2 times Turkey, 2.7 times the Italian south and 1.4 times Spain.

When did the north–south gap open up?

When did these gaps open up? Did it happen during the globalization boom after 1870, some exploiting it well, some exploiting it badly, and some exploiting it not at all? Did they open up instead during the century containing the first industrial revolution after the 1770s? Or did they open up even earlier?

The Mediterranean vs Scandinavia shortly before 1850

One paper in this volume explores the size of the north–south gap at two points along the periphery shortly before 1850. Jaime Reis (Chapter 2) documents standard-of-living differences between Denmark and Sweden on the one hand, and Portugal, Spain, Greece and some pre-unification Italian states on the other. Reis (Table 2.7) documents that by the 1840s infant mortality was already 45 per cent higher in the east and central Mediterranean (Spain, Portugal and Italy) than in Scandinavia (Denmark, Norway, Sweden and Finland); the adults who survived were significantly shorter (Table 2.6); and agricultural output per capita was almost 50 per cent lower (Table 2.4). Of course the gaps between the east and central Mediterranean and the more industrial European northwest were even bigger. But what about the eastern part of the Mediterranean, and what about before the 1840s?

A century of Mediterranean experience 1770s–1870s

There are two long real-wage time series documenting performance in urban labour markets in the central and eastern parts of the Mediterranean, dating from about the time when Adam Smith's *Wealth of Nations* first appeared. They are both plotted in Figure 3.2.

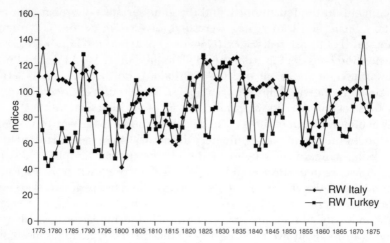

Figure 3.2 Real wage indices for Turkey and Northern Italy, 1775–1875 (1875 = 100).

The Turkey time series 1775–1875 is from Şevket Pamuk and refers to the real daily wages of unskilled construction workers in Istanbul, where 1875=100. The series is described in the next section, but it is not extended beyond 1875 in Figure 3.2 since I believe the source – palace and pious institutions – no longer reflects private labour markets beyond that point. The northern Italy time series 1775–1875 is from Robert Allen (1998a) and it too refers to the real daily wage of unskilled construction workers in towns. The series documents labour markets in Florence and Milan, and 1875=100 here as with the Istanbul series.

Figure 3.2 makes two important points. First, there is absolutely no evidence of persistent real-wage growth over the century at either location in the Mediterranean. The evidence seems, therefore, to confirm the prediction of the pre-industrial classical model restated some time ago by W. Arthur Lewis in terms of elastic labour supplies (Lewis 1954).[4] Second, there is considerable real-wage instability in both time series, and that instability gives us the opportunity to explore whether these labour markets were integrated or segmented.

There are, of course, many ways to test the labour market integration hypothesis,[5] but the time series on real wages in northern Italian towns and in Istanbul clearly favour segmentation: although not reported here, the correlation is never statistically significant after 1820, and before 1820 it is negative. The breakdown of real-wage correlations into nominal and cost-of-living correlations is also interesting. While nominal wages between the two regions were never significantly correlated, the cost of living was, at least most of the time. There were distinct regimes of cost-of-living correlations between urban labour markets in Turkey and northern Italy: during the French Wars (here 1775–1819), the cost of living was positively correlated,

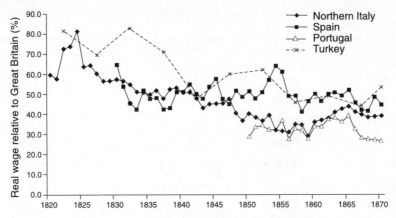

Figure 3.3 Urban real wages relative to Great Britain, 1820–1870 (in per cent).

and significant at the 5 per cent level; between 1820 and 1854, the correlation is again positive, and significant at the 10 per cent level; however,
between 1855 and 1874, the correlation is negative, but insignificant. This is
a puzzling statement about the behaviour of commodity markets, since intu-
ition would have predicted the opposite. I would have expected segmentation during the French Wars and integration during the globalization boom
after 1850. Future research will have to sort this puzzle out. However, the evidence supporting labour-market segmentation between the central and eastern Mediterranean is powerful, a finding which is certainly consistent with
the facts of very low over-the-border labour migration in this part of the
Mediterranean prior to the 1870s (see below).

Figure 3.3 and Table 3.2 differ from Figure 3.2 in two ways. Figure 3.2 sets
the wage series 1875 = 100. In contrast, now we use the Table 3.1 (Panel B)
purchasing-power-parity estimates to establish explicit wage relatives
throughout the period. Thus, the gaps between the wage series are meant to
reflect true differences in urban workers' living standards around the Mediterranean basin.[6] All the series plotted in Figure 3.3 are relative to Britain,[7] so
the figure actually measures the real-wage gaps between these four locations
around the Mediterranean and the European industrial leader. Furthermore, we now add real-wage time series for Spain (1830–70) and Portugal
(1850–70), both taken from my own database. The two critical points which
emerged from Figure 3.2 seem to be confirmed by the addition of the
shorter Spanish and Portuguese time series in Figure 3.3. First, there was no
real-wage catch-up on Britain between 1830 and 1870 in Spain, or between
1850 and 1870 in Portugal: indeed, the wage gap between Iberia and Britain
increased up to 1870. What was true of the western part of the Mediterranean was also true of the central and eastern parts: real wages in urban
Turkey and northern Italy fell relative to Britain over the half century after
1820. However, most of the decline (a further rise in the north–south gap

Table 3.2   Urban real wages relative to Britain in the Mediterranean Basin, 1820–1870 (per cent)

Years	Turkey	Northern Italy	Spain	Portugal
1820–24	81.5	69.0	—	—
1825–29	69.7	60.3	—	—
1830–34	82.4	54.0	51.6	—
1835–39	71.0	51.0	46.4	—
1840–44	48.5	47.4	51.4	—
1845–49	59.9	42.9	50.0	—
1850–54	62.1	37.3	54.2	32.1
1855–59	46.0	32.2	49.3	31.3
1860–64	49.2	38.9	49.3	36.0
1865–69	44.2	40.5	46.0	31.0
1870	53.4	38.8	44.8	26.9

Sources:
The Turkish (Istanbul) and northern Italian (Florence and Milan) data come from the sources described in Table 3.3. In particular, the Turkish figures here refer to an Istanbul vs London comparison (in terms of deflated silver wages) constructed using the same technique as in Table 3.3.
The data for Britain, Spain and Portugal are taken from a revision of my 1995 database (O'Rourke and Williamson 1997).
The relative-to-Britain benchmark is from the data underlying Table 3.1.

and thus greater real-wage divergence) took place from 1820 to mid-century. Second, formal statistical tests, not reported here, show that real wages across these countries are very poorly correlated in the middle third of the nineteenth century. Of the six possible pairwise correlations involving Turkey, Italy, Spain and Portugal over the four decades 1830–70, none shows a significant correlation. In short, there is absolutely no evidence of labour-market integration in the Mediterranean, and plenty of evidence of segmentation. This was not the case for the Atlantic economy (Williamson 1995; O'Rourke and Williamson 1999), and I suspect the reason is that the Iberian and the eastern Mediterranean economies were simply not participating in the mass migrations during most of the nineteenth century. I return to this issue below.

In the century following 1775, were real wages fixed at some low-level steady state everywhere around the Mediterranean? Even if they were so fixed, modern growth theory can now show (Barro and Sala-i-Matin 1995) that such "equilibrium" need not imply the same steady-state living standards everywhere around the Mediterranean. Table 3.2 and Figure 3.3 cannot speak to this issue since they report living standards *relative* to Britain. However, and as we shall see in a moment, Table 3.3 deals with *absolutes* and does not report any long-run stability in real wages or living standards anywhere around the Mediterranean. Furthermore, the evidence in Tables 3.2 and 3.3, as well as Figure 3.3, also suggests that there was considerable short-run instability around the long-run trends in the real wage, and the absence of correlation between real wages from these four urban parts of the Mediterranean is consistent with the hypothesis of labour-market segmentation already cited. Finally, the real-wage evidence suggests the secular rise in the north–south gap ceased around mid-century, remaining stable up to 1870.

The north–south gap since the Middle Ages

In two recent papers, Robert Allen (1998a, 1998c) has exploited wage and price data which scholars first started collecting for Strasbourg and southern England. In 1929, the International Scientific Committee commissioned similar studies covering all of England, Germany, France, Austria, Poland and Spain (Cole and Crandall 1964). Belgium and Italy were added later. Allen was able to find sufficient material to reconstruct real wages over the four centuries 1500–1913 for London, Florence, Milan, Naples, Valencia, Madrid and ten other European cities, many of the remainder in central and eastern Europe. The wages are for urban labourers and craftsmen, the rates of pay are daily, and they are expressed in grams of silver. The same is true of commodity prices, but Allen uses those prices and fixed market baskets to construct true purchasing-power-parity adjusted wages across these cities. His market baskets contain a wide range of commodities including oils, animal fats, grains, bread, meats, wine, beer and fuel.

Allen's careful attention to these purchasing-power-parity issues makes it possible for him (and us) to say something concrete about living standard convergence and divergence over the very long run in Europe. Allen's real-wage evidence that speaks directly to the north–south gap is summarized in Table 3.3. Note in particular the series for three Italian cities relative to London – Florence and Milan in the north and Naples in the south – plus two Spanish cities – coastal Valencia and inland Madrid. Note also the addition of a penultimate column which reports real (daily) wages in Istanbul, and an ultimate column which reports Istanbul relative to London. These Istanbul real wage figures are from Şevket Pamuk and are based on construction accounts of the palace and semi-official pious foundations for wages and consumption goods. Pamuk makes his purchasing-power-parity benchmark calculations for 1500–50, where he has (silver) prices for commodities in both Valencia (Hamilton 1934) and Istanbul, and where the fixed market-basket weights in both cities are taken to be the food budget shares implied by the accounts of Istanbul soup kitchens for the poor. The cost-of-living calculation is based on nine commodities ranging from lard, mutton and rice to olive oil and firewood. On this basis, Istanbul's consumer price index is taken to have been 25 per cent higher than Valencia's, an adjustment which is then

Table 3.3 The north–south gap since the Middle Ages

	London	Florence & Milan	Valencia	Madrid	Naples	Relative to London (%) Florence & Milan	Valencia	Madrid	Naples		Istanbul	Istanbul relative to London (%)
A. Fixed-budget-deflated urban unskilled wages, in grams of silver, daily												
1500–49	5.2	4.9	5.3	—	5.3	94.2	101.9	—	101.9	1500–49	3.5	66.7
1550–99	4.8	4.5	3.6	4.2	4.0	93.8	75.0	87.5	83.3	1550–99	3.2	66.5
1600–49	4.7	4.8	3.8	3.9	5.2	102.1	80.9	83.0	110.6	1600–49	2.8	59.7
1650–99	5.7	—	3.3	—	—	—	57.9	—	—	1650–99	2.9	50.6
1700–49	6.3	3.7	3.4	4.7	5.1	58.7	54.0	74.6	81.0	1700–49	3.5	56.3
1750–99	5.7	2.7	2.7	3.4	4.0	47.4	47.4	59.6	70.2	1750–99	3.2	56.7
1800–49	5.7	2.0	—	5.0	2.5	35.1	—	87.7	43.9	1800–49	4.0	70.4
1850–99	8.6	2.5	—	5.0	—	29.1	—	58.1	—	1850–99	5.5	63.4

continued on next page

Table 3.3 The north-south gap since the Middle Ages (cont.)

B. Fixed-budget-deflated urban skilled wages (building craftsmen), in grams of silver, daily

						Relative to London (%)						Istanbul relative to London (%)
	London	Florence & Milan	Valencia	Madrid	Naples	Florence & Milan	Valencia	Madrid	Naples		Istanbul	
1500–49	8.0	9.1	8.2	8.4	9.5	113.8	102.5	105.0	118.8	1500–49	5.3	66.7
1550–99	7.1	8.9	4.8	8.3	6.4	125.4	67.6	116.9	90.1	1550–99	4.4	61.4
1600–49	7.4	8.8	4.5	9.6	7.4	118.9	60.8	129.7	100.0	1600–49	3.2	43.0
1650–99	8.6	7.5	5.0	9.4	—	87.2	58.1	109.3	—	1650–99	3.8	44.2
1700–49	8.8	7.0	5.1	10.2	7.4	79.5	58.0	115.9	84.1	1700–49	4.3	48.9
1750–99	8.9	5.1	4.1	6.8	5.9	57.3	46.1	76.4	66.3	1750–99	4.1	45.7
1800–49	9.3	3.9	—	9.0	4.4	41.9	—	96.8	47.3	1800–49	6.1	65.6
1850–99	13.5	4.5	—	9.8	—	33.3	—	72.6	—	1850–99	7.9	58.5

Sources:
All but Istanbul: Panel A from Allen (1998a, Table 6, p.36), Panel B from Allen (1998a, Table 5, p.35). Istanbul is taken from personal correspondence with Şevket Pamuk in June 1998 and again in March 1999, based on construction accounts of the palace and semi-official pious foundations. Pamuk's real wage is calculated for both skilled (weight 2) and unskilled (weight 1) urban construction workers, but the same COL deflator is used for both. The purchasing-power-parity benchmark is for 1500–49 prices and market baskets, and the real wage time series is applied to that base. This yields the result that real wages in Istanbul were 63.4% of those in London in 1850–99. See text.

applied to the nominal wages quoted in silver prices in both places. By this calculation, real wages in Istanbul turn out to be about two-thirds of those in London (3.5/5.2, Table 3.3).[8]

These data certainly may have their flaws. For example, use of a fixed purchasing-power-parity benchmark from the early sixteenth century to the late nineteenth century may stretch the credibility of the Istanbul data. In addition, some readers may believe that recorded wage payments by the palace and pious institutions in Istanbul did not reflect private labour-market conditions, especially in the last century of the series. And we have already seen how by 1850–99 the real wage relative to England was very different as measured in Table 3.3 (Panel C of Table 3.1), compared with Panels A and B of Table 3.1. It is to be hoped that these empirical problems will be sorted out in the near future, but it must be said that Pamuk's Istanbul series in Table 3.3 is truly pioneering.

Whether they are flawed or not, these data certainly speak clearly to the issue. The central message is that the north–south gap was not the product of the late-nineteenth-century globalization surge, and we shall have far more to say about that later in this essay. Instead, the north–south gap was the product of two events: the seventeenth- and eighteenth-century pre-industrial British economic success while the Mediterranean economies underwent retardation; and Britain's industrial revolutionary gains up to the mid-nineteenth century while the Mediterranean economies pretty much stagnated. Retardation in the western and central Mediterranean between 1500 and 1850 was ubiquitous and comprehensive. The only exception was Madrid, where living standards for the urban unskilled fell by only 19 per cent between 1550–99 and 1750–99, and where all of that fall and more was recovered up to 1800–49.[9] Madrid appears to have been atypical. Living standards fell by 59 per cent in Florence and Milan between 1500–49 and 1800–49, by 49 per cent in Valencia between 1500–49 and 1750–99, and by 53 per cent in Naples between 1500–49 and 1800–49. Even the magnitudes of the decline are very similar across these three parts of the Mediterranean, suggesting that there were similar forces at work.

The eastern end of the Mediterranean does not appear to have shared in this retardation. Pamuk's real-wage estimates for Istanbul were stable between 1500–49 and 1750–99, and they even rose a bit up to 1800–49. Why the big difference between Istanbul and the rest of the Mediterranean? The explanation may, of course, lie with flaws in the data. But until such flaws are revealed, we have reason to search for the economic and demographic fundamentals which might account for these patterns. One fundamental might be simply that living standards were so low in Istanbul in the sixteenth century that a further fall was impossible: a low-level subsistence equilibrium trap had been reached. That answer implies another question: why was the eastern Mediterranean so far behind in 1500? The question for the rest of the Mediterranean is why they lost their big economic advantage after 1500. The advantage they lost was not just relative to Britain and the other leaders in the north, but they lost in terms of absolutes as well. Furthermore, they even lost their advantage relative to the eastern Mediterranean, at least based on this comparison with Istanbul.

Naples, Valencia, Florence and Milan seem to have shared a common experience between 1500 and 1850: living standards of urban wage earners were cut about in half. Furthermore, most of the decline took place in two discrete steps: in Florence and Milan, 40 per cent of the decline over the 350 years took place between 1600–49 and 1700–49, while the remaining 60 per cent took place between 1700–49 and 1800–49; in Naples, much like Florence and Milan, 45 per cent of the decline took place between 1600–49 and 1750–99, while the remaining 55 per cent took place between 1750–99 and 1800–49; and in Valencia 77 per cent of the decline took place between 1500–49 and 1650–99, while the remaining 33 per cent took place between 1650–99 and 1750–99. As we have seen, there was no secular decline in Madrid, and unskilled workers in Istanbul simply maintained a miserable living standard.

While urban living standards fell in the western and central parts of the Mediterranean, they rose, although modestly, in London. Thus, while in the early sixteenth century real wages in urban Spain and urban Italy were roughly comparable with those in London when unskilled urban workers are used in the comparison (or even higher than those in London when skilled urban craftsmen are used in the comparison), they had collapsed to less than half that level in the late nineteenth and early twentieth century. Even in Madrid, where living-standard retardation failed to take place, real wages for skilled craftsmen had fallen from above those in London to only three-quarters of them in the late eighteenth century.

Thus, most of the north–south gap which Table 3.1 documents for the 1890s and just prior to World War I was not just the product of some uneven timing of industrial revolutions or of some inability to exploit the globalization boom which started after 1850 or 1870. Instead, the gap was in large part the product of pre-industrial events during the three centuries between 1500 and 1800.

This finding for the north–south gap is consistent with what Allen finds for the European periphery more generally. While I have stressed relative economic decline of the western and central parts of the Mediterranean, Allen (1998a, Tables 5 and 6) shows the same for the eastern European cities of Augsburg, Gdansk, Krakow, Leipzig, Lwow, Strasbourg, Vienna and Warsaw. Meanwhile, Amsterdam and Antwerp shared London's economic success.

What about Istanbul? The eastern Mediterranean seemed to be bucking the retardation tide between 1500 and 1850. Perhaps it was some combination of demography, policy, and globalization forces. Perhaps, but, as I indicated above, a simpler explanation is more likely. Unskilled urban labour in the eastern Mediterranean was at subsistence, so there were no living-standard levels to lose after 1500. Unskilled urban labour in the central and western Mediterranean had far higher living standards, and plenty to lose.

W. Arthur Lewis revisited: did the core pull along the periphery during the first globalization boom?

In his Janeway Lectures given more than twenty years ago, W. Arthur Lewis (1978a) offered a number of arguments and observations on the nature of economic growth around the Third World periphery during the globalization boom prior to World War I. As Lewis pointed out, the Third World had two options in dealing with the industrialization challenge coming from northwest Europe: industrialization and direct competition with European manufactures in Third World home markets, or primary product export to satisfy booming industrial and consumption demands in European markets. Lewis made a number of additional assertions which have motivated much of the research on the Third World since then, but, with the exception of trade data (Lewis 1978a, 1978b; Hanson 1980), the debate has been based on fairly weak evidence. While there may be more, here are three questions suggested by Lewis's work which might usefully organize new comparative research on the Mediterranean:

1   Is there any evidence of catching-up around the Mediterranean after 1870? Did living standards grow faster in the Mediterranean regions that opted to industrialize behind protective walls or in those that opted for liberal policies toward trade and factor flows?
2   Lewis thought that elastic labour supplies implied stable real wages or at least real wages that lagged behind. He also thought that elastic labour supplies were reinforced in the primary-product-exporting tropical countries by immigration. Is there any evidence from the Mediterranean that supports the thesis?
3   The Lewis model implies rising inequality. Is there any evidence of rising inequality in the Mediterranean during the half century prior to World War I? If so, can it be explained by the Lewis model or might it have been driven by something else, and could the something else be globalization?

The new database on real wages and relative factor prices can speak to these questions. This section deals with the first question, while the remainder of this essay deals with the other two.

The real-wage data for 1870–1940 are plotted in Figure 3.4 relative to Great Britain. Those readers who have strong priors about British failure will be reassured by Table 3.4, which suggests that an alternative figure would look pretty much the same if each country's real wage were plotted relative to the average of Britain, France and Germany. The real-wage data for the Mediterranean are reported in Table 3.4 as averages for the 1870s, the 1890s, 1909–13 and the 1930s. The first panel reports each country relative to Great Britain (using the PPP-adjusted benchmarks in Panel B of Table 3.1), the second relative to the United States (where the USA–Britain relative is from my Atlantic economy real-wage database), the third relative to the average of

Britain, France and Germany (where the France–Britain and the Germany–Britain relatives are also from my Atlantic economy real-wage database), and the fourth relative to the average of those three plus the United States. The last panel reports per annum growth rates of the real wages.

The variety in growth performance is considerable. Between the 1870s and the 1890s, three countries were catching up, and two of them were in the east. Turkey and Egypt both recorded real-wage growth at least double that of France, Germany and the United States, and more than Britain as well. This was very strong catching-up indeed. Italy was catching up too, but not at the same fast rate as Egypt and Turkey: Italy's growth rate up to the 1890s was only slightly higher than Britain's, but almost double that of the United States. The others did badly: as we know, Spanish real wages deteriorated; Portugal and Serbia recorded only modest real-wage growth, well below the industrial leaders. There was no catch-up in these three parts of the Mediterranean, but rather fall-back. Why the variety? Was it policy, demography, or luck in world commodity markets?

Thus, there is no consistent evidence of catching-up around the Mediterranean between the 1870s and the 1890s. While Italy, Egypt and Turkey underwent catching-up, Portugal, Spain and the Balkans underwent falling-back. Nor is there any evidence supporting the Lewis thesis that the countries who adopted a more active industrialization strategy did better than those that did not. The more industrial and protectionist Portugal and Spain failed, the latter badly, while Italy did modestly well. The less industrial and open Egypt and Turkey did exceptionally well. A policy of export growth in an environment more open to trade seemed to work much better up to the 1890s than a policy of industrialization in an environment more closed to trade.

To complicate matters, however, growth performance around the Mediterranean changed dramatically between the 1890s and World War I. Real-wage growth in Egypt and Turkey collapsed: both underwent a deterioration in real wages up to 1909–13. Real-wage growth collapsed in Portugal and Serbia too: what modest real-wage growth there was up to the 1890s, evaporated thereafter. In contrast, real-wage growth in Spain surged from a pre-1890s deterioration to a post-1890s growth in excess of 2 per cent per annum, and Italy managed to raise its catching-up growth rate of 2.1 per cent per annum to an even more impressive catching-up rate of 2.4 per cent per annum. Why the dramatic switch in real-wage performance at so many points around the Mediterranean? Did the open economies suffer unfavourable price shocks after the 1890s, or did closed-economy industrialization policies finally begin to pay off? I suspect it was unfavourable price shocks, and the paper by José Morilla Critz, Alan Olmstead and Paul Rhode (Chapter 8) in this volume has much to say about that fact.

Globalization does not seem to have had any consistent positive impact on economic performance around the Mediterranean between 1870 and World War I. There is no evidence of consistent catch-up or of fall-back. Yet,

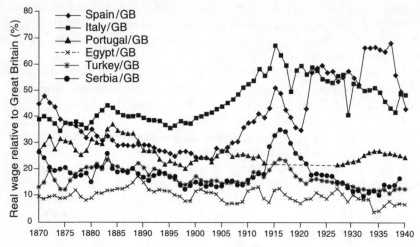

Figure 3.4 Real wages in the Mediterranean Basin relative to Great Britain, 1870–1940 (per cent).

Table 3.4 Real wage performance in the Mediterranean Basin by decades 1870s–1930s

Decade	Spain	Italy	Portugal	Turkey	Serbia	Egypt
A. Relative to Great Britain						
1870s	39.7	37.3	28.7	20.4	25.6	11.9
1890s	27.0	37.7	23.6	21.9	20.4	13.8
1909–1913	38.7	54.7	24.6	21.5	21.2	13.8
1930s	61.8	49.1	25.9	16.2	16.3	9.6
B. Relative to the United States						
1870s	23.3	22.2	17.0	12.3	15.1	7.1
1890s	18.2	25.4	15.8	14.7	13.8	9.3
1909–1913	21.9	30.9	13.9	12.2	12.0	7.8
1930s	32.0	25.6	13.4	8.4	8.3	5.1
C. Relative to average of Britain, France and Germany						
1870s	45.1	42.6	32.7	23.3	29.2	13.6
1890s	33.2	46.3	28.9	26.9	25.1	16.9
1909–1913	43.9	62.0	27.9	24.4	24.0	15.7
1930s	72.7	57.8	30.5	19.0	19.3	11.3
D. Relative to average of Britain, France, Germany and USA						
1870s	36.5	34.6	26.5	19.0	23.6	11.1
1890s	27.5	38.4	24.0	22.3	20.8	14.0
1909–1913	35.1	49.5	22.3	19.5	19.2	12.5
1930s	54.9	43.7	23.0	14.4	14.4	8.6

continued on next page

Table 3.4 Real wage performance in the Mediterranean Basin by decades, 1870s–1930s (cont.)

Period	Spain	Italy	Portugal	Turkey	Serbia	Egypt	France	Germany	Britain	USA
E. Per annum growth rate (%)										
1870s–1890s	−0.14	2.14	0.80	2.51	0.66	3.11	1.26	1.27	2.07	1.22
1890s–1909/13	2.26	2.37	0.03	−0.34	−0.02	−0.21	0.33	0.77	−0.26	0.86
1909/13–1930s	3.63	0.18	0.94	−0.54	−0.46	−0.84	0.50	0.29	0.68	0.06

Sources:
Egypt, Serbia and Turkey are from Appendices 1–3 of the July 1998 working paper cited in the endnote.
The remaining countries are from my revised Atlantic economy database.

in the interwar period, the collapse of growth at the European industrial center *did* translate into an even poorer performance almost everywhere around the Mediterranean except for Spain. Why then would the interwar collapse at the center translate consistently into even bigger economic troubles around the Mediterranean periphery when the pre-war globalization boom had such uneven effects around the same periphery?

Growth was uneven in the Mediterranean from the 1870s to the 1930s, across countries and over time. While this essay does not launch the analysis, it suggests that globalization, demographic pressure, policy and other events must have played complex and probably offsetting roles. Mediterranean economic history seems to offer an especially difficult challenge to conditional convergence analysis. The trick will be to document potential right-hand-side variables, but hopefully they can be approximated in future work by the 1870 real wage, the rate of population growth, proxies for an open commitment to world trade, external price shocks, proxies for the rate of technical change, economic geography variables and others that have appeared recently in the new growth literature.

Mediterranean migration and catch-up

Mass migration helped push real-wage convergence along in the Atlantic economy. The poorest European countries tended to have the highest emigration rates, the richest New World countries tended to have the highest immigration rates, and the European industrial leaders tended to lie in the middle with net migration close to zero. However, and this qualification is very important, the correlation was far from perfect: potential emigrants from poor countries often found the cost of the move more than they could afford; furthermore, many New World countries restricted the inflow from Asia and from certain countries along the poor European periphery. Typically, however, the labour-force impact was very big (Taylor and Williamson 1997; O'Rourke and Williamson 1997; Williamson 1997). Mass migration after 1870 served to augment the 1910 New World labour force by an enormous 49 per cent, to reduce the 1910 labour force in the emigrant countries around the European periphery by a very large 22 per cent, and to reduce the 1910 labour force in the European industrial core by a tiny 2 per cent. Mass migration by itself probably explained about 70 per cent of the real-wage convergence in the late-nineteenth-century Atlantic economy (Taylor and Williamson, 1997; O'Rourke and Williamson, 1999, Ch. 8).

Could the *absence* of mass migration explain the absence of catch-up in the Mediterranean? Kevin O'Rourke and I (1997) concluded recently that emigration from Italy explained an enormous share of its convergence on Britain and America. But the catch-up would have been considerably more impressive had Italian return migration been more modest. One of the reasons why Italian catch-up was delayed until the 1890s and only modest thereafter, was that the *net* emigration rate was modest compared to what a

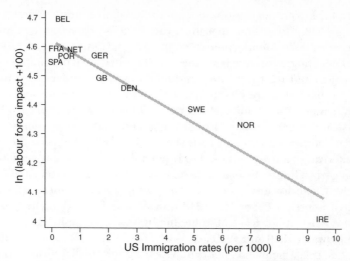

Figure 3.5 The correlation between emigration's labour force impact in the sending country and the US immigration rate from that country, 1870–1910: eleven Atlantic economies.

country that poor should have recorded. We also concluded that the emigration rate from Spain and Portugal was even lower compared to what it should have been. Indeed, a significant share of the rise in the real-wage gap between Iberia and Britain from 1870 to 1910 can be explained by Iberian "under-emigration", as much as a tenth for Spain and a quarter for Portugal. Under-emigration was hardly the only force at work (Tortella 1994; O'Rourke and Williamson 1997), but it was one of the reasons why Iberia missed a chance to catch up on the industrial leaders prior to World War I. Timothy Hatton and I (1998, Ch. 3) have shown that most of the explanation for the low Iberian emigration rates was, quite simply, poverty and the constraints that it placed on the ability of the poor to move. The higher-paid Italian worker was better able to release some of that constraint, but apparently not all of it (Faini and Venturini 1994). The low Iberian emigration rate can also be explained by discrimination and problems of cultural assimilation in the receiving regions. Finally, as Blanca Sánchez-Alonso (Chapter 11) shows so clearly in her paper in this volume, it may also have been due to exchange-rate policy: depreciation of the peseta tended to raise the cost of emigration, by increasing the peseta price of steerage and job search, to the Spanish worker contemplating a move to the New World or to industrial centres in the north of Europe.

What role did mass migration play elsewhere in the Mediterranean? The problem here, of course, is that we have so little solid information for the Balkans, Turkey, Egypt and other regions in the eastern and southern parts of the Mediterranean. Ferenczi and Willcox (1929), for example, were able to document almost nothing useful for our purposes, although the qualitative evidence for Egypt suggests no net emigration at all from that country. But suppose we were to assume that the United States' gross immigration rate from some eastern Mediterranean countries was a good mirror reflecting the total net emigration rate from the same country to all destinations (both "rates" calculated relative to the sending country's population).[10] Indeed, Figure 3.5 shows that, for eleven members of the Atlantic economy, the correlation between the estimated total impact of mass emigration (to all destinations) on the 1910 labour force at home and the gross immigration rate from that country into the USA was very high (0.90).[11] Suppose the regression underlying Figure 3.5 is used to predict the impact of mass emigration from Bulgaria, Greece, Romania, Serbia and Turkey, five eastern regions for which the US authorities reported gross immigration statistics (Appendix 1 in HIER Discussion Paper No. 1842, July 1998)? Point estimates[12] of how much the 1910 labour force at home might have been reduced by net emigration between 1870 and 1910 are: Bulgaria not at all; Romania a tiny 0.27 per cent; Serbia a small 3.38 per cent; Greece a still small 5.81 per cent; and Turkey 15.89 per cent. Based on qualitative evidence, the figure for Egypt is zero. Turkey seems to have exploited emigration possibilities far better than its Balkan neighbours or Egypt, as it also did in the post-World War II guestworker era. But even so, the labour-force impact of emigration from Turkey was lower than the 1870–1910 average around the European periphery, 22 per cent, and that average includes the under-emigrating Iberians and Italians. However approximate these figures are, it seems safe to conclude that all of these countries in the eastern part of the Mediterranean – just like Portugal and Spain in the western part – missed out on an important catching-up opportunity prior to World War I: while poor countries in Europe were sending out a flood of emigrants, the Mediterranean countries were sending out only a trickle. After the US immigration quotas were imposed in the early 1920s, these lagging countries lost their chance for thirty years, since they had to wait for the European postwar revival.

Mass migration in the Atlantic economy played an important role in forging a global labour market prior to 1914, but most of the Mediterranean wasn't part of it.

Hints and hunches about inequality trends 1870–1939

Eli Heckscher and Bertil Ohlin[13] argued that the integration of global commodity markets would lead to convergence of international factor prices, as countries everywhere expanded the production and export of commodities which used their abundant (and cheap) factors intensively. Evidence from the Atlantic economy seems to be consistent with their prediction: the trade boom led to rising wage/rental ratios in labour-abundant Europe, and falling wage/rental ratios in the land-abundant New World.[14] As a consequence, conditions improved for the poor unskilled worker relative to the rich landlord in much of Europe, while the opposite was true of the New World

(O'Rourke *et al.* 1996; Williamson 1997, 1998d). Did the Mediterranean behave more like the New World or the Old World? Was the Mediterranean labour or land abundant? Certainly labour in the Mediterranean was poor compared to the New World and the European industrial core, but the real question is whether the ratio of *effective* labour to *effective* land was big or small in the Mediterranean compared with trading partners in industrial Europe. Guided by the historical insights of Gregory Clark (1987a) and the theoretical insights of Robert Lucas (1990) that poverty does not necessarily mean cheap or abundant labour, as well as by the obvious fact that Mediterranean fruits, nuts and even cotton can only be grown on land with a Mediterranean climate, my guess is that the Mediterranean had large effective land/labour ratios. If the countries in the Mediterranean were relatively land-abundant in this sense, then they should have specialized in land-intensive products and thus should also have undergone a decline in their wage/rental ratios in response to trade booms; that is, the demand for land should have enjoyed a boom compared with labour. All of this is pure speculation, of course, awaiting confrontation with evidence.

Mass migration mattered too, and, in the Atlantic economy, probably a lot more. Immigrants in high-wage countries tended to be unskilled, and became increasingly so as the late nineteenth century unfolded. Thus, they flooded labour markets at the bottom in destination countries, lowering the unskilled wage relative to the skilled wage, as well as relative to white-collar incomes, and land rents. Mass migration implied rising inequality in labour-scarce, resource-rich countries. However, mass migration implied falling inequality in those poor low-wage countries that were sending the emigrants abroad. Both emigration and trade should, therefore, have moderated inequality in poor countries around the European periphery. In contrast, they should have had the opposite effect in the Mediterranean if my assertion about the effective land/labour ratio is correct. On the other hand, the previous section suggests that the emigration forces were likely to have been far weaker in the Mediterranean than they were in the Atlantic economy. Thus, the trade forces may well have dominated in the Mediterranean.

So much for globalization. What about labour surplus? In his famous model of the labour-surplus economy, W. Arthur Lewis (1954) showed how early industrialization could create inequality. Stable real wages implied rising profit shares economy-wide. According to this model, the worker fails to share in GDP per capita growth since elastic labour supplies keep wages and living standards stable. The labour-surplus model has also been used to predict stable real wages in Latin America, since it has been alleged that mass migration from the Mediterranean served to create an elastic labour supply in, for example, both Argentina and Brazil (Diaz-Alejandro 1970: 21–2; Leff 1992: 6). In fact, the model appears to have failed for Latin America (Taylor 1994) and to have failed for Italy and Iberia (Hatton and Williamson 1998, Ch. 3), but perhaps it might do better in the eastern Mediterranean. The Lewis model is quiet about what happens to land rents, but the classical

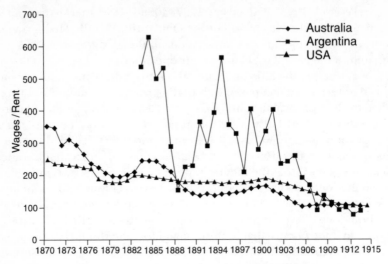

Figure 3.6 New World wage/rent ratios, 1870–1914 (1911 = 100).

model from which it was derived clearly predicted a rise in rents. It follows that trade booms and elastic labour supplies make the same prediction for the Mediterranean, falling wage/rental ratios and rising inequality. Discriminating empirically between these competing views will prove difficult.

Complete income distributions at various benchmarks between the mid-nineteenth century and World War II are available only for a few countries and dates, but even if such data were available, it is not obvious that they would be the best way to search for the underlying causes of changing inequality. Our interest here is factor prices: wages, rents and the structure of pay. How did the typical unskilled worker near the bottom of the distribution do relative to the typical landowner or capitalist near the top, or even relative to the typical skilled blue-collar worker or educated white-collar employee near the middle of the distribution? The modern debate over OECD inequality has a fixation on wages, but since land and landed interests were far more important to late-nineteenth-century inequality trends – especially in the more agrarian Mediterranean – we need to add them to any distribution inquiry. In any case, there are two kinds of evidence available to document inequality trends prior to World War I: changes in the ratio of the unskilled wage to farm-land rents (or land values), and changes in the ratio of the unskilled wage to GDP per worker-hour.

The wage/rental ratio plunged in the New World, where it had been initially high (Figure 3.6). One study estimates that by 1913 the Australian ratio had fallen to one-quarter of its 1870 level, that the Argentine ratio had fallen to one-fifth of its mid-1880 level, and that the US ratio had fallen to less than half of its 1870 level (O'Rourke *et al.* 1996). In Europe, the (initially low) wage/rental ratio surged up to World War I, especially where there was free

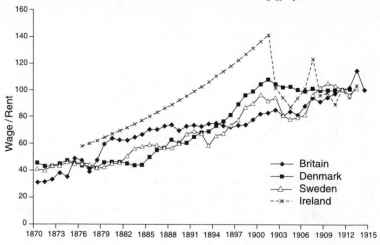

Figure 3.7 Free trade Old World wage/rent ratios, 1870–1914 (1911 = 100).

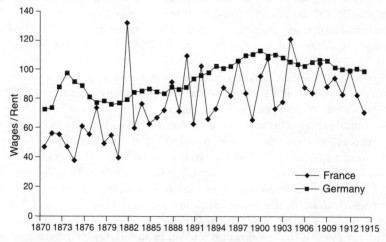

Figure 3.8 Protected Old World wage/rent ratios, 1870–1914 (1911 = 100).

trade (Figure 3.7). The British ratio increased by a factor of 2.7 over its 1870 level, while the Irish ratio increased by even more. The Swedish and Danish ratios both increased by a factor of 2.3. Not surprisingly, the surge was more pronounced in free-trade countries than in the two protectionist countries for which I have documentation: the ratio increased by a factor of "only" 1.8 in France and 1.4 in Germany (Figure 3.8).

Landowners were at the top of the income distribution pyramid in Europe (and, one must assume, the Mediterranean). The falling wage/rental ratio in the rich, labour-scarce New World is consistent with the belief that inequality rose there, while the rising wage/rental ratio in poor, labour-abundant Europe is consistent with the belief that inequality was falling

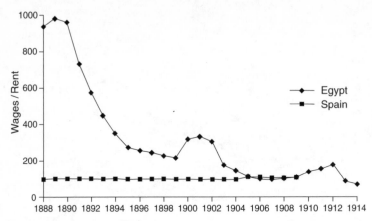

Figure 3.9 Wage/rent ratios: Egypt and Spain, 1885–1914 (1909 = 100).

there. A liberal policy commitment to globalization seems to have mattered: European countries staying open to trade absorbed the biggest distributional hit; European countries retreating behind tariff walls absorbed the smallest distributional hit (Williamson 1997; O'Rourke and Williamson 1999, Ch. 9).

Now, what about the Mediterranean? Here I have evidence for only two countries: Spain, which refused to play the globalization game, and Egypt, which played it with enthusiasm. Figure 3.9 shows that the Spanish wage/rental ratio declined hardly at all from 1888 to 1909,[15] since landlords were protected from the "grain invasion"; the Egyptian ratio, however, underwent a spectacular fall, driven by the cotton export boom which drove up land values and rents. Even if we purge the decline to 1895 as being too steep to believe, the ratio still more than halves from 1895 to World War I. Egypt seems to share the rising inequality witnessed even in the richer primary producers in the New World. However, and in contrast with the New World, my guess is that emigration and other demographic events had very little to do with the collapse in the Egyptian wage/rental ratio, while trade and export prices had everything to do with it.[16]

What about the ratio of the unskilled worker's wage (w) to the returns on all factors per labourer as measured by, say, Angus Maddison's (1995) estimates of GDP per worker-hour (y)? Changes in this ratio (w/y) measure changes in the economic distance between the working poor near the bottom of the distribution and the average citizen in the middle of the distribution. It turns out that the w/y ratio is highly correlated with more comprehensive inequality statistics in the few cases where both are available in the Atlantic economy. In any case, here is the inequality tale that the ratio w/y tells for the Atlantic economy over the four decades prior to World War I. The index rises from 100 to about 153 for Denmark and Sweden, and falls to 53 or 58 for Australia and the United States. An alternative way to

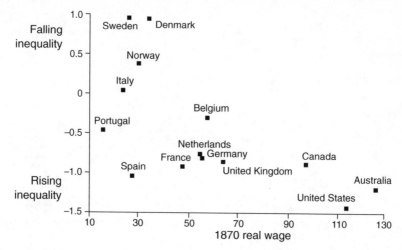

Figure 3.10 Initial real wages vs inequality trends in the Atlantic economy 1870–1913 (average annual percentage change in inequality index).

Note: The real wage in 1870 is relative to the United Kingdom = 100 in 1905.

standardize these distributional trends up to 1913 is to compute the annual percentage change in the index for each country relative to its 1870 base: the per annum rates range from +0.97 and +0.98 for Denmark and Sweden, to −1.22 and −1.45 for Australia and the United States.

This measure of inequality change is plotted against the 1870 real wage in Figure 3.10, and it offers strong confirmation of the globalization hypothesis: between 1870 and 1913, inequality rose dramatically in rich, land-abundant, labour-scarce New World countries like Australia, Canada and the United States; inequality fell dramatically in poor, land-scarce, labour-abundant, newly industrializing countries like Norway, Sweden, Denmark and Italy; inequality was more stable in the European industrial economies like Belgium, France, Germany, the Netherlands and the United Kingdom; and inequality was also more stable in the poor European economies which failed to play the globalization game, like Portugal and Spain.

What about the eastern end of the Mediterranean? Figure 3.11 plots what little evidence we have: Egypt 1880–1939, Serbia 1913–39, and Turkey 1913–39. The w/y ratio declined throughout, and the magnitudes were not unlike those recorded by Australia and the United States. By 1929, the Serbian ratio had fallen to 57 per cent of its 1913 level and to 41 per cent of its 1914 level, enormous declines over such a short period. The Turkish ratio fell by 11 per cent over the same period. While volatile in the short run, the Egyptian ratio fell steadily over the six decades between 1880 and 1939. Between 1880–89 and 1900–9, it fell by more than 28 per cent, and between 1900–9 and 1930–39 it fell by more than 14 per cent. Limited though this evidence may be, it offers support for the view that inequality was on the rise at

Figure 3.11 Real wages/GDP per capita, Egypt, Serbia and Turkey, 1880–1939 (1913 = 100).

Sources: GDP per capita figures for Egypt are from Yousef (forthcoming). The same figures for Turkey and Serbia are from Maddison (1995), suitably interpolated. The real-wage data are taken from the appendix of my HIER Discussion Paper 1842 (July 1998).

the eastern end of the Mediterranean during the late nineteenth century and the interwar years.

What explains the rising inequality? Was it labour surplus, trade booms, or policy? As I argued early in this section, rising inequality is consistent with both Lewis' labour-surplus model and the Heckscher–Ohlin globalization model (revised to accommodate Clark–Lucas *effective* endowment adjustments). This essay will duck this question about the sources of inequality trends, but it is added to that lengthening agenda.

An agenda for the future

Factor-price data is far more abundant for the Mediterranean prior to 1914 than are GDP and other macro-performance indicators. With these new data, we are now able to say quite a bit about the behaviour of real wages in six parts of the Mediterranean during the globalization boom from 1870 to World War I: Portugal, Spain, Italy (north, centre and south), the Balkans, Turkey and Egypt. We are also able to comment extensively on real-wage behaviour in Portugal, Spain, northern Italy and Turkey between 1820 and 1870. Furthermore, we can say plenty about real-wage behaviour over the three centuries before 1820 in Istanbul, Florence, Milan, Naples, Madrid and Valencia. This real-wage performance in the Mediterranean can also be compared with Britain and with what eventually became the rest of industrial Europe.

That's an amazing amount of evidence which previous scholarship has pretty much ignored, but researchers are greedy and they always want more. What's missing is more comprehensive evidence on the returns to other factors of production, such as land. The labour-surplus model and conventional trade theory both predict falling wage/rental ratios in those parts of the Mediterranean where the forces of world trade were allowed to have an impact and where emigration was choked off by poverty, but this prediction can only be documented for Egypt. Where the forces of world trade were not allowed to have an impact one might expect much more stable trends, but this prediction can only be documented for Spain. We need more evidence on farmland rents and values earlier in time and across a wider range of countries. And what about the premium on skills? If Gabriel Tortella is right in asserting that schooling scarcity helps explain poor growth performance in Iberia and Italy, then the premium on skills should have been high, thus reflecting that scarcity. Assuming he is right – which I doubt – was the skill premium driven up even higher when so many economies in the Mediterranean got caught up in the late-nineteenth-century globalization boom? Can the premium be proxied by urban–rural wage gaps? If so, it can be retrieved from the same sources which supply the (urban unskilled) real-wage data reported elsewhere in this essay.

However limited, this new factor-price database can speak to these inequality issues and to a number of growth and labour-market issues which I repeat here in the form of an explicit agenda for the future:

1   How did the Latin part of the Mediterranean, sending emigrants, perform relative to the Latin part of the New World, receiving those immigrants, between 1820 and 1940? Did the rising gap between the north and south in Europe have its counterpart between Latin America and the Mediterranean, Iberia and Italy in particular?[17]
2   While the Mediterranean labour market may have become increasingly segmented from that of the Atlantic economy, what about labour-market segmentation *within* the region? Can the poor correlations between urban labour markets around the Mediterranean after 1820 be explained by "different shocks" or by the absence of migrations working effectively at the margins?
3   Real wages in the western and central parts of the Mediterranean were on a par with real wages in London and Amsterdam around 1500, but they collapsed thereafter. Why the collapse when there was an upward creep in pre-industrial England? And why wasn't the pre-industrial real-wage collapse in the west and central parts of the Mediterranean shared by the east, at least as documented by Istanbul? Was it simply that real wages and living standards there were already at a low-level equilibrium, or did the east avoid the unfavourable economic and demographic shocks which beset the west and central Mediterranean?
4   Why did the interwar collapse at the centre translate into an even bigger collapse almost everywhere around the Mediterranean periphery, while the pre-1914 globalization boom did not translate into ubiquitous catching-up? Why this asymmetry prior to and after World War I?

5   Emigration made an enormous contribution to real-wage growth in the poor sending parts of Europe, and it hastened their convergence on the industrial leaders. Emigration from Iberia was much smaller, and it was tiny from much of the eastern part of the Mediterranean. Does this fact help explain why the Mediterranean failed to undergo catch-up prior to 1914?

6   Why the rise in inequality in the eastern Mediterranean while it was falling in much of the labour-abundant European periphery?

These are only some of the questions suggested by this new factor-price data for the Mediterranean. The list is long, but the answers appear to be within reach.

Notes

This is a revised version of a paper presented to the *Conference on Long-Run Economic Change in the Mediterranean Basin*, Istanbul, Turkey (June 4–6 1998). I would like to thank Tarik Yousef for helping me navigate the Egyptian sources; Şevket Pamuk for helping me navigate the Ottoman and Turkish sources, and for sharing his Istanbul data; Michael Palairet for sharing his Serbian data; Bob Allen for sharing his northern Italian data; and the participants at the Istanbul conference who supplied useful comments. I would also like to acknowledge the excellent research assistance of Maggie Angell, Davin Chor, Ximena Clark, Matt Weinzierl and Pinar Yegin. The database underlying this paper is reported in Appendices 1–3 of a *HIER Discussion Paper* 1842 (July 1998) which is available from the Harvard Economics Department. The data and the *HIER* paper are also reported at my website: http://www.economics.harvard.edu/~jwilliam. However, the data have been revised (spring 1999), and I will make the revisions available on diskette upon request. The *HIER* 1842 working paper has two *HIER Discussion Paper* companions: "Real Wages and Relative Factor Prices in the Third World 1820–1940: Asia" [1998a] and "Real Wages and Relative Factor Prices in the Third World 1820–1940: Latin America" [1998b], which are also available from the same source as *HIER Discussion Paper* 1842. The data from Asia and Latin America are also reported at my website, but since they also have been revised and augmented, I will make them available on diskette too.

1   Robert Allen (1998a, 1998c) argues that the divergence *within* Europe started much earlier. This evidence will be discussed below.

2   Standard trade theory makes the prediction that factor prices converge (or diverge) far faster than does GDP per capita or GDP per worker. See the next section.

3   For a summary, see Williamson (1996a), and O'Rourke and Williamson (1999).

4   When the real wage is regressed on time and time squared, the results reject any evidence of significant and positive real-wage growth over the full century. The adjusted R-squared for northern Italy is zero, and all t-statistics are less than unity. The adjusted R-squared for Istanbul is 0.10, and no t-statistic exceeds 1.2.

5   There are many ways to test *any* market-integration hypothesis, including commodity market integration. See, for example, Persson (1999: Ch. 5).

6   I have already implied, however, that a resolution of the disagreement between the competing benchmarks in Table 3.1 will imply some repair to the gaps plotted in Figure 3.3.

7   The real-wage series for Britain 1830–70 is taken from the revisions of my Atlantic economy database (Williamson 1995, revised). The extension to 1820 relies on Lindert and Williamson (1983: Table 3; 1985: Table 1).

8   Pamuk has time-series data for both wages and prices. The price deflator for the time series is constructed by using an Istanbul worker's fixed market basket which includes coal, wood, nails, imported woolen cloth, local woolen cloth, chick peas, flour, honey, rice and cooking oil.

9   The remainder of this paragraph uses unskilled real wages in Panel A to illustrate the decline, but almost exactly the same figures emerge when those in Panel B for skilled craftsmen are used.

10 Somewhere between 60 and 70 per cent of the overseas migration from Europe went to the United States.

11 The correlation in Figure 3.5 is much higher when the outlier Italy, with its enormous return migration rate, is excluded. Including Italy, the correlation drops to 0.64.

12 These are point estimates, but their credibility must be gauged by the wide ranges which should be embracing those points. The wide ranges are generated by regressions with and without Spain, Italy and Portugal, the bigger numbers without. They can be widened still further by taking one standard deviation on either side of the point estimate, as the Appendix in my *HIER Discussion Paper* 1842 (July 1998) shows.

13 Translated in Flam and Flanders (1991).

14 I am referring to farm rents and farmland values here.

15 The Spanish wage/rental ratio is revised from the earlier one reported in O'Rourke *et al.* (1996), since the wage series itself has been revised.

16 See the pioneering work on this topic by Bent Hansen (1991a, 1991b).

17 I offer the answers to this and related questions in a companion paper (Williamson 1998b).

4   European economic development

The core and the southern
periphery, 1870–1910

James Foreman-Peck and Pedro Lains

Introduction

In relations between states and regions, the rich are the core and the poor
are the periphery. But which countries belong to the so-defined core and
periphery varies with the historical epoch. In some times and places, poorer
economies catch up and even overtake the richer. In others, international
income gaps widen. When and where convergence and divergence of
national incomes per head are found is easier to describe than to predict.
The most ambitious collection of world national income statistics by Angus
Maddison (1995) denies any general pattern of convergence since 1820, or
even between 1870 and 1914. Whereas in western Europe GDP per head
increased by 75 per cent between 1870 and 1914, GDP in southern and eastern European rose by only one half. Incomes in the west were more than
double those in the east, by the outbreak of World War I. The gap had widened
after 1870.

This experience might be explained by the recent flowering of quantitative empirical studies of economic growth, especially since institutions, natural resources and technology have recently entered this literature (e.g. Sachs
and Warner 1995; Barro 1997). Economic historians have traditionally seen
these three variables as mainsprings of growth. They are the fundamental
elements of the model of European core–periphery development in the
later nineteenth century, based on Foreman-Peck (1995), specified and estimated in the present paper. We employ this model to explain why countries
in the Balkans and Iberia showed no ability to catch up with the European
leader, the United Kingdom, in the years 1870–1910, even though some
other economies in the area, as well as in northwestern Europe, were doing
so. The next section compares the two poor peripheries of Europe in a preliminary search for the causes of relative success and failure in economic
growth during the 1870–1910 period. The third section links a selection of
the economic growth literature to the present concerns, while the fourth discusses the ideas behind the model and the fundamental variables. The
parameters estimated for the model and their implications are reported in
the fifth section. The data are presented in an appendix.

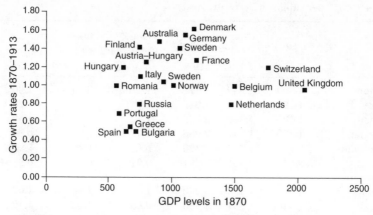

Figure 4.1 GDP levels, 1870, and growth rates, 1870–1913.

The southern European periphery

The southern European periphery seems to have been poorer than the Scandinavian economies even before the mid-nineteenth century, as Jaime Reis' and Jeffrey Williamson's chapters show. Table 4.1 and Figure 4.1 depict the basic data on differences in national GDP per capita by 1870, which our model attempts to explain. Figure 4.1 shows clearly two convergence clubs, one below and one above the line of US$ 1,000 of GDP per capita in 1870 (at 1980 "international dollars"). Among the "rich" converging countries we may include the Scandinavian countries (Finland excepted), as well as France, Germany and the small western European economies. The poor convergers include Finland, Austria and the more successful economies of the southern and eastern peripheries, namely, Italy, Spain, Romania and Hungary. The rest of the countries in Figure 4.1 did not converge at all. Thus, the countries in the southern periphery of Europe fall into two groups: Italy, Spain and Romania on the one hand, and Portugal, Greece, Serbia and Bulgaria, on the other. Our purpose here is to explain the differences in economic performance of these two groups with a model of income and output for the European economies.[1]

Measured by population, there are two large and converging countries (Italy and Spain); one small and slightly converging country (Romania); and four "unsuccessful" and small countries (Portugal, Bulgaria, Greece and Serbia). A small population was not peculiar to the periphery economies and thus was probably not a major cause of economic backwardness. In fact, the five small countries in our sample of poor countries had an average population of 4.6 million, whereas in the centre and northern periphery there were seven small countries with an average population of 4.4 million (Belgium, Denmark, Finland, the Netherlands, Norway, Sweden and Switzerland). Among the Balkan countries, only Serbia, with 60 persons per square

Table 4.1 GDP per capita and growth rates

	GDP per capita (1980 "international" US$)			Trend growth rates (annual, per cent)		
	1870	*1890*	*1913*	*1870–90*	*1890–1913*	*1870–1913*
Belgium	1 500	1 859	2 311	1.08	0.95	1.00
France	1 196	1 436	1 973	0.92	1.39	1.28
Germany	1 101	1 376	2 023	1.12	1.69	1.56
Netherlands	1 469	1 947	2 286	1.42	0.70	0.80
Switzerland	n/a	1 763	2 320	n/a	[1.20]	[1.20]
UK	2 045	2 451	2 991	0.91	0.87	0.97
Denmark	1 172	1 450	2 276	1.07	1.98	1.63
Finland	740	847	1 286	0.68	1.83	1.42
Norway	1 014	1 157	1 550	0.66	1.28	1.04
Sweden	1 057	1 230	1 838	0.76	1.76	1.41
Austria–Hungary	793	987	1 359	[1.10]	[1.40]	[1.26]
Austria	*897*	*1 145*	*1 623*	*1.23*	*1.53*	*1.48*
Hungary	*616*	*752*	*998*	*[1.00]*	*[1.24]*	*[1.20]*
Italy	748	831	1 399	0.53	2.29	1.11
Spain	928	1 188	1 457	1.24	0.89	1.05
Bulgaria	n/a	726	814	n/a	[0.50]	[0.50]
Greece	671	724	840	[0.38]	[0.65]	[0.54]
Portugal	624	746	837	0.90	0.50	0.69
Romania	565	663	872	[0.80]	[1.20]	[1.00]
Russia	n/a	743	893	n/a	[0.80]	[0.80]
Serbia	n/a	646	724	n/a	[0.50]	[0.50]

Notes and sources: Estimates for 1913 as in Table 4A.1. Backward extrapolation with trend growth rates for other years. See Tables 4A.1 and 4A.2 and sources in Appendix.

kilometre, had a population density close to that of France. The population density in the remaining Balkan countries was much lower.[2] Possibly because of the low densities, the Balkan population increased at faster rates than that of western Europe, particularly after the 1870s.[3]

Despite lower population densities in the Balkans, the pressure of agricultural labour on productive land was higher. On average, there were more workers to a given area of agricultural land in the southern periphery than in the countries of the European core and the northern periphery. Although some forms of Mediterranean agriculture, such as viticulture, may have required high labour intensity, the likelihood is that overall labour productivity was depressed in the Balkans, Portugal and Italy, compared with elsewhere in industrialized Europe. The density of agricultural population over productive land in southern Europe fell generally within the range of 46–52 agricultural workers per square kilometre. In France and Denmark that proportion was 32 workers per square kilometre, and even less in the UK. Pressure on the land was higher in Serbia, at 93 workers per square kilometre.

The higher ratio of agricultural population to agricultural land was linked to a lower share of husbandry in agricultural production. Agriculture on the southern periphery was more dependent on crops and less on animal output. In fact, animal production accounted for about one-quarter of agricultural output in Bulgaria, Greece, Italy and Portugal, and even less in Romania. Spain and Serbia had larger shares (30 and 36 per cent, respectively), but still below those of France (44 per cent), Germany (65 per cent) and the UK (72 per cent).[4] The share of animal output positively affects agricultural productivity because animals are a source of manure and traction. It also reflects the income-elastic demand for meat.

The exception to these generalizations, as far as livestock is concerned, is Serbia, but there, producers were catering for the export market. If we compare the share of animals in output with the share of pastures in the use of land, we must conclude that the animal sector had a higher productivity in Bulgaria and Serbia than in the rest of the periphery. Wheat yields in Romania were relatively high, above those in France. Bulgaria, Serbia and Spain also achieved good wheat yields, compared to France's. On the other hand, productivity levels in the wine sectors of Greece, Portugal and Romania were particularly high.[5]

These conclusions about comparative productivity in the agricultural and livestock sectors are compatible with the structure of agricultural exports from the southern periphery. Serbia's exports concentrated on animal produce, whereas Romania and Bulgaria specialized in wheat or other grain exports. Romania exported in 1909–13 half of its wheat output, and Bulgaria 30 per cent. Greece was a large exporter of currants and Portugal of wine; the share of these exports in domestic output fell a little below 30 per cent (Evans 1924: 95; Lampe and Jackson 1982: 170).

The patterns and directions of foreign trade were intimately related with political factors. The political setting defined the economic zones of our peripheral countries. Romania, for instance, exported large amounts of grain to Turkey, although it also sold to the neighbouring Habsburg Empire, as well as to Britain and France (Lampe and Jackson 1982: Table 3.4). The other Balkan countries were also tied to the Ottoman Empire's market. Bulgaria, for example, exported coarse woollen cloth for the Ottoman army. The end of the Ottoman Empire in the Balkans encouraged the redirection of trade links to the west, which was soon followed by western capital imports. Romania benefitted more than Serbia or Greece from that possibility. Portuguese external relations integrated the country into one of the fastest-growing trade zones in Europe, centred on Britain. Although connections between Portugal and Spain and industrial Europe were closer, only in the 1850s did agricultural exports noticeably increase and not until two decades later was foreign capital imported in significant volumes.

The share of exports in GNP was larger in Romania than in the small peripheral countries: Portugal, Bulgaria and Serbia. The available data shows that export shares did not increase in any of the above countries after the late 1870s. An explanation is in the chapter by Morilla Critz, Olmstead and Rhode, showing how Mediterranean fruit and nut exports were hit by American competition. By 1911 Romania exported 25 per cent of its GNP, Bulgaria about 20 per cent, Serbia 15 per cent and Portugal about 13 per cent.[6] Taking the available estimates of the growth of GDP per capita, we conclude that exports may have increased by between 0.5 and 1.0 per cent per year in real per capita terms. In the world as a whole, the growth of exports was above 3 per cent, in real terms. The export sector therefore performed badly in the Balkans and the Mediterranean periphery (Lampe and Jackson 1982: 164–5; Lains 1995: 77).

There is some modern evidence that a certain amount of democracy is beneficial for economic growth (Barro 1997), but political history does not separate the two groups in the southern European periphery that concern us here. The Romanian lands were never a formal part of the Ottoman Empire and in 1821 they were granted limited autonomy. In 1859 the two principalities of Wallachia and Moldavia formed the principality of Romania. After losing the war with Russia in 1878, the Ottoman government granted full independence to the principality, which then proved a good performer. Much earlier, in 1830, Greece won independence and Serbia also became fully autonomous in 1878, but they both lagged behind Romania. Bulgaria, the Balkan country with the closest ties to the Ottoman Empire, which achieved autonomy only in 1878 and full independence in 1908, was also a poor performer. On the other hand, Portugal had been independent for centuries, Spain's boundaries were defined by the seventeenth century, and Italy did not exist before 1861.

Constitutional and representative government was not a western periphery monopoly. True, Portugal was at first ahead of Bulgaria by twenty years or so, but not much more. In both countries the nineteenth century saw the fall of the *ancien régime*, though this happened sooner in Portugal: a revolution imposed a parliament and a constitutional charter in 1820. Yet the Portuguese changes were only fully implemented after a further *coup d'état* in 1851. Only then was a regime based on two major political parties (with factions) in place. Elections were manipulated but there were no governments without parliamentary support until 1907. Bulgaria gained independence from Istanbul in 1878, but a similar parliamentary regime based on two major parties followed immediately. The rapid introduction of the parliamentary regime in Bulgaria is explained by Ottoman rule not totally hindering the formation of the domestic institutions in the region.

Turning to the industrial sector, at the end of our period, Portugal was the most industrialized country, with a share of industry in national income of 25 per cent (*c.* 1910), followed by Romania for which the corresponding figure was 20 per cent. The shares for Bulgaria and Serbia were somewhat lower at

15 and 12 per cent, respectively. In Greece the industrial sector was dwarfed by the service sector and particularly by shipping; industry contributed only 5 per cent of national income by 1910. For most of the above countries the shares of industry in national income were higher than the shares of manufactures in exports (the exceptions are Greece and probably Bulgaria and Serbia, where both figures were low). This means that in Portugal, Romania, Spain and Hungary, the external competitiveness of the industrial sector was lower than that of the economy as a whole. In Portugal and Spain the explanation was industrial protection. In Romania tariff protection was lower and only in the 1890s did the rates there rise to Latin levels. Yet in 1913 tariff protection was rather similar in the above countries. Bulgaria and Serbia had somewhat lower levels of tariffs on manufactured imports (Woytinsky and Woytinsky 1953: 277; Lampe 1986: 40).

The structure of industrial output of Romania and Portugal clearly reveals the impact of protection. In Portugal, the protected textile manufactures accounted for 43 per cent of industrial output. This share was not in accordance with the country's revealed comparative advantages. In fact, by 1910, only 27 per cent of industrial exports from Portugal were composed of textiles and the vast majority of those textiles were sold in the protected colonial markets. The share of textiles in Romania's industrial output was only 15 per cent. There was no equivalent in Portugal of the development of heavy industries in Romania. In 1910 the petroleum sector accounted for as much as 23 per cent of output of the secondary sector (industry and mining) and the flour and sugar industries added 24 per cent of industrial output (or 19 per cent if mining is included with industry).[7]

Although the industrial share in Romania was close to that of Portugal, the pattern of industrial growth in the two countries was remarkably different. In 1870 Portugal was more industrialized than the Romanian lands.[8] From then on, industry expanded faster in Romania than in Portugal and, particularly, Romania saw the rapid expansion of heavy industrial sectors, which were practically non-existent in Portugal down to the 1920s. In Portugal industrial growth was slow and in no period or sector can we find annual growth rates above 4 per cent. Estimates for Romania are probably less accurate, mainly because there is some uncertainty regarding price trends. From 1901–2 to 1911–12 we have information regarding nominal and real growth rates for output of "manufacturing", which are 9.1 and 8.4 per cent per year. In real terms (taking the same inflation rate), mining expanded in the same period at 12.8 per cent per year, and the "artisan and household" sectors at 3.4 per cent per year. Total industry expanded at 6.4 per cent, in real terms, in the same decade. From the mid-1860s to 1912–3, the Romanian industrial sector grew at 4 per cent per year, in current prices. If we assume no inflation between 1860–1900 and take the estimated 1 per cent yearly inflation in the period 1900–12, the above rate would be 3.8 per cent (Jackson 1986: 62 and 82). These rates are much higher than estimated for Portugal.

Romania, Bulgaria and Serbia all specialized in the foodstuffs industries.

Serbia possessed a substantial meat-packing industry and there were large flour-milling industries, as well as tobacco and sugar sectors, in all three countries. The domestic demand for flour and sugar were probably rising by as much as population, if not faster. Among the external drivers, two clearly set the Balkan countries apart from the countries in the southwestern periphery: the favourable export markets in central Europe and direct foreign investment in these industries.

With independence came the opportunity to define national foreign-trade policy. Except for the UK and a few small countries in western Europe, there was a drive towards tariff protection in the later nineteenth century. In the east, tariff policy was somewhat constrained by the international agreements that had granted either autonomy or independence from the Ottoman Empire to the area. Yet, by the early 1890s, Greece, Bulgaria, Romania and Serbia were permitted to raise their tariffs, which they did.

Foreign direct investment was not apparently stimulated by protection, but instead was channelled to the export sector and to railways, which also favoured exports by providing the necessary transport infrastructure. In Romania, in 1914, 82 per cent of industrial joint-stock capital was foreign. In the petrol, gas and sugar industries the proportion of foreign capital was close to 95 per cent. Domestic capital was predominant only in the paper and pulp industries (54 per cent) and foodstuffs (69 per cent). The proportion of foreign-owned bank assets in Romania was 15 per cent. In Greece, 50 per cent of the capital invested in the industrial and banking sectors was foreign. In Serbia, in 1910, 36 per cent of total capital (fixed and working) in industry was foreign, as was 9 per cent of bank assets. Serbia's mining sector was exclusively foreign owned. Finally, the share of foreign investment in Bulgaria was probably lower. In the industries with state protection, 23 per cent of the capital was foreign and 12 per cent of the bank assets were also foreign. Foreign investment originated particularly from France and Germany.[9]

Domestic as well as foreign investors will have been influenced by the size of the public debts, which differed greatly between the periphery countries. In Portugal and Greece servicing the public debt took a large part of state resources, whereas in the other three countries it was considerably lower. The effective rate of interest of foreign loans to Bulgaria, Romania and Greece decreased between 1864–89 and 1900–11 (in Greece, after having increased in the 1890s), converging to 5.0–5.5 per cent. In Serbia, they remained stable throughout, at 5.2–5.5 per cent and in Portugal effective interest rates were slightly higher, above 6 per cent (Lampe and Jackson 1982: 233; Mata 1993: 242). The Portuguese government ran deficits throughout the period, although there was some improvement in the coverage of public expenditure by revenue. The Greek budget was also massively in deficit in the 1890s. Yet foreign intervention ensured that public revenue was higher than expenditures, on average, for the period 1880–1912 in Greece, as in Romania and Bulgaria.[10]

Some quantitative empirical growth studies

From describing the poor southern periphery, we now turn to possible explanatory models. Neoclassical economists expect to find convergence of incomes between states, a conclusion which two schools of thought reach by different routes. One considers national economies as observations generated by neoclassical growth models. The proportion of output devoted to investment cannot accelerate the long-run growth rate because of diminishing returns, but convergence of income per head, conditional upon initial values and other variables, should be observed. The other neoclassical view is that national economic growth is primarily explicable by open economy forces – trade, migration and foreign investment. In the extreme form, with common international technology, trade alone brings about factor-price equalization, transport costs and trade controls permitting.

A development from neoclassical theory, "endogenous growth" theory, does not produce convergence, but the evidence for this formulation is contested. These models have no steady-state income level because they assume increasing returns production functions. A similar conclusion, about the absence of a steady state, can be obtained by other routes, including the denial of the usefulness of an economy-wide production function. In one scheme, the rate of growth of output depends upon gross investment and quality adjusted labour – roughly comparable with a short-run (non-steady-state) neoclassical model (Scott 1993).[11] Investment increases output directly, not through the capital stock of the neoclassical production function. There are no diminishing returns to cumulative investment. Quality-adjusted employment growth for ten leading developed countries showed that on average the adjustments more than doubled the size of the effective labour force, though sometimes they reduced it. These differences were significantly related to growth of output (adding in human capital as a separate variable arguably does the same, though endogenous growth models go for aggregating human and physical capital, rather than labour adjustment).

There is a good deal of evidence that this type of formulation fits many recent economic growth facts well. For instance, there is a robust cross-country relationship in which growth rate depends on investment proportions, starting values and schooling between 1960 and 1988 (Levine and Renelt 1992). With the data suggesting a capital-output ratio of 1.9 and a capital elasticity of 0.33, a rise of one percentage point in the investment rate raises output growth by $0.33/1.9 = 0.174$. Crafts (1996) argues that the relationship is probably not entirely causal, however. Investment responds to growth opportunities, according to causality tests, as well as creating them, in this later period (Islam 1995). For instance, there is evidence that acceleration of work-force growth, after population growth has peaked, boosts both investment and labour-participation rates, thus raising per capita income growth (Bloom and Williamson 1998; Williamson 1998e). Technological progress rates, not surprisingly, vary across countries. The apparent impact of schooling on growth is actually negative, but this might be explained by a correlation between schooling and technical progress.

Technical progress in the neoclassical steady-state model is simply understood as exogenous, that is, determined outside the explanatory system. Each country has a distinctive production function and exogenous savings and population growth (Mankiw, Romer and Weil 1992) (MRW). This implies convergence to different steady-state paths for incomes per worker/head. An economy's income per head will be higher at a point in time in the steady state, the more productive its workers initially, the faster its technical progress, the higher its saving rate and the lower its rates of population growth and depreciation.

In the MRW neoclassical formulation, country-specific influences on income per head, reflecting distinctive national characteristics, such as resource endowments, climate and institutions, are captured by the multiplicative factor in the production function and a random error – which is (questionably) assumed uncorrelated with the savings rate and population growth. All countries are supposed to have the same rate of technical progress. MRW augment the model to allow for a fixed rate of accumulation of human capital, using the percentage of the working-age population in secondary school as a proxy for this rate of investment. As an interpretation of history the model arguably conflates investment rates with national rates of technical progress. Especially for understanding core–periphery relations over time, the problem is to explain different rates of technical progress between countries (Grossman and Helpman 1994). The most convincing evidence may originate from economic historians, but unfortunately it is rarely systematic.

The MRW convergence representation of the neoclassical model shows that the growth rate of an economy's output per worker is a function of the determinants of the ultimate steady state and of the initial level of output or income per worker. This formulation is appropriate if economies are not in steady-state growth. If all countries had the same (ultimate) steady state, then this convergence representation could be interpreted and estimated across a group of nations as "followers", or the periphery, catching up a "leader" or core economy. This fits comfortably with the "leader-follower" approach to European economic history in the nineteenth century (we include Rostow 1960, Gerschenkron 1962 and Landes 1969 in this group).

During the later nineteenth century, when transport costs were falling and European economies were becoming more open, the alternative neoclasssical analysis makes a great deal of sense. The "globalization", or Heckscher–Ohlin, approach to convergence (for example Williamson 1996a; Foreman-Peck 1983, Ch. 2) emphasizes what at first sight is an entirely different process; the international movement of labour, capital and goods, rather than the closed-economy accumulation of, for example, MRW. It is adapted to explain levels of output and income, although Jeffrey Williamson and his collaborators actually explain growth and changes in factor prices.

So for instance, Williamson (1996a) adopts the "conditional convergence" formulation in showing that schooling did not help late-nineteenth-century real-wage convergence in Italy, Spain and Portugal, but did in Scandinavia.

For relations with the core, "Globalization was by far the dominant force accounting for convergence (and divergence) around the periphery" (O'Rourke and Williamson 1997). Globalization here means the integration of international commodity and factor markets. Under what conditions does this dialectical concept produce one result, rather than its opposite? Late-nineteenth-century intercontinental migration can be seen as a response to shocks under fixed exchange rates when domestic European growth was relatively sluggish. Migration helped convergence between the Old and New Worlds (Taylor and Williamson 1997), but only in the sense that it was a consequence of institutions that under some circumstances, encouraged convergence. Moreover convergence of "followers" with "leaders" refers to income per head (or wages), and migration, as in Ireland, can radically reduce the population (and therefore the GDP) of a region. Convergence by depopulation stretches the meaning of the term, but it is certainly a possibility of open economy forces. Suppose transport developments lower grain prices, so a gold-standard, primarily agricultural area of small owner-occupier farmers, can no longer compete. The implicit rent of land falls, farmers sell off and emigrate. Eventually, if there is an equilibrium, diminishing returns should ensure that when sufficiently few people are left, those who remain will be as rich as any in the New World. But the process may take many generations if it works like that at all.

People do not have to migrate. They might take other jobs, importing cheap grains and producing other goods or services, if they can find any that allow them to support a tolerable living standard. Exchange-rate flexibility may accelerate the adjustment process (this thought and what follows is based on Blanca Sánchez-Alonso's chapter in this volume). Cheaper grain imports might depreciate the exchange rate, raising import prices and reducing the prices of export products, both partly insulating the domestic grain-producing sector and encouraging the switching of resources into new export-oriented sectors. External emigration is thus less necessary. Convergence would be reduced, in the sense that if labour was perfectly mobile internationally, the price of labour (allowing for non-pecuniary advantages and disadvantages) would be equalized, and exchange-rate flexibility encourages another sort of adjustment.

Globalization might cause divergence if there was selective migration whereby the more skilled left and were followed by capital, a pattern supposedly identified by, for example, Gunnar Myrdal (1968), and once used to justify regional policy in western Europe. Alternatively, if trade led to unemployment that persisted, divergence might be observed. Either way, a fundamental explanation must be based on something deeper than "globalization".

A historical model of European economic growth

These deeper influences may be classified into natural endowments – especially climate, mineral resources and topography – culture, institutions, policy and technology (Foreman-Peck 1995). Whether technology should be distinguished from institutions is a moot point. If conditions are appropriate, technology can be copied and transferred, assuming it is available to Europe as a whole and that the question is only to explain the European pattern of growth. Financial probity permits economic development; adoption and maintenance of gold, bimetallic or silver standards could be a cause of "globalization" in the process.

Such influences determine the factor supplies and production parameters, both implicitly in the neoclassical model and explicitly in the model described in this section. This second model predicts GDP per head from values of the independent variables. In a model, by contrast with a typology, if a causal pattern is identified then it will support counterfactuals, because the values of the estimated parameters will not change when the explanatory variables alter. These explicit counterfactuals offer tests of some hypotheses regarding the causes of backwardness in the European periphery.

The relationships in our model may be of two types. The reduced-form equation is a summary of all "ultimate" measured explanatory influences, the total impact of the exogenous variables upon the (endogenous) variables to be explained. It is not the explanation itself, which is the mutual interaction of endogenous variables, as well, in the structural equations.

What the historian observes or creates is a set of data from which an explanation is constructed. In principle both structural and reduced-form relationships can be fitted to the data to represent the explanations formally. But although there may be a unique reduced-form equation that fits the data best, there may also be a number of alternative structural relations that could be encompassed by that reduced form. In other words, a variety of explanations may be consistent with the same body of evidence. Supposing a reduced form indicates that coal availability influenced European nineteenth-century GDP, we may still want to know the channels by which it did so, whether directly, through manufacturing consumer goods, or indirectly, through lowering the costs of capital goods and transport. These channels are represented by structural equations.

Whether structural parameters can be inferred from the reduced form is the identification problem. If we are only interested in "retrodiction", forecasting what would have happened had the exogenous values been different, without explaining, then we need pay no attention to the structural relations and their identification, unless to seek confirmation that the reduced form is correct.

Should we explain growth rates or levels of income and output? As noted in the previous sections, much recent discussion has been conducted about growth rates, and relative growth rates in particular. It is not clear that these are the variables on which to focus for an understanding of late-nineteenth-century development. An explanation of income levels of nations could be more effective. If we can explain income levels we can explain income differences, changes in income levels and changes in income differences (convergence or divergence). Moreover, for reasons of accuracy, explaining income levels may be preferable, theory permitting.

Consider three types of errors. The first are those that consistently under- or over-estimate a series. For these, growth rates will be more accurate than the underlying series. But such errors are of no significance for parameter estimation in levels since they do not effect covariation. The second type of error by contrast may take both positive and negative values. Then the maximum value of the measured growth rate is when the error is at its lowest possible value, preferably negative, in t–1 and at its highest possible value, preferably positive, in t. The minimum value of the measured growth rate is when the errors in both periods offset each other, when in t–1 the error is a maximum, large and positive, while in t it is small, preferably negative. Suppose true GDP in year t–1 is 100. With a 10 per cent measurement error, measured GDP may be 90 or 110. Suppose true GDP in t is 120 also with a 10 per cent error in measurement so that measured GDP may be 108 or 132. Then maximum measured growth may be 46.6 per cent compared with a minimum of –1.8 per cent and a true figure of 20 per cent. A bigger true growth rate gets rid of the possibility of negative measured growth. If GDP in t is 140, with a similar 10 per cent error, maximum possible measured growth is 71 per cent and minimum 14 per cent compared with a true figure of 40 per cent.

The third type of measurement error consists of independent random normally distributed variables with means of zero. Then the variance of the errors in the growth-rate series is double the variance of the levels series. A similar calculation as for the second error can be done for independent random normally distributed measurement errors. Suppose there is a 95 per cent chance that the measured value is within 10 per cent of the true value of GDP (100 in t–1 and 120 in t). Hence the standard deviation of the error is 5 in t–1 and 6 in t, and the variances are 25 and 36. For the growth series we must add variances, to get 61, a standard deviation of 7.8 on a growth of 20. There is a 95 per cent chance of the measured growth rate falling between 4.4 and 35.6 per cent, around the true rate of 20 per cent. If the errors are autocorrelated we subtract twice the covariance from the two variances. The case of the same error in both periods corresponds with a covariance of unity and the absence of an error in the growth rate.

These possibly substantial impacts on measured growth rates suggest a case for attempting to explain levels of variables as far as possible, rather than differences. The problem of errors in differences is particularly significant for slow-growing, low-income countries, where GDP measurement errors are high, such as those of the European periphery. Discussion about convergence or divergence in growth rates between a pair of economies compounds the problem of errors by requiring comparison of four series, each with possible errors. Even the preferable analysis of "catching-up" in levels entails two error terms.

Our approach here is to ask how much of the income gap between core and periphery can be explained by systematic factors and how much by country-specific factors and measurement errors. Backwardness or "catching-up" as a positive influence on the potential for raising income in country 2 (Y_2) can be represented by the coefficient on a term $(Y_1 - Y_2)$ where Y_1 is the GNP per head of the core country. But then what is to be explained, Y_2, is also part of the explanation. This can be seen from equation (1), describing the aim of the paper, which explains why one country $(Y_{1,t})$ in time t (the core), was richer than another $(Y_{2,t})$ (the periphery):

$$\ln Y_{1,t} - \ln Y_{2,t} = \Sigma a_j (\ln X_{1,j,t} - \ln X_{2,j,t}) + (e_{1,t} - e_{2,t}) \ldots \tag{1}$$

In the present scheme income differences between any pair of economies are to be explained systematically by two types of influences: differences in values of pan-European variables $(X_{1,j} - X_{2,j})$ and the pan-European parameters (a_j) that linked these variables with incomes. Errors in the measurement of GNP per head are also included in the parameters. The non-systematic part of the explanation is measured by $(e_1 - e_2)$ for the pair 1 and 2 and encapsulates country-specific influences, as well as differences in income-measurement errors.

A distinction can be drawn between globalization and country-specific forces raising income, for international market integration affected all countries in Europe (O'Rourke and Williamson 1997). Education, for example, can be identified as country-specific and idiosyncratic, for education systems differ markedly between countries. The problem is that market integration or globalization did not affect all countries equally because some resisted more than others, with trade barriers of various heights, some specialized in products whose prices changed more or less than others in response to the opening-up of new agricultural lands to the world market, others pursued domestic policies or maintained institutions that were not conducive to capital inflows or capital market integration. It therefore makes much more sense to explain patterns of growth and income by defining systematic forces as those which might be measured tolerably consistently across Europe, and which might be expected to generate a common response in income or growth. So in the present paper we regard education, whether measured by inputs such as schooling, or by outputs, such as literacy, as a systematic – or pan-European – force. Country-specific are those institutions, policies or events that were peculiar to individual countries.

The assumed basic structure of nineteenth-century European economic development is a production function and two factor-supply equations, one for capital and one for labour. The production function is disaggregated between traditional (i.e. agricultural) and modern (i.e. urban or manufacturing) outputs, so that there are four equations. Commonly in nineteenth-century Europe, marginal productivity in the modern sector was higher than in agriculture. An increase in demand for the products of the advanced sector shifts upwards that sector's demand for labour. So long as there is such a gap, labour migration out of agriculture raises the efficiency of the aggregate production function.

Errors in the measurement of the explanatory variables may require the parameter values to be interpreted with some caution since they may be biased. Subject to that proviso, we can examine the properties of the model by simulating it, to show how a poorly performing nineteenth-century European economy, such as those of the Balkans and Iberia, would have developed by 1910 if it had adopted, one by one, the policies of the leader economy, Britain, the human capital and the natural resources. There are two alternative paths to estimating: one is to use the reduced form implied by the structural equations, the other is to retrodict with a reduced form estimated directly. The consistency of the results from the two approaches should offer some check on the appropriateness of the model. In the present paper we restrict ourselves to the reduced form.

The explanatory variables

We now consider the variables that should be included in the structural equations. In the production function we expect to find land, labour and capital, but of greater interest are their particular historical manifestations. Measuring the size of the labour force is always problematic in predominantly agricultural societies. In any case the quality of labour is likely to be more important to output differentials than the quantity. Portugal lay at the bottom of Cipolla's (1965) list of numbers of teachers per head of population in late-nineteenth-century Europe, but coverage of this input index is poor. How else might quality be measured? The desirability of "years of schooling" of the population as a whole as a measure of human capital – assuming it can be measured at all – turns on the homogeneity of schooling in different countries. We know about the heterogeneity in the same country today and that standardized test scores point to great differences in educational achievements at given ages in different national systems (Prais 1995). Thus we might suppose that between European countries in the later nineteenth century, years of schooling did not measure the same thing, and prefer the crude output measure of human capital: literacy. The lack of a strong simple correlation between income and literacy is helpful for the case that literacy may be treated as an exogenous rather than as an endogenous variable in this period (Tortella 1994a).

Turning to the land input, the centrality of agriculture to nineteenth-century European economies implies that climate is a vital (exogenous) factor. As a measure of climate we tried differences in average temperatures (between January and July), which are likely to be less sensitive to the location in the country at which temperatures are measured than average temperatures. Moreover, the differences between winter and summer temperatures also matter more for soil moisture. We also tried the variable rainfall in summer (July). Greece (Athens), Portugal (Lisbon) and Spain (Madrid) were very dry in July, often with zero rainfall. So too was southern France as represented by Marseille, which in July 1910 received 2.7 ml of rain, less than Lisbon's 4.2 ml and almost comparable with Athens. Romania (Bucharest) was not dry in summer, nor was Italy (Rome) – except in 1880, when no rain fell. On the other hand Romania did suffer from large variations in temperature over the year. In 1910 Bucharest averaged –0.1°C in January and 22.3°C in July, whereas Greenwich, London, varied between 4.4°C and 14.8°C. In Iberia, inland Madrid experienced great swings in temperature but coastal Lisbon did not.

Apart from climate, the proxy that we use for natural resources is coal production. Alternative sources of industrial energy were available in nineteenth-century Europe and in some countries charcoal and water assumed an important role. Yet coal was predominant and that is why it is in our model. Coal output per head shows Britain as an outlier, with more than double the 1910 value of its nearest rivals, Germany and Belgium. But Spain mined more than Italy and more than richer Sweden. Greece and Portugal lacked any coal deposits at all. More importantly, by 1910 trade allowed coal consumption per head in Italy of 0.29 metric tonnes, almost matching Spain's consumption of 0.32 metric tonnes. Whereas in recent years natural resources appear to be associated negatively with economic growth (Sachs and Warner 1995), we expect that workable coal deposits conferred an economic advantage, to the extent that transport costs were significant. The reason for this late-twentieth-century difference is that technical change has shifted demand towards oil and gas, which require little labour for their extraction, in contrast to the extremely labour-intensive coal industry, which was central to later nineteenth-century technology. There was therefore less likelihood of radical real exchange-rate appreciation in coal-rich countries damaging the economy by infection with "the Dutch disease".

An important intermediate or endogenous variable is the proportion of the workforce in agriculture. This depends upon agricultural labour productivity, which in turn determines how much energy, raw materials and foodstuffs can be supplied to the non-agricultural sectors. Agricultural productivity is likely to have been affected by climate. The proportion of the workforce in agriculture also depends on the demand for non-agricultural products. Thus, availability of industrial natural resources, infrastructure, general capital supply and policy variables will influence the distribution of labour force.

Infrastructure is another variable determined by the system. We can approximate this type of capital by railways, since they made the greatest demands upon capital (O'Brien 1982). The determinants of national railway sizes can be divided into supply- and demand-side influences. The demand is mainly derived from the production function. Large countries had reason to take more advantage of railways, other things being equal, than small ones. Distances between population centres and natural resource locations were inevitably shorter in small countries and therefore less capital was needed in railways to join them up to create a given productivity level. For two countries with the same-sized railway system, the one with the higher population density would be better served, for willingness to pay for average haul or trip length would be lower; the same number of people can be reached in a smaller area. Denmark, like the Netherlands, was a precocious railway builder between 1860 and 1910, overtaking Spain in the ranking, although by far the densest network at both dates was to be found in Belgium. Bulgaria in 1870 lacked any railways at all, and Romania and Greece only opened their first lines the previous year. Portugal started earlier, in 1856, and in 1875 lay between Italy and Hungary in rail miles per head of population.

The area of a country is also pertinent to foreign trade, for with a given degree of specialization, division of labour and therefore productivity, a larger country would have less foreign trade. Controlling for country size, openness to foreign trade is a good index of productivity and income per head, but it does not indicate what is responsible for the income per head and therefore adds nothing to the explanation. Railways, by contrast, were the means by which the market was widened and productivity boosted.

To account for general capital supplies, the use of interest rates presupposes well developed domestic capital markets, which did not exist outside a few western European economies. Instead there was the international market based in London, Paris or Berlin, where national government bonds traded at interest rates which tend to reflect national domestic conditions. There was a clear pattern depending in part on country risk, in part on the likelihood of exchange-rate depreciation and government default. These factors could be diminished in the eyes of the market by a credible commitment to a metallic standard. Guaranteeing national-currency convertibility into gold or silver markedly increased the availability of capital from abroad and reduced the cost (Gregory 1979; Martín-Aceña 1993). Gold conferred more stability than bimetallism or silver because of the prominence of gold-standard Britain in world trade and the changing relative values of gold and silver after the mid-century. Bimetallic and silver countries experienced serious monetary disorders in the 1860s and 1870s which were likely to deter investment. Greece abandoned bimetallic convertibility in 1868, returned in 1870 and suspended again in 1877, both suspensions a consequence of war. Not until 1910 did Greece successfully achieve gold convertibility (Bordo and Schwartz 1996). Adherence to the silver standard in the early part of the period may have been particularly helpful for countries concerned to attract French capital. For capital exporting countries, a gold standard meant higher returns to capital than in an economy exposed to more exchange-rate uncertainty. Probably of greater significance was the fiscal responsibility implied by a link of the national currency to precious metal. A metallic-standard government could not support excessive spending by printing money, and business confidence at home as well as abroad would have been enhanced.

These considerations suggest that the length of time on any metallic standard may determine how high the availability of capital was. Since the greater investment encouraged by the silver or gold link will have been subject to diminishing returns, the impact of time on adherence will not have increased without limit. Although richer countries were more assiduous in maintaining a gold link for their currencies, one of the poorest – Portugal – adhered to the gold standard from 1854 to 1891, and Spain only abandoned gold in 1883, offering at least two pieces of evidence that causation did not run from income to gold-standard membership.

Apart from the decision to adhere to a metallic standard, the choice of possible policy variables to include in the model is wide. Tariff protection, the most popular industrial policy instrument, was particularly high in the lowest-income countries, Portugal and Russia. Greece began economic independence by taxing exports as well as imports, and like most economies in Europe tended to increase import tariffs towards the later nineteenth century (Minoglou, 1999). The effects of tariff protection in Portugal from 1890 might be captured by the slower transfer of labour from agriculture consequent upon the tariff influence upon the domestic intersectoral term of trade.

State policy may also have influenced the level of literacy by tax-financed schooling but it is the results of (lagged) literacy or illiteracy that we observe in this specification. Equally, policy may determine the agricultural labour productivity differential or the flow of labour into the modern sector, but that will not be identified, nor will the contribution of the state to the spread of railway networks.

Model estimation and implications

A good explanation of the core–periphery gap should fit the facts better than other accounts but should do so parsimoniously and in a manner consistent with knowledge of the way the European economies worked. Unfortunately a truly general model would be enormous in view of the range of possible explanatory variables and the variety of ways in which they might be related. The most general representation adopted in this experiment takes the policy variables tariffs and gold-standard membership, illiteracy as an index of human capital, population, and natural-resource variables temperature, precipitation and coal production (but not consumption) as exogenous to this (but not necessarily to another, higher-level) model.

The structure of the model is shown in Figure 4.2 (Foreman-Peck 1995). Four structural equations – production function, agricultural workforce share, railway supply and coal consumption – underlie the relationship between GDP per capita and the explanatory variables employed to understand the periphery's income gap in Tables 4.2 and 4.3. In the original

Table 4.2 Reduced form OLS regression estimates for the European Income Model, 1870–1910 (dependent variable: log of GDP per capita)

	Illiteracy	Tariff	Metallic standard	Coal production	UK dummy	Climate (temp. diff.)	Area	Pop	R^2	N	Chi
Eq. 1		-0.25	0.045	0.014					0.586	78	2.33
Het		(-9.21)	(5.25)	(2.76)							(3)
Eq. 2		-0.24	0.039	0.008	0.49				0.658	78	7.57
Het		(-10.56)	(4.74)	(1.60)	(7.00)						(4)
Eq. 3		-0.24	0.038	0.015	0.50		0.015	-0.052	0.663	78	10.6
Het		(-6.23)	(4.70)	(1.67)	(7.01)		(0.44)	(-1.14)			(6)
Eq. 4	-0.15	-0.18	0.020	0.013	0.40	-0.16			0.846	70	3.07
Het	(-8.42)	(-10.64)	(3.38)	(4.16)	(7.94)	(-2.22)					(6)

Notes:
All variables in logs. N = number of observations.
Chi = Breusch-Pagan Chi-Squared (D.F.)
Het = White heteroscedastic robust t ratios.
Data are a cross-national panel sampled at decadal intervals.

The Model Structure

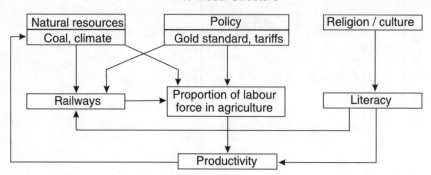

Figure 4.2 The structure of the general model.

Table 4.3 Contributors to the income lag behind the UK, 1870 and 1910 (percentage of income differential).

	Total income gap	Tariff (e = −0.1–0.2)	Metallic standard (e = 0.02–0.04)	Coal production (e = 0.01–0.03)	Climate (e = tempdif = −0.16)	Illiteracy (e = −0.4)
1870						
Bulgaria	n/a	n/a	n/a	n/a	n/a	n/a
Greece	216	6–12	0	12–40	n/a	17
Italy	145	2.5–5	3–6	7–23	4	15
Portugal	218	16–32	0.5–1	12–40	−2	18
Romania	275	1.5–3	16–35	12–40	n/a	18
Spain	133	7–14	5–9	5–17	7	14
1910						
Bulgaria	267	12–26	3–6	7–24	n/a	37
Greece	256	19–41	1.5–3	13–45	9	31
Italy	114	5–9	2–4	6–20	5	28
Portugal	257	17–37	1–2	13–45	0	39
Romania	243	11–22	1.5–3	8–27	13	38
Spain	105	12–26	0.5–1	4–13	10	34

Notes:
e = elasticities.
The percentages need not add up to 100. The total percentages to be explained (i.e. how much each would have to rise to match the UK) are given in the first column.

estimation, two or three variables in the production function relation (agricultural labour-force share, illiteracy and possibly coal consumption) explained from 60 to 80 per cent of the variation in income per head among the European countries in our sample (see the statistical appendix). Although that leaves a considerable proportion to be explained by measurement error and unique individual countries' institutions or policies, it is quite satisfactory compared with the fit of empirical models of more recent economic performance. Illiteracy lagged a decade was intended to capture human capital effects. Railways apparently exercised no direct effect on output, once possible endogeneity was allowed for. The proportion of the male labour force in agriculture measures the impact of the dual economy, which was rather strong. A fall in the agricultural proportion of the workforce from say 60 to 50 per cent raised output per head by almost one fourth. The direct effect of coal consumption on production was significant when it was inappropriately assumed to be exogenous in estimating the function. But the impact was very small and statistically insignificant when the variable was assumed to be endogenous.

Turning to the factor-supply equations, larger railway networks lowered the proportion of the workforce in agriculture, both by integrating markets and proxying the growth of industrial capital. Tariff protection did the opposite, encouraging inefficiency in resource allocation (the contrary result in O'Rourke 1997a is probably to be explained by that different data set including more New World, and few poor Old World, economies).

Wide variations in temperature and/or low July rainfall, during the agricultural year, lowered soil moisture and laid burdens on agriculture that kept productivity low, thus raising the workforce proportion employed.

Abundance of coal both created a need for railways and industrial capital while at the same time providing the raw materials necessary for their cheap supply. Membership of the gold, silver or bimetallic standards guaranteed cheap and secure finance, and low illiteracy ensured the necessary human capital essential to the capital goods industries. Coal consumption per head rose more than proportionately with GNP per head, because of prevailing technology. The coefficient of coal production indicated that international trade was important in compensating for the lack of coal endowments. Transport from the coal-producing areas must have raised coal prices in the consuming areas without coal but, judging by the consumption effect, not apparently by a great deal. Table 4.2 presents estimates of the reduced-form equations for GNP per capita.

Table 4.3 takes the range of elasticities from Table 4.2 and simulates the impact of different causes of backwardness. The harmful impact of tariff protection is small in relation to the income gap – especially so for Italy, as the chapter by Federico and O'Rourke shows, by a different approach. In 1870, Portugal is the biggest loser in Table 4.3 but is overtaken by Greece by 1910. Bulgaria and Romania become more protectionist after 1880 and forgo a higher proportion of income by 1910 than in 1870–80.

Our attempt to measure reputation for financial probity at home and abroad is the number of years on a metallic standard since 1850. Had Romania been able to match the UK's record in this respect in 1870, its income per head may have risen perhaps between 16 and 35 per cent, as a consequence primarily of foreign investment, that did flow in later. That advantage had already been utilized by Greece and Portugal in 1870, but conditions in donor countries then were less buoyant than they were to become. In 1910, Romania and Bulgaria had been virtually on the gold standard for more than a decade, Portugal had abandoned it for twenty years and Greece had just joined. Yet those different experiences did not matter to the income differential *vis-à-vis* Britain.

With Britain's coal production, our periphery economies lacking coal endowments in 1870 would have increased incomes by 26 per cent, and in 1910, Greece and Portugal's incomes would have risen by 28 per cent, according to equation 4 (Table 4.2). In 1910 expanding Bulgaria's and Romania's per head production from respectively 46 and 14 metric tonnes to the UK's 5,893 metric tonnes, raises their incomes by rather less: 15 per cent and 17 per cent. When the climate variable is included in the equations of Table 4.2, the sample size necessarily contracts because of missing data. Greece, Spain and Romania are the losers among our periphery countries, but in comparison with the total income gap, not by much. Comparing the gaps in 1870 with those in 1910 suggests that the weather apparently generated only small national income variations. Human capital as measured by illiteracy was apparently the biggest single contribution to the income gap by 1910 (consistent with Tortella 1994a). We must recognize both the difficulties in measuring illiteracy consistently across countries and the shortcomings of this index of human capital. Subject to these caveats, in illiteracy, Portugal, Greece, Romania and Bulgaria are similar and the relative losses of income from this source more than doubled from 1870 to 1910.

If all the exogenous factors in Portugal had been the same as in Britain then Portuguese income in 1870 would have been perhaps between 45 and 90 per cent higher. But that still leaves more than half the income gap (which was 218 per cent) unexplained with the higher estimate. This remaining difference is to be understood by the distinctive institutions and histories of the two countries compared, together with income measurement errors.

Conclusion

Periphery countries could do nothing about their natural endowments – mineral and climatic – but some developments might have attenuated their impact. Natural resources do have substitutes: irrigation might compensate for dry climates; more investment in water power or mining machinery would have reduced the disadvantage of poor or non-existent coal endowments. Yet, in the conditions of poor economies, such as in the European peripheries, those investments were a further demand on scarce savings.

Importing coal and adapting to the appropriate technology could be cheaper, but not as cheap as coal already on the spot. The same is probably true for climate and its substitute: irrigation/drainage. Periphery countries bore higher investment costs for their agriculture than did northwestern Europe, with its better balance of rain and sun throughout the year; Mediterranean crops – vines, olives and citrus fruits – were no substitute for basic foodstuffs such as wheat.

The spread of railways allowed greater agricultural specialization and productivity, as it did for every sector, and was important for the development of some export branches. That was certainly the case with Bulgaria and Romania, where exports, particularly to Austria and Germany, but also to the Ottoman Empire, had to travel by land. But railways were responses to profit opportunities created by other forces acting on the economies. Agricultural protection or free trade could – and did – make a difference in taking the best advantage of natural endowments. Wheat protection in Portugal led to increased output in a sector with comparatively lower soil productivity. Tariffs, however, could have been a consequence of difficulties in financing the government budget.

Foreign capital brought a positive contribution to investment, particularly in railway construction and direct investment in export industries. By 1910, Romania and Bulgaria had maintained stable currencies for more than a decade, whereas Greece and Portugal had not. Yet, that does not seem to explain income differences. Perhaps foreign investment was too small in terms of the overall investment requirements in these countries, which would explain the unimportance of financial probity. Or, more likely, foreign investment responded to higher risk levels by requiring higher rates of return and the adherence to a metallic standard mattered little.

The model in this paper provides a means for understanding the causes of income differentials in Europe and particularly differences between the core and the periphery in the later nineteenth century. We were able apparently to explain sometimes all of the differentials. The model also provides a tool to "replicate" the structure of the UK economy (or of any other core economy) in the periphery. This is an exercise that is often undertaken only implicitly in the literature, in the guise of "catch-up" or "backwardness", explanations which we have rendered explicit. Our conclusions are that the periphery's income lag is to be explained by tariffs, natural endowments and illiteracy, usually in reverse order of importance, among pan-European influences. Sometimes half of the gap seems to have been due to country-specific factors. Even though we have tried to lift the veil of economic categories, there is a still deeper level of explanation to be reached; one that would help us understand why the periphery was more protectionist and illiterate, and identify the remedial policies.

Data appendix

Table 4.A1 Estimates of GDP per capita, 1913 (1980 "international" dollars)

	A Maddison (1990)	B Maddison (1995)	C Good (1996)	D Bairoch (1981)	E Clark (1951)	F Gini (1959)	G Mean	H Standard Deviation	I Error H/G
1 Austria–Hungary	n/a	n/a	n/a	n/a	n/a	n/a	1 359 (1)	—	—
2 Belgium	2 406	2 417	2 495	2 208	1 976	2 365	2 311	189.7	0.082
3 Bulgaria (1)	756	877	715	772	n/a	951	814	97.0	0.119
4 Denmark	2 246	2 203	2 393	2 398	2 338	2 077	2 276	125.1	0.055
5 Finland	1 295	1 200	1 251	1 423	1 263	n/a	1 286	83.7	0.065
6 France	1 934	2 020	1 867	1 815	1 841	2 360	1 973	203.5	0.103
7 Germany	1 907	2 243	1 875	2 099	2 117	1 894	2 023	151.7	0.075
8 Greece	808	949	794	908	739	n/a	840	86.4	0.103
9 Italy	1 773	1 467	1 531	1 233	1 028	1 360	1 399	256.4	0.183
10 Netherlands	2 400	2 311	2 391	2 005	2 305	2 302	2 286	144.4	0.063
11 Norway	1 573	1 331	1 516	1 666	1 599	1 614	1 550	118.0	0.076
12 Portugal	659	792	683	908	887	1 095	837	162.2	0.194
13 Romania (1)	n/a	n/a	883	1 003	813	788	872	96.3	0.110
14 Russia	973	871	n/a	934	880	806	893	63.8	0.072
15 Serbia (1)	705	602	695	813	679	851	724	91.8	0.127
16 Spain	1 547	1 320	1 575	1 084	1 888	1 326	1 457	276.7	0.190
17 Sweden	1 792	1 812	1 837	1 910	2 097	1 577	1 838	169.2	0.092
18 Switzerland	2 160	2 462	2 231	2 425	n/a	n/a	2 320	146.9	0.063
19 UK	3 065	2 945	3 063	2 899	2 903	3 073	2 991	84.5	0.028
Austria (1)	1 489	1 513	1 453	1 897	1 814	1 574	1 623	186.0	0.115
Hungary (1)	1 052	921	1 004	1 016	934	1 059	998	58.3	0.058

For notes see next page

Notes to Table 4.A1

Column A is from Maddison (1990).
Columns B to F are estimated by taking the data from the authors quoted and converting to 1980 international dollars by using the fitted values of the following regressions:

Madd 90 = 0.585 × Madd 95   R2* = 0.935; DW = 1.888; SER = 173.2; N = 19
    (t = 43.53)

Madd 90 = 1.068 × Good 96   R2* = 0.986; DW = 2.012; SER = 81.6; N = 18
    (t = 91.98)

Madd 90 = 2.710 × Bair 81   R2* = 0.859; DW = 2.122; SER = 254.4; N = 19
    (t = 29.46)

Madd 90 = 6.720 × Clar 51   R2* = 0.829; DW = 1.672; SER = 277.6; N = 17
    (t = 25.69)

Madd 90 = 2.503 × Gini 59   R2* = 0.893; DW = 1.551; SER = 227.0; N = 16
    (t = 31.02)

The original data for columns B to D are in prices of 1960 to 1990, converted with PPP exchange rates.
Data from Clark (1951) and Gini (1959) are based on direct valuation of output. Clark's prices are PPP exchange rates for 1925–34. Gini uses 1913 current French francs.
Column I provides a measure of the error of the estimates. For further details, see Lains (1999).

(1) Maddison (1990 and 1995) and Good (1996) give values for post-1919 borders and in the cases of Austria and Hungary their figures were corrected by a factor of 0.75. Clark (1951) adds Montenegro to Serbia.

Notes to Table 4.A2 (on page 100)

(1) Transylvania only; (2) 1890–1910.

Bold figures are indirect estimates of the authors quoted.
In column F bold figures are from Good and Ma (1998). Trend growth rates are estimated from indices in Maddison (1995) and from Prados *et al.* (1993) for Spain, and Lains (1995) for Portugal. Data for 1880 and 1900 is not reported.
Figures between brackets are from Lains (1999), with estimates based on Good and Ma (1998), for Serbia and the Austrian part of Romania (Transylvania); Berov (1979, 1985, 1987 and 1996) for Bulgaria, Romania and Serbia; Lampe (1989) for Romania; Palairet (1990 and 1997) for Serbia; and Kostelenos (1995) for Greece.

Table 4.A2 Growth of GDP per capita, 1870–1913 (per cent per annum)

	A	B	C	E	F	"Trend" growth rates		
	Bairoch (1976a) 1870–1913	Maddison (1990) 1870–1913	Prados (1993) 1870–1913	Crafts (1983) 1870–1910	Good (1994–98) 1870–1910	1870–1890	1890–1913	1870–1913
1 Austria-Hungary	**1.15**	—	—	—	**1.30**	[1.10]	[1.40]	[1.26]
2 Belgium	1.05	0.80	1.01	1.03	1.03	1.08	0.95	1.00
3 Bulgaria	**0.42**	—	—	—	—	—	[0.50]	[0.50]
4 Denmark	2.19	1.60	1.54	1.57	1.55	1.07	1.98	1.63
5 Finland	**1.19**	1.40	1.31	0.91	1.40	0.68	1.83	1.42
6 France	1.06	1.30	1.01	1.11	1.09	0.92	1.39	1.28
7 Germany	1.30	1.60	1.42	1.27	1.63	1.12	1.69	1.56
8 Greece	**0.60**	—	—	**0.95**	—	[0.38]	[0.65]	[0.54]
9 Italy	0.81	0.80	1.06	0.40	1.00	0.53	2.29	1.11
10 Netherlands	0.93	1.00	0.81	**1.20**	0.90	1.42	0.70	0.80
11 Norway	1.35	1.30	0.99	1.18	1.11	0.66	1.28	1.04
12 Portugal	**0.18**	0.30	0.60	**0.65** (2)	0.30	0.90	0.50	0.69
13 Romania	**1.10**	—	—	—	**1.42** (1)	[0.80]	[1.20]	[1.00]
14 Russia	**0.62**	0.80	—	1.15	—	—	[0.80]	[0.80]
15 Serbia	**0.49**	—	—	—	**1.69**	—	[0.50]	[0.50]
16 Spain	**0.25**	1.40	1.05	**0.84**	1.37	1.24	0.89	1.05
17 Sweden	2.39	1.40	1.29	1.96	1.49	0.76	1.76	1.41
18 Switzerland	**1.32**	1.20	1.23	**1.31**	1.18	0.91	[1.20]	[1.20]
19 UK	1.00	1.00	0.89	0.92	1.00	0.91	0.87	0.97
Austria	—	1.50	1.40	**1.37**	**1.25**	1.23	1.53	1.48
Hungary	—	1.20	—	**1.73**	**1.45**	[1.00]	[1.24]	[1.20]

Table 4.A3 Data for model estimation

	Gnppc	Area	Pop	Illiteracy	Avtarif	Standard	Coalpro	Tempdif
1870								
1 Austria-Hungary	827	241.2	35 730	50.0	0.041	0	8 400	21.3
2 Belgium	1 538	11.4	5 026	37.5	0.019	0	13 700	17.4
3 Bulgaria	—	—	—	—	—	0	0	—
4 Denmark	1 226	14.7	1 785	8.5	0.119	0	0	16.6
5 Finland	766	135.4	1 769	25.0	0.027	0	0	21.1
6 France	1 222	207.7	36 870	31.0	0.027	20	13 300	—
7 Germany	1 103	205.0	40 800	10.5	0.100	0	42 300	18.4
8 Greece	671	19.4	1 458	77.5	0.120	18	0	—
9 Italy	864	110.7	25 860	69.0	0.085	4	100	20.1
10 Netherlands	1 614	12.7	3 580	22.5	0.010	0	0	17.4
11 Norway	1 002	124.6	1 761	10.0	0.116	0	0	22.3
12 Portugal	665	34.3	4 344	82.5	0.270	16	0	13.7
13 Romania	565	50.7	4 270	85.0	0.078	0	0	—
14 Russia	629	1 745.8	84 500	—	0.128	0	700	—
15 Serbia	—	19.1	1 300	—	—	—	0	—
16 Spain	909	195.7	16 220	67.5	0.129	2	600	24.0
17 Sweden	1 057	171.7	4 169	7.5	0.113	13	0	18.4
18 Switzerland	1 234	16.0	2 669	9.5	0.270	20	0	22.4
19 UK	2 118	99.4	31 257	27.5	0.067	19	115 000	18.9
1880								
1 Austria-Hungary	—	241.2	37 883	39.5	0.046	0	16 100	23.2
2 Belgium	1 722	11.4	5 520	31.8	0.013	2	16 900	18.5
3 Bulgaria	—	—	2 008	—	0.125	0	0	—

continued on next page

Table 4.A3 Data for model estimation (cont.)

	Gnppc	Area	Pop	Illiteracy	Avtarif	Standard	Coalpro	Tempdif
1880 (cont.)								
4 Denmark	1 322	14.7	1 969	6.5	0.119	8	0	19.1
5 Finland	771	144.2	2 061	18.8	–	3	0	22.9
6 France	1 318	204.0	37 406	25.5	0.054	22	19 400	17.1
7 Germany	1 208	208.7	45 234	7.5	0.060	8	59 100	20.7
8 Greece	–	19.4	1 679	73.8	0.160	25	0	–
9 Italy	881	110.7	28 460	62.0	0.113	4	100	22.4
10 Netherlands	1 851	12.7	4 013	20.0	0.005	5	0	18.5
11 Norway	1 087	122.2	1 880	8.8	0.111	5	0	21.3
12 Portugal	674	34.3	4 636	80.0	0.295	26	0	9.9
13 Romania	–	50.7	4 540	83.8	0.057	0	0	–
14 Russia	–	1 745.8	97 700	–	0.161	0	3 300	31.4
15 Serbia	–	–	1 724	–	0.080	0	0	–
16 Spain	1 181	195.7	16 900	64.3	0.201	12	800	23.5
17 Sweden	1 143	170.9	4 566	5.3	0.108	20	100	19.9
18 Switzerland	–	16.0	2 846	6.3	–	30	0	24.7
19 UK	2 249	99.4	34 623	20.0	0.049	29	149 000	15.7
1890								
1 Austria-Hungary	987	241.2	41 286	29.0	0.066	0	27 500	17.4
2 Belgium	1 934	11.4	6 069	26.0	0.015	22	20 400	12.5
3 Bulgaria	726	37.2	3 217	82.5	0.165	0	100	–
4 Denmark	1 518	14.7	2 172	4.5	0.105	18	0	13.4
5 Finland	911	144.2	2 380	12.5	0.103	13	0	18.1

continued on next page

Table 4.A3 Data for model estimation (cont.)

	Gnppc	Area	Pop	Illiteracy	Avtarif	Standard	Coalpro	Tempdif
1890 (cont.)								
6 France	1 500	204.0	38 133	20.0	0.081	32	26 100	10.7
7 Germany	1 442	208.7	49 428	4.5	0.089	18	89 200	15.1
8 Greece	724	25.0	2 187	70.0	0.140	25	0	—
9 Italy	947	110.7	30 468	55.0	0.169	11	400	15.3
10 Netherlands	2 010	12.7	4 511	17.5	0.004	15	100	12.5
11 Norway	1 215	124.6	2 001	7.5	0.106	15	0	14.4
12 Portugal	752	34.3	5 060	77.5	0.333	36	0	9.6
13 Romania	663	50.7	5 290	82.5	0.065	9	0	27.4
14 Russia	582	1 745.8	117 800	82.5	0.337	0	6 000	28.0
15 Serbia	*646*	19.1	2 162	—	*0.080*	—	0	—
16 Spain	1 223	194.7	17 718	61.0	0.164	15	1 200	19.1
17 Sweden	1 308	172.9	4 785	3.0	0.108	30	200	14.5
18 Switzerland	*1 763*	15.5	2 933	3.0	0.033	40	0	15.5
19 UK	2 597	99.4	37 485	12.5	0.047	39	185 000	8.9
1900								
1 Austria-Hungary	1 200	241.2	45 177	*23.0*	0.069	0	39 000	20.0
2 Belgium	2 107	11.4	6 694	*19.7*	0.019	32	23 500	17.2
3 Bulgaria	—	37.2	3 744	*72.4*	0.149	3	100	—
4 Denmark	1 843	14.7	2 450	*3.8*	0.081	28	0	18.1
5 Finland	1 103	117.8	2 656	*6.8*	0.111	23	0	22.1
6 France	1 811	204.0	38 451	*16.0*	0.090	42	33 400	14.4
7 Germany	1 759	208.7	56 367	*3.8*	0.085	28	149 500	19.8
8 Greece	—	25.0	2 575	64.9	0.144	25	0	15.5

continued on next page

Table 4.A3 Data for model estimation (cont.)

	Gnppc	Area	Pop	Illiteracy	Avtarif	Standard	Coalcon	Julytemp
1900 (cont.)								
9 Italy	1 039	110.7	32 475	47.2	0.123	12	500	15.6
10 Netherlands	2 188	12.7	5 104	12.5	0.005	25	300	17.2
11 Norway	1 337	124.6	2 240	5.3	0.110	25	0	20.7
12 Portugal	863	34.3	5 423	73.2	0.272	37	0	12.1
13 Romania	—	50.7	5 957	73.8	0.077	19	100	25.4
14 Russia	766	1 745.8	132 900	68.8	0.341	5	16 200	30.9
15 Serbia	—	19.1	2 493	—	0.150	3	200	—
16 Spain	1 410	194.7	18 594	56.6	0.149	15	2 700	20.7
17 Sweden	1 582	172.9	5 137	2.3	0.111	40	300	20.6
18 Switzerland	2 013	15.5	3 300	2.3	0.045	50	0	17.6
19 UK	2 923	99.4	41 155	10.0	0.054	49	229 000	14.5
1910								
1 Austria-Hungary	1 359	241.2	49 458	17.0	0.071	9	47 900	16.6
2 Belgium	2 311	11.4	7 424	13.4	0.015	42	25 500	12.8
3 Bulgaria	814	37.2	4 338	62.2	0.159	13	200	—
4 Denmark	2 276	14.7	2 757	3.0	0.053	38	0	16.1
5 Finland	1 286	117.8	2 943	1.1	0.128	33	0	19.6
6 France	1 973	204.0	39 192	11.9	0.087	52	38 400	13.4
7 Germany	2 023	208.8	64 926	3.0	0.076	38	222 500	15.2
8 Greece	840	24.4	2 698	59.7	0.270	25	0	17.5
9 Italy	1 399	110.7	34 671	39.3	0.080	21	600	14.5
10 Netherlands	2 286	12.7	5 858	7.5	0.004	35	13 000	12.8

continued on next page

Table 4.A3 Data for model estimation (cont.)

	Gnppc	Area	Pop	Illiteracy	Avtarif	Standard	Coalpro	Tempduf
1910 (cont.)								
11 Norway	1 550	124.6	2 392	3.0	0.124	35	0	21.2
12 Portugal	837	34.3	5 958	68.9	0.236	37	0	10.2
13 Romania	872	50.7	7 038	65.0	0.134	29	100	22.4
14 Russia	893	1 745.8	160 700	55.0	0.286	15	25 400	26.0
15 Serbia	724	19.1	2 900	77.5	*0.150*	13	200	—
16 Spain	1 457	194.7	19 927	52.2	0.154	15	4000	19.1
17 Sweden	1 838	173.0	5 522	1.5	0.090	50	300	18.0
18 Switzerland	2 320	15.9	3 753	1.5	0.046	60	0	15.1
19 UK	2 991	99.4	45 649	7.5	0.049	59	269 000	10.4

Note: Figures in italics are linear interpolations.

Notes

Financial assistance from Nuffield Foundation and Banco de Fomento Exterior is gratefully acknowledged. The authors wish to thank the editors, Şevket Pamuk and Jeffrey Williamson, for their detailed comments on the first draft of this paper, and Williamson for editing the last drafts. They also wish to thank George Dertilis, Konstantinos Kostis, David Good, Michael Palairet and Max-Stephan Schulze for help with statistical information. The usual caveat applies.

1   For lack of data, Serbia will be dropped from our model computations.
2   For population totals and density figures, see League of Nations (1914: Tables 2 and 3).
3   See Stoianovich (1994: 206–7).
4   See Lampe and Jackson (1982: 162), Kostelenos (1995: 75 and 95), Lains (1995: 53), Simpson (1995: 36) and Palairet (1997:187 and 302).
5   See Mitchell (1992: Tables C1, C2 and C3) and Lains (1995: Table 2.5 and Appendix).
6   See among other references Preshlenova (1994) and Lains (1995).
7   See Lampe and Jackson (1982: 251) and Lains (1995: Table 2.11).
8   There are no data for 1870 for the two countries. Yet, industrial output increased faster in Romania and the share in 1910 was still smaller than in Portugal.
9   See Woytinsky and Woytinsky (1955: 195), Lampe (1972: 146; 1975b: 74) and Damjanov (1979: 20; 1980).
10 Lampe and Jackson (1982: Tables 7.2 and 7.8) and Mata (1993: Table 36).
11 Scott's (1993) 26-observation regression (including a "catch-up" term) explained 95 per cent of the cross-country and time variation. He estimates his equation from an unbalanced panel of growth observations with data going back to 1856 for Britain, but his data are confined to wealthier countries and most are in the post-1945 period. He also weights observations by reliability and importance.

Part 3

Long-run growth

Country studies

5 Growth and retardation in Ottoman Macedonia, 1880–1910

Ahmet O. Akarlı

Introduction

Over the last three decades our understanding of the nineteenth-century Ottoman economy has improved considerably. Painstaking research undertaken by a group of devoted scholars such as Issawi, Eldem, Karpat, Owen, Pamuk, Quataert, Toprak, Güran and more recently Palairet have rectified our vision of that economy.[1] For instance, we can now boast quite comprehensive estimates of foreign trade, terms of trade, balance of payments and population growth (Pamuk 1987, 1994a; DIE 1995; Karpat 1985). We also have a better understanding of the dynamics of structural change in a number of key economic sectors such as agriculture and manufacturing.[2] Finally, our knowledge of the financial and economic reform policies instituted by the Ottoman government has improved greatly.[3] In short, we now have a better understanding of the structural features and the general direction of the nineteenth-century Ottoman economy. Briefly put, all the above contributions seem to agree that the general direction of the Ottoman economy was towards full-blown integration with the expanding world economy. In this process, important transformations took place which can be briefly summarized as varying degrees of *peripheral* specialization, commercialization, urbanization, infrastructural innovation and the consolidation of European financial control over the economic sources of the Empire.

However, there still exist important gaps in our knowledge of the nineteenth-century Ottoman economy. First, we are still operating in a relative statistical vacuum which often prevents us from putting the Ottoman experience into a solid comparative perspective. We therefore get only a limited glance at the performance of the nineteenth-century Ottoman economy. For instance, output and income estimates are virtually non-existent for the crucial *Tanzimat* years (1839–76). The available Ottoman sources pertaining to this period are still largely unprocessed, dispersed between countless archives and libraries, and technically difficult to use, all of which makes direct measurement of performance exceedingly problematic. For the *Hamidian* (1876–1908) and the *Unionist* years (1908–18), the situation is slightly better and the available archive sources do allow for a relatively more plausible measurement of Ottoman economic performance. In a now classi-cal contribution, Vedat Eldem (1994) estimated Ottoman national income for a number of benchmark years between about 1890 and 1910. Eldem's data suggest that the Ottoman national income as measured by 1913 prices grew at a steady rate of 1.7 per cent between 1890 and 1910, with a probable trend acceleration after the turn of the century (Table 5.1). Also, Eldem maintains that per capita income grew at an annual rate of 0.8 per cent, to reach 1,090 kurus, or 248 francs, in 1910.[4] These estimates suggest signifi-cant dynamism and growth in the Ottoman economy throughout the *Hamidian* and *Unionist* periods.

Since its first publication in 1970, Eldem's contribution has been used widely by Ottoman economic historians and even led some optimistic schol-ars, such as Osman Okyar (1987: 47), to the conclusion that the Ottoman economy had entered a process of modern economic growth or a probable "take-off", which was only to be shattered by the destructive effects of eight years of constant warfare from 1914 onwards. However, Eldem himself was somewhat more pessimistic about the developmental potential of the Otto-man economy. First, he maintained that the Ottoman economic perfor-mance lagged seriously behind the leading industrial powers such as Britain, USA and Germany, and also fell short of the performance of successful late industrializers such as Japan, Denmark and Hungary (Eldem 1994: 235). According to Eldem, the gap between the Ottoman economy and industrial-ized nations remained stable at best and probably widened throughout the period, despite significant economic dynamics and growth.[5] Second, Eldem maintained that the financial insolvency of the Ottoman state blocked the Gerschenkronian path to late industrialization and economic development. Also, growing dependency and intensifying European financial control seri-ously curtailed the Ottoman potential for take-off. Thus, drawing heavily on post-war theories of economic development, Eldem diagnosed developmen-tal failure or sustained relative backwardness in the Ottoman economy, which did not necessarily exclude the possibility of sporadic dynamism and growth.

Available data on nineteenth-century Ottoman living standards also con-firm Eldem's conclusions. Until very recently, we only had a limited under-standing of the changes in Ottoman wage levels. Research undertaken by Boratav, *et al.* (1994: 391) suggests a 118 per cent rise in nominal wages between 1839 and 1913, with a trend acceleration especially after 1896. According to their estimates, Ottoman wages increased by about 40 per cent between 1896 and 1913, or by 2 per cent per annum. However, their esti-mates are only expressed in nominal terms and do not reflect trends in real wages. In this volume, Williamson uses this series in conjunction with a com-prehensive cost-of-living index to compute Ottoman real wages. William-son's analysis suggests that Ottoman real wages declined by 19 per cent between 1890–4 and 1906–10. More importantly, he maintains that the real wage gap between Turkey and the leading industrial powers, i.e. Britain,

France, Germany and the USA, had notably widened between the early 1890s and the early 1910s.[6] If these figures are correct, then it might be possible to seriously maintain the "falling behind" thesis. Indeed, in tune with the suggestions put forth by Jaime Reis (Chapter 2) and James Foreman-Peck and Pedro Lains (Chapter 4), it might be a good idea to perceive the late-nineteenth-century Ottoman economy as a much troubled one, standing at the outer rim of a southeastern Mediterranean "convergence" or, perhaps more accurately, "divergence" club.

When we take a closer look at certain structural features of the Ottoman economy the divergence thesis appears even more plausible. First it is important to note that a robust process of economic growth emerged predominantly within sectors that articulated well with the world economy. Export-oriented cash-crop production and the associated processing industries grew especially fast throughout the century. Also, urban service and construction industries expanded to support and to accommodate spatially the intensifying "peripherization" process. This growth dynamic was particularly visible in port-cities and in (rail-served) interior towns which linked the hinterland economies with the world market.[7]

To a large extent, the sectors serving the domestic market remained defensive throughout the nineteenth century. As correctly pointed out by Quataert, certain sectors less favoured by the conjunctures of the world economy did in fact benefit from the growth of domestic demand. For instance, textile industries, cereal production and a number of sectors specializing in the production of non-durable consumer goods, such as horticulture and dairy-product industries, undoubtedly profited from the growth of domestic (i.e. urban) demand. Still, it must be pointed out that the liberal trade regime of the empire, high overland transportation costs, exorbitant railway tariffs and internal custom duties that remained in effect until the 1870s, held back these domestic sectors from fully reaping the benefits of growing home demand. Thus, the long-term growth potential of the domestic sectors was circumscribed by a combination of foreign competition and high transaction costs. On the supply side, regressive taxation practices, high interest rates prevailing in private credit markets, endemic rent-seeking motives (see below) and the practical difficulties encountered in the diffusion and maintenance of productivity-enhancing techniques, forced the domestic sectors, especially traditional agriculture, into a Schumpeterian standstill for a good part of the long nineteenth century. Hence, a static compartment of the Ottoman economy co-existed with booming cash-crop production and booming sectors.

The evident contrast between the "propulsive/incorporated" sectors and the "retarded/excluded" sectors highlights the growing dualism of the Ottoman economy throughout the nineteenth century. Surely, this dualism must be perceived as the structural manifestation of the ongoing "peripherization" process *par excellence*. However, it is also important to bring into perspective the role played by the Ottoman state in consolidating this dual economic structure. Firstly, the financial insolvency of the Ottoman state appears to have been highly consequential. As has already been noted, the growing indebtedness of the Ottoman state and intensifying European control over the economic sources of the Empire certainly prepared the macroeconomic basis for underinvestment within the Ottoman economy.[8] More importantly perhaps, the financial insolvency of the Ottoman state created certain political and administrative vacuums within which rent-seeking could be liberally manifested. The rent-seeking agents, i.e. local notables, landlords, usurers and influential merchants, regularly generated lucrative incomes through their privileged access to and at times exclusive control over redistributive processes within the public domain (Kiray 1993). Probably, the practice of tax-farming was the rent-seeking activity *par excellence* throughout the empire, where speculators could expect to earn up to 30 per cent in profits. Also, subcontracting to provincial armies and local municipalities for the provision of goods and services and the regular extortion of public credits were other means of income generation through the exercise of political power and influence.[9] When combined with the attraction of moneylending, financial arbitrage and urban real-estate speculation, rent-seeking activities seem to have increased the opportunity cost of growth-generating investments in agriculture and manufacturing, thus exacerbating the Schumpeterian standstill in these core economic sectors. Thus the consolidation of the dual economic structure outlined above.

Turning back to the divergence/convergence debate, we can confidently maintain that the overwhelming weight of the excluded domestic sectors in the Ottoman economy probably undermined its growth performance over the longer term, especially on a per capita basis.[10] In this respect, the scenario of divergence appears more realistic.

However, the degree of falling behind is yet to be measured. We certainly need to bring the *Tanzimat* years into quantitative perspective. For the *Hamidian* and *Unionist* periods there is an acute need to improve the precision of Eldem's estimates. Eldem based his agricultural income estimates primarily on fiscal (tithe) data and on the official output statistics published by the Ottoman government in 1897, 1907, 1913 and 1914. Both data sets had weaknesses. First, the 1897 figures were far less comprehensive. They did not incorporate certain agricultural products and a few important provinces which were included in later statistics. In order to make up for this deficiency, Eldem (1994: 33) complemented the 1897 statistics with the output statistics published in Ottoman provincial yearbooks (*salnames*). However, the statistics in the *salnames* were not entirely reliable. The Ottoman authorities based their output estimates on fiscal data. They mainly took the tithe returns at a sub-provincial (*kaza*) level and deflated them with current agricultural prices to reach indicative output figures. All the *kaza* figures were in turn aggregated to reach provincial output estimates. However, available fiscal data was far from ideal in estimating output levels, as the fiscal records often incorporated an indeterminate margin of underestimation emanating

Table 5.1 Eldem's estimates of Ottoman "national" and per capita incomes, 1889–1910 (1913 prices)

Year	GNI	P	GNI/P	Sub periods	GNI growth (%)	GNI/P growth (%)
c.1890	16 190	17.389	931	1890–1900	1.27	0.35
c.1900	18 370	19.050	964	1900–1910	2.19	1.25
c.1910	22 820	20.897	1 092	1890–1910	1.73	0.80

Source: Eldem (1994: 231). Population figures were taken from DIE (1996: 46). For c.1890, the results of the 1881/1893 census were used as rough approximations; for c.1900, the 1897 census; and for c.1910, the 1906/7 census. All population figures are expressed in '000s.

Note:
Growth rates were calculated as exponential.

from common tax evasion and poor reporting.[11] As such, Eldem's 1897 estimates appeared somewhat lower than they should have been. Obviously, the subsequent juxtaposition of inconsistent data sets presumably led Eldem to overstate agricultural performance in the post-1897 period.

Secondly, Eldem used tithe data to determine the trends in agricultural performance for the period 1889–1914 and to cross-check the reliability of his output estimates which were based on the official statistics. This time, however, he used the tithe data nominally and did not take into account the general increase in agricultural prices, which according to our estimates could have risen by 40 per cent between 1889 and 1913.[12] Besides, there is no evidence to suggest that Eldem allowed for the rise in the official tithe rate, by 20 per cent in 1894 and by another 0.6 per cent in 1900 (Akarli 1976: 164). Finally, Eldem did not appear to take account of the government's changing capacity to tax. This capacity improved especially in the European and Anatolian provinces of the empire following the establishment of more structured provincial administrations and the arrival of railways and telegraphic services. Overall, therefore, Eldem almost certainly overestimated the performance of Ottoman agriculture, and possibly, therefore, of the Ottoman economy as well.

The overestimation inherent in Eldem's estimates is, in fact, consequential. Consider the figures presented in Table 5.1. For example a likely 5 per cent upward bias in his 1910 estimates might suggest lower annual percentage growth rates both on aggregate (1.4) and especially on per capita (0.5) terms. A probable 10 per cent overestimation would yield even lower annual growth rates of 1.1 and 0.26 per cent respectively. At any rate, both alternative growth rates would move the Ottoman economy off the outer rim of the eastern and southeastern European league and relegate it down to the modest-growing Asian and African leagues (Maddison 1995: 60). Therefore, it is imperative to maintain a critical distance from Eldem's estimates in determining the degree of falling behind.

In what follows we will be concentrating on the dynamics of growth and retardation in the Ottoman economy in a more focused regional context. Here our case study will be Ottoman "Macedonia" from about 1885 to about 1910.[13] The choice of Ottoman Macedonia as our case study is mainly linked to a number of empirical and historical reasons. First of all, available sources on the economic history of Macedonia are abundant and allow for a relatively comprehensive historical and quantitative analysis. Secondly, Ottoman Macedonia was one of the most dynamic regions of the late-nineteenth-century Ottoman economy, and embodies all the aspects and contradictions of Ottoman economic life in miniature form. Especially, the above-mentioned duality is possibly best seen in the Macedonian economy. In this context, we will mainly concentrate on the core agrarian sector. Other sectors will be considered only in passing.

We will also make a deliberate effort to support our discussion of the dynamics of growth and retardation in late-nineteenth-century Macedonian agriculture with a robust quantitative analysis. In this context, we will develop alternative estimation methods which will enable us to measure output performance in key agricultural sectors, i.e. cereal and cash-crop production, with relative accuracy. For practical reasons, the technical discussion will be kept at a minimum and will be brought together in the appendix below. Also, the statistical data used in computations will not be presented here due to limitations on space. However, both the relevant database and the technical details of the underlying computations are available from the author on diskette, MACSTATS.

Growth and retardation in Macedonian agriculture, 1875–1910

The worldwide construction of railway networks and the appearance of steamships in international waters from the 1850s onwards marked a breakthrough in transport history signified by a drastic decline in costs of transportation (Pollard 1981; Hugill 1993). The costs of conveying bulky cereals declined especially rapidly throughout the last quarter of the nineteenth century. This development brought the cereal producers of North America, the Black Sea basin and the Indian subcontinent within easy reach of the rapidly expanding European consumer markets (Harley 1980: 228; Malenbaum 1953: 238–9). In this sense, the "transport revolution" destroyed the economic significance of distances somewhat and led to enhanced integration in world cereal markets. Consequently, "peripheral" grains rapidly glutted the European markets and caused prices to decline from the 1870s onwards.[14] The continental economies responded to the emergent challenge by heavily protecting their agrarian economies and by introducing cost-cutting techniques in cultivation.[15]

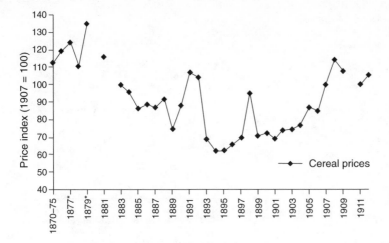

Figure 5.1 Cereal prices (f.o.b.) in Salonica, *c.*1870–*c.*1910.

Source: MACSTATS.

These developments worked much to the disadvantage of Macedonian cereal producers.[16] Prior to the 1860s, cereals were the leading export item of the region (Themopoulou 1994). The emergence of vigorous American and Russian competition and the subsequent reversion to protectionism in Europe, effectively pushed Macedonian cereal producers into a marginal position in overseas markets. Throughout the following four decades, cereal production turned increasingly towards the regional markets. As a result, it gradually lost its importance as a major export item, to be replaced by alternative cash crops such as tobacco, silk, opium and, to a lesser extent, cotton. In what follows, this process of transformation is considered in full historical detail.

The post-1873 price depression in Macedonian cereal markets was quite severe. Due to a combination of inflationary incidents, the depression in prices did not reach Salonica markets until the early 1880s. However, the Russo–Ottoman War of 1876–7 and the disastrous crop failure of 1879, both helped to maintain local cereal prices for a while.[17] However, from 1881 onwards Salonica cereal prices declined for a decade and a half almost without disruption. The only exception to this secular downward trend was the speculative leap generated by the withdrawal of Russian cereals from the world markets due to the severe famine of 1891 (FOAS 1893: N. 1310: 5–6). Otherwise the descent was uninterrupted until the mid-1890s and in 1896 Salonica cereal prices stood at about 55 per cent of their pre-1875 levels (Figure 5.1). Thus, *ceteris paribus*, Macedonian farmers saw their incomes accruing from cereal production dwindle significantly within a decade and a half. In this respect, the adverse income effect of the crisis in cereal trade cannot be denied.

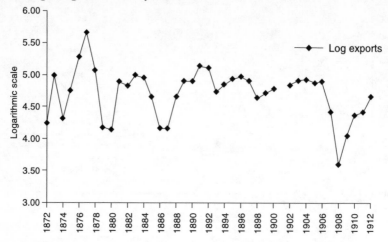

Figure 5.2 Macedonian cereal exports, 1875–1910 (Logarithmic scale).

Source: MACSTATS.

The depth and persistence of the price depression made it extremely difficult for Macedonian cereal producers to take innovative steps to break the
depression's grip by shifting to new products and technologies. First of all,
the dire income effects of the depression ultimately pushed many cereal producers into a circle of growing indebtedness and distressing mortgages.
Under the circumstances, most Macedonian farmers found it ever more difficult, in fact undesirable, to undertake investments to enhance productivity
in cereal production. Besides, the difficulties encountered in the introduction and diffusion of modern farming techniques throughout the region
constituted another serious obstacle to making progress on the productivity
front. These circumstances ultimately held Macedonian cereal production at
a technological standstill throughout the 1880s and 1890s.[18] Thus it became
very difficult, in fact almost impossible, to respond to the challenge of American,
Russian and Indian competitors in the overseas markets.

Not surprisingly, throughout the depression years the export performance of Macedonian cereals remained quite sluggish. Even the completion
of the Salonica–Üsküp railway line in 1872 did not produce a permanent
upward movement in cereal exports. Prior to the railway connection the
annual cereal exports of the region varied between 60,000 to 80,000 tons per
annum,[19] while between 1880 and 1896 they fluctuated around 70,000 tons
per annum (Figure 5.2).[20] The only significant (short-term) upward movements were caused by the Russo–Ottoman War of 1876 and the Russian
famine of 1891.

Three additional factors held Macedonian cereal exports at bay during
this period. The first retarding factor was frequent harvest failure, which seriously disturbed regular export trade in cereals: 1874, 1879 and 1885 were
years of severe crop failures throughout the Macedonian countryside.[21] In

each case, a combination of low supplies and the ensuing government restrictions on foreign trade squeezed exports down to a minimum of 15,000–20,000 tons for a number of years.

In addition, high transportation costs created insurmountable difficulties for Macedonian cereal producers. The main river systems of the region were not navigable, and bulky cereals had to be transported overland from the interior to the port of Salonica. However, Macedonian roads were at the time in poor condition and did not allow for easy wheeled transportation better suited to the carriage of bulky goods. The trade caravans had to rely on more expensive animal transportation which inflated the costs of conveyance. More importantly, the tariffs on the Salonica–Üsküp railway line were set at exorbitantly high rates due to the high kilometric guarantees given by the Ottoman government to the Oriental Railway Company.[22] For instance, during the years of sustained price depression and mounting protectionism in European markets, the railway tariffs amounted to as much as a third of the wheat price and a half of the price of oats, rye, barley and maize in Salonica.[23] This situation placed Macedonian cereal producers at a serious disadvantage in world markets and squeezed them into ever narrower profit margins. In fact, despite successive tariff reductions in the late 1880s and the early 1890s, many producers failed to send their harvests to Salonica and instead the surplus produce of the hinterland ended up in warehouses waiting for a substantial recovery in prices.[24] A transportation constraint seems to have kept the region from fulfilling its export potential.

The other, equally consequential problem was the poor marketing quality of Macedonian cereals. At the time, the farmers and the intermediary merchants of the interior were in the habit of debasing the produce to widen their profit margins. Consequently, the produce sent from the hinterland often appeared heavily debased in Salonica markets. This situation undermined the commercial reputation of Macedonian cereals and led European merchants to favour the better-marketed Russian and American grains.[25] As such, Macedonian produce was pushed further into a subsidiary position in European markets and was traded in considerable amounts only in times of great scarcity, such as wars and crop failures.

However, it seems that throughout the 1880s and 1890s Macedonian cereal producers could resist the tide of depression and managed to maintain levels of cereal production. We estimate that Macedonian cereal production lingered around 1,000,000 tons and possibly rose slightly, by as much as 2.4 per cent, between the mid-1880s and the mid-1890s (Table 5.A3).

During this period two factors seem to have helped secure the perpetuity of cereal production in the region. The first was the apparent rise in domestic demand. Between 1885 and 1895 the population of the three Macedonian provinces Salonica, Manastir and Kosovo, rose by about 5 per cent due mainly to the influx of refugees from the Balkans following the removal of Thessaly to Greece in 1885 (Ipek 1994). Also, urban populations grew in this period. While we do not know the exact magnitude of urban growth for

Macedonia as a whole in the pre-1895 period, available urban statistics for the province of Salonica suggest that the share of urban population residing in towns with more than 5,000 residents rose from 11 per cent in 1880 to 16 per cent in the mid-1890s. Probably similar trends prevailed in greater Macedonia. In fact, Palairet considers this period as one of urban growth and notes that the share of towns with more than 2,000 residents accounted for 26.6 per cent of the Macedonian population around 1895.[26]

The growth of the region and especially of the urban population clearly generated fresh demand for locally grown cereals,[27] since the provision of supplies for the dependent urban populace created special opportunities for local cereal producers. Our calculations suggest that urban wheat consumption rose from 95,000 to 127,000 tons between the mid-1880s and the mid-1890s. During this period cereal imports into the region remained insignificant, which in turn suggests that the domestic market remained the preserve of local farmers at least until around 1895.

This is a telling observation. Unlike the continental economies, the Ottoman trade regime was quite liberal at this time and domestic markets were by and large unprotected from the winds of foreign competition.[28] Under such liberal policy circumstances, we would normally expect the cheap American, Russian and Indian grains and flour to capture a commanding position in the domestic urban markets. However, the exorbitant railway tariffs and the high overland transport costs seem to have worked both ways, providing the sector with some degree of *de facto* protection until the early 1890s. As we shall see, later in the 1890s the reduction of railway tariffs created grave difficulties for the domestic producers. Especially after the turn of the century, wheat and flour coming from the Black Sea basin increasingly forced Macedonian cereal producers to retreat in the domestic markets. For the 1880s and 1890s, however, growing domestic demand and the buffering effect of high transport costs can be considered as the key market factors that helped maintain cereal production in the region.

The second factor that secured the perpetuity of regional cereal production was the well executed and well timed crisis management policies of the Ottoman government, which had a considerable stake in maintaining cereal production throughout the provinces. Tithes accruing from cereal production constituted a substantial source of income for the government. Therefore, prolific cereal cultivation was essential for the wellbeing of Ottoman state finances. Besides, the provision of supplies for the local armies and the growing urban areas, which constituted the actual power base of Ottoman rule in the provinces, was indispensable for the maintenance of the Ottoman *status quo.*[29] The limited financial and administrative means of the Ottoman government were not sufficient to institute extensive modernization projects that would generate a substantial recovery in cereal trade (Quataert 1973, 1975, 1993b). However, public efforts were particularly effective in offsetting the potentially destabilizing and retarding impact of the harvest failures triggered by frequent droughts, floods and other natural calamities. In every crop failure that plagued the Macedonian countryside during the 1880s and 1890s, the Ottoman authorities assumed an active role in restoring regional "balances" in cereal production. On each occasion the authorities distributed seeds, granted tax exemptions and extended cheap credits to the unfortunate farmers throughout the Macedonian provinces. In addition, upon orders from Istanbul, the local authorities executed a strict policy of trade prohibitions that eliminated the potentially destabilizing impact of grain exports.[30] As such, in the short term the Ottoman bureaucracy played an important role in holding back the harvest failures from reaching famine proportions. In the medium term, it helped maintain levels of cereal production through years of sustained price depression.

In the meantime cash-crop production was making steady progress in the region. Silk production recovered from the malignant pebrine disease that had severely undermined sericulture throughout the 1860s. In this process of recovery, the importation of disease-free silkworm eggs from France, Japan and the United States and the encouragement schemes instituted by the Ottoman government and the Ottoman Public Debt Administration (PDA hereafter) played crucial roles in the restoration of sericulture throughout the region.[31]

Subsequently, both the production and exports of silk cocoons almost doubled between the early 1880s and the 1890s (Table 5.A4). Similarly, opium production grew rapidly and rose from near insignificance in the early 1870s to 70 tons in the early 1890s.[32] Strong overseas demand for high-quality Macedonian opium and the handsome prices offered by European and American merchants certainly account for the rapid expansion of poppy cultivation in Macedonia throughout the 1880s and 1890s.[33] Furthermore, tax-exemptions and the introductory schemes carried out by the Ottoman government encouraged farmers to take up the cultivation of this highly profitable crop (PPAP 1883: V.72, 101). Similarly, cotton production recovered from the onslaught of American competition, which had seriously undermined Macedonian cotton cultivation in the earlier decades of the nineteenth century (Themopoulou 1994: 512). The recovery of the post-1880 period was linked to the establishment of a number of mechanized spinning concerns in Salonica and Agustos (Nausta) and to the subsequent rise in the demand for domestically grown cotton varieties.[34]

Tobacco was the problem cash crop of the 1880s and 1890s. The establishment of a new tobacco monopoly, the Société de la Régie Cointéresée des Tabacs de l'Empire Ottomane (Régie hereafter) in 1884 initially gave way to a contraction in tobacco production.[35] The Régie's tight control over the production and marketing of tobacco and its regressive pricing policies initially scared a number of farmers away from tobacco cultivation.[36] Nevertheless, tobacco production recovered somewhat in the 1890s (Table 5.A4). This recovery was partially linked to a series of bountiful harvests between 1891 and 1895.[37] However, there is evidence to suggest that the rise in output emanated from the expansion of tobacco cultivation.[38] It seems that buoyant

Table 5.2 Relative cereal, tobacco and cash crop prices, *c.*1880–*c.*1910

Period	Cereals	Tobacco	Cash crops	Cereals vs tobacco	Cereals vs cash crops
1880–84	100	100	100	100	100
1885–89	82	90	85	91	97
1890–94	83	70	72	118	115
1895–99	70	88	74	80	95
1900–04	71	109	100	65	71
1905–09	95	136	98	70	97
1910–12	99	192	148	52	67

Source: MACSTATS.

overseas demand and the liberal credit policies of the Régie and Hertzog, the Austrian tobacco monopoly, were important factors that facilitated the quick recovery in Macedonian tobacco production.[39]

The advent of the late 1890s brought about important transformations in Macedonian agriculture. First and foremost, the economic conjecture turned entirely against cereal producers from about 1895 onwards. The post-1896 recovery in cereal prices was quite gradual and by 1905 depressed Macedonian cereal prices had only recovered by a modest 15 per cent. In this later period even strong exogenous shocks such as the Spanish–American and the Greco–Turkish Wars could not initiate a jump-start for the long-depressed cereal prices (Figure 5.1). However, the rise in cash-crop prices was considerably faster. Relative prices turned rapidly in favour of cash crops, especially of tobacco, throughout the period (Table 5.2). Even the Russo–Japanese War and the successive crop failures between 1907 and 1910 could not generate an inflationary moment in cereal prices that could keep up with the rapid ascent in tobacco prices.[40] This relative price effect certainly constituted a strong incentive to switch to the production of cash crops, especially tobacco, in the region.

Also, the 21 per cent increase in the tithe rate that took place between 1894 and 1900 further exacerbated the unfavourable conditions in cereal production. According to our calculations, the real tax-burden of the tithe-paying farmers may have risen by as much as 100 per cent on a per capita basis between the late 1880s and the early 1900s (Table 5.3). The rising fiscal burden undoubtedly had an adverse impact on depressed cereal production and encouraged farmers to switch to the cultivation of lucrative cash crops, where the tax-burden was probably more tolerable.

Another serious problem that undermined cereal production in the region was the unidirectional reduction of freight rates on goods

Table 5.3 Real per capita tax burden of Macedonian farmers, late 1880s and early
1900s

Period	Tithe receipts	Rural population	Per capita	Cereal prices	Real tax burden
1888–1890	41 487 000	2 037 000	20	100	100
1901–1903	58 374 000	1 701 000	34	85	200

Source: MACSTATS.
Note: The tithe receipts are given in kuru.

transported from Salonica towards the hinterland from 1891 onwards. The
rate reductions brought urban markets within closer reach of Russian and
American cereals and undermined the market position of local cereal producers.[41] The crucial interior urban markets came within the orbit of import
trade.[42] From the mid-1890s onwards grain stocks were piling up in the interior warehouses and an increasing number of local mills were facing closures
or under-capacity utilization, which was symptomatic of serious stagnation in
local cereal trade.[43]

Finally, a series of successive harvest failures caused mainly by unusually
bad weather conditions between 1897 and 1910, proved detrimental to the
perpetuity of cereal production in the region. Not surprisingly, after depression and drought cereal producers turned to the production of alternative
cash crops, which were better suited to the arid climate of the region.[44] Thus,
cereal production contracted by 11.5 per cent between the mid-1890s and
the mid-late 1900s (Table 5.A3).

The rapid growth of cash-crop production in the post-1896 period was not
solely linked to the depression in cereal production. The demand conditions
remained quite favourable for cash-crop producers. European and American demand for high-quality Macedonian opium continued to expand
throughout and encouraged local farmers to increase the cultivation of pop-
pies.[45] Similarly, the buoyancy of overseas and especially domestic demand
facilitated the growth of silk-cocoon production in the region.[46] Likewise,
the establishment of a number of new cotton-spinning concerns in Salonica,
Vodine, Agustos and Karaferye underlined the growth of cotton production
in Macedonian provinces, especially in the province of Salonica.[47]

The forceful entry of American trading companies into Salonica tobacco
markets following the Spanish–American War and the subsequent Cuban
Civil War gave way to a substantial boost in tobacco cultivation in Salonica.
The American presence quickly undermined the quasi-oligopolistic position
of the Régie and the Austrian tobacco monopoly, Hertzog, and led to a substantial increase in tobacco prices.[48] As relative prices turned swiftly in favour
of tobacco, many farmers switched to the cultivation of this most lucrative

cash crop. Subsequently both the production and export of tobacco more than doubled throughout the late 1890s and early 1900s.

The institutional support of the Ottoman government and the PDA in promoting the cultivation of alternative cash crops constituted a further incentive to step out of cereal production. The encouragement schemes and tax exemptions for producers of opium, cotton and silk continued throughout the period.[49] Similarly, tobacco producers continued to benefit from the liberal credit policies of the tobacco concerns operating in the region, namely the Régie, Hertzog, the Commercial Company of Salonica and the American company Johnston Mayer Co.[50] Under these favourable circumstances, cash-crop production grew by leaps and bounds, often at the expense of cereal production.

However, the dynamism in cash-crop production was difficult to maintain. The primary cash crops produced in the region were all exceedingly labour-intensive. Similar to many other Ottoman regions, late-nineteenth-century Macedonia had long been characterized by high land/labour ratios.[51] Moreover, after the turn of the century, the continuing growth of the urban population and the accelerating emigration to Bulgaria, Serbia, Greece and especially to the USA, led to the depopulation of rural areas throughout the Macedonian provinces.[52] Undoubtedly, depressed cereal prices, a rising tax-burden and successive harvest failures reinforced the processes of rural–urban migration and foreign emigration, thus accelerating Macedonian rural depopulation. In addition, mounting political tensions throughout the Macedonian countryside further exacerbated the problem of the growing labour scarcity.

Under these circumstances, it became exceedingly difficult to maintain levels of cash-crop production in the region. Only the burgeoning tobacco industry could assume a certain degree of vibrancy and could attract farmers and seasonal labourers from the Macedonian highlands.[53] The production of other cash crops either came to a standstill or declined in this later period (Table 5.A4). Thus, Macedonian agriculture entered a period of crisis, *en masse*, in the late 1900s, with the exception of tobacco production. The advent of the Balkan Wars and the ensuing political and economic turmoil simply brought the entire regional economy to a halt.

Overall, the price depression of 1873–96 seems to have triggered a dramatic transformation in the Macedonian economy. Simply put, it seems that the agrarian sector gradually but inevitably moved towards a new pattern of specialization. The terms of this (re)specialization were more or less dictated by the conjunctures of the "world economy". The crisis in cereal production and the growth of cash-crop production in the region were indeed a clear manifestation of this transformative process. In this respect, resistance, retardation and growth seem to have gone hand in hand in the Macedonian countryside, especially throughout the 1890s and 1900s. However, the growth dynamic generated by cash-crop production had its structural limits. In fact, cash-crop production was not ideally suited to the factor endowments of the region. Given the high land/labour ratios and the rapid depopulation of rural areas, especially after the turn of the century, the dynamism in labour-intensive cash-crop production could not be indefinitely maintained. It seems that the attraction of tobacco production reinforced this constraint and brought the cultivation of other cash crops to a relative decline, if not a standstill, in the post-1905 period.

Conclusion

The Macedonian experience illustrates the overwhelming power of the world economy in the last quarter of the "long" nineteenth century. Simply stated, the reduction in global transportation costs and the subsequent collapse of global cereal prices gradually pushed the regional economy towards a new pattern of specialization, which emphasized the production of cash crops, especially tobacco and opium. In this respect, the transformative impact of the world economy cannot be denied.

However, the Macedonian experience also confirms that the effective demand generated by the process of urban growth secured the perpetuity of regional cereal production between 1873–96. The decline in cereal production came with a conjunctural time-lag and materialized only in relation to mounting foreign competition in domestic markets and to the growing attraction of cash-crop production, especially of tobacco. This point is significant, both historically and methodologically. One of the important criticisms raised against the "World System Analysis" (WSA) in Ottoman economic history has been its omission of the dynamic of the domestic market (Quataert 1993a). This criticism is historically justified by the Macedonian experience. Without the dynamic of domestic (urban) demand, the crisis in Macedonian cereal production would probably have been deeper and would have pushed the region towards cash-crop production earlier and at a much faster pace. It is interesting to note however that the growth of the urban areas was in fact largely linked to the dynamic of the world economy itself.[54] So are we really observing a process in which the tide of globalization simultaneously acts as both a retardant and a growth generator for the core agrarian sector of the regional economy? If so, can we really understate the dynamic of the domestic, especially the urban, markets even if we were to subscribe to the standard WSA narrative? It seems therefore that a more integral demand-side analysis will certainly improve our understanding of the dynamics of structural transformation in key agricultural sectors.

Nevertheless, despite the new opportunities created by the growth of domestic demand, cereal production remained at a Schumpeterian standstill throughout the period. Little progress could be made to increase productivity. Sluggish prices and the landlords' disinterest and, at times, inability to introduce productivity-enhancing techniques were important factors that highlighted the persistence of extensive cultivation methods in cereal production. Also, the lack of effective agencies in technological diffusion and the limited fiscal and administrative sources at the disposal of the local governments contributed to the steadfastness of the extensive pattern. The important consequence of this situation was that cereal production became overwhelmingly dependent on labour input, which was the scarce factor of production in the region. In fact, high and rising land/labour ratios seem to have held Macedonian agriculture at a Pareto optimal situation, in which the production of one crop could not be extended without extracting labour from, and hence reducing the production of, another crop. Considering the adverse effects of growing labour scarcities even on cash-crop production later in the post-1900 period, we can maintain that the factor endowments did matter in Macedonia and undermined the growth potential of the entire agricultural sector. In this respect, it is imperative to consider factor endowments as a crucial determinant of sectoral performance in the broader Ottoman economy.

At this point, another important question emerges. Was the conjunctural direction dictated by the world economy always ideally suited to the structural outlets of Ottoman economic regions? Macedonian experience provides us with a negative answer. Land-abundant Macedonian provinces might have been better off if cereal production had been modernized, productivity increased, the domestic market protected, transportation costs reduced, and if regulations to control the quality of marketed produce could have been instituted. However, given the fiscal, political and diplomatic weakness of the Ottoman government, all these adjustments were very difficult to achieve. Under the circumstances, the regional economy was pushed and pulled towards labour-intensive cash-crop production. Mounting political instability, the growing rural tax-burden and the increasing attraction of (under-taxed) urban areas exacerbated the labour-scarcity problem and ultimately put a break on the expansion of Macedonian cash-crop production. This basic observation points towards the difficulty of sustaining the growth processes generated within the export-oriented compartments of the regional economy. In this respect, Macedonia stands in strong contrast to western Anatolia and the Adana region. The active immigration and rural settlement policies of the Ottoman government and the general political stability in the countryside seem to have been instrumental in maintaining a degree of agrarian dynamism in these regions. In fact, the contention of the current author is that factor endowments, the relative effectiveness of government policies and political stability constitute the key to understanding the reasons for the variance in Ottoman regional performance. Nevertheless, it is important to note once again that the conjunctures of the world economy set the broad framework for growth and retardation within the Ottoman economy. Political processes apparently determined margins of flexibility within that framework.

Appendix

Estimation of output levels in cereal production

In estimating levels of Macedonian cereal production we used two methods. The first was quite similar to that of Eldem and entailed the use of fiscal data in conjunction with official statistics published by the Ottoman government. The second method was based on the estimation of regional cereal consumption for three benchmark years. We then added the foreign-trade balance to the consumption estimates to reach indicative output estimates. Finally we brought the results of the two estimation methods together to compute a range of probable output estimates for about 1885, 1895 and 1905.

The fiscal approach

We used the tithe returns of provincial governments to estimate the trends (not levels) in cereal production. Here we were forced to make two crucial assumptions:

1   the degree of under-reporting and number manipulation embedded in tithe returns reported in provincial government budgets did not significantly change over time;
2   accounting methods remained more or less unchanged throughout the period.

The first assumption is justified as there is no way of accounting for the distortion contained in the budgets. The second assumption is based on ignorance: the literature cannot yet report the results of extensive research into accounting methods used by the Ottoman government.

We mainly used the expected (*tahakkukat*) rather than the actual (*tahsilat*) tithe revenues as proxy to determine the growth rates. The choice of *tahakkukat* values was linked to the fact that the expected tax returns were more representative of the tax base, as they did not respond swiftly to short-term shocks, such as harvest failures. There is evidence to suggest that the authorities used a combination of population registers together with the previous three years' actual revenues to estimate the *tahakukkat* values. Therefore, we interpreted the *tahakkukat* values as a three-year moving average. That is, the estimated value of the 1890 budget, say, would be based on the revenues of 1887–9. Therefore we took the 1890 values to indicate "production" levels around 1888. In other words, actual trends in output would lag two years behind the expected tithe revenues.

The data contained in the provincial budgets was relatively comprehensive and we managed to construct a series of *tahakkukat* values between 1888 and 1903. From this point on we followed a three-step procedure to account for the changes in cereal prices, the changes in the tithe rate, and the government's changing capacity to tax. First, based on the price data extracted from

Table 5.A1 Macedonian cereal production (fiscal estimates), *c.*1885–*c.*1905 (tons)

Year	Output
*c.*1885	1 148 000
*c.*1895	1 166 000
*c.*1905	935 000

Source: MACSTATS.

Notes: The *c.*1905 is based on 1907 statistics.

British consular reports, the contemporary journal, *Asır*, and the Journal of the French Chamber of Commerce of Istanbul, *Revue Commerciale du Levant*, we constructed a three-year moving average Laspeyres price index to deflate the tithe values. The weights used in the construction of the price index were based on the relatively reliable 1907 statistics published by the Ottoman government. The computations yielded a "real" tithe index. Second, we brought down the post-1894 values by 20 per cent and the post-1900 values by another 0.6 per cent, to account for the rise in the tithe rate. Thus, we assured consistency within our data set. Finally, we used the percentage ratio of the actual tithe values to the expected tithe values as proxy to measure the government's changing capacity to tax. We divided the consistent real tithe values with this "taxation" deflator to reach a tithe index net of price, tax-rate and taxation effects. Then we chose three relatively stable sub-periods, i.e. 1888–90, 1893–5 and 1901–3, as benchmarks to determine trends in output performance. The adjusted trend index stood at 100 for 1885, 98.4 for 1895 and 80.2 for 1905. Therefore, the long-term trend would be one of slight decline, 1.6 per cent, until 1895 and a rapid decline thereafter, by as much as 19.5 per cent. Assuming that the relatively comprehensive 1907 statistics would constitute a good benchmark to determine output levels around 1905, we estimated cereal production for 1885, 1895 and 1905. The results of our computations are presented in Table 5.A1.

The consumptionist approach

This was a more roundabout method that estimated output levels based on the following simple model:

> Total Output = Total Domestic Cereal Consumption + (Exports – Imports). Assuming zero waste, Total Domestic Cereal Consumption (TDCC) would have three components: TDCC = Human Consumption + Animal Consumption + Seeds.

The estimation of the foreign-trade balance was relatively straightforward. The relevant export/import figures were extracted from British consular

Table 5.A2 Macedonian cereal production (consumption estimates), *c.*1885–*c.*1910 (tons)

Period	TDCC	X	M	TP
*c.*1885	949 224	51 000	0	1 000 224
*c.*1895	983 872	74 000	4 000	1 053 872
*c.*1905	974 754	66 000	30 000	1 010 754

Source: MACSTATS.

Notes:
TDDC = Total Domestic Cereal Consumption;
X = Exports;
M = Imports;
TP = Total Production.

reports (Gounaris 1993). The only difficulty was to convert flour export/import ratios into wheat terms. In the conversions we assumed that 1 kg of hard wheat yielded about 750 g of flour and 250 g of bran.[55]

The estimation of TDCC entailed difficulties. The key assumptions were as follows:

1   Human wheat consumption was dominant in urban areas and the consumption of other cereals were prominent in rural areas. Thus, the rate of urbanization would determine the share of wheat in total human cereal consumption;
2   The rate of urbanization went up from about 25 per cent in *c.*1885 to 40 per cent in *c.*1905;
3   Human per capita (urban) wheat consumption stood around 140 kg per annum;
4   Human per capita (rural) non-wheat cereal consumption stood around 260 kg per annum;
5   Only large animals, i.e. cows, buffaloes, horses, etc., were fed with cereals. Each animal consumed approximately 175 kg of non-wheat cereals per annum;
6   The seed ratio was 15 per cent.

The above assumptions are based on contemporary Ottoman and European sources.[56] Certainly there is room for improvement on these assumptions. Nevertheless, we maintained them to estimate TDCC for three benchmark years for which regional human (Palairet 1997: 13) and animal population[57] figures are available. Incorporating the foreign-trade balance into our calculations we finally reached an estimate of Macedonian cereal production for around 1885, 1895 and 1910 (Table 5.A2). The trend suggested by the consumptionist output estimates indicates slight growth until 1895, 5.3 per cent, followed by a decline of 4.1 per cent thereafter.

Table 5.A3 Macedonian cereal production (range estimates), *c.*1885–*c.*1905 (tons)

Year	Maximum	Average	Minimum
*c.*1885	1 148 000	1 074 500	1 001 000
*c.*1895	1 166 000	1 100 000	1 054 000
*c.*1905	1 011 000	973 000	935 000

By bringing together the output estimates obtained from both estimation procedures, we determined a range of probable output estimates. The results are presented in Table 5.A3. We consider the average estimates as representative of both trends and output levels. Accordingly we suggest that Macedonian cereal production grew slightly, 2.4 per cent, between *c.*1885 and *c.*1895 and then declined considerably, by as much as 11.5 per cent, between *c.*1895 and *c.*1905. Certainly neither the results nor the estimation methods are conclusive. Nevertheless we believe that the use of two alternative methods maintains the relative reliability of the estimates. However, we still underline the fact that the entire procedure is suggestive and is mainly intended to generate further discussion to improve our estimation methods.

Estimation of output levels in cash-crop production

Available output statistics on cash-crop production are relatively reliable and more comprehensive. First of all, the PDA's and the Régie's tight control over the production, taxation and sale of silk and especially of tobacco assures the relative reliability of the official output estimates. Secondly, opium, tobacco and, to a lesser extent silk, were export-oriented crops. Therefore, available export figures enable us to roughly determine trends in output performance and also provide us with a solid basis to test the reliability of the official output estimates. Hence, we use the official output and foreign-trade statistics published by the Ottoman government, the PDA, the Régie and the European consuls quite liberally to determine output levels. The data is presented in the first three columns of Table 5.A4. All figures are the averages of available observations for each sub-period.

The case of cotton is slightly more complex. First, the statistics are relatively less reliable, due to the (apparently) fiscal origins of the official figures. Second, the predominant importance of the domestic market in the cotton trade prevents us from using export figures as proxy to determine trends in production. In order to overcome these difficulties, we produced similar "consumptionist" output estimates. The trade balance was calculated on the basis of import–export statistics regularly published in European consular reports. In estimating consumption levels we had to make two assumptions.

Table 5.A4 Macedonian cash crop production and exports, 1875–1910 (tons)

Years	Tobacco		Cocoons		Opium		Cotton		
	Q	X	Q	X	Q	X	Q	X	M
1870–75	6 800	2 850	650	210	n/a	0.25	n/a	2 850	0
1885–89	5 500	4 950	n/a	330	60	43	1 400	600	0
1890–94	6 250	5 300	1 300	400	70	60	2 550	390	0
1895–99	8 000	7 950	1 600	355	n/a	75	2 850	280	0
1900–04	13 000	12 000	1 700	320	151	145	3 000	310	515
1905–10	14 000	11 050	1 770	400	66	65	2 000	0	1 400

Source: See text.
Notes: Q = Output; X = Exports; M = Imports.

We assumed that the share of hand-spinning in total cotton consumption was relatively limited, about 5 per cent, and remained unchanged through time.[58] Thus, we could take factory consumption of cotton as proxy to determine levels of cotton consumption. Contemporary European consular reports often published the total weight of yarn produced in local spinning mills. Based on this evidence we estimated the weight of mechanized yarn production in Macedonia. Then we assumed that the local factories consumed 1.25 lb of raw cotton to produce 1 lb of coarse yarn.[59] Based on these assumptions we estimated the total factory consumption of cotton. Finally we incorporated the trade balance into our calculations to estimate levels of cotton production in the region between around 1885 and 1910. The results are presented in Table 5.A4.

Notes

I would like to thank Engin D. Akarlı, Peter Howlett, Şevket Pamuk and Donald Quataert for their comments and criticisms on earlier versions of this paper, and Jeffrey Williamson who not only edited this final version but who also resurrected the manuscript after an electronic disaster involving my computer. I would also like to express my appreciation for the comments made by the participants at the April 10 1998 LSE economic history workshop, especially Guillaume Daudin. Finally, I would like to acknowledge Emilie Themopoulou for generously sharing with me the results of her unpublished research on nineteenth-century Macedonian trade.

1   This literature is vast. However, the key contributions can be cited as follows. Issawi (1980a, 1980b, 1982, 1995); Eldem (1994); Karpat (1985); Kasaba (1987, 1992, 1994); Owen (1981); Toprak (1982, 1992, 1995); Pamuk (1984, 1987, 1994a); Quataert (1973, 1993a, 1994); Palairet (1997); Güran (1998). For published Ottoman statistics see DIE (1995, 1996, 1997a, 1997b).
2   For agricultural trends see Issawi (1980a); Eldem (1994a); Owen (1881); Toprak (1992); Pamuk (1984, 1987, 1994a); Quataert (1973, 1994); Güran (1998) and Palairet (1997). For

manufacturing see Issawi (1980a); Eldem (1994); Pamuk (1987, 1994a); Quataert (1988, 1992, 1993a); Owen (1881) and Palairet (1997).

3   Quataert (1973, 1975, 1993b, 1993c, 1994); Akarlı (1976) and Güran (1998). For fiscal aspects of reforms also see Shaw (1975); Akarlı (1976, 1992); Cezar (1986); Shaw and Shaw (1988); Şener (1990) and Kıray (1993).

4   Lampe (1975b: 59–60) and Lampe and Jackson (1982: 160–2) maintain that Balkan per capita incomes stood around 200 to 250 francs in 1913. Recent estimates put forward by Palairet also support Lampe and Jackson estimates. Palairet suggests 193 francs for Serbia and 266 francs for Bulgaria around 1910. If these figures are accurate, it is possible to maintain that on a per capita basis the Ottoman economy stood close to its Balkan counterpart around 1910. The currency conversions were based on the exchange rates given by Pamuk (1994b: 972).

5   This conclusion is also supported by Maddison (1995: 60) and it seems that the Ottoman economic performance as suggested by Eldem lagged behind the leading industrial powers and stayed roughly at par with eastern and southeastern European economies.

6   In fact in this period it seems that among all the retreating peripheral countries (such as Portugal, Serbia, Turkey and Egypt), Turkey did relatively poorly.

7   See Fawaz (1983); Kasaba *et al.* (1986); Kasaba (1987, 1988a, 1992); Keyder *et al.* (1994); Dumont and Georgeon (1996); Palairet (1997).

8   Blaisdell (1929); Suvla (1966); Parvus (1970); Kıray (1993); Eldem (1994); Pamuk (1987, 1994a).

9   For the extortion of public credits by provincial notables, see Quataert (1973) and Güran (1998).

10   Eldem's estimates suggest that the share of propulsive sectors of the Ottoman economy – more specifically cash-crop production, mining, construction, transport, commerce and private services – accounted for 29 per cent of national income (Eldem 1994: 31–2, 225–6).

11   For the details of the preparation of the provincial output statistics and their weaknesses, see *Dersaadet Ticaret Odasi Gazetesı* (*DTOG* hereafter), 7. Za. 1316 (19.3.1899), No. 699: 169.

12   According to our estimates, the prices of agricultural products including cereals and cash crops in Salonica rose by about 40 per cent between *c.*1889 and *c.*1912. This conclusion is also supported by Pamuk's series of Ottoman export prices, which increased by more than 20 per cent between 1889 and 1913 (Pamuk 1994a: 86–187). The relevant data set pertaining to Salonica prices is available from the author.

13   Here the term "Macedonia" is used only metaphorically to denote an Ottoman economic region, encompassing the three provinces of Salonica (Thessaloniki), Manastir (Bitola) and Kosovo. All the place names that will be used in what follows will be based on the ones used in Ottoman sources.

14   Harley (1980: 220–221): Pollard (1981: 264–270); Malenbaum (1953: 34–35); Bairoch (1989b: 69–94).

15   Between 1880 and 1910, French wheat production increased by 56 per cent, German by 43 per cent, Italian by 28 per cent and Austria-Hungarian by 130 per cent (Harley 1980: 228).

16   For a discussion of the impact of the post-1870 price depression on Ottoman agriculture see Akarlı (1976: 1993); Quataert (1973, 1993b, 1994); Pamuk (1984, 1987, 1994a) and Güran (1998).

17   UK *Foreign Office Annual Series* (*FOAS* hereafter), 1883, N. 6: 93; Public Record Office (PRO hereafter), *FO*195/1256, 17.10.1879, Blunt to Layard.

18   For complaints of Macedonian farmers concerning the practical difficulties of importing and maintaining new farm tools and machines see *Asır,* 19.B.1313 (4.1.1896), N. 35:2; *Asır,* 6. S.1314 (10.1.1897), N. 141:4; *Asır,* 11.S.1317 (14.12.1899), N. 440:1; *DTOG,* 26.B.1302 (11.5.1885), N. 10:4. Similar concerns are also supported by contemporary European observers. See *FOAS,* 1886, N. 24:5, and Baker (1877: 415–6). For the technological stagnation of the 1880s and 1890s, see also *FOAS,* 1887, N. 75:8; *FOAS,* 1897, N. 1837:3; *FOAS,* 1898, N. 2111:20.

19 Themopoulou (1994: 339–44). Themopoulou's figures are given in Istanbul bushels (*kile*). To convert these figures bushel/kg parities cited in the 1907 statistics were used for each and every cereal crop.

20 Between 1880–96 exports from the port of Salonica averaged 69,000 tons per annum (MACSTATS).

21 For 1874 see *UK Parliamentary Papers Accounts and Papers* (*PPAP* hereafter), 1874, V. 33: 952; *PPAP*, 1875, N. 17: 447–9; Public Record Office (PRO hereafter), *FO* 195/1007, 12.6. 1874, Blunt to Eliot. For 1879 see PRO, *FO* 195/1256, 17.10.1879, Blunt to Layard; PRO, *FO* 78/3018, 17.10.1879, Blunt to Layard; Basbakanlik Arsivi (BBA hereafter), SD-Selanik, 2008/41, 6Ra. 1296 (27.2.1879). Finally for 1885 see *FOAS*, 1887, N. 75:2; *FOAS*, 1888, N. 254:2.

22 For an excellent discussion of Macedonian railway tariffs and kilometric guarantees, see Gounaris (1993: 74–86).

23 *DTOG*, 16.R.1313 (5.10.1895), N. 562: 472.

24 *FOAS*, 1888, N. 394: 2–3; *DTOG*, 15.N. 1305 (26.5.1888), N. 178: 255–7; *DTOG* 16.R.1313 (5.10.1895), N. 562:472.

25 *PPAP*, 1873. V. 29:735; *Asır*, 20.Za.1318 (11.3.1901), N. 566:2; *Asır*, 28.S. 1319 (10.12.1901, N. 640: 2–3; *Asır*, 20.c.1320 (15.9.1902), N. 717: 2.

26 Palairet (1997: 27). Also see Adanır (1984/5); Veinstein (1992); Gounaris (1993, 1994); Yeralimpos (1996); Lory and Popovic (1996); Anastassiadou (1997).

27 As in many other parts of the Balkans and the Middle East, cereals constituted the main food staple for the Macedonian populace (Baker 1877: 86; Stoianovich, 1994: 209). Surely, this "basic needs" dimension to cereal production assured vibrant business in domestic markets.

28 See Issawi (1980a: 74–5); Quataert (1994: 825–7); Pamuk (1994a: 17–22) for details of the Ottoman trade regime and tariffs.

29 See Quataert (1973, 1993c) and Güran (1998) for the provisionist concerns of the Ottoman government.

30 For the details for crisis-management policies implemented by the Ottoman government see sources cited in note 21.

31 *PPAP*, 1873, V. 29: 748; *FOAS*, 1886, N. 24: 6; *FOAS*, 1888, N. 254: 2; *DTOG*, 11.L.1304 (3.7.1887), N. 131: 184; *1307 Selanik Vilayet Salnamesi* (*SVS* hereafter) (1890: 52); *FOAS*, 1893, N. 1310:7–8; *1312 SVS* (1895: 300, 309).

32 Poppy cultivation was introduced into Macedonia in the late 1860s (*PPAP*, 1883, V.72: 101). Therefore it is reasonable to assume that the cultivation of the crop remained to a large extent limited in the early 1870s and took off after about 1875 (1305 *Kosova Vilayet Salnamesi* (*KVS* hereafter), 1888: 173). The low level of opium exports in this period confirms this contention (Table 5.A4).

33 Macedonian opium had a phenomenally high morphine content which often reached up to 13 per cent (*PPAP*, 1883, V.72: 101; *FOAS*, 1887, N. 75: 3).

34 *FOAS*, 1886, N. 24: 6; *FOAS*, 1887, N. 75: 3; *FOAS*, 1888, N. 348: 2; PRO, *FO* 78/4119, extract from the Salonica Gazette, 1.5.1888.

35 For details concerning the establishment of the Régie, see Parvus (1970), Quataert (1973) and Blaisdell (1929).

36 *FOAS*, 1888, N. 254: 2; *DTOG*, 15.N. 1305 (26.5.1888), N. 178: 255. For the Régie regulations governing the production, taxation and sale of tobacco throughout the Empire see *DTOG*, 3.C.1304 (26.2.1887), N. 113: 59–60; *DTOG*, 12.N. 1304 (4.6.1887), N. 127: 156–7; Abdurrahman 1911: 314–81); Quataert (1973: 265–7; 1983: 13–4).

37 *FOAS*, 1893, N. 1310: 10; *FOAS*, 1896, N. 1663: 3–4; *FOAS*, 1898, N. 2111: 7.

38 *DTOG*, 4.Za.1307 (21.6.1890), N. 286: 295; *Asır*, 21.B.1314 (26.12.1896), N. 137:1.

39 *DTOG*, 15.N. 1305 (26.5.1888), N. 178: 203; *DTOG*, 4.Za.1307 (21.6.1890), N. 286: 295; *FOAS*, 1893, N. 1310: 10–11; *FOAS*, 1896, N. 1663: 3–4.

40   For the impact of the Russo–Japanese War see *Asır*, 20.Z.1321 (7.3.1904), N. 959: 1; *Asır*, 2.S.1322 (18.4.1904), N. 974: 1. For crop failures of 1907–10 see *FOAS*, 1908, N. 4040: 5; *FOAS*, 1909, N. 4359: 5, 7–8; *FOAS*, 1910, N. 4579: 9; *FOAS*, 1911, N. 4797:8.

41   PRO, *FO* 195/1768, 14.4.1892, Blunt to Clareford. This tariff reduction was the outcome of Britain's diplomatic pressures to circumscribe the rapid advance of Austrian commercial interests in the Balkans.

42   *Asır*, 5.Za.1313 (18.4.1896), N. 66: 1–2. For similar complaints also see *Asır*, 13.N. 1313 (26.2.1896), N. 52: 1; *Asır*, 11.L.1313 (27.3.1896), N. 59: 1–2; *Asır*, 9.Za.1313 (22.4.1896), N. 67: 1.

43   *Asır*, 5.Za.1313 (18.4.1896), N. 66: 1–2.

44   Annual rainfall in Macedonia varied between 45–55 cm per annum (Adanir 1984/85: 45). An average of 50 cm of annual rainfall is even below some Middle Eastern and Mediterranean regions which are generally known to be exceptionally arid. For instance Alger (76 cm), Istanbul (73 cm), Antalya (103 cm) received more rain than Macedonia. The Macedonian average rainfall can be compared with Beirut (50 cm), Tripoli (38 cm) and Shiraz (39 cm) (Richards and Waterbury 1990: 54–5).

45   *FOAS*, 1898, N. 2111: 8; *Asır*, 12.B.1318 (5.11.1900), N. 531: 1; *FOAS*, 1901, N. 2730: 23; *Asır*, 15.Ca.1322 (29.7.1904), N. 899: 1.

46   Macedonia had an active textile-weaving industry, which manufactured a range of cotton and silken cloth varieties. Possibly the sector grew in response to rapid urbanization and the subsequent expansion of domestic demand (Quataert 1993a). The growing disparity between silk-cocoon production and exports confirms the increasing importance of the domestic markets (Table 5.A4).

47   *Asır*, 22.L.1322 (29.12.1904), N. 943: 2: *Selanik*, 3.Za.1322 (9.1.1905), N. 1888: 2. See Gounaris (1993); Quataert (1993a; 1993d; 1995) and Palairet (1997) for the development of cotton textile concerns throughout the Macedonian provinces.

48   *Asır*, 16.Za.1913 (24.2.1902), N. 661: 2:*Asır*, 28.B.1320 (30.10.1902), N. 728: 1; *Asır*, 3.Za.1320 (2.2.1903), N. 754: 1; *Asır*, 12.Ra.1321 (8.6.1903), N. 789: *FOAS*, 1904, N. 3250: 4; BBA, *TFR.1.A.*, 2/177, 23.10.1320 (5.1.1905).

49   Most efforts were concentrated around seed and plant distributions. For cotton-seed distributions, see PRO, *FO* 78/4119, 1.5.1888, Blunt to White; BBA, *ŞD-Selanik*, 2003/27, 23.S.1287 (24.5.1870); BBA, *ŞD-Ticaret*, 1213/17, 26.S.1316 (11.12.1898); *Asır*, 23.N. 1322 (1.12.1904), N. 935: 2; *Asır*, 21.Z.1323 (15.2.1906), N. 1051: 1; *Asir*, 12.M.1324 (8.3.1906), N. 1057: 3. For opium-seed provisions, see *Asir*, 12.B.1318 (5.11.1900), N. 531: 1. For the distribution of mulberry trees by the Ottoman government authorities and the PDA, see *FOAS*, 1893, N. 1310: 8; *Asır*, 5.L.1317 (5.2.1900), N. 454: 1–2; *Asır*, 24.M.1319 (13.5.1901), N. 582: 2; *Ticaret ve Ziraat Nezareti Mecmuası* (*TZNM* hereafter), 20.IV.1328 (3.7.1912), V. 18: 263.

50   *Asır*, 29.Za.1319 (10.3.1902), N. 665: 2; *Asır*, 10.Z.1319 (20.3.1902), N. 668: 2. *Asır*, 30.L.1320 (29.1.1903), N. 753: 2.

51   Palairet (1997; 20–1); Karpat (1985: 210-211).

52   The wave of emigration from the region accelerated, especially after the turn of the century, due to a combination of adverse conjunctural trends and political turmoil in the Macedonian countryside. For Macedonian emigration to the USA, see Gounaris (1989; 1993).

53   *Asır*, 3.Za.1320 (1.2.1903), N. 754: 2–3; *Asır*, 9.Z.1320 (3.3.1903), N. 764; *Asır*, 12.Ra.1321 (8.6.1903), N. 789: 1.

54   See Kasaba *et al.* (1986); Keyder *et al.* (1994).

55   This is the average estimate given to me by a Turkish baker from a small fishing village on the western coast of Turkey, who has been baking bread in the village for over thirty years. He warns that the flour yield would depend on the weight and the hardness of wheat to be used, but still, he argues, it would be around 4/3.

56   Assumptions 1, 2, 3, 4 and 5 are based on *Revue Commerciale du Levant, Bulletin Mensuel de la chambre de commerce française de Constantinople* (*RCL* hereafter), 31.1.1909, No. 262: 133–5.

Assumption 2 is also based on the urbanization estimates of Palairet (1997) and Yeralimpos (1996). Assumption 6 is based on the following sources: *Asır*, 4.C.1314 (10.11.1896), N. 124: 1. *Asır*, 11.C.1314 (17.11.1896), N. 126: 1; *1307 SVS* (1890: 49).

57 *1299 SVS* (1882: 173); *1307 SVS* (1890: 69–73); *1305 Manastır Vilayet Salnamesi* (*MVS* hereafter) 1888: 438–41; *1308 MVS* (1891: 177); DIE (1997b: 160–3); *1323 Senesi Avrupa-i Osmani Ziraat Istatistiği* (*OZI* hereafter) (1907: j, 162–3).

58 *Asır*, 23 N. 1322 (1.12.1904), N. 935:2.

59 *FOAS*, N. 3250, (1904: 5); PRO, *FO* 78/3343, 1881, General Report on the Province or the *sancak* of Seres by vice-consul to Seres, Mr Langdon.

6 The choice of technology
Spanish, Italian, British and US cotton mills compared, 1830–60

Joan Ramon Rosés

Introduction

Studies on the cotton industry proliferate. Remarkably, the cotton industry has figured in recent debates over the amplitude and significance of the British Industrial Revolution, the loss of British competitive advantage, and the wealth and the poverty of nations in the nineteenth and the early twentieth centuries. As research moves forward, it seems obvious that the comparative history of the European cotton industry in the period before the "cotton famine" has been grossly neglected. There have been several splendid books and articles on some national cases but the comparative perspective has barely been touched. In particular, to date no study has systematically analyzed the cotton textile industry in the Mediterranean basin during the early industrialization period. This chapter fills that gap by adopting a comparative perspective. More specifically, this chapter concentrates its energies on providing a careful analysis of the technological choices of four cotton industries: the two largest producers in the Mediterranean basin and the two largest producers in the world, from 1830 to 1860.

Before the arrival of the "cotton famine" in the 1860s, the most important settlements of the modern cotton industry in the Mediterranean basin were in Catalonia (Spain) and in the Kingdom of Piedmont-Sardinia.[1] Simultaneously, the world leadership in cotton textiles was in the hands of Lancashire (Britain), while New England (United States) occupied the second position. In these regions, the cotton industry represented the first large-scale application of modern technology and the factory system. However, these four cotton industries differed strongly. In the beginning, the new cotton mills followed the British model but within a few years each country had developed its own practices and adapted the British technology to its own needs. Therefore, it seems that there is a strong case for placing primary stress on the cotton industry as the first example of how technological choice is influenced by local conditions.

Few economic historians believed in the absolute tyranny of fixed factor proportions and fixed attribute bundles; that is, in the argument that the choice of technology is technologically determined. Hence, the majority recognized that there existed a fairly wide range of alternative technology choices. However, economic historians vary in the reasons they stress. For Habakkuk (1962) the choice of different technologies reflects differences in factor endowments. In particular, he argued that land abundance and labour scarcity in the United States led to high relative wages and the substitution of capital for labour. Instead, for North (1981) institutions had crucial importance for technological change since their historical development will decide the outcome of any economic activity in a community. Institutions should be seen in terms of cultural norms, written rules and unwritten codes of conduct that provide the framework within which economic agents function. Finally, David (1985) posits more emphasis on the path-dependence of technological choices. Divergence on technological choices has occurred, in this view, but not simply because of differences in factor endowments or institutions. Rather, the argument is that successive developments depend on prior events. Consequently, it seems that by focusing explicitly on technological choice, one can open the door to a deeper understanding of how prior history, institutions and factor prices could affect technological innovation and long-run growth.

The recent literature on the history of the cotton industry contains three broad perspectives as well. One maintains the unimportance of alternative technological choices in the cotton industry. In particular, Clark (1987) diminished the importance of alternative technology, thereby asserting that countries with different factor prices showed no evidence of any difference in cotton-spinning techniques at the beginning of the twentieth century. According to his view, the effort of workers was the major determinant of the performance of cotton industries. A second view stresses that patterns of adoption of technology are basically consistent with a rational response to prevailing factor costs. For Von Tunzelmann (1978) the technological choices of British, Belgian, and American manufacturers were constrained in the first place by the price they had to pay for energy. For example, he pointed out that in the United States the abundance of (cheap) water power was the incentive offered to develop a new, more power-intensive technology (the ring throstle). For Saxonhouse and Wright (1984), the choice of technology was driven by geographical factors and the capacity to innovate. In particular, they argued that the diffusion of ring-spinning was constrained by the availability of high-quality cotton and subsequently by ingenuity in devising alternatives like cotton-mixing. Instead, Harley (1992) considered implicitly a larger set of factors in his comparison between the British and American cotton industries in the mid-nineteenth century. Thus, he included the relative prices of raw cotton, energy, skills and labour as determinants of the technology. A third interpretation posits a more fundamental role in institutional factors. Lazonick (1990) claimed the importance of entrepreneurial failures for the choice of technology. In particular, he censured the British entrepreneurs for their alleged failure to choose the correct techniques in spinning and weaving during the late nineteenth and early twentieth centuries. According to his arguments, the fundamental error was retaining the British industry's horizontal specialization into spinning and weaving factories. Similarly, Fisher emphasized the reluctance of Swiss textile entrepreneurs to adopt the new spinning machinery. He argued that these entrepreneurs were more risk avoiders than profit maximizers (Fisher 1991: 151). Finally, for Otsuka *et al.* (1988) differential technological performance between the Japanese and Indian cotton industries emanated from differences in market structure and government intervention. They pointed out that in Japan the relative absence of market-intervention policies helped to both ensure an efficient choice of imported technology and to have it adapted in appropriate directions.

While I recognize the importance of institutional and cultural differentials across countries, my basic premise is that labour-force skills and factor endowments are of crucial significance to the choice of technology in cotton textiles. In the period before the "cotton famine", alternative technological choices were relatively important. However, these technology alternatives cannot be interpreted without consideration of the heterogeneity of cotton cloth. In other words, the production of different kinds of cotton cloth employed a particular amount of physical and human capital, labour, energy and raw cotton. Moreover, some types of machinery were more adept than others in the production of some kinds of cotton goods. For instance, the throstle employed more energy and less skilled labour, and was better at spinning coarse yarn than the mule. In consequence, one can argue that the choice of product and machinery was intimately connected with the availability of skilled labour and relative factor prices in this early period of the factory-based cotton industry.

The remainder of this chapter is organized as follows. In the next section, the main characteristics (size, quality-mix and export performance) of these four cotton industries are discussed. The third section provides an analysis of technological developments in cotton textiles during the period. The fourth section discusses the process of diffusion of the cotton-textile technology in Lancashire, New England, Catalonia and Piedmont. This is followed by a section which develops a framework for understanding how technological choices and quality-mix were interrelated and how quality choices were decided by factor endowments, especially workforce skills. The last section concludes and summarizes.

Main characteristics: size, quality-mix and export performance

For the sake of comparison, it is useful to know how large the cotton industries of Catalonia, New England, Britain and Piedmont were. To answer this question, I rely on the amount of cloth produced more than on the number of spindles or raw-cotton import figures. The number of spindles is not a good indicator of the size of the cotton industry because the productivity of

Table 6.1 Production of cotton cloth: Catalonia, New England, Britain and Piedmont, 1830–1860 (in thousands of m², average per year)

	Catalonia	New England	Britain	Piedmont
1830–40	21 291	229 440	680 614	9 690
1840–50	51 430	414 972	1 140 804	17 701
1850–60	109 132	612 815	1 852 892	34 165
1830–60	60 500	420 345	1 233 122	20 519

Notes and Sources:
Numbers subject to rounding errors.
New England's data is drawn from Davis and Stettler (1966: Table 4, 221).
The procedure to compute the Catalan and British figures was the following. First, according Huberman's (1996) method, a disaggregated yarn output series was constructed for Catalonia and Britain. Then, under the assumption that yarn exports and yarn inventories had the same distribution as yarn production, I derived the amount of yarn consumed in the weaving industry where the figures on British yarn exports are drawn from Ellison (1968: Table 2). That is, total yarn production minus exports of yarn, inventories, and wastage (5 per cent) during weaving. To arrive at output in m², I multiply the weight of the cloth consumed by a fixed coefficient. The coefficients are different for each quality also different for Catalonia and Britain. The Catalan coefficients are derived from Comisión Especial Arancelaria (1867) and the British coefficients from the figures on cotton fabrics from *The Economist* (1845). Then I sum across qualities to compute total estimates.
Piedmont's figures on raw cotton imports were drawn from Quazza (1961: 221). After deleting re-exports with coefficients furnished by Castronovo (1965: 282–283), these figures have been transformed into raw cotton consumption. Then, with quality figures of Table 6.3 and Catalan weights, I convert raw cotton consumption into m² of cotton.

spindles varies strongly with yarn quality (count). Similarly, the level of raw-cotton consumption does not furnish information on the real amount of production since, for example, wastage and the weight of the product vary according to yarn quality.[2] For the reasons above, my choice was to compare cloth produced in square metres (m²). Table 6.1 shows the results.

This table immediately reveals that the British cotton industry was gigantic when compared with its rivals. In particular, on average, it was about three times as large as the second-largest cotton industry, New England. Moreover, in comparison with Britain or New England, both the Catalan and the Piedmont cotton industries were minuscule. Thus, by the 1850s, the British cotton industry was about seventeen times the size of the Catalan cotton industry and about fifty-four times the size of the Piedmont cotton industry. Finally, it should be noted that the cotton industry of New England did not progress in the same way as the cotton industry in Great Britain, Catalonia and Piedmont.

A common characteristic of these four regions was that they contained most of the cotton industry of their respective countries. By 1861, Catalonia produced about 75 per cent of Spanish cotton textiles.[3] However, some years earlier these indices of concentration were even higher when Catalonia

Table 6.2 Quality distribution of cloth production: Catalonia, Lombardy, New England and Britain, 1830–1860 (in average per cent per year)

Catalonia	<20	20–40	40–60	60–80	
1830–40	68.37	31.44	0.10	0.09	
1840–50	25.94	71.89	1.83	0.35	
1850–60	18.06	76.43	4.04	1.47	
1830–60	25.93	70.31	2.77	0.99	
Lombardy	*<20*	*20–40*	*40–60*	*60–80*	
1856	66.73	33.00	0.26	0.01	
New England	*<16*	*>18*			
1830–40	75.99	24.01			
1840–50	73.44	26.56			
1850–60	76.12	23.88			
1830–60	75.27	24.73			
Britain	*<20*	*20–40*	*40–60*	*60–80*	*>80*
1830–40	17.12	45.24	24.16	8.03	5.44
1840–50	14.82	48.66	27.87	4.44	4.21
1850–60	8.10	48.79	34.29	4.60	4.22
1830–60	11.76	48.12	30.55	5.17	4.40

Notes and Sources:
Numbers subject to rounding errors.
Spanish figures corresponded to Spanish counts and British, Lombardy's and New England's to English counts. Therefore, since the Spanish counts were slightly finer than the corresponding English counts, Spanish figures understated the quality of the Spanish production. When it has been possible, figures are computed as arithmetic averages to avoid cyclical variation in quality due to changes in the prices of raw cotton and short-term market adjustments.
New England data are drawn from Davis and Stettler (1966: Table A.2). Note that the New England figures are based on a sample of firms but in the entire population.
Lombardy's data are drawn from Zanelli (1967: Table 42).
For sources of the Catalan and British data see the previous Table 6.1.

enjoyed a *de facto* monopoly of the factory-based cotton industry in Spain. Thus, in the 1850s, new factory-based cotton industries emerged in the Province of Málaga (Andalusia) and the Basque country (Nadal 1974: 218–25). Due to the political fragmentation and the presence of important trade barriers, the Italian cotton industry was less concentrated than the Spanish. By the 1850s, Piedmont produced about 43 per cent of Italian cotton cloth but gradually lost its share of Italian production with the emergence of the cotton industry in other regions (Castronovo 1965: 284). Thus, other important settlements of cotton mills in Italy were in Lombardy, Liguria, Campania, Veneto and Tuscany (A'Hearn 1998: 736ff). In 1850, New England produced about 67 per cent of US cotton textiles (DeBow 1970: Table CXCVI, 180). It should be noted, however, that since the 1820s the development of the cotton industry in the southern and the mid-Atlantic regions had reduced New England's share in the US figures (Harley 1992). In 1856, about 68 per cent of British employment in cotton mills was in Lancashire. By sharp contrast with the other three regions, from 1822 to 1856, Lancashire increased its share in national output.[4]

It should be emphasized that the disparities in the quality of cloth among these countries were as notable as their differences in size. Table 6.2 shows that New England and Lombardy produced heavier fabrics than Catalonia and Britain.[5] For the period as a whole, the quality of the New England cloth did not change considerably because about 75 per cent of production was always of the coarsest quality.[6] Similarly, in Lombardy about two-thirds of the cotton cloth was of that quality. In a sharp contrast, Britain and Catalonia tended to concentrate their production in the medium range (counts from 20 to 60). By the 1850s more than three-quarters of their production was in these counts, thus abandoning the production of the heaviest qualities. In Catalonia sharp decreases in the production of coarse cloth took place in the 1840s, whereas in Britain this happened in the 1850s. Finally, it should also be noted that British industry reduced its share of the finest qualities (over 60 count) although Britain was the country with the largest share of that type of cloth.[7]

Differences in export performance were also important. The weakness of the international position of Spanish, Italian and American cotton textiles during this early period should be emphasized. The export of cotton textiles from Spain or Italy was practically negligible and British exports were about thirty times as great as American exports, though America was the world's second-largest cotton textile producer (Harley 1992: 576–9). On balance these three countries imported cotton textiles, mainly from Britain. By direct contrast, through the antebellum years, the British exported about two-thirds of what they produced. Nevertheless, as Sandberg previously noted, from 1845 Britain gradually lost its share of the world market, being replaced by the new European and US cotton industries (Ellison 1968: 97ff; Sandberg 1968).

Table 6.3 shows the evolution of cotton textiles exports from Britain to these three countries and the Mediterranean basin.

Overall cotton exports from Britain grew faster than cotton exports to the United States, Italy and Spain. From the 1820s to the 1850s, total figures for British cotton exports more than doubled whereas exports to the United States only increased by about 78 per cent, exports to Spain practically halved, and exports to Italy grew by a mere 32 per cent. The Spanish and Italian experience is also striking when compared with the rest of the Mediterranean basin, where British exports experienced a sudden increase. More specifically, in the early 1820s over 80 per cent of British cotton textiles exported to the Mediterranean basin were concentrated in the countries of the Iberian and Italian peninsulas, whereas by the end of 1850s this figure was only about 50 per cent.

Interestingly, Sandberg has proposed a quality-related explanation to the persistence of British exports in the countries with emerging cotton factory-

Table 6.3 British cotton textile exports, 1820–1858 (in thousands of £, average per year)

	World	Mediterranean Basin	United States	Spain	Italy
1820–29	16 948	3 544	1 825	808	1 422
1830–39	20 914	4 120	1 874	537	1 710
1840–49	24 361	5 207	1 359	584	1 537
1850–58	34 197	5 154	3 263	421	1 881

Notes and Sources:
Numbers subject to rounding errors.
Figures are in current values. The data are drawn from Mann (1968).
Spanish figures include smuggling which has been computed according to the procedures described in notes to Figure 6.1.

based industries. According to him, Britain continued to export high-quality goods to the American and western European markets while very cheap goods went to the rapidly expanding low-income markets (Sandberg 1968). Thus, the British cotton industry lost almost all of the markets for coarse and medium-quality cloth in Europe. Note that the evidence presented in Table 6.2 gives some support to Sandberg's arguments since the American, Spanish and Italian cotton industries produced coarser quality than Britain's. The evident questions are why European producers and the United States specialized in relatively low-quality and not in high-quality cloth? And why these important differences in quality-mix among Catalonia, Piedmont and New England?

Technology in cotton textiles

In this section I will show that in the pre-cotton famine period several alternative technologies were available to entrepreneurs in cotton textiles.[8] Some technologies required more power than others, some were suitable for domestic production and others simply not, some relied on a skilled workforce whereas others were suitable for unskilled labour. Equally important is the relation between machinery and the quality of goods because only a narrow range of machinery could be used to make each quality. Consequently, the range of "appropriate" technological options was more limited than the large list of machines might suggest.

Both spinning and weaving machines of the mid-nineteenth century were improvements on pioneering machines that dated from the Industrial Revolution. Power costs, and innovations in power sources, strategically affected these improvements (Von Tunzelmann 1978: 175–240). However, the phases of development in fine and coarse spinning showed important differences, both in comparison with weaving and between themselves.

The mid-nineteenth-century cotton-spinning machinery is clearly recognizable as the descendant of the two spinning machines invented in the 1760s. The jenny was invented by James Hargreaves and the water frame was developed by Richard Arkwright. Hargreaves' jenny spun intermittently whereas Arkwright's water frame was based on continuous methods of spinning. While the jennies were made of wood and their small size made them appropriate for use in domestic units, the water frames were used in large factories. However, these two primitive spinning machines proved to be complementary rather than competitive because of their wide differences. The water frame was at least five times as productive as the jenny but could not produce fine counts; therefore, it was used basically for the production of warps. On the other hand, yarn from the jenny was most suitable for wefts but this machine suffered a sharp decline in cost-efficiency when used for anything above quite coarse counts of yarn. In consequence, factory production of warp yarn on water frames also increased cottage production of weft yarn on jennies.

In the following decades, new intermittent spinning machines meant the demise of Hargreaves' jenny but not the ruin of continuous methods, which could produce coarse yarn faster and more cheaply than these new machines. Samuel Crompton invented the mule in 1779. This new spinning machine broke through the technical barrier to permit the economical spinning of fine yarns by machine methods. The first mules were made of wood and their small size made them suitable for use in domestic production. However, by 1790 new large mules made of metal and powered by waterwheels were being used in large factories which specialized in spinning fine yarns (Von Tunzelmann 1978: 224). By the 1830s, the mule was improved by Richard Roberts, who invented the self-acting mule. Until this new device appeared, a man's strength had been required for pushing the mule spindles back and forth on their carriage. When the self-actor removed this requirement, one spinner could now work up to 1,200 spindles, compared with about 300 on a traditional mule. Several constraints limited the universal use of the self-acting mule: it required more power, more repairs, more technicians, and was less flexible (since it had greater difficulty in changing quickly from one grade of yarn to another) than the hand-mule. In effect, until the 1850s, the self-acting mule could only spin yarn below the count number 50. Extremely fine yarn was spun on the older hand-mules into the 1880s.

The continuous method of spinning was also improved in the first half of the nineteenth century. In 1828, John Thorp and Charles Danforth developed independently the throstle, a variant of the water frame, in the United States.[9] This spinning machine automatically and continuously performed the drawing, twisting, and winding of yarn. The only intervention in the spinning process required from workers in throstles was to mend yarns when they broke and to replace bobbins. It should be noted that these tasks could be easily learned in a few days of training. In sharp contrast, the self-acting mule required specific skills and continuous attention from operatives.[10] By the 1850s, the Americans made other important improvements in continuous spinning. For example, the development of cap-spinning and ring-spinning allowed continuous spinning to achieve higher speeds than before. These primitive ring throstles required very great motive power and it was not possible to spin yarn of fine grades of sufficient quality on them. Because of these disabilities, the self-acting mule was not eclipsed by early ring throstles. For example, in the 1860s, only the American industry had almost as many ring throstles as mule spindles (Saxonhouse and Wright 1984: 274).

At the beginning, the diffusion of the new machinery in cotton spinning – which lowered the price of yarns – expanded handloom weaving. The first serious efforts to mechanize the operation of the handloom date back to the attempts of Edmund Cartwright in 1787. In 1803, Horrocks patented the first truly workable powerloom. But it was not until after 1815 that power-driven machinery (i.e. powerlooms) began to play more than an insignificant role in cotton weaving. As with the mule, the primitive powerloom technology was modified over many years, and it was not until the 1850s that weaving by machine triumphed over traditional handloom weaving in England. It took considerably longer in other countries and textile industries.[11]

Technological choices

During the first half of the nineteenth century, technological leadership remained in the hands of the British cotton industry. As shown above, a great part of the progress in cotton technology during the period was due to British engineers.[12] Though some European regions, and later New England, made many technological advances, Lancashire supplied all or most of the textile machinery to most factories in Europe. The first European cotton mills were completely British in design and equipment. Many skilled British workers, including women, performed important technical functions in the new factories. For example, they provided technical advice and guidance as well as supervision and management, and trained local workers in the new technology. According to Bruland (1989), British machinery suppliers provided foreign textile firms with a complete array of information, equipment, and labour. In other words, they provided the technological capability to new cotton factories. However, once they got this technological capability, non-British factories ran by themselves.

In Britain, at the very beginning of the nineteenth century, the fine-spinning branch was the most technologically advanced because, for example, it was the first to apply steam-power to the new textile machinery. These substantial improvements cheapened finer yarns, which had noticeable effects on both exports and cloth fashion. In particular, British firms produced cotton more cheaply than Indian ones (Von Tunzelmann 1978: 224). By the 1830s, however, technological leadership in cotton spinning moved to the production of coarse yarn (Von Tunzelmann 1978: 184ff). Robert's self-acting mule, along with cheaper steam-power and refinements in powerlooms in the following decade, greatly reduced prices of ordinary cloth. Therefore, by the mid-nineteenth century, the British cotton industry remained organized in two different branches: fine- and coarse-spinning mills (Gatrell 1977). Also, many coarse mills integrated vertical powerloom weaving (Gatrell 1977; Lyons 1985).

The first modern spinning machinery (i.e. Arkwright's water frames) appeared in the United States during the last years of the eighteenth century.[13] The embargo and the war with Great Britain had favoured the settlement of the cotton industry in the United States. But the first great expansion of the industry took place from the end of the War of 1812, when the industry was protected by high tariffs (Zevin 1971; Stettler 1977). In this early period, American cotton-textile mills, which were known as the Rhode Island type, were comparable to British coarse-spinning factories.

In a few years, American practices diverged from Britain's. American cotton mills preferred water-driven to power-driven machinery and worked their machines more quickly than the British (Montgomery 1840; Von Tunzelmann 1978: 266ff). As noted above, American engineers not only ran the same British machinery at faster speeds but also improved continuous methods of spinning, which required more installed power. Perhaps more interestingly, by the 1820s the Americans had introduced their own new type of cotton mill: the Waltham-type. They integrated power-spinning on throstles and powerlooms and a new form of organization of the workforce. According to Jeremy, these new mills succeeded in lowering the cost of production for the coarsest products (Jeremy 1981). However, until the American Civil War, both types of mills survived (Cohen 1990). Rhode Island-type mills and hand-weavers specialized in the segments of the market where fashion and flexibility were more important while the Waltham-type dominated the market for standardized products (Harley 1992).

The Catalan cotton industry was older than New England's. The first enterprises devoted to printing cotton cloth were established in Barcelona in the late 1720s.[14] These calicoes were sold in the protected markets of the Metropoly and the Spanish colonies in America.[15] Because for most of the eighteenth century all cotton yarn was imported (mainly from Malta), as well as a large part of the grey cloth consumed, cotton spinning and weaving were not important. It took about sixty years for Catalonia to develop cotton-spinning. In 1802, the new spinning industry was heavily protected since the import of foreign yarn and cloth was forbidden. Through the thirty years that followed the ban, domestic production and out-working were common practice in cotton-spinning. Thus, cotton-spinning tended to remain dispersed in the villages and small towns of the lower Pyrenees, where they could rely upon a good supply of cheap female and child labour, rather than becoming concentrated in the calico centre of Barcelona.[16] Initially, due to its unskilled workforce and the use of jennies and water frames, Catalan spinning concentrated on the low grades of yarn (below 20 count). During the same period, hand-weavers proliferated in the major Catalan manufacturing towns (Sánchez 1989). Catalan cotton cloth was also coarse due to the ban on cotton yarn imports. Nevertheless, skilled hand-weavers produced a wide range of qualities by using other textile fibres such as wool, linen and silk.[17] This development of the domestic industry was accompanied by the scattered adoption of the steam engine.

In 1832, the Bonaplata mill introduced the new forms of organization, the steam engine, and the most recent British machinery (e.g. the powerloom Nadal 1974: 198). In a few years, the new machinery was universally employed in cotton-spinning and dominated cotton-weaving. The Catalan industry was characterized during this period by the rapid adoption of mechanical innovations. For example, Catalan cotton mills made the transition from hand to self-acting mules in only a decade, so that by the 1850s more than 75 per cent of spindles were moved by self-actors (Ronquillo 1851–7; Maluquer de Motes 1976). The diffusion of the new machinery paralleled the increase in the quality of local production since the average count increased to 30 count from about 15 count (Figuerola 1968; Madoz 1846). Moreover, the vertically integrated cotton mills expanded rapidly and captured the market for coarse–medium cloth. However, well before the 1860s, some horizontal spinning mills and domestic hand-weaving survived by producing for more fashion-oriented segments of the market (Rosés 1998b: Ch. 8).

In the first phases of the adoption of the new machinery, during the 1830s and the early 1840s, British and French technicians and workers played a leading role but, by the 1840s, the foreign workers had been completely substituted in their tasks by local technicians. Therefore, after the initial period, the Catalans developed the capacity to maintain their own machinery, adopted the new technologies and, obviously, ran them without any foreign help. Through the post-adoption phase, Catalan firms incorporated a stream of incremental developments and modifications to improve and adapt foreign technology to local requirements (Rosés 1998a). For instance, like the Americans, they developed their own type of centralized, vertically integrated, water-driven cotton-spinning and weaving factory: the *colonia* (Carreras 1983; Nadal 1991).

The cotton industry in the Piedmont was less developed than in the other three regions that are considered in this study.[18] During the eighteenth century, several regulations and laws protecting the wool and silk industries prevented the expansion of cotton textiles. Up to the second decade of the nineteenth century, cotton textile firms had not adopted some modern spinning machinery (i.e. hand-mules). In this early period, the cotton industry was predominantly domestic and rural, employing an unskilled workforce. Moreover, capital for this early development came from foreign entrepreneurs, mainly Swiss and French. These foreign entrepreneurs also introduced the technology and production methods of their countries of origin.

Therefore, most of the Piedmont cotton mills bought almost all their machinery from Alsatian and Swiss engineering firms. It should be noted, however, that the machines did not differ from original British designs (Fisher 1991: 145ff). By the 1830s, economic policy increasingly benefitted cotton textiles since the government established high tariffs on cotton imports. As happened in Catalonia before 1832, these protective measures increased production but failed to stimulate the adoption of power-driven machinery.[19]

Certainly, the turning point in the history of the Piedmont cotton industry was in 1842. The government of Piedmont drastically reduced tariffs on cotton goods. Contrary to the most pessimistic observations, these free-trade measures did not ruin the industry but contributed to its modernization since they eased the substitution of factories for small units of production (Castronovo 1965: 24–5). In addition, by the same year, modern waterwheels and throstles were introduced in Piedmont. Only a few years later, by the 1850s, several spinning factories adopted self-acting mules. In a sharp contrast, cotton weaving did not show signs of modernization. This branch of cotton textiles did not experience any kind of mechanical breakout until the 1870s, when the first powerlooms were used by the new vertically integrated cotton-spinning and weaving factories. Therefore, up to the 1870s, cotton-spinning took place in factories whereas the domestic system and putting-out predominated in cotton-weaving (Castronovo 1965: 164).

Labour management in the very early factory period was similar in Catalonia, Piedmont, Lancashire and New England because all cotton factories combined two forms of factory management: subcontracting and foremanship.[20] More specifically, workers in the preparatory section and spinners on throstles were supervised by foremen, whereas spinners on mules were organized into autonomous, subcontracted work teams. In particular, these spinners had functional autonomy because the craft-oriented machinery ran intermittently. Thus, they decided the pace of their work, organized their own work teams, had the authority to hire and fire assistants, and were paid by piece.

However, by the 1850s, US practices moved towards a new system of production with a workforce mainly formed of women and children controlled by foremen (Cohen 1990). The adoption of powerlooms and self-acting mules in the United States went hand in hand with the transition from subcontracting to foremanship (Cohen 1990: especially Ch. 6). In Piedmont, where the division of labour had been less important (Castronovo 1965: 222ff), the adoption of throstles and self-acting mules signified the elimination of piece-rate payments among spinners. According to Castronovo, operatives in Lombardy's cotton factories were subject to rigid norms and only foreign technicians and foremen had any autonomy (Castronovo 1965: 224–6). By sharp contrast with the United States and Piedmont, the main consequence of the diffusion of the self-acting mule in Catalonia and Britain was the reduction of the number of helpers, but not the dislocation of craft control from the shop floor. Similarly, it seems that Catalan and Lancashire weavers managed to retain their autonomous position in production even if the introduction of the powerloom could have increased foremanship practices in some weaving factories.[21]

The difference in the technological development of the four cotton industries is indeed quite startling. We have seen that there are marked differences in the adoption of the factory system, labour management, the new machinery, and even in the type of machinery preferred. At first glance, the American, Spanish and Italian cotton industries employed during several decades machinery and techniques inferior to Britain's. However, by the 1850s, this technology gap had been practically cut by these followers. Then, the typical American, Spanish, or Italian cotton mill possessed the same machinery as the most modern British cotton mill. Energy costs were partly responsible for this delay in the adoption of new machinery, which was more power-intensive. Thus the invention of the high-pressure steam engine, which decreased coal costs, might ease the adoption of self-acting mules and powerlooms in Spain.[22] However, at this point, many readers can agree that it seems difficult to explain the choice of technology only in terms of technological gaps and energy costs.

Explaining technological choices

The discussion thus far suggests that the choice of technology and quality were closely connected in cotton textiles before the "cotton famine". For instance, American producers preferred throstles to hand-mules because they produced coarse fabrics. Meanwhile, fine-spinning mills in Britain never employed throstles and preferred hand-mules. Therefore, it can be argued that one can interpret technological choices by explaining the final determinants of quality-mix. It should be noted that several alternative explanations for quality choices have been advanced in the literature on cotton textiles.

Sandberg pointed out that it is possible that quality-mix was a consequence of the life-cycle of the cotton industry. Young cotton industries produce low-quality goods because they did not require skilled or experienced labour and there was a large domestic market for them (Sandberg 1968: 15). Instead, mature cotton industries were able to specialize in high-quality cloth as a consequence of their skilled labour. However, the same history of the New England cotton industry gives little support to this argument because the industry matured but was still producing coarse goods.

It is often maintained that the characteristics and sizes of markets shaped the product choice of the cotton industry. For example, Sandberg has argued that only a worldwide exporter such as Britain was likely to have a large market for high-quality goods (Sandberg 1968: 15). Therefore, according to this line of reasoning, all small countries should only develop the production of heavy cloth. The obvious counter-example is the small Swiss cotton industry that produced high-quality cotton goods and could success-fully compete with Britain in some European markets for expensive cloth (Dudzik 1987). On the other hand, many authors have argued that the cotton mills in the USA were biased towards standard and cheap products because of the size and income of their home demand.[23] Following the same logic, one would expect Catalan cotton mills to produce cheap cotton goods since the Spanish home market for textiles was poorer and smaller than other European and American markets.[24] However, the Catalan cotton industry produced more medium-range than cheap goods. Therefore, it seems that the size of the home market does not by itself furnish a convinc-ing explanation for the quality-mix of the cotton industries. It would be more appropriate, however, to relate the characteristics of home production to the preferences of the home consumers. According to this line of reasoning, consumers in the USA would be more prepared to buy standard products than European consumers. However, this argument cannot be verified quantitatively.

It is sometimes argued that barriers to free trade modify the quality of the local production and foreign imports.[25] During the nineteenth century, two types of tariffs were employed: *ad valorem* and fixed duties. The *ad valorem* duties have several relevant properties. First, *ad valorem* duties were higher on cheap than on expensive goods and, therefore, the level of protection was higher for the local production of heavy (low-quality) goods (Sandberg 1968: 15). Second, it is perfectly clear that, *ceteris paribus*, countries with higher *ad valorem* duties would exclude from their home markets finer goods than countries with lower barriers. Third, increases in *ad valorem* duties aug-mented the range of protected goods towards fine (expensive) qualities. Finally, the quality range of foreign production excluded from the home market rests on the price of local production and the amount of the duty. For the same reason, when local costs fell and the duty actually remained con-stant, both the level of protection and the range of goods protected rose. In fixed duties, instead, when local costs decreased and the duty was not modi-fied, the level of protection grew but not necessarily the range of goods protected by the tariff.

Several studies have discussed the influence of tariffs on the development of the cotton industry in the USA.[26] Through the antebellum period, the US tariffs were in *ad valorem* terms. Duties on cotton textiles imports were estab-lished in 1789 and changed no less than twenty times up to the Civil War. The first tariff on cotton goods was relatively lower (5 per cent *ad valorem*) and comparable to tariffs on other manufactured products. In the period 1790–1811, the *ad valorem* duty grew in successive reforms up to 15 per cent. The first great reform happened in 1812 when duties were practically dou-bled (27.5 per cent) to finance the war. Moreover, in 1816, a law was passed by Congress that established the minimum valuation for all pieces of cloth imported into the United States. Note that the system of minimum values reinforced the fact that duties rested more on coarse than fine cloth. In 1832 the system of minimum values was dropped and rates were generally lowered although the *ad valorem* rate was still higher (25 per cent). From 1842 to 1846 there was another protective bubble and *ad valorem* rates were increased to 30 per cent. Finally in 1846 Congress lowered the tariff to 25 per cent and eliminated the minimum valuation.[27] The US tariff had disproportionate effects on the various cotton goods because it gave more protection to heavy than to light cotton cloth. However, Harley has recently shown that the level of protection of the industry in the USA, even after the reform of 1846, was enough to protect the production of coarse and medium-range cotton cloth (Harley 1992: Table 2, 562). Therefore, the level of protection was so high that it probably had negligible effects on the New England cotton mills' choice between coarse and medium products.

The Spanish cotton industry was protected from 1802 by the ban on cotton yarn and cloth imports (Nadal 1974). In theory, obviously, the level of protection in Spain was higher than in the United States. By the 1840s the scope of the ban was limited to yarn below 60 count and cloth produced with that type of yarn.[28] This modification of the structure of the tariff might not have directly affected Spanish production since the domestic industry produced very little yarn above 60 count. Therefore, the level of protection was so high that it probably had negligible effects on the Spanish cotton mills' choice between coarse and medium products. However, one must be aware that the ban on foreign imports was difficult to enforce during these years. As a consequence, smuggled British fabrics reached a large portion of the Spanish market (Prados 1984).

The obvious question is whether changes in the enforcement of the ban can explain changes in the choice of quality of the Catalan mills. Specifically, if the movement towards the medium-range fabrics in the 1840s was caused by an increase in the "real" level of protection (i.e. in the risk of smuggling due to an increase in the repression of the illegal trade). Note that the quantity of foreign goods illegally imported was a function of the margin received by smugglers, the premium risk obtained by consumers, and the risk involved in this illegal activity. For example, when the risk increases and the margin remains constant, smuggling decreases (i.e., the "real" level of protection and, therefore, the market for home industry increases). Moreover, if the risk of smuggling was little or unvaried over time, one could expect that, over the long run, the quantity of smuggled goods paralleled the margin received by smugglers and was independent of the risk incurred in illegal trade. Here, the hypothetical margin of smugglers is easy to compute since the premium risk received by consumers in Spain was negligible. The reason for this was that Spanish law punished only the smuggler and not the buyer, and the seizure of smuggled goods could only take place within the frontier zone. Thus, the margin of smugglers was equal to the domestic price of cotton goods minus transport costs and the foreign price of those goods. Figure 6.1 shows the relationship between the amount of smuggling and the margin of smugglers.

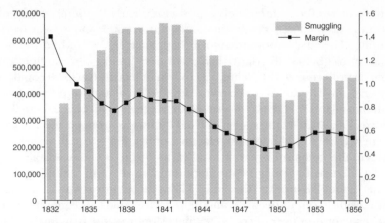

Figure 6.1 Smuggling of British goods in Spain (in £) and margin of smugglers (five-year averages).

Notes and sources:
The value of smuggling has been computed according to the formula proposed by Prados (1984). That is, British smuggling of cotton goods in Spain = 0.2 × exports to Portugal + 0.8 × exports to Gibraltar. The data on the value of exports to Gibraltar and Portugal is furnished by Mann (1968), table 25. The margin of smugglers is defined as the difference between the Spanish and British prices of printed cloth minus transport costs divided by British prices. For Spanish and British prices see Rosés (1998b), chapter 9.

If Figure 6.1 shows the true trend in smuggling and the smugglers' margin, one can reasonably infer that the quantity of smuggled cotton goods relies on the changes in the price gap between home and foreign goods. That is, the ban worked like an *ad valorem* tariff fixed at a (high) rate. In particular, the rapid decrease in the early 1840s of the quantity smuggled was due to the decrease in the price gap (margin), not to an increase in the repression of the illegal commerce. However, Figure 6.1 must be read and interpreted with caution since the data is highly imperfect. First, short-run variations cannot be captured by the formula that was used to compute the smuggling of British cotton goods because the formula was based on fixed coefficients. Second, the margin has been estimated as the difference between the prices of printed cloth in Spain and Britain. But it is possible that the difference between other types of Spanish and British cotton cloth did not evolve in unison with printed cloth. Third, Figure 6.1 cannot explain why smuggling increased faster during the 1830s. In any case, it seems implausible to link the movement of the Catalan cotton industry towards medium-range goods with a hypothetical increase in the repression of illegal trade. The level of protection grew due to the increase in the efficiency of the local production and, therefore, the local improvements were the main reason for the shift of production towards medium-range cotton fabrics.

In Piedmont, duties on cotton textile imports were first established in 1815 and were reformed several times up to 1860.[29] These tariffs were based on fixed duties for each kind of yarn or cloth. Early Piedmont tariff policy gave more protection to coarse than finer cotton goods and to weaving than spinning. The first important reform happened in 1830 when duties on coarse yarns (below 26 count) increased to 2 lire/kg, on medium yarns (from 26 to 49 count) to 1.50 lire/kg, and on fine yarns (up to 50 count) to 1 lire/kg. Similarly, duties on cotton cloth also grew and were fixed from a minimum of about 4 lire/kg on grey cloth to a maximum of 5–5.5 lire/kg on printed cloth. In 1842 the system of fixed duties was dropped and rates were generally lowered although the effective protection was still higher.[30] For instance, the common price of local yarns of the 8 count was about 2.5 lire/kg whereas the price of the imported British yarn, including duties, reached about 2.8 lire/kg (that is: 1.94 lire plus 0.9 lire of duty).[31] Finally in 1851 Cavour lowered the tariffs and signed a free-trade agreement with Belgium, a major producer of cotton textiles. Moreover, the structure of duties was modified, imposing higher duties on the fine qualities. After these reforms, duties on yarn were fixed from a minimum of 0.2 lire/kg in coarse yarn to a maximum of 0.6 lire/kg in fine yarn while duties on cloth were fixed from a minimum of 0.75 lire/kg on grey cloth to a maximum of 1.5 lire/kg on printed cloth. In spite of these reforms, the level of protection of the industry in Piedmont was enough to preserve the home production of coarse and medium-range cotton yarn.[32] Likewise, duties on cloth were so high that foreign cloth encountered many problems in Piedmont markets.[33] Consequently, the level of protection was so intense that it presumably had insignificant effects on the Piedmontese cotton firms' option between coarse and medium products.

It should also be considered that tariffs were endogenously, not exogenously, determined. In other words, the government did not establish duties independently of the pressure of local groups. Spain and Italy furnished many examples of duties influenced by local industrialists. In Spain, when the ban on foreign cotton imports was reformed in the 1840s, the employers' organization (the Junta de Fabricas de Cataluña) showed little opposition to reducing the ban to yarn up 60 count. The reason was that local spinners produced little yarn above 60 count and mixed-fabrics weavers needed this type of yarn (Comisión Especial Aranceleria 1867). Similarly, in Piedmont, Ligurian weavers specializing in fine cloth promoted lower tariffs on fine yarn because of the scarce local production of that good (Castronovo 1965: 302). Moreover, protection on cloth was higher than on yarn because the numerous hand-weavers could exert strong pressure on successive governments (Castronovo 1965: 305ff). Thus, one can argue that some cotton goods received more protection than others, simply because they were produced by the local industry. In consequence, duties were not established to modify the quality of home production.

The three interpretations traditionally advanced in the literature have to be rejected. Neither the life-cycle of the industry, nor home-market

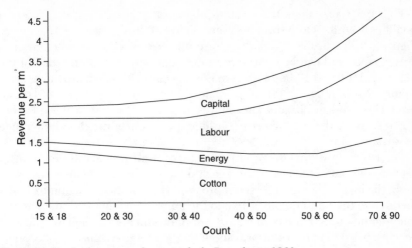

Figure 6.2 Producing costs of cotton cloth: Barcelona, 1860.

Notes and sources: Count refers to the count of yarn used in producing the cloth. The source is Comisión Especial Arancelaria (1867). The figures are drawn from the answer of the España Industrial S.A. The cost of the weaving in the quality 20&30 and 50&60 has been estimated. The cost of yarn in 15&18 counts is drawn from the answer of José Ferrer & Cía. This last figure has been modified to eliminate the transport costs of raw cotton and other materials from Barcelona to Vilanova, where the second firm was settled. Note that cotton comprises the wastage. Energy comprises not only coal for light and power but also other minor raw materials. Labour includes all labour cost even those outside the shop floor. Finally, capital costs comprise depreciation, profits and capital taxes.

Table 6.4 Share of inputs in total costs of cotton cloth: Barcelona, 1860 (per cent)

	Coarse	*Medium*		*Fine*		
Yarn count	*15 & 18*	*20 & 30*	*30 & 40*	*40 & 50*	*50 & 60*	*70 & 90*
Cotton	53.41	47.00	38.51	27.70	18.98	18.31
Energy	8.94	10.10	11.76	13.77	15.21	15.58
Labour	24.39	27.84	31.26	37.37	42.92	42.16
Capital	13.25	15.06	18.47	21.16	22.90	23.95

Notes and Sources: See Figure 6.2.

characteristics, nor barriers to free trade provide a sufficient explanation of the quality-mix of the three cotton industries summarized in Table 6.2.

Anyone who attempts to analyse the choice among different cloth qualities is immediately confronted with the fact that the combination of inputs changes through the quality range. As mentioned above, a different combination of energy, raw cotton, labour, and human and physical capital was employed to produce each quality of cloth. Therefore, it should be relatively straightforward to relate product-mix to factor endowments.

Figure 6.2 and Table 6.4 illustrate the costs of producing the different qualities of cotton cloth from the point of view of the Catalan manufacturers. Figure 6.2 practically covers the entire universe of Catalan production of cotton cloth and can be considered to be representative of the state of the industry at the end of the 1850s. A major objection, however, might be raised against this cost figure. It is impossible to assess the importance of labour-force skills and machinery alternatives in the production of the different qualities, since the two factories considered could produce the whole range of yarn and cloth.

Figure 6.2 shows that the production cost of cloth grew at different rates at each point; that is, the cost–quality relation was not a straight line.[34] Interestingly, the increase in total costs is more important in the transition from the medium to the finest qualities than in the transition from the coarsest to the medium qualities. For example, the cost of producing one square metre of coarse fabric (15 & 18 count) was about Rv 2.40. Whereas the cost of producing one square metre of medium-range fabric (30 & 40 count) was about Rv 2.56 (i.e. only about 6.6 per cent more). More specifically, raw cotton costs per square metre decreased throughout the spectrum of coarse–medium qualities, although wastage increases with count. In the fine qualities, particularly above 60 count, the raw cotton costs grew again due to the use of a large-staple and, therefore, expensive fibre. On the other hand, labour, capital and energy costs rose with count increases.

Table 6.4 displays the fact that the share of different inputs in total costs varied according to quality. Thus, the coarsest quality was the most raw-materials intensive and least labour-intensive, whereas the opposite holds for the finest qualities. Note that the two factories in the sample could produce the whole range of goods given their stocks of human and physical capital.[35] For that reason, the ratios of capital to labour and energy to labour are rather constant. However, they actually produced more medium-quality than other types of cloth (e.g. the share of medium-quality cloth in the production of España Industrial SA was about 80 per cent of the total). In other words, it seems that they were better prepared, given their stock of physical and human capital, to produce medium-range goods.

Figures for the whole Catalan cotton industry would probably diverge by some amount from the sample figures. Thus, firms specializing in the coarsest qualities used throstles instead of self-acting mules and, therefore operated with relatively more capital and energy per worker than the sample firms. Conversely, cotton mills specializing in the finest qualities used mule-jennies instead of self-acting mules and employed less capital and energy per worker.[36] In a few words, the figures presented above presumably overstate the share of labour in the cost of coarse qualities whereas the contrary holds for finest qualities.

Manufacturers in Catalonia were constrained by the price they had to pay for raw cotton and for coal, which was primarily influenced by geological and geographical factors.[37] The problem was alleviated by producing more fine cloth, which was less raw-materials intensive than coarse cloth. Thus, the efficient firm on the frontier of the local best-practice tried to produce cloth as fine as was possible with the level of skills of its workforce. The more skilled the workforce, the finer the production, and the high cost of raw materials was less important. In other words, cotton mills with less-skilled labour specialized in products in which the inferiority of their workforce had relatively little impact on the final price (i.e. in coarse cloth), whereas cotton mills with a highly skilled labour force did exactly the opposite. The constraint on this movement towards fine cloth in Catalonia was the efficiency of the local labour force, because the finest qualities were generally beyond the abilities of the Catalan workers.[38] However, it is not clear whether one should speak about the human capital constraint or the climatic constraint. The fact is that the thread breakages varied with the count level (high counts broke more often than coarse counts) and the dampness of the climate. Because Catalonia is less damp than Lancashire it is clear that thread tended to break more often in the former than the latter. For instance, during the summer, many spinning firms were at a standstill in Catalonia due to the low levels of dampness.[39]

Differences in the workforce skills facing the four countries at the time give strong support to the arguments advanced in the previous paragraph. During the first half of the nineteenth century, British and Catalonian workers were employed in different positions according to their skills. In hand and self-acting mules workers were skilled, whereas in throstles and preparatory machines workers were unskilled. Thus, in the production of coarse yarn workers were unskilled whereas the contrary holds for the finest qualities. Instead, the US and Piedmontese mills used self-acting mules and throstles, and an unskilled labour force to produce coarse cotton cloth. In particular, a contemporary described the situation of the cotton factories in Italy with the following words: "when a factory is unable to specialize in its working, then fewer, low-quality goods are produced, since it is forced to use what could be called *generic* machinery... and has *generic* workers as well".[40]

Conclusions

Despite the fact that the data reported on the previous pages have their limitations, one can argue that they provide an explanation for the technical choice and quality-mix of the Catalan cotton firms and, by extension, of the Piedmontese, British and US cotton mills. On average, Catalan cotton mills produced cloth that was in the middle of the extreme choices; the unskilled and raw-materials intensive production of the coarse-cloth New England mills, and the skills-intensive and raw-materials-saving choice of the fine-spinning Lancashire cotton mills. Therefore, one can argue that it is likely that Catalonia had a scarce supply of raw materials, but that its labour force was on average more skilled than those in the USA but less skilled than the British. Piedmontese cotton mills, with similar raw-materials restrictions to

Catalonia, produced slightly finer cloth than US cotton mills. However, these cotton mills could not produce so fine a cloth as Catalan or British cotton mills, due to their unskilled workforce. Thus, there is strong evidence that the efficiency of labour, which is mainly the result of prior human-capital accumulation, is important in determining the drift of best-practice technology in cotton textiles.

The other components of the quality choice must, however, be allowed their due. Plant and equipment costs were higher in Spain, Italy and the USA compared to Britain. This by itself lowered their optimal quality because it raised their relative operating speeds. Labour costs were higher in the USA and lower in Spain and Italy. In isolation this would have had the effects actually observed: lower quality in the former than in the latter. These aspects along with the particular characteristics of the consumers' choices are not perfectly disentangled.

Notes

The first version of this paper was written while I was visiting scholar at UC Berkeley, financed by the exchange programme between IUE and UC Berkeley. I gratefully acknowledge comments by participants in seminars at UC Berkeley, the European University Institute, Universidad Carlos III, and the Conference on Long-Run Economic Change in the Mediterranean Basin at Istanbul. I am particularly indebted to Jaime Reis for his very useful criticism, and to Jeffrey Williamson and Şevket Pamuk for their editorial assistance at the final stages. Research funding was provided by the Spanish Ministry of Foreign Affairs and the European University Institute. The usual disclaimer applies.

1   Specifically, in the regions of Piedmont and Liguria.
2   See, for example, Blaug (1961), Huberman (1996) or Comisión Especial Arancelaria (1867).
3   Gimenez Guited (1862) gives national figures on cotton industry production.
4   For example, its share in employment in cotton textiles grew from about 55 per cent to about 68 per cent. See Von Tunzelmann (1978: Table 7.18, 239).
5   Unfortunately, quality data for Piedmont are not yet available though Lombardy's figures can be considered similar to those of Piedmont. Particularly, many literary testimonies tend to support the view that all Italian regions produced low-quality cotton goods. See, for example, references given in Zamagni (1993: 89ff).
6   This result is similar to the evidence presented by Temin (1988) for the 1830s.
7   This sharp drop in the finest qualities can explain the drop in the quality index constructed by Sandberg (1968).
8   This section is based on Ellison (1968), Ure (1836) and Von Tunzelmann (1978).
9   The classical account of the American inventions in throstle and ring technology is Copeland (1912). See also Jeremy (1981).
10   See, for example, Cohen (1990) and Huberman (1996).
11   The extended co-existence between powerloom and handloom has led to an intense debate. For Von Tunzelmann (1978), some improvements in the application of power to cotton textiles production, particularly the adoption of high-pressure steam engines, reduced power costs substantially, significantly enhancing the profitability of power weaving. Moreover, the diffusion of the powerloom was partially interconnected with that of self-acting since this spinning machine produced regular yarn such as was required by primitive powerlooms. Instead, for Lyons (1987, 1989) the delay in the triumph of

mechanized weaving had a different explanation since powerlooms were more profitable than handlooms from about 1820. According to his view, handloom weavers adapted to the misfortunes of technological displacement because they moved to areas of rising economic opportunity, had their children earn higher incomes, and maintained family cohesion. In other words, to compete with more efficient powerlooms, handloom weavers squeezed their wages. Therefore, it seems that the triumph of powerlooms depended on the relative costs of energy and labour.

12   On the British advances during the period see, for example, Chapman (1987), Von Tunzelmann (1978), Ellison (1968), and Mann (1968).

13   On the early history of the US cotton industry see, among others, Cohen (1990), David (1970), Harley (1992), Jeremy (1981), Nickless (1979), Temin (1988) and Zevin (1971).

14   On the history of the cotton industry in Catalonia before 1830 see Thomson (1992), and Sánchez (1989).

15   There is a large debate on the role played by the colonial and home markets in the development of the Catalan cotton industry. See the review of the literature in Delgado (1995).

16   Gutiérrez (1834, 1837), Sánchez (1989) and Thomson (1992).

17   In Rosés (1998a), there is a full discussion of the skills differences between hand-spinning and hand-weaving.

18   This account of the Piedmont cotton industry is based on Quazza (1961) and Castronovo (1965).

19   Castronovo (1965) argued that, during this early period, coal costs made the adoption of steam power in cotton textiles uninteresting.

20   Cohen (1990) on the United States, Huberman (1996) and Clark (1994) on England, and Camps (1995) and Rosés (1998a) on Catalonia.

21   Cohen (1990: 73–4) gives inconclusive evidence on this aspect of the British cotton-weaving industry. By contrast, Catalan sources such as the Comisión Especial Arancelaria (1867) or Cerdá (1968) clearly stated that weavers were paid by piece during this period.

22   Von Tunzelmann (1978) relates the adoption of self-actors and powerlooms in England to the invention of high-pressure steam engines.

23   See criticism on this argument in Temin (1988).

24   On the Spanish home market for textiles see Sánchez-Albornoz (1981) and Prados (1983).

25   See, for example, Sandberg (1968) or Temin (1988).

26   David (1970), Stettler (1977), Temin (1988) and Harley (1992).

27   On tariff history in the cotton industry in the United States see Taussig (1931) and Stettler (1977: especially Ch.5).

28   Ronquillo (1851–7) and Gimenez Guited (1862).

29   On Piedmont's duties see Castronovo (1965: 305–12).

30   New duties were 0.9 lire/kg on coarse yarn, 2 lire/kg on grey cloth, 0.75 lire/kg on fine yarn, and 2.5–4 lire/kg on printed cloth.

31   These prices are drawn from Castronovo (1965: 249–50). British prices were prices at the Port of Genoa; thereby they comprised transport and insurance costs.

32   After 1852, the price of Piedmont yarn of 8 count was about 2 lire/kg whereas the price of the same British yarn, including duties, in Genoa was about 2.2 lire/kg. Similarly, the price of local yarn of 30 count was about 2.8 lire/kg while the price of the same British yarn, including duties, in Genoa was about 2.9 lire/kg. All prices are drawn from Castronovo (1965: 249–50), except for the price of the British yarn of 30 count which has been extrapolated from the data on Milan of Zanelli (1967: Table 15, 94).

33   For example, the duty represented about 30–40 per cent of the home price of grey cloth. The prices and duties are drawn from Castronovo (1965: 295–6 and 310).

34   This result invalidates the argument of Bils (1984) on the straight-line relation between costs and quality in cotton cloth.

35   They used steam-powered self-acting mules and powerlooms and organized their workforce into work-teams, as was typical in Catalan cotton firms.

36   Von Tunzelmann (1978: Table 7.3, 185) demonstrates this for Lancashire. See also Gattrell (1977).
37   In Rosés (1998b) costs differentials among Catalan, British and US cotton mills are fully discussed. On average, raw cotton prices in Barcelona were 47 per cent higher than in New York and 28 per cent higher than in Liverpool. Similarly, the price of coal in the Port of Barcelona was about 76 per cent higher than in Britain.
38   Contemporary and recent studies stressed the importance of human capital formation in determining the level of workers' efficiency in the early cotton industry. See, for example, Boot (1995) and Rosés (1998a).
39   See Farnie (1979) and the contemporary, Ferrer Vidal (1875).
40   Ellena cited by Zamagni (1993: 89).

Part 4

Trade, transport and domestic production in the century before World War II

7 Specialization in the international market for olive oil before World War II

Ramon Ramon-Muñoz

Introduction

A new pattern of international specialization emerged between the mid-nineteenth century and the outbreak of World War I. The process is well known. The reduction of transport costs enabled wide areas in the Americas, Asia and Africa to export low-cost primary products to Europe. Labour and capital movements from Europe to the New World increased enormously compared to previous periods. At the same time, Germany, America and other countries industrialized, challenging Britain's industrial supremacy. Although less spectacular, new patterns of international specialization also emerged in markets for individual commodities as new countries entered the market and demand conditions changed in the traditional importing countries.

This chapter aims to contribute to the understanding of these processes of international specialization by analysing the case of the world olive-oil market between 1870 and 1938. Olive oil was, and still is, a Mediterranean commodity. Although olive trees grow in some American and Australian regions, the cultivation of olives takes place principally in the countries bordering on the Mediterranean Sea. On the eve of World War I, Spain, Italy, the Ottoman Empire, Greece, the French colony of Algeria, the French protectorate of Tunisia and Mediterranean France, in descending order, produced more than 90 per cent of the olive oil exported in the world. Olive oil was also a major export commodity for most of these countries. While it is true that generally it never accounted for more than 8 per cent of their total exports, a small percentage when compared with other foodstuffs, it is also true that during long periods it was one of the five major goods exported by the Mediterranean countries.[1]

Mediterranean olive-oil producers did not occupy, however, the same position in the international market of the product. This chapter shows that by the first decade of the twentieth century, the international specialization that characterized the Mediterranean olive-oil industry until World War II was well established. France and Italy had specialized in exporting brand-name olive oil, which was regarded as a "superior" sort of product. Spain had concentrated on exporting bulk olive oil of high and medium quality, although one-third of its exports also consisted of brand-name olive oil. By contrast, southern and eastern Mediterranean producers exported almost exclusively bulk olive oil of medium and low quality, used as a raw product for refining and blending purposes. This chapter argues that differences both in relative costs and in technology, which probably reflected Mediterranean differences in factor endowments, led to the emergence of these distinctive patterns of specialization among olive-oil producers.

These results are not only intrinsic to understanding the Mediterranean olive-oil industry itself but can also throw some light on more general issues. They suggest that although Mediterranean countries traded similar goods they probably tended to cover different segments of the international demand. The existence of different economic structures within the Mediterranean basin, which in turn influenced the position of the producing countries in the international market, is another aspect that this chapter seeks to show. Finally, this study can also throw some light on the general determinants of the patterns of trade, a question that has recently attracted the interest of economic historians.[2]

The chapter is organized as follows. The next section contains a general view of international markets for olive oil. It focuses on three main aspects: the heterogeneity of the product itself; the changing conditions in the importing markets; and the increasing competition among Mediterranean olive-oil producers. The third section documents the existence of different patterns of specialization by looking at data on export orientation and prices. This is followed by a section which explores possible causes for specialization by analysing cross-country information on labour costs, land productivity, labour skills and technological progress. The last section is devoted to the main conclusions of this chapter.

International markets from the 1870s to 1938

Specialization in the international markets for olive oil took place mainly at the time when patterns of demand were being modified and new olive-oil producers were entering the market. Therefore, after examining the heterogeneous nature of the product itself, this section documents both the changing patterns in world olive-oil demand and the increasing competition among the producers of olive oil between 1870 and 1938.

Olive oil: a differentiated product

On the eve of World War I, the olive-oil industry, like many other industries, produced a relatively wide set of products, which differed one from another in final uses, quality, and methods of production. International demand for olive oil was also characterized by the existence of relatively well-differentiated

Table 7.1 Prices of Spanish bulk olive oil in Marseille, 1898, 1913, 1929 (francs/100 kgs)*

Quotation	1898	1913	1929
Fine–Extra	120–130	—	945–998
Fine–High	110–120	160–165	—
Fine	100–110	150–155	—
Ordinary	—	140–145	—
For refinement	—	—	794
For industrial purposes	60–70	—	—

Source: Ramon-Muñoz (2000).

Notes
* Minimum and maximum prices.
Tariffs are included with the exception of olive oil for industrial purposes.

import markets: olive oil was imported for industrial purposes; it was sold as an edible olive oil in bulk, either to be consumed by the population or to be used as a raw material by the food industry; and, finally, it was traded under brand names as a salad-oil and for other cooking purposes. In accordance with this heterogeneity, the characteristics of the product were also different. Thus, while olive oil for industrial purposes was of poor quality, had high levels of acidity, was produced by primitive methods and commanded the lowest prices in international markets, brand-name olive oil was just the opposite. Most important, however, is that the three types of oil corresponded also to three different stages in the process of olive-oil production. In particular, the processes used for bulk and brand-name olive oil differed greatly.

After the planting of olive trees and the gathering of the fruit, the first stage was the production of bulk olive oil. This was a relatively simple operation consisting mainly of crushing the olives, which were reduced to a uniform pasty mass by means of millstones, of pressing the pulp and, finally, of collecting and storing the olive oil after the pressing in tanks and deposits. Pressing was a central operation in the production of bulk olive oil. A first-pressing olive oil, generally called extra-fine or virgin oil and obtained with low pressure, was a product of superior quality. The oils obtained from the second or third pressings, which were made by using the residue of the previous pressings and, in some Mediterranean regions, by adding boiling water to these residues, were instead of inferior quality. They also commanded lower prices in the consuming markets and, in the case of third-pressing oils, might be used for industrial purposes. Table 7.1 gives the prices of Spanish olive oil in Marseille between 1898 and 1929, and illustrates the range of qualities and prices characterizing the product.

Producing brand-name olive oil was, certainly, a marketing strategy of the firms, but it also represented a final stage in the process of making olive oil for food consumption. To some extent, brand-name olive oil was a finished product, which was adjusted to the different tastes of the final consumers through the use of refining methods, blending techniques and packaging operations. Refining, for example, allowed the removal of the excess of free fatty acid, the excess of colour and the objectionable odours and tastes existing in bulk olive oil of medium and low quality. And, by means of blending techniques, different types of olive oils (i.e. fine olive oils from different origins together with refined olive oils) were mixed in order to create suitable varieties of the product. Both refining and blending facilitated, in turn, the production of uniform types of olive oils, which were packed in tins and bottles to be sold direct to the consumer.

The processes required in the production of brand-name olive oil also differed both in complexity and in nature to those used in making bulk olive oil. Indeed, refining and blending olive oil were considered, as will be explained in detail later in this chapter, as more skilled activities than crushing or pressing olives. With regard to the nature of the activity itself, making bulk olive oil was fundamentally a rural activity, while producing brand-name olive oil, which was mainly carried out by dealers and exporters, clearly had an industrial and commercial nature.

There is a final consideration to be made, concerning the added value of the product. Making brand-name olive oil also implied adding value to the olive oil itself. By means of refining methods, some of the deficiencies existing in olive oils of low and medium quality were eliminated, which increased the value of the product. And thanks to blending and packaging operations, the final value of the product could increase even more. As a consequence, brand-name olive oil was a commodity of higher added value when compared to bulk olive oil.

According to the foreign trade statistics of France, Italy and Spain (Table 7.2), over the period 1890–1938 the unit values of olive oil traded under brand names were substantially higher than the olive oil traded in bulk.[3] In fact, contemporaries regarded the former as a "superior" sort of production and export.

Changing patterns in the world demand for olive oil

During the period 1870–1938, international markets for olive oil experienced two key changes, as can be deduced from the estimates presented in Table 7.3. First, demand for industrial olive oil fell dramatically, whereas import markets for edible olive oil, either in bulk or under brand names, increased rapidly, becoming predominant on the eve of World War I. Second, from the late nineteenth century, geographical patterns of trade were totally modified, due mainly to the collapse of northern European markets as well as the expansion of American demand. Like many other changes

Table 7.2 Bulk and brand-name olive oil: unit values, 1890–1938 (five-year averages, in national currencies and percentages)

	France[1,2] (francs/100 kgs)			Italy[1,3] (lire/100 kgs)			Spain[4] (pesetas/100 kgs)		
	Bulk	Brand	% of increase	Bulk	Brand	% of increase	Bulk	Brand	% of increase
1890–94	85	105	23.5	nd	nd	nd	nd	nd	nd
1909–13	135	147	8.3	nd	nd	nd	nd	nd	nd
1925–29	854	1 008	18.1	690	873	26.5	nd	nd	nd
1935–38	nd	nd	nd	433	684	57.9	89	109	22.5

Source: Ramon-Muñoz (2000).

Notes

[1] The bulk olive oil corresponds to the olive oil imported in the regime of temporary admission, whereas the brand-name one is the olive oil re-exported after being refined and manipulated;

[2] 1890–94 excludes 1891; 1925–29 excludes 1925;

[3] 1935–38 excludes 1937 in the particular case of brand-name olive oil;

[4] The bulk olive oil corresponds to the olive oil exported in packages weighing more than 20 kilograms, whereas the branded one is that exported in packages weighing less than 20 kilograms; 1935–38 is 1931–35;

nd: no data.

in the late nineteenth century, the changing pattern in the world olive-oil market was determined by the fall of transport costs, the integration of new areas to the international economy and, finally, the southern European mass migration.

Industrial markets for olive oil, which were mainly in the United Kingdom and continental Europe, were enormous by the 1870s, accounting for almost 80 per cent of the total world olive-oil imports. Olive oil was in demand as a lubricant in machinery, for oiling wool after scouring by the textile industry, as a raw material for soap making, and, finally, as a fuel in lighting. From the 1870s, however, cheaper and more efficient seed oils, animal fats and mineral oils coming from the Americas, India and Western Africa started to replace olive oil in its industrial applications.[4] Although by the eve of World War I industrial markets had already fallen dramatically, olive oils with high degrees of acidity were still in demand in Russia, for lighting in Orthodox churches as well as of the images that religious families had at home; in England, for oiling wool; and in the United States, for technical purposes.[5] These last two countries continued to demand olive oil for industrial purposes until the eve of World War II.[6]

On the other hand, international markets for edible olive oil in bulk became extremely important from the last decade of the nineteenth century. As Table 7.3 shows, France and Italy became the main import markets for bulk olive oil. At least from the last two decades of the nineteenth century, in response to the continuous decline of domestic production, traders from the French cities of Marseille and Nice began to import olive oil for refining or for mixing with some of their own olive oils. They also adjusted the product to the requirements of the final consumption markets, many of which were situated abroad. From the first decade of the present century, the northwestern Italian exporters of Porto Maurizio, Oneglia and Genoa followed the pattern initiated by the neighbouring cities of Marseille and Nice (Ministerio de Estado 1923). The Italian exporters, however, demanded bulk olive oil in order to supply their American markets.

Although less important than the French and Italian markets, the market for bulk olive oil was significant in the United States, where a packaging industry was developed during the years of World War I. With the principal establishments situated near the North Atlantic seaboard cities, namely New York, Baltimore, Boston and Philadelphia, bulk olive oil was used for blending with other vegetable oils, for packing fish or other food products, or was simply repackaged in smaller containers for final consumption in the domestic market (US Tariff Commission 1931: 8). In another large market of the New World, Argentina, the domestic seed oils industry also required olive oil for blending with other vegetable oils (Ministerio de Estado 1920: 32–3; 1922: 8–9).

Perhaps one of the main features of international markets for bulk olive oil was the wide variety of uses to which it was put. Indeed, French and Italian olive-oil exporters used it as a raw material; in the United States, and also in

Table 7.3 Import markets for olive oil: annual rate of growth and share, 1870–1938 (original data in volumes)[1]

	Annual rate of growth (%)				Share of the import markets (%)				
	1870/74–1890/94	1890/94–1909/13	1909/13–1925/29	1925/29–1934/38	1870/74	1890/94	1909/13	1925/29	1934/38
1. The main import markets for industrial olive oil									
United Kingdom	-2.5	-5.1	-2.3	1.8	26.2	15.8	4.5	2.1	3.5
Russia and Central Europe	-1.5	-3.7	—	—	41.3	30.6	11.6	—	—
France	-4.3	—	—	—	10.8	4.5	n/a	—	—
United States	—	—	4.4	6.6	—	—	1.6	2.1	6.9
Total	-2.1	-4.2	-6.3	4.6	78.4	50.9	17.8	4.2	10.4
2. The main import markets for bulk olive oil									
France	6.1	1.4	-1.0	-0.2	6.4	20.6	21.0	11.8	15.3
Italy	-1.3	8.2	6.7	-2.4	6.2	4.8	16.8	31.3	29.7
Norway and UK	n/a	1.7	0.4	-0.3	n/a	5.2	5.6	3.9	5.0
Romania and Bulgaria	5.5	-0.1	-8.5	-8.9	1.8	5.0	3.9	0.6	0.4
United States and Argentina	7.0	10.9	8.4	-0.2	0.2	0.8	3.9	9.3	12.1
Total	4.7	3.1	3.3	-1.4	14.6	36.4	51.2	57.0	62.5

continued on next page

Table 7.3 Import markets for olive oil: annual rate of growth and share, 1870–1938 (original data in volumes)[1] (cont.)

	Annual rate of growth (%)				Share of the import markets (%)				
	1870/74–1890/94	1890/94–1909/13	1909/13–1925/29	1925/29–1934/38	1870/74	1890/94	1909/13	1925/29	1934/38
3. The main import markets for brand-name olive oil									
Argentina	2.2	8.5	3.8	-6.1	3.2	4.9	16.5	19.6	10.8
United States	4.7	10.9	5.1	-5.0	0.6	1.5	7.8	11.4	7.4
Cuba	-1.9	-0.3	1.6	2.8	1.2	3.0	2.3	1.9	3.7
Brazil	1.9	5.4	2.3	-1.8	1.2	2.1	3.1	2.9	3.0
Uruguay	n/a	2.4	8.5	-4.2	n/a	1.1	1.3	3.0	2.2
Total	3.0	5.4	4.0	-4.5	7.0	12.7	31.0	38.8	27.1
Total imports in the main markets	0.0	1.3	2.7	-2.0	100.0	100.0	100.0	100.0	100.0
					(in metric tonnes)				
					103 772	104 007	132 929	202 276	151 507

Source: Ramon-Muñoz (2000).

Note
[1] The original data corresponds to five-year averages in the periods specified in this table. For exceptions to this rule, as well as for other methodological aspects relating to the construction of the table, see sources. Figures always refer to the national boundaries pertaining in each period.

Norway, it was used by the canned-fish industry; and, finally, many importers sold it to low-income consumers. This was the case, for example, in the east European markets.

Another feature was the wide range of qualities demanded by import markets. This was especially true in the interwar period. While the United States, Norway and the United Kingdom demanded exclusively fine olive oils of low acidity, Italy and, to a lesser extent, France increasingly imported high-acidity oils for refining. The increasing demand for the latter was a clear result of technical change in the industry. From the eve of World War I, industrial refineries, which expanded rapidly in northern Italy, allowed the removal of impurities and acidity from the olive oils of poor quality. This meant that some olive oils which because of their high acidity had previously been used for industrial purposes could now be used for food consumption.

Aside from the expansion of international demand for bulk olive oil, import markets for brand-name olive oil also developed rapidly in the twentieth century. Between 1890/94 and 1909/13, the annual rate of growth was greater than 5 per cent, and by 1925/29 brand-name markets accounted for almost 40 per cent of total world olive-oil imports. Mass migration from southern Europe towards the American continent was partly responsible for this expansion. The use of olive oil as a food is, among other factors, highly dependent on consumption patterns and cultural experience. While in other regions butter, fats or other edible vegetable oils were preferred, it was an essential product among the population living in the Mediterranean basin. Therefore, it is not surprising that import markets for edible olive oil expanded as thousands of southern European citizens left their home countries in the direction of the Americas.

The reasons the markets of the Americas tended to import large amounts of brand-name olive oil are, however, more difficult to explain. According to the Italian consular reports, crediting a brand name was a means of entry into these new markets. This information suggests that once the brand was established, potential entry barriers were created by product differentiation; and, finally, the established firms could be favoured by the existence of niche markets.[7]

The marketing strategies of firms might have been one explanation for the massive imports of brand-name olive oil, but they were not the only one. It must be added that brand-name olive oil shipped from Europe offered consumers a certain security in product quality and taste, an important factor when considering that fraud was not uncommon in American markets for olive oil. Information concerning the olive-oil market in the United States during the 1920s stresses that the

> consumer knows that every shipment of olive oil imported in the containers in which it is sold, is protected by careful and stringent examinations by the Department of Agriculture. The buyer knows that he has an assurance that the oil these tins contains, is pure olive oil; that the

volume of the contents is as specified on the tins; that it is full in measure; that it is absolutely free from illegal mixtures; that the possibility of
fraud is minimized to the point of zero.

(Committee on Ways and Means 1929: 716).

According to the same source, this could not always be said of the olive oil
packed, and also labelled, in the United States.

The fact that the main import markets for brand-name olive oil were in the
Americas did not mean that other markets were non-existent. In continental
Europe, the wealthiest classes made some use of a fine and a smooth olive oil,
brand-named in bottles and, mostly, coming from the regions of Tuscany
(Italy) or Provence (France).[8] But taken as a whole, these were weak markets
in contrast to the Americas.

Increasing competition among the Mediterranean olive-oil producers

The changing pattern in international demand was a central aspect explaining the transformation of the world olive-oil market over the period
1870–1938. However, it was not the only one. During the same period, traditional olive-oil producers had to face increasing competition from more
dynamic countries. This did not only occur in the olive-oil market; Morilla
Critz, Olmstead and Rhode, for example, illustrate in this volume the
increasing competition among the dried-fruit producers, especially after the
appearance of California in foreign markets.

In the olive-oil market, this competition took place mainly within the
Mediterranean basin, bringing about relevant changes among the olive-oil
producers. One of the most impressive was, as shown in Table 7.4, the collapse of Italy's leading position in the world olive oil market, both as a producer and as an exporter, and the emergence of Spain as an olive-oil power.
Indeed, Spanish production increased, relative to Italy's, 1.6 times between
the 1890s and the eve of World War I, while its exports increased by almost
three times over the same period. By 1909/13, Spain was already the
world's major olive-oil producer, and by 1925/29 its exports were higher
than any other competitor.[9]

In the interwar period, most of the Mediterranean countries listed in
Table 7.4 were able to increase domestic production and exports.[10] Among
them, the most dynamic were Tunisia and Greece. Indeed, their output,
taken together, almost doubled between 1909/13 and 1934/38, and their
exports tripled. This not only contributed to the erosion of the former Italian hegemony, but also challenged the new Spanish position in the international markets of the product.[11]

The Italian decline was influenced not only by the competition of other
Mediterranean olive-oil producers, but also by other factors. Product substitution in foreign markets was the first one. The southern Italian regions had
oriented their production towards markets demanding industrial olive oil, a

Table 7.4 Area, production and exports of olive oil in the Mediterranean Basin by countries, 1870–1938

Panel 1: Area of olive growing

	In thousand of hectares					Relative to Italy (Italy = 100)				
	c.1870	c.1890	c.1913	c.1929	c.1938	c.1870	c.1890	c.1913	c.1929	c.1938
France	152	133	125	92	80	17	13	12	8	7
Italy	895	1 039	1 009	1 160	1 154	100	100	100	100	100
Spain	n/a	1 154	1 427	1 738	1 903	n/a	111	141	150	165
Tunisia	n/a	185	203	275	300	n/a	n/a	20	24	26
Algeria	n/a	n/a	68	n/a	81	n/a	n/a	7	n/a	7
Greece	168	n/a	200	394	500	19	n/a	20	34	43
Turkey	n/a	n/a	n/a	n/a	750	n/a	n/a	n/a	n/a	65
Syria/Lebanon	n/a	n/a	n/a	61	70	n/a	n/a	n/a	5	6
Portugal	150	n/a	n/a	481	n/a	17	n/a	n/a	34	n/a
Others	n/a	n/a	n/a	n/a	256	n/a	n/a	n/a	n/a	22

Panel 2: Olive oil production (yearly averages)

	In thousand of metric tonnes					Relative to Italy (Italy = 100)				
	1870/74	1890/94	1909/13	1925/29	1934/38	1870/74	1890/94	1909/13	1925/29	1934/38
France	21.6	13.0	9.9	7.0	5.6	7	6	6	3	3
Italy	305.7	230.1	163.2	201.8	209.1	100	100	100	100	100
Spain	213.0	202.4	226.3	415.0	352.6	70	88	139	206	169
Tunisia	n/a	n/a	29.3	40.0	42.0	n/a	n/a	18	20	20
Algeria	n/a	n/a	29.9	22.0	12.1	n/a	n/a	18	11	6

continued on next page

Table 7.4 Area, production and exports of olive oil in the Mediterranean Basin by countries, 1870–1938 (cont.)

	1870/74	1890/94	1909/13	1925/29	1934/38	Relative to Italy (Italy = 100)				
						1870/74	1890/94	1909/13	1925/29	1934/38
Greece	44.3	50.6	45.6	75.4	112.9	15	22	28	37	54
Turkey	n/a	n/a	n/a	15.8	21.3	n/a	n/a	n/a	8	10
Syria/Lebanon	n/a	n/a	n/a	10.6	13.2	n/a	n/a	n/a	5	6
Portugal	16.4	22.2	24.0	46.1	46.3	5	10	15	23	22
Others	n/a	n/a	n/a	18.6	28.8	n/a	n/a	n/a	9	14

Panel 3: Olive oil exports (yearly averages)

In thousand of metric tonnes

	1870/74	1890/94	1909/13	1925/29	1934/38	Relative to Italy (Italy = 100)				
						1870/74	1890/94	1909/13	1925/29	1934/38
France	3.6	11.0	15.5	13.7	14.8	6	21	36	23	38
Italy	63.5	51.1	43.5	58.6	38.8	100	100	100	100	100
Spain	23.5	16.2	39.2	74.5	57.2	37	32	90	127	147
Tunisia	2.1	8.0	8.2	22.4	33.5	3	16	19	38	86
Algeria	3.4	1.7	4.6	12.9	10.1	5	3	11	22	26
Greece	6.4	6.5	7.7	11.2	10.7	10	13	18	19	27
Turkey	n/a	15.1	10.8	5.9	4.6	n/a	29	25	10	12
Syria/Lebanon	n/a	n/a	n/a	2.1	6.5	n/a	n/a	n/a	4	17
Portugal	3.7	0.7	2.6	2.5	4.4	6	1	6	4	11
Others	n/a	n/a	n/a	0.6	0.3	n/a	n/a	n/a	1	1

Source and notes: see Table 7.3.

catastrophic choice when cheaper and more efficient vegetable oils and fats were substituted for olive oil in industry.[12] Olive-tree disease was the second major factor fomenting the crisis in Italy, especially in the south. The causes and the remedies were unclear at that time, but the fact was that around 1900, and through the first decade of the present century, many trees were infected by the *Dacus oleae*, reducing olive harvests, yields and, of course, olive-oil production (Federico 1992: 31).

Competition, product substitution and diseases finally forced Italian farmers to abandon olive cultivation and to allocate resources to more profitable crops.[13] They also increasingly mixed olive trees with other crops and by 1909/13 more than 50 per cent of olives were harvested in mixed areas (Zattini 1921: 247). It is true that over the interwar period both its area and its production also increased.[14] However, in the mid-1930s, Italian output was still 65 per cent lower than Spanish output, and was also losing ground compared to Greece and Tunisia.

Patterns of specialization in the international market for olive oil from the late nineteenth century to World War II

As a consequence of both the deep transformation in the international demand for olive oil and the increasing competition among olive-oil producers, a process of specialization also took place within the Mediterranean basin. Table 7.5 reports estimates on export orientation for the leading olive-oil exporters in three benchmark periods, namely 1909–13, 1925–9 and 1934–8.

The construction of this table requires further comments. In Panel 1, the basic data have been taken from the foreign-trade statistics of the exporting countries, which since the mid-1920s usually specify the amount of olive oil traded for industrial or edible purposes as well as the size of the package used in trading the product, a good proxy to know whether olive oil was traded in bulk or under brand names.[15] Where foreign-trade statistics of importing countries have offered more detailed information, data from the latter have been combined with that of the exporting countries.[16] Finally, when when no statistical information has been found, either from the foreign-trade statistics of the exporting countries or from those of the importing ones, consular reports and specific publications, which offer general descriptions on marketing for most of the olive-oil importing markets, have been used.[17] In order to improve the reliability of our estimates, calculations have also been made by considering exclusively data on olive-oil imports from a sample of twenty importing countries for the period 1909–13 and a sample of seventeen countries for the period 1925–9. This calculation might also help to reduce two common problems affecting accuracy in foreign-trade statistics, namely compilation criteria and inaccuracy in the registration of countries of origin and destination (Federico and Tena 1991; Tena 1992; Pamuk 1987: 153–8). With the exception of France, the sample covers, on average, 90 per cent of the destinations of the olive oil exported by the countries considered here.[18] The

Table 7.5 Estimates on exports orientation, 1909–1938 (five-year averages, in percentages)

Panel 1: Estimates using data from the foreign trade statistics of the exporting countries

	1909–13			1925–29			1934–38		
	Industrial markets	Bulk markets	Brand markets	Industrial markets	Bulk markets	Brand markets	Industrial markets	Bulk markets	Brand markets
France	1	12	87	2	14	84	0	8	92
Italy	6	37	57	1	18	81	1	13	86
Spain	7	65	28	4	66	30	6	60	34
Tunisia	0	100	0	2	98	0	6	94	0
Algeria	0	100	0	9	91	0	16	84	0
Greece	15	85	0	21	78	1	15	83	3
Turkey	19	81	0	10	88	2	17	81	2

Panel 2: Estimates using data from the foreign trade statistics of the importing countries

	1909–13			1925–29		
	Industrial markets	Bulk markets	Brand markets	Industrial markets	Bulk markets	Brand markets
Italy	10	15	75	1	15	84
Spain	5	68	27	5	52	43
Tunisia	0	100	0	2	98	0
Algeria	0	100	0	5	95	0
Greece	10	89	1	14	86	0
Turkey	32	67	1	13	87	0

Sources and notes: see text, endnotes and Table 7.3.

results are presented in Panel 2. Although they are not coincident with those shown in Panel 1, the general picture emerging from both estimates is not so different.

According to these very approximate estimates, the international specialization that characterized the Mediterranean olive-oil industry until World War II was well established by the first decade of the twentieth century. France, and to a lesser extent, Italy, supplied import markets for brand-name olive oil, a product of higher added value as shown previously. Spain sent the larger part of its exports towards markets demanding bulk olive oil, although one-third of the total exports also consisted of brand-name olive oil. Tunisia and Algeria were even more specialized in the export of bulk olive oil. Finally, Greece and Turkey seem to have been more oriented towards markets demanding a low-quality product. By 1909/13, between 10 and 30 per cent of their olive oil was exported to industrial markets, and twenty-five years later their olive-oil exports in bulk seem to have still been characterized by high levels of acidity, as contemporary views stress.[19] In fact, most Greek and Turkish bulk olive oil was used in the Italian refineries.

Table 7.5 (Panel 2) suggests that some modest changes took place after World War I. Perhaps the most obvious are that Spain and Italy seem to have moved towards markets demanding a product of higher added value, since their exports seem to have been more oriented towards brand-name markets. However, it is difficult to take these conclusions any further, partly because the estimates are highly tentative and partly because in the interwar period international markets for olive oil were distorted by tariffs and other import barriers.

Prices provide further evidence about the various countries' places in the world olive-oil market. They are a good proxy of quality. Table 7.6 shows average prices of edible olive oil in four import marketplaces, namely Marseille, Genoa, Buenos Aires and New York, for the years around 1895, 1913 and 1929. It must be mentioned, however, that quotations include transport costs, which might distort the analysis. For example, Greek and Turkish prices in New York can reach higher levels than some of their competitors, not because of their higher quality but because of their higher transport costs. Finally, prices of exporting countries are expressed as a percentage of the prices obtained by French olive oil in each import market.

Price data complement what has been deduced from foreign-trade statistics. Indeed, the first observation to be made refers to the highest prices enjoyed by the French firms both in Buenos Aires and New York, which shows that they not only exported a brand-name product with high added value but also that they specialized in high-quality olive oil. The second point to note concerns Greece and Turkey; as prices suggest, these two countries were exporting low-quality olive oil in bulk. In Marseille and Genoa, for example, they were never able to reach the prices of Spain, not to mention those achieved by French and Italian olive oils. The last observation concerns Spain; its olive oils achieved higher prices in the European markets

Table 7.6 Price ratios in selected import markets around 1895, 1913 and 1929
(French olive oil = 100; for Genoa, Italian olive oil = 100)

c. 1895

	Marseille (14.5.1892)	Genoa (14.11.1891)	Buenos Aires (1895)	New York* (1894/96)
France	100	n/a	100	100
Italy	96	100	91	56
Spain	85	n/a	90	51
Tunisia	72	81	n/a	n/a
Algeria	74	n/a	n/a	n/a
Greece	n/a	83	n/a	31
Turkey	n/a	n/a	n/a	48

c. 1913

	Marseille (1913)	Genoa (1913)	Buenos Aires (1912)	New York* (1913)
France	100	n/a	100	100
Italy	n/a	100	85	82
Spain	96	94	85	61
Tunisia	89	86	n/a	54
Algeria	84	n/a	n/a	54
Greece	n/a	83	n/a	50
Turkey	87	n/a	n/a	50

c. 1929

	Marseille	Genoa	Buenos Aires	New York*
	(from January to June, 1929)			*(1927/1929)*
France	100	n/a	100	100
Italy	n/a	100	62	99
Spain	93	96	n/a	92
Tunisia	90	90	n/a	88
Algeria	86	83	n/a	88
Greece	n/a	89	n/a	84
Turkey	86	80	n/a	90

*Unit values from the American foreign trade statistics.
Source and notes: see Table 7.3.

when compared with those of Tunisia, Algeria, Greece or Turkey. However, they failed to achieve the same success as the Italian and French ones did in both the European and American marketplaces. The only exception to this refers to the Buenos Aires market, where in 1895 and 1912 olive oils under Spanish brand names were similarly quoted to those exported by Italian firms.

Both the estimates on export orientation and the information on prices show that on the eve of World War I a process of specialization had already taken place within the Mediterranean basin. Despite the fact that any producing country tended to occupy a concrete place in the international market of the product, data reported in Tables 7.5 and 7.6 also seem to indicate that olive-oil exporters followed two general patterns of specialization. Indeed, northwestern Mediterranean producers specialized in exporting a product that was "superior" in terms of quality, stage of production and added value. Southern and eastern Mediterranean producers, instead, exported almost exclusively bulk olive oil of lower quality, used as a raw product for refining and blending purposes. The obvious issue is, therefore, to establish the reasons why Mediterranean olive-oil producers specialized in this way.

Explaining specialization in the first third of the twentieth century: some hypotheses

International trade theory offers various explanations for specialization in the international markets. Theories based on the law of comparative advantage suggest that specialization takes place mainly because some countries are more efficient in the production of certain commodities than others. The Ricardian model assumes that comparative advantage arises because of international differences in labour productivity, which can be explained, in turn, by international differences in technology. The Heckscher–Ohlin theory argues, instead, that patterns of specialization in international markets are explained by differences in countries' relative factor endowments. On the other hand, theories based on monopolistic competition suggest that countries tend to specialize in a relatively restricted range of goods in order to take advantage of economies of scale. These theories also assume the existence of market imperfections, differences in tastes, product differentiation and market power to the level of the firm.[20]

The interaction of all these factors influenced patterns in the olive-oil trade, but probably not to the same degree. The next two parts of this section outline in some detail the main characteristics of the bulk and brand-name olive-oil production and provide quantitative and qualitative evidence on farm wages, yields of olive oil, labour skills and technology for a relatively wide sample of Mediterranean countries. This evidence, together with other available information, suggests that Mediterranean producers tended to export the type of olive oil in which they had a comparative advantage. It also suggests that differences both in relative costs and in technology, which probably reflected differences in factor endowments, led to the emergence of distinctive patterns of specialization among olive-oil producers.

Table 7.7 Costs of growing olives and making bulk olive oil in southern Spain, 1920–21

Cost of growing 3.8 hectares of olive trees			Manufacturing costs in 1 metric tonne of olive oil		
	Dollars	%		Dollars	%
Ploughing and cultivation	43	24.0	Olives	177	89.2
Guarding	4	2.2	Labour	5	2.5
Harvesting	39	21.9	Power	6	3.1
Total labour	85	48.1	Grass press bags	2	1.0
Transport	3	1.5	Taxes	1	0.7
Taxes	6	3.6	Interest of variable capital	2	1.2
Interest of variable capital	3	1.9	Depreciation and interest of fixed capital	5	2.3
Rent of land	80	44.9			
Total	177	100.0	Total	199	100.0

Source and notes: Ramon-Muñoz (2000).

The production of bulk olive oil: labour costs and yields

The production of bulk olive oil was a land–labour intensive activity and its production costs were extremely dependent on farm wages and agricultural yields. Table 7.7 presents the costs of growing olives and making bulk olive oil in the early 1920s for southern Spain. It shows clearly an essential point: labour costs, together with the rent of land, had an enormous influence both on the final price of the olive and on the final price of the bulk olive oil.

Labour, for example, accounted for half of the costs of growing olive trees, but it also represented a great percentage in making bulk olive oil. The reason is obvious. Manufacturing costs added only about 10 per cent to the final price of the bulk olive oil; the rest of the cost was constituted entirely by the olives, and, therefore by farm labour and other farm costs. Although these estimates are based on information available for Spain in the early 1920s, Spanish and Portuguese data for the late nineteenth century suggest that relative costs seem to have been similar in previous periods and for other countries.[21]

Table 7.7 does not show the factors affecting farm-labour productivity and yields of olive oil per hectare or per tree, which in fact determined enormously the cost per unit of output in the production of bulk olive oil. James Simpson (1995: 168) has suggested that labour productivity varied according to the method used in harvesting olives, the form of labour contract established and, finally, the harvest size. In fact, olives could be harvested by hand, by means of long rods, by gathering the olives from the ground once the fruit had fallen from the tree, or by a combination of these methods. While labour productivity, i.e. olives collected per worker, was relatively low if olives were gathered by hand, it increased substantially when trees were beaten with long rods. It is true that in this case, however, the olives were easily damaged, and it is also true that the quality of olive oil was negatively affected. Nevertheless, the use of long rods was a more cost-effective method.[22]

Farm-labour productivity in harvesting olives was also affected by the form of labour contract. Workers could be paid either by time or by task, usually depending on the quantity of olives to be harvested. If paid by task, they tended to maximize earnings by increasing the number of olives collected by unit of time. There is no doubt that this form of labour contract meant less care in the collecting of the fruit, but it is also clear that it increased the output per worker.[23]

However, the major influence in increasing labour productivity was perhaps the size of the harvest itself and the productivity of the land. Indeed, when a harvest doubled from one year to the next – something that could occur easily due to the annual fluctuations of the crop – the harvester was able to collect approximately 50 per cent more per hour. In other words, by increasing yields of olives, either per hectare or per tree, the productivity of the harvester could rise enormously (López Ontiveros 1978: 129–34 and 192–3).

Agronomists, experts and contemporary writers mentioned a large number of factors influencing yields of olive oil per hectare or per tree. Some of them dealt with biological and natural facts. For example, from different species of trees, yields of both olives and olive oil varied substantially. However, the same species of trees yielded differently, depending on the quality of the soil as well as the climatic conditions. Growing methods were considered a relevant source of productivity too. Apparently, the shorter the distance between trees the lower the yield. The same could be said regarding the mix of the olive tree with other crops. An orchard mixing olive trees with vineyards or wheat was said to yield less output per tree than an unmixed orchard. Finally, the care of the tree, which included fertilizing, ploughing and regular and careful pruning, was seen as essential in determining yields of olive oil. Although experts did not always agree in stressing one factor over the others, the care of the tree, and probably the quality of soil, appear to be the most relevant factors determining yields.[24] Contrary perhaps to expectations, the use of modern presses in crushing olives did little to increase the yields of olive oil. According to Zambrana's calculations, Spanish industrial yields in the olive-oil industry remained stagnant during the first third of the twentieth century despite the fact that modern machinery had been introduced in the mills (Zambrana 1987: 71).

It can be concluded, therefore, that in terms of costs per unit of output, the production of bulk olive oil was extremely sensitive both to farm wages

Table 7.8 Daily wages for olive harvesters in the Mediterranean around 1907, 1927 and 1933

Period 1907/1908

Country	Region	Year	Hours worked	Male Wages US dollars			Italy = 100
				Maximum	Minimum	Average	Average
France	Provence	1907	n/a	0.77	0.68	0.73	145
Italy	Naples	1907	n/a	0.60	0.40	0.50	100
Spain	Seville	1907	n/a	0.58	0.42	0.50	100
Tunisia	Sfax	1908	n/a	0.43	n/a	0.43	86
Turkey	Broussa	1908	n/a	0.28	0.24	0.26	52

Period 1927/1928

Country	Region	Year	Hours worked	US dollars		Weighted average		Italy = 100	Weighted average	
				Male	Female	I	II		I	II
France	Languedoc	1927–28	7.5	0.87	0.48	0.55	0.69		136	153
Italy	Puglia	1927–28	7.5	0.51	0.38	0.41	0.45		100	100
Spain	Andalusia	c. 1927	n/a	0.67	0.42	0.47	0.55		115	123
Greece	n/a	1928	n/a	0.78	0.39	0.47	0.60		114	133

continued on next page

Table 7.8 Daily wages for olive harvesters in the Mediterranean around 1907, 1927 and 1933 (cont.)

Period 1933/1936

| Country | Region | Year | Hours worked | US dollars | | | | Italy = 100 | |
| | | | | Male | Female | Weighted average | | Weighted average | |
						I	II	I	II
France	Marseilles	1933	n/a	1.27	0.70	0.81	1.00	183	202
Italy	Naples	1933	7.5	0.57	0.41	0.44	0.50	100	100
Spain	Andalusia	1936	n/a	0.73	0.46	0.51	0.60	116	121
Greece	Creta/Corfu	1933/34	n/a	0.55	0.28	0.33	0.42	74	85
Tunisia	Sfax/Susa	1933	n/a	0.52	0.29	0.33	0.41	75	83
Palestine	n/a	1933	7.5	0.39	0.22	0.25	0.31	57	62

Sources: see text, endnotes and Ramon-Muñoz (2000).

Notes:
I It is assumed that the total hours required in harvesting are distributed as follows: men 19% and women 81%.
II It is assumed that the total hours required in harvesting are distributed as follows: men 53% and women 47%.

and to land and labour productivity in the countryside.[25] Tables 7.8 and 7.9 provide information on both aspects for a relatively wide sample of Mediterranean countries.

Table 7.8 compares harvesters' daily wages in the Mediterranean olive oil industry for three benchmark periods: 1907–8, 1927–8 and 1933–6. Certainly, these data have several limitations. The most important concerns the nature and homogeneity of the wages themselves. Sources available do not always report either the number of hours worked by harvesters or the proportion of male and female harvesters. The first problem, i.e. working hours, is extremely difficult to solve and it is likely that, with the exception of Italy and France, cross-country comparisons have to assume a margin of error of around 10 per cent.[26] The second problem refers to gender distribution in harvesting. Women and, to a lesser extent, children were largely employed both in gathering the olives which had fallen to the ground and in collecting the fruit from the tree. Since their wages were lower than those of men, a different intensity in the employment of women and children relative to men also implied differences in labour costs and, thus, in final costs. This problem can perhaps be overcome by considering two alternative estimates, namely that female workers were intensively employed (estimate I) and that male and female workers were employed in similar proportions (estimate II). Estimates are presented in the table and tend to show the upper and lower limits of the possible gap in labour costs.

Table 7.9, on the other hand, provides information on yields of olive oil over the period 1890–1938, expressed both in kilograms of olive oil per hectare and in kilograms per tree. It should be noted that the former indicator, product per hectare, may be misleading because the number of trees planted per unit of land is extremely variable. Instead, product per tree appears to be a more appropriate measure of productivity and, when data are available, it is preferred. Once again, it must be stressed that data reported in the table are not always satisfactory. Although they have been mainly computed from information elaborated by the reputable International Institute of Agriculture, they still remain as rough indicators rather than definitive figures.

Despite all these limitations, the picture emerging from these tables is enormously suggestive. At first glance, the tables show the existence of a substantial difference in costs per unit of output among the Mediterranean olive-oil producers, ranging from the highest in France to the lowest in Tunisia. Of the northwesterners, Spain was the lowest-cost producer of bulk olive oil whereas among the southerners and easterners, Tunisia had the leadership in terms of low unit cost per output. However, a closer examination of these tables also suggests the existence of common features among the northwestern Mediterranean countries on the one hand, and the southerners and easterners on the other. The former appear to be characterized by having higher wages, lower yields and, therefore, higher costs per unit of output than most of their Mediterranean competitors. The contrary holds

Table 7.9 Olive oil yields per hectare and per tree in selected Mediterranean countries 1890–1938

| | *Yield per hectare** | | | | | | | |
| | *In kgs* | | | | *Relative to Italy (Italy = 100)* | | | |
	c.1890	*c.1913*	*c.1929*	*c.1938*	*c.1890*	*c.1913*	*c.1929*	*c.1938*
France	98	79	77	70	44	56	39	41
Italy	222	142	197	168	100	100	100	100
Spain	175	158	206	174	79	111	105	104
Tunisia	n/a	144	145	140	n/a	101	74	83
Algeria	n/a	n/a	n/a	n/a	n/a	n/a	n/a	n/a
Greece	n/a	228	191	226	n/a	161	97	134
Turkey	n/a	n/a	n/a	28	n/a	n/a	n/a	17
	*Yield per tree in bearing**							
	In kgs				*Relative to Italy (Italy = 100)*			
	c.1890	*c.1913*	*c.1929*	*c.1938*	*c.1890*	*c.1913*	*c.1929*	*c.1938*
France	n/a	0.5	0.5	0.4	n/a	46	30	33
Italy	n/a	1.2	1.8	1.3	n/a	100	100	100
Spain	n/a	1.7	2.3	1.9	n/a	146	128	143
Tunisia	n/a	3.9	3.8	3.3	n/a	325	212	244
Algeria	n/a	4.3	n/a	1.5	n/a	360	n/a	110
Greece	n/a	n/a	2.6	2.3	n/a	n/a	146	169
Turkey	n/a	n/a	n/a	1.3	n/a	n/a	n/a	97

* Yields only refer to olive trees growing in unmixed areas.
Source and notes: see Table 7.3.

for the latter. This general pattern seems clear for the years prior to World War I. Indeed, Tunisia produced bulk olive oil at lower costs than France, Italy and, probably, Spain. Data on yields of olive oil per tree around 1913 suggest that unit costs were also relatively lower in Algeria,[27] and perhaps also in Turkey, where harvesters' wages were around 50 per cent lower than Italian ones. For the interwar years, it is more difficult to establish clear conclusions on account of the lack of economic stability. In general, however, the situation was probably not so different from that found for the years before 1913. Tunisia maintained its cost-advantage over the northwestern Mediterranean producers. This was also true for Greece when compared to France and Italy. Greek productivity differential seems large enough to compensate

Table 7.10 Estimated costs of refining and packaging olive oil in Italy and the United States, 1928–30

Cost of producing 1 metric tonne of refined olive oil in Italy			Cost of packaging 1 metric tonne of olive oil in the United States		
	Dollars	*%*		*Dollars*	*%*
Oil for refining	327	85.4	Olive oil	497	79.9
Labour	9	2.5	Direct labour	11	1.8
Power	2	0.5	Administrative expenses	20	3.2
Factory overheads	11	2.9	Cans and cases	65	10.5
Depreciation and interest on capital	34	8.7	Factory overheads	20	3.2
			Interest on investment	9	1.4
Total	383	100.0	Total	622	100.0

Source and notes: Ramon-Muñoz (2000).

for its high wages during the mid-1920s. By contrast, cost-advantages for Algeria and Turkey are more difficult to assess on account of a lack of information about wages.

Luckily, the cost evidence seems to be supported by qualitative information. For example, the relative Italian disadvantage in producing bulk olive oil after World War I coincides with the view of some Italian contemporaries.[28] The cost data also agree with the Spanish historiography, which for the interwar period has stressed both the Greek and Tunisian low-cost competition relative to Spain (Zambrana 1987: 306; Simpson 1995: 217).

Technology and labour skills in the production of brand-name olive oil

Mediterranean differences in farm wages and yields are only a part of the story, however. Technology and labour skills were also different among olive-oil producers, as the analysis of the production of brand-name olive oil will immediately show. This analysis will also show another major aspect: relative to bulk olive oil, the production of brand-name olive oil was a more capital and labour-skilled activity.

Refining, blending and packaging were the main operations carried out in the production of brand-name olive oil, an activity located mainly in coastal cities. Table 7.10 offers data on production costs for two of these operations, i.e. refining and packaging, in the late 1920s. The data are not, however, comparable as they refer to two different countries: Italy and the United States. In spite of this, what is striking is the enormous importance that the raw material, i.e. bulk olive oil, had in the final cost of the product, accounting for 80 per cent or more. The two other major costs, namely depreciation and interest on capital and cans and cases, accounted for 11 and 9 per cent respectively, while the costs of labour appear comparatively insignificant, both in refining and packaging.

Unfortunately, no comparative evidence for costs has been found, either in refining and blending or in packaging. At the present stage of research, almost nothing can be said. Contemporary data shows that in the 1920s tins were supplied to the Italian exporters at better rates than to the Spanish ones and, probably, than to other southern and eastern Mediterranean export-ers.[29] And, unlike eastern Mediterranean producers, cost advantages associ-ated with the economies of scale seem to have benefitted Italian refiners, since large refining plants had been set up after World War I.[30]

The fact is, however, that the main input required by the refining industry, i.e. bulk olive oil, was produced by most of the southern and eastern Mediter-ranean producers at lower costs. Despite this, they did not develop a solid industry of refining, blending and packaging olive oil. This makes it neces-sary to explore in more detail other areas influencing efficiency, and also competitiveness, in international markets for brand-name olive oil. Technol-ogy and labour skills seem to be two of the best candidates. Both have been considered key factors explaining countries' leadership in the world econ-omy. Literature in the field has also suggested that they were essential in the production of brand-name olive oil, not only because they lowered costs per unit of output but because they guaranteed quality and product homogeneity.

Indeed, a firm competing in the international market had to focus its ini-tial attention on one key aspect: the quality of the bulk olive oil employed in producing brand-name olive oil and, of course, on its regular supply. The quality of the olive oil employed was important, because olive oils of lower quality, or those with a deficient filtering, rendered the final product rancid, thereby damaging the credit of the firm among consumers.

Certainly, there was a wide range of factors influencing the quality of bulk olive oil, including the nature of the soil, the climate, the species of the olive tree cultivated and its care, the method used in harvesting or the length of time for which olives remained stored. But as the Spanish literature has pointed out, the speed and modernity of the machinery used in pressing the olives, which in turn affected the time that olives had to remain stored, had a major influence on the final quality of the product (Zambrana 1987: 145–51; Simpson 1995: 171). The substitution of the old wooden presses with new hydraulic ones, especially when they employed mechanical power, was prob-ably one of the major events in the modernization of bulk olive-oil produc-tion prior to World War I.

From the eve of World War I, technology became even more essential, this time due to the expansion of industrial refining plants, which implied switch-ing from manual techniques to mechanized filtering and refining. This mechanization was probably a response to the expansion of the demand for brand-name olive oil. Between 1890 and 1913 world demand for brand-name olive oil grew by around 5 per cent per year. To avoid shortages in the supply of raw materials, especially of virgin oils, exporters set up industrial refining plants, which allowed the use of olive oils of medium and low quality and, therefore, an increase in the supply of edible olive oils. Establishing refining plants had another consequence: through the production of neutral olive oils the standardization of the final product was improved, something extremely important for a brand's reputation. As a final result, once industrial plants were expanded, most of the brand-name olive oil was made by blending refined olive oil with a fine one. The latter gave the final product a suitable flavour, taste and colour; and the percentage of fine olive oil contained in the tin was a good indicator of the quality of the product itself. Of course, regular supplies of fine and refined olive oils were essential to maintain the brand in the market.

There can be little doubt that over the first third of the twentieth century the production of brand-name olive oil became a capital-intensive activity. The replacement of old olive-oil presses with modern ones required a considerable cash investment, not only because of the higher price of the presses themselves, but also because the scale of the mills had to be adjusted to their larger capacity. According to James Simpson, mills using modern machinery required an initial investment 50 per cent higher than those using old presses. The use of hydraulic presses had a second consequence: it reduced the demand for labour by around 35 per cent per unit of olive oil produced (Simpson 1995: 170; 1985: 186 and 239). In fact, substituting old presses with modern ones also implied substituting labour with capital.

However, it was in refining that the initial capital investment was more important. The first Italian refineries were set up by an association of single olive-oil exporters, which suggests the amount of capital required; Zunino, in his book on the Italian olive-oil market on the eve of World War II, observed that in fact the magnitude of the capital to be invested in the plants led, generally, towards the formation of joint-stock companies (Cerisola 1973: 37–8; Zunino 1939: 85–7). There was an important reason explaining the dimensions of the refineries: the plants should have a minimum scale to benefit from the economies of scale existing in this industry.[31] On the other hand, it has to be added that the costs of the variable capital were also substantial in refining, partly because of the large stocks of olive oil to cover yearly needs.[32] This contrasted with the production of bulk olive oil, since mills did not work for more than four months and stocks of olives tended to be relatively low.

If technological change was a first step towards the production of brand-name olive oil, the ability to produce uniform types of the product, adjusted to the foreign market's taste, was equally significant. Branding olive oil was intended to differentiate the product from that of the competitors, but also to assure that it would remain homogeneous over time, especially in taste. It also implied that it was adjusted to consumers' taste, and it was not uncommon for the same firm to market different brands according to the country or to the segments of the market where it was sold. Therefore, both in order

Table 7.11 The mechanization of olive oil factories: Italy, Spain and Greece, 1903 and 1911

		1903			1911		
		Number of firms		*%*	*Number of firms*		*%*
		Mechanised (1)	*Total (2)*	*(1)/(2)*	*Mechanised (1)*	*Total (2)*	*(1)/(2)*
Italy		2 963	18 732	15.8	1 693	7 274	23.3
Spain	(a)	340	4 975	6.8	484	4 250	11.4
	(b)	634	4 975	12.7	844	4 250	19.9
Greece		n/a	n/a	n/a	174	5 721	3.0

Sources: see text, endnotes and Ramon-Muñoz (2000).

Notes
(a) Firms using hydraulic presses driven by mechanical power.
(b) Firms using hydraulic pressses whatever the power employed.

to produce different commercial types of olive oil and to keep them homogeneous, it was necessary to properly blend many varieties of fine and refined olive oil. In these areas, specific skills were considered essential. Indeed, before the expansion of modern refineries, tasters seem to have played a crucial role in evaluating varieties, qualities and uniformity of olive oils. The same could be said regarding olive-oil packers, who tended to use filtering processes.[33] With the expansion of the industrial refineries, the control of product homogeneity was improved, but this did not mean that labour skills were neglected in the olive-oil business. As late as 1923, a report on the olive oil industry of Málaga, in southern Spain, pointed out that blending virgin olive oil with refined oil was a process that had to be verified by "the expert tasting of the skilled cellar man".[34] This report also mentioned that skills in tasting, blending and establishing the final quality of the product were mainly acquired after long experience, which shows the importance of accumulation of labour skills in this industrial activity.

Were southern and eastern Mediterranean olive-oil producers more reluctant to accept technical change? Were skills more abundant in the northwestern Mediterranean? Table 7.11 presents the approximate levels of mechanization in the olive-oil industry before World War I.[35] Although the sample of countries listed in the table is clearly insufficient, it suggests that technological change had been extremely slow among eastern Mediterranean producers. It also shows the Italian technological leadership compared to Spain.[36] Consular information complements and confirms this picture. The American consul of Constantinople, for example, said that "in many regions the system of olive pressing is most rudimentary and in some districts is very similar to that employed by the ancient Jews";[37] from Tunisia it was stressed that "two-thirds of the oil produced comes from Arab mills, where the processes are most rudimentary";[38] and consular information for Algeria said that "there are 30,000 small native oil presses (...), while there are only 1,300 to 1,400 establishments with modern equipment" (Thompson 1913: 29).

As for the industrial refineries, there is a conspicuous absence of clear references for most of the Mediterranean olive-oil producers. The only clear information refers to Italy, where in the region of Liguria at least two industrial refineries were set up before 1914,[39] and to France, where one company was formed in Nice by 1912 and many manufacturers of seed oils installed plants for the deodorization of olive oil in Marseille (Thompson 1913: 9). In Spain, there were factories employing refining processes, but it is not known whether they adopted industrial and mechanical methods, nor is anything known about the real success of these new technologies (Zambrana 1993: 78). For Greece, an Italian report says that in some factories olive oil was refined, but the information suggests that this was not done in industrial refining plants (MAIC 1912: 117). It is likely that prior to World War I, the Italians and the French remained the leaders in modern methods of refining.

The interwar period did not substantially modify the pre-war technological gap. Although Tunisia, followed by Greece and Turkey in the late 1920s, had made significant improvements, the technological gap within the Mediterranean basin persisted. In 1920, 22 per cent of mills were driven by mechanical power in Tunisia, but by the mid-1920s this country had only one industrial refining plant (Ferrara 1927: 132 and 178–9). In Greece the number of factories using mechanical power almost quadrupled between 1911 and 1931, but on the eve of World War II it was still possible to find descriptions stressing the small size of the Greek mills, the low power of their machinery and their rudimentary equipment (Statistique Général de la Grèce 1933: 165; Zunino 1939: 168). The same could be said for Turkey. In the olive-oil regions bordering on the Aegean Sea, i.e. Balikestir, Manisa, Izmir, Aydin and Mugla, new factories using mainly oil as motive-power had been set up after the Greek–Turkish War, but only one of them had incorporated the modern methods of production.[40] Furthermore, in both Greece and Turkey the presence of industrial refineries was relatively insignificant, and contemporaries writing in the late 1930s described two countries exporting a product with high levels of acidity.[41]

In terms of technical change, the Spanish performance is perhaps the most remarkable. If during the decade prior to 1913 Spain had been falling behind the western Mediterranean producers, by the early 1920s it had already caught up with them. In 1927, the modernization of the mills was similar to Italy's, and by 1935 it had already overtaken Italy in both the number and the capacity of its refineries.[42]

Besides technology, the possession of techniques and skills was another important step towards the production of brand-name olive oil. It is difficult to evaluate these factors, and, in fact, here the evidence is scarce and only refers to four countries: France, Italy, Spain and Greece. Although references are extremely superficial, they suggest that France, Italy, and, after World War I, Spain were also the most developed countries in terms of labour skills. In 1907, for example, an American report concluded that in Spain "refining is also done on a large scale, but the results are not comparable with those obtained by Italian and French refineries" (Manufactures Bureau 1907: 110). This was even worse in Greece, since refining methods were just starting on the eve of World War I and deficiencies in the bulk olive-oil industry were negatively influencing the quality of the final product (MAIC 1912: 119). In 1924 a documented study from the University of California also confirmed "the more rapid progress made in Italy and France in the refining, blending, packaging, and foreign marketing of olive oil" (Cruess 1924: 3). The same study recognized, however, that Spain had overcome its initial inferiority by the early 1920s.

A closer look at the French and Italian experiences also shows that labour skills tended to develop in those areas of olive-oil production with initial advantages in product quality. Indeed, in the first half of the nineteenth century, the regions of Provence in southern France, and of Tuscany and Liguria in northern Italy, were already producing fine olive oils. It is difficult to establish the causes of these early improvements, since the more relevant changes in the technology of the industry did not take place until the second half of the century. Natural endowments might have played a significant role in the quality of the product, as an American report about Tuscany suggested (Rosenthal 1896: 317–8). The fact is, however, that as a consequence of their quality, olive oils from these regions could penetrate more easily into foreign markets for edible olive oil. By the mid-nineteenth century several brands from the French city of Marseille were already being widely accepted abroad.[43] By the 1870s and 1880s, as Spanish and Italian consular reports noted (Dirección General de Aduanas 1876; MAIC 1890), there was a notable presence of brands from Liguria and Tuscany both in South America and Europe. If the increase in olive-oil exports is a good indicator of product acceptance abroad, then there is little doubt that the olive oil of these regions was being widely accepted. Between the periods 1870–4 and 1895–9 the French exports tripled and the quantity of Italian olive oil sent to the Americas more than doubled.

This increase in the demand challenged, in turn, the activity of French and Italian exporters. First, domestic supply of fine olive oils became occasionally insufficient, which made it necessary to blend olive oils from other regions or countries. Second, variety in tastes and preferences among foreign consumers grew as demand increased, which imposed the production of several varieties of olive oil. As a response to these challenges, exporters started to develop methods of filtering, refining and blending as well as techniques of product standardization.

To some extent, before the expansion of the international markets for brand-name olive oil, Provence, Liguria and Tuscany were already leading regions in terms of refining and blending techniques. By the end of the nine-teenth century they were also the model for many Mediterranean exporters to imitate. It is highly illustrative that the Catalan, Manuel Porcar y Tió, one of the few Spanish olive-oil exporters who had been able to gain credit for his brand name in the Argentine market by 1880, had started his industrial and commercial activity with "previous knowledge acquired personally in the counties of Tuscany and Provence" (Aguiló 1918: 65).

In conclusion, available information suggests that on the eve of World War II most of the southern and eastern Mediterranean producers were too far behind France, Italy and even Spain to catch up easily. It is true that they had improved their mills and mechanized presses, thus improving the quality of the product; Tunisia, with the help of French investments, was probably lead-ing these processes of technological change. However, it is also true that in the southern and eastern Mediterranean, the olive-oil industry could still be char-acterized in general by its slow adoption of up-to-date methods of producing bulk olive oil, its reluctance in setting up industrial refineries and, last but not least, its relative absence of labour skills and techniques in blending olive oil.

The causes of specialization: some hypotheses

Although much research is still needed, the quantitative and qualitative evi-dence presented previously shows the existence of significant differences in farm wages, yields, technology and labour skills among the Mediterranean olive-oil producers during the first third of the twentieth century. The same evidence stresses two main aspects which are especially relevant for the under-standing of patterns of specialization in the international market for olive oil.

The first aspect deals with efficiency and, therefore, with relative costs. Unfortunately, at the present stage of research it is impossible to measure the units of labour, capital or land required in the production of one unit of bulk olive oil relative to the production of one unit of brand-name olive oil. This makes it impossible to obtain accurate measures on relative efficiency among the Mediterranean olive-oil producers. Despite this important limitation, the information presented in the first two parts of this section suggests that not all Mediterranean countries were equally efficient either in the production of bulk olive oil or the production of brand-name olive oil. France and Italy appear to be more efficient in refining, blending and marketing olive oil than in making bulk olive oil, which was produced at relatively high costs. The contrary holds for the southern and eastern Mediterranean producers, not only because some of them enjoyed both high yields in olive oil and low farm-wages but mainly because of their relative resistance to technological change, especially in refining methods, as well as the relative scarcity of labour skills. The interwar Spanish experience results, instead, more diffi-cult to define, as will be discussed below. Considered as a whole, however, these are interesting findings since they would indicate that olive-oil produc-ers generally tended to export the type of olive oil they could produce more efficiently and, thus, at a relatively lower cost. In other words, they tended to specialize in exporting the type of olive oil in which they had a comparative advantage.

The second aspect has to do with the sources of this comparative advantage. This is a difficult matter. However, the information on farm wages, yields, technology and labour skills, together with other available evidence, suggests that the price of the factors of production and, therefore, factor endowments were different around the Mediterranean basin. Indeed, as already shown, labour skills in refining and blending were relatively abundant among the northwestern Mediterranean producers, especially in Mediterranean France and northern Italy. On the contrary, the existing evidence on farm wages, although scarce, seems to indicate that labour costs tended to be lower in most of the southern and eastern Mediterranean economies, showing either the relative abundance of the workforce engaged in agriculture or the existence of under-utilized labour in the rural areas of the economy.[44] Shortage of physical capital was probably another characteristic of the southern and eastern Mediterranean when compared to the northwest. Estimates on Gross Domestic Product, for example, suggest that in 1913 and 1929 countries like Greece or Turkey tended to have a relatively modest and investment-saving potential, as a result of their lower income and, perhaps, their less equal income distribution.[45]

Although it cannot be tested, both the existence of low-cost farm labour and a relatively modest potential investment might have negatively affected the modernization of the olive-oil industry in southern and eastern Europe. This does not mean, however, that other complementary factors have not played their role in explaining this slow modernization. Domestic tastes, which, of course, can be related to income levels, appear to be the most evident. According to Italian taste standards in the mid-1920s, Greeks, Tunisians and Turks tended to consume olive oils of an acidity higher than 3°.[46] In France, Italy and Spain, these olive oils tended to be used for refining purposes. With such preferences in the domestic markets, southern and eastern Mediterranean olive-oil producers probably felt little encouragement to introduce modern machinery and industrial refining plants, which, as has been repeatedly said, were essential to export "superior" sorts of product.[47]

Finally, it is also interesting to note that some under-utilized land was still available in these countries, as is suggested by the fact that during the 1920s and 1930s Tunisia, Greece and Turkey substantially enlarged both their total cultivated area and their olive-growing area, which remained virtually unchanged among the northwesterners.[48]

If, as shown previously, the production of bulk olive oil was a land–labour intensive activity whereas the production of brand-name olive oil made more intensive use of physical and human capital, differences in endowments may have had important implications in determining trade patterns among the olive-oil exporters. Perhaps not surprisingly, the southern and eastern Mediterranean countries concentrated on exporting bulk olive oil. In other

Table 7.12 The importance of improvement trade in olive oil: France and Italy, 1870–1938 (percentages)*

	France				Italy			
	Imports		Exports		Imports		Exports	
	I	II	III	IV	I	II	III	IV
1870–74	94.3	5.7	73.3	26.7	100.0	0.0	100.0	0.0
1890–94	83.9	16.1	65.1	34.9	100.0	0.0	100.0	0.0
1909–13	62.5	37.5	33.8	662	162	834	56.7	43.3
1925–29	70.5	29.6	44.7	553	1.2	988	19.5	80.5
1934–38	nd	nd	nd	nd	9.0	91.0	4.7	95.3

Source: Ramon-Muñoz (2000).

Notes
* Original data in quantities, five-year averages.
I Olive oil imported for domestic consumption as a percentage of total olive oil imports.
II Olive oil imported for refining and blending purposes under the regime of temporary admission as a percentage of total olive oil imports.
III Domestic olive oil exports as a percentage of total olive oil exports.
IV Refined and blended olive oil re-exports as a percentage of total olive oil exports.

words, they concentrated on the first stages of olive-oil production, those requiring, apart from land, a relative abundance of farm labour. By contrast, the production of brand-name olive oil, which in turn was associated with the production of good-quality bulk olive oil, would have required a more intensive use of physical capital, i.e. modern olive-oil presses and industrial refining plants, and human capital, i.e. specific labour skills in refining and blending olive oil.

Regarding northwestern Mediterranean exporters, trade patterns also appear to have been mainly conditioned by their different factor endowments. Relative scarcity of low-cost farm labour (together with low yields in olive oil) but relative abundance of physical and human capital, compared to the rest of the Mediterranean producers, appear to be essential to explain the northwesterners' specialization in exporting "superior" sorts of olive oil. These facts can help us to understand, for example, why Mediterranean France tended to import, instead of producing, massive quantities of bulk olive oil to be refined, blended with domestic olive oils, packaged and, finally, re-exported. They can also explain why the area devoted to olive trees and olive-oil production was decreasing in France while in its "dominions" of Tunisia (and to a lesser extent Algeria), with cheaper labour costs, more land availability and higher yields, olive cultivation was being extended.[49] Finally, comparatively low efficiency in producing bulk olive oil would explain why the northern Italian exporters behaved similarly to the French ones, i.e. importing bulk olive oil and exporting brand-name oil.[50] Table 7.12 illustrates the importance of this trade pattern for France and Italy.

Spain deserves further comment. A relative unit-cost advantage in producing olives and bulk olive oil had contributed to the expansion of its olive-growing area; and remarkable improvements in technology and techniques had allowed it not only to export bulk olive oil of medium and superior quality but also to sell the product under brand names. This trade pattern differed, however, from the French and, what is even more significant, the Italian ones. This divergence is not surprising for the period prior to World War I. The Spanish position in international markets probably reflected its relatively lower levels of physical and human capital accumulation in the olive-oil industry. However, the same is not true for the interwar years. In this period, Spain's technology and labour skills appear to be quite similar to those of Italy. Although this issue will require a closer analysis, it is likely that Spain paid the cost of being a latecomer in international markets for brand-name olive oil. In 1924, W. Cruess from the College of Agriculture at the University of California, affirmed,

> In recent years, Spain has made great progress in oil making and refining. She now possesses modern mills and up-to-date refineries. As a result, the average quality of her oils has been greatly improved and her fine oils rank with the best of Italy and France. The difficulty has been to convince consumers and dealers of this fact. Consequently large quantities of Spanish oil are still exported to Marseilles, Genoa, and other foreign refining centers for blending purposes.
>
> (Cruess 1924: 3)

Five years later, M. Longoria, a reputed Spanish exporter, also recognized that being a latecomer acted as an entry barrier to the market. According to him, the American consumers' taste "was created both by the Italian and French competitors (...). They dominated markets many years before our exports started. At the beginning, we were trying, [without success], to impose on the American markets our natural olive oils, which have a stronger taste and flavor".[51]

There is another aspect that needs to be mentioned. Most brand-name olive oil was consumed in the Americas by Latin emigrants. And, as Blanca Sánchez-Alonso shows in this book, the Spanish migration towards the Americas was relatively low compared to the Italian. This fact might have influenced the weaker Spanish penetration in markets for brand-name olive oil. Table 7.13 provides information on foreign-born population and market shares in the United States and Argentina, the world's largest import markets for brand-name olive oil, and Spain and Italy, the world's largest exporters of olive oil, in three benchmark periods: 1890, 1913 and 1929. The table shows clearly the relatively small size of the Spanish-born population in these two markets as well as the modest Spanish presence in the market for olive oil around 1890. Between that year and 1929, the Spanish-born population increased, especially in Argentina, but even in this importing market Spain

Table 7.13 Migration and market penetration in the United States and Argentina, 1890–1930

Panel 1:	Foreign-born population							
	United States		Argentina		United States		Argentina	
	Italian	*Spanish*	*Italian*	*Spanish*	*Italian*	*Spanish*	*Italian*	*Spanish*
	(in thousands)				*(as % of Mediterranean born population)*			
c. 1890	187	6	493	199	58.0	1.9	62.7	25.3
c. 1913	1 343	22	930	830	77.4	1.3	50.2	44.8
1930	1 790	59	n/a	n/a	76.0	2.5	n/a	n/a

Panel 2:	Olive oil imports and share in the market							
	United States		Argentina		United States		Argentina	
	Italy	*Spain*	*Italy*	*Spain*	*Italy*	*Spain*	*Italy*	*Spain*
	(in metric tonnes)				*(as % of total olive oil imports)*			
1890/94	1 431	10	3 791	190	59.6	0.4	75.1	3.8
1909/13	10 273	907	14 082	6 247	66.2	5.8	64.3	28.6
1925/29								
Brand	20 885	1 353	—	—	90.5	5.9	—	—
Bulk	5 448	6 867	—	—	35.5	44.7	—	—
Total	26 334	8 220	30 298	9 953	68.5	21.4	70.1	23.0

Source and notes: Ramon-Muñoz (2000).

achieved relatively modest shares. It might be that the massive and earlier presence of Italians in the American markets had long-term consequences; for example, by facilitating the control of the commercial networks or by giving Italian firms a certain market power as first entrants. However, further research at firm level should confirm this hypothesis.

Conclusions

This chapter has analysed patterns of specialization in the international markets for olive oil before World War II. It has shown that within the Mediterranean basin, northwesterners on the one hand, and southerners and easterners on the other, tended to export different types of olive oil in terms of quality, uses, stage of elaboration and added value. While the former specialized in exporting a "superior" sort of product, the latter exported olive oil of lower quality and less added value. The analysis of quantitative and qualitative information on farm wages, yields in olive oil, technology and labour skills indicates that Mediterranean countries specialized in the export of the type of olive oil produced at a relatively lower cost and, therefore, more efficiently, as the theories of comparative advantage would predict. Although much research is still needed, this information, together with other available evidence, also suggests that differences in relative costs and technology among Mediterranean countries roughly reflected differences in factor endowments. In other words, olive-oil producers appear to have exported the type of product that best suited their endowment.

Having said this, it is also true that both northwestern and southern and eastern Mediterranean olive-oil producers formed a heterogeneous group of countries; in fact, within these two groups no country occupied exactly the same position in the international market for the product, despite their similarities in labour skills, farm-labour costs or technology. Of the north-westerners, the case of Spain in the interwar period is the most apparent, and it suggests that an explanation of these different performances within the groups will probably need to take into account other factors in addition to those stressed by the theories of comparative advantage.

Our findings are still tentative. They only refer to olive oil, which was an important commodity in the exports of the countries considered here, but it was not the dominant one. Despite this, they suggest two general remarks on economic performance before World War II. First, it seems that remarkable processes of specialization took place within the Mediterranean basin in the period under consideration. Research available for other Mediterranean products, such as wine and cork, seems to provide evidence in the same direction.[52] If these processes of specialization were really so widespread, one might conclude that while Mediterranean countries were trading similar goods, they tended to cover different segments of the international demand.

The second remark is of a more general nature. Literature on international trading patterns has noted that the character of goods which countries export and import informs about their level of economic development. Federico's research on the world silk industry, a first and excellent example of commodity analysis in historical perspective, has arrived at similar conclusions.[53] If true, the findings in the case of olive oil, a major export commodity in the countries bordering on the Mediterranean basin, can provide further evidence to illustrate the existence of both different economic structures and different levels of economic development among Mediterranean countries.

Notes

I am grateful to Isabel Bartolomé, Jordi Catalan, Alfonso Herranz, Miguel Gutierrez, Jordi Nadal, Şevket Pamuk, Vicente Pinilla, Jaime Reis, James Simpson, Carles Sudrià, Daniel Tirado and Jeffrey Williamson for their help and useful comments on earlier versions of this paper. I am also indebted to the participants at the Istanbul conference on *Long-Run Economic Change in the Mediterranean Basin* who have contributed enormously to improve a previous version of this article. All remaining errors are mine. A working paper with appendix materials, notes and sources is available upon request, cited here as Ramon-Muñoz (2000).

1   For example, between 1882 and 1913 raisins accounted for 40 per cent of total Greek exports, and for 24 per cent of the Turkish ones (Morilla 1995: 269). For a general view on levels of export concentration in four Mediterranean countries, i.e. Italy, Spain, Portugal and Turkey, see Federico (1988: 182). By the 1880s, olive oil ranked third among Italian exports, and fifth among Turkish ones; and by the late 1920s it had become the third-largest commodity exported by Spain and Tunisia, and the fourth-largest exported by Greece. The percentage share of olive oil in total value of national exports was: Italy (1886), 7.6; Ottoman Empire (1880–4), 4.3; Spain (1925–9), 7.4; Tunisia (1925–9), 17.3; Greece (1927–9), 3. For Italy, see Zamagni (1990: 17). Trends on Italian olive-oil exports between 1863 and 1913, both in values and as a percentage of total agricultural exports, can be found in Federico (1979). For the Ottoman Empire, see Aybar (1939: 55). For references to olive oil as a major export commodity in the Ottoman Empire between the late nineteenth century and World War I see also Pamuk (1987: 99, 150, 156). For Spain, see Prados de la Escosura (1982, 1988: 237). For Greece, Statistique Générale de la Grèce (1930: 249–50). For Tunisia, see Direction Générale de l'Agriculture, du Commerce et de la Colonisation (1931).

2   Crafts and Thomas (1986), Estevedeordal (1993), Wright (1990). See also O'Rourke and Williamson (1994).

3   Always attributing a lower quality to bulk olive oil when compared to brand-name oil might, however, be a mistake. As mentioned, there was a wide range of qualities and prices in the case of bulk olive oil. From the end of the nineteenth century at least, the largest import markets of this product distinguished clearly between extra, high, fine or ordinary olive oil. The best one, i.e. extra-fine or virgin olive oil, obtained from the first pressing of olives, was greatly appreciated and, in fact, could command better prices than any other brand-name olive oil. Of course, in the case of brand-name olive oil, international markets also differentiated between qualities through price discrimination.

4   For world trade in oilseeds and fats during the first half of the present century see Yates (1959: 91–5) and Zambrana (1987: 282–7). Olive-oil substitution for industrial purposes has been largely documented. See, for instance, Pierrein (1975: Ch. 3), for the soap industry in Marseille.

5   Ministero di Agricultura, Industria e Commercio (hereafter MAIC 1912: 158); *El Aceite de oliva de España*, (1931: n. 37, 8; 1934: n. 70, 311); and Institut International d'Agriculture (hereafter IIA 1939: 152).

6   The United Kingdom and the United States also imported sulphured oil. Olive oil production generated an after-pressing residue, referred to as olive stones. At the end of the nineteenth century, it was possible to easily obtain oil from olive stones by using chemical processes. The new product, called sulphured oil, began to replace the olive oil itself, especially in the manufacture of soap.

7   For the market of Argentina, see MAIC (1913: 186–7). Several examples of importers' preference for having their own brand name can be found in *Mercurio. Revista Comercial Iberio-Americana* (1913: n. 169 and 182).

8   See MAIC (1913) for Belgium (p. 29), Germany (p. 89), United Kingdom (p. 106), Norway (p. 136) and Switzerland (p. 196).

9   For detailed information about area and production in Spain, see Zambrana (1987: 51–110).

10   This general growth since the 1920s has to be stressed . Mediterranean olive-oil producers, however, also suffered from the competition of other vegetable oils, such as cotton, palm, copra and peanut. As mentioned, in the years prior to World War I vegetable oils began to replace olive oil for industrial purposes. In the 1920s, some of these vegetable oils were made edible by means of refining and deodorizing processes, which allowed them to compete with olive oil in the food market. Data provided by Yates (1959: 62), IIA (1911–39,

and IIA (1944: 304) show that oil seeds, vegetable oils and fat exports grew, in quantities, to an annual growth rate of 3.0 per cent between 1913 and 1929. According to the figures from the IIA, this was roughly the rate of growth experienced by the world olive-oil exports.

11 The Greek expansion is deceptive because it reflects territorial changes after World War I. However, the government also played an important role in promoting olive-oil cultivation during the interwar period (Zunino 1939: 164–8).

12 De Felice (1971: 135–45). See also Bevilacqua (1988: 277–86; 1989: 651–4).

13 Franciosa (1940: 5 and 35), and, for the region of Bari, De Felice (1971: 39).

14 This was a partial result of government intervention. Bacon and Schloemer (1940: 819 and 838–9).

15 Olive oil traded in small packages can be identified as traded under brand names. From the mid-1920s onwards, the foreign-trade statistics of Spain, Greece and Turkey detail the kind of package used in exporting olive oil. For Spain, statistics distinguish between packages weighing less than 20 kg and those weighing more than 20 kg. For, Greece the distinction is between bottles and packages weighing less than 5 kg and barrels. For Turkey the statistics distinguish between packages weighing less than 10 kg and those weighing more than 10 kg. On the other hand, in the interwar period Algerian foreign-trade statistics distinguish between edible and industrial exports of olive oil.

16 For example, from 1905 onwards British foreign-trade statistics distinguish between unrefined (industrial) and refined (edible) olive oil. United States foreign-trade statistics also give detailed information on imports of olive oil both for edible and industrial purposes in the years following 1906. From 1924 onwards, they also detail the size of package used in the imports. In this connection, packages of less than 40 lb have been identified as containing brand-name olive oil.

17 Ministerio de Estado (1899, 1900, 1920, 1922), MAIC (1907, 1912, 1913), and Istituto Nazionale per l'Esportazione (1927). According to these sources, and with the exception of the United States, olive oil exported to the Americas was mostly in small packages and under brand names, whereas it was mainly exported to the largest European markets in bulk. By 1913, olive oil exported to Russia was mainly for industrial purposes. Finally, according to the IIA and other available information, it is considered that most of the olive oil exported by France consisted of high-quality olive oil, which was mainly traded under brand names. The only exceptions are for the olive oil exported to Norway and Italy, which is considered to be bulk olive oil. Information from the United Kingdom and the USA has also been considered in order to estimate French exports of bulk and industrial olive oil.

18 The importing countries are: (a) for the period 1909–13, Argentina, Austria–Hungary, Belgium, Brazil, Bulgaria, Chile, Cuba, Egypt, France, Germany, Italy, Mexico, Norway, Peru, Romania, Russia, Switzerland, the United Kingdom, the United States and Uruguay; (b) for the period 1925–9, the following countries have not been included in the calculations: Egypt, Romania, Russia and the central European states established after World War I, such as Czechoslovakia, Poland and Hungary, formerly part of the Austro–Hungarian monarchy, and Germany. The importing countries covered, in the period 1909–13, the following share of the total olive oil exported by the exporting countries: Italy, 98 per cent; Spain, 84 per cent; Greece, 94 per cent; the Ottoman Empire, 93 per cent; Algeria and Tunisia, more than 95 per cent. For the period 1925–9, the percentages were: Italy, 93 per cent; Spain, 85 per cent; Greece, 75 per cent; Turkey, 97 per cent; Algeria and Tunisia, more than 95 per cent.

19 For the Greek case, see, for example, MAIC (1913: 118), Mears (1929: 60–2) and Zunino (1939: 168). For Turkey, see IIA (1939: 185).

20 For surveys on empirical evidence on trade theories see, for example, Deardoff (1984) and Leamer (1994). Leamer adopts a broader perspective by considering that models based on monopolistic competition also explain comparative advantage. According to him, "the sources of comparative advantage are: (a) differences in technology, (b) differences in factor supplies, (c) economies of scale, (d) differences in tastes and (e) barriers to trade"

(p. 68). For models of trade with economies of scale and monopolistic competition see, for example, Helpman and Krugman (1985) and Grossman (1992).

21   For Spain, see Zambrana (1987: 178), and for Portugal, see Ministerio das Obras Publicas, Commercio e Industria (1889: Ch. 6). As late as 1970, manufacturing costs were still adding only some 10 per cent to the final price of the bulk olive oil (Parejo and Zambrana 1994: 21).

22   In the main areas of production, such as Andalusia (in southern Spain), olives were largely harvested by means of long rods. However, in the Greek island of Corfu, where olive oil was of considerable importance, olives were gathered from the ground. The same can be said for some areas of southern Italy. In the regions of Provence (southern France) and Tuscany (central Italy), the product was harvested by hand. For Spain, see Ministerio de Fomento (1923: 271–371); for France and Italy, see IIA (1939: 59 and 84–95), and for Greece, see Manufactures Bureau (1908b: 131). A brief survey on the methods used in harvesting as well as a valuation of them can be found in Skinner (1903: 407).

23   For Spain, see, for example, Ministerio de Fomento (1923: 279).

24   Confederazione Fascista degli Agricoltori e Settore della Olivicoltura della FNCPPA (1941), part I.

25   The costs of bulk olive oil were also affected by the use of modern machinery, which substantially increased labour productivity and reduced manufacturing costs. But since manufacturing costs only added 10 per cent of the final costs, as already said, its influence was also limited.

26   The working day used in the estimates is 7.5 hours. This was the working day in late-nineteenth-century southern Spain (Simpson 1992: 229).

27   For the case of Algeria, the American consul in Algiers stated that "there is no established daily wage, the natives picking their own olives" (Manufactures Bureau 1908: 73).

28   In 1922, Frezzoti (1922: 26), the director of the experimental olive-oil station in Porto Maurizio, argued that most olive-oil producers were able to supply cheaper bulk olive oil than Italy. By 1930, Borrelli (1930: 31), author of several essays on the olive oil industry, also suggested that costs of producing olive oil were higher in Italy than in Spain because of differences in land productivity.

29   In 1921, a wooden case containing 24 tins of 1.8 kg cost 28 pesetas in Spain but 19 pesetas in Italy. Casa de América (1922: 13). See also Ministerio de Trabajo, Comercio e Industria (1924: 7–11 and 66–71).

30   By 1935, Italy had 32 refining plants, with a production capacity averaging yearly 6,250 metric tonnes of refined olive oil per plant, whereas in the regions of Turkey bordering on the Aegean Sea, there were only two refineries with a capacity averaging 250 metric tonnes. Zunino (1939: 77) and *El Aceite de Oliva de España* (1934: 17).

31   According to Mariani's study, plants should have a refining capacity never lower than 7.5 metric tons of olive oil per day. Società Nazionale degli Olivicoltori Italiani (1927: 164).

32   Zunino (1939: 85–7). He also stresses that investment in variable capital is even higher because refineries tend to maintain stocks of different varieties of olive oils as well as of tins or cans, in order to satisfy consumer tastes and preferences. See also Manjarrés (1872: 156).

33   The American consul in the French city of Nice reported that "some of the packers make a great secret of their filtering process, but I am quite sure that it consists simply in some particular way of arranging the filters and in the number of layers of cotton used" (Manufactures Bureau 1907: 106).

34   According to Málaga's provincial agronomist, "the blend is made taking into account the origin of the fine [olive oil] and the refined [olive oil]. It is also made taking into account the right proportions and according to its [chemical] properties, which are distinguished by the expert tasting of the skilled cellar man (*maestro bodeguero*). The delicate sensibility of his palate can not be given to anybody; and he does not want to divulge his knowledge, which has been acquired after long experience ..." (Ministerio de Fomento 1923: 302).

The translation is mine. In this report, it is possible to find references for other Spanish places confirming the importance of skills.

35 Unlike Spain, Italian and Greek sources do not only refer to the presses employed in producing olive oil but also to the type of energy used by the firms. If it is considered that the hydraulic presses were mainly driven by mechanical power (steam or electricity), data presented in Table 7.11 reflect the modernization of the industry in the countries considered.

36 Table 7.11 presents two alternative calculations for Spain, and should be considered as lower (a) and upper (b) bounds. The actual figure should, therefore, fall between the two calculations.

37 Manufactures Bureau (1909: 122). The American consul of Beirut also insisted that "the mills most used are of primitive character and identical with those in vogue four thousand years ago" (Ravndal 1909: 82).

38 The consul also noted that the system of storing olives was deficient, which "gives a rancidity to the oil that renders it unpalatable to all except the native" (Manufactures Bureau 1908: 71–2).

39 According to Cerisola, the first one, called SAIRO (Società Anonima Italiana Raffinazione Olii), was established in 1912, and two years later, in 1914, the RIO (Raffineria Italiana Olii) was set up, both in the coastal city of Porto Maurizio. (Cerisola 1973:37–8).

40 *El Aceite de Oliva de España* (1934: 16–7). Information based on a Consular Report from the Italian Embassy in Istanbul.

41 For Greece, see Zunino (1939: 168) and for Turkey, see IIA (1939: 185).

42 Both in Spain and Italy, 30 per cent of the factories employed mechanical power in 1927. In 1935, Spain had 53 refineries with a production capacity of around 300,000 metric tonnes, whereas Italy had 32 refining plants with 200,000 metric tonnes of capacity. See, for Spain, Dirección General de Contribuciones, Impuestos y Rentas (1927) and Federación de Fabricantes de Aceite de Orujo de España (1937: 275) and for Italy, Franciosa (1940: 65) and Zunino (1939: 77).

43 Galula (1985: 126). For more references about the olive-oil trade in Marseille between 1725 and 1825, see Boulanger (1996).

44 For example, Şevket Pamuk shows in this volume that 80 per cent of the labour force was still engaged in agriculture as late as 1929, and Lampe and Jackson estimated that 68.3 per cent of the Greek population was dependent on agriculture around 1928–30. It is likely that other olive-oil exporters, like Tunisia or Algeria, also had relatively high percentages of their workforce engaged in agriculture. By contrast, in both Italy and Spain this percentage was around 50 per cent, and around 30 per cent in Mediterranean France. See Lampe and Jackson (1982: 334); Zamagni (1990: 49), data refers to 1936; Nicolau (1989: 79); Toutain (1992: 199), data refers to the Département of Provence in 1931. Land/labour ratios, namely cultivated area per male worker employed, would be better indicators of relative abundance or scarcity of farm labour, but they are unavailable for most of the southern and eastern Mediterranean countries. For France, Italy and Spain see O'Brien and Prados de la Escosura (1992: 529).

45 For levels of GDP per capita, see Maddison (1992) and the alternative estimates of Prados de la Escosura (1998). In 1929, and according to Prados de la Escosura's estimates, per capita levels of GDP relative to the United States (USA = 1), were the following: France, 0.59; Italy, 0.47; Spain, 0.47; Greece, 0.29 and Turkey, 0.28.

46 By the mid-1920s, it was said that the Greeks consumed olive oils having an acidity of 2–7 degrees; the Tunisians preferred olive oil around 5 ; and the Turks consumed a product of even higher acidity. For Greece and Turkey, see Camera di Commercio Italo-Orientale (1927: 216 and 246–8). For Tunisia, see Ferrara (1927: 178–9).

47 Ferrara's book on Tunisia stresses the importance of domestic market preferences regarding the types of olive oils produced: "Olive oil pressed in the old mills is not refined despite its bad quality and its high acidity. The reason is that natives prefer this olive oil and, therefore, they pay a good price, making its refinement not profitable" (Ferrara 1927:

248). For Turkey, the Italian Chamber of Commerce in Eastern Europe wrote "Due to the lack of industrial refineries and taking into account that in Turkey a rudimentary product is consumed, it can be understood why this country is only able to export unrefined olive oil, which is used as a raw material that needs further improvements" (Camera di Commercio Italo-Orientale 1927: 248). The translation is mine.

48   In Greece, Turkey, Tunisia and Algeria fallow land, meadows and new areas were brought into cultivation. In Greece, for example, the cultivated area increased by 5 per cent per year between 1922 and 1931; in Spain this rate was only 1 per cent during the same years, and the figures for Italy and France were even lower or negative. In Tunisia, the area of main arable food crops (wheat, barley and oats) expanded at 6 per cent per year and so also did the other crops, like olive oil. In fact, the total number of olive trees in Tunisia grew at 7 per cent per year between 1921 and 1931. The area devoted to olive trees in Spain and Italy only grew between 1 and 1.5 per cent. For Greece, see Mazower (1991: Table AI.I); for Spain, GEHR (1983: 243); for Tunisia, Mitchell (1982: 129) and IIA (1923: 367) and IIA (1939: 227); for Italy, Zattini (1921) and IIA (1939: 81). In the case of Italy, it has been considered that four hectares of mixed area were equivalent to one hectare of unmixed area.

49   In the concrete case of Tunisia, it was common for French investors to make contracts of partnership with Tunisians. The custom was that the French would supply the capital and the implements required for purchasing and planting olive trees, whereas the Tunisians would be in charge of the manual work needed for maintaining and harvesting the orchard (Manufactures Bureau 1908: 71).

50   Interestingly, domestic specialization also took place in Italy. The south exported a superior quality of bulk olive oil, required either for the fish-canning industry or for blending purposes. It also provided northern Italian exporters with fine olive oils, used in blending operations, but also with other olive oils of inferior quality, used in the refineries. By contrast, northwestern Italy specialized in exporting brand-name olive oil (Zunino 1939: 187; Borrelli 1930: 16).

51   Longoria wrote (*El Aceite de Oliva en España* 1929: n. 5, 31) "as a general rule, the American consumer demands a light colour olive oil, with smooth taste and flavour, fine, clean and brightening ...; he also relies on reputable brand names, which guarantee him a good product and a standard olive oil. The requirement of supplying an 'almost neutral' type of olive oil is the result of the consumers' taste, which was created both by the Italian and French competitors ...". As he explains, the only large American market consuming the *Spanish natural types of olive oil* was Cuba, a Spanish colony until 1898. The translation is mine.

52   In the case of wine, for example, it is clear that Spain was largely oriented toward exporting cheap table wines rather than fine and high-quality wines, whereas France had taken exactly the opposite direction. Similar considerations can be made by considering the case of cork, which could be exported as raw cork or manufactured (cork stoppers), looking at the cases of Portugal and Spain. As Pedro Lains has stressed, in the peak decade of the 1900s, Portugal exported 25 per cent of its cork in manufactures. In the same years, some 95 per cent of the cork exported by Spain was in manufactures. See Simpson (1995: 207) and Lains (1995: 101).

53   Giovanni Federico's research on the world silk industry has stressed that "silk production is a labour-intensive production, that rich countries leave to the poor. The rich concentrate themselves on the 'noble' phases of the silk industry (i.e. textile manufacture)" (Federico 1994: 21). The translation is mine. See also Federico (1997).

8 International competition and the development of the dried-fruit industry, 1880–1930

José Morilla Critz, Alan L. Olmstead and Paul W. Rhode

Introduction

When he arrived in Fresno, California just before 1900, Paul Mosesian had come a long way from his birthplace in eastern Anatolia. Born to Armenian parents in 1870, Mosesian joined the wave of migration to the United States in the early 1890s. In America he worked as a cutter in a Boston shoe factory for several years before striking out in search of his fortune in the Klondike gold fields. But Mosesian did not get rich in the Yukon. Instead he became seriously ill on the journey and was forced to return, nearly broke, to San Francisco. Upon hearing the glowing accounts of a fellow countryman, Mosesian decided to make a new start in the Fresno area where there was a small, thriving Armenian community. In 1900, he was able to purchase 320 acres of raw land near Parlier. This land he planted as vineyards, first in Zinfandel grapes for wine-making and later in Thompson Seedless for raisins. Building on his business ties in New England, Mosesian developed a "large trade in raisins and table grapes" over the next two decades. By 1917, he owned a modern packing-house and cold-storage plant in Fresno and was engaged in extensive real-estate transactions involving vineyards and fruit lands in the surrounding countryside (Vandor 1919: vol. II, 2061).

Paul Mosesian was one of thousands of migrants who, over the late nineteenth and early twentieth centuries, transformed California into one of the world's leading producers of horticultural crops. Together, these newcomers introduced new crops, experimented with new cultural techniques, and created new marketing institutions. They also built a complex infrastructure that included modern processing plants and quality-control procedures, vast irrigation systems, and transportation networks that linked them to distant markets in the eastern United States and western Europe.

This chapter examines the world that Paul Mosesian helped to make – the world in which horticultural crops traditionally grown in the Mediterranean basin spread to regions with similar climates around the globe. With the diffusion of production, international markets for these products became more closely integrated, flows of labour and other factors became increasingly responsive to differentials in returns, and production/processing techniques developed in one producing region became the subject of close study in other regions. The globalization of production also had significant distributional effects as Californians competed vigorously with Mediterranean producers.

The chapter concentrates on the globalization of production and marketing of dried fruit, in particular, raisins, currants, and prunes. These were the first horticultural products grown in California to achieve a truly important position in world markets. The growers, packers, and shippers of these crops established the model that would be successfully emulated in later decades by the growers of oranges, lemons, almonds, walnuts, and a number of other crops. Raisins, currants, and prunes were also by far the most important horticultural crops in Turkey and the neighbouring areas of recent Ottoman rule in the Balkans. In the eastern Mediterranean, dried fruits played a surprisingly important role in the region's economic development, often comprising a significant share of exports. For Turkey the most important horticultural export was raisins, for Greece currants, and for Serbia and Bosnia prunes. These are the countries, along with Spain (a major raisin exporter) and California, that will comprise the subject of our study.

Although important structural transitions were taking place at about the same time in California and in the Mediterranean basin, there has been little analysis detailing the similarities and differences among various regions and asking how the events occurring in one area affected those underway elsewhere. For the most part, the histories of this structural transformation are quite parochial, blessed with a wealth of local detail and lore, but largely uninformed by the insights that might be gained from a more global perspective. In addition, the effect of the integration of commodity markets and of the international exchange of ideas, technologies, labour, and capital on producers and on specific regions has received little attention to date. Of special interest is the important role that dried fruits played in the economic development of the various regions and how Mosesian and his fellow immigrants in California succeeded in competing with producers in the Old World. In addition, we assess the impact of the growth in international competition, stemming from the emergence of California and other new regions of production, on Mediterranean growers.

In many ways, the story of the globalization of Mediterranean horticulture echoes familiar themes found in the literature on the European grain invasion. The schematic "blackboard" diagram presented in Figure 8.1 helps make this point. It represents the world as divided into an "Old" labour-abundant region and a "New" land-abundant region. With the reduction of transportation costs, goods and factors begin to flow between the two regions. Panel 1 offers a simple sketch of the impact of New Area competition in grain on late-nineteenth-century Europe. Wheat from the New Areas flows to the Old, reducing the value of labour (and land) in its agricultural sector and inducing rural out-migration. This labour, in part, flows to urban/industrial jobs in the Old region and, in part, moves overseas to

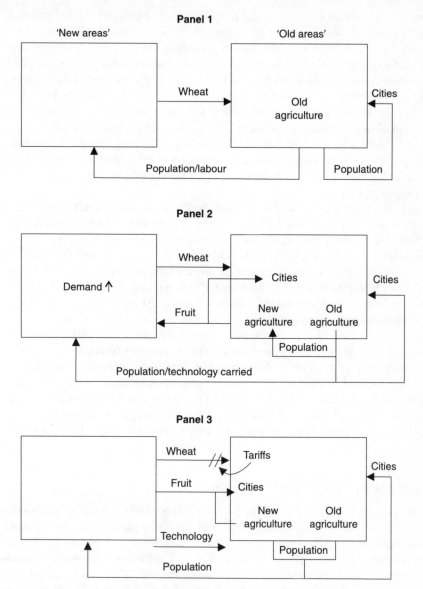

Figure 8.1 Factor and commodity flows between old and new areas.

people the New Lands. The standard classroom interpretation of this diagram is that the opening of the New Lands in some sense creates its own labour supply.

Extending the discussion to consider the globalization of Mediterranean horticulture leads to several additional insights, which are reflected in Panels 2 and 3. First, the competition of the New Lands' wheat and the growth of urban demands for horticultural products pushed farmers in selected pockets of the Old Areas out of cereal production (here labelled Old Agriculture) and into fruit and nut cultivation (labelled New Agriculture). Second, people raised in the Old Areas often had special tastes for home-style products. When they moved to the New Lands, the migrants carried their preferences with them, enlarging the markets there. At least initially, the growth of the New Areas' demand was associated with rising imports of Mediterranean horticultural products (flowing counter to the shipments of cereals). Third, the migrants to the New Lands also carried with them specific knowledge regarding cultural and processing techniques for the Mediterranean crops. Their migration increased the capacity of the New Lands to produce these specialty crops.

In time, as indicated in Panel 3, selected regions of the New Lands shifted into cultivation of fruits and nuts. These producers at first captured their domestic markets, driving out imports, and eventually began to export to the urban markets of the Old Area. In both cases, the rising competition affected Old-Area producers of fruits and nuts much as the earlier grain invasion had. Labour began to flow out of the New Agriculture as well from the Old. There was at least one important difference – most of the major horticultural producing countries in the Old Area remained exporters. In contrast to the story for grains, raising tariffs and other trade barriers were ineffective in dampening the impact of rising competition from the New Lands. Finally, it is useful to take account of the reversal of the flow of technological information. As noted in Panel 2, in the early years, most of the flow of techniques and crop varieties was from Old to New. But as we shall see, as time progressed, producers in the New Areas often developed distinctive and arguably more advanced practices, which those in the Old Areas later adopted in order to compete.

The rise of Californian horticulture

When Paul Mosesian landed in San Francisco just before 1900, California was already in the midst of its great transformation from being a region of extensive grain cultivation to becoming a large-scale producer of horticultural crops. The transition required a lengthy and involved period of experimentation and adaptation as the stories of the rise of the state's raisin and prune industries make abundantly clear.

Raisins

Agostin Haraszthy of San Diego reportedly brought the first vines especially suited for producing raisins to California in 1851. This is one of several "firsts" credited to the flamboyant Hungarian immigrant who imported hundreds of thousands of vines to the state in search of commercially valuable varieties. Most traditional histories date the first commercially successful raisin production in California to the establishment of vineyards by G. G. Briggs of Davisville and R. B. Blowers of Woodland, both in Yolo County (located near Sacramento), in the late 1860s. The intervening two decades witnessed considerable experimentation and several important developments. These included the introduction of the two varieties, the white Muscat of Alexandria and the Muscatel de Gordo Blanco, that would form the backbone of the industry over the late nineteenth century. The former was imported into the state by A. Delmas of San Jose in 1855; the latter in 1861 by the ever-active Haraszthy, now working in the San Francisco Bay Area. Another crucial achievement was Blowers' invention of a workable drying machine that used a fan to move air. This allowed farmers, who normally sun-dried their raisins, to save their crop in years of early rains.

Over the 1870s and 1880s, raisin cultivation spread extensively across the state, north and south. Around 1885, Yolo County, the early centre of production, accounted for only 14 per cent of the state's raisin output. Activity in Southern California experienced more rapid expansion. The Los Angeles–Orange region produced about 30 per cent of the state's crop and the Riverside–San Bernardino region made up another 27 per cent. The Fresno–Tulare region, where G. Eisen first introduced the Muscat grape for raisin production in 1873, comprised about 24 per cent of output.

In the late 1880s, the Fresno area, located in the heart of the San Joaquin valley, became the predominant centre of production. This was associated with the absolute decline of raisin production in the southland. Beginning in 1883, a mysterious epidemic (first known as Anaheim Disease and later as Pierce's Disease) ravaged the vineyards of Los Angeles and Riverside. In addition, the attraction of citrus cultivation induced a shift in the region's cropland to oranges and lemons (California State Board of Agriculture, *Statistical Report* 1911: 144, hereafter *Report*).

But more important was the growing realization of the unique advantages of the San Joaquin valley for raisin production. As M. T. Kearney, a prominent figure in the local industry, noted in the 1899 *Transactions of the State Agricultural Society*:

> Ten or fifteen years ago raisin vineyards were planted in many parts of California, and in the northern and southern districts to a far greater extent than in the central district, but experience has shown that the country around Fresno is peculiarly favored in the matter of climate, and the raisin-growers there find their crops mature and are ready to pick several weeks earlier than in adjoining counties. This difference in time is of great importance, because it enables the grower to cure his crop in the sun and with much less risk of damage from early rains.

By 1916, Fresno County produced over 78 per cent of the state's crop and neighbouring Tulare and Kings counties accounted for an additional 15 per cent (California State Agricultural Society *Transactions* 1888: 13, [hereafter *Transactions*]; *Transactions* 1918: 183).

In addition to the rise of Fresno as the core area of production, the California raisin industry experienced several other important developments over the late nineteenth century. In the early 1870s, George Pettit of San Francisco invented a machine to remove the grapes' seeds and stems, improving quality and reducing the weight by 10–12 per cent. The device was largely ignored until popularized by William Forsythe, a pioneer raisin grower in Fresno, in the 1880s and 1890s. By 1904–6, roughly one-half of the state's raisin crop was processed through seeding machines (*Report* 1911: 155; *Report* 1919: 167). Another change was the growing favour in California for seedless raisin grapes, which originated in Asia Minor and were grown extensively in the Izmir region of Turkey. Among Haraszthy's many vine imports was the sultana which he first introduced in 1861. Of greater long-term significance for the industry, W. Thompson, Sr of Yuba City obtained cuttings of an improved variety, the sultanina, in 1878. Honouring the local man's efforts and adding to confusion over appellation, the Sutter County Horticultural Society renamed the newly imported variety "Thompson Seedless". On the eve of World War I, about 76 per cent of California's crop was muscats, 14 per cent Thompson Seedless, 9 per cent sultanas, and the remainder minor varieties. But by the 1930s, Thompson Seedless grapes made up almost 90 per cent of the state's raisin output (*Report* 1911: 146, 151; *Report* 1918: 183; *Report* 1921: 217; Tufts 1946: 209–11).

Figure 8.2 charts the spectacular growth of California's raisin production over the late nineteenth and early twentieth centuries and indicates how this rapid expansion led to a dramatic shift in the US trade position. As the figure shows, California's raisin output grew from about 120,000 lb in 1873 to 90 million lb in 1893 and then to roughly 180 million lb two decades later. The growth rate of Californian production over the 1873–92 period averaged about 33 per cent per annum – consistent with a doubling of output in just over two years – whereas over the 1892–1914 period the growth rate was about 3.3 per cent per annum, with a doubling of output about every 21 years. US raisin imports had been growing robustly (about 5.1 per cent per annum over the 1867–84 period) before California came on line, but by 1884, imports peaked at 53,000 lb and, after domestic production captured over half of the US market in 1890, imports began their secular decline. By the mid-1900s, the USA had shifted from the status of a net importer to that of a net exporter of raisins.

California's rapid growth propelled it past the several traditional centres of production. In the mid-1890s, the state's raisin output surpassed Spain's and a decade later it exceeded Turkey's. By 1909–13, California accounted for over 38 per cent of the volume of world commercial output and by the 1920s over 63 per cent of the world's supply – more than three times the combined output of the traditional producers. Also significant was the growth of Australian raisin output, which rivalled Spanish production by

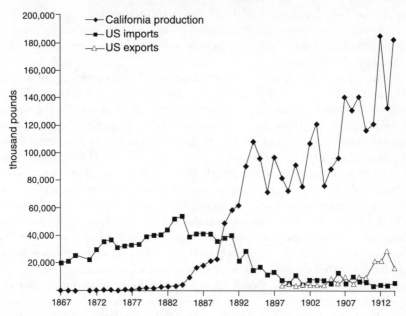

Figure 8.2 US raisin production and trade.

1925. In the late 1920s, New Area growers supplied about one-half of northern European imports.[1]

Prunes

The rise of the Californian prune industry, in many ways, parallels that of raisins. The brothers Pierre and Louis Pellier are credited with importing the first prune scions to the region in 1856 (US Department of Agriculture [USDA hereafter] 1897: 314–16; Tufts 1946: 203). Over the next several decades, growers across the state experimented with myriad different varieties of plum trees including German, Hungarian, Italian and Japanese varieties. But varieties from France, such as the d'Agen, Petite, Impériale, and Robe de Sergeant, dominated local production.

In the 1870s, growers began to plant large orchards at San Jose and the surrounding Santa Clara Valley. This region, which is located at the southern end of the San Francisco Bay and is better known today as Silicon Valley, emerged as the leading centre of Californian production. The degree of geographic concentration of prune cultivation was marked, though not as great as that of raisin production. Around 1928, this region, which included Santa Clara, Alameda, Santa Cruz, and San Benito counties, accounted for about 44 per cent of total prune acreage in the state. A second producing region in Sonoma and Napa counties, located at the northern end of the San Francisco Bay, made up another 20 per cent. Most of the remainder was scattered across the broad expanses of California's Central Valley. In that valley's heavier soils and hotter summers, the prune orchards tended to produce higher yields but lower-quality crops than in the coastal regions (Shear 1928: 8–11; Tufts 1946: 204–5).

Further north, a smaller centre of commercial production arose around Salem, Oregon. In the US Pacific Northwest, Italian varieties such as Fellenberg predominated. These varieties had a tart flavour as opposed to the sweeter flavour of the Californian crop and were closer to the prunes exported from Yugoslavia, the prunes most familiar to Americans of recent European origin. Over the 1898–1913 period, California typically accounted for about 87 per cent of national output and the Pacific Northwest produced the remainder.

Although they grew many of the same varieties as the French, Californian prune producers developed a different set of processing techniques which resulted in a somewhat different product. The French typically subjected their fruit to a succession of light "cookings" followed by exposure to air, and then dried their prunes completely in crude ovens. The product was not so much dehydrated as cooked; much of the prune's sugar was caramelized and its colour turned to black. Pioneer San Jose growers who tried to imitate this process found their fruit could not compete with French imports. Dissatisfied but not defeated, they struck out in a different direction. They quickly learned that California's long dry summers usually made it unnecessary to employ artificially heated evaporators. So they adopted practices similar to those used in the Valencia raisin industry, dipping their fruit in boiling lye to crack the skin (and hasten the loss of moisture) and then setting them on trays to dry in the sun and open air. The resulting prunes remained amber in colour, their sugar did not caramelize, and they could be sold to consumers as a differentiated product.

Over the late nineteenth and early twentieth centuries, the state prune producers made great strides in mechanizing cleaning, grading, processing, packing, and shipping operations. In fact, one of California's foremost agricultural scientists, Edward Wickson (1900: 536–8), observed that in 1910 Californian prune farmers could buy "very capacious appliances for continuous dipping, rinsing, puncturing, and spreading on the trays so that the fruit is handled in large quantities at a minimum cost. In no branch of our fruit industry perhaps has there been greater advance in labour-saving devices than in prune-handling". The widespread use of machines belies the general perception that fruit culture was labour intensive. This may be true relative to wheat production, but focusing on the lack of harvest mechanization can be misleading (Couchman 1967: 13–16). By combining sun-drying and machine processing, Californian prune growers could project an image of their product that was at once more "natural" and more "modern" (and sanitary) than the European imports.

Figure 8.3 graphs the growth of prune production on the Pacific Coast and the corresponding changes in the US trade position. The process of import substitution advanced even faster for prunes than for raisins. In the

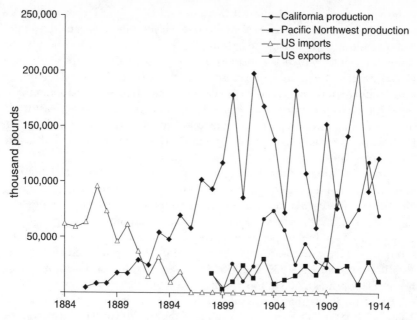

Figure 8.3 US prune production and trade.

early 1890s, prune growers in California and Oregon were able to expel imports and capture nearly the entire domestic market. By 1900, the USA had become the world's foremost commercial producer of prunes, accounting for about 55 per cent of the volume of marketed output. As growth continued, the USA soon emerged as the world's premier exporter. By the mid-1920s, it sold roughly 78 per cent of world output and supplied over 60 per cent of all prunes entering international trade.[2]

The puzzling success of labour-intensive crops in a high-wage economy

Paul Mosesian probably never heard of the doctrine of comparative advantage and was obviously unfamiliar with the Heckscher–Ohlin theorem, but as a shrewd businessman he undoubtedly worked hard to invest in crops that offered the chance to turn a profit in the international marketplace. Why is it that he and so many others succeeded in growing labour-intensive crops in a high wage region in apparent violation of the predictions of the Heckscher–Ohlin theorem? Besides addressing the issue of how production of dried fruit could compete with extensive crops such as wheat, we are also interested in understanding why these industries took hold before other horticultural activities.

There is no doubt that the west coast of America was a high-wage economy in the national, not to mention global, context. For example, in 1910,

Californian farmers paid monthly agricultural labourers 71 per cent more than did their counterparts nationally; day harvest labour was paid a 36 per cent premium. (Of course, the national wage rates are weighed down by the American South, which is considered a low-wage region in the high-wage USA. Even if we focus on a comparison with the east-north-central region, we find Californian farmers paid 25 per cent more for harvest day labour and 47 per cent more for monthly labour.) The differentials in wages with traditional producing countries were obviously much larger, with Californian farmers paying roughly four to eight times the wages commanded in the Mediterranean basin.

In addition, most fruit and nut crops were characterized by high labour-to-land ratios. For example, the USDA estimated that in 1939 producing almonds on the Pacific Coast required 96 hours per bearing acre, dates 275, figs 155, grapes 200, prunes 130, and walnuts 81 hours; this compared with only 6.6 hours of labour per acre of wheat. As another indication of the differences in factor-intensities across crops, the USDA estimated that on the Pacific coast over the 1935–9 period the average value of output per man-hour of labour was $2.03 in food-grain production, whereas it was only $0.58 for fruits and nuts, that is roughly 29 per cent as high (Hecht and Barton 1950: 38 and 98). (The value of output per hour in fruit and nut crops on the Pacific coast was close to the average for all agricultural production activity in the region and well above that for all agricultural production in the country as a whole.)

Underlying this analysis is the notion that wheat farmers competed directly with fruit and nut growers for the labour, but this conclusion needs to be qualified. On the Pacific coast, the labour requirements of both activities were highly seasonal and their peak harvest demands did not fully overlap. In California, for example, the wheat harvest was typically complete by early July whereas the raisin and wine grape harvest did not commence until September and continued through late October. Hence, a worker could, in principle, participate fully both in the grain and grape harvests. Rather than conceiving of the different crops as being competitive in labour, we might be better served by considering them as complementary. As an example, in the lush Santa Clara Valley harvest workers would migrate from cherries to apricots to prunes to walnuts and almonds over a roughly six-month season. Adding other Mediterranean crops such as cotton and navel oranges, stretched the harvest season in large sections of California into the winter months. Thus, by filling out the work year and reducing seasonal underemployment, the cultivation of a range of crops in reasonably close proximity increased the attractiveness to labour of working in Pacific coast agriculture relative to other activities.

There is a second, somewhat cross-cutting argument. Under the prevailing production practices, most of the work on grain operations was performed utilizing machines whereas much of the fieldwork on fruit and nut farms remained hand labour. The traditional historiography sometimes asserts that the two types of work were performed by separate, non-competing groups of labourers and that more specifically the horticultural sector relied primarily on "cheap labour" from Asia (China, Japan, and the Philippines) and southern Europe (Spain, Portugal, and Italy), and later from Mexico. Such arguments tend to overdraw the differences in skill levels, ethnicity, and labour as well as the reliance on short-term workers in the two agricultural sectors. For example, we know that in the 1870s Chinese labourers worked on both wheat and fruit farms. And even if the "hand versus machine" distinction makes some sense with respect to field labour, it ignores the extensive use of machinery in the pre- and post-harvest operations – ploughing, spraying, sorting, dehydrating, packing, and other processing activities – associated with commercial fruit production.

One valuable aspect of this argument is that it draws attention to the important role of labour mobility in the region's agricultural development, and in particular to the manifold and often conflicting efforts of local authorities to encourage, discourage, and otherwise control the migrant flows of specific ethnic groups. By focusing on the political economy of migration, this literature helps undermine the notion that labour scarcity was a "natural" immutable feature of the region. Rather it was in part an outcome of collective political decisions. The migrant flows presumably would have been far larger but for exclusionary agitation and legislation. Nonetheless, the traditional literature's emphasis on the reliance of horticulture on "cheap labour" misses a key point: even if wages on the Pacific coast fruit operations were below those paid in the industrial and commercial sectors, they were still among the highest wages paid to agricultural workers anywhere in the world.

A stronger case can be made that the land used for the various crops was "non-competing". Prime quality fruit lands, with the accompanying climatic conditions, were so different from the lands that remained in grain production that they constituted a "specific input". Indeed, as the discussion above about the localization of individual crops suggests, the soils and climate best suited for raisin production appear quite different from those best suited for prunes. This was true more generally with special niches emerging for most crops.[3]

Differences in the land values help bring these points home. According to R. L. Adams' 1921 Californian farm manual, the market value of "good" wheat land in the state was approximately $100 per acre in the period immediately before World War I. "Good" land for prune production was worth $350 even before planting and valued at $800 when bearing. The "best" land for prunes had a market value of $500 not planted and $1,000 in bearing trees. Similarly, "good" land for raisin grape production was worth $150 raw and $300 in bearing vines; the "best" sold for $250 not planted and $400 bearing. Focusing on physical labour-to-land ratios in comparing wheat and fruit production can be seriously misleading because the acreage used for

Table 8.1 US tariffs on dried fruits, 1867–1930

Tariff Act	Currants	Raisins	Prunes	General tariffs as a share of the value of imports:	
				All	Dutiable
Average ad valorem rate (per cent)					
1867	132	69	88	45	47
1871	56	69	44	39	43
1873	28	41	20	29	42
1883	30	35	31	30	45
1890	0	52	43	24	48
1894	96	36	29	21	44
1897	85	43	19	26	47
1909	60	31	16	20	41
1913	23	16	5	10	29
1922	28	20	6	14	39
1930	35	22	14	18	49
Specific duty (cents per pound)					
1867	5.0	5.0	5.0	n/a	n/a
1871	2.5	5.0	2.5	n/a	n/a
1873	1.0	2.5	1.0	n/a	n/a
1883	1.0	2.0	1.0	n/a	n/a
1890	0.0	2.5	2.0	n/a	n/a
1894	1.5	1.5	1.5	n/a	n/a
1897	2.0	2.5	2.0	n/a	n/a
1909	2.0	2.5	2.0	n/a	n/a
1913	1.5	2.0	1.0	n/a	n/a
1922	2.0	2.0	0.5	n/a	n/a
1930	2.0	2.0	2.0	n/a	n/a

Source:
Compiled from US Department of Commerce *Foreign Commerce and Navigation* (various years).

fruit cultivation was of a different quality (and ultimately higher market value) than that used for grain growing.[4]

Horticultural crops were unusual because unlike the key agricultural staples, many enjoyed effective tariff protection during the late nineteenth and early twentieth centuries. Table 8.1 offers an overview of American tariffs on dried fruits.[5] These tariffs almost surely sped up the growth of Mediterranean agriculture in the USA and were strongly supported by domestic producers, railways, and packers. But it is worth noting that these tariffs served revenue as well as protective purposes. Indeed, the *ad valorem* US rates were actually higher before California and Oregon emerged as important players,

and most northern European nations also had tariffs on horticultural products. Even "free-trade" Britain had duties on currants and raisins in this
period.[6] Prunes and raisins successfully competed in international markets
by the mid-1890s, suggesting that, in the known absence of dumping policies
that discriminated between domestic and foreign markets, the tariffs on
these crops had little remaining impact.[7]

One of the recurrent justifications for tariffs offered by domestic growers
was to help offset high transportation differentials. Almost across the board,
Mediterranean producers enjoyed lower freight rates to the key markets of
the northeastern USA (not to mention northern Europe) than their American rivals did. For example, *c.* 1909, shipping currants from Greece to New
York cost 17 cents per hundredweight while the freight on an equivalent
quantity of Californian dried fruit averaged about one dollar.[8]

The early success of raisins and prunes, relative to other horticultural
products, was in part a result of the transportation costs. Most consumers
preferred their fruit fresh; dehydrating and canning were adopted primarily
as means of overcoming problems of transportation and storage. By processing their fruit, Californian growers and packers raised their product's value-
per-weight ratio – according to E. Wickson, raisins and other dried fruits had
a selling price per pound roughly twice that of fresh deciduous fruit *c.* 1900 –
and reduced its perishability and liability to damage in transit. In the words
of one local observer in the mid-1880s, "Raisins bore transportation better,
and could better await sale than green fruits."[9]

As transcontinental freight rates fell and the quality of service increased
(with the spread of refrigerator cars and the establishment of special fruit
trains beginning in the late 1880s), the composition of Californian fruit shipments shifted from a mixture dominated by processed goods to one comprised mainly of fresh deciduous and citrus fruits. For example, in 1879–81,
canned goods made up 53.2 per cent of the value of the state's fruit exports;
raisins, prunes, and other dried fruits 17.2 per cent; and fresh products 29.4
per cent. By 1909–11, citrus and other fresh fruits accounted for over 70 per
cent of shipments and canned fruits about 8.2 per cent. Raisins, prunes, and
other dried fruits witnessed a small increase in their share to 20.8 per cent.
This shift appears, in part, to be a re-enactment of the classic story in American economic history of the maize-growing farmers of the old northwest.[10]

For the Pacific coast fruit industry, the cost of transportation remained an
important factor, shaping production and processing practices. This is
reflected in an observation that has entered textbook economics, that the
best apples are exported because they can bear the cost of shipping. It also
helps explain one of the defining characteristics of the region's fruit industry, its emphasis on quality. Local producers and packers devoted exceptional efforts to improving grading and quality control, removing culls,
stems and dirt, reducing spoilage in shipment, and developing brand names
and high-quality reputations. This focus makes sense given the high

transportation cost that western producers faced in reaching the markets of the US Atlantic coast and Europe.

A plain statement of this line of thinking comes from Yuba City fruit grower, R. C. Kells. At the Tenth California State Fruit Growers' Convention in 1887, Kells complained that there was as yet

> too much carelessness on the part of the average fruit grower in preparing his dried fruit for market. The cost of selling a pound of poor fruit is greater than that of good, while the freight is the same; at the same time (we are) losing our reputation as growers and packers. Let us, when drying our fruit, do away with the Grecian or Spanish system ... of swindling our eastern customers with so much filth and dirt, while with a trifling cost more we can supply all the markets with good, clean, and wholesome fruit, whereby we will find ready sales at living prices; and our eastern friends will say to the Turkish prune, the Spanish raisin, and the Grecian currant importers: "Thank you, we are done buying dirt and trash, we will try, for a change, the California prunes, raisins, ... etc. and take less chance of contracting some loathsome disease."

At the same meeting, General N. P. Chipman of Red Bluff observed that "There will come a day when people who can have clean fruit, will cease buying imported prunes that are handled by dirty peasants and finally tramped into barrels and kegs with the bare feet; and so with currants." Over the next several decades, the state's fruit growers began collectively to adopt the marketing strategy suggested by Chipman and Kells (Transactions 1888: 316 and 319).

To a large extent, the ability of Paul Mosesian to compete with the growers in his homeland depended on capturing the higher end of the market. With only a few exceptions, Californian dried fruits earned higher prices than their European competition because the state's growers gained a reputation for quality and consistency. As an example, US and French prunes were far superior to those from Serbia and Bosnia (with the Bosnian fruit being of better quality than the Serbian), with American and French prunes commanding twice the price of the Balkan product. In the USA prunes were graded into ten categories ranging from 20–30 prunes per pound to 120 and over per pound. The price differentials were substantial with the top-quality fruit selling for over fifteen times the price of the lowest quality in the mid-1920s. The price of the best prunes was roughly double that of the middle grades. Between 1912 and 1927 there was a significant improvement in the average quality of Californian prunes, with fruit in the 20–40 range increasing from about 1 to 13 per cent of the crop. More generally, fruit in the 20–60 range increased from about 17 to 63 per cent of the crop. These improvements were the result of a systematic application of scientific methods and the relative shift of prune acreage to areas that had provend capable of producing larger fruit. By comparison, in 1910 (the only year for which we have data) the highest grade available for Serbian prunes was 60–65 per pound. Given the subsequent wars and the continued references to quality and price differentials, it seems highly improbable that the quality of Balkan prunes kept pace with the changes underway in California. In addition to the size differences the Californian fruit had other significant quality advantages stemming from better dehydrating, packing, and shipping methods (Shear 1928: 5 and 37–57; Stroykowitch 1910: 186–93).

Accounts of the quality problems of Mediterranean producers fill the US tariff hearings. In testimony in 1909, importers complained that European raisins and currants often arrived with stems attached and "mixed with a great deal of dirt and sand"; they typically required cleaning in the USA before being sent to market.[11] The quality advantage applied across the board to other Californian crops. As a related example, C. C. Teague, President of the Walnut Protective League in Los Angeles, testified in 1921 that foreign nuts "frequently arrive in a musty, damp condition, [with] cracked shells, and [are] sometimes wormy and not good for anything. On the other hand, in California we cultivate our orchards intensively ... . We irrigate them, we spray them for insects, and then ... we put them through expensive processing plants".

Remarkably, Teague's opponent, James McGlone of the Dried Food Association of New York, agreed: "to-day the California walnut is practically in a field by itself. The foreign varieties are not so well graded. I have tried with the growers in France to get them to grade their walnuts, select the imperfect nuts, and bleach them, and to pack them so that we could compete with California, but they won't listen. They just simply ship them now as they did". What is surprising about this exchange is that France was a relatively advanced country within the Mediterranean world; the problems of quality control were apt to be more acute in the less-developed regions.

After the Californian horticultural industry established its strong market presence, the message eventually got through. The extensive efforts that producers in other New Areas and in Europe applied to studying and, with widely varying degrees of success, copying the Californian model provides another indicator of the importance of superior technology and organization in establishing California's comparative advantage.

Global perspectives on market integration

The impact that the rise of Californian production had on European producers was a function of the basic characteristics of the market, including the relative growth of supply and demand, elasticity conditions for dried fruits, and changing transportation costs. Many of these market fundamentals suggest that the expansion of production onto vast new tracts of land would have dire consequences for established growers. As the output of dried fruit from the New Areas rapidly expanded over the late nineteenth and early twentieth centuries, the global rate of growth of supplies began to equal or exceed that of demand. Consumption data for leading markets hint that demand growth was weak. For example, British consumption of currants and raisins per head grew only at 0.2 per cent per annum between 1880 and 1910. For the United States, growth was also flat before 1900, but picked up by the 1910s. Bennett and Pierce estimate that per capita consumption of all dried fruit in the USA climbed from about 1 lb per year in the 1878–80 period to 1.3 lb in 1898–1900 before jumping to 4 lb in 1909–11. A survey of other leading markets suggests demand growth was generally sluggish.[12]

There are grounds for elasticity pessimism. Richard Stone included selected dried fruits in his classic study, *Measurement of Consumers' Expenditure and Behavior in the United Kingdom, 1920–1938*. He found that their "own-price ... elasticity is never significant" and the income elasticity was "the smallest ... of all the fruit groups analyzed ... ." These findings suggest that both the price and income elasticities for dried-fruit products were low, at least in the interwar UK.

Further evidence regarding the relative rates of supply and demand growth appear in the movements of real prices of dried fruits in Britain and New York over the 1880–1914 period, which are presented in Table 8.2. As it shows, the New York price for prunes fell dramatically over the late nineteenth century. Raisin and currant prices, especially in the British market, display greater stability. Real prices rose over the 1870s and 1880s as the phylloxera epidemic reduced European supplies of grape products. With the recovery of the vine sector in the early 1890s and the entry of California into the world scene, real raisin and currant prices dropped, declining by about 38 per cent between 1889 and 1894 before recovering later in the decade.

Declining transportation costs explain some of the fall in prices in the major consuming markets, but in contrast to Knick Harley's story for wheat over the 1850–1913 period, these movements were not consistently associated with rising prices in the producing areas.[13] The available evidence suggests that most of the changes in ocean-freight rates occurred before the mid-1880s when the USA was not yet a major fruit producer. Isserlis reported that the real rates for shipping fruit from the Mediterranean ports to New York City were roughly constant between 1884 and 1899. By way of contrast, real railway rates on fruit from California to New York fell by an average of 3 per cent annually from 1890 to 1910. Though quite rapid, the decline explains only 10 per cent of the fall in the New York wholesale price of prunes or only 31 per cent in that of raisins. Indeed, we know that real wholesale fruit prices in California declined during most of the late nineteenth and early twentieth centuries. The dependence of European horticultural producers on railways varied from region to region, but none shipped very far. In general, most growers were located in close proximity to the sea and its relatively cheap water transportation.[14] For many European growers distances to local ports would not have exceeded that required to get to the railhead in California. Thus, European growers were not so greatly affected by

Table 8.2 Indices of real prices of dried fruits in leading consumer markets, 1880–1914

| | Britain | | United States (New York) | | |
	Currants	Raisins	Currants	Raisins	Prunes
1880	103	104	110	181	268
1881	111	106	116	152	206
1882	106	107	99	152	262
1883	110	102	118	163	260
1884	112	103	92	159	212
1885	118	107	104	232	226
1886	124	114	122	291	160
1887	129	111	131	189	226
1888	127	104	105	215	158
1889	115	109	112	229	187
1890	109	118	87	221	179
1891	108	113	79	171	169
1892	113	106	60	150	182
1893	72	95	52	169	184
1894	71	96	37	130	149
1895	79	100	53	156	130
1896	83	110	74	118	119
1897	100	117	106	159	111
1898	90	109	121	150	104
1899	84	103	91	127	101
1900	194	126	130	141	86
1901	100	108	151	136	89
1902	86	121	84	148	86
1903	78	101	83	128	76
1904	81	103	83	128	71
1905	80	90	82	103	71
1906	97	117	101	136	99
1907	97	101	108	129	84
1908	104	105	97	148	87
1909	95	84	89	97	72
1910	108	105	92	89	82
1911	103	112	118	113	166
1912	99	107	107	105	97
1913	95	91	94	96	84
1914	95	94	93	128	119

Sources:
Statistical Abstract for the United Kingdom (various years);
Mitchell 1988;
US Bureau of Labor Statistics *Wholesale Prices 1890–1920* Bulletin No 296 (Washington DC: GPO 1922);
US Senate *Report on Wholesale Prices on Wages and on Transportation* 62nd Cong, 2nd Sess (Washington DC: GPO 1893) Pt 1 p. 32 and Pt 2 pp. 80-84.

railway charges as their counterparts in California, and the decline in US railway rates contributed significantly to the American's ability to compete.

The dried-fruit industry in the Mediterranean basin

Contemporary observers on both sides of the Atlantic were keenly aware that the emergence of the USA as a major supplier was restructuring international markets and posing serious challenges for the older producing areas. The Mediterranean world had long been known for its production of a rich variety of horticultural crops. But the second half of the nineteenth century witnessed a significant expansion in output as numerous regions around the basin moved into the intensive production of high-value fruit and nut crops destined for the booming export markets of North America and northern Europe. Across Europe's southern rim, horticultural producers began to adopt new ways of doing business. For example, the old practice of planting a mixture of trees along roads or interspersed among other crops gave way to intensive orchards and vineyards. With this growing specialization and commercialization often came a revolution in cultural methods including the increased use of fertilizer, irrigation, and higher-yielding varieties. The new crops also opened a window to the outside world, attracting foreign capital and technologies and stimulating investments in internal transportation systems, processing plants, and better port facilities. These crops became important earners of foreign exchange and in many cases the fortunes of horticultural producers became a key ingredient in determining regional or even national prosperity. In addition, the new export crops represented a harbinger of modernity, setting examples that contemporaries hoped would eventually transform the more backward sectors of the rural economy. In many cases these hopes went unfulfilled in large part because of the increased competition from California and other new areas of horticultural production. The development of the raisin and currant industries in the Mediterranean basin illustrates many of these points and is indicative of a more general pattern.

Raisins and currants

Before the rise of competition from California and other New Areas, Spain and Turkey were the leading areas of raisin production, and Greece dominated the world currant trade. The development of all of these countries was deeply affected by the twin shocks resulting from the growing competition for export markets and from the devastating impact (rippling effects) of the phylloxera epidemic. Almost all Spanish raisin exports emanated from Málaga and Alicante. During the 1870s, raisins were Málaga's chief staple crop, often accounting for about one-third of the area's total (not just agricultural) exports. Basic trends in Málaga's (and Alicante's) raisin trade are displayed in Table 8.3. In the 1870s, nearly 60 per cent of Málaga's raisin

Table 8.3 Exports of Spanish raisins, 1865–1914 (in thousand pounds)

	Malaga total	*To USA*	*Alicante total*	*To USA*
1865	42 231	21 160	18 228	—
1866	43 487	26 912	23 342	—
1867	42 121	28 588	15 208	2 667
1868	49 328	36 148	21 689	—
1869	35 795	23 187	20 829	—
1870	53 891	37 316	19 551	—
1871	49 527	31 607	25 347	—
1872	65 595	31 166	29 998	—
1873	55 235	35 354	21 975	—
1874	44 590	30 373	44 149	—
1875	41 768	25 458	42 231	—
1876	62 641	33 062	42 892	—
1877	50 915	26 273	39 101	—
1878	55 654	30 814	58 035	—
1879	51 599	27 441	31 100	—
1880	51 599	28 081	27 111	18 382
1881	42 848	23 364	49 262	20 807
1882	47 301	26 780	60 900	43 179
1883	35 575	18 889	47 521	33 437
1884	32 864	17 302	39 586	19 374
1885	32 753	14 657	47 058	21 049
1886	28 455	13 996	55 390	31 387
1887	22 218	9 147	70 047	31 784
1888	26 868	—	56 293	30 880
1889	21 733	1 984	51 334	33 635
1890	13 203	1 499	98 260	42 716
1891	12 652	882	54 927	20 829
1892	11 990	1 367	71 282	22 019
1893	8 155	617	50 695	14 393
1894	11 902	661	59 556	14 900
1895	10 932	727	51 070	6 679
1896	17 104	1 322	50 210	9 588
1897	16 575	904	49 505	7 516
1898	14 371	1 080	56 756	8 596
1899	18 316	3 306	58 277	8 883
1900	11 946	1 124	63 964	8 750
1901	9 897	—	50 541	7 362
1902	5 554	—	43 730	2 138
1903	7 516	—	47 565	8 199
1904	8 023	—	42 914	6 127
1905	15 297	—	49 703	11 814
1906	11 263	—	32 313	5 290
1907	14 966	—	44 832	—

continued on next page

Table 8.3 Exports of Spanish raisins, 1865–1914 (in thousand pounds) (cont.)

	Malaga total	To USA	Alicante total	To USA
1908	12 564	—	44 237	—
1909	12 806	—	49 637	—
1910	12 718	—	40 490	—
1911	18 250	—	44 237	—
1912	12 057	—	26 736	—
1913	—	—	29 910	—
1914	—	—	26 185	—

Sources:
Data has been comprised from the following primary and secondary sources:
Instituto de Estudios Fiscales, 1975-1976. *Cuentas del Estado Espanol.* "Desarrollo que ha tenido la exportacion de los principales articulos." Ministerio de Hacienda, Madrid.
Morilla Critz, J. 1989. "Cambios en la viticultura de Andaluceia Oriental durante la crisis de finales del siglo XIX". *Revista de Historia Economica* VII, 1. pp. 180–181. XIX.
Piqueras, J. 1985. *La Economia Valenciana de Exportacion y su Evolucion Historica.* M.A.P.A. Madrid, pp 226–222.
British Consular Reports: 1897, Annual Series no. 2065, p. 23; 1911 Annual Series no. 4981, p. 53; 1913 Annual Series no. 5440, p. 43.
Other British Parliamentary Papers: 2nd Report of the Royal Commission on Depression of Trade and Industry. 1886–XXII, p. 312.

exports were marketed in the United States. But with the rise of production in California, the share of Málaga's exports sold to the USA fell to less than 10 per cent by the 1890s. The loss of the American market was only one of Málaga's misfortunes; in 1878 phylloxera appeared, leading to a precipitous decline in the region's output and exports by the mid-1880s. Raisin shipments fell from an average of about 23,000 metric tonnes annually in the period 1873–82 to roughly 5,000 metric tonnes annually in the period 1890–1913.[15]

Although the initial decline in production was due to the phylloxera infestation, the weak recovery was primarily the result of declining market opportunities. Málaga farmers chose not to replant their vineyards with American rootstocks, as did growers of grapes for the wine and fresh market trades in neighbouring regions. The area devoted to vines in Málaga fell from about 250,000 acres in 1881 to about 42,000 in 1897, with much of the land left idle for decades. A steep fall in Málaga's real raisin prices and the growing unmarketable surplus after 1900 signalled the key role of market forces in the collapse of the raisin economy. Occasionally, when the US raisin or the Greek currant crops were light, Málaga's raisin exports temporarily soared, but for all practical purposes what had been the world's primary raisin exporter had become a bit player after 1890. Málaga's commercial press, led by the Union Mercantile, regularly blamed California for the region's malaise. Foreign consuls stationed in Málaga echoed these sentiments. As an example, the British Consul noted that "the remarkable falling off [of Málaga's raisin exports to the USA] is due, first, to the development of California as a raisin-growing State...". Between 1887 and 1897 Málaga experienced the highest emigration rate in all of Spain, which recent studies have tied to the crisis in the raisin sector.[16]

Spain's second raisin-producing area was the province of Alicante in the region of Valencia. Most output came from the hinterland of the port city of Denia, leading the area's product to be called "Denia" or "Valencia" raisins. Both Málaga and Alicante made raisins from muscatel grapes, but faced with a greater risk of rain, Alicante farmers (like Californian prune producers of the day) dipped their fruit in lye to cut the drying time. These differences are significant for our analysis because Californian raisin producers competed primarily with the Málagan product; much of Alicante's output was used for cooking and was a closer substitute for Greek currants (US Consular Report 1884: 685).

The Alicante industry continued to grow even after Málaga's began to decline, as the data in Table 8.3 reveal. Alicante shipments rose until 1890, with the USA taking 56 per cent of the region's exports during the 1880s. Alicante benefitted from Málaga's phylloxera problems, and its cheaper product was better able to compete in northern European markets. But it would suffer the same fate as Málaga in the important American market, with shipments to the USA plummeting after 1890. Contemporaries had a clear understanding of the source of their problems: "...to the mind of the Dianenses the bitterest rivalry is that of the California raisin, originating from Spanish vine cuttings introduced into America about 1880, which are rapidly killing in the country of their adoption the trade in the Denia raisin." In Alicante, these competitive pressures led to significant out-migration and a gradual substitution by citrus production.[17]

The experience of the Turkish raisin industry over the late nineteenth and early twentieth centuries was closely linked to the fortunes of Spanish producers. Although vineyards were located throughout much of Turkey, commercial production was concentrated around Smyrna (now Izmir). This was Anatolia's leading port, and it handled nearly all of the country's raisin-export trade (Ravndal 1928: 104). Raisins represented the region's single most important export crop, typically making up one-quarter of the total value of exports in this period.[18] But in contrast to the Spanish industry, raisins were a relatively new activity in Turkey. Based on the dearth of references in early sources, Quataert infers that the crop was probably not commercially important before the mid-nineteenth century.

Information on the Turkish industry can be gleaned from US and British commercial reports and a variety of Turkish sources. Although these sources often focus on different entities ranging from a given port or region, to "Anatolia," or "Turkey," or the "Ottoman Empire", a fairly consistent picture emerges. Table 8.4 draws together a number of the more reliable statistical series, which form the basis of the analysis below.

Responding to the growth in foreign demand, raisin production in the Smyrna area expanded rapidly with annual output typically in excess of

Table 8.4 The Turkish raisin trade (in thousand pounds)

	Exports	Izmir exports		Exports	Izmir exports
1868	—	38 000	1900	116 959	—
1869	—	—	1901	—	—
1870	—	—	1902	—	—
1871	—	96 000	1903	—	152 400
1872	—	62 000	1904	—	79 400
1873	—	—	1905	171 519	120 600
1874	—	—	1906	—	60 800
1875	—	—	1907	106 091	95 200
1876	—	—	1908	175 963	125 600
1877	—	—	1909	131 495	120 400
1878	118 492	—	1910	87 674	98 200
1879	133 827	150 000	1911	91 170	49 000
1880	111 758	—	1912	—	120 400
1881	81 776	98 000	1913	154 775	137 800
1882	127 801	—	1914	—	114 200
1883	171 992	—	1915	—	101 400
1884	195 552	190 000	1916	—	76 200
1885	168 589	—	1917	—	63 400
1886	189 251	—	1918	—	57 000
1887	182 466	—	1919	—	67 200
1888	197 198	—	1920	—	40 600
1889	160 133	—	1921	—	74 800
1890	117 295	—	1922	—	82 400
1891	158 962	—	1923	—	80 800
1892	174 955	—	1924	—	108 600
1893	154 573	—	1925	—	66 200
1894	152 795	—	1926	—	78 200
1895	199 288	—	1927	—	105 800
1896	158 874	—	1928	—	100 400
1897	145 398	—			
1898	135 437	—			
1899	162 241	—			

Sources:
Turkish exports from *Osmanli Imparatorlugunun Ticaret Muvazenesi* 1878-1913, p. 66.
Izmir Exports from *Republique Turque Annuaire Statistique 1929*, p. 130.
University of California Experiment Station, *Foreign Production and Trade in Raisins*, p. 41.

50,000 tons by the 1870s. As phylloxera damaged the vineyards of Spain, Turkish raisin output roughly doubled between the early 1870s and the mid-1880s. By the later date, Turkey surpassed Spain as the world's leading raisin producer. In addition, there was a significant increase in the average quality of Turkish raisin production as market-conscious farmers planted seedless sultanas at the expense of the black and red varieties.

But in the early 1890s, just as the Californian product began pouring into the market, phylloxera struck the vineyards of Anatolia. The quantity of Turkish raisin exports stabilized and, after the mid-1890s, started to fall. Despite these setbacks, raisins continued to rank second among all commodity exports shipped from Anatolia for most of the late nineteenth and early twentieth centuries (Quataert 1981: 69–70). The combination of rapidly rising Californian output and falling Turkish output allowed California to capture the position of global leadership *c.* 1905, and by the mid-1910s, Californian output regularly exceeded that of Turkey at its peak.

The Turkish government attempted to redress the depressed conditions in its raisin industry with tax breaks, subsidies, and efforts to develop derivative markets, but such policies could do little to address the fundamental problem arising from the increased supply from California and Australia.[19] As is often the case, government policies had contradictory results. Some demand-side programmes such as the encouragement of derivative markets were designed to raise prices. But other supply-side policies, such as special tax breaks and a free supply of American rootstocks to counter the ravages of phylloxera, contributed to the market glut.[20] In the 1920s and 1930s, raisin output continued to languish, in part due to the expulsion of the Greeks and Armenians but also to unfavourable market conditions. Increased competition from the USA and Australia depressed prices and edged Turkish raisins from their principal market in Britain, forcing Turkish exporters to develop new outlets in northern Europe. Turkey's share of world output continued to decline over the 1920s (Basbakanlik Istatistik 1937: 234–8; Wheeler 1927: 1–19 and 58–62; Bauer 1933: 6; US House of Representatives 1929: 3,664–3,665 and 4,489–4,497).

These efforts were hampered because, like most European fruit producers, Turkey suffered from a persistent inability to match the quality and consistency offered by their American competitors. In some extreme cases foreign consuls stationed in Smyrna threatened to deny import certificates because of unsanitary conditions. Other reports of shipments of Turkish raisins being "utter rubbish and quite unsaleable" when they arrived in European ports, undoubtedly hurt the reputation of the country's exports in the international marketplace (British Consular Report AS No. 2,641, June 1901; AS No. 3,722, Oct. 1906: 7; AS No. 4,598, Nov. 1910: 12).

No country involved in the dried-grape trade experienced sharper swings than Greece. None became so specialized in a single crop – currants made up almost 55 per cent of the value of all Greek exports between 1886 and 1890 (Premier Congrès 1936: 72–3; Morilla Critz 1995: 303–4; Lampe and Jackson 1982: 169; Dakin 1972: 320–1). Currant vineyards represented the major growth sector of Greek agriculture in the second half of the nineteenth century, with production and acreage increasing more than threefold between 1860 and 1890. In the centres of production in Zante, Cephalonia and northwestern Morea, the industry dominated economic life. Figure 8.4

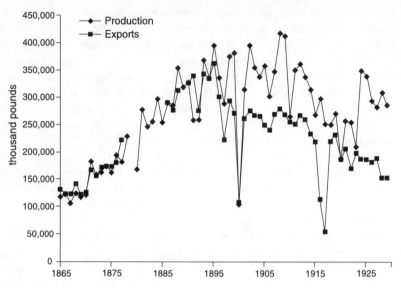

Figure 8.4 Greek currant production and exports.

provides a quantitative picture of the evolution of Greek currant production and exports from 1870 to 1930.

The vast majority of currant exports went to the United Kingdom where they were used in cakes, puddings, and breads. But the growth in output over the late 1870s to the early 1890s was also fuelled by massive exports to France where the currants were used for wine-making during the phylloxera epidemic; between 1880 and 1892, about 31 per cent of Greek currant production went to France. When its vineyards recovered, France imposed a high tariff (1892) on Greek currants and soon thereafter banned their use in wine production; almost overnight, Greece lost one of its largest markets. In early 1896, the British consul in Patras offered a sense of the despair: "The cessation of the French demand caused prices to drop 50 per cent at once, property lost nearly all its value, and, although the growers have been fighting manfully, hoping against hope for the last three years, they are now at the end of their resources ..."(British Consular Report AS No. 1682, April 1896: 5).

The collapse of the French market devastated the Greek economy, unleashing widespread agricultural failures, bankruptcies of commercial houses and financial institutions, and a series of government attempts to monopolize the currant trade, limit production, and divert output to the making of wine and spirits. This was truly a national crisis that contributed to the bankruptcy of the Greek government in 1893 and to the massive emigration over the next two decades (US Consular Report L, 185, Feb. 1896: 243–5; Petmezas 1995: 427–87; Andréadés 1909: 3–25). Greece experienced a second major blow when Russia, which had recently become an important consumer of currants, imposed a prohibitive duty in 1897 (Martin 1913: 274–5). It was in the 1890s that California was beginning to have an impact on world raisin markets.[21] Greek currant exports to the United States remained relatively steady for the next two decades, but the enormous growth of Thompson Seedless production in California (and of currant output in Australia) eroded prices and undercut the long-run prospects for the Greek industry (US Tariff Commission 1929: 1263–7; 1939: 166).

Prunes

By the middle of the nineteenth century, millions of plum trees dotted the countryside of Bosnia–Hercegovina and northern Serbia, and by the 1870s Bosnia had developed a lucrative export trade in prunes. In 1884, the British consul in Sarajevo reported that "with the exception of plums the exports are unimportant" and the "abundant plum crop, which more than any other brings money into the country, was the principal reason for the improvement" in the region's trade over the previous year.[22] A decade later, another British consul noted that "plums are not only the article of commerce which brings the most money into the country but the one which affects nearly the whole population ... . Plums are to the inhabitants of Bosnia ... the one all important crop ..." (British Consular Report AS No. 1,494, April 1895: 8).

Serbia was also a major plum producer, with most of its output converted to plum brandy for local consumption and for export to the Ottoman and Habsburg Empires. This export trade received a serious blow in 1880 when both empires imposed stiff tariffs on Serbian brandy. The resulting supply of plums available for conversion into prunes attracted a number of Bosnian entrepreneurs who had experience with both prune production and export markets. The Bosnians introduced simple mud-brick ovens into northern Serbia and established a network of rural agents throughout the plum-growing regions to supervise construction, provide credit, and manage the preparation and trade in prunes (Lampe and Jackson 1982: 177). This led to rapid changes in the Serbian economy, because according to Lampe and Jackson, about half of the peasant families in northern Serbia soon produced prunes for export. Between the 1840s and 1908, Serbian plum production increased about threefold, with much of the growth fuelled by the new export opportunities for prunes and jam. "These new products transformed plum raising from a peripheral non-money activity ... to a high-yield, highly commercialized form of production ...". To offer a sense of the importance of prunes to the Serbian economy, in 1886 the crop accounted for one-quarter of all Serbian export revenue, and from 1896 to 1909 prunes and prune marmalade accounted for about 17 per cent of the value of all Serbian exports.[23]

In the context of our earlier discussion of the quality differential between Balkan and Californian prunes, from the outset Serbian prunes suffered from quality problems associated with improper drying and packaging. One of the first forays into the English market was a financial failure because Serbian prunes were "regarded as inferior, and so realised an inferior price." Trying to introduce modern methods and equipment and to inculcate better practices among the Serbian peasantry proved to be a difficult challenge. In 1883 the government introduced programmes "so that in the future Serbian prunes will be fit for the best market" (British Consular Report Aug. 1883: 1609). But decades later observers were still commenting on the inferior quality of Serbian fruit and of the inability to develop the type of brand-name recognition that was so important for their competitors in the United States (Patton 1928: 149–51).

Until the late 1880s, the USA was the primary consumer of Balkan prunes, with imports averaging about 46 million lb a year between 1885 and 1889; this probably represented about half of all the combined Serbian and Bosnian exports.[24] With the explosion in Californian production and the doubling of the duty on prunes with the McKinley Tariff in 1890, the Balkan producers were rapidly expelled from the American market. Over the years 1896 to 1900, US imports from Austria–Hungary averaged only 77,000 lb a year; less than 2 per cent of the imports a decade earlier.[25] Bosnian and Serbian producers redirected their exports to Austria–Hungary and Germany, but even in these markets Californian prunes soon competed vigorously. By the early twentieth century, Germany was the world's largest importer of prunes, with California supplying over one-third of the market. The dynamic implications of the increased competition from California must have depressed the potential returns to Balkan producers, retarding the development of commercial agriculture. To get a handle on this distributional question is our next task.

The distributional impact of New World competition

Traditional producers often complained about competition from New Areas. In a counterfactual world without this production, how much higher would the prices and European revenues have been? Examining the question more fully involves measuring the quantitative effect of global production on fruit prices, which depends critically on the elasticities of demand and supply.[26] Elsewhere we have provided a detailed assessment of the impact of US competition on traditional producers, which may be briefly summarized here.

Around 1910, the USA produced 138.5 million lb of prunes and 169.2 million lb of raisins, with a wholesale value in the New York market of roughly $8.7 and $10.4 million, respectively. If the price elasticity of demand was unitary, the sum (about $19.1 million) would have been spent on imports in a counterfactual world in which the US industry disappeared. Of course, not all the revenue would accrue to Mediterranean farmers, labourers, packers, and merchants. Shipping and marketing expenses, including freight, wharfage, insurance, dock labour, and auction charges, and US duties would each claim a share. The available evidence suggests a 35 per cent freight-marketing-tariff markup is reasonable. The added net revenue for the traditional sectors would equal roughly $14.1 million per year. To put this number into perspective, the lost prune and raisin revenues would have been sufficient to support about 98,000 people at the average per capita income levels prevailing in western Mediterranean (Spain and Italy) *c.* 1910.[27]

To the extent that the demand was inelastic, as several econometric studies suggest, the impact of US production would have been greater still. Exactly how many jobs would have been created in the traditional horticultural industries in the absence of the USA or how the added earnings would have been divided among labourers, landowners, merchants and others would, of course, have depended on local supply conditions. Nonetheless, this simple exercise illustrates that the impact of US competition was substantial. Such static calculations, in any case, fail to capture the multiplier effects resulting from the higher regional incomes or the dynamic impacts of the investment possibilities that might have flowed from a more prosperous agricultural export economy.

Conclusion and conjectures

By examining the globalization of the dried-fruit industry, this chapter provides fresh insights into the development of both California and of a number of Mediterranean countries. In addition, by showing how the economies of the two regions were linked through factor flows and competition in output markets, the chapter should add to a rich literature dealing with the growth of the international economy in the nineteenth and early twentieth centuries. In the light of the relatively diversified economies that hug the northern rim of the Mediterranean today, it is easy to forget that roughly a century ago dried fruits played a crucial role in the development of several regions and in some cases whole nations. During much of the late nineteenth century, raisins were a leading cash crop and the most important export for the regions of Málaga and Alicante in Spain and for some years raisins were the leading export for all of Anatolia. For several decades, currants dominated Greek economic life, and prunes held a roughly similar position in Bosnia and northern Serbia.

The increased specialization and trade in fruit and nut crops reflected the more general pattern of an increase in the division of labour that was a hallmark of modern economic development. For all the benefits, the growth of specialization and trade also increased risks by exposing the growers, processors, and shippers of specialty crops to the vagaries of market shocks. There was more involved than the risk associated with the movement away from self-sufficiency. The owners of the new orchards, vineyards, and packinghouses often financed their investments by borrowing, thereby exposing themselves to debt risks. Once made, these investments represented fixed costs that by agricultural standards had relatively long payoff periods. If output prices did not meet expectations the effect could be devastating for investors, labourers, and the broader community.

Benjamin Franklin purportedly once advised "put all your eggs into one basket and then protect that basket". Much like the American South with respect to cotton, the raisin and prune regions of the Mediterranean world put a lot of their eggs into one basket; and like the American South, they were not able to protect their baskets when demand growth withered relative to the growth in supply. The rise of production in California and other New Lands was a primary reason for the long-run deterioration (especially relative to expectations and what might have been) in the fortunes of Mediterranean growers. But coupled with the onslaught of new supplies was a series of shocks which intensified the deeper structural problems and at times precipitated outright crisis. The advent of phylloxera could be absolutely devastating to one area while leading to boom conditions in another. As an example, the early phylloxera epidemics in France and Málaga initially contributed to the prosperity of currant growers in Greece and raisin producers in Alicante, Turkey, and California. This stimulated huge investments in new plantings that eventually contributed to the problems of "over supply". In time, the French vineyards were replanted; the resulting loss of the French market caused shock waves that swept across Greece and were felt in Turkey and California. In time the phylloxera scourge afflicted new areas resulting in local and even regional crises. In addition, the increase in tariffs in the United States and in various European nations also shocked Mediterranean producers, causing financial crises and in some cases widespread political unrest.

As we noted above, the experience of fruit producers was similar in many ways to that of European wheat farmers who saw their markets captured by low-cost producers in the Americas, Russia, and Australia. But there was a significant difference because European wheat growers could protect their home markets by erecting high tariff barriers. This would not work for Mediterranean fruit growers who were dependent on export markets for their livelihood. Friendly domestic governments could provide subsidies and create programmes to try to hold fruit off the market or channel it into derivative uses; but for the most part these policies were ineffectual, and fruit growers had to absorb the full fury of the marketplace. This had the beneficial effect of forcing Mediterranean growers and the middlemen who served them to adapt and modernize. But this was an inexplicably difficult and uneven process.

The puzzle of how Paul Mosesian successfully competed with Mediterranean growers in northern European markets in spite of paying substantially higher labour and transportation costs can most easily be solved by pointing to the higher quality of the American product. But this answer raises an intriguing question. Why is it that Mediterranean producers could not simply copy Paul Mosesian's methods? In fact, they tried. In the fruit trade, countless journalists and technical missions observed Californian methods and enthusiastically reported to their countrymen back home. American and British entrepreneurs and advisers were quick to point out how procedures could be improved, but without dramatic results. Is this a case of entrepreneurial failure? Heaven forbid that we fall back on that thoroughly discredited bromide.

A plausible answer to the puzzle might be found in Ramon Ramon-Muñoz's analysis of the olive-oil market in this volume. Ramon-Muñoz found enormous and persistent differences in the quality of olive oil with France, Italy, and to a lesser extent Spain, dominating in the production of high-quality and high-unit-value brand-name oil destined for table use. Next on the quality scale was bulk oil. At the other end of the spectrum was the low-quality and low-unit-value oil intended for industrial applications. Around 1910 Algeria, Turkey, Greece, and Tunisia were confined to the bottom two markets. Even though there were huge price incentives for breaking into the branded market, these low-end producers were not able to penetrate this lucrative business in the pre-World War II era. Spain's share in this high-end market remained fairly constant at about 30–35 per cent. Ramon-Muñoz attributes the differences to a rational international division of labour reflecting the relative abundance (and prices) of capital, labour, and skills.

Activities such as building brand-name recognition were costly and required a consistency of quality – ingredients that were more within the reach of capital-abundant countries. To a significant extent this reasoning may help explain the quality advantages that California had for a wide spectrum of crops. Certainly, there was a similar rough correlation in the relative abundance of factors of production to that which Ramon-Muñoz observed for olive oil. In California, the pursuit of quality often depended on a systematic coordinated effort of many parties – growers, labourers, packers, and shippers. A failure due to improper handling anywhere along the line could mean ruin. In addition, the contributions of university and government scientists along with a local and highly focused chemical industry were invaluable in the quest for quality. Many of the chemical and mechanical innovations needed to control the pests and diseases that sapped orchard productivity and could turn prized fruit into a gooey mush (both in the fields and during shipment) came from California. This scientific infrastructure had the dynamic effects of pouring out new ideas and methods, and providing a vehicle for transferring this information to the private sector. No Mediterranean country came remotely close to developing a government–scientific infrastructure that could begin to rival what emerged in California.

The political economy of Californian agriculture had a significant impact on product quality. Californian growers, through their co-ops, had an understanding and a significant degree of control over all segments of the production chain. Through collective action, Californians were not only able to visualize fruit production and marketing as an integrated system, they were able to influence the entire process, from pre-harvest spraying to setting packing standards. This helped ensure quality in ways that could only be dreamed of in the Mediterranean basin. There, one individual who gave special attention to quality might expect his efforts to be wasted because of sloppy handling after the fruit left his control.

But this reasoning only takes us so far; given the enormous price differentials between the low- and high-quality oils and fruits, why didn't it pay for some entrepreneurs in Bosnia, Turkey, or Spain to invest in producing higher-quality output. Why did French walnut growers and shippers continue to send moldy, worm-infested nuts? (Recall that in the olive-oil trade, France was a quality pacesetter.) Why, for decades, did Turkish and Greek growers persist in marketing raisins and currants contaminated with dirt and stems. The puzzle is all the more intriguing because packers in many instances could have used labour-intensive methods for activities such as sorting and cleaning fruit.

The situation is somewhat akin to what Gregory Clark described in his analysis of international productivity differences in the textile industry (Clark 1987a). Transport British machines, plant designs, and managers to any number of less-developed countries and the local workers will still have low levels of productivity compared to the UK. But when workers from poor countries migrate to the UK or the United States, they adopt new work standards and their productivity roughly equals the norms of their new country. The same general pattern appears to have applied in the horticultural industry. We doubt that if Paul Mosesian had remained in Turkey, and somehow managed to employ American technology and managers, that he could have achieved American production standards. Clearly, he would not have had the infrastructure that we described above. But in addition, one can reasonably doubt that the illiterate peasant growers that he would have had to work with would have been as diligent and as responsive to market signals as the relatively highly educated Californians. The quality problems in the Mediterranean basin are probably a reflection of just how significant the nebulous "skill" or human-capital component of the production process was.

In addition, cultural factors may have hampered the flow of information and the improvement of standards. In California, growers, packers, and shippers were generally of the same social class and could relatively easily communicate with one another as equals. This would not have been the case in many areas of peasant agriculture, where cultural divides added to the barriers that illiteracy and the lack of a scientific infrastructure already created for the efficient transfer of information and technologies. Notwithstanding these speculations, understanding the sources of the quality and productivity differences remains a hard nut to crack that is deserving of more attention.

Notes

We have received valuable comments from Maurice Aymard, Bridget Biscotti Bradley, Susan Carter, Lisa Cappellari, Giovanni Federico, James Foreman-Peck, Avner Greif, Lovell Jarvis, Naomi Lamoreaux, John Lampe, Peter Lindert, Shelagh Matthews, Michael Palairet, Şevket Pamuk, Socrates Petmezas, Vicente Pinilla, Jean-Laurent Rosenthal, James Simpson, Kenneth Sokoloff, Jean Stratford, Richard Sutch, Jeffery Williamson, and from the seminar participants at UC Davis, UC Berkeley, UCLA, Oxford University, Stanford University, University of Western Australia; and at the conference on "Los impactos exteriores sobre la Agricultura y el Mundo Rural Mediterráneo a lo largo de la Historia," held in Madrid, Spain and the conference on "Long-Run Economic Change in the Mediterranean Basin", held in Istanbul, Turkey.

1   Our estimate of the US share of the world's commercial raisin output is based on Bauer (1933). We exclude Persian and Russian Turkestan's production. In this period almost all of the raisins exported from these areas went to Russia and nearly all of Russian imports came from these two producers. The raisins entering this trade were heavily seasoned to satisfy the distinctive Russian taste and were unmarketable elsewhere, such that they essentially constituted a separate market. Bauer (1933: 84–101 and 118–9); Critz (1995: 303–4); Wheeler (1927:19–24).

2   It is important to note that much of the available data about market shares deal with quantities instead of values and thus understate the relative importance of the American fruit industry (Shear 1928: 19 and 24).

3   The geographic concentration of commercial prune and raisin production activity appear to be primarily the result of "natural advantage". But there was undoubtedly some role for what may be called "artificial advantage", for agglomeration economies arising from better access to specialized inputs and services – packing houses etc. – and to evolving knowledge about best practices. A prune grower located in the Santa Clara valley was likely to have had a far easier time finding suitable drying facilities in a wet year than one located far from the centre of production.

4   For an analysis of the competition between wheat and fruit for an earlier period see Rhode (1995b). See also Adams (1921: 53, 81 and 97).

5   For most years the tariffs on horticultural crops were specific duties. Growers (and tariff takers) preferred specific tariffs because it was harder for importers to understate the value of their shipments and, in times of depressed conditions resulting from a sudden decline in prices, specific duties increased the level of protection. We calculated the *ad valorem* rates to provide rough indices that allow for comparisons between different commodities. These rates are based on the ratio of duties collected to the *declared* values in the port of shipment, but they must be used with caution because these values may not reflect actual market prices. The *ad valorem* rates do not include shipping and marketing commissions and thus they overstate the cushion provided to domestic producers. We should also emphasize that growers had to share the benefits of the tariffs with packers, railroads, and commission agents.

6   Hitchcock (1903) indicates that US tariffs tended to be above the median, but well within the main range – 1.5–2.6 cents per pound for dried fruit – of the duties imposed by other major consuming countries. In addition to creating barriers to US exports, the European tariffs also lowered the "international" price for Mediterranean horticultural products, reducing the net effectiveness of the US protective wall.

7   These cases conform nicely to the prescriptions of those favouring infant industry protection. The tariffs helped the industries, comprised a large number of small producers, and overcame high learning costs, but via market forces ceased to have significant adverse efficiency or distribution effects once the industries matured. By contrast, the tariffs on fresh grapes, figs, dates, and the nut crops appear to have had a continuing impact on imports, prices, domestic production, and growers' profits through the 1930s. Our reading of the tariff hearings over the late nineteenth and early twentieth

centuries supports this conclusion regarding the differential impacts of the tariffs. The advocates for the raisin, prune, and orange producers became far less prominent than the lobbyists for lemon, grape, fig, and nut producers.

8   The US competitive disadvantage was declining over time. Transportation rates on Greek currants declined by roughly one-third in real terms between 1889 and 1909; those on Californian raisins by more than half.

9   Latham (1885: 186) and Wickson (1900: 56).   Lower processing requirements undoubtedly also played a role in the early success of raisins and prunes. Grapes could be left in the sun to turn into raisins without extensive preparation, and prunes were considered unique among stone fruits because they "dry readily without spoiling without the pit being removed … (the) high sugar content of the prune varieties … inhibits fermentation". To dry peaches, apricots, and most other stone fruits required manual labour to cut each fruit in half or quarters and remove the pit. In the early years, the cut fruit were typically dried in evaporators. Over the course of the nineteenth century, Californian growers increasingly adopted the sulphur and sun-drying method. By exposing the cut fruit to sulphur fumes before placing them in the open air and sun to dry, Californian growers found they could preserve their fruit's colour and flavour, protect against insects, and reduce the evaporation time by half. Even with these methods, figures from the 1890s suggest that drying peaches or apricots cost 2.5–3.5 times more per green ton than drying prunes. Couchman (1967: 3 and 30); Wickson (1900: 530–2).

10   Given the very high transportation costs of the pioneer period, these midwestern farmers found it economical to export corn only in high-value processed forms such as whisky. As freight costs dropped, exporting their grain embodied in hogs and other livestock products became profitable. Eventually transportation costs fell low enough to allow midwestern farmers to economically ship their grain directly.

11   US House of Representatives, Committee on Ways and Means, *Tariff Hearings* (1909: 3,937), (hereafter *Hearings*). *Hearings* (1921: 2,027 and 2,035).

12   *Statistical Abstract for the United Kingdom,* various years; Bennett and Peirce (1961: 114–6).

13   Numerous studies have noted how declining transport costs led to an integration of world grain markets that helps explain the success of American wheat producers in capturing European markets: e.g. Harley (1980); Williamson (1996a); O'Rourke and Williamson (1994); and O'Rourke (1997b). Over the period from 1867/72 to 1910/13, the cost of transporting wheat from Chicago to Liverpool fell from 40 cents per bushel to 11.1 cents, or by 28.9 cents; two-thirds of this decline occurred by 1880–4 and 95 per cent by 1895–9.

14   The raisin-producing regions of Málaga, Alicante, and Smyrna were all a short distance from the coast, although new railroads did extend the area of production. This was probably a more general phenomenon that applied to a broader spectrum of cash crops. As an example, in this volume Ahmet Akarli notes in his discussion of Ottoman Macedonia that most cash-crop production was concentrated in Salonica.

15   *California Fruit Grower and Fruit Trade Review* (April 23 1892: 265; May 7 1892: 298), (hereafter *Fruit Grower*); US Consular Report (No. 44, August 1884, SS 2,219: 658; No. 208, January 1898, SS 3,574: 129); Wheeler (1927: 18–22); Aguado (1975: 32); Ignacio Jiménez Blanco (1985: 25). In 1882 raisins made up almost 80 per cent of Málaga's total exports to the United States (US Consular Report 1884: 686).

16   Lacomba (1980: 328); Carnero i Arbat (1980: 128–33); Guisado (1983: 178); Justicia Segovia and Ruiz Sinoga (1987: 175–7); Mignon (1982: 204 and 235). Foster (1938), who surveyed the region in the 1930s, noted: "Changes in world trade argue against the costly replanting of destroyed Málaga vineyards with raisin grapes." The region never fully recovered from the twin shocks of phylloxera and Californian competition. Málaga's raisin exports to the United States more than tripled in 1899, when California experienced a short crop, only to fall again in 1900. US Consular Report (1902: 102–3); US Tariff Commission (1939: 177–8; *La Unión Mercantil* (1887–8); British Consular Report (No. 453, December 1888: 2 and 6; No. 802, Oct. 1890: 3); and in the *Parliamentary Papers* (1886,

vol. LXV: 344); Consejo Superior de Emigración (1916: 410); Robledo (1988: 227–8); Pellejero (1988: 630–1); Sánchez-Alonso (1995: 187).

17 British Consular Reports (AS No. 4,157, Nov. 1908: 32 and 101). Also see: British Consular Reports (AS No. 1672, March 1906: 13; AS No. 2110, May 1898: 20) Costa Mas (1974: 11–21); Robledo (1988: 212–44). Our discussion of Spanish raisins bears on Blanca Sanchez-Alonso's analysis of Spanish emigration elsewhere in this volume. Citing Simpson (1995), she notes that "farmers were slow to switch resources out of cereals ... because of limited opportunities for the export of alternative crops, especially for olive oil and wine". The fact that even the relatively successful export crops like raisins (as well as oranges and fresh grapes) faced a crisis stemming in large part from the growing competition from New World producers further reduced the ability of the Spanish economy to transfer workers within the agricultural sector.

18 Data on exports for 1882–4, 1886, 1898–1906 are compiled from US Bureau of Foreign Commerce (1884: 527–39; 1886: 1,057–66; 1888: 1,012–19; 1899: 1,167–73; 1901: 1,151–4; 1903: 1,158–61), and for 1899, 1901, 1903–6 from British Consular Reports (AS No. 2,462, June 1900: 14; AS No. 2,854, July 1902: 7; AS No. 3,170, May 1904: 16–7; AS No. 3,467, August 1905: 19; AS No. 3,722, October 1906: 15–6; AS No. 3,921, September 1907: 13–4; AS No. 4,141, October 1908: 14). In the 1870s raisins alone constituted about 10 per cent of exports to Britain (Kasaba 1988b: 92; also see, Quataert 1994: 831–3).

19 Quataert (1981: 71–2; 1980: 40–3); US Bureau of Foreign Commerce (1899: 1,168); Basbakanlik Istatistik (1937: 234–8); Istatistik Umum Müdürlügü (1939: 55–9 and 66–7).

20 British Consular Reports (AS No. 3,722, October 1906: 4–5). Supply-side inducements were not limited to grape growers: Akarli (in this volume) describes how the Ottoman government encouraged the production of cash crops in Macedonia by introducing improved seeds, offering special financial incentives, and developing educational programmes to provide cultural information.

21 Costa Mas (1974: 15 and 18). Consumption patterns also changed as housewives, bakers, and other industrial users began substituting more freely between Spanish and Californian raisins and Greek currants; later studies discuss the competition between currants and small seedless raisins. Wheeler (1927: 38); US Tariff Commission (1929: 1,266).

22 British Consular Report (no. 26, May 1884: 777). For Austria–Hungary, see Great Britain Sessional Papers, Microprint (1884, Vol. LXXX); also see the report for Sarajevo in Great Britain Sessional Papers (1886, Vol. LXVI: 425).

23 Lampe and Jackson (1982: 177); Palairet (1977: 582–601, esp. 587); US Department of Commerce and Labor (1909: 263): *Statistical Abstract* (1914: 178–9); Stroykowitch (1910: 3–14 and 184–93).

24 Palairet (1977: 588) shows average Serbian exports of about 52 million lb over this period. His sources indicate that the USA took at least half of Serbia's output in 1883 and about two-thirds in 1889. British Consular Report (AS No. 1,046, May 1893: 12) claims that Serbia had already lost its US market to the higher-quality Bosnian prunes and sold less than $50,000 worth of prunes to the USA over the two years 1889 and 1890. The British Consul in Serbia reckoned that about one-third of Serbian prune exports went to the USA in 1886 (AS No. 176, June 1887: 2–8; AS No. 102, March 1887: 2).

25 France was also squeezed out of the vast US market. Between 1886 and 1895 the USA imported about $700,000 of French prunes annually; over the subsequent decade, the figure dwindled to about $40,000 per year. This, along with the growing competition in European markets, contributed to an absolute decline in French prune acreage and output. Production fell from an average of 45,700 short tons in 1904–8 to 12,300 short tons in 1923–7. Over these years, France's share of world output fell from 26 to 5 per cent, and one of the world's largest prune exporters had become a net importer by the interwar years (Shear 1928: 19 and 52–3).

26 Richard Stone (1954) included selected Mediterranean products in his classic study of consumer expenditures. For dried fruit, he concluded that the "own-price ... elasticity is

never significant" and the income elasticity was "the smallest ... of all the fruit groups analyzed ...".

27   We are using an average income of $668 per capita in 1970 US dollars, based on data from Tortella (1994a: 2). Also see Molinas and Prados de la Escosura (1989: 387 and 397–9). We multiply our 1909/10 citrus revenue data by the change in the US GNP price deflator (4.73) to align them with the Spanish and Italian income data. Using the national per capita income significantly understates the number of farm labourers and their family members who could have been supported in the growing districts.

9 International shipping in the eastern Mediterranean and the Black Sea

Istanbul as a maritime centre, 1870–1910

Gelina Harlaftis and Vassilis Kardasis

Introduction

The emergence and development of an international economy from the last third of the nineteenth century can best be described in terms of the international trade that brought incredible prosperity compared to the past. This was the era of industrial revolution, an increase of world production, technological achievement, quicker communications and cheaper transport costs. Trade and shipping were organized by transnational commercial and maritime networks that contributed to the globalization of the international economy. An international economy, however, still based around Europe. The most important characteristic of international sea trade was the flow of raw materials and foodstuffs to Europe and the flow of industrial goods from Europe to the rest of the world.

Particular bulk cargoes such as grain and its sea-transport determined the organization of international sea trade. The abolition of the European corn laws, navigation acts and other state constraints since the 1840s promoted the process of the internationalization of world markets. The Ottoman Empire adjusted to these trade-liberalization trends by eliminating state monopolies and removing many of the barriers to European merchants, with the famous Anglo–Turkish convention of 1838, which was soon followed by similar agreements with the other European powers. The eastern Mediterranean and the Black Sea had been dominated for centuries by the Ottoman Empire. Its defeat in the Russo–Turkish wars in the late eighteenth century meant the opening-up of the Black Sea to international shipping, which was consolidated with the Treaty of Adrianople in 1829. The ambitious colonization schemes of Catherine II developed the northern and eastern shores of the Black Sea which, together with the fertile lands of the Danube, became the main source of grain for western Europe.

Throughout the nineteenth century the Ottoman Empire experienced a period of decline and readjustment, losing large parts of its territory in the north and south of the eastern Mediterranean. All the sultans, from Mahmud II to Abdulhamid II, tried to open up to western culture and ideas, to reform and modernize the ageing Ottoman system by supporting the empire's international trade. For the expanding colonization systems of industrialized western Europe, the eastern Mediterranean lands became a large unexploited market to penetrate and a desirable and resourceful sphere of influence to manipulate. Moreover, the opening of the Suez Canal in 1869, in conjunction with the introduction of steamships to the area, gave the Mediterranean sea-routes a primary role; a role they had lost three centuries earlier, with the expansion of Europeans to the oceans of the world. The result was an exponential increase in trade and shipping in the eastern Mediterranean during the second half of the nineteenth century.

The increase of the bulk sea-trade brought a direct link and integration of the commodity markets from these eastern lands with the international market of the Atlantic economy. Moreover, it brought the eastern Mediterranean lands and the Black Sea to play a protagonistic role in the international sea-trade, next to the Atlantic. To what extent did integration bring globalization and hence convergence between these two areas?[1] How did eastern Mediterranean countries compare with other parts of the world in the export commodity trades and bulk shipping? What were the effects of the increased activities on the surrounding lands? What were the effects of the thousands of ships ploughing back and forth across the Black and White Seas, at Istanbul, the city that connected this east–west trade, during the period of Abdulhamid II?

Bulk trade and shipping in the Mediterranean

The history of seaborne bulk trade in the Mediterranean basin from the 1870s to the eve of World War I was written mainly by grain and coal and to a lesser extent by cotton. Grain from southern Russia and the Danube was shipped to British and northern European ports, with return cargoes of coal from the British coalfields to the industrialized Mediterranean cities and coaling stations. Cotton from the fertile lands of the Nile was exported from Alexandria to British ports and the ships returned to the Mediterranean with cargoes of coal.

Grain became the main export commodity and the main source of income for the Black Sea lands. The cultivation of the steppe hinterland and the rise of its yields made the Black Sea the paramount granary of Europe. Figure 9.1 pictures the total exports of grain from southern Russia and the Danube and the grain exports from the US Atlantic ports. Although there is an evident steeper upward trend of Black Sea grain exports, the levels of grain exports in both areas were more or less equivalent. Russian wheat, in particular, had managed to stay at the top of western preference before 1861, due to its low prices *vis-à-vis* other competitors, but soon the United States emerged as its main competitor. When, after the American Civil War, farming in the United States improved its yields and the quality of its produce remarkably, while also succeeding in diversifying crops, nothing could compete with it. Russian grain production could not

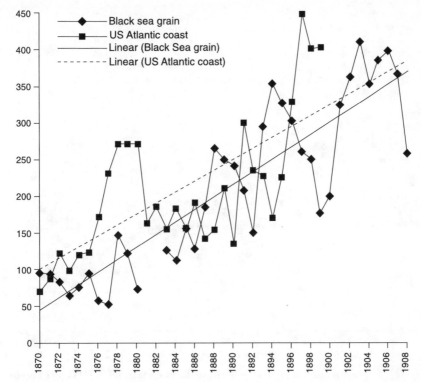

Figure 9.1 Total exports of grain from the Black Sea and US Atlantic Coast (million bushels of 60 lbs).

objectively hold out against American penetration and was destined to be confined to sales in markets with a high demand for second-quality wheat. It managed to keep its position, however, due to certain changes and read-justments. The vast Black Sea wheat-growing regions from the Odessa area to the Azov and the Danube areas proceeded to cultivate different qualities and types of grain and redirected their exports to the continental ports of northern Europe and the western Mediterranean.

As the grain trade continuously increased, the prices of transport, freight rates, continuously declined. This was the period of the second industrial revolution and the introduction of ground-breaking technological changes. In sea-trade this was expressed by the massive adoption of steamships for carrying bulk cargoes, which meant a steep decline in transport costs. Western Europe, which was the main recipient of foodstuffs and raw materials, the bulk commodities of world shipping, proved the main beneficiary of the lower transport costs. Cheaper freights meant cheaper prices of food and products. The reduction of freight rates reinforced the expansion of the export commodities, not only from the Black Sea and the USA but also from India and other new production areas such as South America, promoting

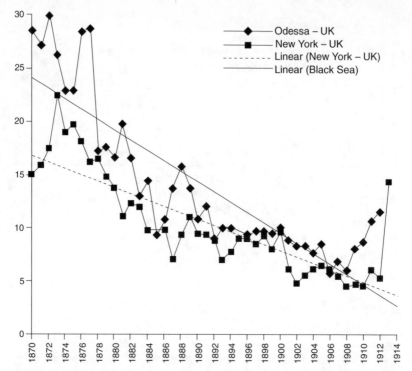

Figure 9.2   Freight rates on grain shipped from the Black Sea and the US East Coast to British ports, 1870–1914 (shillings per ton).

their rapid regional development. As Figure 9.2 indicates, the downward trend of freight rates was steeper in the case of the Mediterranean routes, but the main comparative advantage of the US east coast was that freight rates remained steadily at a lower level. The differences decreased and the freight rates converged in the 1890s.

Coal was the last of the staple industries to develop as a principal bulk commodity in the seaborne trade; on the eve of World War I almost half the tonnage of world coal exports was British and its share of seaborne exports amounted to about 70 per cent. From 1870 to the 1900s, 80–85 per cent of British coal exports were diverted to the Mediterranean and the Baltic. In the Mediterranean, with no alternative sources of quality coal, Welsh steam coal reigned supreme, and continued its rising trend throughout the period under examination (Figure 9.3). In contrast, coalfields in North America kept British exports to the other side of the Atlantic at low levels; they dropped from 6 per cent in 1870 to 1 per cent in 1900. Dramatic increase of British coal exports to South America however, made up for their minimal significance in the northern Atlantic routes, although neither the quantities involved nor the trend could be compared with that of the Mediterranean (Figure 9.3). From 1.5 million tons in 1885, British coal directed to

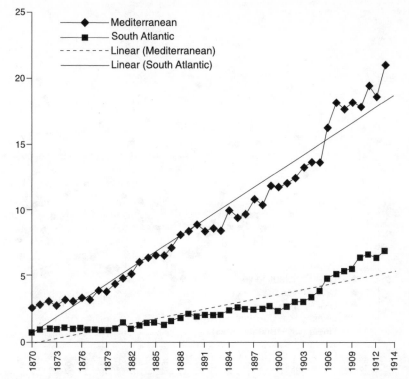

Figure 9.3   Total exports of coal from British ports to the Mediterranean and South
            Atlantic, 1870–1914 (million tons).

Argentina increased to 7 million tons in 1914; it provided return cargoes for
the increasing grain trade from the River Plate during the same period. It is
evident that the availability of coal cargoes from British ports to share the
costs of a round voyage was pivotal for the decrease in freight rates in bulk
shipping. In the Mediterranean, British coal was shipped to the port-cities of
urban industrialized regions in southern Europe, like Marseille or Genoa,
and to coaling stations for steamers, in the Bosporus, Piraeus, Alexandria,
Port Said and elsewhere. Association with both the large grain export trade
from the Black Sea and India's exports through the Suez Canal contributed
also to the steep decline of freights.[2] Figure 9.4 demonstrates the same downward trend of freight rates to both regions, in the eastern Mediterranean and
the South Atlantic routes. Freight rates to Constantinople and Alexandria
coincided and were at significantly lower levels than those to South America.

Cotton is the next bulk-export commodity from the eastern Mediterranean. By 1860, King Cotton was the New World's leading export commodity
and US production was two-thirds of the world total. At the same time Britain
accounted for more than half of the world's consumption of cotton and
American growers supplied it with three-quarters of the cotton it consumed

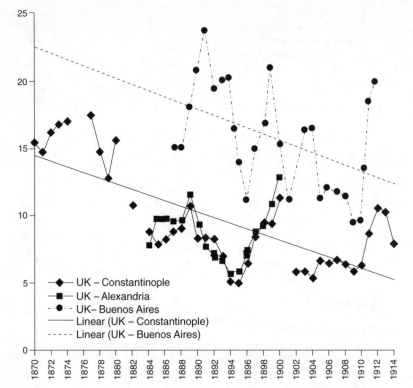

Figure 9.4 Freight rates on coal shipped from British ports to the Eastern
Mediterranean and South Atlantic, 1870–1914 (shillings per ton).

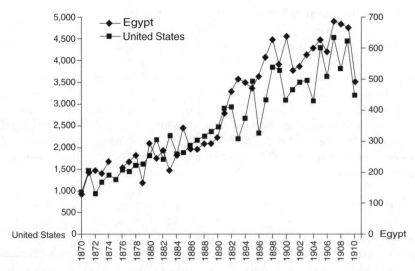

Figure 9.5 Total exports of cotton from Egypt and the United States (million lb).

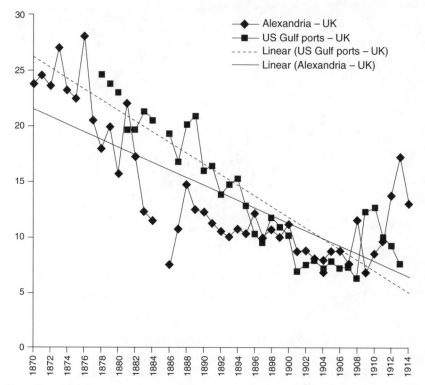

Figure 9.6 Freight rates on cotton shipped from the Eastern Mediterranean and US Gulf ports, 1870–1914 (shillings per ton).

(Cohn 1956). In 1860, Egypt was the sixth most important exporter to Britain, which absorbed 65 per cent of its cotton crop. The American Civil War provided a short-term incentive for Egyptian cotton producers, and between 1864 and 1866 the cultivation of grain was almost completely abandoned in favour of cotton. The United States continued to be by far the biggest cotton exporter, producing six to eight times as much as Egypt from 1870 to 1914, although both production areas indicated the same upward trend (Figure 9.5). However, Egyptian cotton exports enjoyed a continuous growth from 1867 to 1914, increasing sixfold; half of the Egyptian produce was directed to Britain during this period.[3] Cotton freight rates are shown in Figure 9.6 and, as in the case of grain and cotton, indicated clear downward trends. Freight rates from the US Gulf ports such as New Orleans and Charleston to UK ports showed a more rapid decline; freight rates from both areas converged in the 1890s.

Apart from grain and cotton, the eastern Mediterranean was competing with North America in another extremely important bulk cargo that defined the seaborne trade in the twentieth century: oil. In fact the Russian oilfields of Baku in the Black Sea and those of the US east were the world's main oil-

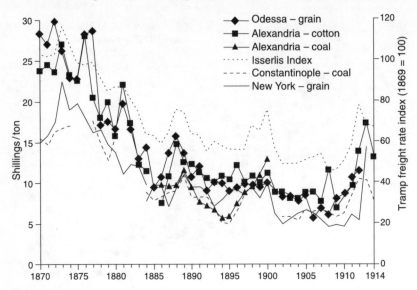

Figure 9.7   Freight rates in Mediterranean and Atlantic routes and the Tramp Freight
Rates Index, 1870–1914.

producing areas in the last third of the nineteenth century. The amounts of
oil involved, however, were at this stage not as significant in defining the seaborne bulk trades in either area, so we are not going to examine them any
more closely.

Although there is a consensus among historians on the decline of freight
rates in the nineteenth century, there is a certain debate as to the timing and
the causes. Douglass North (1958, 1968) had first indicated a rather earlier
decline of freight rates, prior to the introduction of steam, and concluded
that its main causes were the improved economic organization and the establishment of mature commercial networks. C. Knick Harley (1988) in a more
recent article has clearly demonstrated that it was the new industrial technology, metal ships and steam propulsion, that caused a general decline in
freight rates after 1850. Yrjo Kaukiainen (1998) agrees with this view but also
stresses the importance of the increase of speed of communication. He supports the view that the most advanced segment, the western European one,
possessed many of the features and practices – separate freight and commodity markets, advanced chartering, specialized shipbrokers – that were
important for the globalization of markets.

Figure 9.7 combines raw data of freight rates on five eastern Mediterranean and north Atlantic routes for grain, cotton and coal, and an index of
freight rates of tramp trades, meaning bulk shipping (see Appendix). Freight
rates on all routes reveal a remarkable coincidence in the timing of the fluctuations – represented also in the index – indicative of the globalized economy of the second half of the previous century. The decline of freights is

evidently steeper from the mid-1870s to the mid-1880s, and hence follow a steady but slower decline until the eve of World War I.

Just how important were bulk cargoes in the overall trade of the Mediterranean? At this point we consider it necessary to examine the maritime geography of the eastern Mediterranean trade in order to identify the bulk-export trade and to distinguish it from the rest of the trade in the area. We make two categorizations: the first distinguishes between general and bulk cargoes, and the second divides the ports of the eastern Mediterranean into three main groups: the Black Sea ports, the northeastern and the southeastern Mediterranean ports. The cargoes carried by sea between the eastern Mediterranean/Black Sea and the western Mediterranean/northern Europe can be distinguished into general and bulk. General cargo consists mainly of packed expensive goods of limited volume, while bulk cargoes are unpacked cheap goods that occupy a sizeable space. The industrialization of western Europe made this distinction more evident throughout the nineteenth century and general cargo from industrialized countries was usually packed manufactured goods. The distinction of cargoes to be carried by sea into general and bulk also determined the shipping markets of the twentieth century to the present day and defined the organization of shipping companies into liner and tramp shipping, as we shall examine further on.

Shipowners are more concerned with volumes than values.[4] A shipowner rents to the shippers space in the holds of his ship and is not concerned at all about the value of the goods he carries. So bulk cargoes were all the more important for the development of shipping in the area. From 1870 to 1910 bulk cargoes constituted an average of 45 per cent of the total volume of shipping arriving at Marseille from the eastern Mediterranean (Harlaftis 1996: Figure 1.4). For the same period 80 per cent of the tonnage of ships entering British ports from the eastern Mediterranean were loaded with bulk cargoes (Harlaftis 1996: Figure 1.5).

The main port of the eastern Mediterranean remained the large capital of the Ottoman Empire: Istanbul. During the last third of the nineteenth century the movement of ships in this port tripled. This was also the case with the Black Sea ports of Odessa and Taganrog; Alexandria comes next, another port that tripled the movement of ships. The ports of the Archipelago showed a particularly dynamic face: Smyrna (Izmir) quadrupled the movement of its ships, while Piraeus rose from the ashes, replacing Syros as the main Greek port of the eastern Mediterranean with a tenfold increase in traffic (Table 9.1).

The distinction of exporting ports in the eastern Mediterranean into three main groups stems from their geographical positions. Their participation in the export trade of the area has been derived from the arrivals of all ships under all flags from the eastern Mediterranean/Black Sea at the main port of the western Mediterranean, Marseille, and the equivalent arrivals at the main group of ports of northern Europe, the British ports. The Black Sea ports exported bulk cargoes, mainly grain (wheat, maize, barley, oats) along

Table 9.1 Arrivals at the main ports of the eastern Mediterranean, all flags ('000 net tons)

Port	1870	1880	1890	1900	1905
Istanbul*	5 090	6 054	9 996	9 821	14 786
Alexandria	1 199	1 142	1 632	2 376	3 591
Syros	746	833	1 039	839	1 240
Smyrna	630	1 040	1 405	1 578	2 334
Odessa	570	1 092	1 413	1 017	1 394
Danube	550	658	1 539	1 252	1 756
Taganrog	455	—	633	779	918
Salonica	282	376	813	760	922
Piraeus	235	1 158	2 070	2 188	2 845

Sources: British Consular Reports, various years; Folin (1987).

Note
*Excluding coastal craft

with rapeseed, linseed, tallow, wool and wood. These ports are, from west to east, Anchialo (Aktarpolee), Burghaz, Constanza and Varna in Bulgaria, Sulina, Braila and Galatz in Romania, Odessa, Nicolaieff, Sevastopol, Eupatoria, Theodosia in Ukraine, Kertch, Berdiansk, Mariupol, Taganrog, Yeisk and Achtary on the Sea of Azov, Novorossisk, Poti and Batum on the Circassian coast, and Zongouldak on the southern coast of the Black Sea. From the coal mines of Zongouldak coal was exported, while Batum was the main export port from the oilfields of Baku. The Black Sea ports on the whole exported almost exclusively bulk cargoes and formed the most important export area of the eastern Mediterranean. In fact, throughout the period 1870 to 1910, an average of 55 per cent of the total tonnage of ships that left from all ports of the area, destined for Marseille and the British ports, departed from the Black Sea (Table 9.2). The main recipient ports of Black Sea grain after the 1880s were not the British ports but the large continental ports of Antwerp, Rotterdam and Hamburg (Harlaftis 1996: 9–24 and 70–89).

The other main group of exporting ports was in the southeastern Mediterranean, with Alexandria and Beirut standing out by far from the other minor exporting ports of the area, such as Limassol, Jaffa, Latakia, Mersina and Port Said. After the Black Sea ports this group forms the second main exporting area, keeping an average of 30 per cent of the total tonnage of ships destined for Marseille and the British ports. Apart from cotton, other bulk cargoes from Alexandria were cotton seed, wool, wheat, beans, lentils and sugar. There was a great variety of general cargo since Alexandria was an export

Table 9.2 Arrivals of ships at Marseille and British ports from the eastern
Mediterranean, 1870–1910 (net tons)

A. *From the Black Sea*

Year	Arrivals to Marseille	Arrivals to British ports	(A) Total arrivals to both areas	(B) Total arrivals to Marseille and British ports from all ports	% (A)/(B)
1870	334 235	174 823	509 058	1 111 061	46%
1880	419 971	193 206	613 177	1 282 242	48%
1890	484 747	726 261	1 211 008	1 922 506	63%
1900	373 536	314 624	688 160	1 325 735	52%
1910	671 340	423 037	1 094 377	1 731 324	63%

B. *From the north-eastern Mediterranean ports*

Year	Arrivals to Marseille	Arrivals to British ports	(A) Total arrivals to both areas	(B) Total arrivals to Marseille and British ports from all ports	% (A)/(B)
1870	100 583	109 919	210 502	1 111 061	19%
1880	121 454	140 463	261 917	1 282 242	20%
1890	124 351	131 590	255 941	1 922 506	13%
1900	28 941	94 873	123 814	1 325 735	9%
1910	44 606	132 018	176 624	1 731 324	10%

C. *From south-eastern Mediterranean ports*

Year	Arrivals to Marseille	Arrivals to British ports	(A) Total arrivals to both areas	(B) Total arrivals to Marseille and British ports from all ports	% (A)/(B)
1870	157 764	233 737	391 501	1 111 061	35%
1880	112 082	295 066	407 148	1 282 242	32%
1890	99 923	349 098	449 021	1 922 506	24%
1900	195 041	314 514	509 555	1 325 735	39%
1910	162 881	297 442	460 323	1 731 324	27%

Source: See Appendix

port for African and Indian Ocean goods. (Harlaftis 1996: Figure 1.3). In the
1870s and 1880s one-third of the tonnage leaving Alexandria was destined
for Marseille and Britain, and in the 1890s almost one-quarter. It is clear
though that these two areas formed important exporting areas for the southeastern Mediterranean ports up until 1900.

The northeastern ports formed the last group of exporting ports in the
eastern Mediterranean area. The group included some of the main ports of

the area such as Istanbul, Smyrna, Piraeus, Syros, and Salonica as well as a number of smaller Greek ports. The fact that they formed the smallest exporting group in terms of bulk trade does not diminish their importance, because they primarily exported general goods that took up less volume; second, and more importantly, they were on the heaviest passenger sea-traffic routes. Moreover, the fact that they involved some of the most densely populated areas meant that a large part of the shipping was coastal: cargo and passenger coastal shipping. Bulk cargoes such as grain and cotton from the area were also exported from Istanbul, but to quite a limited extent. It is thus evident that the rise of Istanbul as the maritime centre of the area depended very little on its exporting capacities and much more on the increasingly heavy traffic from the Black Sea ports in conjunction with the passenger traffic within the eastern Mediterranean. And this brings us to the other important cargo on which much of the north Atlantic shipping was based: immigrants. Nevertheless, as Williamson suggests in this volume, mass immigration mattered a lot more to the Atlantic economy than to the Mediterranean. Mass migration to the USA from the eastern Mediterranean increased rapidly at the turn of the century and did not affect the development of the trade and shipping of the area in the last third of the nineteenth century.[5] It could also be that there was an important intra-regional migration that has not been considered properly. Throughout the nineteenth century, the northern Black Sea regions with the formation of new cities and the increasing grain trade received a large number of immigrants from Italy, Greece and the Ottoman Empire along with those from Poland and Germany. The economic prosperity of the Black Sea ports encouraged immigration that lasted until the end of the century. The incentives to live there were so great that the population of southern Russia increased from 163,000 in 1782 to 3.4 million in 1856. In a way, the newly developing Black Sea regions were viewed by the poor inhabitants of the Mediterranean lands as the United States by the Irish and the Scottish. Equally, however, Americans seem to have been impressed by the development of southern Russia. An American traveller in the mid-1850s came to Odessa. As he walked about the place he felt that he was in some big city in the USA or Europe, a feeling that his narrative vividly conveys. He was struck by the town plan, the architecture and the grand public buildings. In his opinion the theatre, the casino and the bank of Odessa were superior in aspect to anything comparable in the USA (Kardasis 1998: 84).

It should be noted that Greek commercial houses played a leading role in this extensive trade between eastern and western markets. Already from the mid-eighteenth century the Greeks had penetrated and were engaged in a wide range of activities in other regions that included the Balkan peninsula and southern Russia, while they had expanded their business in central Europe as far as Leipzig (Stoianovich 1960). In the nineteenth century, within the framework of the Ottoman Empire, the Commercial Treaty of 1838 – which contributed decisively to the liberalization of its export–import trade – favoured greatly the Christian minorities, the Greeks and Armenians, who became the bourgeoisie of the cities (Kancal 1983: 361). Thus the immigrants from the Archipelago formed powerful and effective commercial houses, with epicentres in the main mercantile centres of the empire, Istanbul and Smyrna, and branch offices in the main markets of the east (Alexandria, Odessa, Syros), southwestern Europe (Marseille, Trieste, Livorno) and the far-off industrialized west (London, Amsterdam). The cornerstone of this expansion was without doubt the mutual trust between the directors of the branch offices, an indispensable prerequisite for the close cooperation of the various branches of the firms that led to the formation of a closely knit network. The keystone of this network was the common origin or kinship of an extended family enclave. The Greeks developed a commercial know-how that was based on a system of communication and information about the prices, the level of production and the consumption of goods, which meant the exchange of information on a normal basis between the different knots of the network. They also successfully maintained a system of debit and credit accounts which allowed the regular movement of cargoes to and fro, the exchange of the agricultural products of the east with the industrial goods of western Europe. The involvement of these commercial houses in the grain trade was precisely the axis of the development of Greek commercial and shipping activities throughout the nineteenth century (Kardasis 199, Ch. 5; Harlaftis 1996, Ch. 2 and 3). The establishment of numerous Greek commercial houses in London in the world's main grain market as early as the 1820s contributed to the integration of the Black Sea grain trade in the international market.[6] It is our belief that the successful practice of such international commercial and maritime networks led the Greeks to become among the main traders of Istanbul, a fact recognized by the foreign consuls established in the capital of the Ottoman Empire.[7] The same was true of the Black Sea ports of Odessa, Taganrog and Rostoff, of the commercial triangle of the Danube (Galatz, Braila and Sulina), and of Alexandria in the south.

From sail to steam

In 1870 there were fifteen countries involved in the sea transport of the growing trade of the Atlantic economy and 80 per cent of the world tonnage was concentrated in the area with 14 million net registered tons, an amount that reached 25 million n.r.t. in 1914. The countries that formed this fleet were Great Britain (with 45 per cent of the fleet in 1910), the United States (second with 12 per cent in 1910), Germany, Norway, Canada, France, Italy, Sweden, Spain, Russia, Holland, Denmark, Finland, Belgium and Greece (Fischer and Nordvik 1986). This is the period during which the transition from sail to steam took place. It was Britain that started first and replaced its sailing-ship fleet with steamships in the mid-1880s, but by the eve of World War I all the aforementioned countries had completed this transition.

The great upsurge in trade from the eastern Mediterranean and the Black Sea was accompanied by an unprecedented increase in shipping in these areas. Even today, in the age of airplanes, highly advanced highways and railways, at least 80 per cent of the world's international trade is carried on sea lanes. In an era and an area in which road transportation, and, even more, railway transportation were still in their infancy, increase of trade meant sea-trade. Although the introduction of steam into the eastern Mediterranean took place in the late 1820s, the presence of steamers became evident from the 1840s and its massive penetration into the eastern Mediterranean and Black Sea routes after the 1880s. Sailing vessels, however, continued to operate until the end of the century – although increasingly restricted to coastal shipping – despite the great competition they encountered from the new "iron beast". Sailing ships continued to carry bulk cargoes like grain and coal, and the new "unwanted" cargoes like oil, at low rates, and were still preferred, especially when freight rates were low. It was only when freight rates became so low that they could not cope that sail was driven out of business.

The introduction of steam in the Mediterranean brought the increasingly clear distinction of the shipping market into three sectors: liner shipping, tramp shipping and coastal shipping. It is the type of cargo, the type of ship and the area in which it trades that determine the market in which a ship works. Liner shipping emerged from the establishment of regular steamship lines on regular schedules, calling at many ports at specific dates and times. The main advantage of the liner companies is based on their regularity and organization on a wide range of ports regardless of the existence of cargoes. Steam made possible what was impossible for sail: regularly scheduled sailings. Passengers became a prime cargo for liner steamship lines, particularly on the Atlantic routes that served the migration wave from western Europe to the Americas throughout the nineteenth century. The Mediterranean became the arena of fierce competition between European steamship lines; there was also a large wave of immigration from the Mediterranean to the Atlantic towards the end of the century. The introduction of steamships and their evident advantages over sailing ships brought most European nations into wild competition for the control of the seas by establishing steamship companies on state subsidies. These subsidies were given mostly in the form of mail subventions by their states. The steamship companies of a certain nationality that carried the mail of particular countries, with which they traded for free, enjoyed particular advantages with tax exemptions from these countries; their obligation was to serve a particular route a certain number of times per week or month and also to carry the country's mail. Britain, France, Germany, Italy, Austria, Holland, Denmark, the Ottoman Empire, Russia and Greece all established such steamship companies between the 1830s and the 1850s, which competed for cargo and passenger transportation in the Mediterranean. In this way, the British Peninsular & Oriental, Cunard, Leyland, Burns and MacIver, Moss, Papayanni, Prince, Johnson, and Westcott & Laurence steamship liner companies traded regularly between the eastern Mediterranean/Black Sea and Britain. The same happened with the French Messageries Maritimes, Fraissinet, Paquet, Transatlantique and Franco–Belge steamship companies, that traded between the eastern Mediterranean and French ports, the German Deutsche–Levante–Linie and Freitas company, the Austrian Lloyd–Austriaco, the Italian Florio–Rubatino, the Danish Danoise Ferenede Damps Kids, the Dutch Hollandaise Navigation à Vapeur, the Russian Steamship company, the Ottoman Idarei Massousieh, the Ottoman Greek Courtgi Steamship and Hadji–Daout Farkouh steamship lines, the Hellenic Steam Navigation company and a number of smaller steamship lines.

The ships of these liner companies carried mainly general cargo and passengers (although until the end of the century some also carried bulk cargoes); they usually loaded most of their cargo in one port and added small amounts or passengers and small parcels of cargoes from other ports. Each steamship of the above-mentioned companies called at from one to twelve ports. In this way their importance in the trade of a particular port becomes rather blurred. The amount of tonnage counted in each port's shipping statistics involves the whole tonnage of a steamship, exaggerating the importance of the steamships of a certain nationality in the trade of a particular port. For example, the 1,417-ton steamer *Roumelia*, belonging to the Papayanni Steamship Company, called at Odessa, Constantinople, Smyrna and Syros in January 1890. In Syros it might have unloaded "20 packages of sweets" when at the same time a Greek sailing ship, *Agios Panteleimon* of 250 tons, may have unloaded a full cargo of grain. The aggregate shipping statistics recorded, however, the arrival of 1,417 British tons and 250 Greek tons, which really emphasizes the importance of Syros as a port of call for a number of European steamship lines and rather underestimates the main carriers of the bulk cargo of the area. The British steamship lines of course dominated the carriage of passengers and general goods. Furthermore, the opening of the Suez Canal in 1869 made the eastern Mediterranean the main artery for British and other European steamship companies with their colonies in the east and Far East.

Noteworthy is the competition between the foreign liner companies in their scheduled sailings to Istanbul. In fact, what was taking place beyond Gibraltar on the Atlantic routes was also evident in the sea-routes to and from the Ottoman capital. The entry of the German companies at the end of the nineteenth century upset the long-term existing balance imposed by Austrian Lloyd, Messageries Maritimes and the British companies. The Germans, by establishing an incredible collaboration between German railways and their steamship lines, aimed to promote German industrial products in the east through the establishment of Deutsche–Levante–Linie that sailed between Hamburg and Turkey. The same methods were adopted by the other German company that inevitably followed, the Atlas Line of Bremen. A further innovation that they implemented, giving them an advantage over their competitors, was the establishment of a regular monthly sailing between Istanbul and New York at the beginning of the twentieth century; the vessel coming from New York called at Malta, Alexandria, Piraeus, Smyrna, Istanbul, Novorossisk and Odessa. It was really a show of cooperative spirit between the powerful Hamburg–American Line and the Deutsche–Levante–Linie.[8] In this way two important prospects opened up: on the one hand, access to the Levant for the wide American market; the increase of American trade to the area was actually important in the following years, a fact that impressed the British consul in Istanbul. [9] Evidently the German companies earned good profits from this business. On the other hand, the German initiative aimed to exploit the increasing migration wave from the eastern Mediterranean to the United States. Inalcik talks about 1.2 million Ottoman subjects emigrating to North America between 1860 and 1914. It is logical to suppose, on the basis of our knowledge of the Greek experience, that most of this population left during the early years of the twentieth century (Inalcik and Quataert 1994; Kardasis 1997).

The main volume of the area's trade however, the bulk cargoes, was carried by the so-called tramp ships. If liner companies have regular schedules, tramp ships work entirely on demand on an irregular basis. And it was on tramp ships that all grain, cotton, wool and other minor bulk cargoes (like lumber for example) were carried. Tramp ships were owned by a large number of steamship owners and formed half of the large British fleet in the last third of the nineteenth century (Harlaftis 1996: 31–8 and 70–88). The Greeks were also involved, indeed almost exclusively, in tramp shipping and in the period under examination sailing and steam ships coexisted. The main carriers of bulk cargoes from the Black Sea and southeastern ports were the Greeks and the British. In fact it has been calculated that more than half the tonnage carrying bulk cargoes to Marseille from the eastern Mediterranean and the Black Sea was chartered by Greek merchants or carried by vessels under the Greek flag. Similarly, Greek participation in the bulk trades from the area to England, from 1860 to 1880, was about 50 per cent, although after the 1880s it saw a significant decrease. Until the 1880s Greek ships carried grain from the Black Sea to Britain and brought back coal for the Mediterranean. But after 1890 Greek vessels brought grain to ports like Antwerp, Rotterdam, Le Havre and Dunkirk, before sailing to British ports in ballast to load coal for the Mediterranean (Harlaftis 1996: 21–2).

Coastal shipping constitutes another important section of shipping in the eastern Mediterranean. The geography of the area, the existence of a large number of big cities, and the increasing internationalization of the trade from the main port-cities increased the passenger traffic to an unprecedented degree. On the other hand the lack of road transport and the existence of hundreds of islands made necessary the thousands of small craft engaged in the trade over small distances within the Ionian and Aegean Seas, the Dardanelles and the Black Sea. This chapter however, deals with long-distance trade, and the coastal trade of the area is beyond its scope although it really deserves future attention. It is very interesting to note that cargo coastal shipping continued to be conducted by sailing ships to a much higher degree than it is thought, to the eve of World War II.

Istanbul, the maritime centre of the eastern Mediterranean

By the end of the nineteenth century more than 10,000 ships arrived at Langually and departed from the port of Istanbul and many thousands more called at minor ports along the Dardanelles. What were the effects of this intense commercial and maritime activity on the capital of the Ottoman Empire? Istanbul, a transit centre that responded to the economic developments and choices of far-away markets, emerged as an economic centre of international importance transcending the commercial needs of the empire. We shall trace here this transformation through its maritime aspect. First we shall look at the development of Istanbul's maritime infrastructure to serve the increasing shipping needs, second we will examine the nature of maritime services at Istanbul and its surrounding area, and third we will consider Istanbul as a maritime centre of Ottoman and foreign shipping companies.

Istanbul is bounded by water and this great city has always been connected with the sea and ships. The hills upon which it is built provide sea-views from any part of the city. Its three main districts in the nineteenth century, Stambool, Pera and Scutari, were at once separated and connected by the Golden Horn Bay and the Bosphorus. Its unique position has of course ensured its importance as a capital of empires and given it a cosmopolitan character throughout its existence. In 1885 more than half of its 850,000 population belonged to Christian ethnicities; the largest non-Muslim communities were of Greeks and Armenians, followed by the Jews.[10] And all these minorities lived and worked in Galata or Pera, neighbourhoods where the most affluent sections of the population were so concentrated, that it was only natural that the use of gas for lighting and the improvement of public roads took place early there.[11] Pera, "the City of the Giaours", was really a European city transplanted into Anatolia, unconnected with the surroundings and the rest of Ottoman life, evolving entirely by linking the east with the west (Wheatcroft 1993: 185). The whole of the nineteenth century saw serious efforts to westernize this very different Ottoman city. The *Tanzimat* ideology was prevalent in a continuous attempt to adopt change and reform based on western models. It was during this period that Istanbul was connected by railway with Vienna, as if to exorcize the ghosts of the old rivalry between the Muslim and the Christian capitals. It was during this period that tramways were laid in the city, and a regular steamship service was inaugurated; before, hundreds of rowboats carried commuters along its water routes and barges connected its shores (Celik 1986: 82–3).

The construction of bridges and the establishment of regular steam services had very important ameliorating effects on the city's communication system. In the last third of the century long modern quays and warehouses were constructed to secure the traffic and the trade of the foreigners. The increase of shipping enforced systematization and organization in the dock-lands, which were still far from efficient in the late 1860s. The problems at the port were threefold: first of all, the shallow water caused problems for the approach of large sailing vessels and steamships. Second, the lack of wharves appropriate for the loading and unloading of large vessels, along with the lack of basic dock organization at the waterfront, were a source of continu-ous complaints and delays. And lastly, an important problem with social implications was that port services were under the control of guilds of por-ters and boatmen. This was really a closed profession that had the right to monopolize the port movements, to control the entry of new workers in the sector and, of course, to determine the remunerations. It was a common sight at times of congestion of ports, for cargoes to remain on barges or on the docks waiting to be loaded. Delays of ships at the waterfront of Istanbul were all too common, a fact that had negative effects on shipping and the integration of commercial activities.[12]

However, the complaints of the foreign companies through their consuls brought results in dock developments in the city. For example, for the issue of traffic inside the port, a twenty-member Port Committee was established in 1875 with the participation of the British consul; the committee placed buoys and drafted port regulations.[13] But the dock problems were only resolved at the end of the century. In 1890 a French company undertook the construction of docklands, a project that was completed in 1895. These developments covered the need to berth steamships of large tonnage. Major confrontations and problems with the guilds of porters and boatsmen fol-lowed, because, as expected, the French company was granted the right to exploit the docks and was not prepared to settle for the demands of the port workers.[14]

All these problems were prevalent because Istanbul was a port of call for thousands of ships from many places loaded with all kinds of cargoes; how-ever, industrial goods and textiles from the west, and grain from the Black Sea accounted for the largest section in the city's trade. The first, the prod-ucts of Manchester – metals, hardware, colonial produce – were destined for consumption in the wide market of Anatolia. In 1865 Istanbul remained the main supplier of industrial goods to regions like Persia, Georgia and Circassia. Even more, of course, it was the supplier of the whole Ottoman Empire. The imports of the Turkish state and particularly the inflow of mili-tary equipment and supplies should not be overlooked either. Wheat figured at the top of the imports of agricultural products, a decisive component in the smooth functioning of the large population of the capital. But generally grain, seeds, wool, silk, mohair, hides, fruit, dyes, wood, minerals, drugs and other agricultural goods were brought to the city either for local consump-tion or for shipping to the markets of the west that processed raw materials. The appeal to the foreign markets, to the Danubian Principalities and southern Russia, even for products produced in the Ottoman hinterland, was necessary because of lack of any infrastructure of internal communications within the Ottoman dominion, that is access to the places of local production.[15]

So Istanbul was a transit port, for many decades. This role did not decrease as dramatically with the penetration of the steamship, as has been noted in other studies of similar activities in the intermediary commercial ports of the Mediterranean (Kardasis 1987: 102; 1993: 127–140). Rather its nature changed; its proximity to the production area and the increasing sailings from the Black Sea, enhanced its position as a central node of maritime intelligence, even though new technological developments made commercial communications with the west more direct. We have already noted the comparative advantages of the new means of transport over the traditional vessels on sea routes; particularly after the implementation of technological innovations (like the compound engine and steel) which led to savings in fuel consumption, improvements in shipbuilding design and vessels of larger carrying capacity. It was the penetration of liner steamship companies in the eastern Mediterranean that hit the old commercial centres of the area, bringing the decentralization of international trade, since it facilitated direct access to places of production and consumption. The local Anatolian merchant could now order merchandise from abroad more easily, in a shorter period of time and, what is important, at a lower cost.[16] Political developments in the lands of the Ottoman Empire intensified the new situation. The loss of territories had a marked effect on the decrease of commerce of Istanbul and the encouragement of local markets. For example, according to the British Consul General Fawcett, in 1886 Macedonia and Albania imported textiles directly from Manchester via Salonica, from eastern Rumelia via Dedeagatch, from southern Asia Minor via Beirut and Mersine, and from Persia via Bushire. For the importers of Istanbul there remained the southeastern lands of the Black Sea (Trebizond, Samsun), Bourgas in Bulgaria and far Azerbaijan.[17]

On the whole, the period 1879–98 has been described as a phase of relative stagnation in Ottoman foreign trade, as a result of the great depression of the economies of the western states. This situation changed completely with the opening of the railway lines.[18] The railway issue generated a great debate in the rival countries of the east, in that the routes were shaped according to military considerations in Turkey and Russia, an argument that is difficult to avoid.[19] Despite the existence of military plans in both areas, we cannot disregard the fact that railways changed the economic face of wide regions and in this respect produced direct economic results. We mention indicatively that the Anatolian Railway moved the sources of grain supplies for the Istanbul market. The cargoes now came mainly from the grain-producing areas of Anatolia, thus diminishing the importance of the traditional markets of Russia, Romania and Bulgaria.

If the introduction of steam on land routes changed the local trade of the area, the introduction of steam on sea routes brought dramatic changes in the navigation of the straits (Dardanelles) and the international trade of the area. Navigation through the Dardanelles is a complex operation *per se.* The straits are forty miles long, varying from three-quarters of a mile to two miles in width, with a strong current that always runs through to the south, at a rate of two to four miles per hour. The wind that often blows in the same direction proved a great hurdle for sailing ships that wanted to proceed to the north towards the Black Sea and they frequently had to wait at the entrance to the straits. Access from the Black Sea ports to the northern side of the straits could prove even more tricky. The flat and rugged coast could become very dangerous in foggy conditions, when the master could not locate the passage. Signals and lifesaving boats were of little help in sailing the straits.[20] But lack of wind is an even worse enemy to the sailing ship. To help these vessels to proceed, the inhabitants of some villages at the entrance of the Dardanelles, like Khardi-Kioi, had boats or barges led by tow horses against the stream. The introduction of tugs revolutionized the passage through the straits, but this was costly and to the end of the century negotiating the Dardanelles was a difficult task for sailing-ship owners. As late as 1892 the Greek brig *Anastassia,* of 163 tons and registered in Syros, on its way from Genova to Taganrog took twenty-six days to pass through the Dardanelles. When the wind was favourable, however, the passage took one day: "Having the wind northerly we sailed the Dardanelles on the same day and fortunately reached Constantinople, and anchored at Bouyouk Dere of Bosphorus on that same day [25 September 1897]."[21] The large and varied craft that sailed the straits needed different types of services. Ships that entered either from the White Sea or the Black Sea had to pay lighthouse dues, port dues, custom dues, sanitary regulations, to obtain free pratique: "We reached Constantinople on the 3rd of October [1892] at 11:00 a.m. and anchored in Kaminia where we passed sanitary control and obtained free pratique... Next day we received all our papers and we are ready for departure." The information from the logbook gives us no details of sanitary control or quarantine. It is true that Istanbul was always a port that suffered from epidemics because of the frequent appearance of contagious diseases in the eastern Mediterranean basin. In the same period that Master Elias Kulukundis reports in his logbook, the British Consul Wrench expresses his deep concern on the lack of any rationalism with respect to the procedure of sanitary surveillance by the port authorities of Istanbul. According to Wrench, the doctor examined the patient, an infected seaman from a sailing ship, by boat without going aboard the ship.[22] It is evident that the margins of an erroneous diagnosis were rather large and many a crew suffered tremendously. What is more, the Ottoman government reacted against the request of foreign consular representatives to establish a hospital on a laid-up ship, or even on the coast, in order to attend to seamen infected by cholera, the cursed disease of the nineteenth century.[23]

Istanbul provided an endless source of seamen and a convenient place for the change of crew by the master. After loading grain at Yeisk, the *Anastassia* came back to Istanbul and on September 12 1884: "we anchored at Koui-Koule. On the 13th of the same we received our shipping papers and we changed our crew, as is evident from the crew list, and all the necessary supplies for our journey and we proceeded to Malta..." Ships break down and need repair. They need spare parts and maintenance services. Istanbul had available workers even for steamships. Captain Anastassios Syrmas, Master of the s/s *Andriana*, wrote in the logbook on 11 March 1908:[24] "According to the orders of the shipowner we stayed here [in Constantinople] to clean and paint the holds and quarters of the ship, for this and for every safety of the ship we moved from Kapatas to Pasha-Baxe of Bosphorus."[25]

Istanbul was also the place where ships were sought for chartering. The daily arrivals of ships brought news from all ports and news of freight rates and availability of cargoes; Istanbul and the Bosporus provided an excellent central point for ships waiting to be chartered. The years 1883 and 1884 witnessed a shipping crisis when freight rates had reached rock-bottom levels. On 30 March 1884, Captain Elias Kulukundis of the *Anastassia* sought charter and wrote in his logbook "Because of no charter we waited in Constantinople, firing the crew we stayed there around 110 days, that is until 20 July on which day we were able to charter the ship with a whole cargo of grain of Mr Ambanopoulo at Yeisk to bring it to a Mediterranean port." During these difficult years it was in Istanbul that Captain Demetrios E. Catzulis from Galaxidi also sought to charter his brig the *Assimoula* of 308 tons. He did find a rather new cargo from a new port. He transported empty barrels to Batum and returned them to Istanbul filled with petroleum from Baku. A smelly, slippery and unwanted cargo from leaky barrels was also a dangerous cargo for these first sailing tankers: "On 24 May of the year 1883 day Thursday we left from Constantinople for Patoum [sic]... On Saturday the winds are strong... On Sunday the sea is calm...3 June we are in Patoum...We loaded barrels with petrol under the deck 1,887 and 173 on the deck. On 20 June we leave the damned Patoum... Dead calm, as much as you can imagine... Little wind... Days of hell... Disgraceful Thursday.. More calm.. God has no mercy on us... I am sick... for eight days we can not move..."[26] The furious and expressive captain, who took six days to reach "Patoum" from Istanbul, did a "disgraceful" return journey of thirty-three days to unload petroleum. "The Black Sea that blackens the hearts"[27] was a menace to the masters not only in its wildness but also in its calmness.

Although Marconi applied for the world's first patent for wireless in England in 1896, it took almost another fifty years for all ships to acquire wireless apparatus. Tramp ships loaded cargo in the Black Sea and headed, according to their charter parties, to Constantinople, Malta, Gibraltar or Falmouth for orders, because their cargo was sold by branch offices in Marseille or London while the ship was en route. At beginning of the artery of the grain trade, Istanbul became an important port of call for receiving orders from shipowners and ship agents. "On the 1st of June 1883", wrote Captain

Kulukundis, master of the sailing ship the *Anastassia*, "we received orders from Mrss Petrocockino and Company... to sail to Falmouth". Twenty-five years later Captain Syrmas, master of the steamship *s/s Andriana*, wrote in his logbook: "[on 27 June 1908] we arrived in Constantinople and anchored in Kapatas (Galata) where we obtained free pratique waiting for orders from our shipowner in Braila. On Sunday 29 June I received orders from the shipowner in Braila Alcibiades Embiricos through our agents Foscolo and Mango". However, stopping at Istanbul for orders became rarer and rarer for the *Andriana*: "We were on steam in Kavak and we had our sanitary certificates surveyed and we left Kavak, sailing down the Bosphorus with care because of many steamships that were sailing upwards. We sailed the Bosphorus and Constantinople, we left Propontis with a speed of 8 miles per hour we entered the Hellesponte near Gallipoli. We stayed on steam and we gave the fireman to the patrol boat and then we left from Nagara. We sailed through the Dardanelles and left the Hellespont behind..." The *Andriana* did not stop as frequently at Istanbul because it made short stops at Andros for change of crew. Nevertheless, most of the European tramp ships continued to stop in Istanbul before embarking on the long trip to the north. The steamship *s/s Tregenna*, nine years old and of 2,623 gross tons, belonged to Edward Hain from St Ives in Cornwall. During 1901–2 it made five return voyages to the eastern Mediterranean, carrying cargoes from the Black Sea to northern Europe and coal on return voyages. On four of its five voyages it stayed in Istanbul more than one week at a time (Craig 1973: 33–48, Appendix).

The heavy sailing and steamship traffic that went through Istanbul, giving it the most prominent position among the ports of the eastern Mediterranean, also made it the indisputable maritime centre of the Ottoman Empire. Obviously Istanbul owed this position to the passing through of thousands of vessels, most of which, however, were not linked in any way with the port's trade that, as we have already indicated, had declined considerably.

As Wrench noted characteristically: "It must not be supposed that the amount of shipping is any indication of the trade of this port; as all vessels passing through the Straits, to and from Black Sea ports, pay the Turkish dues, and are included in the table, although many of them pass through the Straits in quarantine without touching at Constantinople."[28] Table 9.3 gives an indicative picture of the nationality of the steamships that participated in the trade of the city.

As is directly evident from Table 9.3, barely one-third of the ships and less than one-quarter of the tonnage of steamships that departed from Istanbul had loaded at this port. The rest of the craft just passed through the Ottoman capital. In addition, the powerful position of the Greek flag in terms of number of ships is also evident; this is the period of the formation of the Greek cargo steamship fleet that ploughed the Mediterranean and the Black Sea engaged in bulk trading. These were smaller vessels, at least in comparison to liner steamers, bought second-hand in the British markets, that were also able

Table 9.3 Departures of steamships from the port of Istanbul having loaded cargoes

	1902		1903		1904	
Flag	Number	Tons	Number	Tons	Number	Tons
Turkish	693	390 000	884	367 000	1 017	1 620 000
Greek	472	206 000	634	293 000	652	296 000
Russian	468	386 000	513	456 000	572	440 000
Austrian	278	369 000	354	486 000	372	531 000
British	223	293 000	243	350 000	264	388 000
French	210	316 000	224	356 000	264	419 000
Italian	154	239 000	224	325 000	236	403 000
Rumanian	73	57 000	109	79 000	110	90 000
Bulgarian	70	44 000	82	54 000	76	51 000
Others	54	48 000	46	49 700	38	39 000
German	51	78 000	86	131 000	88	131 000
A. Departures of loaded ships	2 746	2 426 000	3 399	2 946 700	3 689	4 408 000
B. Total departures	8 880	12 148 000	10 450	15 239 000	10 796	16 247 000
(A)/(B)%	31%	20%	32%	19%	34%	27%

Source:
F.O., No. 2813, 12.5.1902, p. 26, No. 2950, 9.3.1903, p.28, No. 3140, 21.3.1904, p. 27.

to sail in the shallow waters of the Danube and the Azov Sea. The relative decline of the British ships and tonnage is also characteristic of the period, if we consider that a decade earlier the British constituted over 50 per cent of the ship movements of Istanbul (excluding coastal craft). There are two reasons for this development: first, the invasion of American grain in the London market, in other words replacing the supplies from Russia, which undoubtedly influenced the range of activities of the British fleet. Second, the internationalization of markets and trade with the exploitation of new markets in South America and the Far East, also contributed to the relative decrease of the presence of British steamers in the Mediterranean markets.[29]

In Table 9.3 the dominance of the Ottoman flag in the movements of the port in terms of ships and tonnage is evident. How big was the Ottoman merchant fleet and where was it based? As expected, Istanbul concentrated half of this tonnage (Table 9.4). In fact, in 1890 the Ottoman fleet comprised of 858 ships of 192,000 net registered tons, which did not compare badly with the Russian fleet but was far behind the leading maritime nations of Europe such as Britain and Germany (Appendix). Almost all of the steamship fleet was concentrated in Istanbul, while most of the Ottoman sailing fleet was concentrated along the southern coast of the Black Sea. In 1890 this consisted of a large number of independent vessels whose owners were in most cases also their captains. Ottoman sailing-ship owners profited from the great upsurge of sea trade and a large number of sailing vessels emerged from Rizeh, Trebizond and Terebolee to Samsun, Sinope, Amasra, Bartin and Heraclee during the last third of the nineteenth century. Bartin and Heraclee concentrated the largest number of these vessels because of the nearby coalmines that provided cargoes for them. The Ottoman Greek sailing-ship owners formed an important group and were concentrated on the southwestern coast of the Black Sea, in Vassiliko and Aktarpolee, in Istanbul and the Aegean islands of Lemnos, Chios and Cassos. In fact the last two became the main cradles of twentieth-century Greek shipowners (Harlaftis 1996: Ch. 4).

Ottoman, or Ottoman Greek, sailing-ship owners, however, were mainly involved in the trade within the eastern Mediterranean, continuing the methods of shipping and trading prominent at the beginning of the century, and were not involved in the area's long-distance trade with western Europe. Table 9.5 has been compiled from data from the Lloyd's Register books which include vessels of 100 tons and above. This means that a large number of the few thousand sailing craft that were the indispensable feature of the whole complex of ports and islands of the Ottoman part of the eastern Mediterranean, are excluded. However, this article deals not with the intra-empire coastal trade but with the international trade of the area, which was mainly carried on vessels of 100 tons and above.

Istanbul between 1890 and the eve of World War I became the entrepreneurial centre of a large number of shipping companies. Furthermore it concentrated almost all the Ottoman steamship fleet from 1890 to 1910 (see Table 9.4).[30] This was the era of the transition from sail to steam, of the telegraph, of fast communication and the concentration of maritime intelligence in big ports, of specialization shipowning and focus on sea-transport services instead of the combined activities of trade and shipping. It is the era of bigger steel ships, of large companies, and of the entry of new entrepreneurs, ex-sailing-ship owners, into steam. Throughout this period there were two major shipping companies, the Idarei Massousieh (Ottoman Steam Navigation Company) and Sirket-i Hayriye (Bosporus Steam Navigation Company). From 1890 to the 1900s these two companies formed two-thirds of the Ottoman steamship fleet. Sirket-i Haryriye was established in 1851 as the first Ottoman corporation issuing bonds, with the full support of the sultan and the ruling elite that became its major shareholders. It was given the concession of the exclusive transport of passengers between Istanbul, Uskudar and the Asian and European sides of the Bosporus. The corporation was also held responsible for building and maintaining its own quays. It functioned throughout the period under examination and reached the number of thirty-six steamships in 1910. Its services proved invaluable in connecting all parts of the city, serving as the first mass transportation system (Celik 1986: 84–5). As the British Vice Consul Wrench reported in 1873: "In short, the direction merits the confidence of the public and the revenues being

Table 9.4 The Ottoman fleet according to ports of registry, 1890

Port of Registry	Ships	Tons	%
Istanbul	293	86 966	45
Chios	60	13 865	7
Bartin	52	7 482	4
Heraclee	30	7 068	4
Oonia	28	5 924	3
Cassos	16	3 330	2
Trebizonde	16	3 204	2
Lesbos	3	2 918	2
Lemnos	17	2 882	2
Abahnah	15	2 770	1
Rizeh	12	2 283	1
Terebolee	12	2 003	1
Kerrasunde	10	1 681	1
Vassiliko	15	1 879	1
Aktarpolee	8	1 540	1
Other*	256	43 473	23
Total	858	192 038	100
A. Ottoman	569	127 558	66%
B. Ott. Greek	289	64 474	34%

Source: *Lloyd's Register of Shipping*, 1890, compiled data.

immense the Cherket Company may safely be described as the only Turkish enterprise existing that is in all respects a success." The establishment and extension of network services within the Dardanelles proved crucial for the development of commercial and maritime services in the city.

On the other hand the story of the Idarei Massousieh (Ottoman Steam Navigation Company) is not such a happy one. Following the European trend for the formation of state-supported steamship companies, it was formed in the early 1840s under the auspices of the Armenian employees of the Imperial Mint. The use of company vessels for government purposes and corrupt administration brought it into bankruptcy and it was taken over by the state. Vice Consul Wrench reported in 1873: "The Government itself has now become the proprietor of the fleet, many of the English engineers have been dismissed and the direction of the concern has been placed in the hands of naval authorities. The result is that the public has completely lost what little confidence it had, either in the punctuality or, indeed, in the safety of a Turkish steamer..." This company owned larger vessels that approached the ports of the Black Sea and the eastern Mediterranean, thus competing with the European steamship companies, although it seems that it limited its activities to intra-empire services. From fifty vessels in 1890 it reached seventy-three in 1900. Even though it showed a decline in number of vessels and tonnage, with ships of an average size of 520 tons, it retained its position as the main shipping company in the fleet.

Apart from these two main Ottoman steamship companies the rest of the Ottoman steamship fleet belonged to another important economic group: Greeks based in Istanbul. This group is important because its members were involved in the foreign trade of the area. They can be divided into three categories, indicating clearly the trends of this period. The first category consists of the most powerful members: the merchants and bankers. The invasion of steam and its evident advantages in sea transport meant the first purchases of steamships by the most powerful Greek commercial houses of the Black Sea and Istanbul. Many of the Istanbul Greek merchants with commercial houses that extended from south Russia to Marseille and London became part of the so-called Galata bankers, who, having access to European credit, provided loans to the Ottoman state at high interest rates (Exertzoglou 1986: 116–8; Pamuk 1987: 56). Such were the merchant land banker L. Zarifi and the oil merchants J. Arvanitidi and S. A. Sideridi, who also invested in steamships, as is evident from Table 9.5. Sideridis, who appears in 1910 as owning the second-biggest shipping company in the Ottoman fleet, invested heavily in ships and in a way "financed" what eventually became some of the most prominent twentieth-century Greek shipowners. These were Chiot sailing ship owners from the families of Lemos, Pateras, Hadjipateras, Livanos and Carras, all masters, who were able to purchase their first steamships in co-ownership with the capitalist Siderides and eventually bought them off. The same subsequently applied to the sailing-ship owners from Cassos, Rethymnis, Yannaghas and Pneumaticos who purchased steamships in co-ownership with the merchant and banker Arvanitides.

The second category of Greek steamship owners was associated with the increasing formation of steamship companies in this big port-city. The seven Greek shipping companies based in Istanbul in 1890 had risen to thirty-seven by 1914. It meant that Greeks did not have to be in areas of production in the Black Sea but could find all they needed in Istanbul, which had become an important maritime centre, in the artery of sea-trade. P. M. Courtgi, who came from Mytilene, established the Aegean Navigation Company in Istanbul in the 1880s. By 1890 it was the second-largest company in the city. He used the Ottoman flag on his ships, which had crews of Greek seamen from the small traditional maritime town of Galaxidi and served lines embracing a range from the Black Sea ports to Alexandria.[31] It is interesting to note that the Courtgi Company owned coalmines in Heraclee. Coal was used to fuel the steamships of the company but was also sold to steamship companies in Istanbul engaged in coastal transports.[32] The exploitation of these mines evidently gave the Courtgi Company an advantage; it managed to survive despite competition from Massousieh and other foreign companies. Pandeli Bros, which established the Pandeli Bros Steamship Company in 1908, also served lines that served the eastern Mediterranean basin. The other steamship owners who bought their vessels in the 1890s and 1900s, and were

Table 9.5 Steamship owners and agents based in Istanbul in 1890, 1900 and 1910

Steamship owners and agents	1890		1900		1910	
	Ships	Tons	Ships	Tons	Ships	Tons
Adore Massousieh (Ottoman Steam Navigation Co)	50	23 792	73	37 955	55	31 152
Courtgi P.M.*	7	2 910	10	5 947	5	4 136
Chirket i Hairie (Bosphorus Steam Navigation Co)	21	2 598	25	3 618	36	5 224
Michalinos*	2	2 407	—	—	—	—
Foscolo, Mango & Co*	3	1 252	4	6 071	—	—
Caramania	1	1 183	—	—	—	—
Essavan	1	1 096	—	—	—	—
Michel C.*	2	956	—	—	—	—
Giustiniani*	1	495	—	—	—	—
Giordiadi*	1	431	—	—	—	—
Stamadiadis*	2	210	—	—	—	—
Zarifi L. (I. Fitilis) *	—	—	6	6 554	2	2 534
Lambros Const.*	—	—	1	442	—	—
Lambros P.*	—	—	1	442	—	—
Oppenheim H.	—	—	1	333	1	333
Societe eu Tombac	—	—	1	288	—	—
Siniossoglu S. *	—	—	2	2 283	1	1 245
Compagnie de Remorquage, de Pilotage et de Sauvetage (Pandermaly)*	—	—	7	222	16	5 940
Saliaris A.K. & Co*	—	—	2	1 813	—	—

continued on next page

Table 9.5 Steamship owners and agents based in Istanbul in 1890, 1900 and 1910 (cont.)

Steamship owners and agents	1890		1900		1910	
	Ships	Tons	Ships	Tons	Ships	Tons
Evlia Effendi	—	—	1	1 380	1	1 380
Dandria Fratelli*	—	—	1	1 202	1	2 244
Siderides S.A.*	—	—	—	—	5	7 066
Destouni & Yannoulatos*	—	—	—	—	14	4 605
Pandeli Bros*	—	—	—	—	4	2 296
Arvanitidi J.*	—	—	—	—	2	1 475
Cosmetto N.*	—	—	—	—	2	1 100
Abadjis Per. A.*	—	—	—	—	2	912
Petzalis & Dounias*	—	—	—	—	2	765
Pandermaly St.*	—	—	—	—	2	457
Gumuschian M.	—	—	—	—	1	1 272
Ambatiellos P.*	—	—	—	—	1	1 220
Cardiacopulos*	—	—	—	—	1	1 151
Andreou G.*	—	—	—	—	1	953
Hatab Kapouli Kadri	—	—	—	—	1	945
Mihran Effendi	—	—	—	—	1	935
Ramsey & Co	—	—	—	—	1	915
Negroponte D.A. & Carousi*	—	—	—	—	1	903
Musta Bey	—	—	—	—	1	891
Nicolaou George*	—	—	—	—	1	859
Papadakis George*	—	—	—	—	1	755
Morello G.	—	—	—	—	1	533

continued on next page

Table 9.5 Steamship owners and agents based in Istanbul in 1890, 1900 and 1910 (cont.)

Steamship owners and agents	1890		1900		1910	
	Ships	*Tons*	*Ships*	*Tons*	*Ships*	*Tons*
Gira M. & Vernadaki*	—	—	—	—	1	453
Cambi A.	—	—	—	—	1	444
Nicolau M.*	—	—	—	—	1	422
Lagoutaki Agat.*	—	—	—	—	1	418
Potamianos J. & Co*	—	—	—	—	1	314
Ahmed Hadji & Hadji Ismail	—	—	—	—	1	297
Levantis E.*	—	—	—	—	1	247
Byron*	—	—	—	—	1	192
Lambros Pericles*	—	—	—	—	1	188
Vernico Nichol.*	—	—	—	—	1	124

Source: See Appendix

Note
* Greek origin

involved in tramp shipping, like Saliaris, Yannoulatos, Nicolaou, Papadakis, Potamianos and Vernicos, became important twentieth-century shipowners. They all moved to Piraeus during and after the Balkan Wars.

The third category involves the new profession developing in the main maritime centres of the time, that of shipping agents/shipbrokers. Such shipping agents/brokers were Foscolo & Mango, established in 1878, who had branch offices in Piraeus (Mango & Sons established in 1898) and London (Mango, Doresa & Co established in 1899). They advertised themselves as shipbrokers and coal merchants, agents of steamship lines, owners of steamships and shipowners, and inspectors of insurance companies. Others were Fitilis, Michalinos and Ambatiellos; the latter two opened successful shipowning/shipbroking offices in London. These were what has been called today "infomediaries", the *sine qua non* agents of the new internationalized world economy that works through networked exchange of exclusive information.[33] Market information via telegraphic transmission influenced trade and shipping to an unprecedented degree. It was a business built on no capital, based on trust and connections; most of the shipbrokers started as employees in commercial companies that also administered ships, they then became independent using their knowledge. The ones who knew the business gained the trust of some merchants and shipowners who had ships to charter and capital to invest. They earned a good living from commissions on chartering, brokerage, sale and purchase and insurance. Selling information and administering all the details of the shipping business proved quite lucrative. Some of today's biggest international broking offices, like Clarksons in the UK, started in the 1850s, while Fearnley and Eger of Norway started in 1869 (Fischer 1992). Knowledge of shipping markets, vessel-management skills, access to the world's maritime centre, London, were primary factors for the successful operation of the Greek brokers of Istanbul.

It is evident from the above that international trade and shipping witnessed major changes in the last third of the nineteenth century. We can distinguish three main categories of the causes of such changes. The first concerns trade *per se*, and particularly the increase of the seaborne bulk trade. The second concerns shipping, or more specifically the transition from sail to steam and the changes brought to the organization of the sea trade by the introduction of cargo steamers. The third also stems from technological advances and deals with their effects on the eastern Mediterranean sea-routes, from the introduction of the telegraph to the opening of the Suez Canal in 1869. The Mediterranean Sea in the nineteenth century provided the busiest sea-lanes, comparable only to those of the north Atlantic. The two areas dealt with the world's leading commodities: grain, cotton and coal, and even to the one with the most incredible future in the following century: oil. The increase in the export of raw materials from the eastern Mediterranean and the Black Sea and the general upsurge of trade to and from the area, in combination with the above technological changes enhanced the importance of Istanbul as a maritime centre. By the last decade of the nineteenth century a large number of suppliers, ship-repairers, shipping agents and shipowners was established in this great capital. Istanbul became the meeting point for all western European and eastern Mediterranean shipping and seamen, where all necessary information about purchases and sales of ships, of chartering, insuring, financing, manning, and equipping their ships could be found. It was the commerce with western Europe that brought British, Austrian, German, Russian, Greek, Italian and French captains on big steamships and sailing ships full of cargoes to Istanbul. It was the development of commerce from the Black Sea, and more particularly the development of bulk trade and shipping that made Istanbul the maritime centre of the eastern Mediterranean. The internationalization of the port of Istanbul and the Dardanelles, however, was almost entirely dependent on the transit bulk sea trade and its recipients in western Europe. When the sea-routes to the Black Sea were blocked soon after the beginning of the Balkan Wars, and the Russian grain sources ceased to export after the Russian Revolution, followed by the closure of Romanian and Bulgarian exports after World War II, the port of Istanbul returned to its eastern isolation for most of the rest of the twentieth century.

In this chapter we have not been concerned with measurements of economic growth through particular factors of production. We have rather identified at a macro-level, the vehicles that brought economic change in the area by tracing the trends of bulk sea trade and shipping. We then proceeded to investigate the micro-level: how the people who dealt with this trade and shipping in the busiest port of the area experienced the impact of these developments. We had only a quick glimpse of merchants, shipowners, shipping agents, captains and port workers at Istanbul. We did not see the people inland. Grain – and indirectly the return cargo of coal – brought unprecedented development in the Black Sea area. It helped to build the port and the warehouses in Odessa, to pave its streets, to construct its opera house, to build quays in Nicolaieff and Novorossisk, to bring the railway to Mariupol, Taganrog and Rostoff, to bring wealth and "Europeanization" of the major Danubian ports of Romania, to make some Greek and Jewish merchants incredibly rich. Still, however, until the 1880s and 1890s the Russian and Romanian peasants were heavily in debt to the grain merchant, and the sacks of grain continued to go to Odessa and Taganrog through muddy roads on ox-carts. Cotton fields in the Nile did not much improve the living conditions of the fellah but made the Greek community of Alexandria and the pashas of Egypt incredibly wealthy. The increase of shipping made maritime communities in some Aegean and Ionian islands extremely prosperous. Truly, one of the big winners of the development and the internationalization of bulk trades from the eastern Mediterranean lands has been Greek shipping, which grew on carrying grain, coal and cotton from the southern to the northern European waters, and in the twentieth century, the same cargoes – from different sources – to the Atlantic, Indian and Pacific routes. The increase of the bulk trade and shipping from the eastern Mediterranean and the Black Sea certainly brought obvious economic change to particular sectors of all the economies involved. But bulk sea trade from the eastern lands also contributed to the further development of the Atlantic economy. Whether integration of the bulk trades from the Black Sea and the eastern Mediterranean lands led to globalization and convergence with the Atlantic economy is something that still remains to be investigated.

Appendix

A background paper which is available upon request from the authors at gelina@unipi.gr includes the data used in this paper. This appendix lists the kind of data reported in that paper: (1) Black Sea exports of grain, 1870–1914; (2) US exports of wheat, 1870–1914; (3) freight rates on Mediterranean and Atlantic routes; (4) coal exports; (5) coal freight rates from the British ports; (6) Egyptian and US cotton exports; (7) cotton freight rates from Egypt and the USA to British ports; (8) tramp freight rate indices; (9) Table 9.2 sources; and (10) Tables 9.4 and 9.5 sources.

Notes

We are grateful to Jeffrey Williamson and Şevket Pamuk for their useful comments and to Professor Lewis R. Fischer for providing valuable information and advice on various aspects of our research. This paper relies heavily on the following archives: Foreign Office, *British Consular Reports*, Constantinople, 1870–1914; the Private Archive of Admiral Anastassios Zografos; and the Archive of the Maritime Museum of Galaxidi; *London Customs Bills of Entry*, 1870–1910; *Semaphore de Marseilles*, 1870–1910.

1   We are using these terms in the way Jeffrey Williamson suggests in Globalization, Convergence, and History (1996a) and in Chapter 3 of this volume.
2   See also Harley (1989).
3   For a detailed analysis on Egyptian exports see Owen (1969).
4   See also Alexander and Omer (1979).
5   For example, there were 2,400 immigrants from Greece to the USA in 1899 and almost 50,000 in 1907. For more details on passenger shipping in the eastern Mediterranean see Kardasis (1997).
6   Kardasis (1998) and Harlaftis (1996) have discussed at great length this integration by the formation of extensive commercial networks. Goodwin and Grennes (1998) give the erroneous impression that such integration took place only in the last third of the century. Greek grain merchants were the first to establish links with western Europe early in the century and by the mid-nineteenth century were the main exporting commercial houses; they collaborated and were replaced by Jewish firms in the late nineteenth century. See also Herlihy (1986) and Chapman (1992).
7   F.O. No. 2196, 14.11.1898, p. 10, Report of Vice Consul Sarell, referring to the importance of the commercial networks of the Greeks and Armenians who controlled the import trade of Istanbul. For Odessa, in the period 1833–60, there are specific estimates that the entrepreneurial activity of the Greeks in the city's exports was as high as 40 per cent. See Kardassis (1998: Appendix).
8   FO No 2,813, 12.5.1902, p.27, Report of Vice Consul Waugh.

9   FO No. 3,140, 21.3.1904, p.23, Report of Vice Consul Waugh.
10   More specifically, 44.06 per cent were Muslim, 17.48 per cent Greek Orthodox, 17.12 per cent Armenians and 5.08 per cent Jews; the remaining were other western European foreigners. See Celik (1986: 38).
11   F.O. Report of the General Consul Logie dated 30.6.1865, p.929.
12   F.O. 26.6.1883, p. 1,730, report of Consul Wrench. Detailed wages and port dues are found in the detailed report of Consul General Sir P. Francis, FO, March 1870, p. 301.
13   More on port facilities in other commercial ports of the empire during the period 1860–1900, that is Izmir, Salonica, Beirut (Inalcik and Quataert 1994: 802).
14   See the relevant article by Quataert (1983: 459-470). In Inalcik and Quataert (1994: 803) the deterioration of the porters' guilds is attributed to the establishment and exploitation of the docklands by foreign companies at the main ports in the empire.
15   FO Report of General Consul Logie, 30.6.1865, pp. 926–9. See also the Report of Consul General Sir P. Francis of 25.1.1869, p.137. The British representative informs that merchandise from Manchester reaches Istanbul and is distributed in the whole area. Moreover he reports that this trade is almost entirely in the hands of the Greeks.
16   There are multiple references to these developments by the British consuls. Indicatively, see FO 20 April 1874, p.1,539, Report of Vice Consul Wrench.
17   A different and more likely reliable conclusion for the same period can be found in Turgay (1983). According to the author British exports took place directly to and from Trebizond from the first decades of the nineteenth century because of the port's vicinity to the Persian market. These exports continued to the end of the century, having German industrial goods as their only rival.
18   Şevket Pamuk (1987: 33–4) supports the view that the introduction of railways promoted the economic development of Turkey.
19   This is reported in the case of Turkey by Inalcik and Quataert (1994: 807), while on Russian railways we have references by Cameron (1971: 227) and Knowles (1967: 226).
20   Report of Vice Consul Wrench on 20 March 1877, p. 826.
21   Sailing Directions for the Euxine or Black Sea and the Seas of Marmora and Azov; embracing also the navigation of the Dardanelles and Bosphorus, London, James Imray, 1853, p. 2.
22   FO No. 1,384, 10 May 1894, p. 12, Report of Consul Wrench.
23   FO No. 1,224, 24.4.1893, p.11, Report of Consul Wrench.
24   *Andriana* belonged to the House of the Embiricos Bros, merchants and shipowners with branch offices in Braila, Piraeus and London.
25   Logbook *Andriana*, Private Archive of Admiral Anastassios Zografos.
26   Logbook *Assimoula*, Maritime Museum of Galaxidi.
27   Andreas Syngros, Memoirs, p. 286.
28   FO No. 1,384, 10 May 1894, p. 17, report of Consul Wrench.
29   FO No. 1,224, 24.4.1893, p. 9, Report of Consul Wrench. For the decline of British ships in the region and the emergence of new maritime powers in the area see FO, No. 2,650, 15.5.1901, p. 5, Report of Consul Sarell.
30   There were two steamship lines based in Smyrna belonging to Ottoman Greeks: that of Daoud Farkouh Hadji and of Pantaleon.
31   There were other Greek liner companies based in Smyrna, Daoud Farkouh Hadji and Pantaleon.
32   FO, No. 2,813, 12.5.1902, p. 33, Report of Consul Waugh.
33   For an interesting account of today's new infomediaries, see Hagel and Rayport (1997).

Part 5

Pre-1914 policy choices and the political economy of growth

10 Much Ado About Nothing?

Italian trade policy in the late nineteenth century

Giovanni Federico and Kevin H. O'Rourke

Introduction

At the time of its political Unification in 1861, Italy was a poor and backward country with a per capita GDP of about $1,400–1,500 (1990 US dollars), less than half the British level, and slightly more than that of present-day India (Maddison 1995). Fifty years later, on the eve of World War I, Italy was still poor and backward, but it had undoubtedly started its modern economic growth, and could aspire to becoming one of the great European powers. Its GDP per capita was two-thirds higher, at some $2,400 (slightly less than that of Indonesia). On the other hand, Italy's position relative to other advanced European countries had barely improved, unlike other peripheral European economies, notably the Scandinavian countries (O'Rourke and Williamson 1997). Its per capita GDP was still half that of Britain, and three-quarters that of France. This mixed record aroused many controversies among political observers at the time, and among historians subsequently (Zamagni 1993; Cohen and Federico forthcoming). Arguably the most controversial issue in the debate is the role of the state, especially with regard to trade policy. Like most European countries, Italy switched to protection in the late 1880s after a spell of free trade in the 1860s and 1870s. The first tariff approved in 1878 protected only a few industrial goods (mainly textiles) while the more protective and comprehensive 1887 tariff covered a fairly wide range of manufactures (notably iron and steel products) and, crucially, wheat. In the following years, individual duties were changed several times, sometimes as a result of trade treaties, but the basic framework of the 1887 tariff lasted until World War I.

The causes of Italian trade policy are not really controversial. Historians seem to agree on a very crude political economy model based on sector-specific interests. Industrialists had always complained of foreign competition, and asked for protection, often with the (organized) support of workers. However, they were too weak politically to get it: after all, the Parliament was elected by a very small minority of the population (about 2 per cent), among whom landowners outnumbered any other group.[1] The switch to protection was caused, as in most European countries, by the threat of foreign wheat. Some industries were more able than others to exploit this opportunity, either because they were better organized (e.g. cotton and wool) or, as in the case of the steel industry, because they could claim to be indispensable for a great power. Subsequent industrial development increased the political power of industrialists, whose lobbying was instrumental in drafting a new tariff in 1921–3.

The debate, consequently, focuses on the effects of this policy. Some regard protection as causing a misallocation of resources, thereby wasting precious opportunities for development. The most extreme statement of this thesis was put forward by nineteenth-century economists. Pareto and Einaudi strongly campaigned for free trade (Cardini 1981), arguing that Italy should have left industrial growth to spontaneous market forces. More recently, Alexander Gerschenkron (1962) has heavily criticized the choice of activities protected. In his opinion, wheat-growing and steel production were totally unsuited to Italian factor endowments, and the textiles industry was old and had little growth potential. It would have been more sensible to protect engineering and chemicals, the industries of the Second Industrial Revolution. His criticism of the duty on wheat is widely shared, and recently Stefano Fenoaltea (1993) has argued that it indirectly caused emigration by lowering the domestic purchasing power of wages so much as to make (exogenous) world wages highly attractive. But Italian tariff policy has its supporters, too, such as Vera Zamagni (1993) and Guido Pescosolido (1998). They both argue (Pescosolido more vehemently) that without protection Italian industry would never have been able to withstand foreign competition, and that therefore Italy would not have developed at all. Both sides, however, agree on one point: trade policy deeply shaped Italian economic growth.

Until very recently, the debate has relied mainly on anecdotal evidence on duties (mostly from contemporary sources), sometimes supported by data on trade flows, and without systematic research and statistical testing. The first comprehensive set of estimates of nominal and effective protection has only recently been published (Federico and Tena 1998, 1999). Aggregate protection turns out to have been quite low, except perhaps for a brief period in the 1890s, and the highest duties were raised on sugar, oil and coffee (i.e. they were revenue-raising, rather than directly protective). Protection on wheat and steel products was higher than average, as traditional accounts suggest, but duties on other manufactures were rather low (and effective protection was sometimes negative). Giovanni Federico and Antonio Tena therefore query the conventional wisdom that Italy was a severely protectionist country. Trade policy seems to have been inspired by the pressing need for fiscal revenue as much as by the desire to protect the incomes of landowners, or by the aim of fostering industrialization, and its long-run effects on growth and structural change may consequently have been much smaller than usually assumed.

These inferences may be plausible, but a simple look at nominal or effective tariff rates is not sufficient. One has to consider the overall effects of protection and by definition this requires a general equilibrium approach. This chapter aims to fill this gap in the literature. It makes use of a computable general equilibrium (CGE) model of the Italian economy in 1911 – the first year for which the available data are abundant and reliable enough for such an exercise. The model is described in the next section, while the results are presented in the third and fourth sections. The third section reports in some detail the results of the basic (static) model. The discussion will focus on the potential effects of free trade, the most extreme alternative, but we will deal briefly with other tariff counterfactuals which have been suggested in the literature. As is typically the case, the static model predicts that protection had a small overall impact on welfare. However, static trade models do leave open the possibility that tariffs can have large effects on individual sectors and on the distribution of income, and this will provide the focus for our discussion. The fourth section presents a preliminary dynamic version of the model. The growth model we use is a traditional classical one *à la* Ricardo, with savings being a constant share of the income of capitalists, although we also consider briefly an alternative, Solovian specification. The fifth section sums up the argument regarding Italy, while in the last, highly speculative, section we ask whether and to what extent our Italian results might be useful for understanding the economic histories of other Mediterranean countries.

The basic (static) model

The model is a fairly standard neoclassical one. There are nine production sectors, each producing one commodity. Four of these are agricultural: wheat and sugar (WHEAT), non-wheat tillage crops (TILL), Mediterranean products (MED) such as wine and oil, and animal production (ANIMAL). The latter two sectors are clearly distinguished by their production technologies, which implied distinctive factor shares. On the other hand, wheat and sugar shared many technical features with other tillage crops. They are lumped together in a different sector because they enjoyed a high level of protection and wielded sizeable lobbying power. Five sectors are non-agricultural: the "military-industrial complex" (MIC), which comprised the activities most supported by the state (steel-making, the production of rolling-stock and shipbuilding); other capital-intensive industries (KII) such as chemicals and the rest of engineering; textiles (TEXT); other industries (OTHER), which consisted mainly of the production of consumer goods (food processing, clothing, wood and leather); and non-tradables (NT), including utilities, services and the civil service. In addition, exotic goods (EXOT) such as tea and coffee are imported, but not produced domestically.

There are four factors of production, unskilled (raw) labour (L), capital (K), land (R) and skills (H). All sectors use unskilled labour and capital, while land is used in agriculture only, and skills in industry and services. Various assumptions are made concerning the mobility of factors of production

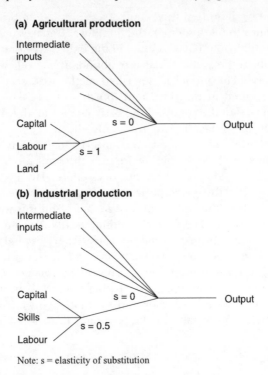

(a) **Agricultural production**

Intermediate inputs

Capital

Labour

Land

s = 0

s = 1

Output

(b) **Industrial production**

Intermediate inputs

Capital

Skills

Labour

s = 0

s = 0.5

Output

Note: s = elasticity of substitution

Figure 10.1 The structure of production.

across sectors. In the benchmark case, "Mediterranean land" is specific to the Mediterranean sector, while non-Mediterranean land is assumed to be perfectly mobile between the other three agricultural sectors. Capital is fully mobile between all sectors, while skills are sector-specific. Labour is assumed to be imperfectly mobile between agriculture and the rest of the economy, implying that wages can differ (as they in fact did) between town and country.[2] In some counterfactual scenarios we let capital be freely available to the economy at a fixed world price (from abroad); in others (including the benchmark specification) we let all factor supplies be exogenous.

Production in each sector takes place in a two-stage fashion (Figure 10.1). In the first stage, primary factors of production are combined to form a value-added aggregate, via a constant elasticity of substitution (CES) production function; in the second stage, the value-added aggregate is combined with intermediate inputs in a Leontief fashion to produce gross output. Initially, the CES elasticity of substitution is set equal to unity in agricultural sectors (which implies Cobb–Douglas production functions) and to one-half in non-agricultural sectors. The gross output is either used at home (D) or exported (X). Following standard practice in the applied general equilibrium literature (the so-called Armington assumption) we assume that

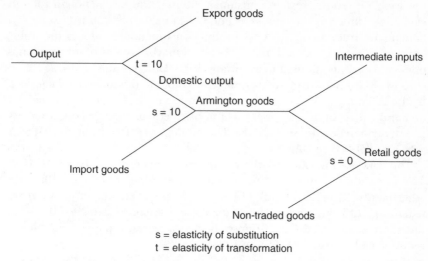

s = elasticity of substitution
t = elasticity of transformation

Figure 10.2 Trade and retail markups.

domestic output, exports and imports for a given sector are not identical: this implies that domestic prices are not fully determined by world prices, and allows for the reality of two-way trade in particular sectors.[3] Domestic output and exports can be transformed into each other via constant elasticity of transformation (CET) production functions, with benchmark elasticities of transformation equal to ten.

Exports are used to get the foreign exchange with which the economy buys imports. Imports and domestic products are combined via CES production functions (with initial elasticities of substitution equal to ten) to produce "Armington aggregate" goods (Figure 10.2). These Armington aggregate goods are either used as intermediate inputs, or are combined with non-traded goods (representing wholesale and retail services) to produce "retail goods". It is these goods which are consumed, either by the private consumer, or by government.

Government levies taxes; in the benchmark scenario these are on outputs, factor inputs, trade and consumption. Government also pays fixed lump-sum transfers to the private consumer, and consumes fixed quantities of the MIC and non-traded retail goods. Government purchases of most goods are thus effectively treated as intermediate inputs into the non-traded sector. We model purchases from the military-industrial complex separately because they include rolling stock, which is classified as an investment good. The distinction will become important in the dynamic version of the model. In counterfactual scenarios, in which tariff revenues are altered, lump-sum taxes are adjusted to keep the government on its budget constraint. The private consumer owns primary factors of production, pays lump-sum taxes, receives lump-sum transfers, consumes "utility", and owns enough foreign exchange (which is the *numéraire* good) to enable the country to run its benchmark trade deficit. A CES production function produces the utility good using retail goods as inputs. The benchmark elasticity of substitution is one – obviously equivalent to assuming Cobb–Douglas utility.

As in all competitive general equilibrium models, this one is characterized by the following equations: for every commodity (or factor of production) demand equals supply; for every sector, price equals average cost; for every agent, income equals expenditure. The model was solved using the MPSGE solver available with GAMS.

The data used to calibrate the model are presented in Tables 10.1–10.3. The value-added figures and the input–output table are taken (with some adjustments) from Rey (1992). Other data (e.g. on taxation, tariffs, etc.) are taken from official sources. The factor shares have been estimated by us. All the sources and methods are described in a working paper available on request (Federico and O'Rourke 1998).

The basic results

Before we begin discussing the impact of protection, it is worth pausing briefly to examine the structure of Italy's trade in 1911 (Table 10.2). Italy was a net exporter of Mediterranean products, textiles and (barely) other industrial products, and a net importer of wheat, other tillage, animal products, MIC and other capital-intensive goods, and exotic goods. This pattern conforms fairly well with the predictions of the Heckscher–Ohlin model of trade, which suggests that labour-abundant countries such as Italy should export labour-intensive commodities and import capital- and land-intensive commodities (Table 10.3 gives factor shares in each sector). In common with the rest of Europe, Italy could not compete with the wheat and animal exports of the land-rich New World and Ukraine. The production of Mediterranean crops was rather land-intensive, but in this case land embodied long-term investments in vines and fruit trees. Furthermore, these sectors were favoured by the Italian climate. Within industry, the military-industrial complex and the capital-intensive industries (as befits their name) were capital-intensive; other industrial goods were labour-intensive. Interestingly, textiles were both (raw) labour- and capital-intensive. In fact 80 per cent of the workforce consisted of low-paid women, and the share of skilled labour was correspondingly very low.

Table 10.4 gives average tariffs for the nine imported goods in our model for 1897 and 1911. As can be seen, duties in 1911 were especially high for exotic goods, reflecting the government's desire to raise revenue. While such revenue tariffs clearly have an impact on consumers' decisions, and thus on welfare, they will have almost no effect on resource allocation or income distribution. Among other commodities, wheat and sugar (which for brevity will henceforth be referred to as "wheat") and the military-industrial

Table 10.1 Italian Input–Output Table for 1911 (millions of lire)

From/To	WHEAT	TILL	MED	ANIMAL	MIC	KII	TEXT	OTHER	NT	SUM
WHEAT	5.8	0	0	0	0	4.2	0	1 317.7	28.2	1 355.9
TILL	40.5	6.7	0	0	0	5	363.1	429.2	66.8	911.3
MED	0	0	0	0	0	78.5	0	176.7	63.9	319.1
ANIMAL	0	0	0	0.5	0	9.2	307.9	1 481.9	85.2	1 884.7
MIC	0.5	0.6	1.2	1.2	59.9	230.3	0	12.4	188.8	494.9
KII	65.8	36.7	93.6	9.6	96.4	451.4	64	433.4	883.2	2 133.2
TEXT	1.1	1.3	2.4	2.3	0	28	256	487	26	804.1
OTHER	2.8	2.3	4.4	253.3	9.9	91.1	7	373.2	723	1 467.9
NT	26.7	16	18.5	13.9	94.0	134.2	73	164	925	1 465.3
EXOT	0	0	0	0	0	0	0	0	0	0
SUM	143.2	63.6	120.1	280.7	260.2	1 032	1 071.0	4 875.5	2 990.0	10 836.2

Source: Federico and O'Rourke (1998).

Table 10.2 End uses of commodities, Italy, 1911 (millions of lire)

Sector	OUTPUT	IMPORT	TARIFFS	EXPORT	MARKUP	TAXES	SUBS	GOV	CTAX	INV
WHEAT	1 391.4	300.3	94.4	0.3	204.6	113.1	0	0	0	0
TILL	1 456.7	625.2	31.2	172.3	201	3.5	0	0	0	10
MED	2 888.5	13.4	2.5	197.6	398.6	7.0	0	0	119.7	375
ANIMAL	2 723.4	164.4	7.8	90.6	375.8	6.6	0	0	0	16
MIC	516.3	134.1	23.1	28.2	44.1	4.3	5	95.1	0	98.5
KII	2 311.6	1 153.9	89.4	359.7	653.1	33.6	0	0	0	1 282.3
TEXT	1 500	390.2	24.1	748.5	305	12.4	0	0	0	0
OTHER	6 894.2	610.8	61.1	634.7	1 189.7	111.5	0	0	179.5	419
NT	11 150.0	0	0	0	0	108.7	64	1 944.0	508.7	1 202
EXOT	0	40.2	30.2	0.4	10	0	0	0	0	0
SUM	30 832.1	3 432.5	363.5	2 231.9	3 381.9	400.8	69	2 039.1	807.9	3 402.9

Source: Federico and O'Rourke (1998).
Note
Variables are defined as follows:

OUTPUT: gross output
IMPORT: imports valued at world prices
TARIFFS: tariffs and other taxes on trade
EXPORT: exports
MARKUP: retail markup (modelled as an input from the non-traded sector)

TAXES: taxes on output
SUBS: output subsidies
GOV: government demand
CTAX: consumption taxes

Table 10.3 Factor inputs and factor taxes, Italy, 1911

Panel A. Factor Inputs (millions of lire)

	L	K	LAND	LMED	H	LTAX	KTAX
WHEAT	468.7	153.5	626	0	0	49.5	3.7
TILL	836	99.1	458.1	0	0	26.1	0
MED	1 115.8	162.2	0	1 490.4	0	118.5	0
ANIMAL	996.9	528.9	916.9	0	0	72.3	0
MIC	79.1	114.3	0	0	62.7	0	10.1
KII	365.6	737.7	0	0	176.3	0	65.1
TEXT	194.3	181.8	0	0	52.9	0	16.0
OTHER	1 010.2	580.7	0	0	427.7	0	51.2
NT	2 099.9	3 071.9	0	0	2 988.3	0	390.4
SUM	7 166.5	5 629.9	2 001.0	1 490.4	3 603.3	266.4	536.5

Panel B. Factor Shares (per cent)

	L	K	LAND	LMED	H
WHEAT	37.6	12.3	50.2	0.0	0.0
TILL	60.0	7.1	32.9	0.0	0.0
MED	40.3	5.9	0.0	53.8	0.0
ANIMAL	40.8	21.7	37.5	0.0	0.0
MIC	30.9	44.6	0.0	0.0	24.5
KII	28.6	57.7	0.0	0.0	13.8
TEXT	45.3	42.4	0.0	0.0	12.3
OTHER	50.0	28.8	0.0	0.0	21.2
NT	25.7	37.6	0.0	0.0	36.6
TOTAL	36.0	28.3	10.1	7.5	18.1

Source: Federico and O'Rourke (1998).

Note: variables are defined as follows:
L: labour input
K: capital input (including capital taxes)
LAND: land input (including land taxes)
LMED: input of Mediterranean land (including land taxes)
H: input of human capital
LTAX: taxes on labour
KTAX: taxes on capital

complex enjoyed the highest levels of protection, reflecting the power of large landlords and the desire of the state to build up strategic sectors. These sectors would have been the most likely to contract under a free-trade policy. Mediterranean products apparently enjoyed a high level of protection as well; however, imports in this category were in fact very small, and consisted of tropical fruits and luxury wines, which were seen by the authorities as a non-controversial source of revenue.

Table 10.4 Italian tariff levels, 1897–1911 (*ad valorem* equivalents, per cent)

Sector	1897	1911
WHEAT	97.7	29.6
TILL	5.7	4.0
MED	17.8	8.1
ANIMAL	2.9	3.6
MIC	26.1	15.7
KII	15.8	6.6
TEXT	6.8	4.1
OTHER	8	8.4
EXOT	95.4	74.5

Source: Federico and O'Rourke (1998).

Table 10.3 shows that wheat-growing was much more land-intensive than the rest of agriculture. We would therefore expect that a move to free trade would have mainly hurt the owners of land – a wide category, which included some peasants (especially in the mountains), but consisted mainly of rural and urban elites. The effects on other factors are less easy to predict. Heckscher–Ohlin logic suggests that the impact on wages should have been positive, as (raw) labour-intensive activities such as tillage, textiles and other industries were likely to expand. The impact on capital is unclear. Profits could have been hurt by the reduction in size of the MIC, which was relatively capital-intensive. However, the sector was small, and in absolute terms it accounted for less than 5 per cent of total capital in tradables (Table 10.3). The effects on profits of MIC contraction might have been counterbalanced by the effects of free trade on capital-intensive industries and textiles, which used much more capital and were likely to gain, as protection in those sectors was comparatively low (Table 10.4).

Table 10.5 begins testing these intuitions by exploring sectoral outputs under a range of counterfactual tariff scenarios. Column 1 asks how outputs would have changed if Italy had adopted free trade in 1911. The overall structure of the economy would not have changed greatly. The production of non-tradables, which accounted for about 40 per cent of GDP, would hardly have been affected. The gross output of agriculture would have contracted by 2 per cent, and that of industry would have grown by 6 per cent. Contrary to the protectionists' direst predictions, free trade would not have destroyed Italian industry – maybe because the protection it enjoyed in 1911 was quite low. But free trade would nevertheless have brought about substantial changes *within* agriculture and industry. Perhaps the most important one (but of course hardly unexpected) would have been a dramatic contraction

Table 10.5 Impact of tariff reforms on sectoral outputs (percentage changes)

	(1) Free trade	(2) Exotic tariffs only	(3) Zero wheat tariff	(4) Zero wheat & MIC tariff	(5) 30% KII tariff & exotic tariff	(6) Uniform 10.6% tariff	(7) 1897 tariff vs 1911 tariff	(8) Free trade vs 1897 tariff
WHEAT	-53.2	-53.2	-57.1	-57.1	-54.5	-38.7	23.1	-62.0
TILL	21.5	21.4	23.5	23.6	19.8	21.7	-7.0	30.6
MED	-0.8	-0.8	-0.6	-0.6	-0.8	-0.8	0.1	-0.9
ANIMAL	9.8	9.8	9.6	9.7	6.2	5.7	-6.4	17.3
MIC	-14.2	-14.3	-0.8	-19.2	-23.0	-8.0	7.5	-20.2
KII	-1.8	-1.9	-1.0	2.2	24.7	2.8	7.7	-8.8
TEXT	27.0	26.8	12.0	12.4	11.5	2.0	-7.8	37.7
OTHER	5.0	5.0	6.8	6.9	1.1	2.5	-4.8	10.3
NT	-0.3	-0.3	-0.3	-0.3	-1.0	-0.2	-0.3	0.0

Source: See text.

of wheat-growing and sugar-producing. Domestic output would have halved, imports (not shown) would have more than tripled and the total consumption of these goods (in real terms, also not shown) would have increased by over a quarter. This would surely have increased the welfare of a population which still widely used inferior cereals for bread-making and had the lowest consumption of sugar in Europe – 3.9 kg per head per annum in 1909 versus 41.1 in the UK and 6.2 in Russia (Bianchi 1988, Table 2). The decline in wheat-growing would have released land for alternative uses, and consequently, both animal output and (especially) tillage output would have increased, the latter by over 20 per cent. The tiny decline in Mediterranean output (just under 1 per cent) may seem surprising, but is easily explained: it is due to our assumption that land was immobile between this sector and the rest of the economy. With the land input fixed, only labour and capital could leave the sector, and thus output would only contract by a small amount.

As expected, free trade would have hit the military-industrial complex, but less than the literature implies. It would not have been wiped out, as predicted or feared by historians believing in steel-making as the key to industrialization (Amatori 1997). Actually, its output would have contracted by less than 15 per cent. Surprisingly, the big winner would have been the textile industry: it would have grown more than any other activity, both in relative and in absolute terms (almost 30 per cent). This makes sense given that tariffs on textiles were particularly low (Table 10.4) and that textiles were a labour-intensive (Table 10.3) export good (Table 10.2). Tariffs might have been instrumental in the development of the textile industry in the 1880s, as argued (in a critical mood) by Gerschenkron, but by the eve of World War I they had become a hindrance to its further growth. Interestingly, this counterfactual growth under free trade would have been achieved by a 53 per cent surge in exports (not shown). In 1911, Italy exported 750 million lire worth of textiles, half of which consisted of raw silk, its traditional staple. Exports accounted for half the output (Table 10.2), and this share would have increased to three-fifths with free trade. Yet Italy would have remained only a minor player in world textile markets – except for raw silk, where its market share would have increased from about 20 per cent to something between 27 and 30 per cent.[4] It can be shown that the growth of the textiles sector was mainly hampered by the protection of agriculture and "other industries". The abolition of these duties would have increased textiles output by 25 per cent (not shown), not so much less than the 27 per cent increase brought about by free trade (Table 10.5, column 1). As a relatively small sector (see for example the labour input figures in Table 10.3, Panel A) textiles stood to gain considerably from any reduction in the output of other, much larger, labour-intensive sectors.

The other columns of Table 10.5 experiment with alternative counterfactuals. Column 6 reports the impact of imposing a uniform tariff on all sectors; not surprisingly, this would have had similar, but smaller, effects as would have a move to free trade. Column 2 establishes that tariffs on exotic goods were irrelevant to the structure of output in the economy; reintroducing them from an initial situation of free trade produces no discernible change in outputs (compare columns 1 and 2). Column 3 shows that within agriculture, it was the wheat tariff that was crucial: abolishing wheat tariffs alone would have produced the same decline in wheat production, and the same increases in tillage and animal production, as would have a complete switch to free trade. Moreover, abolishing the wheat tariff alone would have led to textile output increasing by 12 per cent, and to other industrial output increasing by 7 per cent, as labour was reallocated to industry, favouring the labour-intensive sectors there (and dis-favouring the capital-intensive sectors). Within industry, abolishing the MIC tariff alone (in addition to abolishing the wheat tariff) would have reduced its output by almost 20 per cent (column 4), more than a complete move to free trade, which would also have reduced the output of capital-intensive industries, thus boosting MIC output. However, abolishing the MIC and wheat tariffs would only have led to textiles output increasing by 12.4 per cent, little more than the 12 per cent produced by free trade in wheat alone (compare columns 3 and 4). As should be evident from their very different factor proportions, textiles and the military-industrial complex were not in direct competition with each other for resources.

Column 5 shows that Gerschenkron's strategy for development might have been successful on his own terms. A heavy dose of protection (30 per cent) would have boosted capital-intensive industry, which he deemed appropriate for a latecomer such as Italy, by almost a quarter. As he envisaged, the MIC would have lost most – more than in the free trade alternative (compare columns 5 and 1); and textiles' growth would have been severely curbed (relative to free trade) by the competition for resources from engineering or chemicals.

Finally, column 7 asks what the economy would have looked like if protection had stayed at its 1897 level, the historical peak in aggregate protection (Table 10.4). Tariff levels almost halved between 1897 and 1913, as price increases reduced the impact of specific duties, and the latter were reduced by trade treaties (notably a round in 1904–6) and by autonomous government actions (Federico and Tena 1998: Table 2). The greatest tariff cut involved the duty on sugar, which fell from a staggering 314 per cent in 1897 to a still high 120 per cent in 1913. The duty on wheat also diminished (from 40 per cent to 29 per cent): without these reductions, the output of wheat and sugar would have been almost a quarter greater than was actually the case. In contrast, the differences for other sectors would have been small, outputs changing by less than 10 per cent. Of course, it is difficult to judge the impact of the 1897 tariff with a model of the Italian economy in 1911, but a comparison of columns 7 and 1 yields a rough estimate of the impact of protection in the earlier year (column 8).[5] A move from the 1897 tariff to free trade would have reduced wheat output by 62 per cent, and MIC output by 20 per cent, while it would have increased tillage output by almost a third, and textiles output by over 35 per cent. These are quite large figures, which suggest a substantial impact of protection in its heyday. As in the "basic" case, however, resources would predominantly have been reallocated within agriculture and within industry, leaving the overall agricultural/industrial output mix almost unchanged.

What was the impact of protection on income distribution? As we will see, the answer to this question is sensitive to assumptions made about the mobility of factors across sectors. Table 10.6 gives the answers when the benchmark assumptions are made: it reports the real returns to factors of production, as well as real GDP (i.e. the sum of all factor incomes), for the same counterfactual tariff scenarios as the previous table. The impact of protection on Italian welfare was negative but small. Moving to free trade would have boosted real Italian GDP by a mere 2.4 per cent. Even abolishing the higher 1897 tariffs would only have increased real incomes by 3.1 per cent: the fall in protection in the 1900s increased national income by a modest 0.7 per cent. These findings are consistent with those of other researchers; for instance, Harley (1992b) finds that the removal of antebellum tariffs in the United States would have increased income by only 0.5 to 2.1 per cent. Any significant overall welfare effects of protection must have come from its dynamic effects, rather than its static resource allocation effects.

In spite of its modest macroeconomic effect, protection did change the distribution of income substantially. As might be expected, the biggest changes involved factors that were "stuck" in particular sectors, and whose fortunes were thus tied to those sectors – in the benchmark model, skills. The impact of a move to free trade on the returns to sector-specific human capital was in some cases dramatic, with the return to skills in the military-industrial complex declining by almost a third, and those to human capital in the textiles sector increasing by four-fifths. However, in the latter case, the starting point was extremely low (Table 10.3).

The impact of tariffs on intersectorally mobile factors was much less dramatic. Rents on non-Mediterranean land would have fallen by 8 per cent, not an insubstantial decline, but perhaps less than might have been expected, given the dramatic 50 per cent plus fall in wheat cultivation. The explanation is simple: in the basic model, land is assumed to be mobile between wheat and other agricultural activities, such as tillage, which would have expanded under free trade.[6] (Non-Mediterranean) landlords would have lost some 135 million lire out of a total income (rents and profits) of 2,783 million; landlords in general would have lost 106 million lire out of a total of 4,435 million. Interestingly, this is about the order of magnitude estimated by advocates of free trade in the early 1900s. The sum was equivalent to a hefty 90 per cent increase in state taxation on non-Mediterranean land (or a 40 per cent increase in overall land taxation: see Table 10.3); however, land taxes had fallen in real terms by a third from the 1870s to the 1890s (Repaci 1966: Table 13), while agricultural output rose by 40 per cent over the same

Table 10.6 Impact of tariff reforms on factor returns (percentage changes)

	(1) Free trade	(2) Exotic tariffs only	(3) Zero wheat tariff	(4) Zero wheat & MIC tariff	(5) 30% KII tariff & exotic tariff	(6) Uniform 10.6% tariff	(7) 1897 tariff vs 1911 tariff	(8) Free trade vs 1897 tariff
L	3.5	3.3	2.2	2.3	0.4	1.4	-1.4	5.0
K	3.4	3.2	2.1	2.3	5.7	0.9	-0.2	3.6
LAND	-8.1	-8.3	-10.5	-10.3	-13.5	-5.9	3.4	-11.1
LMED	1.6	1.5	0.7	0.9	-0.8	-0.4	-1.1	2.7
H-MIC	-30.3	-30.7	0.0	-40.8	-46.9	-18.8	20.4	-42.1
H-KII	-0.8	-1.3	-0.2	7.6	75.1	7.8	18.3	-16.1
H-TEXT	80.4	79.2	32.4	33.7	32.1	5.9	-17.5	118.7
H-OTHER	17.2	17.0	20.9	21.3	5.1	7.7	-12.4	33.8
H-NT	2.4	2.4	1.3	1.2	0.2	0.4	-1.8	4.3
GDP	2.4	2.2	1.1	1.2	1.1	0.4	-0.7	3.1

Source: See text.

Note: variables are defined as follows:
L: returns to labour
K: returns to capital
LAND: returns to land
LMED: returns to Mediterranean land
H-X: returns to human capital in sector X
GDP: real GDP

period (Ercolani 1969: Table XII 1.1.A).[7] Probably Italian landowners could have afforded to pay it.

Wages and profits would both have increased slightly. The returns to unskilled labour would have increased by 3.5 per cent. Abolishing only the duty on wheat, the Fenoaltea (1993) counterfactual, would have increased real wages by just 2.2 per cent, not enough to have a big impact on migration (Hatton and Williamson 1998: Table 6.2). The cost of protection for workers only increases marginally when returns to human capital are included in the calculation. Protection reduced the total wage bill in industry and services (including skills) by about 300 million lire: in other words, it cost the average worker the equivalent of 10–12 days of work.[8] The sum was not negligible, but neither was it so large as to induce trade unions and the Socialist Party to accept the repeated pleas by free-traders to join their campaign in the 1900s (Inghirami 1991); and without some outside support, the campaign was doomed to failure from the beginning. The contrast with the British case is instructive: Jeffrey Williamson (1990) estimated that repealing the Corn Laws in the 1830s would have raised unskilled wages by 12–23 per cent.

Free trade would have boosted profits by 3.4 per cent, which is at first sight surprising: the positive effect on profits of the free-trade expansion in textiles would have dominated the negative impact of the decline in the KII and MIC sectors. As Gerschenkron might have predicted, protecting the KII sector alone (in addition to placing duties on exotic goods) would have boosted the profit rate by even more (5.7 per cent), at the expense of both labour and land. Whether this would have been sufficient to produce dynamic gains from protection will be explored in the next section.

On balance, the results so far suggest that the effects of protection were not that large, with some exceptions. A free-trade Italy would perhaps have been more similar to the country in the 1920s – with less wheat-growing and a bigger export-oriented textile industry – but not fundamentally different. We tried a variety of alternative specifications to see to what extent our results are sensitive to assumptions about factor mobility. For example it might be argued that capital was fairly mobile between Italy and the rest of the world in the late nineteenth century, a period characterized by the gold standard and high levels of international financial market integration (Obstfeld and Taylor 1998; O'Rourke and Williamson 1999: Ch. 11). Free trade, by raising the returns to capital, would thus have attracted capital imports. It turns out, however, that allowing capital to be perfectly mobile between Italy and the rest of the world makes almost no difference to the results, since free trade had such a small impact on the returns to capital in Italy.[9]

Most other assumptions about factor mobility made almost no difference either: for example, assuming that capital was immobile between agriculture and the rest of the economy (in fact, there is no evidence of any such capital market segmentation), or assuming that land was mobile between Mediterranean agriculture and the rest of agriculture (which seems implausible, since "Mediterranean" land embodied vines, olive trees, terracing and so on). The only alternative plausible specification which would have made a difference assumes that skills were mobile between sectors; in that case, while the overall impact on agriculture and industry would have been largely the same, there would have been a much more dramatic reshuffling of resources within industry, the MIC contracting by almost 50 per cent, and textiles output more than doubling.[10] Again, however, we doubt that this assumption is more appropriate than our own, given the limited extent of formal education, and the extent to which skills were learned on the job, implying that those acquired not of much use in retailing, or even engineering.[11]

The dynamic effects of trade policy

In this section we present some preliminary results generated by a simple dynamic model of the Italian economy. The model is identical to that outlined in the second section, with the addition of a number of features designed to capture the process of accumulation and growth. The basic growth mechanism is classical: growth is due to investment, which adds to the capital stock. The private sector invests a fixed share of profits each period, reflecting the common nineteenth-century assumption that it was capitalists who accounted for the bulk of investment spending. (It would be a simple matter to allow for a fixed share of profits plus rents to be invested, or indeed to allow for a fixed share of national income to be invested, which is of course what the Solow growth model assumes, and later we implement such a model.) Investment is modelled by having the private sector purchase an investment good. The investment good is produced by an artificial sector which uses Armington aggregate goods as inputs in fixed proportions (the proportions being those implied by the final column of Table 10.2). In addition, the government purchases rolling stock from the military-industrial complex each period; these public investment purchases are treated as exogenous.

The model is solved as follows. First, the static model is solved for 1911. The capital stock is then updated: the 1912 capital stock is taken to be the 1911 capital stock, plus the total amount of private investment, plus the total amount of government purchases of rolling stock, minus depreciation. Depreciation is assumed to be a fixed proportion of the previous year's capital stock; following Vitali (1969, Table XIII B.4), we assume that the depreciation rate was equal to 2 per cent. Labour-force growth is taken as exogenous; following ISTAT (1965), total population growth between 1911 and 1938 is taken to be 25.3 per cent, and we assume that this growth occurred at an even pace over time (implying that each year the labour force grew by 0.8 per cent).[12] With the new (1912) capital stock and labour force in hand, the model is again solved, yielding the static 1912 equilibrium, including equilibrium values for profits and investment; the 1913 capital stock and labour force are derived from the 1912 capital stock and labour force as before; and so on. In principle, this procedure could be followed for as many years as

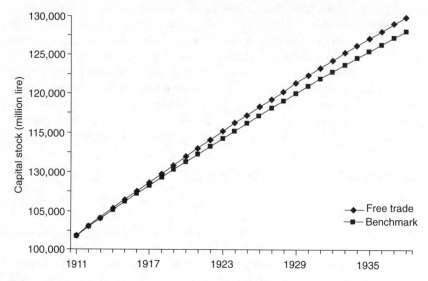

Figure 10.3 Accumulation of capital with benchmark and zero tariffs.

Source: See text.

desired; we have traced out the resultant growth process as far as 1938. The method yields the growth path for the economy which would have ensued had there been no changes (other than accumulation and population growth) affecting the economy over the time period in question. In particular, this version of the model assumes away technological progress (although the dynamic implications of an exogenous technological shock could easily be investigated).

The process just described can trace out the growth path assuming that 1911 tariffs were in place. Alternatively, the 1911 static model can be solved for some counterfactual tariff scenario, and the dynamic consequences of such a tariff reform can be explored.

This model does not on its own generate large amounts of growth, which is not surprising, given that it ignores technical change.[13] Between 1911 and 1938 Italian GDP grew by 60–80 per cent (depending on the estimate) and the capital stock by 70 per cent (Ercolani 1969: Table XII.3.5).[14] Our model predicts a 16–19 per cent growth in gross output, and a 26–8 per cent increase in the capital stock between 1911 and 1938, depending on the assumptions made about tariff policy (Table 10.7, Figure 10.3); that is, it can account for roughly one-quarter to one-third of output growth over the period.

Table 10.2 shows that gross investment in 1911 (including government purchases from the MIC) amounted to 3,498 million lire. Capital income (net of capital taxes) amounted to 5,093.4 million lire in the same year (Table 10.3). Assume that the rate of return on capital was 5 per cent; the

Table 10.7 Comparing static and dynamic effects of free trade

	1 1911 Free trade Static effect	2 1938 1911 tariffs Dynamic effect	3 1938 Free trade Dynamic effect	4 1938 Free trade vs 1911 tariffs
Panel A. Sectoral outputs				
WHEAT	–53.2	8.3	–54.9	–58.4
TILL	21.5	24.4	51.9	22.1
MED	–1.0	12.0	10.4	–1.4
ANIMAL	9.5	18.5	30.3	10.0
MIC	–14.5	14.9	1.2	–11.9
KII	–2.0	24.9	26.4	1.2
TEXT	26.7	30.7	60.9	23.1
OTHER	4.8	16.6	22.7	5.2
NT	–0.1	12.4	12.7	0.3
Panel B. Real factor returns, endowments, and GDP				
L	3.5	–10.1	–6.4	4.1
K	3.6	–12.9	–10.9	2.3
LAND	–8.3	15.4	5.9	–8.2
LMED	1.3	14.5	15.3	0.7
H-MIC	–31.0	28.6	–6.2	–27.1
H-KII	–1.1	49.0	57.8	5.9
H-TEXT	79.3	65.2	183.2	71.4
H-OTHER	16.7	32.2	57.0	18.8
H-NT	3.4	29.1	34.4	4.1
GDP	2.6	15.7	19.4	3.1
Capital stock	0.0	25.6	27.5	1.5
Labour force	0.0	25.3	25.3	0.0

Source: See text.

Note: Variables as defined in Table 10.6.

capital stock in 1911 was then equal to 101,868 million lire, which would have yielded a figure for total depreciation (assuming a 2 per cent depreciation rate) of 2,037.4 million lire. Net investment would then have been 1,460.6 million lire, which would have increased the capital stock by a

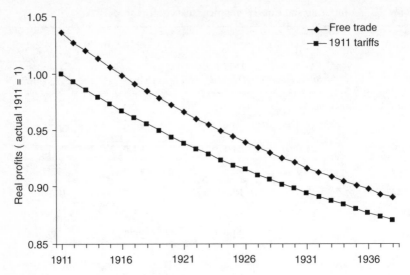

Figure 10.4 Real profits with benchmark and zero tariffs.

respectable if not enormous 1.4 per cent. So why the slow growth over the period as a whole? First, as is well known, the Solow model predicts that growth based on accumulation will eventually run out of steam, as diminishing returns to capital set in. In addition, in the classical model there is an extra mechanism at work, emphasized by Ricardo and others. As capital accumulates, the profit rate declines (Figure 10.4): since investment is funded out of profits, the rate of investment declines sharply.

More importantly for our purposes, Table 10.7 indicates that the dynamic effects of protection are no larger than the static effects. Column 1 reports the static effects of a move to free trade in 1911.[15] Columns 2 and 3 compare the 1938 equilibrium with the 1911 equilibrium, under two sets of assumptions: that the 1911 tariff schedule remained in place throughout the period; and that the economy switched permanently to free trade in 1911. The final column compares the 1938 free-trade equilibrium (column 3) with the 1938 tariff equilibrium (column 2); that is, it gives the long-run effects of a switch to free trade in 1911. As can be seen, the long-run and the short-run effects of protection were almost identical; for example, whereas a move to free trade would have boosted 1911 GDP by 2.6 per cent, it would have boosted 1938 GDP by 3.1 per cent.

It does not appear that these conclusions are crucially dependent on the assumption that savings were financed out of profits rather than out of general income. In the classical model just described, and in the absence of any tariff reform, capital stocks grow by 25.6 per cent between 1911 and 1938, while real GDP grows by 15.7 per cent. We also implemented a Solow growth model, where savings were a constant proportion of total income. In this case, the capital stock grows by 27.9 per cent in the absence of tariff reforms, and GDP by 16.3 per cent; while a move to free trade increases 1938 real GDP by 3 per cent, or by less than in the classical growth model. It appears that in our classical model, the Solovian mechanism of diminishing returns to capital is more important in slowing the economy than the Ricardian mechanism of a declining profit rate leading to a declining savings rate.

What would have been the dynamic effects of a Gerschenkronian strategy of protecting capital-intensive industries only? As it happens, capital would have been accumulated slightly more slowly than under the free-trade scenario; by 1938 it would have increased by 26.4 per cent, as compared with the 25.6 per cent recorded with the 1911 tariffs in place, or the 27.5 per cent with free trade. This implies that there were no dynamic gains (relative to free trade) that would have compensated for the static loss associated with protection; the Gerschenkron strategy was better than what actually happened, but it was still worse than complete liberalization.

Late nineteenth-century Italian trade policy: conclusions

Despite the occasional sensitivity of our results to elasticity values and factor mobility assumptions, there are some conclusions that seem to be fairly robust.

First, as long as we stay within a broadly neoclassical framework, we are unlikely to find that protection had a significant negative effect on aggregate welfare, either in the short run or the long run. The static impact of a move to free trade (increasing real GDP by 2.4 per cent) is larger than many other static trade models have found. Even the dynamic effects of protection on real GDP were small, within the context of neoclassical models in which growth is due to accumulation alone. Endogenous growth models might, however, produce different conclusions.

Second, protection did not change the overall structure of the economy: if anything, it promoted the growth of industry as a whole, but the effect is very small. However, protection did affect the distribution of output within agriculture and industry, and it did matter for individual sectors. In particular, it doubled the output of wheat and sugar and lowered the output of the Italian textile sector by over one-fifth. It also had a significant negative impact on other tillage production, and a significant positive impact on the output of the Italian military-industrial complex. These figures refer to the low duties of 1911: the impact of protection was substantially larger in the 1890s, when duties were twice as high.

Third, the impact of protection on income distribution was, on the whole, surprisingly small. The big potential losers from free trade were landlords, whose rents would have fallen by a quarter had they persisted in growing wheat.[16] By switching their land to alternative uses, they could however have significantly moderated this decline (by up to two-thirds, in fact). The impact of protection on the other factors of production also depended crucially on how mobile they were between sectors. If all factors of production were mobile (simulation not shown), then no factor returns would have increased or declined by more than 5 per cent, quite a small number. To be sure, a 5–10 per cent increase or decrease in one's own income was not negligible, but still protection in 1911 did not seem vital for any large social group. And in fact it was not a big political issue in Italy, as it was in Germany or Great Britain: these results reported here help us understand why.

There is, however, an important potential caveat to the last point. As is well known, Italy was (and still is) distinguished by wide regional disparities: in 1911, GDP per capita in the northwest exceeded the national average by 40 per cent and was almost double that of the south.[17] Industries were heavily concentrated in the so-called "industrial triangle" in the north, and agriculture was also more advanced in the north, with a larger share of animal production. In addition, labour was not particularly mobile between Italian regions, with the result that large income differentials persisted throughout the period. All this implies that, in principle, large movements in the output of individual sectors could have had an important impact on the regional distribution of income.

To evaluate this possibility we would need a regional model of the Italian economy in which factors of production were not perfectly mobile between regions. However, the output results presented above suggest (yet again) that the (regional) impact of tariffs may not have been so great as is commonly thought. The biggest impact of protection was on wheat production, but wheat-growing was in fact widely diffused (with 36 per cent produced in the north, 20 per cent in the centre and 44 per cent in the south). Moreover, the winners and the losers from industrial protection were all in the north. Perhaps free trade would have been marginally better for the north, as industry would have grown a little at the expense of agriculture, and 57 per cent of animal production was in the north.

On the whole, our results point to a well-defined conclusion, which runs strongly against the conventional wisdom. Trade policy was neither the villain (*à la* Gerschenkron) nor the saviour (*à la* Pescosolido) in Italian industrialization. It was at most a fairly marginal actor. The sources of Italian industrialization, growth and regional inequality have to be found elsewhere.

The Mediterranean basin in an Italian mirror: some speculations

To what extent might these conclusions apply to other Mediterranean countries? The answer will depend on how similar were their economies and their tariff policies.

One would expect that Mediterranean countries shared at least a similar climate and environment, with long dry summers, mild winters, and rainfall heavily concentrated in time. And this was undoubtedly true, even if there

Table 10.8 Characteristics of some "Mediterranean" countries, c. 1910

	GDP per capita	Total population (thousands)	Share of agriculture in total labour force (%)
Italy	2 407	35 146	59
Greece	1 621°	2 693	57*
Portugal	1 354°	6 004	57
Spain	2 223	19 994	66
Turkey	979	25 500	n/a
France	3 219	43 065	41
Germany	3 602	65 359	35[#]

Sources: GDP per capita: Maddison (1995: Table D-1). Population: Maddison (1995: Table A-3, 1911 boundaries, adjusted with coefficients from Table H.1), except for the Ottoman Empire (Pamuk 1987: Table 6.2) and Italy (ISTAT 1958). Share of agricultural labour force: Kaelble (1989), except Italy (Zamagni 1987: Table A.1).

Note
° 1913; * 1920; # 1907.

were also extensive "non-Mediterranean" areas within these countries, such as the Po Valley in Italy, and the north of Spain (Galicia, Asturias, Navarra). Factor endowments were broadly similar: capital was scarce, and labour abundant. However, Italy had a lower land/labour ratio than did other Mediterranean countries: the population per square kilometre of productive land was 145 in Italy, about the same as in Switzerland or Germany, but much higher than in Portugal (100), Spain (82), or Greece (66).[18] Because of the scarcity of capital, the structure of the economy was quite similar in all countries, with a huge agricultural sector, which was to shrink only after World War II (Table 10.8). Yet the level of development differed quite markedly: according to Maddison's (1995) data the gap between Italy, the richest country of the group, and Portugal, the poorest, was almost as large as that between Italy and the UK,[19] and this despite Italy's lower land/labour ratio. The country most similar to Italy, in terms of development and size, was Spain, which also happens to have the most detailed data on the composition of value added (Table 10.9). The structures of the two economies appear quite similar, with one major difference: the higher percentage of services in Italy, which *ceteris paribus* must have muted the impact of protection. Given these structural similarities, it is not surprising that the composition of imports and exports in these countries was also fairly similar (Table 10.10), with the exception of Turkey, which emerges as notably more specialized in non-manufacturing activities.

Thus, by and large, the first condition necessary for our conclusions to be generalizable to the rest of the Mediterranean is fulfilled: the similarities

292   *Pre-1914 policy choices and the political economy of growth*

Table 10.9 The structure of the Italian and Spanish economies (per cent of value added)

	Spain 1913	Italy 1911
Cereals	12.66	7.77
Other tillage	7.97	5.01
Wine	8.53	13.43
Animal	11.29	12.30
Capital-intensive industry*	9.64	8.62
Labour-intensive industry[o]	25.80	15.81
Non tradables	24.11	37.06

Sources: Italy: Rey (1992); Spain: Prados de la Escosura (1993).

Notes
* sum of military-industry complex and capital-intensive industries.
[o] sum of textiles and "other industries".

Table 10.10 Foreign trade around the Mediterranean, *c.* 1910

	Exports/GNP	Share of manufactures in imports (%)	Share of manufactures in exports (%)
Italy	12.0	35.1	34.5
Portugal	13.6	22.1	11.5
Spain	11.8	43.5	34.6
Turkey	14.0	56.0	9.0

Source: Federico (1992a: Tables 9.1 and 9.2).

Note:
The Italian data differ from those in Table 10.2, because of the different classifications used. For example, in Table 10.2 processed food belongs to "other industries", mineral products to "capital intensive industries" and silk to textiles. The table here uses the GATT classification, for the sake of comparability with other countries, and therefore these goods are included among primary products.

among Mediterranean countries seem to prevail over the differences. The real disparity was in size, as proxied by total population (Table 10.8).

However, it appears difficult to speak of a "Mediterranean" pattern of protection. The history of trade policy differed quite markedly from one country to another. Turkey was not free to set its own duties, being bound by treaties with western powers to a flat rate on all imports (8 per cent from 1861 to 1907, and 11 per cent thereafter). Egypt maintained an open trading policy throughout this period, as did other southern Mediterranean countries with strong metropolitan links, as Şevket Pamuk reports in this volume

Table 10.11 Levels of protection around the Mediterranean, *c.* 1911

	Tariff revenues/ imports	Unweighted average tariff	Dispersion of tariffs (CV)
Italy	9.6	14.9	1.09
Greece	24.8°	n/a	n/a
Portugal	24.7	34*	1.6*
Spain	14.9	25.2	0.97
Turkey	11.0	n/a	n/a
France	9.2	n/a	n/a
Germany	6.3	n/a	n/a

Sources: Italy: Federico and Tena (1998); Spain: Tena (1998a); Portugal: Lains (1987), Confraria (1999: Table 11.6); Turkey: Pamuk (1987); Greece, France and Germany: Mitchell (1975: Tables F1 and H5).

Note
* 1892; ° 1903

(drawing on the work of Tarik Yousef and others). Greece (Minoglu 1999) raised its tariffs (for fiscal purposes) in the 1860s, and then again, in a disorderly way, in the 1880s–1890s; Spain (Tena 1998) followed a cyclical pattern, with peaks in 1891 and 1906. Portugal never experienced a period of free trade, even if, as in Italy, its duties increased substantially in the 1890s and fell in the years before World War I. As a result, the levels of protection in 1911 differed quite widely among the five countries (Table 10.11), with Italy the least protected of the group in 1911, and the least protected after Turkey for most of the period. The data also permit us to compare the structure of protection in Italy with that in Spain and (with a lot of caveats) Portugal (Table 10.12).[20] Italy and Spain had a similar structure, but the Spanish levels were consistently higher, while the Portuguese structure was quite different. Pepelassis Minoglu (1999: 111) emphatically denies that tariffs were used for promoting manufacturing in Greece, in apparent contrast with the situation in Iberia. While these conclusions all rely on fairly crude measures of average protection, it should be noted that Antonio Estevadeordal (1997), who develops estimates of protection based on Edward Leamer's (1988) methodology, also finds that Italy was more open than the Iberian economies, with the difference being particularly marked in manufacturing.

On the whole, therefore, the available evidence suggests that the structure and level of protection in Mediterranean countries differed widely. Therefore it seems likely that protection had a greater impact in Spain or Portugal than in Italy. How much greater remains to be seen, although in their contribution to this volume, James Foreman-Peck and Pedro Lains suggest that tariffs adversely affected the development of the poorest European countries,

Table 10.12 The structure of protection in three Mediterannean countries, c. 1910
(average nominal duties, percent)

	Italy	Spain	Portugal
Primary products	10.0	15.5	—
Foodstuffs	23.4	20.6	40.2
Raw Materials	—	—	4.1
Intermediate	8.3	12.0	7.7
Iron and steel	21.9	30.4	3.3
Chemicals	4.9	6.7	10.1
Manufactures	9.3	15.5	25.9
Consumer goods	10.8	20.3	—
Equipment goods	8.0	13.6	—
Total	9.6	14.9	—

Sources: Italy: Federico and Tena (1998); Spain: Tena (1998a); Portugal: Lains (1987: Tables 5 and 6).

including Greece and Portugal. Their argument is that tariffs lowered incomes by retaining labour in low-productivity agriculture. By contrast, Kevin O'Rourke (1997a) finds that tariffs are positively correlated with growth in a sample of ten mostly rich Atlantic economies. One possible explanation for this finding is that, on balance, tariffs in these economies shifted labour out of agriculture, with this effect being particularly strong in the New World. In Italy, protection had no great impact on the relative fortunes of agriculture versus industry (on balance leading to a slight decline in agriculture's share of GDP); in this respect, it may have been closer to core Continental European countries, such as France and Germany, than to the rest of the Mediterranean.

Notes

1   Until the late 1880s, the right to vote was limited to the literate males who paid a (rather large) sum in taxes and a handful of other carefully listed categories (university graduates, clerks, civil servants, etc.). In the late 1880s, the right was extended to all literate males, including most urban industrial workers, and in 1911 to all males.
2   This is modelled by endowing the economy with "raw" labour, which can be transformed into agricultural and non-agricultural labour using a constant elasticity of transformation production function. The benchmark elasticity of transformation in this pseudo-sector is taken to be 10.

3   It also surmounts the well-known problem of over-determination in open economy models: where the number of exogenous commodity prices (n) exceeds the number of factors of production (m), the system is over-determined, and typically only m traded commodities will end up being produced. We treat exotic commodities differently, however. They are assumed to be imported, but not exported: the small quantity of re-exports are netted out to yield net imports.

4   Based on the data in Federico (1997: Table AII). All data refer to market shares by weight (those by value being slightly higher). The computation assumes a 53 per cent increase in total exports of silk – and hypothesizes that Italian silk either substituted for exports from other countries (upper bound) or added to them (lower bound).

5   For example, under free trade, wheat output would have been 46.8 per cent of its 1911 level, while wheat output would have been 123.1 per cent of its 1911 level under 1897 tariffs. Thus, the impact of free trade on wheat output, relative to an initial equilibrium involving 1897 tariffs, was to reduce it by 62 per cent.

6   The impact of a 29 per cent decline in grain prices on land rents would have been very similar in Britain, France and Sweden in the 1870s if land had been perfectly mobile between alternative uses there (recall from Table 10.4 that the wheat tariff in 1911 was 29.6 per cent): real rents would have declined by 9.4 per cent in Britain, 4 per cent in France and 14.4 per cent in Sweden (O'Rourke 1997b: Table 7). Land was probably more mobile in Italy than in Britain, where there were pronounced regional differences in the percentages of land devoted to grain.

7   There are no data on local-authority land taxes, which in 1911 accounted for about two-thirds of the total charge. However, local taxes closely followed national taxes, and their total receipts increased as much as state receipts (Brosio and Marchese 1986).

8   Industry and services occupied about 7.3 million people (Zamagni 1987: Table A.1) at an average daily wage of some 3.3 lire.

9   All simulation results cited in the following paragraphs are available from the authors on request.

10   The increase in textile output would have led to unskilled labour's wages rising 4.8 per cent, rather than 3.5 per cent; the return to economy-wide skills would have increased by 3.8 per cent.

11   The results were also fairly robust to assumptions about elasticities; as always, however, Armington elasticities mattered a lot for output levels in traded sectors, and by implication for sector-specific returns in those sectors (for a good discussion aimed at an economic-history audience, see Harley 1992b). Our benchmark assumption that these elasticities were equal to 10 is designed to reflect the view that domestic and foreign goods were extremely close, but not perfect substitutes.

12   We thus assume that population and labour-force growth rates are identical.

13   Indeed, in some sense this is not a "growth" model at all, since (like the Solow model) it cannot be used to derive long-run (steady-state) growth rates.

14   The 1938 data include the areas "liberated" after World War I – which however only accounted for about 4 per cent of GDP (Svimez 1961).

15   These are slightly different to those presented in Tables 10.5 and 10.6, as the static version of the dynamic model contains investment demands, which the earlier static model did not.

16   Based on a simulation (not shown) in which all land and capital is sector-specific.

17   Zamagni (1978).

18   Rogowski (1989: Table 2.6, p. 27). Productive land includes land under crops and pasture, but excludes forests.

19   The Turkish data are not really comparable, as the Maddison figures refer to the country as defined by its 1990 borders, which included only about a half of the population of the pre-1914 empire.

20 The figures for Portugal are not strictly comparable with those of the two other countries. These latter cover all trade, and are classified according to the GATT classification. The Portuguese data cover only 75 per cent of trade, and use a somewhat different classification (for instance, oil is included among manufactures instead of among primary products). Last but not least, in Portugal since 1892 wheat-growing was protected by a system of regulated markets, while duties were levied mainly for fiscal reasons (Reis 1992).

11 What slowed down the mass emigration from Spain before World War II?

A comparison with Italy

Blanca Sánchez-Alonso

Mass migration from Spain?

This chapter compares Italy and Spain during the years 1880-1914 in order to examine a potential and major obstacle to a greater international integration of the Spanish economy. In particular it enquires why emigration from Spain was so low at the end of the nineteenth century compared to other European countries such as Italy, the largest supplier of emigrants in southern Europe. Spanish historiography suggests that one of the major impediments to the mobility of Spanish labour was the tariff imposed on agriculture. In contrast, this chapter takes the view that the tariff on wheat exercised positive effects on external emigration, which is not a surprising result if the Spanish economy of the late nineteenth century operated as predicted by the Heckscher–Ohlin model and the Stolper–Samuelson theorem. However, when the effect of a currency depreciation is added to the already high cost of movement for potential emigrants from Spain, the low out-migration rate at the end of the nineteenth century is virtually explained. Currency depreciation at the end of the nineteenth century and early twentieth century, actively discouraged Spanish external emigration, something that did not happen in the Italian case. The calculations presented here show that in the absence of depreciation, Spanish emigration could have been almost 60 per cent higher during the period 1892–1905. The difference is significant and, because of "chains" that these potential emigrants might have developed, it accounts in great part for the differences between Spain and Italy in labour emigration. Such effects operated because Spanish emigration at the end of the nineteenth century was income-constrained. Many potential emigrants could not afford the costs of external migration. Hence, the importance of pioneer migrants to help finance the move and start-up costs overseas for subsequent emigrants.

It is notable that Italian historiography has hardly debated the effects of the agrarian tariffs on emigration, but Italy imposed tariffs as Spain did in the late nineteenth century and a comparison between the countries might, therefore, be illuminating. Italy took advantage of an evolving global economy which was entirely friendly to labour emigration, while Spain lost the

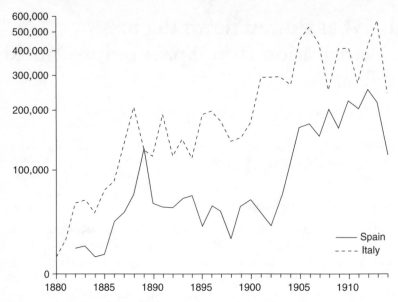

Figure 11.1   Gross emigration from Spain and Italy, 1880–1914.

potential economic benefits derivable from a higher rate of external emigration. In the absence of the depreciation of the peseta, the Spanish and Italian emigration rates would have been very similar over the last decade of the nineteenth century.

The next two sections discuss the effects of the late-nineteenth-century agricultural depression on labour mobility and briefly review the literature, both historical and theoretical, on the effects of tariffs on labour mobility. The third section discusses the effects of currency depreciation on emigration. In the fourth section the hypotheses of this chapter are tested econometrically for both countries. Conclusions are included in a short final section.

Emigration and protection for agriculture

As the integration of the international economy occurred from the 1870s onwards, movement of capital and labour between the Old and the New World increased. Competition from the New World primary producers (especially in cereals) had a strong impact on European agriculture (Bairoch 1976b: 48–56). Unable to compete with the New World, European agriculture entered a period of depression and structural crisis in the late nineteenth century. One of its effects was massive emigration. When we compare the emigration trends of Spain and Italy during the period 1880–1914 interesting similarities and differences can be observed between these two classical cases of emigration.

Table 11.1 Rates of gross emigration: Spain and Italy, 1882–1914 (per thousand population)

	1882–1891	1892–1905	1906–1914
Spain	3.4	3.9	9.5
Italy	3.8	6.6	11.2

Sources:
For Spain, Sánchez-Alonso (1995: Appendix A.3).
For Italy, Rosoli (1978).

For example, there are two similar periods in both series (Figure 11.1): the late 1880s which exhibit a rising trend, and the years 1904–13, which witnessed a more sharply rising trend and was the period when emigration from Spain and Italy peaked.[1] But Spain was different from Italy in the 1890s and the early 1900s: the Spanish series fell while Italian emigration started to boom (Table 11.1).[2] Spanish emigration rates remained low and stable between 1892 and 1905, while Italian emigration almost doubled in relation to the previous period (Table 11.1). It has been argued that Spanish emigration levels were low during the 1890s because the Baring crisis had a strong negative impact on Argentina, the main country of destination, and Spain's colonial war against Cuba also discouraged emigration. But Argentina was a common destination for both Italians and Spaniards, and Italian emigration recovered much faster after the Baring crisis (Ford 1962). Furthermore, Spanish emigration to Cuba had been relatively low before the revolution and only became significant after independence and during the sugar boom of the first decade of the twentieth century (Sánchez-Alonso 1995: Ch. 4).

In comparative and historical perspective the central problem is to explain the stagnation of Spanish emigration in the 1890s and its strong acceleration in the early twentieth century. After all, the 1880s and 1890s included years in which the agrarian depression was felt intensely across European agriculture and when competition from New World grain imports exercised a serious influence on emigration from Europe.[3] Unfortunately, there are very few studies which examine the effects of the depression on agricultural employment in any detail. Agricultural historians tend to agree that the fall in agricultural prices (especially cereals) affected rural employment adversely and the rise in emigration rates in several European countries during the decade of 1881–90 seems to confirm their perception.[4] Nevertheless, the direct impact of the agricultural depression on European emigration is more difficult to establish, because studies of whether the emigrants in the 1880s and 1890s belonged to groups most directly affected by the depression (namely small landowners, tenant farmers or smallholders) are scarce.[5] In the Spanish case, R. Garrabou (1985: 535) refers to "the brutal impact of the crisis in rural society" and points out that, "dispossessed of their lands and facing a weak demand for their labour, smallholders and tenant farmers had as their only alternative emigration". J. Fontana (1975: 190) also states that "the consequence of the agricultural crisis was the huge rural emigration flow at the beginning of the twentieth century". Spanish emigration grew at an annual rate of 2.1 per cent during the period 1880–1900 and at an extraordinary rate of 11.7 per cent over the years 1900–13. For Italy the figures are 6.6 per cent and 4.7 per cent respectively.[6] Why then was Spanish mass emigration only a twentieth-century phenomenon? Why were the outflows relatively low during the agrarian depression of the late nineteenth century while Italy maintained high rates of emigration during the 1880s and the 1890s?

Faced with a sharp fall in agricultural prices at the end of the nineteenth century, most European governments opted for protection and imposed tariffs on imported agricultural goods, particularly on wheat. The exceptions, Great Britain, Holland, Denmark and Switzerland, continued importing wheat at low prices and shifted their agricultural production into livestock farming and dairy production (O'Rourke 1997b). Spain also opted for protection and the effects of this policy on Spanish agriculture, especially on cereals, has been much debated among Spanish economic historians.[7] Following increases in tariffs (first in 1891, then in 1906 and finally in 1922), the price of Spanish wheat far exceeded world levels. In a period of falling international prices, cultivated area and output for wheat increased in almost all of Spain's agricultural regions (Simpson 1995; GEHR 1980). Around 1910 cereals were 33 per cent of Spanish agricultural final output.[8] According to the historiography, tariffs helped to maintain traditional agriculture, which was inefficient, kept Spanish wheat prices at artificially high levels and retarded structural change within the agricultural sector. The consequences over the long-run growth of Spanish economy were considerable (Prados de la Escosura 1988; Tortella 1994b). Spanish historians have also wondered how Spanish agriculture would have performed without the tariff. According to Tortella,

> if the protection on wheat had not been so high, the growing imports of cereals would have caused a decrease in the number of wheat farmers, weeding out the less efficient,

and he continues,

> the absence of tariffs would undoubtedly have forced peasants and landowners to switch to crops other than cereals .... and a massive exodus of farmers to the urban centres and to foreign countries would have followed.[9]

Prados de la Escosura has also pointed out that policies for the protection of cereals resulted in an inefficient allocation of resources and help to explain the persistently high share of the labour force in Spanish agriculture over time.[10]

Recently, James Simpson (1997) has developed a different view and argued that tariffs were not sufficient in themselves to explain the poor performance of Spanish agriculture. Farmers were slow to switch resources out of cereals, not so much because of tariffs, but rather because of the limited opportunities for the export of alternative crops, especially for olive oil and wine. Although, in his view, the rural exodus was determined by factors other than the tariffs, Simpson does not deny that without protection rural emigration could have been higher, but suggests that the impact of policy on Spain's agricultural performance has been exaggerated. However, neither the consensus view that tariffs slowed down the rural exodus nor critics of that view (such as Simpson) have formulated an explicit model of their critique of agrarian protectionism in Spain or tested it econometrically.

Protectionist policies as a response to falling agricultural prices in the international market were not limited to Spain. Italy is another example of the many countries in Europe adopting new tariffs at the end of the nineteenth century. Although there are many similarities between the two countries, differences concerning the level of protection in the Italian economy and its effects on economic development are also quite remarkable (Estevadeodal 1997). Italian historiography has also paid less attention to the protectionists' policies on agriculture and the potential effects on labour mobility. Debates and controversies (if any), concentrate mainly on the effects of protection in the industrial sector, especially in the steel and cotton industries. Gerschenkron (1962: 81) remarked that Italian industrialization could have been more dynamic if a more rational tariff policy in the industrial sector had been carried out. He deemed the duty on wheat harmful to industrialization as it unnecessarily increased the price of a basic wage good, and regarded tariffs as "one of the obstacles in the road of the Italian industrialization", a view shared by Fenoaltea (1978). Italian historiography has basically criticized not so much a protectionist policy in order to promote industrial development, but *the* kind of protection Italy had and the way tariffs were applied. Toniolo (1988: 231) states that the economic history of Italy, namely its industrial development, would not have been essentially different with a more liberal tariff policy; Italian tariff policy has also its supporters such as Zamagni (1990). Federico and Tena (1998) have recently shown that Italy had low levels of aggregate protection which, in any case, had more impact on primary products than on industrial ones. The protection on wheat and steel products was higher than average, but duties on other manufactures were low. Trade policy seems to have been inspired by the pressing need for fiscal revenue as much as by the desire to protect the income of landowners, or by the aim of fostering industrialization. The tariff imposed on wheat in Italy was raised following the 1887 tariff and, according to Federico's (1984) estimates, ensuring a protection of 33–38 per cent of the average import price in Italy. The price to pay was probably high but difficult to quantify (Federico 1994).

The effects of protection on agriculture, especially the consequences for rural exodus, have hardly been studied in the Italian case. Regarding the 1887 tariff and its effects on agriculture, Galassi and Cohen (1992: 145) remarked, in agreement with some of the opinions expressed for the Spanish case, that "the tariff provoked a misallocation of resources; these were allocated more to wheat production than it would have been without the tariff and wheat prices were higher than would have been otherwise". As their data show, the amount of land dedicated to cereals increased after the tariff, although to a lesser extent than in the case of Spain. Federico considers that the optimal policy would have been a combination of a free cereals import policy and some form of compensation for wheat producers (maybe a tax reduction). A temporary tariff would have been a second best.[11] In any case, Italian agriculture showed greater dynamism than Spain's. Farmers switched more quickly to crops other than cereals and there was an increase of fruit and citrus production (51 per cent increase between 1884 and 1909–13). Vegetable and industrial products also grew 145 per cent in the same period.[12] In relation to the effects of tariffs on labour mobility, Zamagni suggests that, without tariffs, rural exodus, which had already involved large numbers of the population, would have imposed unbearable social costs for Italian society (Zamagni 1990: Ch. 2).

Fenoaltea (1993) has focused on the effects of the agrarian protectionism for Italian economic development from a new perspective.[13] According to Fenoaltea, it is surprising how little attention Italian historiography has paid to the *dazio sul grano*, because, he thinks, if one has to blame a protectionist policy for the slow industrial and economic growth in Italy, it should be the agrarian tariff and not the peculiarities of the industrial tariffs. Taking the Ricardian model as a starting point, Fenoaltea develops an alternative model based on the assumption that capital and labour are mobile both in the domestic and in the international market. If factors of production are just mobile in the national market, an agrarian tariff would displace them from industry to agriculture, cutting down their real income. If, on the contrary, capital and labour are mobile both in the domestic and the international market, as was the case of Italy at the turn of the century, they would be less prone to bear a decrease in their real income and would fly overseas; the result is lower employment in agriculture, a higher exodus from industry and a net loss of resources towards the international market. Protection of cereals altered the structure of relative prices in Italy in favour of agriculture and increased the cost of labour for industry so, in the end, a decrease in marginal productivity reduced the demand for labour both in industry and in agriculture. Thus Fenoaltea maintains the hypothesis, but without any empirical testing, that one of the main reasons for the high level of Italian emigration in the early twentieth century was the tariff on grain. In Fenoaltea's words: "The tariff on cereals could have prevented not the, inevitable, rural exodus but the development of alternative activities; instead of blocking peasant migratory movement, it could have redirected them abroad."[14]

In any case, Italian historiography has paid little attention to the effects of agrarian protection on labour mobility. Fenoaltea's article is the exception and there are various reasons for that. First, industrial development in Italy from 1890 to World War I was remarkable and greater than Spain's, in spite of regional differences between the north and the south. Second, given the high rates of Italian emigration between 1880 and 1913, one of the highest in Europe, it seems rather pointless to wonder about the effects of more potential emigrants from Italy under free trade. Moreover, emigration in Italy was never considered, either by contemporaries or by historians, a negative fact for Italian economic development, as was frequently the case in Spain.[15] In Italy historians, politicians and contemporaries realized very early that emigration had several positive effects for such a densely populated country. Underemployment and overpopulation have been frequently mentioned as characteristics of Italian agriculture. O'Brien and Toniolo estimated that agricultural production during 1908–11 could have been obtained with only half of the labour force, fully employed, because of the existence of a large group of workers whose marginal productivity was close to zero (O'Brien and Toniolo 1986). Emigrants' remittances also had a positive impact on the Italian balance of payments. In such a context it is hardly surprising that external Italian emigration can be considered as a relief. In Toniolo's view, massive emigration accelerated the rural exodus from agriculture, which would otherwise have been delayed due to weak demand from the urban and industrial centres (Toniolo 1988: 179).

However, most Spanish and Italian historians have an implicit "sector-specific model" in mind.[16] The basic assumptions of the model are that there are two sectors: agriculture and industry, producing two commodities: food and manufactures. Agriculture produces food using land and labour; industry produces manufactures using capital and labour. Land and capital are factors *specific* to a particular sector and labour is mobile across sectors. If food is the imported good and its price falls either because of cheaper transportation or production costs (both of which happened in the late nineteenth century), the demand for labour in agriculture decreases and the level of employment in agriculture falls. Labour would then migrate to the industrial sector which would benefit from low wages due to an increase in labour supply. Industry is better off and capitalists gain because their wage costs fall and their profits rise. Thus, through migration Spanish economic growth could have proceeded more rapidly.[17] On the contrary, tariffs would reduce migration from agriculture to urban centres or abroad. In this model free trade means a loss for landowners because their rents fall. For this reason, the majority of European landowners, especially cereal producers, lobbied for an agrarian tariff and were against free trade. The "sector-specific model" clearly predicts a conflict between land and capital because free trade has an uneven impact on returns to different factors of production. Capitalists should have become free traders. Though that happened in Britain it did not in the cases of Italy or Spain where, according to historiography, protectionist alliances of industrialists and landowners dominated the making of commercial policy in the late nineteenth century. It has been argued that the shape of commercial policy in different countries depends upon political alignments. Nevertheless, from the perspective of the sector-specific model, there is a paradox in land and capital being protectionist to which I shall return later.

What happens, in turn, to wages and employment in the sector-specific model? The consequence for labour as a result of free trade is not so clear. Labour is mobile across sectors and given free trade will move from agriculture to industry. Wages decline (which is good for industry) but food prices also decline due to cheaper imports (which is good for labour). We have then two different effects: the labour-demand effect and the cost-of-living effect. O'Rourke demonstrated that in Britain the positive cost-of-living effect of cheap grain outweighed the negative labour-demand effect.[18] However, in two protectionist countries, Sweden and France, his model suggests that tariffs offset the impact of cheap cereals on agricultural incomes. Protection turned out to be good for landowners and bad for capital in both countries but had different effects on labour (O'Rourke 1997b: Tables 8 and 9).

It is hard to believe that Spanish and Italian governments tried deliberately to hurt capital and benefit landowners, when they introduced the 1891 and 1887 tariffs respectively, although the landowners were a powerful pressure group at the time in both countries (Varela Ortega 1978; Cardini 1981). Some historians have argued, however, that the Spanish government had no clear view of commercial policy and that the shape of the protectionist regime in Spain was the outcome of pressure groups' activity in an Olsonian way (Fraile 1991). Federico and Tena (1998) suggest that Italian trade policy was shaped more by the need for revenue than by a deliberate policy to foster industrialization, by sectoral interest, or by international relations.

But how can we explain the paradox that Spanish and Italian capitalists demanded protection for industry and conceded protection for agriculture? If instead of thinking about free trade and protection within the framework of the specific-factor or classical Ricardian models, a simple Heckscher–Ohlin model might be a more useful and illuminating approach to the case of protection during 1890–1914.

In the Heckscher–Ohlin model both capital and labour are mobile. In the sector-specific model only labour is mobile, and changes in commodity prices produce effects on rents and wages.[19] The crucial assumption here is the *intensity* of factors used to produce food or manufactures. The Heckscher–Ohlin model can be briefly summarized. First, patterns of trade reflect the relative endowment of productive factors. Thus, relatively labour-abundant countries tend to export labour-intensive commodities, and relatively capital-scarce countries tend to import capital-intensive commodities.

Second, free trade tends to equalize commodity prices among countries and also tends to equalize wages and rents in the home country with those abroad. This is the so called "factor-price-equalization theorem". What matters for Spanish and Italian economic history is the Heckscher–Ohlin model insight that commodity trade can serve as a substitute for factor mobility. In other words, international trade and international labour migrations are partial substitutes.

Although the Heckscher–Ohlin model has been criticized on empirical grounds, from Leontief onwards, economic historians have shown recently that for the late nineteenth century and early twentieth century the model is useful for the explanation of world trade patterns. The model also accounts for trends in relative factor prices over the decades before World War I (O'Rourke and Williamson 1994; O'Rourke, Taylor and Williamson 1996). By opening up new regions of the international economy to trade and settlement, new technologies (especially steamships and railways) altered relative factor endowments around the world. For example, Europe was transformed, relative to the rest of the world, from having a relative abundance to having a relative scarcity of land.

An important extension to the Heckscher–Ohlin model was the Stolper–Samuelson theorem which predicts that "any interference that drives up the local import price must unambiguously benefit the productive factor used intensively in producing the import competing good" (Stolper and Samuelson 1941: 68). Thus, protection will benefit owners of factors of production in which (relative to the rest of the world) a given society is poorly endowed, as well as producers who use that scarce factor intensively. Conversely, protection depresses the income of relatively abundant factors of production.[20] European workers, as the abundant factor, should, according to Stolper and Samuelson, have favoured free trade and resisted tariffs. In fact, a majority of Socialist parties in Europe opposed agricultural protection. Furthermore, impediments to trade (for example, a tariff) operate to stimulate factor movements (for example, labour). This is most clearly stated in Mundell's work: "The effect of any trade impediment is to increase the scarcity of the scarce factor and, hence, make more profitable an international redistribution of factors" and therefore, he concludes, "tariffs will stimulate factor movements." (Mundell 1957: 330). Economists generally assume that capital is more mobile than labour, but over the period 1870–1914, we can fairly say that labour was also highly mobile.

If we consider the Spanish and the Italian case in the light of a Heckscher–Ohlin model, land as the relatively scarce factor should have benefited from the introduction of a tariff, and at the same time, we would expect increased levels of protection to be *positively* related to labour outflow.[22] Thus, it could be the case that the agrarian tariffs stimulated the international migration of labour, the abundant factor in the Spanish and Italian economy. By the end of the nineteenth century Italy and, particularly, Spain were not only economies in which land was relatively scarce but also economies short of capital. The Heckscher–Ohlin model and the Stolper–Samuelson theorem predict that protection benefits land and capital (the scarce factors) and harms labour (the abundant factor of production). Thus, the paradox of a protectionist alliance between land and capital is resolved. Rogowski's work shows that in countries where both land and capital were the scarce factor and labour the relatively abundant factor, coalitions of capitalists and landowners were likely to arise.[23]

Prados de la Escosura and Tena (1994) have also noticed that, at the turn of the century, Spain's scarce factor (land) benefited from an increased demand flowing from protection as it was the factor used intensively in the import competing sector. Spain and Italy can be represented as labour-abundant and land- and capital-scarce countries, relative to the New World. Furthermore, since in theory international trade is a substitute for international factor mobility, it might well be the case that tariffs stimulated the export of the abundant factor: labour. This is an unexpected and counterintuitive implication of widely accepted theories.

To sum up: relations between protection and emigration are not so clear cut as historians suggested. Only by thinking in terms of a specific-factor model and assuming that the negative effect on demand for labour dominated, can an inverse relationship between tariffs and emigration be expected. O'Rourke and Williamson (1997) suggest, however, that in peripheral countries with large agricultural sectors the labour-demand effects might have dominated when cheap imported grain lowered real wages. Yet, even in that case, relations with external emigration are still not clear because lower wages make it difficult to finance the costs of moving abroad. Cheap grain could have stimulated internal migration by lowering real wages, but at the same time, that would have reduced external migration by increasing the cost of long-distance moves. In a Heckscher–Ohlin model, tariffs, as impediments to trade, stimulated international factor mobility. In the context of the late-nineteenth-century international economy, we should expect a direct relation between tariffs and emigration.

Currency depreciation and emigration: the peculiarities of the Spanish case

Tariffs were not the only phenomenon that contributed to the Spanish economy's isolation from international markets. The Grupo de Estudios de Historia Rural (hereafter, GEHR) have called attention to the role that the depreciation of currency value had on reinforcing the impact of the 1891 tariff, and Cortés Conde also pointed out that between 1890 and 1904, the protection derived from the depreciation of the peseta turned out to be more significant than the impact of the tariff delaying emigration from agriculture (GEHR 1980; Cortés Conde 1988). Thus, it was a combination of the 1891 tariff and currency depreciation, from 1895 till 1905, that reduced external emigration (Sánchez-Alonso 1995: Ch.5).

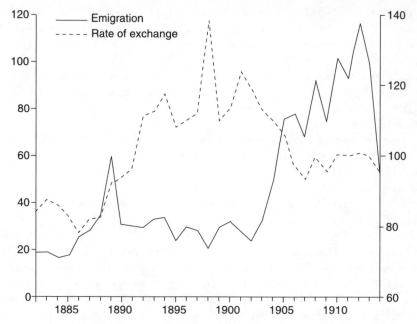

Figure 11.2 Spanish emigration and PTA: real rate of exchange, 1880–1914.

Sources: For emigration, Sánchez-Alonso, Causas de la emigración, Appendix, A-3; For the real rate of exchange, Prados de la Escosura and Tena, Protectionism in Spain.

The external value of the peseta remained stable between 1883 and 1895, in spite of the abandoning of gold convertibility in 1883.[24] While Spain had a *de facto* fiduciary standard during those years, the government tried hard to maintain a fiscal and monetary discipline similar to what it might have been under the Gold Standard (Tortella 1994b: Ch. 7). Furthermore, and until 1891, the stability of the peseta was also linked to net inflow of foreign capital.[25] Unfortunately, from 1895 (the beginning of the Cuban War) until 1905, the peseta depreciated by approximately 30 per cent, due to a combination of fiscal disorder, monetary expansion and a flexible exchange rate (Martín Aceña 1994). Martín Aceña (1994) suggests that to be off the Gold Standard detached Spain from the world economy, especially from the inflows of international capital investment in the 1880s and 1890s. They resumed after 1904–5 when the peseta's value recovered rapidly following a conversion of the external debt and a fiscal reform.

The combined impact of devaluation and tariffs made imports more expensive from the mid-1890s through the mid-1900s. According to GEHR, before 1890 and after 1906, tariffs played the leading role in protecting Spanish farmers from cheap grain but between 1892 and 1905, devaluation of the peseta was more important. Those years became "a period of absolute protectionism" (GEHR 1980: 98) The effects of depreciation were not alleviated by differential rates of inflation between Spain and the rest of the world (Prados de la Escosura and Tena 1994). When the peseta recovered after 1904, foreign wheat once again became a serious threat to Spanish farmers and the government raised tariffs in 1906. Figure 11.2 correlates fluctuations of emigration and the rate of exchange. In spite of the new 1906 tariff, emigration reached its peak when the peseta began to recover its value after 1904. This view implies that Spain enjoyed "exchange rate protection" during those years.[26]

Italy experienced a net outflow of foreign capital after 1887 that also provoked a depreciation of the exchange rate of the lira, together with a crisis in the banking sector and a decline in investment and industrial output. This depreciation of the currency was, however, very brief. From 1896, the Italian economy entered a period of significant growth, the so-called "Giolitian boom", which lasted until World War I.[27]

From the theoretical point of view depreciation changes the relative prices of traded goods as a whole, exports and imports, relative to non-tradables. Furthermore, devaluations are supposed to have a clearly expansionary effect on output and employment. Devaluation increases tradables' prices and hence lowers real wages, if nominal wages are sticky. Migration theory predicts that the lower the wage, the higher the emigration, but if emigration is income-constrained the relationship between low wages and low emigration will be positive. The inverted-U-model for external emigration, developed by Hatton and Williamson (1994), predicts a direct relation between low real wages and low levels of emigration. Thus, large wage gaps between home and a foreign country can be consistent with low emigration rates. Previous research has shown that Spanish wages in some regions were so low that they hindered external emigration.[28] Spanish emigration was clearly income-constrained. Up to the 1880s Spanish emigration levels had remained very low, so few pioneers sent remittances or pre-paid tickets to finance the moves of relatives and friends. In Italy, higher levels of emigration from the 1870s created early migratory chains and the process of sending remittances. In the Spanish case, chain migration was mainly a twentieth-century phenomenon as the process of diffusion took place.

In microeconomic terms, the effects of currency depreciation on individual emigrants are complex. On the one hand, the depreciating home currency benefits immigrants already working in the country of destination and already sending remittances home; it does not benefit future emigrants or previous emigrants who do not intend to return home with savings. Indeed, for potential emigrants still at home, currency depreciation can be viewed as adverse and an obstacle. It clearly increased the price of the steerage ticket, bearing in mind that the main shipping companies fixed their prices in currencies attached to gold.[29] It also lowered the value of emigrants' savings while they searched for new jobs in their countries of destination. Spanish emigration had long been low because low wages provided inadequate surpluses to finance emigration. Currency depreciation made the situation worse for potential emigrants. Since the peseta depreciated on average nearly 30 per cent between 1892 and 1905, we can assume that emigration costs in those years were 30 per cent higher. Ticket fares from Galicia to the River Plate were around £9.8 in 1880/1889. In current pesetas fares increased, due to depreciation, from 250.9 Ptas in the 1880s to 321 Ptas in 1892/1905.[30] For an agricultural worker in Galicia and Asturias (regions of high emigration rates) whose daily wage was around 1.65 Ptas in 1896/97, the cost of the trip, measured in number of working days, increased from 153 working days in 1880/89 to 195 working days in 1892/1905 over a working year of around 250 days.[31] This is without making any allowances for lost earnings during the trip (around 20 extra days) and installation costs in the receiving country.[32] Furthermore, the Baring crisis in Argentina (a favoured destination for Spaniards in the late 1880s) led to a marked depreciation of the Argentinean peso during the years 1891–9 (Cortés Conde 1979: 95–100). The depreciation of the peso clearly affected the remittances (including pre-paid tickets) from Argentina. Once the peso recovered, Argentina regained its position as an attractive destination for Spanish emigrants, although then the depreciation of the peseta increased the costs of moving.[33]

Currency depreciation in late-nineteenth-century Spain could be inversely related to external emigration. At the macro level, depreciation could have had the effect of "exchange-rate protection" and maintained levels of employment in agriculture. Depreciation also lowered real wages and as emigration was income-constrained it lowered migration to the New World, an effect compounded by the depreciation of the Argentine peso in the 1890s.

Econometric tests

The aim of this section is to test the two main hypotheses outlined above: (a) the tariff protection of agriculture had a negative impact on labour mobility and retarded Spanish emigration, and (b) currency depreciation, by increasing the costs of emigration for potential emigrants, also operated to slow down Spanish emigration at the end of the nineteenth century. The same hypotheses will be tested for the Italian case.

Table 11.2 includes the regression equation for the period 1882–1914 for the Spanish case. Other variables which try to capture major determinants of Spanish emigration have also been included: these relate to the main country of destination, Argentina, as well as Spain.[34] Protection is proxied by the nominal tariff on wheat.[35] Wheat was the most important crop produced by Spanish agriculture, and agriculture was the most important sector of the Spanish economy. Trends in agricultural and industrial protection look very similar. Tena's (1998b) recent work confirms that nominal protection was very similar to effective protection. The coefficient for the real depreciation

Table 11.2 Determinants of Spanish external emigration, 1882–1914

C	−13.750
	(−4.828)
Argentinean Construction Output	0.744
LCONARG	(9.155)
Wage differential Spain–Argentina	0.563
DRWSPARG3	(2.195)
Real depreciation of the Pta	−1.593
LDPRL(−1)	(−3.905)
Nominal wheat protection	1.670
LPROTRI	(2.247)
Agricultural Output	−3.186
LAGSP13	(−2.937)
GDP per head	5.846
LYPC13	(3.433)
AR (1)	−0.306
	(−1.651)

Sources:
LMIGRATE from Sánchez-Alonso (1995: Appendix A.3);
LCONARG is the Argentinean construction output. Cortés Conde (1997);
DRWSPARG3 is the real wage differential between Spain and Argentina. Williamson (1996b);
LAGSP13 is Spanish output in agriculture, forestry and fishing;
LYPC13 is Spanish GDP per capita: both from Prados de la Escosura (1997b);
LPROTRI is the log of wheat tariff divided by the wheat price in Spain plus one. GEHR (1980);
LDPRL(−1) is the coefficient of the real depreciation of the peseta, i.e. adjusted by the inflation differential and with a lag of one year. Prados de la Escosura and Tena (1994).

Notes
R^2 adjust.	0.828
S.E. regress.	0.222
D.W.	2.063
F-stat.	22.321

Dependent variable is the ratio of transatlantic gross emigration to population (LMIGRATE)
All the variables are expressed in natural logarithms.
LCONARG, LDPRL(−1), LAGSP13 and LYPC13 are normalised 1913 = 100.
t statistic in brackets

of the peseta is lagged one year because it is assumed that the potential emigrants had a delayed response to currency depreciation.[36]

Several conclusions can be drawn from Table 11.2. Emigration displays a negative and significant relation with the depreciation of the peseta. The protection variable shows also a positive sign although less significant.

Nevertheless a positive sign would not be anticipated by most Spanish historians and would not be predicted by the sector-specific model even though it could be suggested that the tariffs of 1891 and 1906 were not high enough to protect Spanish agriculture from the world market forces.[37]

But the result is predictable in terms of the Heckscher–Ohlin and Stolper–Samuelson models. As elaborated above, these models predict a direct relation between tariffs and emigration. The results set out in Table 11.2 confirm the suggestion that tariffs, by preventing trade, promoted emigration particularly for the years after 1900. An increase in protection would lead to a more than proportional increase in external emigration.

Table 11.2 also makes clear that tariffs exercised a weaker impact on emigration than currency depreciation. Indeed, the depreciation of the peseta proves to be highly significant in explaining the low emigration rates during the period 1891–1904. It turns out to be the distinctive feature of the Spanish economy at the turn of the century compared to economies like Italy.[38] Currency depreciation increased the price of tickets and reduced emigrants' savings while they searched for new jobs in their countries of destination. Currency depreciation was particularly adverse for the majority of potential emigrants, due to low levels of income. Finally, the emigration variable displays rather high elasticities in relation to fluctuations in the international value of the peseta, as is the case for protection.

Economic conditions in Argentina, which absorbed the majority of Spanish emigrants, were also significant. For example, the influence of a variable such as output construction (a sector prone to short-term fluctuations in its demand for unskilled labour force), is highly significant. The results indicated an elasticity of around 0.7 for the estimated Spanish emigration response to fluctuations in construction output in Argentina. Furthermore, the wage differential between Spain and Argentina is not as significant as the construction output although it presents the expected positive sign. It could be that referring to just one of the many countries of destination for Spanish emigrants, the variable does not fully capture the effects of wage differentials on Spanish out-migration. What seems more plausible, however, is the suggestion that the variable reflects the fact that Spanish emigration was income-constrained.[39]

GDP per capita shows a positive and significant relation with external emigration in the equation presented in Table 11.2.[40] Fluctuations in agricultural output are inversely correlated with external emigration. Bad conditions in agriculture tended to stimulate emigration because of lack of employment opportunities, while a better situation delayed or avoided emigration by providing agricultural jobs.

In order to quantify the effects of depreciation on emigration I have carried out a simulation exercise based on the counterfactual that the value of the peseta had remained as in 1883, that is, before the abandonment of gold convertibility and with the level of protection remaining at pre-1891 levels. This static simulation exercise generates lower-bound estimates for the

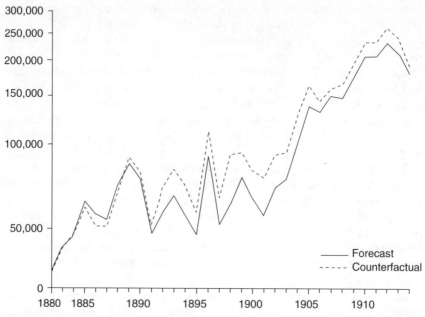

Figure 11.3 Forecast and counterfactual emigration, 1882–1914.

volume of additional emigration that might have taken place in the absence of currency depreciation and with no changes in the tariff.

The peseta fell sharply in 1892–1905, and the values in column 3 of Panel A (Table 11.3) show that, in the absence of depreciation, emigration could have been almost 60 per cent higher. Approximately 600,000 more people might have emigrated, and they represent some 20 per cent of the population between 15–24 years old according to the 1900 population census, the age group most likely to emigrate.[41] Figure 11.3 suggests that far higher emigration rates could have been attained between 1892-1905 in the absence of depreciation. The Spanish gross rate of emigration could have been 5.7 per thousand of population, very similar to the Italian rate over the period 1890–1904 (Table 11.1).

For reasons already elaborated, under the counterfactual scenario of no protection, emigration could have been reduced by about 400,000 during the period 1892–1914. Panel C of Table 11.3 displays emigration under the counterfactual of no depreciation and no increases to levels of protection. Currency depreciation exercised more powerful restraints on emigration than higher tariffs. According to this exercise, Spanish emigration could have been 14.5 per cent higher in the period 1882–1914 and as much as 36.5 per cent higher in the years of rapid depreciation. Nearly half a million more people would have emigrated from 1882–1914 if tariff levels and the external value of the currency had remained stable.

Table 11.3 Counterfactual emigration under no depreciation and no increase in protection after 1882*

Panel A. Hypothesis of no depreciation

	(1) 1882–1914	*(2)* 1882–1891	*(3)* 1892–1905	*(4)* 1906–1914
Per cent change over the forecast value	33.3	1.6	59.3	28.4
Emigration change in absolute terms ('000)	1 093	9	612	472

Panel B. Hypothesis of no increase in protection

Per cent change over the forecast value	–13.8	–7.5	–14.2	–15.8
Emigration change in absolute terms ('000)	–453	–45	–146	–261

Panel C. Hypothesis of no depreciation and no increase in protection

Per cent change over the forecast value	14.5	–6.2	36.5	8.3
Emigration change in absolute terms ('000)	478	–37	377	138

Note
* Forecast values were computed by applying the equation parameters to the annual values of each independent variable. Counterfactual values were computed by the same procedure, except for the depreciation and protection variables for which the 1883 value was fixed. Spain abandoned gold convertibility in 1883 and adopted a high protectionist tariff in 1891.

The counterfactual estimates are, however, a lower-bound conjecture. It is plausible to think that agricultural output per worker and wage rates in Spain would have increased with higher emigration rates. The extra emigrants would also have pulled still more emigrants abroad in their wake due to remittances, pre-paid tickets and chain migration. One of the problems for Spanish economic development in the long run was the slow release of labour from agriculture. Thus, higher external emigration during years of favourable international conditions for international labour mobility could well have had positive effects both on agricultural development and on the overall macroeconomic performance of the Spanish economy. Due to currency depreciation, Spain missed an opportunity to raise its standard of living by emigration. However this is not the sole explanation for low levels of exodus from the countryside. Institutional factors in Spanish agriculture must also be taken into account. Slow urban and industrial development was also and perhaps mainly responsible for the lack of pull from the industrial and urban sectors (Pérez Moreda 1985; Prados 1988).

Table 11.4 Determinants of Italian emigration, 1880–1913

	(1)	*(2)*
C	–7.490	–15.181
	(–0.654)	(–8.843)
USA Construction Output	0.629	0.803
LCONUSA1	(1.933)	(4.008)
Wage differential Ital–USA/Argentina	0.829	0.928
DRWUSARG	(2.257)	(2.388)
Nominal depreciation of the Lira	–1.615	
LDPRIT1(–1)	(–0.680)	
Nominal wheat protection	2.048	1.815
LPROTRITA	(3.666)	(4.154)
Italian GDP per head	1.304	1.195
LYPCIT1	(2.419)	(2.344)

Sources:
LMIGRATIT from Rosoli (1978, Appendix); LCONUSA1 is the USA construction output. Tafunell (1989); DRWUSARG is the real wage differential between Italy and USA and Argentina weighted by the share of Italian emigration to each country. Williamson (1995); LDPRIT1(–1) is the coefficient of the nominal depreciation of the lira with a lag of one year, Fenoaltea (1992); LPROTRITA is the log of wheat tariff divided by the wheat price in Italy plus one. Federico (1984);   LYPCIT1 is the Italian GDP per capita from Bardini, Carreras and Lains(1995).

Notes

R^2 adjust.	0.88	0.88
S.E. regress.	0.22	0.22
D.W.	2.02	2.10
F-stat.	0.00	0.00

Dependent variable is the ratio of transatlantic gross emigration to population (LMIGRATIT)
All the variables are expressed in natural logarithms.
LCONUSA1, LDPRIT1(–1) and LYPCIT1 are normalized 1913 = 100.
t statistic in brackets

Table 11.4 presents the equations carried out for the Italian case.[42] I have tried to select a group of variables similar to the ones used for the Spanish equations. However, in the Italian case, the United States (Construction Output) has been included as the main country of destination for Italian emigrants instead of Argentina, although this country also received a large number of immigrants from Italy. The wage differential between Italy and a weighted average for the USA and Argentina has also been included and it shows, as does construction output in the United States, a significant and positive relation with Italian transatlantic emigration. This is an expected result also confirmed by recent research on Italian emigration (Hatton and Williamson 1998: Ch. 6). I have also included the nominal depreciation of the lira, lagged one year as in the Spanish case, although the Italian lira depreciated much less than the Spanish peseta and during a shorter period of time. The depreciation variable included in equation (1) is not significant but it shows a negative relation with external emigration as it happened in the Spanish case. Obviously, since the depreciation in Italy was not as high as in Spain, its effects on emigration must have been smaller. Nevertheless, the Italian case seems to confirm that even a small depreciation of the currency was inversely related to external emigration.

In turn, nominal protection on wheat presents a positive and significant relation to emigration, suggesting that Fenoaltea's interpretation of the duty on grain stimulating emigration might be correct. It also confirms for the Italian case that in a Heckscher–Ohlin framework tariffs can be positively related to the labour-force mobility. Finally, the GDP per head variable shows a positive relation to emigration in the Italian case. Brinley Thomas (1954) suggested in his classic work that emigration rates in Italy were higher during the booming years of the Italian economy and not otherwise as conventional theory predicts. Italians were able to leave the country in large numbers only when conditions at home were favourable and the population could afford the cost of emigration. The same happened in the Spanish case (Table 11.2), since in both countries emigration seems to be income-constrained. Both Faini and Venturini (1994) and Hatton and Williamson (1998: Ch. 6) have also tested emipirically this positive association beteeen GDP and emigration in Italy although with different results.

Conclusions

By the eve of World War I, Italy was much more integrated in the international economy than Spain. This chapter has compared Italian and Spanish emigration in order to isolate the potential obstacles to Spain's closer integration into the world economy between 1880–1914. It is focused on international labour mobility and has two central hypotheses: first, protection of agriculture restrained labour emigration particularly in the Spanish case; second, currency depreciation increased the cost of moving abroad and slowed down Spanish emigration in the late nineteenth century.

Spanish historiography regards the protectionist policies adopted and followed from 1891 onwards, as a major source of the slow out-migration from agriculture. But Italy also adopted agricultural protection in the late nineteenth century and Italian emigration reached one of its peaks in those years. Furthermore, Spanish historiography is based upon an implicit sector-specific model and assumes that the negative labour-demand effect dominated; it concludes that relations between tariffs and emigration must have been inverse. If, however, we represent the Spanish economy, and the Italian economy as well, in the late nineteenth century in terms of the Heckscher–Ohlin model and the Stolper–Samuelson theorem, tariffs impeded trade and stimulated labour mobility. Something similar seems to be happening in Europe at the present time when restrictions on trade imposed by the European Union operate to promote labour migration from the other side of the Mediterranean.

Nevertheless, the most important element in the explanation for the slow emigration from Spain between 1892 and 1905 was not so much the tariff, but the depreciation of Spanish currency. This was the crucial factor differentiating the Spanish and Italian emigration rates in the late nineteenth century. Currency depreciation in Spain was strong and increased the cost of moving for income-constrained potential emigrants. This also seems to be the case for Italy although depreciation of the lira was smaller and therefore its effects were weaker. Unfortunately for Spain, favourable international conditions for intercontinental emigration came to an end with World War I. Econometric calculations suggest that if the peseta had not depreciated Spanish emigration rates would have been 30 per cent higher and similar to Italian rates. These "counterfactual Spanish emigrants" could, in turn, have pulled even more workers across the Atlantic through chain migration, prepaid tickets and remittances. Since the large proportion of labour employed in agriculture is one of the enduring features of Spanish backwardness, higher external emigration could only have exercised positive effects on long-term economic development. Spanish emigrants had to wait until the second age of economic convergence after 1950, when they travelled to destinations within Europe.

Notes

I gratefully acknowledge the helpful criticisms and comments of James Simpson, James Foreman-Peck, Agustín Llona and, especially, Patrick O'Brien, Kevin O'Rourke and Jeffrey Williamson. Participants in the Economic History Workshop at the LSE also made useful suggestions. Leandro Prados de la Escosura kindly let me use his unpublished data on Spanish GDP and Jeffrey Williamson his new data base on Spanish real wages. I also acknowledge the comments and suggestions from all the participants at the Conference "Long-Run Economic Change in the Mediterranean Basin" (Istanbul, June 1998). Financial support was provided by Ministerio de Educación y Cultura PF9705253090.

1 I am using gross emigration data since the main interest is the trends and fluctuation of emigrants' departures.
2 Hatton and Williamson's (1994b: 66) explanation that what really made Spain different after the 1890s was the delayed demographic transition and economic failure at home seems insufficient.
6 For the Italian case, Sori (1979); for Portugal, Pereira (1984).
4 For the Spanish case, Garrabou (1988) where Italy and Portugal are also included.
5 Baines (1985: 205–10) suggests that in England and Wales, the high emigration of the 1880s cannot be related to the agricultural depression, because the majority of the emigrants in those years came not from the rural counties, but from the urban ones.

6   Sánchez-Alonso (1995: 140–2). In fact, the rate of gross emigration per thousand population in 1910–13 was 11 for Spain and 11.7 for Italy.

7   The coming of the conservative party to power, led by Prime Minister Canovas, imposed a protectionist policy which was to last until the second half of the twentieth century. But even with Canovas' rise to power, protection was not new to the Spanish economy (Serrano Sanz 1987: 140 and *passim*).

8   Measured in national currencies and compared to 21 per cent in Italy, 19 per cent in Germany and 22 per cent in France. O'Brien and Prados de la Escosura (1992: Table 3).

9   Tortella (1994b: 59). (The translations for all the Spanish quotations are mine.) But, still, one can consider that the migration of labour to the towns in response to a negative agricultural shock would depress urban wages, lowering the incentive to move.

10   Prados de la Escosura (1988: 102). However, although it is true that protecting a sector does attract resources from other sectors, this does not necessarily mean that overall employment will rise. It depends on what happen to employment in other sectors, for example, the export sector.

11   Federico (1994: 104). Those who defend the tariff in Italy use the same arguments as in the Spanish case: there was no alternative because of the severity of the agricultural depression, and its absence would have created a serious deficit in the balance of payments. Federico himself supported the balance of payments argument in an early work. Federico (1984).

12   Cereal output increased 37 per cent in those years (Toniolo 1988: 166).

13   Fenoaltea (1993).

14   Fenoaltea (1993). My translation.

15   In Italy, some politicians and writers spoke against emigration but never with the same intensity as in the Spanish case. See Sánchez-Alonso (1995: Ch. 2).

16   Caves, Frankel and Jones (1996: Ch. 6). For a good summary of this model applied to historical events, see O'Rourke (1997).

17   The idea is clearly stated in Prados de la Escosura (1988). It follows very much the line of Kindleberger (1967:106) who stated that emigration "is the force, which above all others (rising exports, closer association with the rest of the world, capital investment and foreign aid) has been responsible for the rapid growth of all Mediterranean countries" in the post-war period.

18   If food is a sufficiently important part of a worker's budget then real wages increase, if not, they decline. O'Rourke (1997).

19   Here, I am following Caves, Frankel and Jones (1996).

20   It is important to note that whereas the assumption that countries share identical technologies is crucial for the factor-price-equalization theorem, it is not necessary for the Stolper–Samuelson theorem.

22   Land/labour ratios were 6.9 in 1890 and 6.7 in 1910 for Spain compared to 39.2 and 44.1 for the United States in the same years. O'Brien and Prados de la Escosura (1992: Table 3). The ratio of wages to land values was 123.2 in 1890 and 67.5 in 1910 for Spain (1901=100) compared to 84.9 and 115.4 for Britain in the same years (free trader in the Old World) and 103.2 and 64.0 in the same two years for the United States. O'Rourke, Taylor and Williamson (1996: Table 2).

23   Rogowski (1984: Ch.1). His model is quite convincing for the German, Italian and Spanish case, but less so for France. France, he says, "is a case where you realized that *other things* also mattered" (p. 69). This model also predicts class conflict: workers will end up being politically radical and, where much of the labour is rural, demanding an agrarian reform. (Rogowski 1984: 38 and *passim).* For a much more political-science-oriented model applied to French commercial policy, see Verdier (1994).

24   Spain never officially adopted the gold standard. Convertibility of paper money into gold and/or silver was maintained until 1883, when eventually it was suspended. Resumption never took place. Martín Aceña (1994).

25   As shown by a recent estimate of the Spanish balance of payments by Prados de la Escosura (1997a).
26   Corden (1981). For the purpose of the present argument, the distinction between currency depreciation and devaluation is irrelevant.
27   Toniolo (1988). In the case of Spain, a net outflow of foreign capital has also been confirmed for the 1890s by Prados de la Escosura (1997a).
28   Even at the turn of the century an increase in agricultural wages between 1896 and 1908 had a strong direct effect on provincial rates of external emigration. Sánchez Alonso (1995: Table 6.1, 257).
29   From the 1880s onwards most of Spain's emigrants were transported by British, German and French companies: Royal Mail Steam Packet, Pacific Steam Navigation Company, Nelson Steam Navigation Company, Hamburg Amerika Line, Nordeustcher Lloyd and Chargeurs Réunis. Only two companies flew the Spanish flag. See Vázquez Gonzalez (1988: 92–3).
30   Prices refer to the cheapest fares from Galicia to Buenos Aires (Vázquez Gonzalez 1988: 92–3).
31   Daily wages in Sánchez-Alonso (1995: Appendix). Average working days in Vandellós (1925: 119).
32   The length of the trip hardly changed (23 to 20 days) between the 1880s and the 1890s (Moya 1998: 38).
33   Even during the crisis of the 1890s Argentina remained the major destination for Spanish emigrants. After 1894 Cuba became less attractive because of the war of independence and Brazil and Uruguay continued to be secondary destinations (Sánchez-Alonso 1995: Ch. 4).
34   I also introduced a demographic variable, the rate of natural increase of the population lagged 20 years, as it is commonly used, but it was not significant. The same result is to be found with the demographic variable in a cross-section analysis of Spanish regional patterns of emigration in 1911/1913 (Sánchez-Alonso 1995: Ch. 6).
35   I also tried nominal average protection, that is, customs revenues as a share of imports, which did not give significant results. It is well known that this is a poor index of protection as it can conceal the prohibitive effects of a tariff.
36   Unit Root Tests for the variables in the equation were carried out. In all cases the variables considered are integrated of order one. The Johansen Cointegration Test for the combination of the variables in the equation was also computed accepting the hypothesis that the residuals are cointegrated.
37   GEHR (1988: 59–62) has pointed out that, in spite of protection, the grain-producing landowners were forced to make some adjustments facing increasing competition from abroad, although the whole process of agrarian change was delayed.
38   Although the Italian lira also depreciated at the end of the nineteenth century, it did so less than the Spanish peseta and during a shorter period of time.
39   This appears to be a common feature for Spain and Portugal (O'Rourke and Williamson 1997).
40   This hypothesis is also confirmed by the higher coefficient obtained for the GDP per capita variable, reported in this equation, as compared to the one yielded if the variable is introduced in absolute terms.
41   The figure would be much higher if we considered only male emigrants in that age group. I acknowledge David Reher for the annual data of population according to sex and age.
42   As in Table 11.2, Unit Root Tests for the variables included in the equations were carried out on all the variables and were considered integrated of order one. The Johansen Test for the combination of the variables in both equations was also computed accepting the hypothesis that the residuals are cointegrated.

Part 6

Interwar policy choices and the political economy of growth

12 Intervention during the Great Depression

Another look at Turkish experience

Şevket Pamuk

Introduction

Many developing countries around the world experienced a turning point during the 1930s. The contrast between "before and after 1929" may often be exaggerated, but there is little doubt that in many parts of the developing world the decade witnessed a decline in international trade and capital flows and a relative rise in import-substituting activities. The crisis also changed the nature of political power with a weakening of the large landowners and export-oriented interests and the commitment to the liberal order that prevailed until World War I. In many countries control fell into more populist hands, with nationalist leanings towards autarky and import-substituting industrialization.

During the 1980s Carlos Diaz Alejandro (1984) and Angus Maddison (1985) showed that, whatever the outcomes may be in the longer term, developing economies that shifted to protection and inward-looking policies generally fared better during the Great Depression than those that adhered to the earlier strategy based on primary exports. Diaz Alejandro also offered a list of policy instruments adopted by the interventionist governments in Latin America during the 1930s. These were, in order of decreasing importance, exchange-rate policies, import repression and import diversion, expansionary monetary and fiscal policies and a variety of other measures ranging from wage repression and public-works programmes to debt repudiation. These should not be viewed as a comprehensive set of measures, however. In the absence of a unified body of theory, they were mostly *ad hoc* measures adopted by the different governments in response to the specific conditions in each country.[1] The shift towards an interventionist, inward-oriented regime was not complete in the 1930s, but emerged fully after World War II when the export pessimism of Raoul Prebisch and the ECLA arguments of structuralist and interventionist development provided the necessary theoretical support.

Not all regions or countries experienced these trends to the same degree, however. For one thing, shocks, policies and capacities differed substantially from country to country. On the whole, colonies of European powers adhered more closely to the orthodox regimes. Similarly, countries where the landed interests were more powerful or where they could not be challenged tended to remain more passive and adhere to the earlier model. On the other hand, ability and willingness to actively manipulate policy instruments such as exchange rates, tariffs and domestic credit were greatest in countries which were either large or had relatively autonomous public sectors.

Most Latin American countries adopted the new, inward-looking strategies, while the experience of developing countries in Asia was more heterogeneous. Around the Mediterranean, policy outcomes were also more diverse. In southern Europe, where the inflationary impact of World War I was still well remembered, governments tended to remain fiscally conservative while embracing protection and stronger bilateral relations with Germany. In Fascist Italy the government moved slowly towards a controlled economy. An orthodox policy of tight money was accompanied by tariff measures to protect those domestic industries that stood to lose the most from an overvalued currency. Coercive measures typical of consolidated dictatorship were taken, both to reduce wages and control prices. Recovery from the Depression was therefore slow until the orthodox policies were reversed in 1935 by the decision to conquer Abyssinia (Feinstein, Temin and Toniolo 1997: 175–7).

In Greece macroeconomic policy was more interventionist. In addition to providing early support for tobacco and wheat producers, the government was forced to move away from the gold standard and devalue the drachma in 1932, the first country in the Balkans to do so. It also defaulted on its external debt and adopted exchange controls the following year. With protection and other forms of government support for import-substituting activities, the industrial sector in Greece registered during the 1930s one of the highest rates of expansion anywhere in Europe (Mazower 1991: 115–270). Similarly, the Great Depression also led to a rise in state intervention and an expansion of the economic role of the state in Yugoslavia, Bulgaria and Romania (Lampe and Jackson 1982: 434–519; Barlas 1998: 14–28).

On the other hand, colonial administrations in Syria, Lebanon and Palestine did relatively little in response to the Depression. The same was true of the countries of the Maghrib – Morocco, Algeria and Tunisia. Writers on the British and French empires have identified a number of basic principles underlying colonial economic practice, all of which were in evidence in the management of these countries. Most importantly, colonies were expected to pay for themselves without recourse to special financial assistance from the metropolis. This produced pressures for fiscal conservatism, including the need to balance the budgets. Secondly, the colonial currencies were tied closely to that of the metropolis to facilitate trade and payment flows. Typically, a colonial currency was managed by a currency board in London or Paris (Owen and Pamuk 1998: 51–3).

With the help of British pressure, large Egyptian landowners enjoyed decisive influence over the nominally independent government. They exercised control through their association with the various parties as well as their strong presence in the parliament. Under the circumstances, the emerging manufacturing interests could hope to obtain government support only to the extent allowed by the landed groups. Hence, support for the domestic textiles industry was the logical choice. The extent of protection for this and other branches of industry remained limited in relation to other, more interventionist countries, however (Owen and Pamuk 1998: 34-45).

This paper will re-examine the economic policies and the performance of the Turkish economy during the Great Depression from the comparative perspective offered by Diaz Alejandro and Maddison. The Depression was sharply felt, especially in the foreign-trade oriented regions of the country. In response, the policies of the government controlled by an urban-based bureaucracy were strongly interventionist. Protectionist measures of the early years were followed in 1932 by the adoption of etatism or import-substituting industrialization led by the state. The recovery of the 1930s was stronger in Turkey than in most other countries around the eastern Mediterranean, as I shall show.

The legacy of the 1930s profoundly influenced attitudes toward international trade in Turkey. Per capita foreign-trade indicators reached in the 1920s were not surpassed until the 1960s. Similarly, the degree of openness of the 1920s as measured by the exports/GDP ratio was not exceeded until the 1980s. Unfortunately, because of the absence of long-term macroeconomic series until recently, it has not been possible to study analytically and quantitatively the 1930s and more generally the first half of this century. Partly because of this deficiency, debates about the 1930s have focused overwhelmingly on etatism or state-led industrialization as a model for the post-World War II era.

The next section will link the published statistics and the existing estimates for the national income accounts of the Ottoman Empire to those of Turkey to construct, for the first time, reasonably uniform series for the period 1913–50. The rest of the paper will then examine the reasons for the relatively strong performance of Turkey's economy during the period 1929–39. Turkey belonged to the camp of interventionist regimes during the 1930s. The commonly accepted explanation has long emphasized that etatism or state-led industrialization was responsible for the strong performance of the urban sector. While etatism significantly contributed to the country's industrialization after World War II, it is difficult to accept that argument for the 1930s, in view of the limited numbers of state economic enterprises and their output levels in comparison to the overall size of the Turkish economy at that time.

I will show that, as was the case in many developing countries, government economic policies were rather eclectic during the 1930s. While exchange-rate policies resulted in the appreciation of the currency, fiscal and monetary policies were not expansionary until the very end of the decade. Instead, the government preferred balanced budgets and a stable money supply. We thus have an apparent puzzle on our hands. How can such a cautious approach to macroeconomic policy be consistent with the strong performance of the urban sector and the national economy ?

I will argue that severe import repression was one of the most important reasons behind the performance of the urban sector during the 1930s. The protectionist measures adopted by the government included an increasingly restrictive foreign-exchange regime and bilateral trading arrangements that sharply reduced the import volume, creating attractive conditions for the mostly small and medium-sized domestic manufacturers.

There is another explanation for the overall performance of both the urban and the national economy, which has frequently been ignored by economists and economic historians in their often heated debates over etatism and its implications. For that I will turn to agriculture, the largest sector of the economy employing more than three-quarters of the labour force during the 1930s and accounting for close to half of the GDP. I will show that despite the sharp deterioration of the intersectoral terms of trade, agricultural output registered significant increases during the 1930s. I will argue that this strong performance can be explained in terms of the availability of marginal lands combined with the demographic and economic recovery of the countryside after a decade of wars lasting until 1922. All of this inevitably raises questions about the effectiveness and contribution of the state sector to the strong economic performance of the 1930s.

The growth record, 1913–50

The period from 1913 until 1945 was exceptionally difficult for Turkey's society and economy. In addition to the world depression, the country suffered through two world wars and a radical redrawing of the borders accompanying the process of transition from an empire to a nation state.

Until recently it was not possible to assess the impact of these events on the Turkish economy. Utilizing the official statistics, Tuncer Bulutay and his colleagues had constructed national income accounts for the period 1923–48. However, these series were not linked to the official production, tax-collection and foreign-trade series of the Ottoman period, or to the reasonably detailed estimates for national income prepared by Vedat Eldem for the years before World War I (Bulutay *et al.* 1974; Eldem 1994).

Isik Özel (1997) linked these two sets of evidence for the first time, producing comparable series for the area within the present-day borders of Turkey for the period 1907–39. Thanks to this work, it is now possible to assess the macroeconomic performance of the Turkish economy during the first half of the twentieth century, and for the purposes of the present paper, insert the 1930s into a long-term context (Özel 1997; see also Güran 1997).

The results are summarized in Figure 12.1 and Tables 12.1 and 12.2. They indicate that Turkey's GDP per capita in 1950 stood approximately 30 per

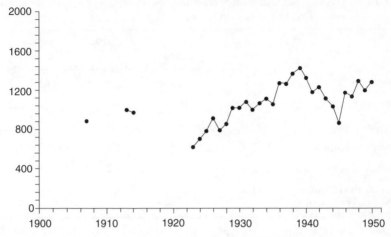

Figure 12.1 GDP per capita in Turkey, 1907–1950 (in 1990 PPP dollars).

Table 12.1 Turkey: basic economic indicators, 1923–1946

	1923	1929	1939	1946
Population in millions	13	14	17.5	19
Share of agriculture in the labour force	n/a	80	77	77
GNP per capita in 1990 PPP dollars	615	1 015	1 425	1 180
Share of agriculture in GNP (per cent)	40	52	39	46
Share of manufacturing in GNP (per cent)	12	9	17	13
Share of total industry including construction in GNP	16	14	22	18

cent higher than its level in 1913, an average annual rate of increase of 0.7 per cent. Not surprisingly, there were sharp fluctuations in between, in population, GDP, and GDP per capita. Periods of expansion (before 1914, 1923–9 and 1929–39) were disrupted by wars (1914–22 and 1939–45). For more than a decade beginning in 1912, Anatolia had been ravaged by a series of wars. Total casualties, military and civilian, of Muslims, Armenians and Greeks during this decade are estimated at close to 3 million. Moreover, in the largest peacetime agreement of population exchange between two governments, approximately 1.2 million Greeks left Anatolia, and in return, approximately half a million Muslims arrived from Greece and the Balkans

Table 12.2   Turkey: a periodization of economic growth 1923–1946 (average annual rates of growth in per cent)

	1923 to 1946	1923 to 1929	1929 to 1939	1939 to 1946
Population	1.9	1.7	2.2	1.2
GNP	4.6	10.3	5.2	-2.0
GNP per capita	2.6	8.4	3.0	-3.2
Agricultural output	4.9	13.6	4.4	-1.4
Manufacturing output	3.3	7.2	5.2	-3.0
Total industrial output including construction	4.5	10.2	5.7	-2.6

Sources: Calculations based on Turkey, State Institute of Statistics (1994); Bulutay *et al.* (1974) and for the conversion to 1990 PPP dollars, Maddison (1995: 184–185). The Bulutay *et al.* estimates for the growth rates of manufacturing output and other related aggregates for 1929–39 were revised downwards following the calculations by Zendisayek (1997: Ch. 4).

after 1923 (Behar 1995; Shorter 1985; Eldem 1994; McCarthy 1983). As a result of these massive changes, the population of Turkey stood at 13 million at the end of 1924, a decrease of almost 25 per cent from a decade earlier. Accompanying these dramatic changes was the sharp decline in the levels of production. In agriculture where the evidence is more detailed, total production may have declined by more than 50 per cent from its 1914 levels.[3]

The former military officers, bureaucrats and intellectuals who assumed the positions of leadership in the new nation state founded in 1923 strove, from the outset, to create a national economy. Industrialization and the creation of a Turkish bourgeoisie were viewed as the key ingredients of economic development (Tezel 1986: 389–97; Keyder 1987: 91–101). The economy recovered sharply during the 1920s. Sectoral growth rates summarized in Table 12.2 indicate that agricultural output almost doubled from 1923 to 1929. Comparisons of Ottoman and Turkish statistics suggest that per capita production levels within the boundaries of Turkey exceeded their pre-World War I levels in 1929 (Özel 1997: Ch. 3).

The available series also indicate that the economy performed strongly during the decade of the Great Depression. From 1929 to 1939 GDP and GDP per capita are estimated to have increased at average annual rates of 5.2 and 3.0 per cent, respectively. Even though Turkey did not participate in World War II, it maintained a large army and the economy came under enormous pressure as imports were disrupted and the diversion of resources for the military placed enormous strains on both industry and agriculture. GDP fell by about 35 per cent from 1939 to 1945 (Boratav 1981: 63–72).

From a comparative perspective, the overall trend of 0.7 per cent annual

Table 12.3 Mediterranean economic growth in comparative perspective, 1913–50
(GDP in 1990 PPP dollars)

Country or Region	GDP per capita		Average annual rate of change
	1913	*1950*	*(per cent)*
France	3 450	5 220	1.1
Portugal	1 350	2 130	1.1
Yugoslavia	1 030	1 550	1.1
Italy	2 510	3 430	0.9
Turkey	995	1 300	0.7
Greece	1 620	1 950	0.5
Spain	2 260	2 400	0.2
Egypt	510	520	0.0
Latin America	1 520	2 610	1.5
Asia (excl. Japan)	700	640	−0.3

increase in GDP per capita for the period 1913–50 puts Turkey's economic performance in the middle of the spectrum spanned by the southern European and Mediterranean countries for which GDP series are available. According to the estimates prepared by Angus Maddison in 1990 Purchasing Power Parity dollars, GDP per capita remained unchanged in Egypt between 1913 and 1950, increased by 0.2 per cent per annum in Spain and by 0.5 per cent per annum in Greece. At the higher end of the spectrum, GDP per capita increased by 0.9 per cent per annum in Italy and by 1.1 per cent per annum in Portugal, Yugoslavia and France. GDP series are not available for the other eastern and southern Mediterranean countries. Between 1913 and 1950, GDP per capita increased by an average of 1.5 per cent per annum in Latin American countries where the impact of the two world wars was limited. In contrast, the developing countries of Asia experienced a decline in per capita GDP of about 0.3 per cent per annum during the same period (Table 12.3).

The Great Depression

The principal mechanism for the transmission of the Great Depression to the Turkish economy was the sharp decline in the prices of agricultural commodities. Prices of wheat and other cereals declined by more than 60 per cent from 1928–9 to 1932–3 and remained at those levels until the end of the decade. Prices of the leading export crops – tobacco, raisins, hazelnuts and

Table 12.4   Turkey's foreign trade, 1924–1946

	1924–5	*1928–9*	*1938–9*	*1945–6*
Exports (million dollars)	92.5	81.5	107.5	192.0
Imports (million dollars)	114.5	97.0	105.5	108.5
Exports/GNP (per cent)	12.8	11.4	6.9	5.2
Imports/GNP (per cent)	15.8	14.4	6.8	2.8
Trade balance/GNP (per cent)	–3.0	–3.0	+0.1	+2.4
External terms of trade (export prices/import prices)	129	100	79	68

Sources: Turkey, State Institute of Statistics (1994) and calculations based on Bulutay *et al.* (1974).

cotton – also showed declines averaging around 50 per cent, although they recovered somewhat later in the decade. Since these decreases were greater than the decline in the prices of non-agricultural goods, the external terms of trade of the country deteriorated by more than 25 per cent and the domestic terms of trade shifted against agriculture by 31 per cent from 1928–9 to 1932–3 (Tables 12.4 and 12.5). In contrast, the physical volume of exports continued to rise after 1929, perhaps reflecting the continued recovery in output levels. Nonetheless, the result was a sharp decline in the real incomes of most market-oriented agricultural producers. The adverse price movements thus produced a sharp sense of agricultural collapse, especially in the more commercialized regions of the country.[4] Also in 1929, the economy went through a severe foreign-exchange crisis, both real and speculative, arising in part from the sharply higher import volume ahead of the expected tariff increases and in part due to the anticipation of the first annual payment on the Ottoman debt (Tekeli and Ilkin 1977: 75–90; Tezel 1986: 98–106).

   In response, the government moved quickly towards protection and greater control over foreign trade and foreign exchange. A new tariff structure was adopted in October 1929 as soon as the restrictions of the 1923 Lausanne Peace Treaty on commercial policy ended. Average tariffs on imports are estimated to have increased from 13 to 46 per cent in 1929 and to more than 60 per cent by the second half of the 1930s. Equally importantly, tariffs on imports of foodstuffs and manufactured consumer goods were raised substantially but were kept lower for agricultural and industrial machinery and raw materials. For this reason, the effective rates of protection on many of the final goods selected for protection were substantially higher. In addition, quantity restrictions were introduced on the imports of a long list of goods in November 1931. The lists were updated frequently and

Table 12.5   Turkey: agricultural production and prices, 1928–1946 (all indices, unless indicated otherwise)

	1929–30	1938–39	1945–46	
Labour force	100	119	125	
Cultivated land	100	142	135	
Total crop output	100	146	120	
Total yields	100	103	89	
Wheat output in million tons	2.4	3.8	2.6	
Wheat output	100	160	110	
Wheat yields	100	113	81	
Cereals output	100	148	99	
Non-cereal output	100	148	146	
Relative prices	1928–9	1932–3	1938–9	1945–6
Internal terms of trade agricultural prices/non-agricultural prices	100	69	81	95
Cereal prices/non-agricultural prices	100	55	57	80
Prices of non-cereal crops/non-agricultural prices	100	90	104	109

Source: Calculations based on Bulutay *et al.*(1974).

some of the tariffs were raised further during the 1930s as import substitution spread to new sectors (Yücel 1996: 74–84 and 105–13). The immediate beneficiaries were the small and medium-scale manufacturing enterprises in many parts of the country consisting of textile mills, flour mills, glassworks, brick factories, tanneries and others which began to experience high rates of growth. A recent study estimated the average rate of growth of this manufacturing sector at 6.3 per cent per annum during the period 1929–33.[5]

The crisis that began in 1929 had a number of other important repercussions as well. First, concern for trade deficits and balance-of-payments problems moved the government increasingly towards clearing and barter agreements and bilateral trade. By the second half of the decade, more than 80 per cent of the country's foreign trade was being conducted under clearing and reciprocal quota systems. These bilateral arrangements also facilitated the expansion of trade with Nazi Germany, which offered more favourable prices for Turkey's exports as part of its well-known strategy towards southeastern Europe. Germany's share in Turkey's exports rose from 13 per cent in 1931–3 to an average of 40 per cent for 1937–9. Similarly, its share of Turkey's imports increased from 23 per cent in 1931–3 to 48 per cent in 1937–9 (Tezel 1986: 139–62 ; Tekeli and Ilkin 1982: 221–49).

It is significant that the government did not use exchange-rate policy to improve the balance of payments and soften the impact of the Depression. On the contrary, the existing parity of the Turkish lira *vis-à-vis* was strictly maintained even as the leading international currencies were devalued. As a result of the actions of other governments, the lira was revalued by a total of 40 per cent against both sterling and the dollar between 1931 and 1934 and the new parities were maintained until the end of the decade.[6]

Even though the export volume continued to rise in absolute terms, these far-reaching changes in the structure of foreign trade combined with the adverse price movements and the increases in GDP later in the decade to lead to a sharp decline in the share of exports in GDP from 11.4 per cent in 1928–9 to 6.9 per cent in 1938–9 (Table 12.4). It is thus clear that exports did not act as a source of recovery for the national economy during the 1930s. The causes of that recovery have to be sought elsewhere.

Government concern with the balance of payments also led to a cessation of payments on the external debt and a demand for a new settlement after the first annual payment in 1929. The subsequent negotiations, aided by the crisis of the world economy and demands for resettlement by other debtors, produced a favourable result, reducing the annual payments by more than half for the rest of the decade. During that period the Kemalist regime sought foreign funds and expertise for its industrial projects. Due to the world economic crisis, however, inflows of foreign capital remained quite low during the 1930s (Tezel 1986: 165–89).

Etatism

The difficulties of the agricultural and export-oriented sectors quickly led to popular discontent with the single-party regime, especially in the more commercialized regions of the country: in western Anatolia, along the eastern Black Sea coast and in the cotton-growing Adana region in the south. The wheat producers of central Anatolia who were connected to urban markets by rail were also hit by the sharply lower prices. As the unfavourable world market conditions continued, the government announced in 1932 the beginning of a new strategy called *etatism*, or state-led import-substituting industrialization.

Etatism promoted the state as a leading producer and investor in the urban sector. A first five-year industrial plan was adopted in 1934 with the assistance of Soviet advisers. This document provided a detailed list of investment projects to be undertaken by the state enterprises rather than an elaborate text of planning in the technical sense of the term. A second five-year plan was initiated in 1938 but its implementation was interrupted by World War II. By the end of the decade, state economic enterprises had emerged as important, and even leading, producers in a number of key sectors such as iron and steel, textiles, sugar, glass, cement, utilities and mining.[7]

Etatism involved the extension of state-sector activities and control to other parts of the urban economy as well. Railways which were nationalized from European ownership, as well as the newly constructed lines, were transformed into state monopolies. Most of the state monopolies which had been handed over to private firms in the 1920s were taken back. In transportation, banking, and finance, state ownership of key enterprises was accompanied by increasing control over markets and prices. At the same time, the single-party regime maintained tight restrictions on labour organization and labour-union activity. These measures paralleled the generally restrictive social policies of the government in other areas. It is significant that despite considerable growth in the urban sector during the 1930s, real wages did not exceed their levels of 1914 (Pamuk 1995: 96–102).

Etatism has undoubtedly had a long-lasting impact in Turkey. For better or worse, this experiment also proved to be inspirational for other state-led industrialization attempts in the Middle East after World War II.[8] From a macroeconomic perspective, however, the contribution of the state sector to the industrialization process in Turkey remained modest until World War II. For one thing, state enterprises in manufacturing and many other areas did not begin operations until after 1933. The total number of active state enterprises in industry and mining on the eve of World War II did not exceed twenty. Official figures indicate that in 1938 total employment in manufacturing, utilities and mining remained below 600,000 or about 10 per cent of the labour force. State enterprises accounted for only 11 per cent of this amount, or about 1 per cent of total employment in the country. Approximately 75 per cent of employment in manufacturing continued to be provided by small-scale private enterprises (Tezel 1986: 233–7).

It would be difficult to argue, however, that the private sector was hurt by the expansion of the state sector during the 1930s. The largest private enterprises were in the foreign trade sector, and these were adversely affected by the contraction of foreign trade. This was, however, due more to the disintegration of international trade than to etatism itself. Elsewhere in the urban economy, most of the private enterprises remained small in size. By investing in large, expensive projects in intermediate goods and providing them as inputs, the state enterprises actually helped the growth of private enterprises in the manufacturing of final goods for the consumer. Private investments continued to be supported and subsidized during the 1930s. Nonetheless, the private sector remained concerned that the state sector might expand at its own expense. Tensions between the two sides continued.

There is some admittedly crude evidence on the rates of investment by the state and private sectors which sheds additional light on their respective roles. These estimates show that total gross investment in Turkey averaged more than 12 per cent of GDP during 1927–9. Private investment accounted for about 9 per cent, and the rest came from the state sector, primarily in the form of railway construction. With the onset of the Depression, private investment dropped sharply to 5 per cent of GDP and stayed at that level for the rest of the decade. State investments, on the other hand, rose modestly to an average of 5 per cent of GDP by the end of the decade (Tezel 1986: 362–88). These estimates suggest that the state sector made up for some of the decline in private investment during the Depression but was not able to raise the overall rate of capital formation. It is also possible that the investment rates of the late 1920s were unusually high due to the post-war reconstruction and recovery. If so, one may conclude that the aggregate rate of investment fully recovered in the second half of the 1930s even though it had declined after 1929.

Sectoral breakdown of public-sector investment is also instructive. Close to half of all fixed investments by the public sector during the 1930s went to railway construction and other forms of transportation. This substantial commitment reflects the overriding desire of the single-party regime to create a politically and economically cohesive entity within the new boundaries. In comparison, industry received limited resources, attracting no more than a fourth of all public investment, or slightly above 1 per cent of GDP during the second half of the 1930s. This low figure supports our earlier argument that the contribution of etatism to the industrialization process remained modest in the 1930s.

Sources of economic growth

It is difficult to be precise about the rate of growth of industrial output and more generally the rate of growth of the urban sector during the 1930s. In their reconstruction of the only series of national income accounts for the period before 1948, Tuncer Bulutay and his colleagues assumed, in the absence of other evidence, that the manufacturing sector as a whole grew at the same rate as those mostly large establishments which received subsidies from the government under the law for the Encouragement of Industry, for which data were available (Bulutay *et al.* 1974). This method sharply overstated the extent of the increase in manufacturing output. In fact, other independent evidence has since become available, showing that the small manufacturing establishments achieved a more modest increase in output during the 1930s. The consequent revisions to the Bulutay calculations bring down the overall annual rate of growth for manufacturing industry from more than 10 per cent to 5.2 per cent per annum (Zendisayek 1997: Ch. 4). This is undoubtedly a significant correction, but the latter rate is still remarkable for the decade of the Great Depression. The revised estimates presented in Table 12.2 still point to a strong performance for the economy as a whole.

We thus have an apparent puzzle on our hands. We have evidence of strong performance by the industrial sector, the urban economy and the national economy. At the same time, aggregate figures show that the contribution of the state sector to the urban economy, both as an investor and as a producer, was rather modest during the 1930s. How can these growth rates be explained?

The experience of other developing countries during the 1930s suggests that one important candidate is exchange-rate policy.[9] However, it has already been shown that rather than using devaluations to soften the impact of the Depression, the government actually allowed the lira to appreciate by 40 per cent against sterling and the dollar between 1932 and 1934. Similarly, fiscal policy can hardly be characterized as expansionary during the 1930s. Government revenues and expenditures increased only modestly from about 13 to 15 per cent of GDP in the late 1920s to a new range of 17–19 per cent during the 1930s. Government budgets remained balanced despite minor yearly fluctuations and no attempt was made to use deficit financing as an additional mechanism for generating savings (Tezel 1986: 368–88; Yücel 1996: 62-73). As a result, the nominal amount of currency (banknotes plus coinage) in circulation also remained stable and was linked closely to the gold and foreign currency reserves of the Central Bank until 1938. Despite this passive stance, there occurred a large increase in the real money supply after 1929 due to the decline of the aggregate price level.[10] The most important reason behind this cautious approach to macroeconomic policy was the bitter legacy of the Ottoman experience with budget deficits and large external debt until World War I and the inflationary experiment with paper currency during the war. Ismet Inönü, a close associate of Atatürk and the prime minister for most of the interwar period, was a keen observer of the late Ottoman period and the person most responsible for this conservative policy stance.[11]

In the absence of the use of currency depreciation, fiscal policy or monetary policy to expand aggregate demand, the strong protectionist measures adopted by the government beginning in 1929 emerge as one of the key causes of the output increases after 1929.[12] In addition to tariffs and quotas on a wide variety of manufactured goods, an increasingly restrictive foreign-exchange regime and a growing reliance on bilateral trading arrangements sharply reduced imports from 15.4 per cent of GDP in 1928-9 to 8.7 per cent by 1932–3 and 6.8 per cent by 1938–9. Even more importantly, the composition of imports changed dramatically. The share of final goods declined from 51 per cent in 1929 to 21 per cent in 1940 while the share of intermediate goods rose from 26 per cent to 54 per cent and machinery and equipment from 9 per cent to 22 per cent during the same period. Severe import repression thus created very attractive conditions for domestic manufacturers after 1929. These mostly small and medium-sized producers achieved relatively high rates of output growth for the entire decade until World War II (Zendisayek 1997: 54–105; Yücel 1996: 89–130).

There is yet another explanation for the overall performance of both the urban and the national economy which has frequently been ignored by economists and economic historians in their often heated debates over etatism and its meaning.[13] For that we need to turn to agriculture, the largest

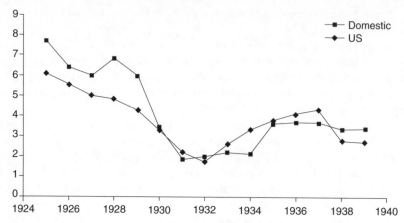

Figure 12.2 Domestic and international prices of wheat in US cents/kg.

Sources: Based on Bulutay *et al.* (1974) and U.S. Bureau of the Census (1974).

sector of the economy, employing more than three-quarters of the labour force during the 1930s and accounting for close to half of the GDP.

Agricultural expansion during the depression

The story of the agricultural sector during the interwar period has two parts: one concerning prices, the other concerning quantities. First, as has already been pointed out, the collapse of commodity prices and the deterioration of the intersectoral terms of trade after 1929 had severe consequences for most producers. Not only did the market-oriented producers, both small and large, in the more commercialized, export-oriented regions of the country experience a decline in their standards of living, but so too did the more self-sufficient producers of cereals in the interior. The decline in the terms of trade of the latter was in fact much greater than that of the producers of non-cereals (Table 12.5). The sharp decline in agricultural prices also increased the burden of the indebted peasantry, forcing many to give up their independent plots and accept sharecropping arrangements.

One of the responses of the government was to initiate, after 1932, direct and indirect price-support programmes in wheat and tobacco. It began to purchase wheat from the producers, first through the Agricultural Bank, and later via an independent agency established for this purpose called the Soil Products Office. Until the end of the decade, however, such purchases remained limited, averaging 3 per cent of the overall crop or about 15 per cent of the marketed wheat (Atasagun 1939; Bulutay *et al.* 1974).

These purchases may have prevented a further decline in wheat prices, but they certainly did not reverse the sharp deterioration of the terms of trade faced by the wheat producers. In fact, a comparison of the Turkish wheat prices with those of the USA shows that the domestic price of wheat had been above international world prices before 1929 when Turkey was a net importer. With the increases in wheat production, domestic prices fell below and remained close to the sharply lower international prices during the 1930s (Figure 12.2). Clearly, the sharply lower agricultural prices were seen as an opportunity by the government to accelerate the industrialization process in urban areas. It is also significant that the prices of export crops, and more generally of the non-cereal crops, did not fare as poorly. The terms of trade faced by the producers of non-cereals improved after 1934, regaining their pre-1929 levels by the end of the decade (Table 12.5).[14]

More generally, the distributional impact of protection during the 1930s can be analysed with a sector-specific factors model. Turkey was a land-abundant, capital- and labour-scarce country during the interwar period. Agriculture used land and labour and the urban sector used capital and labour. Despite the possibility of rural–urban migration, labour and capital were mostly immobile between the rural and urban sectors until 1950. Under these circumstances, the rural–urban dichotomy can best explain the distributional impact of the tariffs. Land and labour in agriculture lost but capital and labour in the urban sector gained from protection.[15]

However, such an analysis needs to take into account second-order effects as well. Most importantly, there were the benefits to the agricultural sector of the growth and industrialization in the urban sector. In addition to increased demand for traditional foodstuffs, the rise of manufactures in textiles, sugar, tobacco and other products created new demand for cotton, sugar beets, tobacco and other cash crops. Domestic prices of these crops may have exceeded international prices during the second half of the 1930s. If so, these second-order effects helped distribute some of the benefits of urban growth to the rural sector.

The second part of the story about agriculture during the Great Depression is less well known, but at least equally important. Evidence from a variety of sources, including the official statistics, shows that agricultural output increased by 50 per cent to 70 per cent during the 1930s, after adjustments are made for fluctuations due to weather. The evidence thus indicates an average rate of growth of more than 4 per cent per year for aggregate agricultural output during the decade. The official statistics suggest that the big jump in agricultural output occurred in 1936 (Figures 12.1 and 12.3), but crop output may have begun to rise earlier. Similarly, foreign-trade statistics indicate that Turkey turned from being a small net importer of cereals at the end of the 1920s into a small net exporter of wheat and other cereals on the eve of World War II, despite a population increase of 20 per cent during the 1930s (Tables 12.1 and 12.5).[16]

The next task would be to explain these substantial increases in output in the face of unfavourable price movements. Two different and not mutually exclusive explanations appear possible, although it may not be easy to assess the contributions of each without more detailed research. First, government policies may have played a role. Most importantly, the abolition of the tithe

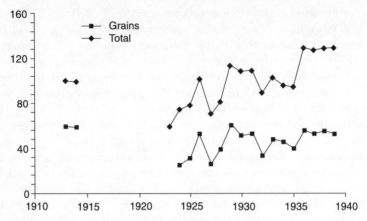

Figure 12.3 Per capita crop production, 1913–1939.

Sources: Based on Bulutay *et al.* (1974), Güran (1997) and Özel (1997).

in 1924 may have contributed to the recovery of the family farm by improving the welfare of small and medium-sized producers and helping them to
expand the area under cultivation or to raise yields. Another important contribution of government policy was the construction of railways, which
helped integrate additional areas of central and eastern Anatolia into the
national market. Railways may have encouraged the production of more
cereals in these areas. The government was also involved in a number of
other programmes in support of the agricultural sector, such as the expansion of credit to farmers through the state-owned Agricultural Bank, promotion of new agricultural techniques and higher-yielding varieties of crops.
Despite the rhetoric from official circles, these programmes did not receive
large resources, however, and their impact remained limited.

The second explanation focuses on the long-term demographic recovery
of the family farms and their response to lower prices. In the interwar
period, Anatolian agriculture continued to be characterized by peasant
households which cultivated their own land with a pair of draft animals and
the most basic of implements. Most of the large holdings were rented out to
sharecropping families. Large-scale enterprises using imported machinery,
implements and waged labourers remained rare. Irrigation and the use of
commercial inputs such as fertilizers also remained very limited. If one
reason for the strength of family farms was the scarcity of labour, the other
was the availability of land, especially after the death and departure of millions of peasants, both Muslim and non-Muslim, during the decade of wars.
Under these circumstances, increases in production were achieved primarily
through the expansion of cultivated area, so that a shortage of labour
emerged as the effective constraint in blocking higher agricultural output in
most parts of the country.

After the wars ended and the population began to increase at an annual rate of around 2 per cent, the agricultural labour force followed suit, albeit with a time lag, thus facilitating the expansion of the area under cultivation. The basic agricultural trends summarized in Table 12.5 confirm this picture. They show that while yields remained little changed, the area under cultivation expanded substantially during the 1930s. Area cultivated per person and per household in agriculture also increased. Numbers of draft animals rose by about 40 per cent during the same period, both confirming the material recovery of the peasant household and facilitating the expansion in cultivated area (Shorter 1985). Comparisons of the late Ottoman and early Turkish statistics indicate that per capita agricultural output did not return to pre-World War I levels until 1929 and the early 1930s. Total agricultural output reached pre-war levels only in the second half of the decade (Figure 12.3). The availability of land also helps explain why land reform and redistribution of land did not become an important issue in Turkey during the interwar period except in the southwest, where Kurdish tribal leaders controlled large tracts of land (Keyder and Pamuk 1984: 61–3).

An additional factor contributing to output growth may have been due to the economic behaviour of peasant households. It is possible that peasant households relying mostly on family labour responded to the lower cereal prices after 1929 by working harder to cultivate more land and produce more cereals in order to reach certain target levels of income. Increases in land under cultivation per household and per person in the agricultural labour force would support this explanation as well as the argument for the demographic and economic recovery of the family farm.[17]

Sharply lower prices and rising output levels in agriculture thus created very favourable conditions for the urban sector during the interwar period. Underlying the high rates of industrialization and growth in the urban areas were the millions of family farms in the countryside which continued to produce more despite the lower prices. These increases in crop output, in turn, kept food prices low for longer periods of time. Without this performance from the countryside, protection of domestic industry alone would not have allowed the urban sector to achieve such high rates of growth (Figure 12.3).

Conclusions

The case of Turkey during the Great Depression is exceptional in the eastern Mediterranean not only because of the extent of government intervention but also because of the strength of economic recovery. Moreover, the policy mix in Turkey was rather unusual in comparison to the activist government initiatives in other developing countries in Latin America and Asia. Government intervention in Turkey was not designed, in the Keynesian sense, to increase aggregate demand through the use of devaluations and expansionary fiscal and monetary policies. The preference for balanced budgets and a strong currency during the 1930s was closely associated with the Ottoman government's unfavourable experiences with external debt up to 1914 and with a paper-currency-driven inflation during World War I. Instead of expansionary macroeconomic policies, the emphasis was placed on creating a more closed, more autarkic economy and increasing central control through the expansion of the public sector. These latter preferences were directly related to the bureaucratic nature of the regime.

This paper has also shown that, contrary to the assertions of much of the existing literature, the contribution of the state sector to recovery and growth during the 1930s was limited. Instead, it was the small and medium-sized private enterprises which benefitted from the severe import repression and the strong performance of the agricultural sector that sustained the economy until late in the decade.

The economic model and strategy for development thus created during the Great Depression worked in the 1930s, and for the most part, through the 1960s when much of the import substitution was technically simple and protection created strong incentives for continued accumulation in the urban sector. The state sector played an important role in the industrialization process during this period. Since then, however, the legacy of the 1930s has been casting a long shadow on Turkey's economic development. Efforts to reduce the extent of government regulations and privatize the state economic enterprises have had a mixed record against the political and legal opposition during the last two decades.

Notes

1   Diaz Alejandro (1984: 17–39). Compare with Bulmer Thomas (1994: 201–37).
3   Based on a comparison of the agricultural statistics of the 1920s as summarized in Bulutay *et al.* (1974) with the Ottoman statistics before World War I as given in Güran (1997). Also Özel (1997: Ch. 2).
4   Since most of the impact of the Great Depression was felt through price effects, national income accounts prepared in constant prices do not reflect the severity of the impact. For example, see Figure 12.1.
5   Zendisayek (1997: 54–106). See also Yücel (1996: 113–30), Boratav (1981: 170–6) and Kazgan (1977: 231–73).
6   Tezel (1986: 144–50). Bent Hansen's (1991a: 374–5) calculations show that the effective exchange rate against the leading trade partners also appreciated sharply during this period.
7   Tekeli and Ilkin (1982: 134–220);Tezel (1986: 197–285); Boratav (1981: 172–89); Hansen (1991a: 324–35); Hershlag (1968: Ch. 4 and 9).
8   For the influence of etatism on the state-led industrialization strategies in other Middle Eastern countries after World War II, see Richards and Waterbury (1990: 174–201).
9   For the close relationship between exchange-rate devaluations and economic recovery in Latin America during the 1930s, see Campa (1990).
10   Yücel (1996: 55–9). It appears unlikely that this *de facto* increase in the real money supply had a significant impact on the level of aggregate demand.
11   The government's reluctance to pursue expansionary policies was, of course, consistent with the orthodoxy of the period. For a recent survey of the restrictive fiscal and monetary policy that prevailed in the United States and western Europe until 1933, see Temin (1989: Ch. 2), and also Eichengreen (1992).
12   See Table 12.2 and Tezel (1986: 102–3).

13 For the debate, see Hershlag (1968: Ch. 4), Boratav (1981), Keyder (1987: Ch. 5) and Tezel (1986: 197–232).

14 In contrast to the studies approaching the 1930s from the perspective of urban economy and etatism, Birtek and Keyder (1975) emphasized the importance of agriculture and the key position of the middle farmer. They argued that a key element in government policy of the period was the political alliance with and the support provided to the medium-sized, market-oriented wheat producer. While the emphasis on the countryside is refreshing, the argument is not consistent with the limited volume of wheat purchases and the trends in relative prices. For a similar criticism, see Boratav (1981: 180–6).

15 See O'Rourke (1995; 1997b: 775–81) and compare with the more general Heckscher–Ohlin framework used by Rogowski (1989).

16 Net imports of wheat averaged 2 per cent of domestic production during 1926–9. Net exports of wheat averaged 2.5 per cent of domestic production a decade later, during 1936–9. The sources are the *Statistical Yearbooks* (1930–1 and 1940–1) for Turkey and Bulutay *et al.* (1974).

17 This would be consistent with the behaviour of the peasant household as analysed by the Russian economist Chayanov (1987).

13 Egyptian commodity markets in the age of economic liberalism

Tarik M. Yousef

This development in transport has had profound and, on the whole, decidedly beneficial consequences by stimulating agricultural and mineral production and facilitating the formation of national markets and integrated states and societies.

Issawi, 1982

Introduction

Over the past quarter century, economic historians have made a concerted effort to examine the role of technological advances and institutional change in promoting the economic transformation of the north Atlantic economies in the late eighteenth and nineteenth centuries. More recently, scholars have turned their attention to the developing regions of the late nineteenth century in search of fresh evidence for earlier hypotheses and, more importantly, to understand the historical origins of the rapid economic growth in the periphery relative to the centre.[1] On the technology side, this literature has by and large focused on the role of railways in reducing transportation costs, facilitating market integration and accelerating income growth. Institutional analyses, on the other hand, have tackled a range of issues centreed on the impact of property rights and transaction costs on, for example, the patterns of financial development, entrepreneurship, industrial organization and agricultural transformation, all of which are believed to have conditioned overall economic performance. The emerging consensus from this line of research has further underlined the importance of technological and institutional factors in determining economic outcomes in the periphery.[2]

With a few exceptions, the countries of the southern and eastern Mediterranean (including the Middle East) have yet to be fully integrated into this research agenda. In particular, the role of transportation and institutions in explaining economic performance has not received adequate analytical attention from economic historians. However, as the chapters in this volume demonstrate, the engines of global economic integration and growth in the late nineteenth century – trade and factor flows – were operating with force in much of the southern and eastern Mediterranean during this period. The expansion of trade with Europe and North America necessitated investments in modernizing transport infrastructure which in turn required capital inflows from abroad. The commercialization of society which accompanied integration into the global economy through commodity markets, capital flows and when present, mass migrations, often induced fundamental changes in the social and economic institutions governing society. These dynamics were at least clearly present in the economic history of Egypt from the mid-nineteenth century through the interwar years. While becoming gradually integrated into the global economy, Egypt was increasingly governed by a liberal economic ideology that fostered the growth of free markets and narrowed the role of the state to building legal institutions and transport infrastructure. Although growth performance was impressive between 1870 and 1914, Egyptian historiography has long been consumed by debates on the failure of this liberal policy to sustain rapid post-1914 growth and to accelerate industrialization before World War II (Tignor 1984). Thus, little attention has been devoted to examining the impact of advances in late-nineteenth-century transportation infrastructure and institutional reform on other aspects of economic performance.

Did Egypt's age of economic liberalism coincide with the rise of a unified market economy? Did the revolution in transport infrastructure and legal systems promote efficiency in local and regional trade? These questions remain largely unanswered despite their centrality to evaluating the achievements of Egypt's experiment with economic liberalism for over a century prior to World War II. This chapter presents empirical evidence on the integration of commodity markets during this unique period in Egyptian economic history. Specifically, we seek to shed new light on the operation of domestic commodity markets that have often been presumed to be inefficient although understudied. In doing so, we provide a critique of the perceived failure of economic liberalism in interwar Egypt in addition to addressing early structuralist thinking on the price mechanism in developing economies. Finally, by focusing on commodity-market integration, we highlight another dimension of the contribution of railways and institutions to economic change that is equally relevant to the study of economic performance in the periphery.[3] Following this introduction, the balance of the chapter is divided as follows: the next section reviews relevant economic and policy developments that conditioned the evolution of Egypt's commodity markets in the late nineteenth century; this is followed by a section which describes the markets, commodities and method of analysis; next, two sections report the main empirical investigation; a final section concludes.

The evolution of Egyptian commodity markets 1800–1939

Much is known about the integration of Egypt into the world economy in the nineteenth century. Roger Owen (1981) has singled out the multiplication of trade links with the expanding industrialized economies of the west as having profoundly changed city and society in Egypt and the rest of the Middle East. Local, regional and long-distance trade were linked and are believed to have expanded as part of the same process of market creation.[4] However, while a great deal has been written about the transformation of long-distance trade with Europe and the Far East, considerably less is known about regional and local trade. By and large, writings on Egyptian commodity markets have taken place as an indirect by-product of other more popular themes in Egyptian history; the few studies that do exist have been conducted by sociologists and anthropologists who were usually more interested in social than economic history (Shirbini 1995; Baer 1969; Larson 1985). Thus, there has never been a systematic study of the integration of Egyptian commodity markets including that of its chief export, cotton.[5]

Organized commodity markets have operated in Egypt for a very long time, mainly in the form of weekly gatherings for local trade in consumer goods.[6] The importance and structure of these markets has undergone rapid change since the early nineteenth century in response to the needs and policies of the state and the openness of Egyptian markets to international trade. Accordingly, one could conveniently classify the historical development of commerce on the basis of the division of production and distribution activities between the state and the market.[7] The past two centuries have witnessed the full spectrum of this division of labour. Beginning with Mohamed Ali's (1802–42) centralization of domestic and external commerce in state monopolies, the balance gradually shifted in favour of the market, especially during the period of British occupation, until the post-World War II period when the state once again controlled production and marketing. In the 1990s, Egypt is once again liberalizing domestic markets while opening up the economy to the outside world. Egypt has passed through a complete policy cycle twice since 1802, it seems.

The second half of the nineteenth century saw a dramatic decline in the domination of the state in trade and increased commercialization of the countryside. Markets penetrated the country, linking Cairo and Alexandria to consumers and producers in towns and rural villages. This process was sparked to a large extent by the rapid expansion of cotton and grain exports and the invasion of Egypt by European imports (Issawi 1947).[8] Peasants sold their cash crops in exchange for imported textiles and foodstuffs that could not be produced locally. Domestic trade in cereals flourished, enabling peasants to shift from subsistence agriculture and to specialize in cash crops like cotton, wheat, rice and onions. The growing, processing, and marketing of cotton and other cash crops involved extensive marketing arrangements between rural peasants, interior merchants, city buyers and export agents in

Cairo and Alexandria (Owen 1969). In particular, it necessitated a revolution in the transportation system that would give the state an active role in the creation and integration of domestic markets.

Egyptian markets had always been accessible by boat due to their proximity to the Nile. The irrigation projects of the second half of the nineteenth century provided additional navigable waterways in the Delta and Nile Valley, a development that was exploited with the introduction of steamboats that sailed as far south as the Sudan (Crouchley 1938). But the greatest of transport developments took place with the introduction of the railway in 1851. Thereafter, the construction of railways expanded on an impressive scale; the length of tracks reached 1,338 km in 1869 and tripled to 5,606 km by 1939. This process paralleled the development of infrastructure in the New World, made possible by the flow of British capital into export-driven economies of the late nineteenth century. As a result, the cost of freight fell by 60 per cent and the tonnage transported by rail expanded by 100 per cent between 1880 and 1910; by the early twentieth century, the bulk of traffic in passengers and goods was transported by railways.[9] The transportation revolution was simultaneously affecting the communications system. The electric telegraph was introduced at the same time as the railway; the first line connecting Cairo to Alexandria was laid in 1854. Over the next three decades, an additional 6,000 km of telegraph were built and a further 9,000 added by 1939. Finally, the mail service organized by Mohamed Ali in 1835 expanded with the addition of 7,000 post offices around the country.

The marketization of the economy received further stimulus with the introduction of reforms affecting private property, administration, regulation, and foreign participation in the economy. With the Land Law of 1858, private ownership of land was instituted and peasants were assessed for taxes directly, eliminating tax farmers and collective village responsibility for tax payments.[10] Whereas under Mohamed Ali peasants sold prescribed crops directly to the state in order to pay taxes, they now had control over what to grow and marketed their produce directly to merchants and export agents.[11] Having lost its marketing monopoly, agricultural produce on public lands became subject to market forces in open auctions. The gradual transition from payment of taxes in kind to cash payments was advanced by the introduction of mortgage laws in the 1870s, stimulating the growth of rural credit markets. The reform of the legal system gained momentum in the 1870s with the promulgation of western-inspired legal systems including the Commercial Code, the Code of Maritime Commerce and the Code of Civil and Commercial Procedure in addition to the new Civil and Penal codes of 1875. Finally, the political right to universal suffrage was accorded to all Egyptians in 1883 as part of a new constitutional framework which provided for establishment of national courts, provincial councils, a legislative council and an assembly (Anderson 1968). In all, the integration of Egypt into the world economy coincided, at least in theory, with the liberalization of the economy and the introduction of a legal framework that would serve the requirements of a modern market economy.

The incentives for foreign participation in domestic trade multiplied in the second half of the nineteenth century. Although Egypt and other Ottoman provinces had been committed under the Anglo–Turkish Convention of 1838 to maintaining an open trade regime with free exchange of products and minimal import duties, the state monopolies of Mohamed Ali made this difficult in practice. The suppression of internal customs, the elimination of the state monopoly on transportation and the *de facto* lifting of the ban on direct purchases by foreign merchants from native growers in the interior in the 1850s, secured the freedom of commerce and stimulated greater foreign presence in agricultural marketing and exports.[12] The formalization of the Mixed Courts in 1876, staffed by foreign and Egyptian judges, with jurisdiction in cases involving foreign and native subjects, provided a considerable measure of judicial order along with the protection of property and enforcement of contracts under the newly passed laws regulating commerce.[13] The increased stability of Egypt together with the high prices commanded by grains and cotton during the Crimean War and the American Civil War, respectively, attracted greater foreign investment in Egyptian agriculture, infrastructure, and commerce (Owen 1969). As a result, the size of the resident foreign community in Egypt increased sharply from 3,000 in 1836 to 68,000 in 1878, and to 152,000 by 1907. With the help of Egyptian minorities, foreigners exploited the open economic system and the westernizing current in the country and soon came to watch over commercial and financial activities, foreigners owning no less than 60 per cent of the total capital invested in public debt and joint-stock companies in 1907 (Crouchley 1936).

The Egyptian Market Company was formed in 1898, a British firm given a concession to build new weekly markets and enclose old ones within walls. By 1938, there were 500 weekly markets in Egypt, all of which were privately owned. With the removal of internal tolls on shipments of goods, the state monopoly on water navigation, and the restrictions on foreign participation in the village economy, wholesale and retail trade links between rural villages and town centres expanded rapidly (Shirbini 1995). The eighteenth-century monopolistic structure where rural markets served primarily as bulking centres for Cairo and Alexandria, was gradually replaced with one structure that fostered horizontal links between villages, cities and export centres (Larson 1985). The traditional organization of village markets changed in favour of retail trading; cities and large towns bustled with department stores resembling those in Europe, which in some cases had branches even in smaller villages.[14] Monopolistic practices of guilds were dismantled by the influx of European goods and a series of government decrees in 1887–90, facilitating the influx of rural labour into all trades in major towns. Those employed in commerce as a percentage of total employment increased from 1.3 per cent in 1880 to 4.6 per cent in 1907 and 7.5 per cent in 1937. Finally, trading activities benefitted from the gradual monetization of the economy and the eventual replacement of gold and silver coins with paper currency in the early twentieth century (Rifaat 1935).

Should the transportation revolution and institutional reforms of the late nineteenth century have facilitated the creation of an integrated national market economy? Since the writings of Adam Smith, economic historians have argued that developments in transportation went hand in hand with greater integration of commodity markets (Metzer 1979; Issard 1949; Kindleberger 1989). Similarly, historical and contemporary debates on market efficiency, including the analysis of village bazaars in traditional societies, have emphasized the role of property rights and transaction costs embedded in formal or informal contractual and marketing arrangements (Geertz 1978; North 1990; Greif 1999). Not surprisingly, similar views are echoed in Egyptian historiography. Crouchley (1938), for example, has gone so far as to suggest that "the great development in production, commerce and foreign trade in this period would not have been possible without the extension of the means of communication".[15] According to Safran (1961), the cumulative effects of the political, social and economic transformation in the late nineteenth century "amounted to nothing less than a complete transformation of the basic character of the life and organization of Egyptian society." One consequence of this transformation, according to Larson (1985), is that towards the late nineteenth and early twentieth century the Egyptian marketing structure contained many elements of what anthropologists refer to as a competitive interlocking vertical and horizontal system.

Surprisingly, most economic historians have been skeptical of the view that Egyptian commodity markets became efficient, even while acknowledging the importance of the transport revolution and legal reforms in stimulating the growth of a dynamic national economy. Hansen (1991a), citing a study by Martin and Levi (1910), conjectured that, with the exception of intermediate wholesalers and cotton markets, consumer markets were non-competitive and inefficient. Others have cited the Egyptian aversion to trading activities, peasant ignorance of market conditions, and excessive reliance on minorities and foreigners to build and operate the commercial system as contributing to the slow integration of rural Egyptian markets.[16] Similarly, nationalist writings appearing from the 1930s onwards tended to reflect structuralist thinking on the failure of the price mechanism in the traditional sector in developing economies (Schultz 1964). As such, it did not take long after World War II before the new political leadership ushered in the era of state-led industrialization and domination of agricultural marketing and pricing (Waterbury 1983).

With no concrete empirical evidence to support these conflicting views of the historical record, our starting point is the claim that the debate on market integration, and its relevance for understanding the impact of the transportation improvements and institutional changes in late nineteenth- and early twentieth-century Egypt, remains open. The remainder of this chapter presents results from an empirical examination of price integration across Egyptian commodity markets. We test the predictions of the law of one price (LOP) in rural and urban markets on a commodity-by-commodity basis. The evidence suggests that Egyptian commodity markets were as well integrated in the 1920s as they are in the United States today.

Geography, markets and commodities

With an area of 1 million square kilometres, or 386,000 square miles, Egypt is deceptively large, almost the size of Texas and New Mexico combined. Yet, the desert covers 97 per cent of the country, leaving just 12,355 square miles, an area the size of Maryland and Delaware combined, where 95 per cent of the population lives. Unlike Brazil, where the introduction of the railways was hampered by mountainous terrain, Egypt's topography is practically flat, offering no natural obstacles (other than waterways) to any form of transportation. Since ancient times, economic life and urban centres have been concentrated along the banks of the Nile in the Valley (Upper Egypt) and the Delta (Lower Egypt).[17] Our sample of thirty-four cities and towns spans the entire administrative and geographical map of Egypt: thirteen are in the Delta, seventeen are in the Nile Valley, and the remaining four are coastal cities on the Mediterranean and Red Seas (Figure 13.1).[18] Virtually all cities were accessible by railways, roads and navigable waterways in the early twentieth century.[19]

In order to track the evolution of price integration across markets over time, one would prefer to examine a panel of prices from the late nineteenth to the early twentieth century. However, such data, even if it existed, would cover only a few commodities and would certainly be of low frequency. Instead, we provide a rich test of the extent of price integration in the early twentieth century, using a high-frequency panel of prices for as large a basket of commodities as possible. Thus, we focus on the 1920s, a period of steep price deflation in Egypt that followed the inflationary episode during World War I.[20] As Figure 13.2 illustrates, the Cairo Commodity Price Index followed a downward trend during the 1920s, although some commodities experienced even more volatility during the decade. The aggregation of prices into a single index masks significant variability in short-term price trends across commodities, a fact that we exploit by examining the extent of price integration across the thirty-four markets on a commodity-by-commodity basis (Figure 13.2).[21]

The sample of twenty-six essential commodities (including twenty-four food items) may be conveniently classified on the basis of their perishability as goods or, alternatively, they may be classified according to whether they entered into international or local trade.[22] We use the perishability criterion, since it helps illuminate the important role of goods' storability in price integration (Williams and Wright 1991). The list of eleven perishable goods includes bread, butter, cheese, eggs, milk, wet beans, fish, chicken, mutton,

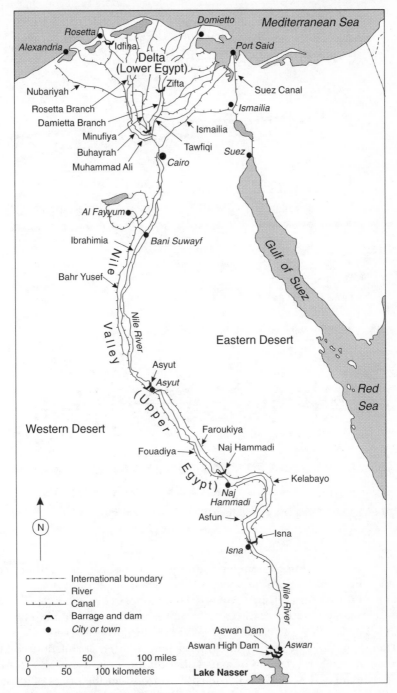

Figure 13.1 Egypt's topography.

Source: *Egypt: A Country Study* (1983).

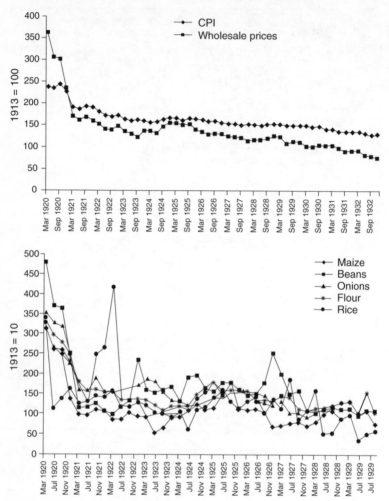

Figure 13.2 Commodity prices and the CPI in Cairo, 1920–29.

Source: Yousef (1999).

veal and beef. The fifteen non-perishable goods are wheat, maize, flour, dry
beans, lentils, rice, onions, potatoes, coffee, sugar, oil, alcohol, soap, petroleum and fissikh (dried fish).[23] We observe retail prices on a quarterly basis
for each market and for each year 1920–29; thus, for every commodity we
have a panel of forty price observations across thirty-four markets.

Traditional tests of market integration have utilized correlation coefficients and simple regressions of spatial prices as the tools of analysis (Metzer
1974; Latham and Neal 1983; Barnett 1995). Consider the prices of a commodity k in two localities i and j, P_i and P_j in logarithmic levels. Market
integration is then examined by running the OLS regression:

$$P_{it} = \alpha + \beta P_{jt} + \varepsilon_{ijt} \qquad\qquad (1)$$

where equation (1) is estimated over time for each commodity and pair of cities, or markets may be pooled together and the equation estimated for each commodity. Estimates of β close to 1 are interpreted as support for the hypothesis of integration. The results using such an approach, however, would be misleading if the price series contained trends, i.e., were nonstationary.[24] The relationship between prices would require the explicit modelling of such trends through a cointegration methodology (Ardeni 1989). Alternatively, we follow the approach adopted in the recent literature which focuses on intercity price differentials: that is, for commodity k we consider $Q_{ijt} = P_{it} - P_{jt}$, the price differential expressed as a percentage difference in prices between cities i and j.[25] With perfect arbitrage, the price differential should be zero. This is the essence of the law of one price, since abstracting from trade barriers, taxation and transportation costs, prices across markets should be equal (Kindleberger 1989). Fortunately, as we observed in the previous section, our data should enable us to abstract from all these factors except transportation costs which we approximate by distance in rail kilometres.[26] Intercity price differentials should be bounded by the costs of arbitrage with the width of this band varying with transportation costs. In consequence, we would expect the variability and absolute deviation of intercity price differentials, $Q_{ij,k,t}$, to be positively related to transportation costs or distance (Engel and Rogers 1996).

Table 13.1 presents the summary statistics of intercity price differentials using the standard deviation and mean absolute size of $Q_{ij,k,t}$ overtime. In the interest of comparative analysis, we compare our results with those obtained in Parsley and Wei's (1996) analysis of LOP across US cities over the period 1972–92. Our benchmark city is Tanta, the largest urban centre in the Delta, located directly north of the fulcrum dividing the Delta from the Nile Valley.[27] Using either measure of price differentials in Egypt and the USA, perishable goods exhibit greater variability than non-perishables. Although Egyptian price differentials from the 1920s appear slightly more volatile than those in the USA fifty to seventy years later, the magnitudes are remarkably similar. Figure 13.3 plots intercity price differentials against the costs of arbitrage, measured by the distance in rail kilometres relative to Tanta. The regression results establish a strong link between transportation costs and intercity price differentials; the results also support the finding of a non-linear relationship between distance and price differentials.[28] Not surprisingly, price variability is more strongly related to distance in the case of non-perishable commodities, which were stored, transported and traded domestically and internationally.

The law of one price in Egypt

We now examine the hypothesis of market integration on a commodity-by-commodity basis and provide estimates of the rates of convergence to the law

Table 13.1 Summary statistics of quarterly retail prices

	Egypt (1921–1929)		USA (1975–1992)	
	Mean	Standard deviation	Mean	Standard deviation
Variability of price differential				
Perishables	0.141	0.074	0.149	0.058
Nonperishables	0.134	0.070	0.129	0.046
Mean absolute price differential				
Perishables	0.146	0.088	0.144	0.066
Nonperishables	0.129	0.076	0.125	0.052

Sources and notes:
1. Price differential variability is defined as the standard deviation over time of the percentage price difference   where $P_{i,k,t}$ and $P_{j,k,t}$ are the prices of good k in cities i and j at time t. Throughout, city j is Tanta. With 11 perishable goods and 33 city pairs, there are 330 observations over which to take the mean and standard deviation. Similarly, with 15 nonperishables, there are 495 observations over which to take the mean and standard deviation.
2. Mean absolute price differential is defined as the mean absolute deviation of $Q_{i,j,k,t}$.
3. The commodity groups are: (1) perishables: bread, butter, cheese, eggs, milk, wet beans, fish, chicken, mutton, veal and beef; and (2) nonperishables: wheat, maize, flour, fissikh, dry beans, lentils, rice, onions, potatoes, coffee, sugar, oil, alcohol, soap and petroleum.
4. The US data are from Parsley and Wei (1996, Table 1).

of one price. We do this by testing the data for the stationarity (mean reversion) of intercity price differentials, $Q_{ij,k,t}$ (Frankel and Rose 1996; Lothian and Taylor 1993). Economically speaking, we ask whether intercity price differentials fluctuate around and return to their hypothetical mean level of zero or if they meander away without a tendency to revert to this long-run mean. Equation (1) may be rewritten in terms of $Q_{ij,k,t}$ in the following way:

$$Q_{it} = \beta Q_{it-1} + \varepsilon_{ijt} \qquad (2)$$

If β is strictly less than one in absolute value, then the process is stationary; if $\beta = 1$, then the process is a random walk, implying that LOP does not hold even in the long run.[29] In all tests, we use the critical values provided by Levin and Lin (1993).

Panel A of Table 13.2 summarizes the empirical findings for perishable and non-perishable commodities. For non-perishables, we are able to reject the random-walk null hypothesis for all but one commodity at the 95 per cent level and for all but two commodities at the 99 per cent level – in percentage terms, 95 per cent and 85 per cent of the time, respectively. Although less overwhelming, we find similar evidence for perishables in eight out of eleven commodities at the 95 per cent and 99 per cent levels. Furthermore, we find that all commodities that are internationally traded,

Table 13.2 Panel tests of commodity price integration

Perishable commodities

	Panel A Test without city effects	Panel B Test with city effects
Commodities that pass the test of price integration	Bread, mutton, chicken, wet beans, butter, cheese, eggs, milk	Bread, mutton, chicken, fish, wet beans, butter, cheese, eggs, milk
Commodities that fail the test of price integration	Beef, veal, fish	Beef, veal

Nonperishable commodities

	Panel A Test without city effects	Panel B Test with city effects
Commodities that pass the test of price integration	Flour, maize, wheat, fissikh, lentils, onions, rice, potatoes, coffee, sugar, oil, petroleum, alcohol, soap	Maize, wheat, fissikh, lentils, dry beans, onions, rice, potatoes, coffee, sugar, oil, petroleum, alcohol, soap
Commodities that fail the test of price integration	Dry beans	Flour

Source: Yousef (1999).

Notes:
1. The test of market integration involves modifying equation (2) by running an augmented Dickey-Fuller test.
2. The null hypothesis is that prices follow a random walk, while the alternative being that the process is stationary, i.e., markets are integrated.
3. Critical values at the 95 per cent level provided by Levin and Lin (1993) are used.

perishable and non-perishable, exhibit the strongest mean reversion behaviour; we interpret this as reflecting a general efficiency of domestic commerce in internationally traded goods and not just in cotton as Hansen (1991a) has suggested. Finally, the role of storability is clearly highlighted by the price behaviour of raw fish versus fissikh; the former commodity is extremely perishable and hence fails the test of stationarity, while the latter is storable for several months and exhibits strong mean reversion properties.

Panel B of Table 13.2 summarizes the results when the empirical specification in equation (2) allows city-specific effects. In other words, we allow for the possibility that the true mean of $Q_{ij,k,t}$ has a city-specific component that is not zero. One justification for this is the possibility that trade in commodities may entail systematic or sunk costs that may vary across cities (Parsley and Wei 1996; Obstfeld and Taylor 1997). In the historical and contemporary context of Egypt, such considerations are plausible given the wide variance in the size, development and accessibility of markets in the Delta and Nile

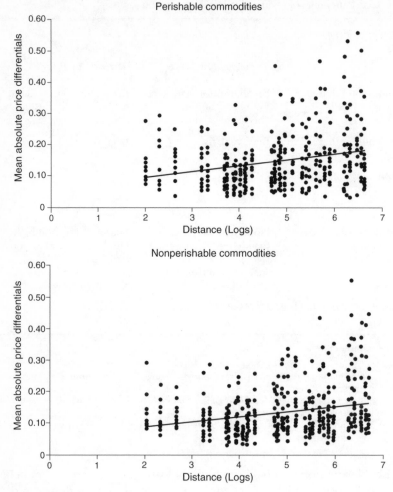

Figure 13.3 Transport costs and price dispersion.

Note: See table 13.1 for definitions.

Valley. For example, many small towns in the early twentieth century did not possess adequate facilities for storage and refrigeration, and their links to the railway system may have given them less flexibility within the transportation system (El Sherbini and El Sherif 1956). On the other hand, entry into trading activities may have also been restricted by existing networks of traders in major cities and may have required investments whose financing would have been difficult in Upper Egypt (Owen 1991). The implications of augmenting equation (2) with city-specific effects are quite surprising given that, in previous studies, the inclusion of these effects tended to weaken results

Table 13.3 Rate of convergence to the Law of One Price

	Perishables	Nonperishables
Without city effects:		
Average half-life	7.5	4.1
Median half-life	3.5	3.5
With city effects:		
Average half-life	0.6	0.5
Median half-life	0.6	0.4

Source: Yousef (1999).

Notes:
1. Rate of convergence to LOP is defined as the half-life of deviations or the length of time (in quarters) it takes for deviations from LOP to shrink by half. For each group of commodities we calculated the median and average half-life.
2. We excluded fish from the perishables and dry beans from the nonperishables.

considerably (Frankel and Rose 1995). In contrast, we are able to reject the random-walk hypothesis as often as previously and with wider margins of significance.

What about the rates of convergence to LOP? That is, what is the length of time it takes for deviations from market integration to disappear? The failure to find high convergence rates in the literature is at the heart of the perceived empirical failure of the Purchasing Power Parity (PPP) doctrine (Frankel and Rose 1995). In time-series or cross-section studies, the typical half-life of deviations from LOP falls in the range of three to five years.[30] In Parsley and Wei's (1996) work, the median half-life for perishables and non-perishables are, respectively, three and five quarters. Table 13.3 presents the implied half-lives by the estimates of β in equation (2). Overall, the half-lives are shorter for non-perishable commodities than for perishables; they are shortest for those goods exported and imported. Without non-zero city means, the average and median half-lives are 7.5 and 3.5 quarters for perishables and 4.1 and 3.5 quarters for non-perishables. With city-specific effects, the average and median are comparable across commodities and range between 0.4 and 0.6 quarters. In other words, if we allow markets to exhibit separate long-run equilibrium price differentials, on average deviations from these equilibria shrink by 50 per cent within two months. Again, the half-lives are shortest for commodities entering external trade.

To summarize, we find very strong evidence favouring the law of one price for the overwhelming majority of our commodities; the implied half-lives for interwar Egypt are comparable to those found in the USA in recent years and are certainly superior to those implied by international purchasing-power-parity studies. Based on these findings alone, we can safely reject previous assertions of Egyptian commodity market segmentation in the early twentieth century.

Upper Egypt versus Lower Egypt

Is the distinction between markets in the Delta and Nile Valley relevant in testing for market integration in Egypt? Already, we have observed that city-specific factors mattered. A priori, an argument could be made that the two regions are different in terms of history and geography. In contrast to the Delta, markets south of Cairo are smaller in size and population, and are more spatially dispersed (Platt and Hefny 1956). With no seaports or border links to neighbouring countries, the Valley has historically lagged behind Lower Egypt in exposure to the outside world, receiving fewer foreigners and less foreign capital in the nineteenth century. Indeed, "the greater proximity of Lower Egyptian villages to the mercantile and cultural centres of the country brought with it greater economic opportunities as well as faster cultural development" (Baer 1968: 141). The resulting social differentiation led to considerable migration from Upper Egypt to Lower Egypt at the end of the nineteenth century.

We begin with the link between transport costs and intercity price differentials already examined. Table 13.4 examines the link by commodity group between price variability and transport costs after introducing regional dummy variables for the Delta and the Nile Valley. Replacing the distance variable with the regional dummy in regression (2) produces essentially the same results; including the regional dummy with the distance variable in regression (3) renders both insignificant. The reason is straightforward: the regional dummy does not have any explanatory power once distance is taken into account, since the two are highly correlated. Thus, distance accounts for the wider price differentials associated with cities in the Nile Valley. However, the relationship between distance and price differentials is different in the two regions as evidenced by the implied elasticities for the two regions when they are allowed to differ in regression (4). The elasticity of the price differential with respect to distance is greater in the Nile Valley, implying that distance gives rise to wider price differentials. In addition to the differences in economic development between the two regions, the nature of transport infrastructure in the Nile Valley is the key to understanding this result. Rail networks in the Nile Valley are much less dense and flexible than in the Delta (Figure 13.1). While goods may be transported between any two cities in the Valley using only one rail track, a typical pair of cities in the Delta has access to several rail tracks. Furthermore, more navigable waters and roads exist in the Delta than in the Valley, thereby providing Lower Egypt with the distinct advantage of lower transportation costs.

If transport costs mattered more in the Nile Valley than in the Delta, does this imply that transport costs might have caused the rates of convergence to

Table 13.4 Transport costs and intercity price differentials by region

Variability of price differential for nonperishables

	(1)	(2)	(3)	(4)
Ln distance	0.004*	—	0.004	0.0157*
	(0.001)		(0.003)	(0.004)
Region	—	–0.008*	0.0004	0.096*
		(0.004)	(0.007)	(0.029)
Region × Ln distance	—	—	—	–0.019*
				(0.005)
Product dummies	yes	yes	yes	yes
R^2	57.4%	57.3%	57.5%	58.4%
No. of observations	495	495	495	495

Variability of price differential for perishables

	(1)	(2)	(3)	(4)
Ln distance	0.003*	—	0.003	0.0148*
	(0.001)		(0.002)	(0.006)
Region	—	–0.009*	0.0006	0.087*
		(0.004)	(0.005)	(0.034)
Region × Ln distance	—	—	—	–0.017*
				(0.006)
Product dummies	yes	yes	yes	yes
R^2	63.1%	62.5%	63.4%	66.1%
No. of observations	330	330	330	330

Notes:
* indicates statistical significance at the 95 per cent level.
The dependent variable is the variability of price differentials or the standard deviation over time of $Q_{i,j,k,p}$ as defined in Table 13.1. Region = 1 if the city is in the Delta and 0 if the Nile Valley. Ln is the natural logarithm of the variable and standard errors in parentheses. The following specification forms the basis for the above regressions: s.d. (Qij,k,t) = B_1ln(distance) + B_3 region × Ln(distance) + Σ product dummies.

LOP to differ across cities in the two regions? We have yet to examine the link between transport costs and the rates of convergence. Our earlier results are open to the criticism that we have estimated rates of convergence to LOP between Egyptian cities which are closer to each other than those in other countries. In fact, this is the case as the average distance between Tanta and other Egyptian markets is 120 miles compared to 850 miles for US cities examined in Parsley and Wei (1996), and in cross-country purchasing-power-parity studies, distances are measured in thousands of miles. To the extent that geography matters to the operation of the law of one price and conditions the rates of convergence, it could then be concluded that transportation costs explain the empirical failure of purchasing-power-parity. To address this issue, we estimated equation (2) after introducing distance separately and interacted with the initial intercity price differentials. We pooled the data together for all commodities but allowed the two groups – perishables and non-perishables – to have separate slopes, i.e. different rates of convergence.

We find that transport costs conditioned the rates of convergence; convergence to LOP is slower in cities that are farther apart, i.e., the rates are now an increasing function of distance. Using the average distance between cities, we approximated the half-life of deviations from LOP for each commodity group.[31] They now range between 0.5–2.5 quarters for perishables and 0.49–2.01 quarters for nonperishables. Even with these calculations, we are still left with mean-reversion tendencies in Table 13.3 that suggest a more rapid convergence to LOP than is found in cross-country studies.

Could the high convergence rates in Egypt be justified by appeal to the transportation revolution alone? The same point has been echoed by Engel and Rogers (1996) who find that price dispersion of similar commodities within the USA is considerably smaller than between Canadian and US cities separated by the same distance.[32] Our measure of transport costs, distance between cities in rail kilometres, overlooks the speed and flexibility gained with the introduction of railways (Landes 1969). Furthermore, we have not factored in the impact of the quality of rail links, communication lines and other developments in road and water transport infrastructure. Imagine the following counterfactual illustration: if we assume that transport costs would have doubled in the absence of the transportation revolution – a reversal of what in fact took place between 1890 and 1910 – then the implied half-life of deviations from LOP would have increased by over 30 per cent for both community groups. If properly measured, perhaps future research will be able to show unambiguously that late-nineteenth-century advances in transportation and communication created the market integration that made it possible for the law of one price to prevail by the 1920s.

Conclusions

Although the empirical results reported here on Egyptian commodity-market integration in the 1920s are still preliminary, a number of conclusions are warranted. First, previous notions of segmented local markets must be rejected in the light of the overwhelming evidence of market integration. Second, Egyptian commodity markets exhibit mean-reversion tendencies that compare very favourably with those obtained for the USA in recent years and in cross-country studies of purchasing-power-parity. We interpret this as evidence of efficiency in the operation of domestic commodity markets. Third, the revolution in transportation and communications contributed to the creation of a nationally integrated economy, although the exact timing and magnitude of this contribution have yet to be quantified. Our knowledge would benefit greatly from estimates of the social savings from the introduction of the railway in Egypt. Furthermore, this paper implies a clear agenda for future research on Egyptian domestic markets. What role did Cairo and Alexandria play in the formation of local markets and in the transmission of price signals? To what extent were local markets integrated with global commodity markets before and after the 1937 tariff reform? What happened to price integration following the end of economic liberalism and the rise of state interventionism in 1952?

Notes

1   This is particularly true for the economic history of Latin America in the nineteenth century; see, for example, the collection of essays in Coatsworth and Taylor (1999), and Haber (1997).

2   For recent surveys of the application of the New Economic History to the study of economic growth and institutional change in the developing world, see the editor's introduction in Haber (1997), and Harris, Hunter and Lewis (1995), respectively.

3   This impact of the introduction of railroads on market integration has been emphasized by Metzer (1974) in Tsarist Russia and Hurd (1975) in India.

4   On the conceptual distinction between local, regional and international trade, see Polanyi (1944). Traditional analyses have focused on transport costs and taxation as the primary factors in distinguishing one type of trade from the other.

5   The one exception here is Owen's (1969) classic study of the Egyptian cotton economy. However, his work deals primarily with the evolution of the cotton sector and its links with the international market, providing little information on the integration of local cotton markets in Egypt. Issawi (1988) provides a compilation of annual grain prices in the Levant in the late nineteenth century but does not assess the trends in spatial integration within the region or across international markets.

6   Civilization has endured in Egypt since ancient times where an agriculture system based on farming villages appeared 5,000 years BC (Allen 1997). Similarly, long-distance trade in the Near East dates back to the predynastic period. Weekly gatherings of markets in Egypt have been known to exist since the sixteenth century at least.

7   Alternatively, one could trace the evolution of markets on the basis of the openness of the Egyptian economy. It turns out that the two approaches coincide: that is, when the state dominated commerce, the economy was closed to the outside world and vice versa. It is possible to project this reasoning much further back in Egyptian history beginning with the formation of the state around 3000 BC, which led to the monopolization of production and trade (Trigger 1993).

8   The external trade regime was made more open starting in the mid-nineteenth century, following the signing of commercial agreements with European powers which until the 1930s guaranteed the free flow of imports into much of the Middle East including Egypt (Issawi 1982).

9   For example, the cost of transporting one qantar (49 kg) of cotton between two markets in Lower Egypt was cut in half between 1892 and 1902 following the opening of a light railway (Issawi 1982: 59). Rail freight rates between Chicago and New York fell by almost 50 per cent during the period 1880–1910 (Harley 1980). A similar decline in transport costs has

been documented in India following the construction of rail networks in the late nineteenth century (Hurd 1975).

10   Other functions of the village as a corporate body were abolished in the 1880s when the corvee and the responsibility to fight locusts and floods became an individual duty (Baer 1969).

11   For a description of the marketing system and the effects of Mohamed Ali's policies on agriculture, see Rivlin (1961).

12   Abdel-Rahim Mustafa (1968) provides a lucid discussion of events leading up to the dismantling of the state monopolies in agriculture. Mohamed Ali and his immediate successors strongly resisted all efforts to liberalize domestic marketing, even after opening Egypt to external trade flows.

13   Since the Middle Ages, the "capitulations" had given foreigners and their protected subjects in the Middle East extraterritorial jurisdictions and immunity from local taxes, including the right to be tried in their own courts. The mixed courts were set up in Cairo and Alexandria to deal with commercial cases between foreigners and Egyptians (Anderson 1968: 210–12).

14   See North's (1990) analysis of markets in traditional societies, which echoes issues raised by Geertz (1978) in his work on Moroccan village bazaars.

15   However, like most writing on nineteenth-century Egyptian economic development, he notes that much of the foreign-financed transport infrastructure, especially the irrigation networks and the Suez Canal, led to large state indebtedness and the debt crisis in 1876 (Crouchley 1938: 107–25), which constrained Egypt's fiscal independence until the 1930s.

16   See Issawi (1954) and el Sherbini and el Sherif (1947). The literature is abundant with accounts of rural wholesale buyers, in coordination with city merchants' buyers and export agents, exercising considerable market power vis-à-vis village producers and consumers. The impression created is that the local and international integration of Egyptian markets has come at the expense of peasants despite the evidence that they received higher prices for crops and increased consumption especially of durable imported goods (Owen 1969).

17   Notwithstanding their common dependence on the river, these two regions have different physiographies, agricultural specializations and even cultural and political histories. Their shares in the population in 1937 were respectively, 36 per cent and 44 per cent, with the rest of the population in Cairo, Alexandria and the desert (Platt and Hefny 1958).

18   The Delta cities are Damanhur, Damietta, Shubrakhit, Aga, Mansura, Mit Ghamr, Tanta, Zifta, Minuf, Shibin el Kum, Tala, Benha, Shibin el Qanatir and Zagazig; the Valley cities are Aswan, Idfu, Kum Ombo, Asyut, Dairut, Mallawi, Beni Suef, Faiyum, Sinnuris, Sohag, Giza, Imbaba, Maghagha, Minya, Luxor, Qena and Qus. The two cities on the Mediterranean are Rosetta and Port Said, and the Red Sea cities are Ismailiya and Suez. At this point, we are not able to include Cairo and Alexandria since their data was collected using a different method.

19   This feature of Egypt's transportation system is well noted. It is not known why the system had been designed in such a way as to bring the various methods of transportation into direct competition with each other (Gammal 1939).

20   Rifaat (1935) has attributed these domestic price movements to the adoption of a sterling standard in 1916 which, together with Egypt's open-door trade policy and intimate trade links with Britain, ensured the transmission of Britain's price trends to Egypt. Interestingly, he observed that the price volatility of basic commodities in Cairo and Alexandria in the 1920s was simultaneously felt in rural markets throughout Egypt.

21   Beginning in 1921, the Ministry of Finance sent out a monthly questionnaire to 355 civil servants and laborers, requesting information on the cost of living in their respective localities. The returns, which also included the costs of housing, utilities and transportation contained the prices of the twenty-six essential commodities including twenty-four food items. The ministry used the data to construct a monthly cost-of-living index for various urban regions in Egypt. The commodity list was assigned a 52 per cent weight in the index and, hence, it provides a reliable indicator not only of inflationary

trends, but also of the extent of price dispersion across markets. See the November 1921 issue of the *Monthly Bulletin of Agricultural and Economic Statistics* for details on the design and use of the monthly survey.

22 According to Egypt's external trade statistics, only ten of these commodities were not traded internationally: bread, butter, soap, wet beans, milk, chicken, fish, veal, beef and cheese (Annuaire Statistique 1924).

23 Note that the classification of goods is to some extent arbitrary, since several perishable commodities (for example, mutton, bread and beef) are easily storable in non-perishable form. Fissikh is dried fish and has been a main food staple in Egypt since ancient times (Allen 1997).

24 This is equivalent to saying that the two price series contain deterministic or stochastic trends that keep them apart from each other even in the long run. Under these circumstances, an OLS regression would be spurious.

25 To be precise, this is the approach used in empirical examinations of PPP where authors examine the behaviour of exchange-rate adjusted differentials of aggregate price indices. In our context, we believe that Q is a legitimate object of analysis since we use prices of identical tradable goods at all locations and throughout the period of analysis (Obstfeld and Taylor 1997).

26 Egyptian city councils never possessed the authority to tax or regulate national trade; their budgets were financed by the central government in Cairo. Since the mid-nineteenth century, the central government relied on land and trade taxes; it intervened after 1952 in agriculture with pricing and production policies.

27 That is, the intercity price differentials will be measured relative to those of Tanta. Tanta is located in the heart of the most productive agricultural section in the Delta; it is the crossroads for railroads and motor roads linking towns within the Delta and between the Delta and the Valley. Hence, since the early nineteenth century at least, it has been the most important centre and transit point for internal trade in the Delta. Other cities were used as a benchmark for comparison (Giza and Beni Suef) without yielding significantly different results.

28 See Yousef (1999) for a full elaboration on these empirical results.

29 It is generally difficult to reject the random-walk hypothesis in tests of PPP using international aggregate price indices (Froot and Rogoff 1995).

30 The half-life is the length of time in quarters that it takes for deviations from LOP to shrink by 50 per cent.

31 See Yousef (1999) for a full elaboration on these empirical results.

32 Once they corrected for the impact of distance on convergence, Parsley and Wei (1997) reach a similar conclusion. Their half-life for perishables and nonperishables are three and six quarters, respectively. In their study of PPP across OECD economies, their distance-corrected half-life is four years.

Part 7

Twentieth-century Palestine

14 Economic growth and external trade in Mandatory Palestine

A special Mediterranean case

Jacob Metzer

Introduction

In a recently published book entitled *The Divided Economy of Mandatory Palestine* (Metzer 1998), I provided a fairly detailed account of the ethno-nationally divided economy of Palestine under British rule. The documentation and analysis in *The Divided Economy* concentrates on the economic performance, socio-economic attributes, and bilateral relations of Arabs and Jews, as well as on the particulars of the segmented factor markets, and on the functioning of the governmental and non-governmental public sectors within each community and in the country at large. The "dual economy" postulate serves as an organizing theme for the treatment of these topics, distinguishing developmental disparities of a general dualistic nature from Palestine-specific ethno-nationally dividing political factors.

While drawing partly on the findings and analysis of *The Divided Economy*, and not ignoring the ethno-nationally distinguishing attributes of economic activity, I intend to shift the focus of this chapter to the country-wide level. In so doing, I shall examine comparatively Palestine's economic performance and trade patterns, and highlight its rather atypical record among the Mediterranean economies.

The next section discusses the country's overall growth record. This is followed by a section which explores fluctuations in economic activity. Next, the pattern and weight of external trade are taken up, followed by a comparative assessment of Palestine's citrus industry, the major source of the country's interwar export earnings. Some concluding remarks are offered in the last section.

The record of economic growth and its sources, 1922–47

The available estimates of aggregate economic performance of the countries in and around the Mediterranean basin in the first half of the twentieth century, crude as they may be, are summarized in Figure 14.1. Each country is plotted by its level of income per capita in 1939 relative to that of France (in index numbers) against its average annual growth rate over the period.

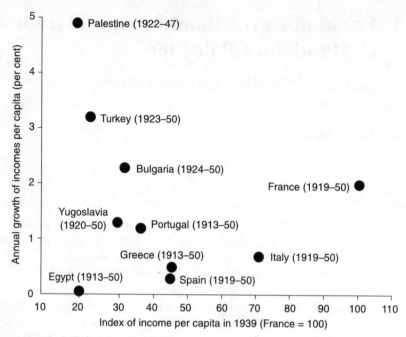

Figure 14.1 Income per capita in the Mediterranean countries.

Sources: Palestine: Metzer (1998: Tables A.1, A.22); All other countries: Maddison (1995: Appendix D).

Figure 14.1 suggests that there is some evidence of "unconditional convergence" in the interwar Mediterranean, with relatively poor countries like Palestine growing faster than relatively rich countries like France and Italy. The figure reveals that on the eve of World War II Palestine was the poorest economy in the region, a position to which it was driven by the extremely low income of the Arab community (Arab income in 1939 reached a level not higher than 11.4 by the index scale of Figure 14.1). The substantially higher level of income per capita in the Jewish community (30.4 in the 1939 index scale) was, on the other hand, comparable to that of Bulgaria and Yugoslavia and well above that of Turkey and Egypt (Maddison 1995: Appendix D; Metzer 1998: Table A.22).

However, as far as the growth record is concerned, Mandatory Palestine grew faster than any other economy in the region over the period 1919–50, with an increase in income per capita of 4.9 per cent annually between 1922 (the first year for which estimates of national income accounts are available for Palestine) and 1947 (the last full year of the British mandatory regime). Moreover, it was not only the country as a whole and the Jewish sector that grew faster than any other country in the region, but also the Arab sector: income per capita in the Jewish sector grew at 4.8 per cent per annum while

Table 14.1 Population growth in Palestine and other Mediterranean countries, 1913–1950 (percentage change per annum)

Palestine*	Arabs	2.7
	Jews	8.5
	All	3.8
Bulgaria		1.1
Egypt		1.4
France		0.0
Greece		0.9
Italy		1.3
Portugal		0.9
Spain		0.9
Turkey		1.3
Yugoslavia		0.5

Sources: Palestine: Metzer (1998: Table A.1); All other countries: Maddison (1995: Appendix A).

Note
* The period for Palestine is 1921–1947.

in the Arab sector it grew at 3.6 per cent per annum (Metzer 1998: Table 1.3).

This impressive rise of income per capita was achieved while Palestine's population increased at an exceptionally fast annual rate of 3.8 per cent over the entire Mandate period (Table 14.1). Note that the second-fastest rising population, that of Egypt, grew only at 1.4 per cent per annum between 1913 and 1950.

As shown in Table 14.1, the enormous increase in Palestine's population was generated primarily by the immigration-driven expansion of the Jewish community, which grew at an exceedingly high annual rate of 8.5 per cent (about 73 per cent of the growth of Jewish population in the Mandate period was due to immigration). But the Arab community, whose increase was primarily natural, rose also at a noticeably fast rate (2.7 per cent annually), unmatched by any other Mediterranean region and almost twice as high as the Egyptian rate.

These observations obviously rule out the operation of some Malthusian mechanism in Palestine.[1] In the Arab sector, the prime factors "responsible" for avoiding the trap of diminishing marginal productivity of labour seem to have been the expansion of land under cultivation, the intensification of its utilization, and the rise of the overall capital/labour ratio, coupled with intra- and inter-industry allocative improvements and technological advances in farming.

These patterns reflected in part a response to the pressure of the growing population and the falling land/labour ratio in the Arab community. But they were also driven by rising export opportunities (primarily of citrus: see below), government technical farm-support programmes, technological spillover from the Jewish sector, and the expanded demand for Arab products generated by the fast-growing Jewish community. These productivity-increasing forces fostered a substantial increase of total factor productivity in the Arab domestic economy (3–3.5 per cent per annum) which accounted for about half or possibly more of its output growth.

The economic absorption of the massive influx of people into the Jewish community was facilitated primarily by the huge, albeit fluctuating, inflow of foreign capital, amounting to about 64 per cent of Jewish output and to 22 per cent of all-Palestine Net Domestic Product (NDP) in 1922–47. More than two-thirds of this capital inflow was either private – mainly in the form of immigrants' unilateral transfers and of private investments made in Palestine by Jews living abroad – or contributions collected by Zionist and other non-profit public institutions from world Jewry. Jewish capital imports were not only induced by immigration but largely embodied in it.

The volume of imported capital was on the whole large enough to allow domestic investment not just to catch up with the increasing labour supply in the Jewish community but to raise the amount of capital per member of the labour force over the entire period at 2.6 per cent annually. The proportion of the immigrants of working age was relatively high: about 78 per cent of the incoming Jews in 1928–45 were in the 15–64 age group, whereas the share of this group in the Jewish resident population of Palestine never exceeded 68 per cent. This fact caused the Jewish labour force to grow even faster than the population (8.8 per cent versus 8.5 per cent per annum).

In view of the spectacular growth in labour and capital inputs in the Jewish economy (at 8.8 and 11.6 per cent per annum, respectively, in 1922–47), it is no wonder that total factor productivity – which grew in the Jewish sector at the enormous rate of 3.5 per cent annually – accounted for "only" 25 per cent of Jewish output growth. But the growth of total factor productivity itself was not independent of immigration. One link between the two was facilitated by the high amount of "imported" educational capital that characterized the immigrants in comparison with the resident Jewish community in Palestine: fragmentary evidence suggests a possible differential of two years between the median years of schooling of the two groups in the Mandate period. Another link to total factor productivity growth was provided by the immigrants' learning by doing and adjustment to their new economic environment.

Economic fluctuations

A strong association between immigration, capital import, productivity and output growth has been established econometrically in a recent study for the Jewish sector (Beenstock *et al.* 1995), suggesting that upswings in the inflows of people and capital, which exhibited swing-like patterns, stimulated short-run upsurges in investment and productivity. The former was mainly driven by the demand for housing and a rising supply of investable funds. The latter

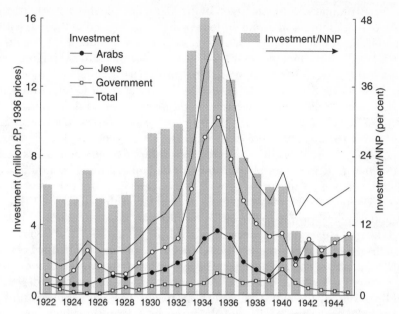

Figure 14.2 Gross investment in fixed capital and investment/NNP ratio in Palestine.

Sources: Metzer (1998: Tables A.22, A.23, A.25, A.26).

reflected, at least in part, the temporary increase in the utilization of resources and intensification of production in response to immediate absorption requirements of newcomers and to the corresponding rise in aggregate demand.

Jewish investment accounted on average for about 61 per cent of Palestine's capital formation, and except for three years this share never went below 50 per cent in any single year over the entire period. The Arabs contributed another 30 per cent, and the remaining 9 per cent consisted of investments made by the Mandatory government (Metzer 1998: Tables A.23, A.25 and A.26).

Figure 14.2 shows that fluctuations of the country's total capital formation coincided pretty much with those of Jewish investment, and the same is true also for the swings in Palestine's overall investment to NDP ratio. The investment swings were analogous to the oscillations in Jewish output growth, making the cyclical profile of the entire economy resemble rather closely that of its Jewish component.

This profile, however, showed little correspondence with the fluctuations in the Mediterranean and world economies. Some information to that effect is presented in Table 14.2, which reports average rates of change of income per capita in Palestine and in the other Mediterranean countries for the 1920s, the first and second half of the 1930s, the entire Depression decade, and the war years.

The 1920s marked the inception of the Mandatory economy, with the first wave of immigrants and capital inflows being concentrated in the first half of the decade and making for an average yearly growth rate of 6 per cent in Jewish per capita income in 1922–9. In the Mediterranean region, only Turkey did better with the remarkable growth performance of 9.3 per cent annually in 1923–9. Note, however, the relatively small weight which the Jewish sector had in the Mandatory Palestine economy at that time, 27 per cent of the country's NDP in 1922–9 (Metzer 1998: Tables A.20 and A.21), and its limited impact on the Arab sector, which grew only at 1.4 per cent in those years. Thus, Palestine registered a growth rate in between, 3.5 per cent annually, pretty much in line with the other Mediterranean economies and close to their median rate of growth (3 per cent per annum) prior to the Great Depression. This leaves the big story of Palestine's deviation from the regional cyclical profile to the 1930s and the war years.

Taking the Depression decade as a whole, Palestine exhibited a very healthy growth rate of income per capita – 4.2 per cent annually between 1929 and 1939 – which placed it at the top of the Mediterranean economies, just above Turkey's 4.1 per cent. However, it is the swings within the 1930s, and particularly the extraordinarily fast growth (11.8 per cent per annum) during the peak years of the global depression (1929–35), which put Palestine in a distinctly unique position *vis-à-vis* the economies in the area and in the rest of the world.[2]

Palestine's uninterrupted path of rising total and per capita output between 1929 and 1935 involved in its early phase (1929–32) the recovery of the Arab economy from the extremely poor crop year of 1928 (which was the main cause of the 14.7 per cent decline in Arab total output in that year) and the cyclical upswing in Jewish economic activity, following the subsidence of the period's first immigration wave and the short-lived slack of 1926–7.

The major factor driving the accelerated continuation of growth in 1932–5 was the increase in demand, resource accumulation, and productivity. These in turn were induced by the revival of Jewish immigration after the lull of the second half of the 1920s, coupled with an intensified inflow of capital. This pattern may have partly reflected a response to Palestine's economic pull effect in those years, but it was mainly induced by the push of the depression-stricken and politically troubled eastern and central Europe and Nazi Germany. Note also that by a special transfer arrangement, the German (Nazi) government allowed emigrating Jews to transfer their private wealth to Palestine in the form of German export goods via a well-defined commercial mechanism. The influx of people and capital caused Jewish population to double and capital stock in the Jewish sector to rise by 2.3 times between 1932 and 1936, with population and reproducible capital in the country as a whole growing by 27 and 67 per cent, respectively, between these two years.

The numbers in Table 14.2 reveal that the growth impetus in the first half of the 1930s was strong enough to generate an exceptional rise in income between 1929 and 1935, for Arabs as well as Jews. This was in sharp contrast

Table 14.2 Income per capita growth in Palestine and other Mediterranean countries (percentage change per annum)

		*1920s**	*1929–35*	*1935–39*	*1929–39***	*1939–45****
Palestine:	Arabs	1.4	8.1	−4.2	3.0	5.8
	Jews	6.0	11.9	−10.4	2.4	6.9
	All	3.5	11.8	−6.4	4.2	6.7
Bulgaria		5.4	0.8	6.7	3.1	−6.5
Egypt		—	—	—	0.2	1.4
France		5.3	−2.3	4.1	0.2	−9.8
Greece		2.4	1.0	1.6	1.2	−15.8
Italy		0.8	0.3	2.8	1.3	−9.6
Portugal		0.8	—	—	1.2	1.9
Spain		3.0	−0.9	−6.6	−3.2	1.4
Turkey		9.3	1.9	7.5	4.1	−7.5
Yugoslavia		2.9	−2.9	5.0	0.3	−0.8

Sources: Palestine: Metzer (1998: Tables A.1 and A.22); Egypt: Hansen (1991a: Table 1–1); All other countries: Maddison (1995: Appendix D).

Notes
* Palestine, 1922–29; Bulgaria, 1924–29; France, 1919–29; Greece, 1913–29; Italy, 1919–29; Portugal, 1913–29; Spain, 1919–29; Turkey, 1923–29; Yugoslavia, 1920–29.
** Portugal, 1929–38,
*** Egypt, 1939–55; Portugal, 1938–45; 1939–47.

to the substantial growth slowdown, or even absolute decline, of per capita income that characterized the other Mediterranean countries at the time. Another asymmetry can be observed in the second half of the 1930s, when Palestine suffered an economic decline while most Mediterranean economies underwent renewed growth.

Although signs of a slowdown-to-come could already have been detected in some of the figures of 1935 (such as the reduction of capital imports and Jewish income per capita), Palestine's economic slump was caused primarily by the Arab revolt of 1936–9, and by a shrinking inflow of immigrants. Palestine became a less attractive destination country in those years of violence and insecurity, but immigration was also curtailed by politically motivated restrictions that the Mandatory government imposed on Jewish immigration from 1937 onward. The only other Mediterranean country to suffer a severe economic downturn in 1935–9 was Civil-War Spain. Here too, a major factor to blame for the short-run economic decline was domestic political turmoil and its economic cost.

It was only during World War II that Palestine managed to recover economically and join Portugal, Spain and Egypt in experiencing an overall rise of total and per capita income between 1939 and 1945. But as shown in Table 14.2, Palestine's remarkable wartime rate of growth (6.7 per cent annually) was 3.5 times faster than that of its runner-up, Portugal (1.9 per cent). This expansion was driven primarily by the demand of the Allied forces in the eastern Mediterranean, for whom Palestine became a major regional supply centre, and by the substitution of domestic production for diminished civilian imports during the war. However, notwithstanding Palestine's impressive wartime growth, recent findings suggest that a narrowly defined "non-war" counterfactual would have yielded an even stronger recovery than the one actually experienced in 1940–45 (Beenstock *et al.* 1995).

External trade

The interwar trade patterns of the Mediterranean economies are summarized in Table 14.3, which reports trade indices for seventeen countries between the mid-1920s and the late 1930s. The picture revealed by the table is quite striking. Imports, exports and total trade all declined sharply in the region towards the mid-1930s after peaking in the 1920s, but the trends for Palestine were precisely the opposite.

Moreover, except for Palestine, none of the Mediterranean economies regained the level of imports reached in the mid- or late 1920s before World War II. Although exports grew in the second half of the 1930s in most countries, only in two of them (Bulgaria and Morocco) recorded exports were larger in 1938/39 than in 1925/26. In Palestine, however, merchandise exports rose continuously from the mid-1920s to the late 1930s, and the levels of import and total trade, although lower in 1938/39 than in the mid-decade, were on the eve of World War II substantially larger than in the late 1920s.

Furthermore, external trade and its components grew in Palestine even faster than output between the mid- and the late 1920s and, except for exports, between the late 1920s and the mid-1930s (Table 14.4). These patterns seem to be consistent with the sharp upswings in economic activity and domestic demand in those years which were largely fuelled by the already-discussed massive influx of people and capital. They may also have reflected, particularly during the peak of the Depression, the policy of non-interference with external trade (but for non-discriminatory tariffs) that the government adopted in adherence with the guidelines of the Mandate.

In the downswing of the second half of the 1930s, imports and trade as a whole fell more than output, suggesting again a high (larger than one) income elasticity of import demand. Needless to say, since the volume of exports actually grew between 1934/35 and 1938/39, so did the export/output ratio in those years of declining economic activity.

Unlike Palestine, however, trade/output ratios were lower in 1934/35 than in 1928/29 in all the Mediterranean countries for which it is possible to calculate them, indicating that import, export and total trade shrank faster than total output in the years of the severe depression. Although rising somewhat in the second half of the 1930s, the trade/output ratios of 1938/39 were, once again unlike Palestine, substantially lower than those of the late

Table 14.3 Indices of external trade in Palestine and other Mediterranean countries (in current prices, 1928/29 = 100)

	1925/26	1928/29	1934/35	1938/39
A. *Import*				
Palestine	100.9	100.0	241.0	177.6
Albania*	66.2	100.0	36.8	64.7
Algeria*	78.7	100.0	58.9	39.3
Bulgaria	88.3	100.0	33.9	65.8
Cyprus*	—	100.0	45.1	68.1
Egypt	103.1	100.0	35.7	38.5
France*	94.1	100.0	40.0	36.4
Greece	95.2	100.0	32.6	41.3
Italy*	90.2	100.0	34.0	31.2
Malta*	—	100.0	53.0	54.1
Morocco*	62.9	100.0	53.7	41.5
Portugal	109.0	100.0	49.3	46.9
Spain*	76.5	100.0	30.1	16.2
Syria	—	100.0	42.9	42.0
Tunis*	71.7	100.0	61.8	36.4
Turkey	107.0	100.0	34.6	52.3
Yugoslavia	104.4	100.0	35.3	48.2
B. *Export*				
Palestine	86.0	100.0	181.3	257.0
Albania*	96.6	100.0	34.5	65.5
Algeria*	83.0	100.0	63.4	58.8
Bulgaria	90.1	100.0	45.7	92.3
Cyprus*	—	100.0	43.8	94.5
Egypt	94.4	100.0	38.0	32.8
France*	104.5	100.0	32.9	26.0
Greece	84.0	100.0	41.5	57.2
Italy*	93.9	100.0	33.8	41.7
Malta*	—	100.0	46.2	46.2
Morocco*	51.0	100.0	51.6	52.2
Portugal	93.6	100.0	52.6	65.1
Spain*	75.5	100.0	28.3	14.7
Syria	—	100.0	40.0	50.2
Tunis*	71.4	100.0	50.7	41.3
Turkey	123.8	100.0	54.4	77.7
Yugoslavia	115.1	100.0	42.5	56.6

continued on next page

Table 14.3 Indices of external trade in Palestine and other Mediterranean countries (in current prices, 1928/29=100) (cont.)

	1925/26	*1928/29*	*1934/35*	*1938/39*
C. *Total Trade*				
Palestine	97.3	100.0	226.7	196.6
Albania*	75.3	100.0	36.1	64.9
Algeria*	80.6	100.0	60.9	47.7
Bulgaria	89.1	100.0	39.2	77.7
Cyprus*	—	100.0	44.5	79.9
Egypt	98.7	100.0	36.8	35.6
France*	99.1	100.0	36.6	31.4
Greece	91.5	100.0	35.6	46.6
Italy*	91.7	100.0	33.9	35.4
Malta*	—	100.0	52.6	53.6
Morocco*	58.7	100.0	53.0	45.3
Portugal	104.6	100.0	50.2	52.1
Spain*	76.1	100.0	29.3	15.6
Syria	—	100.0	42.1	44.3
Tunis*	71.6	100.0	57.0	38.5
Turkey	128.0	100.0	48.0	70.5
Yugoslavia	109.5	100.0	38.7	52.3

Sources: Palestine: *Survey of Palestine* (1946: Vol I, p. 462). The export data were adjusted by replacing the official figures for the value of citrus export (*Statistical Abstract of Palestine* 1940: Table 77) by my revised figures (Metzer 1998: Table A.6); Albania, 1925/26: Trade figures in gold francs were taken from Mitchell (1975: Table F1), and converted into dollars by the convergence rates used by the League of Nations in the *Review of World Trade* (1930: Summary Table IV); Albania in other years and all other countries: League of Nation figures quoted in *Statistical Year Book* (1927: Table 81; 1933/34: Table 104; 1938/39: Table 119; 1941/42: Table 92).

Note
* The trade indices of the last column were calculated for 1938 only.

Sources for Table 14.4 (opposite page)

Palestine: see Table 14.3 for trade figures and Metzer (1998: Table A.22) for domestic product; Turkey: Pamuk in this volume; All other countries: Mitchell (1975: Tables F1 and K1).

Table 14.4 Ratios of external trade and import surplus to domestic product in Palestine and other Mediterranean countries

		1925/26	1928/29	1934/35	1938/39
A. Percentage ratios of import (I), export (E), and total trade (T) to domestic product (DP)					
Palestine	I/DP	43.8	45.7	51.6	42.9
	E/DP	10.8	13.2	11.3	17.8
	T/DP	54.6	58.9	62.9	60.7
Bulgaria	I/DP	13.6	13.7	7.3	9.2
	E/DP	12.0	11.3	8.0	10.6
	T/DP	25.6	25.0	15.3	19.8
France	I/DP	19.1	15.4	8.4	11.1
	E/DP	19.4	14.0	6.4	7.7
	T/DP	38.5	29.4	14.8	18.8
Greece	I/DP	—	28.2	18.1	20.2
	E/DP	—	14.6	11.6	14.4
	T/DP	—	42.9	29.7	34.6
Italy	I/DP	14.1	13.2	6.7	6.2
	E/DP	10.0	8.9	4.6	6.2
	T/DP	24.1	22.1	11.3	12.4
Spain	I/DP	9.2	12.3	3.4	—
	E/DP	6.6	9.2	2.4	—
	T/DP	15.8	21.5	5.8	—
Turkey*	I/DP	15.8	14.4	—	6.8
	E/DP	12.8	11.4	—	6.9
	T/DP	28.6	25.8	—	13.7
Yugoslavia	I/DP	10.8	9.0	7.3	6.8
	E/DP	11.0	8.4	8.0	7.4
	T/DP	21.8	17.4	15.3	14.2
*B. Percentage ratios of import surplus to domestic product***					
Palestine		33.0	32.5	40.3	25.1
Bulgaria		1.6	2.4	−0.7	−1.4
France		−0.3	1.4	2.0	3.4
Greece		—	13.6	6.5	5.8
Italy		4.1	4.3	2.1	0.0
Spain		2.6	3.1	1.0	—
Turkey*		13.0	3.0	—	−0.1
Yugoslavia		−0.2	0.6	−0.7	−0.6

Notes
* The ratios for Turkey are for 1924/25 and not for 1925/26.
** The ratios with the minus sign stand for export surplus.

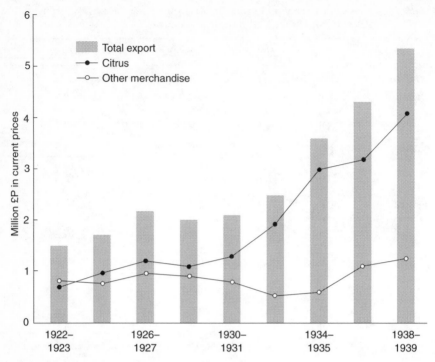

Figure 14.3 Palestine's merchandise export, 1922–39.

Sources: The same as for Figure 14.2.

1920s, pointing to the decline in overall demand, and to the "inward-looking" import-inhibiting policies that most governments adopted in the 1930s in response to the Depression (Table 14.4).

A case in point is Turkey. Şevket Pamuk shows in his contribution to this volume that protection and control over foreign exchange were, among other measures, responsible for Turkey's relatively strong economic performance in the Depression decade of the 1930s. Pamuk estimates that average tariffs increased in Turkey from 13 per cent to 46 per cent of the value of imports in 1929, and further on to 60 per cent by the second half of the 1930s. In Palestine, by comparison, tariffs reached on average no more than 25 per cent of imports during the 1930s (Gross 1984).

Other attributes singling out Palestine were the economic weight of its external trade and the extremely large import surplus. Note that the trade/output ratio in Palestine moved between 0.55 and 0.63, while in Greece, which was the second most trade-intensive economy in the region, the ratio of trade to output did not exceed 0.43. In most Mediterranean countries imports exceeded exports over the entire interwar period, but in none of them did the size of the import surplus relative to the level of output get even close to Palestine's order of magnitude of 25 per cent to 40 per cent (Table 14.4).

The ratio of import surplus (like that of imports) to income moved procyclically in Palestine. This pattern focuses attention once more on the instrumental role that immigration-accompanied capital inflows played in the country's economy. It was this influx which was crucial for the absorption of immigrants, while at the same time enabling the immigration-generated domestic demand to be satisfied by substantial imports and import surplus that did not require an equivalent increase in exports or foreign borrowing. Moreover, the inflow of capital saved Palestine from the typical beggar-thy-neighbour effects of export-inducing policies exercised by the depression-afflicted economies of the 1930s.

Unlike the movement of imports and import surplus, which was mainly related to the swings in Palestine's economic activity, the growing volume of merchandise exports throughout the interwar years was due primarily to the massive expansion of citrus fruits, whose weight in the value of the country's overall export rose from 54 per cent in the 1920s to 77 per cent in the 1930s (Fig 14.3). Particularly noticeable in this respect is the divergence between citrus fruits and other exports during the depressed 1930s.

The pattern of non-citrus exports followed pretty much the swings in world economic activity and trade, with the sharp downturn in demand of the early years of the decade (world export prices and volume shrank between 1929 and 1932 by 48 per cent and 27 per cent, respectively (Maddison 1995: Appendix I), being followed by the recovery later in the decade. In the case of Palestine one should also add to the general demand-reducing attributes of the Depression, the specific effect of the highly protective tariff that Egypt imposed in 1930, thereby curtailing the exports of soap and watermelons that had previously been sold mostly in the Egyptian market. These two items made up 32 per cent of Palestine's non-citrus exports in the late 1920s (Metzer 1998: Ch. 5).

Citrus production and exports

In view of the dreary picture for non-citrus exports, the fast-rising export of citrus fruits from the late 1920s to the end of 1939 becomes all the more remarkable. Moreover, since Palestine's citrus industry was export-dominated (in neither of the years between 1922 and 1939 was the share of exported citrus fruits smaller than 80 per cent of total citrus output; Metzer 1998: Table A.6), little room was left for possible substitution of sales abroad for domestic consumption, and the growth of export thus "required" an analogous increase of production to facilitate it.

Indeed, the expansion of citriculture was the most prominent characteristic of Palestine's agriculture in the interwar years, with the share of citrus fruits rising from 11 per cent of agricultural output in the early 1920s, up to 50 per cent in 1932–5, then declining to 41 per cent in 1936–9. The relatively high, and even slightly rising, export prices of citrus fruits in the first half of the 1920s seem to have generated large enough profits to induce a massive

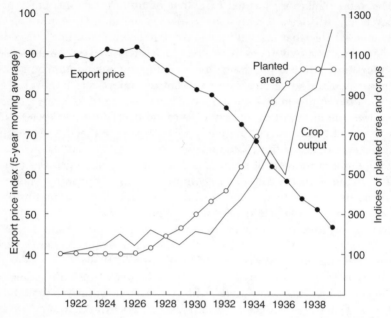

Figure 14.4 Indices of citrus prices, planted area, and crops in interwar Palestine (1921 = 100).

Source: Metzer (1998: Table A.6).

investment in citrus groves, increasing the planted area by more than tenfold (from 29,000 dunams to 298,000 dunams) between 1923 and 1937 (Figure 14.4). Almost two-thirds of the interwar investment in citrus fruits were undertaken by Jewish planters and the rest by Arabs, thereby raising the Jewish weight of the country's citrus production from 37 per cent in 1922 to 62 per cent in 1939 (Metzer 1998: Ch. 5).

From the mid-1920s onward, citrus prices exhibited a continuous decline in export markets, to which Palestine's planters adapted gradually by slowing down the planting of new groves in 1935, bringing it to a complete stop in 1937. However, since it takes a gestation period of about six years before a newly planted citrus grove starts producing marketable quantities of crop, production and export of citrus fruits continued their substantial expansion throughout the decade (Figure 14.4).

Palestine's citrus exports were dominated by shamouti oranges (oranges comprised about 97 per cent of the country's citrus export in the early 1930s and, with the expansion of grapefruits, 85 per cent in 1937–9). The shamouti – commercially brand-named as Jaffa – was a high-quality, much appreciated and, at least partly, demand-differentiated winter and early-spring brand in the export market (Hazen 1938; Metzer 1998, Ch. 5).

It was primarily Europe and particularly the British market that provided an outlet, albeit at declining prices, for the fast-rising supply of Jaffa

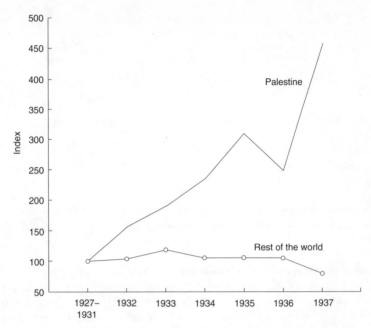

Figure 14.5 Volume indices of Palestine's and world export of citrus, 1927–37
(1927/31 = 100).

Sources: Palestine: Metzer (1998: Table A.6); Rest of the world: Webber and Batchelor (1948: Tables 19, 21, 23).

oranges.[3] While Palestine's citrus exports increased by 4.5 times between 1927/31 and 1937, the rest of the world's exports of citrus fruits grew by only 19 per cent from 1927/31 to 1933, and declined thereafter, making the volume of world exports in 1937 20 per cent lower than that of 1927/31 (Figure 14.5).

These divergent patterns underlay the rising weight of Palestine in the world's total export of citruses (from 4.7 per cent in 1927/31 to 21.9 per cent in 1937), turning Palestine from the fourth-largest citrus-exporting country in 1927/31 to the third-largest in 1932/36 (and surpassed only by the Mediterranean "big two", Spain and Italy). In 1937 Palestine changed places with Italy and became the second-largest citrus-exporting country in the world (Table 14.5).

However, in none of the other major exporting countries did the weight of citrus fruits in total exports come even close to that of interwar Palestine (in which, as indicated above, it was 77 per cent of all merchandise exports in the 1930s). In Spain it reached 26 per cent, in Italy 5.5 per cent, and in each of the other large exporters – the USA, South Africa and Brazil – the export share of citrus was even lower (Hazen 1938: Table 10). Palestine was the only country whose overall export activity depended almost entirely on its ability to sell its citrus fruits abroad.

Table 14.5 Percentage distributions of the world citrus export by origin: the five largest exporting countries and all the rest

	1927–31		1932–36		1937	
	%	Rank	%	Rank	%	Rank
Spain	53.7	1	50.1	1	28.4	1
Italy	22.2	2	17.7	2	21.3	3
United States	9.9	3	9.5	4	7.0	5
Palestine	4.7	4	9.7	3	21.9	2
South Africa	2.5	5	4.3	5	8.3	4
All other exporters	7.0	—	8.7	—	13.1	—
Total	100.0	—	100.0	—	100.0	—

Sources: Palestine: Metzer (1998: Table A.6); the rest of the world: Webber and Batchelor (1948: Tables 19, 21 and 23).

Most of the internationally traded citruses (81 per cent) were oranges; they were destined in the interwar period primarily for the European market, which absorbed more than 80 per cent of the world's total exports, with the UK making up almost half (47 per cent) of the entire European import in 1928–37 (Hazen 1938; Webber and Batchelor 1948: Tables 19, 21 and 23; Mendelsohn 1958: Table A-4). Palestine was an extreme case, selling practically all of its exported citrus fruits (99 per cent) in Europe, 70 per cent of which went to the UK. It was thus the successful penetration of the high-quality Jaffa oranges into the British market (this was done without enjoying any imperial preferences, despite the Mandated status of Palestine) that was the key to the expansion of Palestine's citrus (and overall merchandise) export before World War II (Hazen 1938; Survey of Palestine 1946: Vol I, Ch. IX; Metzer 1998: Ch. 5).

Palestine's oranges were shipped to Britain (and to other European destinations) in the winter and early spring, and as such had to compete in the British market primarily with the imports of relatively cheap oranges from Valencia, Spain. Virtually the entire quantity (95 per cent) of oranges that was shipped to Britain between December and April of each year (which amounted to between three-quarters and two-thirds of the British yearly import of oranges) originated in these two regions (Hazen 1938). However, while the quantity of oranges imported from Spain fell rather sharply from the early 1930s onwards, the import from Palestine grew steadily, and the share of the Jaffa oranges in the sum of the two rose from 15 per cent in 1924/27 to 56 per cent in 1936/39 (Figure 14.6).

Orange prices fell substantially in the British market between the mid-1920s and the late 1930s from both Valencia and Palestine. However, since the decline of the latter was faster than that of the former, the British price ratio of Palestinian to Valencian oranges exhibited a continuous downturn,

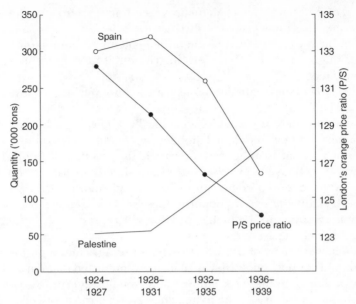

Figure 14.6 Britain's import of oranges from Palestine (P) and Spain (S), 1924–39.

Source: Mendelsohn (1958: Table VI–11).

while maintaining throughout the price superiority of the high-quality Jaffa brand (Figure 14.6).

Additional pieces of evidence relevant for the appreciation of the changes in the British citrus market are: the rise in the overall export supply of Jaffa oranges, the continuous reduction in the output and export of Spanish oranges in the 1930s (due to frosts and bad crops in the first half of the decade and to the political turmoil and civil war in its second half), and some indications of partial substitution of apples and bananas for oranges in British fruit consumption (Hazen 1938; Simpson 1995: Parts IV and V).

This evidence suggests that the quantity and price reduction of Spanish oranges in Britain (by 58 and 32 per cent, respectively, between 1928/31 and 1936/39) was caused by their shrinking supply and even faster declining demand, while the considerable increase in the supply of Jaffa oranges, with some decline in British consumer demand, made for a threefold rise in the volume of Palestine citruses sold in Britain between 1924/27 and 1936/39, coupled with a 40 per cent reduction in their import price (Mendelsohn 1958: Table VI–11).

Concluding remarks

This paper demonstrates that the outstanding record of secular growth, the direction and intensity of swings in economic activity, and the volume and patterns of external trade, set Mandatory Palestine apart from the rest of the Mediterranean. It was primarily the massive inflow of people and capital (most of them Jewish) which distinguished Palestine from the other countries in the region, and they were instrumental in shaping its atypical economic record.

The Mandatory government, on its part, did not pursue an active macro and trade policy, and, except for the imposition of non-discriminating tariffs, allowed in the interwar period for a practically uninterrupted movement of merchandise and for free capital mobility in and out of the country.

In so far as the citrus industry is concerned, the government fulfilled some regulatory functions and provided technical assistance to planters. But in the main it was the entrepreneurship of Jewish and Arab planters which led them to exploit the export opportunities for Jaffa oranges by directing investable resources to the highly intensive citrus production in the 1920s and during a good part of the 1930s.

In a detailed report of the US Department of Agriculture on the Citrus Industry of Palestine, published in 1938, it was predicted that notwithstanding the declining profits in the industry and even the observed losses to marginal producers, the massive planting of new groves during most of the 1930s would assure a continuous increase of production and exports at least up to and including the season of 1943. Moreover the report projected a doubling of the annual exported volume from about 11 million cases in 1937 to 20–23 million in 1942–3 (Hazen 1938). The realized picture, however, was entirely different. The severe disruption to overseas trade brought about by World War II and war-devastation in Europe, caused Palestine's citrus industry to collapse during the war. Exports shrank from 15 million cases in 1938/39 to 170,000 cases in 1940/41, rising to only 2.75 million cases in 1944/45.

By the end of the war, Palestine's international trade (export of citrus fruits included) revitalized, but soon thereafter, the termination of the British Mandate, the war of 1948, the establishment of the State of Israel, and the massive ethno-demographic and economic changes that the country underwent, had transformed the former Mandatory Palestine into a new political and economic realm. With that, a new chapter in the economic history of the country began to unfold, a story that must be told another time.

Notes

1   The discussion in the rest of this section draws on the analysis and figures presented in Metzer (1998: Chps. 1, 3, 4 and 5).
2   The discussion in the rest of this section draws on Metzer (1998: Chp. 1).
3   Since *Jaffa* oranges seem to have faced a downward sloping demand in the world market, supply-reducing policies, or cartel-type marketing could have increased the profits of Palestine's citrus exporters. However, no such policies were undertaken, after which the Mandatory government established the Citrus Marketing Board for the purpose of consolidating and regulating the fruit's export trade following the war-caused collapse of Palestine's citrus exports (*Survey* 1946: Vol I, Chapter IX).

Bibliography

Abdel-Rahim Mustafa, A (1968) "The Breakdown of the Monopoly System on Egypt after 1840", in P Holt (ed.) *Political and Social Change in Modern Egypt*, London: Oxford University Press.

Abdurrahman, V (1911) *Tekâlif Kavaidi* [Rules of Taxation], V.2, Dersaadet, Istanbul: Kanaat Matbaasý

Adams, R L (1921) *Farm Management Notes*, Berkeley: University of California Associated Students' Store.

Adanýr, F (1984–5) "The Macedonian Question: the Socio-economic Reality and Problems of its Historiographic Interpretation", *International Journal of Turkish Studies* 3, N. 1: 43–64.

Aguado, J (1975) "Las exportaciones de pasas de Málaga durante el siglo XIX", *Gibralfaro* 24–7: 23–41.

Aguiló, I (1918) *Notas de actualidad sobre la elaboración del aceite de oliva*, Barcelona: Herederos de Juan Gili.

A'Hearn, B (1998) "Institutions, Externalities, and Economic Growth in Southern Italy: Evidence from the Cotton Textile Industry, 1861–1914", *Economic History Review* 51 (4): 734–62.

Akarlý, E D (1976) "The Problems of External Pressures, Power Struggles, and Budgetary Deficits in Ottoman Politics under Abdülhamit II: Origins and Solutions", unpublished PhD Thesis, Princeton: University of Princeton.

—— (1992) "Economic Policy and Budgets in Ottoman Turkey, 1876–1909", *Middle Eastern Studies* 28: 443–76.

Alexander, D and Omer, R (1979) *Volumes Not Values*, St John's, Newfoundland: Maritime History Group.

Allen, R (1997) "Agriculture and the Origins of the State in Ancient Egypt", *Explorations in Economic History* 34: 135–54.

Allen, R C (1998a) "The Great Divergence: Wages and Prices in Europe from the Middle Ages to the First World War", Department of Economics Discussion Paper N. 98–12, Vancouver: University of British Columbia, Vancouver.

—— (1998b) "Agricultural Output and Productivity in Europe, 1300–1800", Department of Economics Discussion Paper N. 98–14, Vancouver: University of British Columbia.

—— (1998c) "Toward a Simple Model of European Wages, 1300–1910", Department of Economics, Vancouver, Canada: University British Columbia.

Alvarez, L A (1993) "La Modernización de la Industria del Tabaco en España, 1800–1935", Working Paper 9304, Madrid: Fundación Empresa Pública-Programa de Historia Económica.

Amable, B (1993) "Catch up and Convergence: A Model of Cumulative Growth", *International Review of Applied Economics* 37.

Amatori, F (1997) "Italy: The Tormented Rise of Organizational Capabilities between Government and Families", in A Chandler, F Amatori and T Hikino (eds.) *Big Business and the Wealth of Nations*, Cambridge: Cambridge University Press: 246–76.

Anastassiadou, M (1997) *Salonique, 1830–1912, Une ville ottomane à l'âge des Réformes*, Leiden: Köln Brill.

Andersen, D C (1996) "Productivity in Danish Agriculture during the Age of Reform (1750–1850). A Comparative Perspective", in E Buyst, G Dejongh, B van Ark and J L van Zanden (eds.) *Historical Benchmark Comparisons of Output and Productivity, 1750-1990*, CES Discussion Paper, Katolieke Universiteit Leuven: 53–77.

Anderson, J N (1968) "Law Reform in Egypt: 1850–1950", in P Holt (ed.) *Political and Social Change in Modern Egypt*, London: Oxford University Press.

Andréadés, A (1909) "La crise de surproduction des raisins de Corinthe", *Revue Economique Internationale* 7: 3–25.

Angelini, F (1941) "Il lavoro in olivicoltura", in Confederazione Fascista degli Agricoltori & Settore della Olivicoltura della FNCPPA, *Atti del Convegno Nazionale di Olivicoltura* (Bari 21–2 settembre 1938), Rome: Stab. Tipografico del Ramo Editoriale degli Agricoltori: 309–33.

Angier, E A V (1920) *Fifty Years' Freights, 1869–1919*, London.

Anuario Estadístico de España Correspondiente al Año de 1859, (1860) Madrid: Imprenta Nacional.

Ardeni, P (1968) "Does the Law of One Price Really Hold for Commodity Markets?", *American Journal of Agricultural Economics*: 661–9.

[Argentina] (1916) *Tercer Censo Nacional levantado el 11 de Junio de 1914*, Buenos Aires: Rosso y Cía. Vols. II–IV.

Arrighi, G (ed.) (1985) *Semi-Peripheral Development: The Politics of Southern Europe in the Twentieth Century*, Beverley Hills: Sage.

Asýr, Miscellaneous issues, 1313 (1897)–1325 (1907), Salonica.

Atasagun, Y (1939) *Türkiye Cumhuriyeti Ziraat Bankası*, Kenan Basimevi: Istanbul.

Aybar, C (1939) *Osmanli Imparatorlugunun Ticaret Muvazenesi, 1878–1913*, Ankara.

Bacon, L B and Schloemer, F C (1940) *World Trade in Agricultural Products. Its Growth, Its Crisis, and the New Trade Policies*, Rome: International Institute of Agriculture.

Baer, G. (1968) "Social Change in Egypt: 1800–1914", in P Holt (ed.), *Political and Social Change in Modern Egypt*, London: Oxford University Press.

—— (1969) *Studies in the Social History of Modern Egypt*, Chicago: University of Chicago Press.

Baines, D (1985) *Migration in a Mature Economy. Emigration and Internal Migration in England and Wales, 1861–1900*, Cambridge: Cambridge University Press.

Bairoch, P (1976a) "Europe's Gross National Product: 1800–1975", *Journal of European Economic History* 5: 273–340.

—— (1976b) *Commerce exterieur et développement économique de l'Europe au XIXᵉ siècle*, Paris: Ecole des Hautes Etudes en Sciences Sociales.

—— (1977) "Estimations du Revenu National dans les Sociétés Occidentales Pré-Industrielles et au Dix-Neuvième Siècle", *Revue Economique* 28:177–208.

—— (1979) "Ecarts Internationaux des Niveaux de Vie avant la Révolution Industrielle", *Annales ESC* 34: 145–71.

—— (1981) "The Main Trends in National Economic Disparities since the Industrial Revolution", in P Bairoch and M Lévy-Leboyer (eds.) *Disparities in Economic Development since the Industrial Revolution*, London: Macmillan.

—— (1989a) "Les Trois Revolutions Agricoles du Monde Developpé: Rendements et Productivité de 1800 a 1985", *Annales ESC* 44: 317–53.

——(1989b) "European Trade Policy, 1815–1914", in P Mathias and S Pollard (eds.) *The Cambridge Economic History of Europe, The Industrial Economies: The Development of Economic and Social Policies*, V. VII, Cambridge: Cambridge University Press: 1–160.

Baker, J (1877) *Turkey*, New York: Henry Holt and Company.

Bardini, C, Carreras, A, and Lains, P (1995) "The National Accounts for Italy, Spain and Portugal," *Scandinavian Economic History Review* XLV: 115–46.

Barlas, D (1998) *Etatism and Diplomacy in Turkey, Economic and Foreign Policy Strategies in an Uncertan World, 1929–1939*, Brill: Leiden.

Barnett, V (1995) "Soviet Commodity Markets During NEP", *Economic History Review*. 329–52.

Barquin, R (1998) "Primer Aproximacion al Coste de la Vida entre 1814 y 1860", unpublished paper presented at the Conference on La Politica Monetaria e las Flutuaciones de la Economia Española en el Siglo XIX, Barcelona.

Barro, R J (1997) *Determinants of Economic Growth*, Cambridge, Mass: MIT Press.

—— and Sala-i-Matin, X (1995) *Economic Growth*, New York: McGraw-Hill.

Basbakanlik Istatistik (1937) *Istatistik Yilligi 1936/37*, Ankara: Istatistik G D Nesruyatindan.

Baten, J (1997) "Protein Supply and Nutritional Status in Early Ninetenth Century Bavaria", unpublished paper, Munich.

Bauer, R W (1882) *Haandbog i Mønt, Maal og Vægtforhold*, Copenhagen: P G Philipsens Forlag.

Bauer, W (1933) *Foreign Production and Trade in Raisins*, California Agricultural Experiment Station Bulletin No. 566. Berkeley.

Baumol, W J, Nelson, R R and Wolff, E N (eds.) (1994) *Convergence of Productivity. Cross-National Studies and Historical Evidence*, Oxford: Oxford University Press.

Beenstock, M, Jacob, M and Sanny, Z (1995) "Immigration and the Jewish Economy in Mandatory Palestine", Research in Economic History 15: 149–213.

Behar, C. (1995) *The Population of the Ottoman Empire and Turkey, 1500–1927*, Ankara: State Institute of Statistics.

Ben-David, D (1995) "Convergence Clubs and Diverging Economies", Foerder Institute Working Paper No. 40–95, Tel-Aviv.

Bengtsson, T (1987) "Migration och Löner. Tillämpning av Todaros Migrationsteori på 1800-Talets Svenska Urbanisering", in O Krantz and R Ohlsson (eds.) *Ekonomisk-Historisk Vingslag*, Lund: Ekonomisk Historisk Föreningen: 21–38.

Bennett, M K and Peirce, R H (1961) "Change in the American National Diet, 1879–1959", *Food Research Institute Studies* 2: 95–120.

Berend, I and G Ranki (1982) *The European Periphery and Industrialization 1780–1914*, Cambridge: Cambridge University Press.

Berov, L (1978) "La Salaire des Ouvriers Qualifiés dans les pays Balkaniques au Cours de la Periode Capitalisme Manufacturier et de la Révolution Industrielle", *Etudes balkaniques* 1: 30–54.

—— (1979) "Wages in the Balkan Lands during the Period of Manufacturing Capitalism and the Industrial Revolution", *Bulgarian Historical Review.* 91–115.

—— (1985) "The Effect of the West European Economy on the Market Conditions in the Balkan Countries in the Nineteenth and Early Twentieth Centuries", *Etudes balkaniques,* 22–38.

—— (1987) "Trends in the Level and Structure of the Incomes of the Working People in the Balkan Countries in the Eighteenth and Nineteenth Centuries up to 1912", *Bulgarian Historical Review.* 65–83.

—— (1996) "The Industrial Revolution and the Countries of South-eastern Europe in the Nineteenth and Early Twentieth Centuries", in M Teich and R Porter, *The Industrial Revolution in National Context,* Cambridge: Cambridge University Press.

Berthelemy, J C and Varoudakis, A (1996) "Economic Growth, Convergence Clubs and the Role of Financial Development", *Oxford Economic Papers* 48: 300–28.

Bevilacqua, P (1988) "Il paesaggio degli alberi nel Mezzogiorno d'Italia e in Sicilia (fra VIII e secolo)", *Annali dell'Istituto Alcide Cervi* 10: 259–306.

—— (1989) "Clima, mercato e paessaggio agrario nel Mezzogiorno", in P Bevilacqua, *Storia dell'agricultura italiana in età contemporanea. I: Spazi e paessaggi.* Venezia: Marsilio Editori: 643–76.

Bianchi, T E (1988) *L'industria dello Zucchero in Italia dal Blocco Continentale alla Vigilia della Grande Guerra (1897–1914),* Annali di Storia dell'Impresa 4: 211–78.

Bils, M (1984) "Tariff Protection and Production in the Early U.S. Cotton Textile Industry", *Journal of Economic History* 44 (4): 1033–45.

Birtek, F and Çağlar K (1975) "An Inquiry into Agricultural Differentiation and Political Alliances : the Case of Turkey", *The Journal of Peasant Studies* 2: 446–68.

Black, C E (1943) *The Establishment of Constitutional Government in Bulgaria,* Princeton: Princeton University Press.

Blaisdell, D (1929) *European Financial Control in the Ottoman Empire,* New York: Columbia University Press.

Blaug, M (1961) "The Productivity of Capital in the Lancashire Cotton Industry during the Nineteenth Century", *Economic History Review* 13 (3): 358–81.

Boel, J (1985) *Husmaend og Landarbejdere i Danmark ca.1848-1875 med Holbaek og Vejle amter som Eksempler,* Copenhagen: Landbohistorisk Selskab.

Bolletino della Camera di Commercio e Industria di Genova (1913).

Boot, H M (1995) "How Skilled Were Lancashire Cotton Factory Workers in 1833?", *Economic History Review* 58 (2): 283–303.

Boratav, K (1981) "Kemalist Economic Policies and Etatism", in A Kazancıgil and E Özbudun (eds.), *Atatürk : Founder of a Modern State,* London: C Hurst: 165-190.

——, Ökçün, A G, and Pamuk, Ş (1985) "Ottoman Wages and the World Economy, 1839–1913", *Fernand Braudel Center Review* 8: 379–406.

Bordo, M D and Schwartz, A J (1996) "The Operation of the Specie Standard. Evidence for Core and Peripheral Countries, 1880–1990" in J Macedo, B Eichengreen, and J Reis, *Currency Convertibility. The Gold Standard and Beyond,* Routledge: London.

Borrelli, F (1930) *L'Industria degli Olii nel Mezzogiorno.* Bari: Stablilimento Arti Grafiche Cressati.

Boulanger, P (1985) "Huiles blanches ou paillerines? Essai de physiologie du goût au XVIIIe siècle", in Centre National de la Recherche Scientifique, Maison de la Méditerrané, *L'huile d'olive en Méditerranée. Histoire, Anthropologie, économie de l'antiquité à nos jours*, Aix-en-Provence: Institute de Recherches Méditerranéens. Université de Provence: 25–34.

—— (1996) *Marseille, marché international de l'huile d'olive: un produit et des hommes de 1725 à 1825*, Marseille: Institut Historique de Provence.

Bowley, A L (1900) "The Statistics of Wages in the United Kingdom during the Last Hundred Years", *Journal of the Royal Statistical Society* 63, Part III.

Bringas, M A G (1998) "La Produccion y la Productividad de los Factores en la Agricultura Española, 1752–1935", unpublished PhD Thesis, University of Santander.

British Sessional Papers. House of Commons, consular reports (several years).

Brosio, G and Marchese, C (1986) *Il Potere di Spendere*, Bologna: Il Mulino.

Brown, E H P and Hopkins, S V (1955) "Seven Centuries of Building Wages", *Oxford Economic Papers*, New Series, 22: 195–206.

Brown, I (ed.) (1989) *The Economies of Africa and Asia in the Inter-war Depression*, London and New York: Routledge.

Bruland, K (1989) *British Technology and European Industrialization: The Norwegian Textile Industry in the Mid Nineteenth Century*, Cambridge: Cambridge University Press.

Bulmer-Thomas, V (1994) *The Economic History of Latin America since Independence*, Cambridge: Cambridge University Press.

Bulutay, T, Yahya, S T and Nuri, Y (1974) *Türkiye Milli Geliri (1923–1948)*, 2 vols, Ankara: Üniversitesi Publications.

Buyst, E, Smits, J P and van Zanden, J L (1995) "National Accounts for the Low Countries", *Scandinavian Economic History Review* XLIII: 53–76.

California Fruit Grower and Fruit Trade Review, various years.

California State Agricultural Society Transactions. Sacramento: various years.

California State Board of Agriculture *Annual Reports*, Sacramento: State Printing Office, various years.

—— *Statistical Reports*, Sacramento: State Printing Office, various years.

Camera di Commercio Italo-Orientale (1927) "La Produzione ed il Consumo Degli olii nei Paesi Orientali", in Società Nazionale degli Olivicoltori Italiani, *Atti del IX Congresso Nazionale di Olivicoltura*. Bari, 19–22 d'ottobre 1925, Spoleto: Arti Grafiche Pareto & Petrelli: 183-257.

Cameron, R (1971) *La France et le developpement économique de l'Europe, 1800–1914*, Paris.

—— (1985) "A New View of European Industrialization", *Economic History Review* 38: 1–23.

Campa, J M (1990) "Exchange Rates and Economic Recovery in the 1930s: An Extension to Latin America", *The Journal of Economic History* 50: 677–682.

Camps, E (1995) *La formación del Mercado de Trabajo Industrial en la Cataluña del Siglo XIX*, Madrid: Ministerio de Trabajo.

Carani-Donvito, G (1933) "Prezzi e Compensi nel Mezzogiorno e in Puglia ai Primi del Secolo XIX", *Rivista di Politica Economica* XXII: 1135–41.

Cardini, A (1981) *Stato liberale e protezionismo in Italia, 1890–1900*, Bologna: Il Mulino.

Carnero i Arbat, T (1980) *Expansión vinícola y atraso agrario (1870–1900)*, Madrid: Ministerio de Agricultura.

Carreras, A (1983) "Aprovechamiento de la Energía Hidraúlica en Cataluña, 1840–1920. Un Ensayo de Interpretación", *Revista de Historia Económica* 1 (2): 31–63.

Carrión, J (1986) "Estatura, Nutricion y Nivel de Vida en Murcia, 1860–1930", *Revista de Historia Económica* IV: 67–102.

Casa de America (1922) *Memorándum de la Casa de América de Barcelona Sobre el Problema de la Exportación del Aceite de Oliva, en Relación con la Solicitud de la Asociación Gremial de Negociantes de Aceite de Barcelona, Pidiendo la Admisión Temporal de la Hojalata en Blanco para envases del Aceite Destinado a la Exportación*, Barcelona.

Castronovo (1965) *L'industria Cotoniera in Piemonte nel Secolo XI*, Turin: ILTE.

Caves, R E, Frankel, J A, and Jones, R W (1996) *World Trade and Payments. An Introduction*, New York: Harper Collins.

Celik, Z *The Remaking of Istanbul. Portrait of an Ottoman City in the Ninenteenth Century*, Seattle, Wash.: University of Washington Press.

Cerdá, I (1968 [1867]) *Monografía estadística de la Clase Obrera de Barcelona en 1856*, Madrid: Instituto de Estudios Fiscales.

Cerisola, N (1973) *Storia delle Industrie Imperiesi*, Savona: Casa Editrice Liguria.

Cezar, Y (1986) *Osmanlý Maliyesinde Bunalým and Deðiþim Dönemi (XVIII, yy. dan Tanzimat'a Mali Tarih)* [Era of Crises and Change in Ottoman Fiscal Policy, Fiscal History from XVIIIth Century to the Tanzimat], Istanbul: Alan Yayýncýlýk.

Chapman, S D (1987) *The Cotton Industry in the Industrial Revolution* (2nd. Edition), London: Macmillan.

—— (1992) *Merchant Enterprise in Britain From Industrial Revolution to World War I*, Cambridge: Cambridge University Press.

Chayanov, A V (1987) *The Theory of Peasant Economy*, New Edition editted by D Thorner, R E F Smith and B Kerblay, Madison, Wisconsin: University of Wisconsin Press.

Christensen, J (1983) *Rural Denmark 1750–1980*, Copenhagen: The Central Cooperative Committee of Denmark.

—— (1985) *Landbostatistik Haandbog i Dansk Landbostatistik 1830–1900*, Copenhagen: Landboshistorisk Selskab.

—— (1992) "Om Lonudviklingen for Byarbejdere i Danmark 1830–1870", Memo N.188, Økonomisk Institute, Copenhagen University.

Cipolla, C (1965) *Literacy and Development in the West*, Penguin, Harmondsworth.

Clark, C (1951) *The Conditions of Economic Progress*, London: Macmillan.

Clark, G (1987a) "Why Isn't the Whole World Developed? Lessons from the Cotton Mills", *Journal of Economic History* 47: 141–73.

—— (1987b) "Productivity Growth without Technical Change in European Agriculture before 1850", *Journal of Economic History* 47: 419–32.

—— (1994) "Factory Discipline", *Journal of Economic History* 54 (1): 128–63.

——, Huberman M and Lindert P H (1995) "A British Food Puzzle, 1770–1850", *Economic History Review* 48: 215–37.

Coatsworth, J H and Taylor, A M (eds.) (1999) *Latin America and the New Economic History*, Cambridge: Harvard University Press.

Coelho, E (1861) *Estatística do Districto de Vianna do Castello*, Lisboa: Imprensa Nacional.

Cohen, I (1990) *American Management and British Labor. A Comparative Study of the Cotton Spinning Industry*, New York: Greenwood Press.

Cohen, J and Federico, G (forthcoming) *The Economic Development of Italy*, Cambridge: Cambridge University Press.

Cohn, D L (1956) *The Life and Times of King Cotton*, Oxford: Oxford University Press.

Cohn, E (1957–8) *Privatbanken i København gennem Hundrede År 1857–1957*, Copenhagen: Privatbanken.

Cole, A and Crandall, R (1964) "The International Scientific Committee on Price History", *Journal of Economic History* 24: 381–8.

Comisión Especial Arancelaria (1867) *Información sobre el derecho diferencial de bandera y sobre los de aduanas exigibles a los hierros, al carbón de piedra y los algodones, presentada al gobierno de Su Majestad por la comisión nombrada de efecto en Real Decreto de 10 de noviembre de 1865*. Madrid: Imprenta Nacional.

Committee on Ways and Means (1921) *Tariff Information, 1921*. Hearings before the Committee on Ways and Means. House of Representatives. *Schedule A. Chemicals, Oils and Paints*, Washington: Government Printing Office.

—— (1929) *Hearings before the Committee on Ways and Means*. Seventieth Congress. Second Section. Vol. VII. *Schedule 1: Chemical, Oils and Paints and Schedule 7: Agricultural Products and Provisions*, Washington: Government Printing Office.

Confederazione Fascista degli Agricoltori & Settore della Olivicoltura della F.N.C.P.P.A. (1938) *Atti del Convegno Nazionale di Olivicoltura* (Bari 21–22 settembre), Rome: Stab. Tipografico del Ramo Editoriale degli Agricoltori.

Confraria, J (1999) "Portugal: Paternalism and Poverty", in J Foreman-Peck and G Federico (eds.) *European Industrial Policy: The Twentieth Century*, Oxford: Oxford University Press: 268-294.

Consejo Superior de Emigración (1916) *La emigración española transoceánica, 1911-1915*, Madrid: Hijos de T Minuesa de los Rios.

Copeland, M T (1912) *The Cotton Manufacturing Industry of the United States*, Cambridge Mass: Harvard.

Coppa, F J (1970) "The Italian Tariff and the Conflict between Agriculture and Industry: The Commercial Policy of Liberal Italy", *Journal of Economic History* 30: 742–69.

Corden, W M (1974) *Trade Policy and Economic Welfare*, Oxford: Clarendon Press.

—— (1975) "The Cost and Consequences of Protection: A Survey of Empirical Work", in P B Kenen (ed.) *International Trade and Finance. Frontiers for Research*, Cambridge: Cambridge University Press: 51–93.

—— (1981) "Exchange Rate Protection" in R Cooper *et al.* (eds.) *The International Monetary System Under Flexible Exchange Rates: Global, Regional and National. Essays in Honor of Robert Triffin*: 17–34.

Cortés Conde, R (1979) *El progreso argentino, 1880–1914*, Buenos Aires: Sudamericana.

—— (1988) "Migración, cambio agrícola y políticas de protección. El caso argentino", in N Sanchez-Albornoz (ed.) *Españoles hacia América. La emigración en masa, 1880–1930*, Madrid: Alianza: 235–48.

—— (1997) *La economía argentina en el largo plazo (Siglos XIX y XX)*, Buenos Aires: Ed. Sudamericana-Universidad de San Andres.

Costa Mas, J (1974) "Producción y comercio de las pasas de Denia", in *Primer Congreso de Historia del País Valenciano* 4, Valencia: Universidad de Valencia: 11–21.

Couchman, R (1967) *The Sunsweet Story: a History of the Establishment of the Dried Tree Fruit Industry in California and of the 50 Years of Service of Sunsweet Growers, Inc.*, San Jose, Calif.: Sunsweet Growers.

Crafts, N F R (1983) "Gross National Product in Europe, 1870–1910: Some New Estimates", *Explorations in Economic History* 20: 387–401.

—— (1996) "Post-neo-classical Endogenous Growth Theory: 'What Are its Policy Implications?'" *Oxford Review of Economic Policy* 12: 30–47.

—— (1997) "Some Dimensions of the Quality of Life during the British Industrial Revolution", *Economic History Review* 50: 617–39.

—— and Thomas, M (1986) "Comparative Advantage in UK Manufacturing Trade, 1910–1935", *Economic Journal* 96: 629–45.

Craig, R (1973) "Shipowning in the South-West in its National Context, 1800–1914", in H E S Fisher and W E Minchinton (eds.) *Transport and Shipowning in the Westcountry*, Exeter, England: University of Exeter.

Crouchley, A E (1936) *The Investment of Foreign Capital in Egyptian Companies and Public Debt*, Cairo.

—— (1938) *The Economic Development of Modern Egypt*, London.

Cruess, W V (1924) "The preparation and refining of olive oil in Southern Europe", *Circulars. University of California. College of Agriculure. Agricultural Experiment Station*, No. 20, October.

D'ippolito, T (1935) *I costi dei produzioni nelle aziende industriali*, Milano: Dott. Guiffrè Editore.

Dakin, D (1972) *Unification of Greece 1770–1923*, London: Ernest Benn.

Damjanov, S (1979) "Sur le Développement Industriel du Sud-est Européen a la fin du XIXe et du Xxe Siècles", *Etudes balkaniques*: 3–30.

—— (1980) "Sur l'Importance des Investissements Nationaux et Etrangers dans l'Industrie du Sud-est Européen (fin du XIXe début du XXe siècles)", *Etudes balkaniques*: 60–73.

David, P A (1970) "Learning by Doing and Tariff Protection: A Reconsideration of the Case of the Ante-Bellum United States Cotton Textile Industry", *Journal of Economic History* 30 (3): 521–601.

—— (1985) "Clio and the Economics of QWERTY", *American Economic Review* 75 (2): 332–7.

Davis, L E and Stettler, H L (1966) "The New England Textile Industry, 1825–1860: Trends and Fluctuations", in D S Brady (ed.) *Output, Employment and Productivity in the United States after 1800*, New York: NBER: 213–38.

Deardorf, A V (1984) "Testing Trade Theories and Predicting Trade Flows", in R Jones and P Kenen (eds.), *Handbook of International Economics, Vol. I*, Amsterdam: Elsevier Science Publishers: 467–517.

De Bow, J D B (1970 [1854]) *Statistical View of the United States*, New York: Gordon and Breach.

De Felice, F (1971) *L'agricoltura in Terra di Bari dal 1880 al 1914*, Milano: Banca Commerciale Italiana.

De Felice, R (1965) *Aspetti e Momenti della Vita Economica di Roma e del Lazio nei Secoli XVIII e XIX*, Roma: Storia e Letteratura.

Delgado, J M (1995) "Mercado Interno Versus Mercado Colonial en la Primera Industrialización Española", Revista de Historia Económica 13 (1): 11–31.

Dell'amore, G (1938) *Il Commercio dei Prodotti Agrari in Italia. Volume Primo: Le negoziazoni anteriori al raccolto*, Milano: A Giufré Editore.

DeLong, J B (1988) "Productivity Growth, Convergence and Welfare: Comment", *American Economic Review* 78: 1138–54.

Dersaadet Ticaret Odasý Gazetesi, Miscellaneous issues, 1302 (1885)–1323 (1906), Istanbul.

Dertilis, G (1993) *Taxation and Power in the Modern Greek States* [in Greek], Athens: Alexandria Press.

Devlet Istatistik Enstitüsü (DIE) (1995) *Yüzyýlda Osmanlý Dýþ Ticareti* [Ottoman Foreign Trade in the Nineteenth Century], prepared by Ş Pamuk, Devlet Ýstatistik Enstitüsü, Tarihi Ýstatistikler Dizisi, V.1, Ankara: Devlet Ýstatistik Enstitüsü Matbaasý.

—— (1996) *Osmanlý Ýmparatorluðunun ve Türkiye'nin Nüfusu* [The Population of the Ottoman Empire and Turkey], prepared by C Behar, Devlet Ýstatistik Enstitüsü, Tarihi Ýstatistikler Dizisi, V.2, Ankara: Devlet Ýstatistik Enstitüsü Matbaasý.

—— (1997a) *Osmanlý Dönemi Tarým Ýstatistikleri, 1909, 1913 ve 1914* [Agricultural Statistics of Turkey during the Ottoman Period], prepared by T Güran, Devlet Ýstatistik Enstitüsü, Tarihi Ýstatistikler Dizisi, V.3, Ankara: Devlet Ýstatistik Enstitüsü Matbaasý.

—— (1997b) *Osmanlý Devleti'nin Ýlk Ýstatistik Ýýllýðý, 1897* [The First Yearbook of the Ottoman Empire], prepared by T Güran, Devlet Ýstatistik Enstitüsü, Tarihi Ýstatistikler Dizisi, V.3, Ankara: Devlet Ýstatistik Enstitüsü Matbaasý.

Diaz, A C (1984) "Latin America in the 1930s", in R Thorp (ed.), *Latin America in the 1930s, The Role of the Periphery in the World Crisis*, London: Macmillan: 17–49.

Diaz-Alejandro, C F (1970) *Essays on the Economic History of the Argentine Republic*, New Haven, Conn.: Yale University Press.

Diouritch, G (1919) "A Survey of the Development of the Serbian (Southern Slav) Nation. An Economic and Statistical Study", *Journal of the Royal Statistical Society* 82: 293–334.

Direccion General de Contribuciones, Impuestos y Rentas (1903, 1911, 1927) *Estadística administrativa de la contribución industrial y de comercio*, Madrid.

Direccion General Deaduanas (1876) *Memorias comerciales redactadas por el Cuerpo Consular de España en el extranjero*, Madrid: Imprenta de los Señores Iglesias y García.

Direction de la Statistique Générale et de la Documentation (1939) *Annuaire Statistique, 1938*, Paris: Imprimerie Nationale.

Direction Générale de l'Agriculture, du Commerce et de la Colonisation. Régence de Tunis. Protectorat Français (1931) *Statistique Générale de la Tunisie*, Tunis.

Di Rollo, F (1965) *Le Retribuzioni dei Lavoratori Edili a Roma dal 1826 al 1880*, Roma: Archivio Economico dell'Unificazione Italiana.

"Documentos da Casa Real" (1800–1910), *Arquivo Nacional da Torre do Tombo*, Lisboa.

Dovring, F (1956) *Land and Labour in Europe, 1900–59. A Comparative Study of Recent Agrarian History*, The Hague, Martinus Nijhoff.

Drukker, J W and Van Meerten, M A (1995) "Beyond Villermé and Quetelet: The Quantitative Relation between Sex-and Age-Specific Height and Real per Capita Income", in J Komlos (ed.) *The Biological Standard of Living on Three Continents. Further Explorations in Anthropometric History*, Boulder: Westview Press: 25–57.

Dudzik, P (1987) *Innovation and Investition: Technische Entwicklung und Unternehmerentscheide in der Schweizerischen Baumwollspinnerei, 1800 bis 1916*. Zurich: Chronos.

Dumont, P and Georgeon, F (eds.) (1996) "Modernlepme Sürecinde Osmanlý Kentleri",
Ottoman Towns in the Modernization Process, Istanbul: Tarih Vakfý Yurt Yayýnlarý.

Dyrvik, S, Fossen, A B, Gronlie, T, Hovland, E, Nordvik, H and Tveite, S (1979) *Norsk Økonomisk Historie 1500–1970*, Bergen: Universitetsforlaget.

Economist, The (1845) "Markets of the Industrial Districts", *The Economist*, several issues.

Eichengreen, B (1992) "The Origins of the Great Slump Revisited", *Economic History Review* 45: 213–39.

El Aceite de oliva en España, El. Organo de la Federación de Exportadores de Aceite de Oliva de España 1929, n. 5; 1931, n. 37; 1934, n. 70.

Eldem, V (1970) *Osmanli Imparatorlugu'nun Iktisadi Şartlari Hakkinda Bir Tetkik*, Istanbul: Is Bankasi Publications.

—— (1994) *Osmanlý Ýmparatorluðu'nun Ýktisadi Þartlarý Hakkýnda bir Tetkik* [Research on the Economic Conditions of the Ottoman Empire], Ankara: Türk Tarih Kurumu Basýmevi.

Ellison, T (1968 [1886]) *The Cotton Trade of Great Britain*, London: Frank Cass.

El-Sherbini, A and El-Sherif, A (1956) "Marketing Problems in an Underdeveloped Economy", *L'Egypte Contemporaine*: 42–6.

Engel, C and Rogers, J (1996) "How Wide Is the Border?", *American Economic Review*.

Ercolani (1969) "Documentazione Statistica di Base", in G Fua (ed.) *Lo Sviluppo Economico in Italia* Vol. III, Milan: F.Angeli: 379–470.

Essemyr, M (1989) *Bruksarbetarnas Livsmedelskosumtion, Formarks Bruk 1730-1880*, Uppsala: Almqvist and Wicksell.

Estevadeordal, A (1993) *Historical Essays on Comparative Advantage: 1913-1938*, unpublished PhD Thesis. Cambridge, Mass.: Harvard University.

—— (1997) "Measuring Protection in the Early Twentieth Century", European Review of Economic History 1: 89–125.

Evans, I L (1924) *The Agrarian Revolution in Romania*, Cambridge: Cambridge University Press.

Exertzoglou, H (1986) "Greek Banking in Constantinople, 1850–1881", unpublished PhD Thesis, King's College, University of London.

Faini, R and Venturini, A (1994) "Italian Emigration in the Pre-War Period", in T J Hatton and J G Williamson (eds.) *Migration and the International Labor Market, 1850–1939*, London: Routledge: 72–90.

Farnie, D A (1979). *The English Cotton Industry and the World Market, 1815–1896*, Oxford: Clarendon Press.

Fawaz, L (1983) *Merchants and Migrants in Nineteenth Century Beirut*, Cambridge, Mass.: Harvard University Press.

Federacion de Fabricantes de Aceite de Orujo de España (1937) *Memoria*, Madrid.

Federico, G (1979) "Per una Analisi del Ruolo dell'agricultura Nello Sviluppo Economico Italiano: note Sull'esportazione di Prodotti Primari (1863–1913)", Società e Storia 5: 379–441.

—— (1984) "Commercio dei cereali e dazio sul grano in Italia (1861–1913). Una analise quantitative", *Nuova Rivista Storica* LXVIII: 46–108.

—— (1986) "Mercantilizzazione e Sviluppo Economico in Italia (1860–1940)", *Rivista di Storia Economica*, III.

——(1988) "Commercio Estero e 'Periferie'. Il Caso dei Paesi Mediterranei", *Meridiana Rivista di Storia e Scienzie Sociali* 2/4: 163–96.

—— (1992a) "El Comercio Exterior de los Paises Mediterraneos en el Siglo XIX", in L Prados de la Escosura and V Zamagni (eds.) *El Desarrollo Económico en la Europa do Sur: España e Italia en Perspectiva Historica*, Madrid, Alianza Editorial: 269–92.

—— (1992b) "Il Valore Aggiunto dell'Agricoltura", in G M Rey (a cura di), *I Conti Economici dell'Italia. Vol. 2. Una Stima del Valore Aggiunto per il 1911*. Roma-Bari: Laterza.

—— (1994) *Il Filo d'oro. L'industria Mondiale della seta dalla Restaurazione alla Grande Crisi*, Venezia: Marsilio editore.

—— (1997) *An Economic History of the Silk Industry 1830–1930*, Cambridge: Cambridge University Press.

—— and O'Rourke, K (1998) "A Social Accounting Matrix for Italy, 1911", *Centre for Economic Research Working Paper WP98/19*, Department of Economics: University College, Dublin.

—— and Tena, A (1991) "On the Accuracy of Foreign Trade Statistics (1909–1935): Morgenstern Revisited", *Explorations in Economic History* 28: 259–73.

—— and Tena, A (1998) "Was Italy a Protectionist Country?", *European Review of Economic History* 2: 73–97.

—— and Tena, A (1999) "Did Trade Policy Foster Italian Industrialization? Evidences from Effective Protection Rates 1870–1930", *Research in Economic History* 19:

Feinstein, C H, Temin, P and Toniolo, G (1997) *The European Economy Between the Wars*, Oxford: Oxford University Press.

Feliú, G (1991) *Precios y Salarios en la Cataluña Moderna*, Madrid: Banco de Espana.

Fenoaltea, S (1978) "Riflessioni sullésperienza industriale itaiana del risorgimento all prima guerra mondiale", in G Toniolo (ed.) *L´ economía italiana, 1861–1940*, Bari: Laterza: 93–103.

—— (1988) "International Resource Flows and Construction Movements in the Atlantic Economy: the Kuznets Cycle in Italy", *Journal of Economic History* 48: 605–37.

—— (1992) "El ciclo de la construcción en Italia, 1861–1913: evidencia e interpretación", in L Prados de la Escosura and V Zamagni (eds.) *El desarrollo económico en la Europa del Sur: España e Italia en perspectiva histórica*, Madrid: Alianza: 211–52.

—— (1993) "Politica doganale, sviluppo industriale, emigrazione: verso una considerazione del dazio sul grano", Rivista di Storia Economica 10: 65–77.

Ferenczi, I and Willcox, W F (1929) *International Migrations*, Vol. I, New York: National Bureau of Economic Research.

Fernandez, A (1993) *La Argentina, un mercado étnico? Las Exportaciones Españolas al Río de la Plata en un Enfoque Comparativo (1880–1935)*, Memoria de Doctorado. Universitat de Barcelona.

Ferrara, A (1927) *Le Colture Legnose e le Industrie Derivate della Tunisia*, Firenze: Istituto Agricolo coloniale italiano.

Ferrer V J (1875) *Conferencias sobre el arte de hilar y tejer en general y especialmente sobre el de hilar y tejer el algodón*, Barcelona: Establecimiento de Jaime Jepús Roviralta.

Ferro, J P (1995) *A População Portuguesa no Final do Antigo Regime 1750–1815*, Lisboa: Presença.

Figuerola, L (1968[1849]) *Estadística de Barcelona en 1849*, Madrid: Instituto de Estudios Fiscales.

Fischer, L R and Nordvik, H W (1986) "Maritime Transport and the Integration of the North Atlantic Economy, 1850–1914" in W Fischer, R M McInnis and J Schneider (eds.) *The Emergence of a World Economy, 1500–1914*, Wiesbaden: Franz Steiner Verlag.

Fisher, W (1991) "The Choice of Technique: Entrepreneurial Decisions in the Nineteenth-Century European Cotton and Steel Industries", P Higonnet, D S Landes, and H Rosovsky (eds.), *Favorites of Fortune. Technology. Growth and Economic Development since the Industrial Revolution*, Cambridge, Mass: Harvard University Press: 142–158.

Flam, H, and Flanders, M J (1991) *Heckscher–Ohlin Trade Theory*, Cambridge, Mass.: MIT Press.

Flandreau, M, Le Cacheux, J and Zumer, F (1997) "Stability without a Pact? Lessons from the European Gold Standard, 1880–1914", mimeo.

Flora, P (1973) "Historical Process of Social Mobilization: Urbanization and Literacy, 1850–1965", in S N Eisenstadt and S Rokken (eds.) *Building States and Nations: Models and Data Resources*, vol 1, Beverly Hills: Sage.

Flores, A M (ed.) (1986) *Atlas de Historia Económica de la Baja Andalucia (Siglos XVI–XIX)*, Seville: Editoriales Andaluzas Unidas.

Floud, R (1984) "The Heights of Europeans since 1750: A New Source for European Economic History", *NBER Working Paper N.1318*.

Folin, R (1987) "Ports et Navigation en Mediterranée. Essai Statistique 1870–1905", in *Navigations Mediterranéennes au XIXe siècle*, vol. 1, Cahier no 9, Institut de Recherches Mediterranéennes, Université de Provence.

Fontana, J (1975) *Cambio economico y actitudes politicas en las Espana del siglo XIX*, Ariel: Barcelona.

Ford, A G (1962) *The Gold Standard, 1880–1914: Britain and Argentina*, Oxford: Oxford University Press.

Foreman-Peck, J (1983) *A History of the World Economy: International Economic Relations since 1850*, Brighton: Harvester-Wheatsheaf.

—— (1995) "A Model of Later Nineteenth Century European Economic Development", *Revista de Historia Económica* 13: 441–71.

Foster, A (1938) "The Málaga Raisin District: A Study in Mediterranean Agriculture", *Journal of Geography* 37: 1–14.

Fraile, P (1991) *Industrialización y grupos de presión: la economia política de la protección en España*, Madrid: Alianza.

Franciosa, L (1940) *L'olivo nella economia italiana*, Roma: Tipografia Failli.

Frankel, J and Rose, A (1996) "A Panel Project on Purchasing Power Parity: Mean Reversion Within and Between Countries", Journal of International Economics: 209–24.

Frezzoti (1922) "Su la Crisi dell'olivicoltura e del Commercio Oleario. Fatti e Commenti" *Oleum. Rivista mensuale dell'Olivicultura, dell'Oleificio e del Commercio Oleario* 2, Porto Maurizio: 26–31.

Froot, K and Rogoff, K (1995) "Perspectives on PPP and Long-Run Real Exchange Rates", in G Grossman and K Rogoff, (eds.) *Handbook of International Economics*, Vol. 3, Amsterdam: North Holland.

Galassi, F and Cohen, J (1992) "La agricultura italiana, 1860–1930: tendencias de la producción y diferencias en la productividad regional" in L Prados de la Escosura and V Zamagni (eds.) *El desarrollo económico en la Europa del Sur: España e Italia en perspectiva histórica*, Madrid: Alianza.

Galula, R (1895) "Le commerce des huiles d'olive sur la place de Marseille", in Centre National de la Recherche Scientifique. Maison de la Mediterranée (1985), *L'huile d'olive en Méditerranée. Histoire, Anthropologie, économie de l'antiquité à nos jours*. Aix-en-Provence: Institut de Recherches Méditerranéennes. Université de Provence: 125–32.

Garrabou, R (1985) "La crisis agraria española de finales del siglo XIX: una etapa del desarrollo del capitalismo" in R Garrabou and J Sanz (eds.) *Historia Agraria de la España Contemporánea. II Expansión y crisis 1850–1900*, Barcelona: Crítica: 477–542.

—— (1988) "La historiografía de la crisis: resultados y nuevas perspectivas", in R Garrabou (ed.) *La crisis agraria de finales del siglo XIX*, Barcelona: Crítica.

——, Pujol, J and Colomé, J (1991) "Salaris, Ús i Explotació de la Força de Treball Agrícola (Catalunya 1818–1936)", Recerques 24: 23–49.

Gatrell, V A C (1977) "Labour, Power, and the Size of Firms in Lancashire Cotton in the Second Quarter of the Nineteenth Century", *Economic History Review* 30 (1): 95–139.

Geertz, C (1978) "The Bazaar Economy: Information and Search in Peasant Marketing", American Economic Review: 28–32.

GEHR (1980) Grupo de Estudios de Historia Rural *Los precios del trigo y al cebada en España, 1891–1907*, Madrid: Banco de España.

—— (1983) Grupo de Estudios de Historia Rural "Notas sobre la producción agraria española, 1891–1931", *Revista de Historia Económica* 1: 185–252.

—— (1985) Grupo de Estudios de Historia Rural "Contribución al Análisis Histórico de la Ganaderia Española 1865–1929" in R Garrabou and J Sanz (eds.) *Historia Agraria de la España Contemporanea*, Barcelona: Editorial Crítica vol. 2: 229–79.

—— (1988) Grupo de Estudios de Historia Rural "La crisis agrícola en Castilla La Vieja y Andalucia: los casos del trigo y del olivar", in R Garrabou (ed.) *La crisis agraria de finales del siglo XIX*, Barcelona: Crítica.

Gerschenkron, A (1952) "Economic Backwardness in Historical Perspective", in B Hoselitz (ed.) *The Progress of Underdeveloped Areas*, Chicago: University of Chicago Press.

—— (1962) *Economic Backwardness in Historical Perspective*, Cambridge, Mass.: Harvard University Press.

Gimenez G F (1862) *Guia fabril e industrial de España*. Publicada con el apoyo y autorización del gobierno de S.M, Madrid and Barcelona: Librería Española and Librería del Plus Ultra.

Gini, C (1959) *Ricchezza e reddito*, Turin: Unione Editrice Torinese.

Giretti, E (1913) *I Trivellatori della nazione Italiana*, Roma: Libreria Politica Moderna.

Godinho, V M (1955) *Prix et Monnaies au Portugal 1750–1850*, Paris: Armand Colin.

Good, D F (1984) *The Economic Rise of the Habsburg Empire, 1750–1914*, Berkeley: University of California Press.

—— (1994) "The Economic Lag of Central and Eastern Europe: Income Estimates for the Habsburg Successor States, 1870–1910", *Journal of Economic History* 54: 869–91.

—— (1996) "Economic Growth in Europe's Third World: Central and Eastern Europe, 1870–1989", in D H Aldcroft and R E Catterall, *Rich Nations–Poor Nations. The Long-run Perspective*, Cheltenham: Edward Elgar.

—— and Tongshu, M (1998) "New Estimates of Income Levels in Central and Eastern Europe, 1870–1910", in F Baltzarek, F Butschek and G Tichy (eds.) *Von der Theorie zur Wirtschftspolitik ein Österreichischer Weg*, Stuttgart: Lucius.

Goodwin, B K and Grennes, T J (1998) "Tsarist Russia and the World Wheat Market", *Explorations in Economic History* 35: 405–30.

Gounaris, B C (1989) "Emigration from Macedonia in the Early Twentieth Century", *Journal of Modern Greek Studies* 7: 133–53.

—— (1993) *Steam over Macedonia, 1870–1912, Socio-Economic Change and the Railway Factor,* New York: East European Monographs, Boulder, distributed by Columbia University Press.

—— (1994) "Selanik", in C Keyder, Y E Özveren and D Quataert (eds.), *Doğu Akdeniz'de Liman Kentleri, 1800–1914* [Port Cities of the Eastern Mediterranean, 1800–1914], Istanbul: Tarih Vakfý Yurt Yayynlarý: 103–20.

Great Britain. Board of Trade (1914) *Statistical Abstract for the Principal and Other Foreign Countries in Each Year from 1901 to 1912,* Vol. 39. London: HM Stationery Office.

——. Foreign Office. *Diplomatic and Consular Reports,* London: HM Stationery Office, various years.

Gregory, P R (1979) "The Russian Balance of Payments, the Gold Standard and Monetary Policy", *Journal of Economic History* 39: 379–99.

Greif, A (1999) *Genoa and the Maghribi Traders: Historical and Comparative Analysis,* New York: Cambridge University Press.

Gross, N.T. (1984) "The Economic Policy of the Mandatory Government in Palestine", *Research in Economic History* 9: 143–85.

Grossman, G M (ed.) (1992) *Imperfect Competition and International Trade,* Cambridge, Mass.: MIT Press.

—— and Helpman, E (1994) "Endogenous Innovation in the Theory of Growth", *Journal of Economic Perspectives* 8: 23–44.

Guillen, G (1893) *Reglas practicas per a obtenir bons olis,* Barcelona: Victor Verdés.

Guisado, J (1983) "Crisis agraria e invasión filoxérica en la España del siglo XIX. Verificación de algunas recientes interpretaciones sobre problemas de la viticultural en Andalucía y Cataluña mediante un análisis comparativo", *Revista de Historia Económica* 1: 165–84.

Güran, T (1997) *Agricultural Statistics of Turkey during the Ottoman Period,* Ankara: State Institute of Statistics.

—— (1998) *Yüzyýl Osmanlý Tarýmý Üzerine Araptýrmalar* [Research on Nineteenth Century Ottoman Agriculture], Istanbul: Eren Yayýncýlýk.

Gutiérrez, M M (1834) *Comercio Libre o Funesta Teoría de la Libertad Económica Absoluta,* Madrid: M Calero.

—— (1837) *Impugnación a las Cinco Proposiciones de Pebrer Sobre los Grandes Males que Causa la ley de Aranceles a la Nación en General, a la Cataluña en Particular, y a las Mismas Fábricas Catalanas,* Madrid: Imprenta de M Calero.

Habakkuk, H S (1962) *American and British Technology in the Nineteenth Century,* Cambridge: Cambridge University Press.

Haber, S (1997) *How Latin America Fell Behind,* Stanford, Calif.: Stanford University Press.

Hagel, J and Rayport, J F (1997) "The informediaries", *The McKinsey Quarterly* 4.

Hamilton, E (1934) *American Treasure and the Price Revolution in Spain, 1501–1650,* Cambridge, Mass.: Harvard University Press.

Hansen, B (1991a) *The Political Economy of Poverty, Equity, and Growth: Egypt and Turkey,* New York: Oxford University Press for the World Bank.

—— (1991b) "Factor Prices in Egypt and Some Major Developed Countries from 1900 to WWII", in R Ransom (ed.) *Research in Economic History*, Greenwich, Conn.: JAI Press.

Hansen, S A (1984) *Økonomisk Vækst I Danmark*, Copenhagen: Økonomisk Institut.

Hansen, V F (1889) *Stavnbaands-Løsningen og Landboreformerne set fra National-økonomiens Standpunkt*, Copenhagen: Forlagt af Universitetsboghandler.

Hanson, J R (1980) *Trade in Transition: Exports from the Third World 1840–1900*, New York: Academic Press.

Harlaftis, G (1990) "The Role of the Greeks in the Black Sea", in L R Fischer and H W Nordvik (eds.) *Shipping and Trade, 1750–1950: Essays in International Maritime Economic History*, Yorkshire: Lofthouse Publications.

—— (1996) *A History of Greek-owned Shipping. The Making of an International Tramp Fleet, 1830 to the Present Day*, London: Routledge.

Harley, C K (1980) "Transportation, the World Wheat Trade, and the Kuznets Cycle, 1850–1913", *Explorations in Economic History* 17: 218–50.

—— (1988) "Ocean Freight Rates and Productivity, 1740–1913: The Primacy of Mechanical Invention Reaffirmed", *Journal of Economic History* 48: 851–76.

—— (1989) "Coal Exports and British Shipping, 1850–1913", *Explorations in Economic History* 26: 311–38.

—— (1992a) "International Competitiveness of the Antebellum American Cotton Textile Industry", *Journal of Economic History* 52: 559–84.

—— (1992b) "The Antebellum American Tariff: Food Exports and Manufacturing", *Explorations in Economic History* 29: 375–400.

Harris, J, Hunter, J and Lewis, C (1995) *The New Institutional Economics and Third World Development*, London: Routledge.

Hatton, T J and Williamson, J G (1994a) "What Drove the Mass Migrations from Europe in the Late Nineteenth Century?", *Population and Development Review* 20: 533–59.

—— (1994b) "Late Comers to Mass Emigration: The Latin Experience" in T J Hatton and J G Williamson (eds.) *Migration and the International Labor Market, 1850–1939*, London: Routledge: 55–71.

—— (eds.) (1994c) *Migration and the International Labor Market, 1850–1939*, London: Routledge.

—— (1997) "Italian Emigration in a Globally Integrating Atlantic Economy", Department of Economics, Harvard University (June).

—— (1998) *The Age of Mass Migration*, Oxford: Oxford University Press.

Hazen, W N (1938) *The Citrus Industry in Palestine*, Washington, DC: United States Department of Agriculture, Bureau of Agricultural Economics.

Hecht, R W and Barton, G T (1950) *Gains in Productivity of Labor*, USDA Technical Bulletin No. 1,020. Washington, DC: USDA, December.

Heikkinen, S. (1996) "Finnish Food Consumption, 1860–1993", Kuluttajatutkimuskeskus. *JulKaisuja* 1: 1–27.

Helpman, E and Krugman, P (1985) *Market Structure and Foreign Trade*, Cambridge, Mass.: MIT Press.

Herlihy, P (1986) *Odessa*, Cambridge, Mass.: Harvard University Press.

Hershlag, Z Y (1968) *Turkey: The Challenge of Growth*, Leiden: E J Brill.

Historisk Statistik 1968, (1969) Oslo: Statistik Sentralbyrå.

Historisk Statistik för Sverige, (1959) Stockholm: Statistika Centralbyran.

Hitchcock, F H (1903) *Foreign Import Tariffs on Fruits and Nuts* USDA, Division of Foreign Markets, Bulletin No. 36, Washington, DC: Government Printing Office.

Hjerppe, R (1989) *The Finnish Economy 1860-1985: Growth and Structural Change*, Helsinki: Bank of Finland.

Hodne, F and Grytten, O H (1994) "Gross Domestic Product of Norway 1835–1915", in O Krantz (ed.), *Nordiska Historiska Nationalrakenskaper, Occasional Papers in Economic History*, Umea University N. 1.

Hoffman, P T (1996) *Growth in a Traditional Society. The French Countryside 1450–1815*, Princeton: Princeton University Press.

Hohenberg, P M and Lees, L H (1985) *The Making of Urban Europe 1000–1950*, Cambridge, Mass.: Harvard University Press.

Hoppe, G and Langton J (1994) *Peasantry to Capitalism. Western Östergötland in the Nineteenth Century*, Cambridge: Cambridge University Press.

Huberman, M (1996) *Escape from the Market. Negotiating Work in Lancashire*, Cambridge: Cambridge University Press.

Hugill, P J (1993) *World Trade since 1431, Geography, Technology, and Capitalism*, Baltimore: The Johns Hopkins University Press.

Hurd, J (1975) "Railways and the Expansion of Markets in India", *Explorations in Economic History*: 263–88.

Ignacio Jiménez Blanco, J (1985) *Crisis y expansión de la agricultura de Andalucía Oriental, 1874–1936*, Madrid: Fundación Juan, March.

Iliopoulus, P I (1973) *The Evolution of Greece's External Trade, 1830–1972*, [in Greek], Athens: Commercial Chamber of Athens.

Inalcik, H and Quataert, D (eds.) (1994) *An Economic History of the Ottoman Empire, 1300-1914*, Cambridge: Cambridge University Press.

Inghirami, S (1991) *La Predica Inutile dei Liberisti*, Milan: F Angeli.

Institut International d'Agriculture (1911–1939) *Annuaire International de Statistique Agricole*, Rome: Institut International d'Agriculture.

—— (1914) *Annuaire International de Statistique Agricole (1911 et 1912)*, Rome.

—— (1923) *Oleaginous Products and Vegetable Oils. Production and Trade*, Rome: Institut International d'Agriculture.

—— (1939) *L'Olivier dans le Monde. Superficie, Production, Commerce de ses Produits*, Rome: Institut International d'Agriculture.

—— (1944) *Les Grands Produits Agricoles. Compendium de Statistiques Agricoles*, Rome: Institut International d'Agriculture.

Ipek, N (1994) *Rumeli'den Anadolu'ya Türk Göçleri* [Turkish Migration from Rumelia to Anatolia], Ankara: Türk Tarih Kurumu Basýmevi.

Islam, N (1995) "Growth Empirics: A Panel Data Approach", *Quarterly Journal of Economics*, 110: 1127–70.

Issawi, C (1947) *Egypt: An Economic and Social Analysis*, London: Oxford University Press.

—— (1954) *Egypt At Mid-Century*, London: Oxford University Press.

—— (1961) "Egypt since 1800: A Study of Lopsided Development", *Journal of Economic History* 21: 1–25.

—— (1980a) *The Economic History of Turkey*, Chicago: University of Chicago Press.

—— (1980b) "De-industrialization and Re-industrialization in the Middle East since 1800", *International Journal of Middle East Studies* 12: 469–79.

—— (1982) *An Economic History of the Middle East and North Africa*, New York: Columbia University Press.

—— (1995) *The Middle East Economy: Decline and Recovery, Selected Essays by Charles Issawi*, Princeton: Markus Wiener Publishers.

Isserlis, L (1938) "Tramp Shipping", *Journal of the Royal Statistical Society New Series*, 101, pt. 1: 53–134.

ISTAT (1958) *Sommario di Statistiche Storiche*, Rome: ISTAT.

—— (1965) *Sviluppo della Popolazione Italiana dal 1961 al 1964*, Rome: ISTAT.

Istatistik Umum Müdürlügü, Türkiye Cümhuriyeti (1939) *Osmanli Imparatorlugunun Ticaret Musvazenesi, 1878-1913*, Nesriyat No. 132, Tetkiler Seri No. 73. Ankara: Zerbamat.

Istituto Centrale di Statistica (1958) *Sommario di stastistiche storiche italiane, 1861–1955*, Roma.

Istituto Nazionale per l'Esportazione (1927) *La Produzione e il Commercio Mondiali dell'olio di oliva*, Roma: Società Anomia Tipografica, Castaldi.

Jackson, M R (1986) "Industrial Output in Romania and its Historical Regions, 1880 to 1930", *Journal of European Economic History* 15: 59–111 and 231–57.

—— and Lampe, J R (1983) "The Evidence of Industrial Growth in Southeastern Europe before the Second World War", *East European Quarterly* 16: 385–415.

Jensen, E (1937) *Danish Agriculture. Its Economic Development. A Description and Economic Analysis Centering on the Free Trade Epoch 1870–1930*, Copenhagen: J H Schultze.

Jensen, S P (1991–2) "Mennesket, Naturen og Landbrugsreformerne", *Bol og By*: 7–54.

Jeremy, D J (1981) *Transatlantic Industrial Revolution*, Oxford: Basil Blackwell.

Johansen, H-C (1985) *Dansk Økonomisk Statistik 1814–1980*, Copenhagen: Gyldendal.

—— (1998) "Food Consumption in the Pre-Industrial Nordic Societies", Scandinavian Economic History Review XLVI: 11–23.

Jørberg, L (1972) *A History of Prices in Sweden, 1732–1914*, Lund: CWK Gleerup.

—— and Bengtsson, T (1981) "Regional Wages in Sweden during the Nineteenth Century", in P Bairoch and M Levy-Leboyer (eds.), *Disparities in Economic Development since the Industrial Revolution*, London: Macmillan: 226–43.

Justicia S A and Ruiz Sinoga, J D (1987) *Especialización agrícola y desarticulación del espacio: La viticultura en Málaga durante el siglo XIX*, Málaga: Servicio de Publicaciones Diputación Provincial de Málaga.

Justino, D (1988) *A Formação do Espaço Nacional. Portugal 1810–1913*, Lisboa: Vega.

—— (1990) *Preços e Salários em Portugal, 1850–1912*, Lisboa: Banco de Portugal.

Kaelble H (1989) "Was Prometheus Most Unbound in Europe? The Labour Force in Europe During the Late XIXth and XXth Centuries", *Journal of European Economic History* 18: 65–104.

Kancal, S (1983) "La conquête du marché interne ottomane par le capitalisme industriel concurrentiel (1838–1881)", in *Economies et Sociétés dans l'Empire Ottoman (Fin du XIIIe–Debut du XXe siècle)*, Editions du Centre National de la Recherche Scientifique, Paris.

Kardasis, V (1987) Syros. *The Crossroads of Eastern Mediterranean (1832–1857)*, Athens: Cultural Foundation of the National Bank of Greece (in Greek).

—— (1993) *From Sail to Steam. Greek Merchant Shipping, 1858–1914*, Athens: Cultural Foundation of the Industrial Bank (in Greek).

—— (1997) "Greek Steam Liner Companies, 1858–1914", *International Journal of Maritime History* 9:

—— (1998) *The Greeks in Southern Russia (1775–1861)*, Athens: Alexandria Editions (in Greek).

Karpat, K (1985) *Ottoman Population, 1830–1914, Demographic and Social Characteristics*, Madison, Wisconsin: University of Wisconsin Press.

Kasaba, R (1987) *The Ottoman Empire and the World Economy, The Nineteenth Century*, New York: State University of New York Press.

—— (1988a) "Was there a Compradore Bourgeoisie in Mid-Nineteenth-Century Western Anatolia", *Review* 11: 215–88.

—— (1988b) *Ottoman Empire and the World Economy: the Nineteenth Century*, Albany, New York: State University of New York Press.

—— (1992) "Open-Door Treaties: China and the Ottoman Empire Compared", *New Perspectives on Turkey* 7: 77–89.

—— (1994) "Izmir (Smyrna)", in C Keyder, Y E Özveren and D Quataert (eds.), *Doğu Akdeniz'de Liman Kentleri (1800–1914)* [Port Cities in the Eastern Mediterranean (1800–1914)], Istanbul: Tarih Vakfý Yurt Yayýnlarý: 1–22.

——, Keyder, Ç and Tabak, F (1986) "Eastern Mediterranean Port Cities and Their Bourgeoisies, Merchants, Political Projects and Nation-States", *Review* 19, N. 1: 121–35.

Kazgan, G (1977) "Türk Ekonomisinde 1927–35 Depresyonu, Kapital Birikimi ve Örgütlesmeler", in Iktisadi ve Ticari Ilimler Akademisi Derneği, Atatürk Döneminin Ekonomik ve Toplumsal Sorunları: 231–74.

Keyder, Ç (1987) *State and Class in Turkey, A Study in Capitalist Development*, Verso: London.

—— and Pamuk, Ş. (1984) "1945 Çiftçiyi Topraklandırma Kanunu Üzerine Tezler", Yapıt, 8: 52–63.

—— and Quataert, D (eds.) *Doğu Akdeniz'de Liman Kentleri, 1800–1914* [Port Cities of the Mediterranean], Istanbul: Tarih Vakfý Yurt Yayýnlarý.

——, Özveren, Y E and Quataert, D (1994) "Osmanlý Ýmparatorluðu'nda Liman Kentleri, Bazý Kuramsal ve Tarihsel Perspektifler" [Port Cities in the Ottoman Empire, Some Theoretical and Historical Perspective], in C Keyder, Y E Özveren and D Quataert (eds.) *Doğu Akdeniz'de Liman Kentleri, 1800–1914* [Port Cities in the Mediterranean], Istanbul: Tarih Vakfý Yurt Yayýnlarý: 121–57.

Kindleberger, C (1967) *Europe's Post-war Growth. The Role of Labour Supply*, Cambridge: Harvard University Press.

—— (1989) *Economic Laws and Economic History*, New York: Cambridge University Press.

Knowles, L C A (1967) *Economic Development in the 19th Century*, New York.

Koskinen, S, Martelin, T, Notkola, I-L and Pitkanen, K (1994) *Suomen Väestö*, Hämeenlinna: Gaudeamus.

Kosova Vilayeti Salnamesi, Miscellaneous Volumes, 1,296 (1879)–1,318 (1900), Üsküp.

Kostelenos, G C (1995) *Money and Output in Modern Greece: 1858–1938*, Athens: Centre of Planning and Economic Research.

Krantz, O (1988) "New Estimates of Swedish Historical GDP since the Beginning of the Nineteenth Century", *Review of Income and Wealth* 34: 165–81.

—— (1997) "Swedish Historical National Accounts 1800–1990", unpublished paper.

—— and Nilsson, C-A (1974) "Relative Income Levels in the Scandinavian Countries", *Economy and Society* XVII: 52–69.

Krugman, P (1990) *Rethinking International Trade*, Cambridge, Mass.: MIT Press.

Kýray, E (1993) *Osmanlý'da Ekonomik Yapý ve Dýp Borçlar* [Economic Structure and Foreign Debts in the Ottoman Empire], Istanbul: Iletiþim Yayýnlarý.

La Unión Mercantil (1887–1888), Vol. 8–13, Narciso Diaz Escovar Library, Málaga: Spain.

Lacomba, J A (1980) "La filoxera en Málaga", *Agricultura y Sociedad* 16: 323–70.

Lains P (1987) "O Proteccionismo em Portugal (1842–1913): Um Caso Mal Sucedido de Industrialização Concorrencial", Analise Social 23: 481–503.

—— (1990) *A Evolução da Agricultura e da Indústria em Portugal (1850–1913). Uma Interpretação Quantitativa*, Lisboa: Banco de Portugal.

—— (1992) *Foreign Trade and Economic Growth in the European Periphery: Portugal, 1851–1913*, unpublished PhD Thesis, Florence: European University Institute.

—— (1995) *A Economia Portuguesa no Século XIX. Comércio Externo e Crescimento Económico, 1851–1914*, Lisbon: Imprensa Nacional.

—— (1998) "Sources of growth and stagnation of Portuguese agriculture, 1850–1950", paper presented to the workshop on Agricultural Change in Southern Europe in the Nineteenth Century, Florence: European University Institute, 27–28 November.

—— (1999) "Looking for Third Europe, 1870–1913", mimeo.

—— (forthcoming) *L'Economie portuguaise au XIXe siècle*, Paris: L'Harmmatan.

—— and Sousa, P (1999) "Portuguese Agriculture, 1846–1915: What's New?", unpublished paper.

Lampe, J R (1972) "Serbia", in R Cameron (ed.) *Banking and Economic Development*, New York: New York University Press.

—— (1975a) "Finance and pre-1914 Industrial Stirrings in Bulgaria and Serbia", *Southeastern Europe* 2: 23–52.

—— (1975b) "Varieties of Unsuccessful Industrialization: The Balkan States before 1914", *Journal of Economic History* 35: 56–85.

—— (1983) "Debating the Balkan Potential for Pre-1914 Development", *Journal of European Economic History* 12: 187–96.

—— (1986) *The Bulgarian Economy in the Twentieth Century*, London: Croom Helm.

——(1989) "Imperial Borderlands or Capitalist Periphery? Redefining Balkan Backwardness, 1520–1914" in D Chirot (ed.) *The Origins of Backwardness in Eastern Europe*, Berkeley: 177–209.

—— and Jackson, M R (1982) *Balkan Economic History, 1550-1950. From Imperial Borderlands to Developing Nations*, Bloomington: Indiana University Press.

Landes, D S (1969) *The Unbound Prometheus*, Cambridge: Cambridge University Press.

—— (1998) *The Wealth and Poverty of Nations. Why Some Are so Rich and Some so Poor*, New York: W W Norton.

Larson, B (1985) "The Rural Marketing System of Egypt Over the Last Three Hundred Years", *Comparative Studies in Society and History*: 494–530.

Latham, A and Neal, L (1983) "The International Market in Rice and Wheat", *Economic History Review*: 260–79.

Latham, H (Dr) (1885) "Fruit Growing in California", 1885 *Transactions of the State Agricultural Society*.

Lawton, R and Lee, R (eds.) (1989) *Urban Population Development in Western Europe from the Late 18th Century to the Early Twentieth Century*, Liverpool: Liverpool University Press.

Lazonick, W (1990) *Competitive Advantage on the Shop Floor*, Cambridge, Mass: Harvard University Press.

Leamer, E E (1994) "Testing Trade Theory", in D Greenway and L A Winters (eds.), *Surveys in International Trade*, Oxford: Blackwell: 66–106.

—— (1998) "Measures of Openness", in R E Baldwin (ed.), *Trade Policy Issues and Empirical Analysis*, Chicago: University of Chicago Press.

Leff, N H (1992) "Economic Development in Brazil, 1822–1913", *First Boston Working Paper FB–92–02*, Columbia University.

Levine, R and Renelt, D (1992) "Sensitivity Analysis of Cross-Country Growth Regressions", *American Economic Review* 82: 942–63.

Lewis, W A (1954) "Economic Development with Unlimited Supplies of Labour", *Manchester School of Economic and Social Studies* 22: 139–91.

—— (1969) *Aspects of Tropical Development*, Uppsala: Wiksell.

—— (1978a) *The Evolution of the International Economic Order*, Princeton, N.J.: Princeton University Press.

—— (1978b) *Growth and Fluctuations 1870–1913*, Cambridge: Allen and Unwin.

Lindert, P H and Williamson, J G (1983) "English Workers' Living Standards During the Industrial Revolution: A New Look", *Economic History Review*, Second Series, 36: 1–25.

Lindert, P H and Williamson, J G (1985) "English Workers' Real Wages: Reply to Crafts", *Journal of Economic History* 45: 145–53.

Lopez Ontiveros, A (1978) *El sector oleícola y el olivar: oligopolio y coste de recolección*, Madrid: Ministerio de Agricultura, Industria y Pesca.

Lory, B and Popovic, A (1996) "Balkanlarýn Kavþaðýndaki Manastýr, 1816–1918" [Manastyr at the Crossroads of the Balkans, 1816-1918], in P. Dumont and F. Georgeon (eds.) *Modernleþme Sürecinde Osmanlý Kentleri*, [Ottoman Towns in the Process of Modernization], Istanbul: Tarih Vakfý Yurt Yayýnlarý: 60–78.

Lothian, J and Taylor, A M (1996) "Real Exchange Rates: The Recent Float from the Perspective of the Past Two Centuries", *Journal of Political Economy*: 488–541.

Lucas, R E (1990) "Why Doesn't Capital Flow from Rich to Poor Countries?", *American Economic Review* 80: 92–6.

Lyons, J S (1985) "Vertical Integration in the British Cotton Industry, 1825–1850: A Revision", *Journal of Economic History* 45 (2): 419–425.

—— (1987) "Powerloom Profitability and Steam Power Costs", *Explorations in Economic History* 24 (4): 397–400.

—— (1989) "Family Response to Economic Decline: Handloom Weavers in Early Nineteenth-Century Lancashire", *Research in Economic History* 12: 45–91.

Maddison, A (1985) *Two Crises, Latin America and Asia :1929–38 and 1973–83*, Paris: OECD Development Centre Studies.

——(1990) "Measuring European Growth: the Core and the Periphery" in E Aerts and N Valério, *Growth and Stagnation in the Mediterranean World*, Leuven: Leuven University Press: 82–118.

—— (1991) *Dynamic Forces in Capitalist Development*, Oxford: Oxford University Press.

—— (1995) *Monitoring the World Economy, 1820–1992*, Paris: OECD Development Center Studies.

—— and van der Wee, H (1994) *Economic Growth and Structural Change. Comparative Approaches over the Long Run*, Milan: Universitá Bocconi.

Madoz, P (1846) *Diccionario Geográfico-estadístico-histórico de España y sus Posesiones de Ultramar*, Madrid.

Malenbaum, W (1953) *The World Wheat Economy, 1885–1939*, Cambridge, Mass.: Harvard University Press.

Maluquer de Motes, J (1976) "La estructura del sector algodonero en Cataluña durante la primera etapa de la industrialización (1832–1861)", Hacienda Pública Española 38: 133–48.

Manastýr Vilayeti Salnamesi, Miscellaneous Volumes, 1,293 (1876)–1,314 (1896) Manastýr.

Manjarres, R (1872) *Memoria Sobre el Mejoramiento de Nuestros Aceites y Necesidad de Presentarlos bien Elaborados y Clarificados. Informe dado a la Junta Directiva del Instituto Agrícola Catalán de San Isidro por,* Barcelona: Imprenta del Diario de Barcelona.

Mankiw, N G D, Romer, D and Weil, N (1992) "Contribution to the Empirics of Economic Growth", *Quarterly Journal of Economics* 107: 407–37.

Mann, J A (1968 [1860]) *The Cotton Trade of Great Britain,* London: Frank Cass.

Manufactures Bureau (1907) "Olive culture [in France, Spain and Italy]", *Monthly Consular and Trade Reports* 327, December: 104–13

—— (1908a) "Olive Culture [in Tunis, Australia and Algeria]", *Monthly Consular and Trade Reports* 329, December: 70–73.

—— (1908b) "Olive Culture [in Greece, Syria, Spain and Chile]", *Monthly Consular and Trade Reports* 331, April: 130–4.

—— (1909) "Olive Crop Reports [for Turkey, Syria, Palestine and Spain]", *Monthly Consular and Trade Reports* 343, April: 121–4 and 130–4.

Martin Aceña, P (1989) "El Sistema Financiero", in A Carreras (ed.), *Estadísticas Históricas de España, siglos XIX–XX,* Madrid: Fundación Banco Exterior.

—— (1993) "Spain during the Classical Gold Standard Years, 1880–1914" in M D Bordo and F Capie (eds.) *Monetary Regimes in Transition,* Cambridge: Cambridge University Press.

—— (1994) "Spain during the Classical Gold Standard Years, 1880–1914", in M Bordo and F Capie (eds.) *Monetary Regimes in Transition,* Cambridge: Cambridge University Press: 135–72.

Martin, G and Levi, I (1910) "Le marché egyptien et l'utilité de la publication des mercuriales", L'Egypte Contemporaine.

Martin, P F (1913) *Greece of the Twentieth Century,* London: T Fisher Unwin.

Martins, C A (1997) "Trabalho e Condições de Vida em Portugal 1850–1913", Análise Social 142: 483–536.

Mata, E (1993) *As Finanças Portuguesas da Regeneração à Primeira Guerra Mundial, in História Económica,* 4.

Mayer, W (1984) "Endogenous Tariff Formation", *American Economic Review* 74: 971–85.

Mazower, M (1991) *Greece and the Inter-War Economic Crises,* Oxford: Clarendon Press.

McCarthy, J (1983) *Muslims and Minorities, The Population of Ottoman Anatolia and the End of the Empire,* New York: New York University Press.

Mears, E G (1929) *Greece Today. The Aftermath of the Refugee Impact,* London: Stanford University Press.

Medici, G (1941) "Intorno ad alcuni Caratteri Economici dell'olivicoltura Italiana", in Confederazione Fascista degli Agricoltori & Settore della Olivicoltura della FNCPPA, *Atti del Convegno Nazionale di Olivicoltura (Bari 21–22 settembre 1938),* Rome: Stab. Tipografico del Ramo Editoriale degli Agricoltori: 402–12.

Mendelsohn, C (1958) "International Trade in Oranges: Competition for Export Markets", unpublished PhD Thesis, University of California, Berkeley, California.

Mercurio. *Revista Comercial Ibero-Americana,* 1913, ns. 169 and 182.

Metzer, J (1974) "Railroad Development and Market Integration: The Case of Tsarist Russia", Journal of Economic History: 529–50.

—— (1998) *The Divided Economy of Mandatory Palestine*, Cambridge: Cambridge University Press.

Mignon, C (1982) *Campos y campesinos de la Andalucía mediterránea*, Madrid: MAPA.

Minde, K B and Ramstad, J (1986) "The Development of Real Wages in Norway about 1736–1910", *Scandinavian Economic History Review* XXXIV: 90–121.

Ministerio das Obras Publicas, Commercio e Industria (1889) *Inquerito Agricola. Estudo Geral da Economia rural da 70 Regiao Agronomica Executado pelo Commisario Especial da Mesma Regiao Paulo de Moraes en Cumprimento do Decreto de 30 de Dezembre de 1886*, Lisboa: Imprensa Nacional.

Ministerio de Estado (1899) *Centro de Información Comercial. Aceite de Oliva (primera parte)*, Madrid: Imprenta de la Vda. de M Minuesa de los Rios.

—— (1900) *Centro de Información Comercial. Aceite de oliva (segunda parte)*, Madrid: Imprenta de la Vda. de M Minuesa de los Rios.

—— (1920) *Los Aceites en la República Argentina. Por Emilio Boix*, Madrid: Imprenta del Ministerio de Estado.

—— (1922) *Mercado Argentino. Aceite de Oliva. Por Emilio Boix*, Madrid: Imprenta del Ministerio de Estado.

—— (1923) *El Aceite Italiano. Por José María Lamo de Espinosa*, Madrid: Imprenta del Ministerio de Estado.

Ministerio de Fomento (1923) *El Aceite de Oliva. Resumen Hecho por la Junta Consultiva Agronómica de las Memorias de 1921 Remitidas por los Ingenieros del Servicio Agronómico Provincial*, Madrid: Imp. Hijos de M G Hernández.

Ministerio de Trabajo, Comercio e Industria (1924) *La Exportación del Aceite de Oliva. Antecedentes, Resultados de la Información Pública Realizada, Gestiones de la Junta Nacional del Comercio Español de Ultramar*, Madrid: Gràfica Universal.

Ministero di Agricoltura, Industria e Commercio (1888) *Il Commercio degli Oli d'Oliva all'Estero*, Roma: Tipografia Nazionale di G Bertero.

—— (1898) *Annuario Statistico Italiano, 1898*, Roma: Tipografia Nazionale di G Bertero.

—— (1906) *Statistica Industriale Riassunto delle Notizie Sulle Condizioni Industriali del Regno [1903]*, Roma: Tipografia Nazionale di G Bertero e C.

—— (1907) *Gli Imballagi più in uso su Alcuni Mercati Esteri*, Roma: Tipografia Nazionale di G Bertero e C.

—— (1912) *Il Commercio dell'olio d'oliva all'estero. Parte I: Europa*, Roma.

—— (1913) *Il Commercio dell'olio d'oliva all'estero. Parte II: Asia, Africa e America*, Roma.

—— (1914) *Censimento degli opifici e delle Imprese Industriali al 10 giugno 1911*, Roma.

Ministry of Finance, *Annuaire Statistique de l'Egypte, 1909–39*. Cairo.

——, *Monthly Bulletin of Agricultural and Economic Statistics, 1919–39*. Cairo.

Minoglou, I P (forthcoming) "Greece: From Rent-seeking Protectionism to Direct Intervention" in J Foreman-Peck and G Federico (eds.) *European Industrial Policy: The Twentieth Century Experience*, Oxford: Oxford University Press.

Mitchell, B R (1975) *European Historical Statistics 1750–1970*, London: Macmillan.

—— (1986) *International Historical Statistics: Africa and Asia*, London: Macmillan.

—— (1988) *British Historical Statistics*, Cambridge: Cambridge University Press.

—— (1992) *International Historical Statistics. Europe, 1750–1988*, London: Macmillan.

Mokyr, J (1988) "Is There Life in the Pessimist Case? Consumption during the Industrial Revolution, 1790–1850", *Economic History Review* 48: 69–92.

—— (1993) *The British Industrial Revolution. An Economic Perspective*, Boulder, Co.: Westview Press.

Molinas, C and Prados de la Escosura, L (1989) "Was Spain Different? Spanish Historical Backwardness Revisited", *Explorations in Economic History* 26: 385–402.

Montgomery, J (1840) *A Practical Detail of the Cotton Manufacture of the United States of America; and the State of the Cotton Manufacture of that Country Contrasted and Compared with that of Great Britain; with Comparative Estimates of the Cost of Manufacturing in Both Countries*, Glasgow: J Niven.

Moore, W E (1947) *Economic Demography of Eastern and Southern Europe*, League of Nations.

Morilla Critz, J (1995) "La irrupción de California en el mercado de productos vitícolas y sus efectos en los países mediterráneos (1865–1925)", in J Morilla Critz (ed.) *California y el Mediterráneo. Estudios de la historia de dos agriculturas competidoras*, Madrid: Ministerio de Agricultura, Pesca y Alimentación: 255–318.

Morini, U (1930) *L'industria olearia. Manuale Pratico sugli impianti d'estrazione dell'olio dalle sanse di oliva con solventi, raffinazione, ecc*, Torino: G. Lavagnolo Editore.

Mortara, G (1930) *Prospettive Economiche, 1930*, Milano: Università Bocconi.

Moya, J C (1998) *Cousins and Strangers. Spanish Immigrants in Buenos Aires, 1850–1930*, Berkeley: University of California Press.

Mundell, R A (1957) "International Trade and Factor Mobility", *American Economic Review* XLVIII: 321–35.

Myrdal, G (1968) *Asian Drama: An Inquiry into the Poverty of Nations*, New York: Pantheon Books.

Nadal, J (1974) *El Fracaso de la Revolución Industrial en España*, Barcelona: Ariel.

—— (1991) "La Indústria Cotonera", in J Nadal, J Maluquer de Motes and F Cabana (eds). *Història Económica de la Catalunya contemporània* 3, Barcelona: Enciclopèdia Catalana: 12–85.

Nickless, P J (1979) "A New Look at Productivity in the New England Cotton Textile Industry, 1830–1860", *Journal of Economic History* 39 (4): 889–910.

Nicolau, R (1989) "La Población" in A Carreras (ed.) *Estadísticas Históricas de España, siglos XIX–XX*, Madrid: Fundación Banco Exterior.

North, D C (1958) "Ocean Freight Rates and Economic Development 1750–1913", Journal of Economic History 18: 537–55.

—— (1968) "Sources of Productivity Change in Ocean Shipping, 1600–1850", *Journal of Political Economy* 76: 953–70.

—— (1981) *Structure and Change in Economic History*, New York: Norton.

—— (1990) *Institutions, Institutional Change and Economic Performance*, Cambridge: Cambridge University Press.

O'Brien, P (ed.) (1982) *Railways and the Economic Development of Europe, 1830–1914*, London: Macmillan.

—— and Keyder, Ç (1978) *Economic Growth in Britain and France 1780–1914*, London: Allen and Unwin.

—— and Prados de la Escosura, L (1992) "Agricultural Productivity and European Industrialization, 1890–1980", *Economic History Review* 45: 514–36.

—— and Toniolo, G (1986) "Sull arretratezza dell agricoltura italiana rispetto a quella del Regno Unito attorno al 1910", *Ricerche Economiche*: 266–85.

O'Rourke, K (1995) "The Costs of International Economic Disintegration, Ireland in the 1930s", in R Sutch and S Carter (eds.) *Research in Economic History*, Vol 15, Greenwich Conn: Jai Press: 215–59.

—— (1997a) "Tariffs and Growth in the Late Nineteenth Century", *Working Paper, No. 1700*, Centre for Economic Policy Research.

—— (1997b) "The European Grain Invasion, 1870–1913", *The Journal of Economic History* 57: 775–801.

—— and Williamson, J G (1994) "Late Nineteenth-Century Anglo-American Factor-Price Convergence: Were Heckscher and Ohlin Right?", *Journal of Economic History* 54: 892–916.

—— and Williamson, J G (1995) "Education, Globalization and Catch-up: Scandinavia in the Swedish Mirror", *Scandinavian Economic History Review* 43: 287–309.

—— and Williamson, J G (1997) "Around the European Periphery 1870–1913: Globalization, Schooling and Growth", *European Review of Economic History* 1: 153–91.

—— and Williamson, J G (1999) *Globalization and History: The Evolution of a Nineteenth Century Atlantic Economy*, Cambridge, Mass.: MIT Press.

——, Taylor, A M, and Williamson, J G (1996) "Factor Price Convergence in the Late Nineteenth Century", *International Economic Review* 37: 499–530.

Obstfeld, M and Taylor, A (1997) "Nonlinear Aspects of Goods Market Arbitrage and Adjustment", *Journal of Japanese and International Economics*: 441–79.

—— and Taylor, A M (1998) "The Great Depression as a Watershed: International Capital Mobility in the Long Run", in M Bordo, C Goldin and E White (eds.), *The Defining Moment: The Great Depression and the American Economy in the Twentieth Century*, Chicago: University of Chicago Press: 353–402.

Okyar, O (1987) "A New Look at the Problem of Economic Growth in the Ottoman Empire (1800–1914)", *The Journal of European Economic History* 16, N. 1: 7–50.

Orman ve Meadin ve Ziraat Nezareti Ýstatistik Ýdaresi (1907) *1323 Senesi Avrupa-i Osmani Ziraat Ýstatistiki* [1323 Ottoman Agricultural Statistics], Dersaadet, Istanbul: Mvd Matbaasý.

Otsuka, K, Ranis, G and Saxonhouse, G (1988) *Comparative Technology Choice in Development. The Indian and Japanese Cotton Textile Industries*, London: Macmillan.

Owen, E R J (1969) *Cotton and the Egyptian Economy, 1820–1914, A Study in Trade and Development*, Oxford: Oxford University Press.

—— (1981) *The Middle East in the World Economy: 1800–1914*, London: Methuen.

Owen, R and Pamuk, Ş (1998) *A History of the Economies of the Middle East in the Twentieth Century*, London and Cambridge: I B Tauris Publishers and Harvard University Press.

Özel, I (1997) "The Economy of Turkey in the Late Ottoman and Republican Periods: A Quantitative Analysis", unpublished MA Thesis, Istanbul: Boğaziçi University.

Ozmun, E H (1908) "Turkish Olive Industry", Monthly Consular and Trade Reports 335, August: 88–91.

Palairet, M (1977) "Merchant Enterprises and the Development of the Plum-Based Trades in Serbia, 1847–1911", *Economic History Review* 30: 582–601.

—— (1983) "Land, Labour and Industrial Progress in Bulgaria and Serbia before 1914", *Journal of European Economic History* 12: 163–85.

—— (1990) "Real Earnings and National Product in Yugoslavia in the Long-run (1863–1988)", in E Aerts and N Valério (eds.) *Growth and Stagnation in the Mediterranean World*, Leuven: University Press: 63–81.

—— (1997) *The Balkan Economies, c.1800–1914. Evolution without Development*, Cambridge: Cambridge University Press.

Palmer, S (1979) "The British Coal Export Trade, 1850–1913", in D Alexander and R Ommer (eds.) *Volumes Not Values: Canadian Sailing Ships and World Trades*, St. John's, Newfoundland: Maritime History Group.

Palumbo, L (1979) *Prezzi e Salari in Terra di Bari (1530–1860)*, Bari: Grafica Bigiemme.

Pamuk, Ş. (1984) "The Ottoman Empire in the 'Great Depression' of 1873–1896", *Journal of Economic History* 44, N. 1: 107–18.

—— (1987) *The Ottoman Empire and European Capitalism, 1820–1913, Trade, Investment and Production*, Cambridge: Cambridge University Press.

—— (1994a) *Osmanlý Ekonomisinde Baðýmlýlýk ve Büyüme* [Dependency and Growth in the Ottoman Economy], Istanbul: Tarih Vakfý Yayýnlarý.

—— (1994b) "Appendix: Money in the Ottoman Empire, 1326–1914", in H Inalcyk and D Quataert (eds.) *An Economic and Social History of the Ottoman Empire, 1300–1914*, Cambridge: Cambridge University Press: 947–80.

—— (1995) "Long Term Trends in Urban Wages in Turkey, 1850–1990", in V Zamagni and P Scholliers (eds.), *Labour's Reward: Real Wages and Economic Growth in 19th and 20th Century Europe*, Bodmin, Cornwall: Edward Elgar: 89–105.

Parejo, A (1997) *La Producción Industrial de Andalucía (1830–1935)*, Sevilla: Instituto de Desarrollo Regional.

—— and Zambrana, J F (1994) "La Modernización de la Industria del Aceite en España en los siglos XIX y XX", in J Nadal and J Catalan (eds.), *La cara oculta de la industrializacion Española*, Madrid: Alianza: 13–42.

Parsley, D and Wei, S (1996) "Convergence to The Law of One Price Without Trade Barriers or Currency Fluctuations", *Quarterly Journal of Economics*: 1,213–36.

Parvus, E (1970) *Türkiye'nin Mali Tutsaklýoý [Turkey's Financial Dependency]*, Istanbul: May Yayynlarý.

Pasvolsky, L (1930) *Bulgaria's Economic Position. With Special Reference to the Reparation Problem and the Work of the League of Nations*, Washington, DC: The Brookings Institution.

Patton, K S (1928) *Kingdom of Serbs, Croats, and Slovenes: A Commercial and Industrial Handbook*, Washington, DC: Government Printing Office.

Pazzagli, C (1973) *L'Agricoltura Toscana nella Prima Metá dell'800*, Florence: L S Olschki.

Pech, R (1975) *Entreprise Viticole et Capitalisme en Languedoc Roussillon du Phylloxera aux Crises de Mévente*, Toulouse: Publications de l'Université de Toulouse.

Pedersen, J (1930) *Arbejdslønnen I Danmark under Skiftende Konjunkturer I Perioden ca. 1850–1913* Copenhagen: Gyldendalske Boghandel.

Pellejero, C (1988) "Decadencia del viñedo y crisis poblacional en la Málaga de finales del siglo XIX", *Revista de Historia Económica* 6: 593–633.

Pepelassis M I (1999) "Greece: From Rent-Seeking Protectionism to Direct Intervention", in J Foreman-Peck and G Federico (eds.) *European Industrial Policy: The Twentieth Century*, Oxford: Oxford University Press: 295–318.

Perez Moreda, V (1985) "La evolución demográfica española en el siglo XIX (1797–1930): tendencias generales y contrastes regionales" in *La popolazione italiana nell'Ottocento*, Bologna: Clueb.

Persson, K G (1999) *Grain Markets in Europe, 1500–1900: Integration and Deregulation*, Cambridge: Cambridge University Press.

Pescosolido, G (1998) *Unità Nazionale e Sviluppo Economico*, Bari: Laterza.

Petmezas, S D (1995) "Diverse Responses to Agricultural Income Crisis in a South-Eastern European Economy: Transatlantic Emigration from Greece (1894–1924)", in I Zilli (ed.) *Fra Spacio e Tempo: Studi in Onore di Luigi de Rosa, le Novecento*, Napoli: Edizioni Scientifiche Italiane: 427–87.

—— (1998) "Agricultural Change and Export Trade in Greece, ca. 1830–1914", paper presented to the workshop on Agricultural Change in Southern Europe in the Nineteenth Century, Florence: European University Institute, 27–28 November.

—— (forthcoming) "El comercio de la pasa de Corinto y su influencia en la economía griega del siglo XIX (1840–1914)", in J Morilla Critz, J Gómez-Pantoja, and P Cressier (eds.) *Los Impactos Exteriores Sobra la Agricultura Mediterráneos*, Madrid: Ministerio de Agricultura, Pesca, y Alimentación.

Pierrein, L (1975) *Industries traditionnelles du Port de Marseille. Le cycle des sucres et des oléagineaux, 1870–1958*, Marseille: Institut Historique de Provence.

Platt, R and Hefny, M (1958) *Egypt: A Compendium*, New York: American Geographical Society.

Polanyi, K (1944) *The Great Transformation: The Political and Economic Origins of Our Time*, Boston: Beacon.

Pollard, S (1981) *Peaceful Conquest. The Industrialisation of Europe 1760–1970*, Oxford: Oxford University Press.

Prados de la Escosura, L (1982) *Comercio Exterior y Crecimiento Económico en España, 1826–1913*, Madrid: Servicio de Estudios del Banco de España.

—— (1983) "Producción y consumo de tejidos en España, 1800–1913: Primeros resultados", in G Anes, L A Rojo, and P Tedde (eds.) *Historia económica y pensamiento social*, Madrid: Alianza-Banco de España: 455–71.

—— (1984) "El Comercio Hispano-británico en los Siglos XVIII y XIX", *Revista de Historia Económica* 2 (2): 113–62.

—— (1988) *De Imperio a Nación. Crecimiento y Atraso Económico en España 1780–1930*, Madrid: Alianza.

—— (1993) "Spain's Gross Domestic Product, 1850–1990: A New Series", *Working Paper D–93002*, Ministerio de Economia y Hacienda, Direccion General de Planificacion, Madrid.

—— (1997a) "El sector exterior y el atraso económico español, 1815–1913", unpublished paper.

—— (1997b) "Output and Expenditure in Spain, 1850–1995: New GDP Series", Fundación Argentaria (unpublished paper).

—— (1998) "International Comparisons of Real Product, 1820–1990: An Alternative Data Set", paper presented to the Conference on Growth in the 19th and 20th Century: A Quantitative Economic History. Spain: Valencia, December 14–15.

——, Sanchez, T and Oliva, J (1993) "De te Fabula Narratur? Growth, Structural Change and Convergence in Europe, Nineteenth and Twentieth Centuries", *Working Paper No. D–93009*, Ministerio de Economia y Hacienda, Direccion General de Planificacion, Madrid.

—— and Tena, A (1994) "Protectionism in Spain, 1869–1930" in P Lindert, J Nye and J Chevet (eds.) *Political Economy of Protectionism and Commerce, XVIIIth–XXth Centuries*, Milan: Proceedings of Eleventh International Economic History Congress.

Prais, S J (1995) *Productivity, Education and Training: An International Perspective*, Cambridge: Cambridge University Press.

Premier Congrès International du Raisin et du Jus de Raisin (1936), Paris: Librairie Félix Alcan.

Preshlenova, R (1994) "Austro-Hungarian Trade and the Economic Development of Southeastern Europe before World War I", in D F Good (ed.) *Economic Transformations in East and Central Europe. Legacies from the Past and Policies for the Future*, London: Routledge: 231–76.

Quah, D (1997) "Empirics for Growth and Distribution: Stratification, Polarization and Convergence Clubs", *Journal of Economic Growth* 2: 27–59.

Quataert, D (1973) *Ottoman Reform and Agriculture in Anatolia*, unpublished PhD Thesis, Los Angeles: University of California Los Angeles.

—— (1975) "Dilemma of Development: The Agricultural Bank and Agricultural Reform in Ottoman Turkey, 1888–1908", *International Journal of Middle East Studies* 6: 210–27.

—— (1980) "The Commercialization of Agriculture in Ottoman Turkey, 1800–1914", *International Journal of Turkish Studies* I: 38–55.

—— (1981) "Agricultural Trends and Government Policy in Ottoman Anatolia, 1800–1914", *Asian and African Studies* 15: 69–84.

—— (1983) "A Provisional Report Concerning the Impact of European Capital on Ottoman Port and Railways Workers, 1888–1909", in *Economie et sociétés dans l'empire ottoman (fin du XVIIe–début du XXe siècle)*, éditions du CNRS, Paris.

—— (1988) "The Ottoman Handicrafts and Industry in the Age of European Industrial Hegemony, 1800–1914", *Review* 11, N. 2: 160–78.

—— (1992) *Manufacturing and Technology Transfer in the Ottoman Empire, 1800–1914*, Istanbul: The ISIS Press.

—— (1993a) *Ottoman Manufacturing in the Age of the Industrial Revolution*, Cambridge: Cambridge University Press.

—— (1993b) "Agricultural Trends and Government Policy in Ottoman Anatolia, 1800–1914", in *Workers, Peasants and Economic Change in the Ottoman Empire, 1730–1914*, Istanbul: The ISIS Press: 17–30.

—— (1993c) "Limited Revolution: The Impact of the Anatolian Railway on Turkish Transportation and the Provisioning of Istanbul, 1890–1908", in *Workers, Peasants and Economic Change in the Ottoman Empire, 1730–1914*, Istanbul: The ISIS Press: 63–80.

—— (1993d) "Premières fumées d'usine, Some General Factors Favoring the Development of Industry in Salonica", in *Workers, Peasants and Economic Change in the Ottoman Empire, 1730–1914*, Istanbul: ISIS Press: 159–74.

—— (1994) "The Age of Reforms, 1812–1914", in H Inalcýk and D Quataert (eds.) *An Economic and Social History of the Ottoman Empire, 1300–1914*, Cambridge: Cambridge University Press: 759–946.

Quazza, G (1961) *L'industria laniera e cotoniera in Piemonte dal 1831 al 1861*, Turin: Museo Nazionale del Risorgimento Italiano.

Ravndal, G B (1909) "Olive Industry in Turkey", *Monthly Consular and Trade Reports* 345, June : 82–3.

—— (1928) *Turkey: A Commercial and Industrial Handbook*, Washington, DC: Government Printing Office.

Real Associaçao Central da Agricultura Portuguesa (1906) *Congresso de Leitaria, Olivicultura e Industria do Azeite en 1905*. Volume II, Lisboa, Imprensa Nacional.

Reher, D (1990) "Urbanization and Demographic Behaviour in Spain, 1860–1930", in A van der Woude, J de Vries and A Hayami, *Urbanization in History. A Process of Dynamic Interaction*, Oxford: Clarendon Press: 165–185.

—— and Ballesteros, E (1993) "Indicadores de la Dinamica Economica en Madrid: Precios y Salarios, 1800–1991", CSIC, Instituto de Demografía, Serie Documentos de Trabajo, Madrid, no. 9.

Reis, J (1982) "A Economia de Viana de Castelo em 1840: Um Inquérito Esquecido", *Revista de Estudos Contemporâneos* 2/3: 143–98.

—— (1992) "A Lei de la Fome As Origines do Proteccionismo Cerealifero (1889–1914)", in J Reis (ed.) *O Atraso Economico Português*, Lisbon: Imprensa Nacional Casa de Moeda: 33–85.

Repaci, F (1962) *La Finanza Pubblica Italiana nel Secolo 1861–1960*, Bologna: Zanichelli.

Review of World Trade (various years), Geneva: League of Nations.

Revue Commerciale du Levant, Bulletin Mensuel de la chambre de commerce française de Constantinople, Istanbul: Miscellaneous Issues, 1890–1912.

Revue Oléicola, La (1913) Nice.

Rey, G M (ed.) (1992) *I Conti Economici dell'Italia – 2 Una Stima del Valore Aggiunto per il 1911*, Bari: Laterza.

Rhode, P W (1995a) "La intensificación de la agricultura Californiana", in J Morilla Critz (ed.) *California y Mediterráneo: Estudios de la historia de dos agriculturas competidoras*, Madrid: Ministerio de Agricultura, Pesca, y Alimentación: 72–120.

—— (1995b) "Learning, Capital Accumulation, and the Transformation of California Agriculture", *Journal of Economic History* 55: 773–800.

Richards, A and Waterbury, J (1990) *A Political Economy of the Middle East, State, Class, and Economic Development*, Boulder: Westview Press.

Rifaat, M (1935) *The Monetary System of Egypt*, London: Allen.

Rivlin, H (1961) *The Agricultural Policies of Mohamed Ali in Egypt*, Cambridge, Mass.: Harvard University Press.

Robledo, R (1988) "Crisis agraria y éxodo rural: emigración española a ultramar, 1880–1920", in R Garrabou *La crisis agraria de fines del siglo XIX*, Barcelona: Ed. Crítica: 212–44.

Rogowski, R (1989) *Commerce and Coalitions: How Trade Effects Domestic Political Arrangements*, Princeton: Princeton University Press.

Romano, R (1976) *Napoli: dal Viceregno al Regno: Storia Economica*, Torino: Einaudi.

Ronquillo, J O (1851–1857) *Diccionario de materia mercantil, industrial y agrícola*, Barcelona: Imprenta Gaspar.

Rosenthal, A S (1896) "The Olive Tree and Olive Oil in Tuscany", US Consular Reports L, n. 186, March: 317–25.

Rosés, J R (1998a) "Measuring the Contribution of Human Capital to the Development of the Catalan Factory System (1830–1861)", *European Review of Economic History* 2 (1): 25–48.

—— (1998b) *The Early Phase of Catalan Industrialisation, 1830–1861*, unpublished PhD Thesis, European University Institute.

Rosoli, G (ed.) (1978) *Un secolo di emigrazione italiana, 1876–1976*, Roma: Centro Studi Emigrazione.

Rostow, W W (1960) *The Stages of Economic Growth. A Non-Communist Manifesto*, Cambridge: Cambridge University Press.

Ruiz, J (1979) *La Agricultura Española a Mediados del Siglo XIX. Resultados de un Encuesta Agraria de la Epoca*, Madrid: Servicio de Publicaciones Agrarias.

Sachs, J D and Warner, A M (1995) "Natural Resource Abundance and Economic Growth", *Working Paper*, No. 5,398, National Bureau of Economic Research, Cambridge, Mass.

Safran, N (1961) *Egypt in Search of Political Community*, Cambridge, Mass.

Sailing Directions for the Euxine or Black Sea and the Seas of Marmora and Azov; embracing also the navigation of the Dardanelles and Bosphorus (1853), London: James Imray.

Sanchez, A B (1992) *La inmigración española en Argentina. Siglos XIX y XX*, Gijón: Ed. Júcar, Fundación Archivo de Indianos.

—— (1995) *Las causas de la emigración española, 1880–1930*, Madrid: Alianza.

Sánchez, A (1989) "La era de la Manufactura Algodonera en Barcelona, 1736–1839", *Estudios de Historia Social* 48–9: 65–113.

Sánchez-Albornoz, N (1981) "El Consumo de Textiles en España, 1860–1890: una Primera Aproximación", Hacienda Pública Española 69: 229–35.

Sánchez-Alonso, B (1995) *Las causas de la emigración española*, Madrid: Alianza Universidad.

Sandberg, L (1968) "Movements in the Quality of British Cotton Textile Exports, 1815–1913", *Journal of Economic History* 28 (1): 1–27.

—— (1979) "The Case of the Impoverished Sophisticate: Human Capital and Swedish Economic Growth before World War I", *Journal of Economic History* 39: 225–41.

Sanz, A G (1979–1980) "Jornales Agricolas y Presupuesto Familiar Campesino en España a Mediados del Siglo XIX" *Anales del CUNEF*: 49–71.

Sanz, J and Garrabou, R (eds.) (1988) *Historia Agraria de la España Contemporanea*, Barcelona: Critica.

Sarda, J (1948) *La política monetaria y las fluctuaciones de la economía española en el siglo XIX*, Madrid: Consejo Superior de Investigaciones Científicas.

Saxonhouse, G and Wright, G (1984) "Ring and Mules around the World: A Comparative Study in Technological Choice", *Research in Economic History* 3: 271–300.

Schofield, R, Bideau, A and Reher, D (eds.) (1991) *The Decline of Mortality in Europe*, Oxford: Clarendon Press.

Scholliers, P (ed.) (1989) *Real Wages in Nineteenth and Twentieth Century Europe*, New York: Berg.

—— and Zamagni V (eds.) (1995) *Labour's Reward: Real Wages and Economic Change in 19th and 20th Century Europe*, Aldershot: Elgar.

Schön, L (1995) *Jordbruk med Binäringar 1800–1980*, Lund: Studentlitteratur.

Schousboe, K (ed.) (1983) *En Faestebondes Liv: Erindringer og Optegnelser af Gardfoester og Sognefoged Soren Pedersen, Havrebjerg 1776–1839*, Odense: Landbohistorisk Selskab.

Schulze, M (1997) "Reestimating Austrian GDP, 1870–1913. Methods and Sources", *Working Paper in Economic History*, No. 36/97, London: School of Economics.

Scott, M F (1993) "Explaining Economic Growth" *American Economic Review* 83: 421–5.

Selanik Gazetesi, Miscellaneous issues, 1322 (1905), Salonica.

Selanik Vilayeti Salnamesi, Miscellaneous volumes, 1,293 (1876) – 1,324 (1906), Salonica.

Sener, A (1990) *Tanzimat Dönemi Osmanß Vergi Sistemi* [Ottoman Taxation System of the Tanzimat Period], Istanbul: Iþaret Yayýnlarý.

Serrano Sanz, J M (1987) *El viraje proteccionista en la Restauración. La política comercial española, 1875–1895*, Madrid: Siglo XXI.

Shaw, S J (1975) "The Nineteenth-Century Ottoman Tax Reforms and Revenue Systems", *International Journal of Middle East Studies* 6: 421–59.

—— and Shaw, E K (1988) *History of the Ottoman Empire and Modern Turkey, Reform Revolution and Republic: The Rise of Modern Turkey, 1808–1975*, V. 2, Cambridge: Cambridge University Press.

Shear, S (1928) *Prune Supply and Price Situation California Agricultural Experiment Station Bulletin* No. 462, Berkeley, California.

Shorter, F C (1985) "The Population of Turkey after the War of Independence", *International Journal of Middle East Studies* 17: 417–41.

Simpson, J (1985) *Agricultural Growth and Technological Change: the Olive and the Wine in Spain, 1860–1936*, unpublished PhD Thesis, University of London.

—— (1989) "La Producción Agraria y el Consumo Español en el siglo XIX", *Revista de Historia Económica* VII: 355–88.

—— (1992) "Technical Change, Labor Absorption and Living Standards in Rural Andalucia, 1886–1936", *Agricultural History* 66: 1–24.

—— (1995) *Spanish Agriculture. The Long Siesta, 1765–1965*, Cambridge: Cambridge University Press.

—— (1997) "Did Tariffs Stifle Spanish Agriculture before 1936?", *European Review of Economic History* 1: 65–87.

Skinner, R P (1903) "Olives and Olive Oil in France", *Consular Reports* LXXII, n. 274: 403–21.

Smithsonian Institute (1927) "World Weather Records", *Miscellaneous Collection*, 79, Washington.

Soares, R M (1873) *Relatório da Direcção Geral do Commercio e Indústria acerca dso Servios Dependentes da Repartição de Agricultura desde a sua Fundação até 1870*, Lisboa: Imprensa Nacional.

Società Nazionale degli Olivicoltori Italiani (1927) *Atti del IX Congresso Nazionale di Olivicoltura*. Bari, 19–22 d'ottobre 1925, Spoleto: Arti Grafiche Pareto & Petrelli.

Söderberg, J (1987) "Real Wage Trends in Urban Europe 1730–1850: Stockholm in a Comparative Perspective", Social History 12: 155–76.

Soltow, L (1985) "The Swedish Census of Wealth at the Beginning of the Nineteenth Century", *Scandinavian Economic History Review* XXXIII: 1–24.

Sori, E (1979) *L'emigrazione italiana dall'Unita alla seconda guerra mondiale*, Bologna: Il Mulino.

Sousa, P (1996) "Statística e Produçao Agrícola em Portugal (1846–1915)", Working Paper presented in the seminar *Economic History of Portuguese Growth*.

Spinelli, F and Fratiani, M (1991) *Storia monetaria d'Italia. L'evoluzione del sistema monetario e bancario*, Milano: Arnoldo Mondadori Editore.

State Institute of Statistics (1994) *Statistical Indicators, 1923–1992*, Ankara.

Statistical Abstract for the United Kingdom, London: HM Stationery Office, various years.

Statistical Abstract of Palestine (annual issues, 1936–45), Jerusalem: Office of Statistics.

Statistical Year Book (various years), Geneva: League of Nations.

Statistique Général de la Grèce (1930) and (1933) *Annuaire Statistique de la Grèce*, Athens.

Statistk Tabelværk Udgivet af den dertil Allernådigt Anordnede Commission. Femte Heft, (various years) Copenhagen.

Steckel, R (1995) "Stature and the Standard of Living", *Journal of Economic Literature* 33: 1903–1940.

Stettler, H L (1977) *Growth and Fluctuations in the Ante-Bellum Textile Industry*, New York: Arno Press.

Stoianovich, T (1960) "Conquering Balkan Orthodox Merchant", *Journal of Economic History* 20: 234–313.

—— (1994) *Balkan Worlds, the First and Last Europe*, New York: M E Sharpe.

Stone, R (1954) *Measurement of Consumers' Expenditure and Behavior in the United Kingdom, 1920–1938*, Vol. 1, Cambridge: Cambridge University Press.

Stopler, W F and Samuelson, P M (1941) "Protection and Real Wages", *Review of Economic Studies* XI: 58–73.

Storchi, M L (1981) "Un Azienda Agricola della Piana del Sele" in A Massafra (ed.), *Problemi di Storia delle Campagne Meridionale nell'Eta Moderna e Contemporanea*, Bari: Dedalo: 117–41.

Strong, F (1842) *Greece as a Kingdom, or a Statistical Description of that Country from the Arrival of King Otho, in 1833, Down to the Present Time*, London: Longman, Brown, Green and Longmans.

Stroykowitch, W (1910) *Recherches physiologiques sur la prune, et étude des méthodes à employer pour l'amélioration de l'industrie prunière en Serbie*, Nancy: Imprimerie Universelle Marcel Vagner.

Suomen Taloushistoria (1983), Helsinki: Kustannusosakeyhtio Tammi, vol.3.

Survey of Palestine (1946), Jerusalem: Government Printer.

Suvla, R (1966) "The Ottoman Debt, 1850–1939", in C Issawi (ed.), *The Economic History of the Middle East, 1800–1914, A Book of Readings*, Chicago: The University of Chicago Press: 94–106.

Svimez (1961) *Un Secolo di Statistiche Italiane Nord e Sud 1861–1961*, Roma: Svimez.

Szirmai, A, van Ark, B and Pilat, D (eds.) (1993) *Explaining Economic Growth : Essays in Honour of Angus Maddison*, Amsterdam: North Holland.

Tafunell, X (1989) "La construcción residencial barcelonesa y la economía internacional. Una interpretación sobre las fluctuaciones de la industria de la vivienda en Barcelona durante la segunda mitad del siglo XIX", *Revista de Historia Económica* VII: 389–437.

Taussig, F W (1931 [1892]) *The Tariff History of the United States*, New York: G P Putnam's Sons.

Taylor, A M (1994) "Mass Migration to Distant Southern Shores", in T J Hatton and J G Williamson (eds.) *Migration and the International Labor Market, 1850-1939*, London: Routledge.

Taylor, A M (1998) "On the Costs of Inward-Looking Development: Price Distortions, Growth and Divergence in Latin America", *Journal of Economic History* 58: 1–28.

—— and Williamson, J G (1997) "Convergence in the Age of Mass Migration", *European Review of Economic History* 1: 27–63.

Tekeli, I and Ilkin, S (1977) *1929 Dünya Buhranında Türkiye'nin Iktisadi Politika Arayışları*, Ankara: Orta Doğu Teknik Üniversitesi.

—— (1982) *Uygulamaya Geçerken Türkiye'de Devletçiligin Olusumu*, Ankara: Orta Doğu Teknik Üniversitesi.

Temin, P (1988) "Product Quality and Vertical Integration in the Early Cotton Textile Industry", *Journal of Economic History* 48 (4): 891–907.

—— (1989) *Lessons from the Great Depression*, Cambridge, Mass.: MIT Press.

Tena, A (1992) *Las Estadísticas Históricas del Comercio Intenacional: Fiabilidad y Comparabilidad*, Madrid: Servicio de Estudios del Banco de España.

—— (1998a) "Un Nuevo Perfil del Proteccionismo Espanol Durante la Restauracion 1875–1930", *Documento Trabajo* 98–19 (02), Departamento de Historia Economica e Istituciones, Universidad Carlos III de Madrid.

—— (1998b) *Proteccion y crecimiento económico en la España de la Restauración (1870–1930)*, (unpublished manuscript).

Tezel, Y S (1986) *Cumhuriyet Döneminin Iktisadi Tarihi (1923–1950)*, Expanded Second Edition, Ankara: Yurt Yayınları.

Themopoulou, E (1994) *Salonique, 1800–1875: Conjoncture Économique et Mouvement Commercial*, unpublished PhD Thesis, Paris: Université de Paris I Panthéon-Sorbonne.

Thomas, B (1954) *Migration and Economic Growth: A Study of Great Britain and the Atlantic Economy*, Cambridge: Cambridge University Press.

Thompson, E W (1913) "Edible Oils in the Mediterranean District", US Department of Commerce, *Special Agents Series*, n. 75. Washington: Government Printing Office.

Thomson, J K J (1992) *A Distinctive Industrialisation. Cotton in Barcelona: 1728–1832*, Cambridge: Cambridge University Press.

Ticaret ve Ziraat Nezareti Mecmuasý, Miscellaneous Issues, 1328 (Mali) (1912) Istanbul.

Tignor, R L (1984) *Enterprise and Economic Change in Egypt, 1918–1952*, Princeton, N J: Princeton University Press.

Tilly, R (1994) "German Banks and Foreign Investment in Central and Eastern Europe before 1939", in D F Good (ed.) *Economic Transformations in East and Central Europe. Legacies from the Past and Policies for the Future*, London: Routledge: 210–30.

Toniolo, G (1988) *Storia economica dell'Italia liberale, 1850–1918*, Bologna: Il Mulino.

Toprak, Z (1982) *Türkiye'de Millî Ýktisat, (1908–1918)* ['National Economy' in Turkey, (1908–1918)], Ankara: Yurt Yayýnlarý.

—— (1992) "Modernization and Commercialization in the Tanzimat Period: 1838–1875", *New Perspectives on Turkey* 7: 57–70.

—— (1995) *Türkiye'de Ekonomi ve Toplum (1908–1950), Ýttihat-Terakki ve Devletçilik*, [Economy and Society in Turkey (1908–1950), Committee of Union-Progress and Statism], Istanbul: Tarih Vakfý Yurt Yayýnlarý.

Tortella, G (1987) "Agriculture: A Slow Moving Sector, 1830–1935", in N Sanchez-Albornoz (ed.), *The Economic Modernisation of Spain, 1830–1930*, New York: New York University Press: 42–62.

—— (1994a) "Patterns of Economic Retardation and Recovery in South-Western Europe in the Nineteenth and Twentieth Centuries", *Economic History Review* 47: 1–21.

—— (1994b) *El desarrollo económico de la España contemporánea*, Madrid: Alianza.

Toutain, J C (1992) "La production agricole de la France de 1810 à 1990: Départements et Régions. Croissance, productivité, structures", *Economies et Sociétés. Cahiers de l'ISMÉA*, AF n. 17, tome I, 11–12.

Tufts, W (1946) *Rich Pattern of California Crops*, Berkeley: University of California Press.

Turgay, A U (1983) "Ottoman–British Trade through southeastern Black Sea Ports during the nineteenth century", in *Economie et societes dans l'empire ottoman*, éditions du CNRS, Paris: 297–315.

UK *Foreign Office Annual Series*, *(FOAS)*, Diplomatic and Consular Reports on Trade and Finance, 1885–1912, London.

UK *Parliamentary Papers, Accounts and Papers (PPAP)*, Consular Reports, 1870–1885, London.

US Bureau of Foreign Commerce (1884) *Commercial Relations of the United States with Foreign Countries During the Years 1882 and 1883, Vol. II, Africa, America, Asia, Australasia, and Polynesia*, Washington, DC: Government Printing Office.

—— (1886) *Commercial Relations of the United States with Foreign Countries During the Years 1884 and 1885*, Washington, DC: Government Printing Office.

—— (1888) *Commercial Relations of the United States with Foreign Countries During the Years 1886 and 1887*, Washington, DC: Government Printing Office.

—— (1899) *Commercial Relations of the United States with Foreign Countries During the Year 1898*, Vol. I, Washington, DC: Government Printing Office.

—— (1901) *Commercial Relations of the United States with Foreign Countries During the Year 1900*, Vol. I, Washington, DC: Government Printing Office.

—— (1903) *Commercial Relations of the United States with Foreign Countries During the Year 1902*, Vol. I.,Washington, DC: Government Printing Office.

US Consular Reports (1884) "Fruit Culture in the Several Countries", Vol. 41 1/2, Washington, DC: Government Printing Office.

US Consular Reports, Washington, DC: Government Printing Office, various years.

US Department of Agriculture *Yearbook*, Washington, DC: Government Printing Office, various years.

US Department of Commerce and Labor, Bureau of Statistics (1909) *Statistical Abstract of Foreign Countries, Parts I-III, Statistics of Foreign Commerce*, Washington, DC: Government Printing Office.

US Department of Commerce. Bureau of Census (1971) *Historical Statistics of the United States. Colonial times to 1970. Part 1*, Washington, DC: Government Printing Office.

US House of Representatives (1929) *Hearings on Tariff Readjustment, 1929.* 70th Cong., 2d sess., Vol. 7. Washington, DC: Government Printing Office.

US House of Representatives, Committee on Ways and Means (1897) *Tariff Hearings*, 54th Cong., 2nd sess., Vol. 1, Doc. No. 338. Washington, DC: Government Printing Office.

—— (1909) *Tariff Hearings*, 60th Cong., 2nd sess., Vol. 4, Doc. No. 1505. Washington, DC: Government Printing Office.

—— (1921) *Tariff Hearings*, 66th Cong., 3rd sess. Washington, DC: Government Printing Office.

US Tariff Commission (1929) *Summary of Tariff Information, 1929 on Tariff Act of 1922, Schedule 7, Agricultural Products and Provisions*, Washington DC: Government Printing Office.

—— (1931) *Report to the President on Olive Oil*, Washington, DC: Government Printing Office.

—— (1939) *Grapes, Raisins, and Wines*, Report No. 134, Second series, Washington DC: Government Printing Office.

United States, Bureau of the Census (1976) *Historical Statistics of the United States*, Washington DC: Government Printing Office.

Ure, A (1836) *The Cotton Manufacture of Great Britain Systematically Investigated with an Introductory View of its Comparative State in Foreign Countries*, London: C Knight.

Uselding, P (1975) "Wage and Consumption Levels in England and on the Continent in the 1830s", *Journal of European Economic History* 4: 501–13.

van Zanden, J L (1995) "The Beginning of the Kuznets Curve: Western Europe during the Early Modern Period", *Economic History Review* 48: 643–64.

—— (1996) "An Experiment in Measurement of the Wealth of Nations. International Disparities in Agricultural Productivity and GDP per Capita at about 1810", in E Buyst, G Dejongh, B van Ark and J L van Zanden (eds.), *Historical Benchmark Comparisons of Output and Productivity, 1750–1990*, CES Discussion Paper, Katolieke Universiteit Leuven.

Vandellos, J A (1925) "La richesse et le revenu de la Péninsule Ibérique," *Metron* V: 151–86.

Vandor, P E (1919) *History of Fresno County, California with biographical Sketches of the Leading Men and Women of the County who have been Identified with its Growth and Development from the Early Days to the Present*, Los Angeles: Historical Record Co.

Varela Ortega, J (1978) *Los amigos políticos. Oligarquía y caciquismo en la Restauración*, Madrid: Alianza.

Vazquez Gonzalez, A (1988) "La emigración gallega. Migrantes, transporte y remesas," in S Albornoz (ed.) *Españoles hacia América. La emigración en masa, 1880–1930*, Madrid: Alianza: 80–104.

Veinstein, G (ed.) (1992) *Salonique, 1850–1918, La "ville des Juifs" et le réveil des Balkans*, Paris: Editions Autrement.

Verdier, D (1994) *Democracy and International Trade. Britain, France and the United States, 1860–1990*, Princeton: Princeton University Press.

Vinos y Aceites, Los (1878).

Vitali, O (1969) "La Stima degli Investimenti e dello Stock di Capitale", in G Fua (ed.), *Lo Sviluppo Economico in Italia*, Vol. III, Milan: F Angeli: 478–537.

Von Tunzelmann, G N (1978) *Steam Power and British Industrialization to 1860*, Oxford: Clarendon Press.

Webber, H J and Batchelor, L D (eds.) (1948) *The Citrus Industry*, Berkeley and Los Angeles: University of California Press.

Wei, S (1997) "The Law of One Price: Food Markets in China during 1901–1912", Harvard University, unpublished paper.

Wheatcroft, A (1993) *The Ottomans*, Canada: Penguin Books.

Wheeler, L A (1927) *International Trade in Dried Fruit*, US Bureau of Foreign and Domestic Commerce, Trade Promotion Series No. 44, Washington, DC: Government Printing Office.

Wickson, E (1900) *California Fruit*, San Francisco: Pacific Rural Press.

Wilber, D (1969) *United Arab Republic: People, Society and Culture*, New Haven: Hraf Press.

Williams, J and Wright, B (1991) *Storage and Commodity Markets*, Cambridge: Cambridge University Press.

Williamson, J G (1985) *Did British Capitalism Breed Inequality?*, Boston: Allen and Unwin.

—— (1990) "The Impact of the Corn Laws Just Prior to Repeal", *Explorations in Economic History* 27: 123–56.

—— (1995) "The Evolution of Global Labor Markets Since 1830: Background Evidence and Hypotheses", *Explorations in Economic History* 32: 141–97.

—— (1996a) "Globalization, Convergence, and History", *Journal of Economic History* 56: 277–306.

—— (1996b) "*The Evolution of Global Labor Markets Since 1830: Background Evidence and Hypotheses. Revision of Appendix 1: Nominal Wage, Cost of Living and Real Wage series*" (unpublished manuscript).

—— (1997) "Globalization and Inequality, Past and Present", *World Bank Research Observer* 12: 117–35.

—— (1998a) "Real Wages and Relative Factor Prices in the Third World 1820–1940: Asia", *HIER Discussion Paper 1844*, Department of Economics, Harvard University (August).

—— (1998b) "Real Wages and Relative Factor Prices in the Third World 1820–1940: Latin America", *HIER Discussion Paper 1853*, Department of Economics, Harvard University (October).

—— (1998c) "Real Wages and Relative Factor Prices in the Third World Before 1940: What Do They Tell Us About the Sources of Growth?", paper presented to the Conference on 20th Century Growth, Valencia, December 13–14.

—— (1998d) "Globalization, Labor Markets and Policy Backlash in the Past", *Journal of Economic Perspectives* 12 (Fall): 51–72.

—— (1998e) "Growth, Distribution and Demography Some Lessons from History", *Explorations in Economic History* 35: 241–71.

Woytinsky, W S and Woytinsky, E S (1953) *World Population and Production. Trends and Outlook*, New York: The Twentieth Century Fund.

Wright, G (1990) "The Origins of American Industrial Success, 1879–1940", *American Economic Review* 80: 651–68.

Yates, P L (1959) *Forty Years of Foreign Trade*, London: Unwin and Allen.

Yeralimpos, A (1996) "Tanzimat Döneminde Kuzey Yunanistan'da Þehircilik ve Modernleþme" [Urban Planning and Modernization in Northern Greece during the Tanzimat Period], in P Dumont and F Georgeon (eds.) *Modernleþme Sürecinde Osmanlý Kentleri* [Ottoman Towns in the Process of Modernization], Istanbul: Tarih Vakfý Yurt Yayýnlarý: 31–59.

Yousef, T (1999) "Egyptian Commodity Markets Before State Intervention, 1920–1950", *Working Paper*, Department of Economics, Georgetown University.

—— (forthcoming) "De-Globalization, Divergence and Inter-War Egypt", *Journal of Economic History*.

Yücel, Y (1996) "Macroeconomic Policies in Turkey during the Great Depression, 1929–1940", unpublished MA Thesis, Istanbul: Boğaziçi University.

Zamagni, V (1978) *Industrializzazione e Squilibri Regionali*, Bologna: Il Mulino.

—— (1987) "A Century of Change: Trends in the Composition of Italian Labour Force, 1881–1981", *Historical Social Research* 44: 36–97.

—— (1990) *Dalla periferia al centro. La seconda rinascita economica dell'Italia, 1861–1981*, Bologna: Il Mulino.

—— (1993) *The Economic History of Italy, 1860–1990*, Oxford: Clarendon Press.

Zambrana, J F (1987) *Crisis y Modernización del Olivar Español, 1870–1930*, Madrid: Ministerio de Agricultrua, Pesca y Alimentación.

—— (1993) "Las Industrias de los Aceites y Grasas Vegetales en España: un Desarrollo Limitado", *Revista de Historia Industrial* 4: 57–90.

Zanelli, S (1967) *L'industria del Cotone in Lombardia dalla fine del Settecento alla Unificazione del paese*, Turin: ILTE.

Zattini, G (1921) "La produzione delle olive e dell'olio in Italia in base alla statistica del docicennio 1090–1920," *Notizie Periodiche di Statistica Agraria* part 9: 240–8.

Zendisayek, B (1997) "Large and Small Enterprises in Turkish Industrialization during the Great Depression", unpublished MA thesis, Istanbul: Boğaziçi University.

Zevin, R D (1971) "The Growth of Cotton Textile Production after 1815", in R W Fogel and S Engerman (eds.), *The Reinterpretation of American Economic History*, New York: Harper and Row: 122–47.

Zunino, G (1939) *Il mercato italiano degli olii d'oliva*, Milano: Dott. A. Giuffrè.

Index